NUMISMATIC NOTES AND MONOGRAPHS

169

Numismatic Finds of the Americas

an Inventory of American Coin Hoards, Shipwrecks, Single Finds, and Finds in Excavations

John M. Kleeberg

Numismatic Notes and Monographs
169

Printed under the Auspices of the International Numismatic Commission

THE AMERICAN NUMISMATIC SOCIETY
NEW YORK
2009

© 2009 The American Numismatic Society

ISSN 0078–2718
ISBN 978–0–89722–311–9

Library of Congress Cataloging-in-Publication Data

Kleeberg, John M.
  Numismatic finds of the Americas : an inventory of American coin hoards, shipwrecks, single finds, and finds in excavations / John M. Kleeberg.
    p. cm. -- (Numismatic notes and monographs, ISSN 0078-2718 ; 169)
  Includes bibliographical references and index.
  ISBN 978-0-89722-311-9 (hardcover)
  1. Coin hoards--America--Catalogs. 2. Coin hoards--America--History. I. Title.
  CJ277.A45K55 2009
  910.4'52--dc22
                     2009011702

Printed in China

Contents

Introduction	1
Part I: Numismatic Finds in the Americas	15
Part II: Treasury Accumulation and Release of U.S. Silver Dollars	263
Part III: Finds of American Coins outside the Americas	269
References	311
Indices	337
Index of Find Spots	337
Index to Special Types of Finds and to Named Hoards	346
Index to Contents of Finds	349

Introduction

This is an inventory of numismatic finds (chiefly coins, but also paper money, medals, and tokens) from North and South America, plus an inventory of American numismatic items found outside the Americas. This introduction will distinguish among the various types of finds; provide a chronological narrative of the development of coinage in the Americas as it relates to coin finds; discuss the sources for this inventory; and explain its arrangement. This inventory may be abbreviated as "*NFA*," short for *Numismatic Finds of the Americas*.

Numismatic Finds—Defined and Categorized

The term "finds" is the greater term, which includes the more narrow term, "hoards." All hoards are finds; not all finds are hoards. This work will use the following definition of hoards:

> Two or more coins or other valuable objects, removed from circulation and intentionally concealed, usually with the purpose of eventual recovery, but not recovered by the original owner, and not recovered until a substantial period of time has passed, typically a decade or more.

The latter part of the definition is borrowed from the jurisprudence regarding treasure trove. The courts write, "Treasure trove has the air of antiquity."[1] The researcher into numismatic finds in the United States soon discovers that bags of money fall out of armored trucks with alarming frequency,[2] and without that limitation all those incidents would have to be included. The focus of this inventory is on numismatic finds that tell us something of the history of the time. The fact that bags of money are being thrown out regularly onto the American highway tells us interesting information about the competence of the armored truck industry, but a million nickels smeared all over the Garden State

---

1. John M. Kleeberg, "The Law and Practice Regarding Coin Finds: Treasure Trove Law in the United States," International Numismatic Commission, *Compte Rendu* 53 (2006): 13–26 (quotation is on page 16). A separate article discusses the admiralty law pertaining to coins found on shipwrecks: John M. Kleeberg, "The Law and Practice Regarding Coin Finds: United States Laws Concerning Historic Shipwrecks," International Numismatic Commission, *Compte Rendu* 54 (2006): 13–29.
2. E.g., Hoel v. Powell, 904 P.2d 153 (Okla. App. 1995).

Parkway are of little help in analyzing the monetary patterns of the late twentieth century. Walter Breen, in his 1950 inventory of American coin hoards, excluded "hoards made for a numismatic purpose," such as the hoard of flying eagle cents accumulated by John Beck.[3] Despite the ambiguity of the term "numismatic purpose," it is clear what Breen means, namely hoards made by collectors for the collectible value, rather than the monetary value. This inventory excludes those accumulations as well, partly by using the definition "removed from circulation." These collector and dealer accumulations tell us interesting things about the collector habits of the period, but they do not tell us much about monetary circulation.

In addition to hoards, this inventory will also include shipwrecks; single finds; and finds in archaeological excavations.

The common law distinguishes three categories of lost property, namely lost, abandoned, and mislaid. Coin hoards often get treated as a fourth category, "treasure trove." An object is mislaid when someone places it somewhere and then forgets where it was located. The lost/abandoned/mislaid distinction provides a useful framework for describing the various types of coin finds; in analyzing the conduct of the owner it parallels the accidentally/intentionally/negligently distinction.

Many writers use the term hoards loosely, calling a series of finds, or any large group of coins, a "hoard." The following outline, applying the lost/abandoned/mislaid framework, should make the distinction clear:

I. Lost.
    A. Casual losses (e.g., coins dropping out of pockets).
    B. Losses due to disasters:
      1. Shipwrecks.
      2. Volcano (eruption of Vesuvius).
      3. Other disasters (flood, fire, San Francisco earthquake).

II. Abandoned.
    A. Discarding counterfeits (the term discarded has been adopted from the work in Roman numismatics done by Richard Reece).
    B. Discarding base metal coins that no longer circulate (e.g., Garza *jolas*, *NFA* 579).
    C. Abandonment for votive purposes:
      1. Funerary deposits ("Charon's obol").
      2. Foundation deposits (cornerstones, *Bauopfer*).
      3. Religion/Luck (wishing wells).

III. Mislaid (coin hoards).
    A. Emergency hoards.
    B. Savings hoards.

In archaeological excavations, the most common finds will fall into categories I.A and II.A. The characteristic find from United States sites of the early nineteenth century is the Spanish American ½ real, the *medio*, which was worth about six cents, and small and easy to lose. Counterfeits (II.A) are

---

3. Walter Breen, "Survey of American Coin Hoards," *Numismatist* 65, no. 1 (January 1952): 7–24; 65, no. 10 (October 1952): 1005–10.

discarded because possession of a counterfeit is in itself a crime. In a case of II.B, an issuer of tokens (here, José Antonio Garza) redeemed his tokens, and having paid them off wanted to get rid of them; so he dumped them in the San Antonio River, where they were found by later generations (*NFA* 579). II.C.1 refers to a phenomenon often known as "Charon's obol," where a coin is placed with a corpse to supply it with funds for the afterlife; these coins can be placed on the eyes, in the mouth, or in the hand (*NFA* 16, 17). This custom exists in most coin-using cultures. The most important numismatic finds recovered from burials are Indian Peace Medals (*NFA* 711). II.C.2, foundation deposits (in German, "*Bauopfer*") is a custom of placing coins underneath a threshold or in a cornerstone to confer good luck on a building or bridge (*NFA* 774); an ocean-going variant is to place coins when stepping the mast of a ship (*NFA* 403). II.C.3 refers to the habit of throwing coins into wishing wells and rivers for luck (*NFA* 34). Category III, hoards, is divided into the two major categories of emergency hoards and savings hoards. Emergency hoards occur when some disaster impends (war, invasion); the owner grabs what coins there are and conceals them (*NFA* 312, 756). A savings hoard is accumulated over a series of years, and chooses the better coins from circulation; coins in a savings hoard are often skewed towards heavier weights (*NFA* 27, 670).

A "reverse hoard" is a variant of discarding counterfeits (II.A). In the early 1990s, a counterfeit subway token was widely circulated in New York City, nicknamed "the people's token." Token clerks had to pick out the counterfeits every time they emptied the turnstiles, to forestall selling the counterfeits onward. It was not uncommon to see token booths with stacks of a dozen "people's tokens" piled up on the shelf. These accumulations were, in effect, "reverse hoards": the hoarders were not picking out the desirable coins from circulation, but picking out the undesirable coins to prevent their further circulation. The Montclair Hoard has some "reverse hoard" characteristics, since many of the coins in that hoard bear cancellation graffiti (*NFA* 476).

It is possible for finds to move from one category to another. For example, an individual may accumulate a savings hoard in Pompeii, and then get buried by lava from Vesuvius—thus most of the finds at Pompeii will be I.B.2, but there will also be subcategories of III.B. Someone may accumulate coins, believing that they are valuable, but then the passage of time makes them valueless—an example would be state coppers that became valueless after the coppers panic. The finds then move from III.B to II.B. Examples of this phenomenon would be the Stepney Hoard (*NFA* 456) and the Bank of Montreal Hoard (*NFA* 644).

Numismatic Finds of the Americas: a Chronological Overview

I. Early Finds.

The pre-Columbian civilizations of North and South America did not have coinage, but they did create metal objects that appear to have had some coin-like functions. The Aztecs used axe-shaped "hoe money," (*tlacas*), made of thin sheets of copper and shaped like the Greek letter *tau*; they are thought to have played some sort of monetary function, and hoards of these pieces have been found. Finds of non-coin traditional monies (such as cowries, hoe money, and wampum) have not been included in this inventory partly because of the difficulty of drawing the line between a cowry shell that served a monetary function, and one that was used as jewelry. The discoveries of ancient coins in the Americas, thought by some to be evidence of pre-Columbian contact, have been brilliantly debunked by Epstein, who shows them to be later losses by collectors.[4]

The coin evidence of contact begins with a series of tantalizing single finds—a Norse penny in Maine, a Castilian blanca on San Salvador island in the Bahamas, and English sixpences on Roanoke Island and in California, which may be related to the explorations of Leif Ericson, Christopher Columbus, Sir Walter Raleigh, and Sir Francis Drake (*NFA* 1, 2, 24, 35). More secure evidence begins with the excavations at La Isabela, in the Dominican Republic—the site of a settlement established by Columbus and abandoned by 1498—and the coins found on the site of Hernando de Soto's camp of 1539 in Tallahassee (*NFA* 3, 6). The characteristic coins of this period are the blancas of Henry IV of Spain, Portuguese ceitils, and maravedíes struck at Seville in Spain specifically for circulation in the Americas.

II. The Sixteenth Century.

When the Spanish established mints at México (1536), Santo Domingo (1542), Lima (1568), and Potosí (1573), plus a short-lived mint in Panama (1580), the output of coinage from America soared. The output from Santo Domingo was chiefly copper, although a small silver coinage is known. It was the issues in the names of Charles and his mother, the unfortunate Johanna the Mad, from the mint of México that became the predominant coinage. By 1550 a Mexican coin appears in an European hoard (*NFA* A2); by 1576 the coinage of México and Santo Domingo is depicted in the cambist by Parijs and Plantin, published in Antwerp.[5] This resulted from the discovery of vast silver mines by the Spaniards in their viceroyalties of New Spain and Peru, of which the most important was the silver mountain of Potosí.

Another innovation of this period was the fleet system to transport bullion and coinage to Spain and to the Philippines. There were two major Atlantic fleets, the New Spain fleet and the *Tierra Firme*

---

4. Jeremiah F. Epstein, "Pre-Columbian Old World Coins in America: An Examination of the Evidence," *Current Anthropology* 21, no. 1 (February 1980): 1–20.

5. Christoffel Plantin and Guillaem van Parijs, *Ordonnantie Provisonael ons Heeren des Conincx opt stuck ende Tolerantie vanden Prijs ende loop van de gouden ende silveren Munte cours ende ganck hebbende over al des C. Maiesteyts landen van herwertsover.* Antwerp: Christoffel Plantin and Guillaem van Parijs, 1576; John M. Kleeberg, "Paper Chase: The 10 Reales of Santo Domingo," *Money of the Caribbean,* ed. Richard G. Doty and John M. Kleeberg, Coinage of the Americas Conference 15 (New York: American Numismatic Society, 2006), 5–19.

fleet. The New Spain fleet was loaded at Veracruz, and then would follow the currents along the Gulf of Mexico to Havana on the island of Cuba. The silver from Peru was taken via llamas down to the ports of Callao and Arequipa, and then was transported by a Pacific fleet, called the *Armada del Sur*, to the Isthmus of Panama. Mule trains took the silver across the isthmus to two towns, Nombre de Dios (until 1596) and Portobelo (after 1596). During weeklong fairs the silver would be placed on the ships of the *Tierra Firme* fleet, which had also stopped on the coast of what is now Colombia for emeralds. The *Tierra Firme* fleet would proceed to Havana, where it would rendezvous with the New Spain fleet. Finally the joint fleets would leave Havana, pass up through the Straits of Florida between Florida and the Bahamas, and follow the Gulf Stream to Spain. At Spain they would arrive at Cadiz, and proceed up over the sandbars of Guadalquivir River to arrive at Seville, where all treasure from America had to be landed.

The other fleet system was in the Pacific, where one to three galleons a year traveled between Manila and Acapulco. The Manila galleon brought American silver to the Philippines, whence it passed across the Manila straits to China; it brought back porcelain and silks to Acapulco, which were transported by mule train across Mexico to Veracruz, where the porcelain was shipped onwards to Spain. Shipwrecks have been found from all types of fleets, although it is only with the seventeenth century that shipwreck discoveries become abundant. The most important American shipwreck of the sixteenth century is the 1554 Plate Fleet, which was wrecked off Padre Island in Texas, and was excavated in the 1960s and 1970s (*NFA* 13, 14, 15).

III. The Seventeenth Century.

In the seventeenth century, more Spanish mints were established (Cartagena and Santa Fe de Bogotá in 1622, plus the short-lived mint at Cuzco in 1698) and the fleet system operated extensively. Shipwreck evidence becomes more ample from this period with the *Atocha* (1622), *Concepción* (1641) and *Maravillas* (1656), to name only three of the most famous (*NFA* 60, 78, 100). Spain poured troops and treasure into the Netherlands in an unsuccessful attempt to defeat the revolt of 1568–1648. Much of the coin spent by Spain in the Netherlands, including much American coin, ended up in the hands of the Dutch. Three Dutch hoards of 1604–22, Ooselt, Oud-Beijerland, and Sneek, have an American component as high as a third (*NFA* A20, A22, A31). There are more hoards of coins from Spain's American colonies reported from the Dutch northern provinces, which the Spanish lost and which became the Netherlands, than there are from the southern provinces, which the Spanish retained and which became Belgium. In 1580 Spain absorbed Portugal, but neglected to maintain Portugal's vast empire in Brazil and in the East Indies. The Dutch took over both places, temporarily in Brazil, permanently in the East Indies. They supplied their far-flung empire through their own fleet system; the ships were heavily stocked with coin from the colonies of Spanish America. The Dutch East India Company ships would go down the coast of Africa to the Dutch settlement on the Cape of Good Hope. They would use the winds of the Roaring Forties in the Southern Ocean to sail east; then, just before the coast of Australia, they would make a sharp left, and head north to Batavia (now Jakarta). Some of these ships did not turn in time, rammed into Australia, and their wrecks have since been recovered. These shipwrecks include the *Batavia* (1629), the *Vergulde Draeke* (1656), and the *Zuytdorp* (1712) (*NFA* A34, A61, A90).

Spain's troubles reached their nadir in the 1640s. The assayers at Potosí secretly debased the silver coinage. Spain's commercial partners lost their trust in Spanish coinage. This led to extensive countermarking operations in Spanish America and in Antwerp (*NFA* A61, A70), and also to the first coinage in what is now the United States—the New England and the willow, oak, and pine tree shillings from the mint in Boston, Massachusetts.[6] The countermarked coins of Spanish America have been recovered from the *Capitana* (1654) and the *Maravillas* (1656)(*NFA* 93, 100). The Massachusetts silver coins are found in several notable single finds (including a New England sixpence found on Long Island, *NFA* 91), plus hoards (such as the Castine Deposit, *NFA* 178), and in shipwrecks (HMS *Feversham,* 1711, *NFA* 185; *Princess Louisa,* 1743, *NFA* A105).

IV. The Eighteenth Century.

The latter half of the seventeenth century in Europe was overshadowed by the wars of Louis XIV, and in the last decade of the century these wars affected America as well. During the War of the League of Augsburg, Massachusetts undertook an invasion of Canada, and in 1690 it paid off the returning troops with the first government-backed paper money (as opposed to banknotes) in the western world. France's worldwide ambitions had several important numismatic effects in America. One was the competitive distribution of Indian peace medals by the French, the English, and latterly the Spanish in North America, as they sought to win Indian tribes over to their side (*NFA* 317, 416). The French bid for power in North America is reflected not only in site finds from their forts and settlements in Canada and the Ohio and Mississippi valleys (*NFA* 145, 153), but also in the finds of French écus sent over to finance the fur trade (notably the Castine Deposit, *NFA* 178). Noteworthy finds from the French period include the shipwrecks *Le Chameau,* 1725(*NFA* 242), *Saint Michel,* 1745 (*NFA* 287), and *L'Auguste de Bordeaux*, 1761 (*NFA* 343).

The last war of Louis XIV was the War of the Spanish Succession (1701–13), as a result of which the Bourbons replaced the Habsburgs on the throne of Spain. The Spanish reign of the Habsburg pretender Charles III of Spain (also known as Charles VI of Austria) was confined to Barcelona, where he could count on the support of the British Royal Navy. His minting of a debased 2 reales (the pistareen) would greatly influence the monetary circulation of North America.[7] The War of the Spanish Succession interrupted treasure shipments, and the Spanish Plate Fleet of 1715 is thought to have been particularly ample because of these interruptions in the annual fleets (*NFA* 190).

The Bourbons modernized Spain. Among their reforms was the introduction of modern minting machinery in the Spanish colonies. The gradual transition to machine-struck coinage at the mint of México—from cobs to the transitional "klippes" (called in Spanish, *recortados*) to the first milled issues of 1732, and finally the milled issues from 1733—has been documented by several shipwrecks, such as those of the 1733 Plate Fleet, the *Reigersdaal,* and the *Rooswijk* (*NFA* 263, A104, A110). The Spanish also established more mints (Guatemala, Santiago de Chile, Popayán). One of the mints, Guatemala, used superannuated equipment from México, and turned out peculiar cobs with the

---

6. Philip L. Mossman, "The Potosí Scandal and the Massachusetts Mint," *Colonial Newsletter* 48, no. 2 (whole no. 137)(August 2008): 3289–3309.

7. John M. Kleeberg, "'A Coin Perfectly Familiar to Us All': The Role of the Pistareen," *Colonial Newsletter* 38, no. 3 (whole no. 109) (December 1998): 1857–77; Thomas A. Kays, "When Cross Pistareens cut their Way through the Tobacco Colonies," *Colonial Newsletter* 41, no. 1 (whole no. 116)(April 2001): 2169–99.

"dos mundos" type. Another new mint, Santiago de Chile, is important because of its output of gold coins, many recovered from *Nuestra Señora de la Luz,* which sank in 1752 (*NFA* 314).

The large output of Santiago gold may actually have been smuggled over from Brazil. The first big gold strikes were made in Brazil in the 1690s; gold production peaked in 1735–45, much of it produced in Minas Gerais. Oddly, the most extensive recovery of Brazilian 6,400 and 12,800 reis (the "joes") is from a shipwreck of the late nineteenth century, the *Douro,* which sank in 1885 (*NFA* A145).

The American Revolution was accompanied, as are most wars, with some hoarding activity (*NFA* 390). The Butternut Valley hoard, buried in connection with the military operations in upstate New York, is the most notable (*NFA* 400). After the Revolution the period of state coinages led to an increase in the number of mints—Boston, Massachusetts; New Haven, Connecticut; Rupert, Vermont; Newburgh, New York; New York City; Morristown, New Jersey; Rahway, New Jersey; Elizabeth Town, New Jersey; Baltimore, Maryland; and Annapolis, Maryland. The Stepney Hoard is the most important hoard for Confederation issues (*NFA* 456). In 1792 these mints are superseded by the Federal Mint at Philadelphia. A hoard of the last decade of the eighteenth century that shows the work of the early United States Mint is the Goodhue-Nichols find from Salem, Massachusetts, the source of many mint state draped bust large cents (*NFA* 505).

V. The Nineteenth Century.

In 1797, during the French Revolutionary Wars, Britain went off the gold standard, but by revaluing the 8 reales upwards to keep them in the country pegged the pound sterling to the Spanish dollar. The importance of the Spanish-American dollar in the British Isles in this period is evidenced by the Wellington Bridge hoard in Ireland (*NFA* A131). In 1811 this supply of silver was cut off when the War of Independence broke out in Mexico. A large hoard of the copper coins of Morelos documents the War of Independence (*NFA* 566). The Mexican War of Independence led to the establishment of numerous branch mints to supply the armies, many of which continued to flourish after independence. A similar proliferation of mints happened as Central and South America won their independence. The centralized mint system of colonial New Spain and Peru would not be re-established.

The British attempt to enforce their blockade of France led to conflict with the United States, which cut off the British supply of planchets to the United States mint, and led to an interruption in the coinage of cents, so there are no cents dated 1815. A coin find from the War of 1812 is the coins found after Indian village of Thame in Upper Canada was burnt down by the United States forces (*NFA* 563).

The West Indies had a very complex coinage, involving the cutting and counterstamping of Mexican 8 reales and Brazilian joes. As possession of the islands changed hands during the Napoleonic Wars, the French, British, and Dutch regularly cut and counterstamped the coinage. Two hoards, one from Montserrat, another from Bell's Jetty, Dominica, document this process (*NFA* 528, 536).

The United States operated a centralized minting system until the discovery of gold in the southern Appalachian Mountains in Georgia and in North Carolina led local jewelers to begin minting their own coins: these were the coins of Templeton Reid and the Bechtlers. The Treasury set up branch mints at Charlotte, North Carolina and Dahlonega, Georgia (both opened 1838) to compete with the private mints. A third southern branch mint was at New Orleans. The discovery of gold in California led to the establishment of, first, private assayers, and, subsequently, the San Francisco branch mint in 1854. This process is reflected in finds from the *Central America,* 1857(*NFA* 707).

A rich category of hoards comprises those associated with the United States Civil War. A hoard found at Natural Bridge, Virginia, is thought to have been buried just before the Union general David Hunter's raid in June 1864 (*NFA* 752). A hoard found at Fort Leonard Wood, Missouri, in November 1962 is believed to be the treasure of Wilson M. Tilley, who made much money trafficking in mules during the Civil War and who was killed by bushwhackers prior to a Confederate invasion of Missouri in September 1864 (*NFA* 753). A hoard from Columbia, South Carolina, was deposited shortly before the city was captured and burnt in February 1865 (*NFA* 756).

The discovery of the huge silver supplies in Nevada (the Comstock and Bonanza lodes) led to the establishment of the Carson City mint in 1870. It shut down because of the financial crisis prompted by bimetallism in 1893. The large production of silver dollars, required by the Bland-Allison Act, led to the amassing of hundreds of millions of the coins in Federal government vaults, the largest coin accumulation ever put together in the United States. This was then dispersed in the 1960s, 1970s, and 1980. A separate section in this inventory discusses this accumulation of silver dollars (Part II).

VI. The Twentieth Century.

The most important hoarding phenomenon in the Americas in the twentieth century was the hoarding of gold in the United States following the stock market crash of 1929, which was made illegal by the gold turn in order issued by Franklin D. Roosevelt in 1933. The hoard evidence shows that this law was widely flouted (*NFA* 884, 887).

A study of the law reports and the newspapers shows that huge hoards continue to be formed in the late twentieth and early twenty-first centuries, often by the illicit drug trade or to evade the income tax.[8] Most of these hoards are composed of paper currency. In the law reports, however, the notes are described in little detail, with merely the cash total mentioned. Where little revealing detail is reported, the hoards have been omitted from this inventory.

Previous Studies of American Coin Finds and Sources

American coin finds have been of interest to numismatists from the very beginning of numismatic study in the United States. This is clear from the fine reports of coin finds in a nineteenth century antiquarian periodical, the *Historical Magazine*.[9] The literature has grown to be vast and dispersed.

Sydney P. Noe, who contributed much to the study of ancient coin hoards, also wrote about United States hoards, including the Economite hoard and the Castine Deposit.[10] Noe's work was built upon by Walter Breen, who published two articles listing United States coin hoards in the *Numismatist* in

---

8. James LeMoyne, "Talk of a Puerto Rico Town: Buried Treasure, No Kidding," *New York Times,* April 18, 1990; "Goods Linked to Drugs are Seized by Agents," *New York Times,* May 12, 1990.

9. William Elliot Woodward, "Numismatic Notes—Pine Tree Money." *Historical Magazine* 7, no. 10 (October 1863): 318–19.

10. Sydney Phillip Noe, *Coin Hoards,* Numismatic Notes and Monographs 1 (New York: American Numismatic Society, 1920), 41–44, 46; *The Castine Deposit: An American Hoard,* Numismatic Notes and Monographs 100, (New York: American Numismatic Society, 1942).

1950.[11] In 1997, Q. David Bowers published a work on coin hoards from the United States.[12] It built upon the work of Breen and on hoards published in the *Numismatist* and the *American Journal of Numismatics*. The distinctions between this work and Bowers may be summarized as follows. This work includes single finds, Bowers as a rule does not; this work includes non-USA coins found in the Americas, Bowers as a rule does not; this work includes finds in all the Americas, Bowers only covers the USA; this work includes American coins found outside the Americas, Bowers does not. There are also a number of hoards in Bowers that this inventory does not include, such as large accumulations of Lincoln cents. Those hoards have been omitted because they do not tell us much about the history of the period. This inventory uses a concise, standardized, chronological arrangement, modeled after the *Inventory of Greek Coin Hoards*,[13] as opposed to the topical and discursive approach used by Bowers.

In his *Encyclopedia*, published in 1988, Walter Breen mentioned numerous hoards in the catalog listings.[14] When the Breen/Bland/Borckardt *Encyclopedia* of early date large cents came out in 2001, Del Bland's pedigree information made it possible to determine if the hoards reported by Breen were confirmed by the provenance of large cents.[15] If the cents came from a hoard, the higher-grade specimens should trace their provenance to a common source. Except for the well-documented Goodhue-Nichols find (*NFA* 505), none of Breen's hoards could be confirmed by the pedigree information. Breen seems to have attributed the prevalence of many high-grade coins of a particular variety to the existence of hoards, when there are many other possible explanations (such as better mint quality control with that particular variety). Most hoards for which the only evidence is Breen's 1988 *Encyclopedia* have accordingly been omitted. Some hoards in Breen's 1950 articles, such as the "Hidden Find," likewise have been omitted because they could not be verified.

This inventory is based on five different groups of sources—the numismatic literature, the shipwreck literature, the archaeological literature, law reports, and newspapers.

Numismatic literature was covered by reading through most of the major United States numismatic periodicals. The major source for American coin finds is the *Numismatist,* although many other periodicals, such as the *American Journal of Numismatics,* the *Canadian Antiquarian and Numismatic Journal,* the *Canadian Numismatic Journal,* both series of the *Coin Collector's Journal,* the *Historical Magazine,* and the *Numismatic Scrapbook Magazine* are also useful. Other sources, such as auction catalogs and monographs (plus the periodical *Coin Hoards* and the periodical bibliography *Numismatic Literature*), were also examined. F. Gordon Frost tracked down and supplied much of

---

11. Walter Breen, "Survey of American Coin Hoards," *Numismatist* 65, no. 1 (January 1952): 7–24; 65, no. 10 (October 1952): 1005–10.

12. Q. David Bowers, *American Coin Treasures and Hoards* (Wolfeboro, NH: Bowers and Merena Galleries, 1997).

13. Margaret Thompson, Otto Mørkholm, and Colin M. Kraay, eds. *An Inventory of Greek Coin Hoards* (New York: American Numismatic Society, 1973).

14. Walter Breen, *Walter Breen's Complete Encyclopedia of U.S. and Colonial Coins* (New York: F.C.I. Press/Doubleday, 1988). For an example of one such hoard that could not be confirmed, see the hoard of large cents, varieties S-289 and S-290, on page 201 (Breen 1783 and 1784).

15. Walter Breen, Del Bland, and Mark Borckardt, *Walter Breen's Encyclopedia of Early United States Cents, 1793–1814* (Wolfeboro, NH: Bowers and Merena Galleries, 2000).

the shipwreck literature.[16] Archaeological literature was accessed by reading through *Archaeology* magazine to prepare a list of researchers in the field, and then searching Columbia University Library and the New York Public Library for works by those authors. The major source among the newspapers was the *New York Times*, because it has been indexed since 1851. Other indices were also consulted, such as the *Canadian Periodicals Index* and the *Reader's Guide to Periodical Literature*, and indices to other newspapers such as the *St. Louis Post-Dispatch*, the *New York Tribune*, the *New York Evening Post*, and the *Brooklyn Daily Eagle*. The legal literature was accessed by looking through digests under the law of finds and treasure trove. This inventory exploits all these sources more thoroughly than has ever been done before.

Finds in Canada were comparatively easy to locate because of the Canadian numismatic periodicals, the *Canadian Periodicals Index,* and the Canadian numismatic bibliography of Daryl Atchison. Finds in the Americas, outside of the United States and Canada, have been more difficult to track down. There are several Latin American numismatic periodicals, but the coverage is by no means as comprehensive as is the case in Canada and the United States. The major lack is the absence of newspaper indices like that for the *New York Times,* since newspapers are the primary source of information about coin finds. The coverage outside of Canada and the United States is thus more haphazard.

Arrangement

The Inventory is divided into three parts: in the first part are finds of all types in the Americas, in the second part the dispersal of the accumulation by the USA federal government of silver dollars, and in the third part finds of American numismatic items, found outside the Americas. Finds in the first part are designated by simple Hindu-Arabic numerals, dispersals in the second part by Roman numerals, finds in the third part by Hindu-Arabic numerals plus the letter "A" as a prefix.

Each entry begins with the *type of find:* single find, hoard, shipwreck, or archaeological excavation. The type of find can refer either to the circumstances of deposition (hoard, shipwreck) or the method of recovery (archaeological excavation). The coins found in archaeological excavations were usually deposited in the same manner as most single finds, i.e., accidental losses rather than the intentional deposition of a hoard. The intentional discarding of counterfeits also forms a major component of the archaeological record.

The finds are ordered by the date of deposit. The term "date of deposit" is used instead of burial date, since modern hoards are often concealed by methods other than burial. For archaeological excavations, the date of the occupation of the site is used, or, if that extensively antedates the coins, the date of the earliest coin found. The entries are modeled on the *Inventory of Greek Coin Hoards,*

---

16. Examples are: Robert F. Burgess and Carl Clausen, *Gold, Galleons and Archaeology: A History of the 1715 Spanish Plate Fleet and the True Story of the Great Florida Treasure Find* (Indianapolis: Bobbs-Merrill, 1976); Mendel Peterson, *The Funnel of Gold* (Boston: Little Brown, 1975); John S. Potter, Jr., *The Treasure Diver's Guide,* revised ed. (New York: Bonanza, 1972); Sydney Wignall, *In Search of Spanish Treasure. A Diver's Story* (Newton Abbot, England: David & Charles, 1982). The literature is now much more accessible thanks to two bibliographies prepared by David S. Crooks: David S. Crooks, *Bibliography of Sunken Treasure Books* (Clarendon Hills, Illinois: the Author, 2002); David S. Crooks, *Important Shipwreck Auction Catalogs* (Clarendon Hills, Illinois: the Author, 2004).

although the coins are described in more detail, because the underlying sources can be difficult to access. The *Inventory of Greek Coin Hoards* mentions if a hoard is a "pot hoard"; this inventory includes an entry on the container, if any. Each find is referred to by its location (city, state or province, country) and the date of finding, so far as that is known. If the date of finding is not known, then the date of reporting (often the month and year of the periodical where the hoard is mentioned) is used instead.

There can be a lag of several months before a report in local newspapers is published in a national magazine, such as the *Numismatist*. A comparison of ten instances where newspaper reports and reports in the *Numismatist* have been located for the same hoard shows that, assuming that the publication date of the *Numismatist* is the first day of the month, this lag extends from as few as nineteen days to (exceptionally) as many as 117 days (the next longest lag is forty-eight days). The median number of days is thirty-six. Thus if a hoard is reported in, say, the *Numismatist* for November 1926, the researcher in local newspapers should begin looking at the local newspaper for October 31, 1926, and work backwards; the hoard should be reported by the time the researcher reaches the issue for September 12, 1926; to be certain that the researcher has not missed anything, the search should be extended back to the issue of June 16, 1926.

The next entry is the number of items of each material (copper, silver, gold, paper); then the date of deposit. The date of deposit is usually arrived at from the coin with the latest date, or, as some numismatists say, the coin that "closes" the hoard. (Single finds are usually listed at the date of the coin; a 1784 8 reales will be found with the finds from 1784, even though such a coin may have been lost at any time well into the nineteenth century.) Since, however, there are often well-documented historical circumstances that suggest the reason for the burial of the hoard (such as the movements of Confederate or Union armies during the Civil War), this date of deposit has often been used instead. Where the date of deposit is the coin with the latest date, the hoard could have been deposited years later. The date of deposit is often not a precise date, but a *terminus post quem*; and the date of finding, likewise, not a precise date but a *terminus ante quem*. This is then followed by a detailed description of the find, plus the disposition, if known. Bibliographical references conclude each entry. The bibliographical entries do not include every mention of the find (in some cases, such as the *Atocha*, to list every mention would result in a huge book), but the three or five most important, occasionally more if the references are especially interesting. Most sources are referred to by the author-date system, with full entries found in the reference list at the end; however, short articles in the *Numismatist*, the *Numismatic Scrapbook Magazine*, the *New York Times* and other popular publications that are referred to only once are entered in full in the entry referring to the find and omitted from the reference list.

Where a hoard appears to be genuine, but incorrectly described, the description has been amended. An example of this is a report of 3,000 Spanish silver coins, dated from 1763 to 1805, which "included in the find an American silver dollar bearing the date 1804 with the likeness of George Washington." Bowers points out that this is the ultimate rarity, an 1804 dollar showing Washington rather than Liberty.[17] This inventory asks the question, "Is this a real hoard that has been described incorrectly, and if so, what genuine coin could be mistaken for an 1804 dollar with Washington?" The

---

17. Q. David Bowers, *American Coin Treasures and Hoards* (Wolfeboro, NH: Bowers and Merena Galleries, 1997), 405.

conclusion is that Charles IV of Spain does have a distant resemblance to George Washington, and that a Mexican 8 reales of 1804 was described as a United States silver dollar of that year with George Washington on it (*NFA* 535). Similarly, gold hoards of United States coins where the oldest coin is reported as dated 1830 have been corrected to 1834 because people tend to round off numbers (*NFA* 717, 724, 739, 803). These emendations are mentioned in the text. Incomplete descriptions, such as "Spanish silver coin," have been filled out by inserting the name of the likeliest casual loss of the period—e.g., Spanish colonies, ½ real, México. These additions are also mentioned in the text.

Geographical Coverage

In Canada, finds have been reported from the provinces of British Columbia, New Brunswick, Newfoundland and Labrador, Nova Scotia, Ontario, Prince Edward Island, Québec, and Saskatchewan, plus the Northwest Territories and the Nunavut Territory. Finds have been reported from every single one of the fifty states composing the United States of America, except for three: Hawaii, Oklahoma, and Wyoming. In the Caribbean, finds have been reported from the British Virgin Islands, Cuba, Dominica, the Dominican Republic, Haiti, Jamaica, Montserrat, Puerto Rico, and the U.S. Virgin Islands. Among American islands in the Atlantic, finds have been reported from the Bahamas and Bermuda. Finds have been reported from all the mainland countries of Central and South America, except for Belize, Bolivia, British Guyana, French Guyana, Honduras, Paraguay, and Surinam.

Despite this extensive coverage, many gaps remain to be filled, particularly from outside the United States. Comparatively few coin finds have been reported from Latin America. The rich and complex history of Latin America, especially after independence, could usefully be supplemented by hoard evidence.

Outside the Americas, the geographical coverage reflects the extensive circulation of the coins of Spain's American colonies in littoral countries, plus numerous shipwreck recoveries. Finds have been reported from Australia, Belarus, Belgium, Bulgaria, the Cape Verde Islands, China, France, Germany, Greece, Ireland, Italy, Kenya, Latvia, Luxembourg, Mauritius, Mozambique, Namibia, the Netherlands, Norway, the Philippines, Poland, Portugal (that is, Madeira rather than mainland Portugal), Russia, Serbia, South Africa, Spain, Sri Lanka, Turkey, the Ukraine, the United Kingdom, and Vietnam. Particularly valuable series of hoard reports are due to the assiduousness of H. Enno Van Gelder, Pablo I. de Jesus, and Felipe Mateu y Llopis, who compiled hoard reports for the Netherlands, the Philippines and Spain respectively.[18]

---

18. Van Gelder: Enno Van Gelder, "Muntvondsten: De vondst Sneek 1947," *Jaarboek voor Munt- en Penningkunde* 41 (1954): 112–14; Enno Van Gelder, "Muntvondsten: Raamsdonk 1967 en Raamsdonk 1970," *Jaarboek voor Munt-en Penningkunde* 56/57 (1969/70): 159–66; De Jesus: Pablo I. de Jesus, "Buried Hoard in Manila's Walled City," *Numismatist* 65, no. 11 (November 1952): 1082–90; Pablo I. de Jesus, "Cavite Coin Hoard," *Philippine Numismatic Monographs* 15 (1965): 1–6. Mateu y Llopis: Felipe Mateu y Llopis, "Hallazgos Monetarios (IV)," *Ampurias. Revista de Arqueología, Prehistoria y Etnología* 7–8 (1945–46): 233–76; Felipe Mateu y Llopis, "Hallazgos Monetarios (XIX)," *Numario Hispánico* 10 (1961): 141–61.

Acknowledgements

Many people have helped the author greatly in compiling this book, and the author would like to single out two: Q. David Bowers and Oliver Hoover, for they both shared with the author their own research notes into the same field. This was extraordinarily generous. Len Augsburger, likewise, shared his work on the Baltimore Gold Hoard when it was still in manuscript. Dave Ginsburg also shared his primary source materials from his research on the Kerens, Texas gold hoard. Philip Mossman read over the manuscript and made many helpful suggestions. Sarah E. Cox obtained a reference from a library to which the author did not have access, and retraced her steps when the first reference the author had supplied turned out to be incorrect.

The author would further like to thank the following individuals for their assistance and suggestions: Robert Apuzzo, Carmen Arnold-Biucchi, Len Augsburger, Michael L. Bates, Armando Bernardelli, Larry Bolyer, Q. David Bowers, Jeremiah D. Brady, F. Carl Braun, Katarina Briggler, Theodore V. Buttrey, Jr., Francis D. Campbell, Tony Carlotto, Sarah E. Cox, Howard A. Daniel III, Henry Ditmer, Richard G. Doty, Penelope B. Drooker, Michael J. Druck, Leigh Eckmair (Town of Butternuts historian), Leslie A. Elam, Joseph Ettle (Collections Manager, Museum of Science and History, Corpus Christi, Texas), Chris Faulkner, Harold M. Forbes (Associate Curator, West Virginia and Regional History Collection, West Virginia University), F. Gordon Frost, Jay Galst, Dave Ginsburg, Ira Goldberg, Paul M. Green, Henry Grünthal, Howard W. Herz, Robert Wilson Hoge, Wayne Homren, William S. Kable, Jonathan K. Kern, Jennifer L. Kolb (Deputy Director, Wisconsin Historical Museum), John Kraljevich, James Lamb, Joseph Lasser, Frank J. Leon (Federal Reserve Bank, Charlotte, North Carolina), John Lorenzo, Ally McClure, Robert Martin, Andrew Meadows, William E. Metcalf, Philip L. Mossman, Eric P. Newman, Oliver Hoover, William Panitch, Donald G. Partrick, Normand Pépin, Francesca Pitaro (Consulting Archivist, Port Washington Public Library), Arent Pol, Merle Pribbenow, Mike Ringo, Andrea Saccocci, Daniel Frank Sedwick, Wayne Shelby, William Spengler, Alan M. Stahl, Elena Stolyarik, Jesse Teitelbaum (Executive Director, Luzerne County Historical Society), Anthony J. Terranova, Diana di Zerega Wall, Jann Wenner, Byron Weston, and Müşerref Yetim, and the following institutions: the American Numismatic Society, especially its library; Florida Bureau of Archaeological Research (David Dickel, Irina T. Franklin); Florida Master Site File (Vincent Birdsong, Ginny L. Jones); Peabody Museum of Archaeology and Ethnology, Harvard University (Scott A. Templin); the library of the Université de Montréal; the Law Library of the New York University School of Law; the libraries of Columbia University, especially Butler Library, Avery Library, and the Diamond Library of the Law School; and the New York Public Library, especially the microfilm and the Local History divisions.

Abbreviations and Mintmarks

United States Mintmarks

C – Charlotte
CC – Carson City
D – Dahlonega (1838–61)
D – Denver (1906 to present)
O – New Orleans
S – San Francisco
No mintmark – Philadelphia
USAOG – United States Assay Office of Gold, San Francisco

French Mintmarks

A – Paris	M – Toulouse	X – Amiens
B – Rouen	N – Montpellier	Y – Bourges
C – Caen	O – Riom	Z – Grenoble
D – Lyons	P – Dijon	AA – Metz
E – Tours	Q – Perpignan	BB – Strasbourg
G – Poitiers	R – Orléans	CC (addorsed) – Besançon
H – La Rochelle	S – Reims	& – Aix
I – Limoges	T – Nantes	9 – Rennes
K – Bordeaux	V – Troyes	baquette (cow) – Pau
L – Bayonne	W – Lille	

Spanish Assayers

Letter abbreviations for Spanish coins are the names of the assayers. Only initials are used in this listing. The names and the dates of the assayers before milled coinage are listed in these references:

Frank and Daniel Sedwick, *The Practical Book of Cobs*. 4th ed. (Winter Park, FL: the authors, 2007).

Sewall Menzel, *Cobs, Pieces of Eight and Treasure Coins: the Early Spanish-American Mints and their Coinages, 1536–1773* (New York: American Numismatic Society, 2004).

Material Abbreviations

AE, bronze or copper; AR, silver; AV, gold; B, brass; BI, billon; NB, nickel-brass; NI, nickel; P, paper; PB, lead; SN, tin; ZN, zinc.

Other Abbreviations

ND, no date; NDA, no date or assayer.

Part I

Numismatic Finds in the Americas

1. Indian site near Bar Harbor, Brooklin, Blue Hill Bay, Hancock County, Maine, USA, 1961.

Type of find: Archaeological excavation.

Date of site: Ca. 1100?

Contents: 1 AR.

Description: Norway, Olaf III Kyrre, silver penny, [1065–80].

If the date of deposit does indeed precede 1492, this is numismatic evidence for Norse/Indian contact in the eleventh century.

Disposition: Found in shell and bone midden by Guy Mellgren, an amateur archaeologist. Donated to the Maine State Museum, Augusta, Maine.

Bibliography: McKusick and Wahlgren 1980; Rolde 1995; Seaby 1978.

"Coin May Prove Norsemen Beat Columbus to America," *Numismatist* 92, no. 1 (January 1979): 65.

"Expert Says Maine Find Is Genuine Norse Coin," *New York Times,* February 8, 1979, A16.

2. Long Bay, San Salvador (Watling Island), the Bahamas, 1986.

Type of find: Archaeological excavations on what may be the site of Columbus's first landfall.

Date of site: Thought to be October 1492.

Contents: 1 BI.

Description:

Spanish states, Castile and Leon, Henry IV, blanca [1471–74]

Bibliography: Brill 1987, 255–57.

3. La Isabela, Dominican Republic, 1992–93.

Type of find: Archaeological excavation.

Date of site: 1494–98.

Contents: 74 BI, 4 AR. Subsequently, more coins were recovered so that total rose to 112 coins; of these, 109 coins were attributed, breaking down 104 BI, 5 AR.

Description: The attributions of the earlier 78 coins recovered were:

Italian states, Aquilea, Louis II of Teck, soldo

Italian states, Genoa, 15th century, minuto

Spanish states, Navarre, Catherine I and John II d'Albret, ½ blanca

Spanish states, Castile and Leon, Anonymous issue, late 13th century, seisén

Spanish states, Castile and Leon, Henry IV, blancas (60): Avila (13); Burgos; Cuenca (5); Coruña (2); Segovia (5); Seville (16); Toledo (9); uncertain mint (9)

Spanish states, Castile and Leon, Henry IV, ½ reales (2)

Spanish states, Castile and Leon, Henry IV, real

Spanish states, Castile and Leon, Ferdinand and Isabella, ½ real

Portugal, Alphonse V, ceitil (5)

Portugal, John II, ceitil

Unidentified (4)

Other numismatic objects recovered were:

Spanish states, Castile and Leon, Henry IV, blanca, lead counterfeit (attributed as a token, but more likely a counterfeit)

Coin weights (2)

German states, Nuremberg, jetons (2)

Bibliography: Deagan 1992; Deagan and Cruxent 2002a, b; Stahl 1992, Stahl 1993–4.

4. El Mango, on the Cañada Honda Farm of the United Fruit Company, near Barrio Mulas, Cuba, summer 1941.

Type of find: Archaeological excavation.

Date of site: 1400–1600; date of earliest coin, 1505–10.

Contents: 1 AE.

Description:
Spain, Ferdinand and Isabella, maravedí, Seville, 1505–10, struck for Santo Domingo
The denomination is uncertain, since the dimensions of the coin were not provided.

Bibliography: Rouse 1942, 70.

5. El Yayal, Almirantes Region, Báguanos Municipality, Holgún Province, Cuba, 1930 and 1935.

Type of find: Archaeological excavation.

Date of site: 1450–1550.

Contents: 3 AE, 1 AR.

Description:
Portugal, ceitil
Spain, Ferdinand and Isabella, 4 maravedíes, Seville, struck for Santo Domingo
Spanish colonies, Charles and Johanna, 4 maravedíes, Santo Domingo [1542–56] (2)

Disposition: 3 coins were found by J. A. García Castañeda in 1935. What was probably a 4 maravedíes of Santo Domingo (it is not adequately described) was found by Ernesto Segeth in 1930. The artifacts found by Segeth were bought by the Museo Montané of the Universidad Nacional de Cuba before 1938. In 1962 García Castañeda donated the artifacts he had found to the Colección de Piezas Arqueológicas of the Academia de Ciencías de Cuba.

Bibliography: Domínguez 1995; García 1938.

6. Tallahassee, Florida, USA, May 1987.

Type of find: Archaeological excavation.

Date of site: October 1539–March 1540 (De Soto's winter camp at Anhaica, a city of the Apalachees).

Contents: 2 AE, 3 BI.

Description:
Spain, 4 maravedíes, Seville, 1505–10, struck for Santo Domingo
Spain, maravedí, 1505–17
Portugal, Alphonse V, ceitil [1438–81]
Portugal, John II, Manuel or John III, ceitil [1481–1557]
Portugal, John III, ceitil [1521–57]

Bibliography: Ewen and Hann, 1998, 80–81.

7. Puerto Rico, USA, October 1933.

Type of find: Hoard.

Date of deposit: 1542.

Contents: 27 AE.

Description:
Spanish colonies, 4 maravedíes, Santo Domingo, [1542–56] (27)

Disposition: Mrs. E. H. Wildmon; donated in 1933 to the American Numismatic Society in New York, accession number 1933.92.

8. Santo Domingo, Dominican Republic, December 1920.

Type of find: Hoard.

Date of deposit: 1542.

Contents: 3 AE.

Description:
Spanish colonies, 4 maravedíes, Santo Domingo, [1542–56] (3)

Disposition: F. Munro Endicott; donated to the American Numismatic Society in New York, December 14, 1920, item numbers 1920.205.14-16.

9. Dominican Republic, August 24, 1964.

Type of find: Hoard.

Date of deposit: 1542.

Contents: 424 AE.

Description:

Spanish colonies, 4 maravedíes, Santo Domingo, [1542–56] (424)

Disposition: Found after the Dominican Republic was hit by Hurricane Cleo in 1964. Exported into the United States numismatic market, according to W. A. Selfridge, a numismatist of New York City.

Bibliography: "424 4-Maravedis of Charles and Johanna Uncovered by Hurricane," *Numismatic Scrapbook Magazine* 33, no. 11 (November 1967): 2077.

10. Puerto Real, Habitation Montholon, Haiti, 1979–86.

Type of find: Archaeological excavation.

Date of site: 1503–78; date of earliest coins, 1542.

Contents: 560 AE, 2 AR.

Description:

Spanish colonies, 4 maravedíes, Santo Domingo, [1542–56] (560)

Spanish colonies, Charles and Johanna, reales, probably Santo Domingo (2)

Bibliography: Deagan 1995.

11. Sabana Seca, Puerto Rico, USA, December 1996–May 1997.

Type of find: Archaeological excavation.

Date of site: 1542?

Contents: 2 AE.

Description:

Spanish colonies, 4 maravedíes, Santo Domingo [1542–56] (2)

Bibliography: Michael B. Hornum, letter to John M. Kleeberg, May 9, 1997.

12. Taylor Mound, Lawrence Plantation, Saint Simon's Island, Georgia, USA, summer 1971.

Type of find: Funerary deposit.

Date of site: 1540–60.

Contents: 9 AE.

Description:

Spanish colonies, Charles and Johanna, 4 maravedíes, Santo Domingo [1542–56] (6)

Spanish colonies, Charles and Johanna, 4 maravedíes, México [1536–42] (3)

The coins were holed in the center and around their circumference; they had probably been used to decorate a cap.

Bibliography: Pearson 1977.

13. Padre Island, Texas, USA, 1870 and August 1951.

Type of find: Shipwreck. Beach finds on Padre Island from the offshore wrecks of the 1554 plate fleet. This entry comprises finds not attributed to a specific ship. The finds specifically ascribed to the *Espíritu Santo* and the *San Esteban* are in the next two entries.

Sank: April 1554.

Contents: 32+ AR.

Description:

Spanish colonies, Charles and Johanna, 2 reales, México, assayer L

Spanish colonies, Charles and Johanna, 4 reales, México, assayer L

Disposition: In the year 1870 coins, including 2 reales and 4 reales of assayer L, were found on the beach by William Headen; examples of both denominations were given to General Meigs, who donated them in 1883 to the Cabinet of the United States Mint. As of 2007, two coins that correspond to the above descriptions, with a patina characteristic of sea salvage, are in the Smithsonian, where the Mint collection has been since 1923.

In August 1951 Louis Rawalt, then aged 62, found 29 Spanish coins on the beach.

Bibliography: Dubois 1884, 90; Sedwick and Sedwick 2007, 152 (Sedwick 2).

"Discoveries on Padre Island," *American Journal of Numismatics* 5, no. 1 (July 1870): 9 (citing the *New Orleans Picayune*).

"Boat Found After Flood Believed 200 Years Old," *New York Times*, August 3, 1951, 38.

Numismatic Scrapbook Magazine 36, no. 1 (January 1970): 108.

Richard G. Doty, e-mail message to John M. Kleeberg, March 15, 2007.

14. Padre Island, Texas, USA, 1967.

Type of find: Shipwreck.

Ship: Espíritu Santo.

Sank: April 1554.

Contents: 786 AR.

Description: Spanish colonies, coins of Charles and Johanna, México, summarized in the following table:

Assayer	2 reales	3 reales	4 reales
R	1	1	4
G	4		1
P	9		
G with water	7		39
S, R, and A	3		19
L	98		600

A non-Mexican coin was also recovered:

Spanish colonies, Charles and Johanna, 4 reales, Santo Domingo, assayer F

The specific numbers of coins of the "with water" series (assayers S, G, R, A, L) in the table are estimates, because the archaeological report states the number of each denomination, and the number of each assayer, but does not break down the assayer/denomination combinations.

Disposition: Artifacts studied at the Texas Archaeological Research Laboratory during litigation with the treasure salvors (Platoro of Gary, Indiana). After extensive litigation, the salvors were awarded the value of the find; the artifacts remained in possession of the State of Texas. As of 2007, the artifacts are held by the Museum of Science and History, Corpus Christi, Texas, USA.

This ship was one of four in this fleet, which contained 2 million pesos in total. One shipwreck, the *Santa María de Yciar*, was destroyed in the 1940s when the channel was dredged; one ship escaped to Havana; the two other wrecks have been excavated.

Bibliography: Keith 1988, 53; Olds 1976, 109–19; Sedwick and Sedwick 2007, 152 (Sedwick 2); Smith 1988, 89.

Joseph Ettle, Collections Manager, Museum of Science and History, Corpus Christi, Texas, USA, letter to John M. Kleeberg, March 27, 2007.

15. Padre Island, Texas, USA, 1972, 1973, and 1975.

Type of find: Shipwreck.

Ship: San Estebán.

Sank: April 1554.

Contents: 1 AE, 327 AR.

Description: Spanish colonies, coins of Charles and Johanna, México, summarized in the following table:

Assayer	Real	2 reales	4 reales
R		2	
P			1
S		2	4
G with water		14	4
R		4	
A		5	
L	1	59	162
Unknown		28	38

Spanish colonies, Charles and Johanna, 4 maravedíes, Santo Domingo

Spanish colonies, Charles and Johanna, 4 reales, Santo Domingo, assayer F

Spain, Ferdinand and Isabella, real, Seville

Also included 37 silver disks, one gold bar,

and 362 unidentified fragments of silver, some of which may have been coins.

This ship was one of four in this fleet, which contained 2 million pesos in total. One shipwreck, the *Santa María de Yciar*, was destroyed in the 1940s when the channel was dredged; one ship escaped to Havana; the two other wrecks have been excavated.

Disposition: Artifacts studied and published by the Texas Archaeological Research Laboratory. As of 2007, the artifacts are held by the Museum of Science and History, Corpus Christi, Texas, USA.

Bibliography: Arnold and Weddle 1978; Sedwick and Sedwick 2007, 152 (Sedwick 2).

Joseph Ettle, Collections Manager, Museum of Science and History, Corpus Christi, Texas, USA, letter to John M. Kleeberg, March 27, 2007.

16. Spruce Creek, a tributary of the Halifax River, East Florida, USA, winter 1871.

Type of find: Funerary deposit.

Date of deposit: 1550s?

Contents: 3 AR.

Description:

Spanish colonies, Charles and Johanna, real, México (2)

Spanish colonies, Charles and Johanna, 4 reales, México

Excavation of an Indian burial mound. One of the reales was resting in the eye socket of a skull, evidently a "Charon's obol."

Numerous Spanish ships were wrecked on Florida in the sixteenth century; the coins from these wrecks were salvaged by the Indians. Early European explorers in Florida found that the Indians wore gold and silver ornaments, and shipwrecks are thought to have been where the Indians obtained the metal.

Disposition: Frossard wrote: "Mr. G. F. McComb of Lockport, N.Y., has in his possession a 4 reales piece of Carlo and Joanna, struck in México at an early date, and discovered in a Florida Indian Mound."

Bibliography: S. C. C., of Jamaica Plain, Massachusetts, "Opening of a Burial Mound in Florida," *American Journal of Numismatics* 6, no. 1 (July 1871): 16.

Édouard Frossard, "Items of Interest," *Numisma* 4, no. 1 (January 1880): [7].

17. Indian Mound at Bear Point, Perdido Bay, Baldwin County, Alabama, USA 1901.

Type of find: Funerary deposit.

Contents: 1 AR.

Description:

Spanish colonies, Charles and Johanna, real?, México

Found in Burial Number 30 in an Indian mound by Clarence Bloomfield Moore.

Disposition: Moore's collections, originally kept in Philadelphia, were subsequently donated to the Museum of the American Indian (now in Washington, DC).

Bibliography: Moore 1901, 426.

18. Emanuel Point, Pensacola, Florida, USA, October 1992–95.

Type of find: Shipwreck.

Ship: Thought to be one of the ships of the expedition of Tristan de Luna.

Sank: September 19, 1559.

Contents: 1 BI.

Description:

Spanish states, Castile and Leon, Henry IV, blanca [1471–74]

Bibliography: Smith et al. 1995, 117.

19. Henry County, Alabama, USA, June 1984.

Type of find: Single find.

Contents: 1 AR.

Description:
Spanish colonies, Charles and Johanna, 4 reales, México, assayer O [1564–72], holed
The suggestion that this coin was deposited as a result of the Tristan de Luna expedition (1559–61) is not possible, since assayer O is now thought to have been active only from 1564 onwards.
Bibliography: Smith 1984.

20. Saint Augustine, Florida, USA, 1976–79.
Type of find: Archaeological excavation.
Date of site: 1565–1600.
Contents: 1 AE.
Description: Spain, maravedí
Disposition: Florida State University.
Bibliography: Deagan 1980.

21. Parris Island, South Carolina, USA, 1979–85.
Type of find: Archaeological excavation of the site of the Spanish settlement of Santa Elena.
Date of site: 1566–87.
Contents: 1 AR.
Description: Spain, Ferdinand and Isabella, ½ real
The coin is in very poor condition, so the identification is not entirely certain. Clearly a Spanish coin, because the upper quadrant with the castle for Castile is visible, but little else.
Disposition: Excavated by Stanley South.
Bibliography: Judge 1988.

22. South of Savannah, Georgia, USA, November 1993.
Type of find: Single find.
Date of deposit: 1570s?
Contents: 1 AR.
Description: Spain, Ferdinand and Isabella, real
A date of deposit of the 1570s has been chosen on the grounds that the coin would most likely have been lost after the establishment of Saint Augustine in 1565.
Bibliography: Coin World, November 22, 1993, 1, 8.

23. Bayahá, Fort Liberté Bay, Haiti, 1982.
Type of find: Archaeological excavation.
Date of site: 1578–1605.
Contents: 9 AE.
Description: Spanish colonies, 4 maravedíes, Santo Domingo [1542–56] (9)
Bibliography: Deagan 1995.

24. Thirty Miles north of San Francisco, California, USA, November 1974.
Type of find: Archaeological excavation.
Date of site: June 1579.
Contents: 1 B, 1 AR.
Description:
German states, Nuremberg, jeton, 1577
England, Elizabeth I, sixpence, 1567
The coin was found during archaeological excavation of the Olompali Miwok Indian site on the floor of an Indian dance house by Charles Slaymaker, who suggested that the coin had been left during the circumnavigation of Sir Francis Drake. The jeton is mentioned in Hudson's article as having been found in the San Francisco Bay area and thought to be related to Drake, but the specific find spot and discoverer are not given.
Bibliography: Hudson 1979, 112–14; Villiers 1975, 216, 220, 223.
"1567 Silver Coin May Be Clue To Site of Drake's Coast Fort," *New York Times,* November 11, 1974, 39.

25. Bermuda, July 1968.
Type of find: Shipwreck.
Ship: Unknown Portuguese ship.
Sank: 1580.
Contents: 6+ AR, 10+ AV.

Description:
  Portugal, reign unknown, ½ San Vicente
  Portugal, John III, cruzado [1521–57]
  Portugal, Sebastian, cruzados [1557–78] (4)
  Portugal, Henry I, cruzados [1578–80] (4)
  Spanish colonies, Philip II, 2 reales (2)
  Spanish colonies, Philip II, 4 reales (2)
  Spanish colonies, Philip II, 8 reales (2)

Disposition: Found by Harry Cox.

Bibliography: Marx 1971, 299 (and plate); Potter 1972, 287–89.
  "Bermuda Diver Finds Ancient Sunken Gold," *New York Times,* September 20, 1968, 59.

26. Puebla, Mexico, summer 1952.

Type of find: Hoard.

Date of deposit: 1580s.

Contents: 1,000+ AR.

Description:
  Spanish colonies, Charles and Johanna, ½ reales, México (73) (including 2 or 3 early ones)
  Spanish colonies, Charles and Johanna, reales, México, all with water (1,000)
  Spanish colonies, Philip II, real, México
  Spanish colonies, Charles and Johanna, 2 reales, México (232)
  Spanish colonies, Charles and Johanna, 4 reales, México (15)

Disposition: Clyde Hubbard.

Bibliography: Hubbard 1993; Nesmith 1955, 4–5.

27. At the shrine of our Lady of Guadalupe, Mexico City, Mexico summer 1950.

Type of find: Hoard.

Date of deposit: 1580s.

Contents: 3,000 AR.

Description:
  Spanish colonies, Charles and Johanna, ½ reales, México
  Spanish colonies, Charles and Johanna, reales, México, assayers S and A (2,000)
  Spanish colonies, Philip II, reales, México
  They were found in an adobe wall of an old house on church property. The coins were added a little at a time to the hoard (a savings hoard), and so many were in uncirculated condition.

Disposition: Casa Baron; 1,000+ to Clyde Hubbard. Other pieces were acquired by O. K. Rumbel, E. H. Windau, and Victor Lanz. Nesmith saw the pieces in all four collections.

Bibliography: Hubbard 1993; Nesmith 1955, 4–5; Nesmith 1958a, 16; Nesmith and Potter 1968, 37.

28. Mexico?, 1951.

Type of find: Hoard.

Date of deposit: 1580s.

Contents: 300 AR.

Description:
  Spanish colonies, Charles and Johanna, reales, México, assayer O, variety Nesmith 108 (300)

Bibliography: Nesmith 1955, 126.

29. Guatemala City, Guatemala, 1955.

Type of find: Hoard.

Date of deposit: 1580s.

Contents: 275 AR.

Description:
  Spanish colonies, Charles and Johanna, 4 reales, México, assayer O, variety Nesmith 110 (275)

Disposition: Clyde Hubbard.

Bibliography: Hubbard 1993; Nesmith 1955, 126.

30. Ruins of old Panama, Panama, 1997.

Type of find: Archaeological excavation.

Date of coins: 1581.
Contents: 4 AR.
Description:
    Spanish colonies, ½ real, Panama, assayer Xo
    Spanish colonies, real, Panama, assayer Xo
    Spanish colonies, 2 reales, assayer Xo (2)
Bibliography: Proctor 2005, 118, 121, 138–39.

31. Camino Real, Panama, 1970.

Type of find: Hoard? Not clear whether found as a hoard or a series of single finds.
Date of deposit: 1582.
Contents: 4 AR.
Description:
    Spanish colonies, ½ real, Panama, assayers P and M
    Spanish colonies, real, Panama, assayer Xo
    Spanish colonies, real, Panama, assayer Bo
    Spanish colonies, 2 reales, Panama, assayer Bo
Disposition: Discovered by George Chevalier. Freeman Craig Auction, November 17, 1981 (George Chevalier Collection).
Bibliography: Proctor 2005, 115, 122, 128, 142.

32. Nombre de Dios, Panama, 2005.

Type of find: Hoard?
Date of deposit: 1582.
Contents: 3 AR.
Description:
    Spanish colonies, ½ real, Panama, assayer Xo
    Spanish colonies, real, Panama, assayer Bo (2)
    The earliest report of the find is the Proctor monograph, but the coins were probably found several decades before. It is also not clear whether the coins are a series of single finds or a hoard.
Bibliography: Proctor 2005, 119, 134–35.

33. Panama, 2005.

Type of find: Hoard?
Date of deposit: 1582.
Contents: 4 AR.
Description:
    Spanish colonies, reales, Panama, assayer Bo (2)
    Spanish colonies, 2 reales, Panama, assayer Bo (2)
    The earliest report of the find available is the Proctor monograph, but the coins were probably found several decades before. It is not clear whether the coins are a series of single finds or a hoard.
Bibliography: Proctor 2005, 130–31, 147.

34. Rimac River, Lima, Peru, 1980s.

Type of find: Votive deposits.
Date of earliest coin: 1582.
Contents: AR.
Description: Includes:
    Spanish colonies, real, Panama, assayer Bo [1582]
    Spanish colonies, ¼ real, Lima, 1750
    Spanish colonies, ½ real, Lima, 1750
    Coins thrown into the water by lovers making pledges as they walk over the bridge over the Rimac River. Lima children have recovered many ½ real cobs from the mud of the river.
Bibliography: Menzel 1987; Proctor 2005, 132; Sedwick and Sedwick 2007, 198.

35. North end of Roanoke Island and Fort Raleigh, Manteo, North Carolina, USA, 1962.

Type of find: Archaeological excavation.
Date of site: 1585.
Contents: 2 B, 2 AR.
Description:
    German states, Nuremberg, jetons, Hans Schultes [1550–74] (2)
    England, Elizabeth, sixpence, cut half
    England, Elizabeth, sixpence, 1563, holed
    The 1563 sixpence was found at the north end of Roanoke Island.

Disposition: National Park Service Museum, Manteo, North Carolina, USA.

Bibliography: Hudson 1979, 112–14; Leonard 2006, 44; Noël Hume 1984, 236, 238; 1994, 14–15 (includes photograph of the 1563 sixpence).

36. Saint Catherine's Island, Georgia, USA, 1981–82.

Type of find: Archaeological excavation on the site of Santa Catalina de Guale.

Date of site: 1570s–1683.

Contents: 1 B.

Description: Spain, Catholic religious medal with image of the Virgin Mary

Disposition: Fernbank Museum of Natural History, Atlanta, Georgia, USA.

Bibliography: John Noble Wilford, "Excavation of Mission Recalls Clash of Cultures," *Saint Louis Post-Dispatch*, December 21, 1982, D1. Fernbank Museum of Natural History, "St. Catherine's Island Collection," http://www.fernbank.edu/museum/stcatherines/stcatherinesintro.apx.

37. Bermuda, late summer 1955.

Type of find: Shipwreck.

Ship: Probably the *San Pedro*.

Sank: 1596.

Contents: 2,000+ AR.

Description:
France, silver coins
Spanish colonies, Philip II, 4 reales, México
Spanish colonies, Philip II, 8 reales, México
Dates of the coins ranged from 1495 to 1593.
Gold bars (15)
Gold disks (2)
Gold pectoral cross (stolen before 1975)

Disposition: Excavated by Edward B. Tucker. Acquired by the Bermuda Maritime Museum. In 1972 one gold bar was on loan to the Smithsonian Institution.

Bibliography: Kent 1958; Marx 1971, 42, 47, 298, 301; Nesmith 1958a, 178–84; Peterson 1975, 43, 74, 86, 274–77; Pickford 1994, 127, 161; Potter 1972, 92, 280–83; Sedwick and Sedwick 2007, 154; Smith 1988, 89–90; Tucker 1962, 44–47.

38. Yunque, New Mexico, USA, summer 1960.

Type of find: Archaeological excavation.

Date of site: 1598–1610.

Contents: 1 AE.

Description: Spain, gilded bronze Catholic religious medal with the Trinity on the obverse and Saint Jerome in the desert on the reverse, date of object 1519–92

Bibliography: Boyd 1961; Johnson 1961.

39. Walker's Creek, a tributary of the Raritan River, New Jersey, USA, June 1881.

Type of find: Shipwreck?

Ship: Unknown.

Sank: ca. 1600.

Contents: 6+ AR.

Description:
Spain, Ferdinand and Isabella, reales
Spanish colonies, Philip II, 8 reales?, México
Spanish colonies, Philip II, 8 reales?, Lima
Found among the timbers of the wreck of a boat.

Bibliography: "Capt. Kidd's Collection, No. 2," *Coin Collector's Journal* 6 (whole no. 67) (June 1881): 86–87.

40. In the Caribbean between the Yucatan and Cuba, 1993.

Type of find: Shipwreck.

Ship: Unknown.

Sank: 1600.

Contents: 3,000 AR.

Description:
Spanish colonies, Charles and Johanna, reales, México
Spanish colonies, Charles and Johanna, 2 reales, México
Spanish colonies, Charles and Johanna, 4 reales, México
Spanish colonies, Philip II, 4 reales, Lima, assayer D (2)
Spanish colonies, Philip II, 4 reales, Potosí (3): assayer L; assayer R; assayer C/B
It is possible that two different shipwrecks may be involved, one of ca. 1550 and one of ca. 1590. Sedwick ascribes the Charles and Johanna coins to a 1550 shipwreck (sunk off western Cuba, which he calls the "Golden Fleece" shipwreck) and the Philip II to a 1590 shipwreck (sunk off the Yucatan). However, the type of corrosion that Sedwick attributes to the coins from the 1590 shipwreck is also seen on the Charles and Johanna coins, so it seems that these two shipwrecks are actually one. Note that the two findspots that Sedwick gives ("off Yucatan" and "off western Cuba") are also very close together.
Sedwick says the three Charles and Johanna 8 reales known were recovered from the "Golden Fleece" shipwreck. The authenticity of these coins is, however, still under discussion.

Bibliography: Ponterio 1993, lots 1964–68; Sedwick and Sedwick 2007, 153 (Sedwick 1 and 4).

41. Garden in Richmond Road, Williamsburg, Virginia, USA, ca. 1975.

Type of find: Single find.

Date of deposit: 1607.

Contents: 1 AR.

Description: England, Henry VIII, groat, [1526–44] (third bust)
This is the earliest English coin found in Virginia.

Disposition: Found during construction. Photographed by Ivor Noël Hume, and then returned to the finder.

Bibliography: Noël Hume 1995, 19.
"Freshest Advices: Oldest English coin Found?" *Colonial Williamsburg. The Journal of the Colonial Williamsburg Foundation* 19, no. 3 (Spring 1997): 9–11.

42. Southeastern Virginia, USA, January 12, 2008.

Type of find: Hoard.

Date of deposit: 1607.

Contents: 8 AR.

Description:
England, Elizabeth I, sixpence (6): 1569; 1573; 1590; 1593; ND (2)
England, Elizabeth I, shillings, ND (2)
Two of the sixpence are bent ("witch pieces"). One shilling is bent. One sixpence is holed. One sixpence is partially cut.

Disposition: Found by metal dectorists.

Bibliography: Bill D., "American Relic Hunters—Relics Forum: Absolutely unbelievable!!!!!!!!!," http://www.americanrelichunters.com/cgi-bin/relic/webbbs_config.pl/read/86774 (includes photograph of the coins found).

43. Jamestown, Virginia, USA, 1958, 1994–2002.

Type of find: Archaeological excavation.

Date of site: 1607–39.

Contents: 1 PB, 85 AE, 1 BI, 18 AR.

Description:
Courland, Riga, silver coin
Sweden, silver coin
Netherlands, stuiver, Zeeland, 161[-]
Netherlands, 2 stuiver, Zeeland, 1616 (cut into three parts)
Netherlands, jeton, obverse depicts Pope and Philip II, inscription, LIBERR … CIRI LEO PERNEGAT; reverse, mouse gnaws through

rope binding lion, inscription ROSIS LEONEM LORIS … LIBERAT, 1579

Netherlands, jeton, Groningen, 1590

German states, Lübeck, sechsling, 1629

German states, Nuremberg, jeton, Hans Schultes [1550–74]

German states, Nuremberg, jeton, Hans Krauwinckel I [1586]

German states, Nuremberg, jeton, Hans Krauwinckel II [1580–1610]

German states, Nuremberg, jeton, Hans Laufer [1610–60]

German states, Nuremberg, jeton, Hans Krauwinckel [1580–1610], with FAMAM EXTENDE FACTO ET VIRTU

German states, Nuremberg, jetons, unspecified (51)

Scotland, James VI, plack (4 pence) [1583–90]

England, Elizabeth I, threehalfpence cut to make ¾ of a penny

England, Elizabeth I, ½ groats (2): halved to make a penny, hand mintmark [1590–92]; rolled into a bead

England, Elizabeth I, sixpence (5): 1602, whole; 1602, cut into rectangular pendant and pierced; ND (3)

England, Elizabeth, shilling cut into wedge worth 1½ pence

England, James I, silver halfpenny [1606–8]

England, Charles I, farthings (4): Harrington farthing [1613–36] (2); rose farthing [1636] (2)

England, Elizabeth I, lead token, obverse crowned rose, BEATY REGINA, reverse, crowned phoenix, SO PHONIX MVN DYE [1570]

England, king's touch tokens (5): James I, uniface rose and thistle touch token (2); other touch tokens, unspecified (3)

England, religious medals (6)

England, coin weights (4): Elizabeth, weight for gold ryal worth 15 shillings [1583–92], made in Antwerp by PVG; James I, weight for angel (11 shillings) [1612–19]; James I, weight for unite (22 shillings) [1612–19]; James I, weight for double crown (11 shillings) [1612–19]

Ireland, Elizabeth I, copper halfpenny, 1601

Ireland, Elizabeth I, copper pence, 1602 (5)

Spain, maravedí

Spain, 4 maravedíes, counterstamped

Spanish colonies, silver coins, cut (3)

The religious medals excavated at Jamestown are very Roman Catholic in appearance; this reflects the Anglican religion of the period, which had not yet undergone the more thoroughly Protestant reforms that would occur in the mid-seventeenth century.

Disposition: Many of the coins excavated are on exhibition at the Archaearium in Jamestown.

Bibliography: Cotter 1958, 60, 191, 240, and plate 89; Hudson 1979, 112–14; Kelso 2006, 83, 179, 188; Kelso, Luccketti and Straube 1995 (Jamestown Rediscovery I), 14–16; Kelso, Luccketti and Straube 1996 (Jamestown Rediscovery II), 6–8, 36–37; Kelso, Luccketti and Straube 1997 (Jamestown Rediscovery III), 47–53, 55; Kelso, Luccketti and Straube 1999 (Jamestown Rediscovery V), 11; Kraljevich 2007; Noël Hume 1984, 236, 238, 247; Noël Hume and Noël Hume 2001, Part I: Interpretive Studies, 175 n. 2.

44. Saint George's Island, Bermuda, 1958–59 and 1978–86.

Type of find: Shipwreck.

Ship: Sea Venture.

Sank: July 28, 1609 (Old Style).

Contents: 2 AE.

Description: German states, Nuremberg, jeton, Hans Krauwinckel [1580–1610] (2)

Bibliography: Steffy 1988, 111–13; Wingood 1986.

45. Mexico City, Mexico, 1932.
Type of find: Hoard.
Date of deposit: 1611.
Contents: 300 AR.
Description:
　Spanish colonies, Philip II, reales, México
　Spanish colonies, Philip III, reales, México
　Spanish colonies, Philip II, 2 reales, México
　Spanish colonies, Philip III, 2 reales, México
　Spanish colonies, Philip II, 4 reales, México
　Spanish colonies, Philip III, 4 reales, México
　Spanish colonies, Philip II, 8 reales, México
　Spanish colonies, Philip III, 8 reales, México
　Spanish colonies, Philip III, 8 reales, México, assayer F
　Spanish colonies, Philip III, 8 reales, México, 1607
　Spanish colonies, Philip III, 8 reales, México, 1611
　The hoard included some of the earliest dated issues (1607–11) of the México mint.
Disposition: The coins were found when excavations were made while building a new opera house in Mexico City, probably the Palacio de las Bellas Artes, which opened in 1932. Robert I. Nesmith (107).
Bibliography: Nesmith 1958a, 16 (an undated Philip III coin, assayer F, is reproduced as coin no. 41 on plate G); Nesmith and Potter 1968, 37.

46. South shore beach near Port Royal, Bermuda, 1877.
Type of find: Single find.
Contents: 1 AE.
Description: English colonies, Somers Islands, twopence [1616]
Disposition: Washed up on the beach, found by a child. Acquired by General Sir John Henry Lefroy.
Bibliography: Breen 1988, 11 (Breen 7); Lefroy 1878; Sportack 2005, 2883.

47. Saint George's, Bermuda, 1881.
Type of find: Single find.
Contents: 1 AE.
Description: English colonies, Somers Islands, twopence, [1616]
Disposition: Acquired by Colonel Mitchell, Royal Engineers.
Bibliography: Dubois 1885, 66–67; Lefroy 1883; Sportack 2005, 2883, 2886.

48. Saint George's, Bermuda, 1853.
Type of find: Single find.
Contents: 1 AE.
Description: English colonies, Somers Islands, sixpence
Disposition: Found in a garden. Acquired by Benjamin Betts of Brooklyn, NY, USA; illustrated in Crosby.
Bibliography: Crosby 1875, 18; Sportack 2005, 2881, 2886.

49. Saint George's, Bermuda, early 1884.
Type of find: Single find.
Contents: 1 AE.
Description: English colonies, Somers Islands, sixpence, [1616]
　"The coin in question was picked up in the early part of this year on the northeastern slope of the town of St. George's in a garden. My father bought it from the finder's husband. It was unfortunately rubbed by the finder on a brick."
Disposition: 1884 to the Cabinet of the United States Mint; 1923 to Smithsonian.
Bibliography: Dubois 1885, 66–67.

50. Bermuda, November 1861.
Type of find: Single find.
Contents: 1 AE.

Description: English colonies, Somers Islands, shilling, [1616]

Disposition: Bermuda Museum.

Bibliography: "Philadelphia Numismatic Society—Philadelphia, November 7, 1861," *Historical Magazine* 6 (January 1862): 28.

51. Castle Island, Bermuda, July-August 1993, July-August 1994, July-August 1996.

Type of find: Archaeological excavation.

Date of site: 1621–50.

Contents: 19 AE.

Description:
English colonies, Somers Islands, sixpence (16): large portholes (9); small portholes (7)
English colonies, Somers Islands, shillings (3): large sails; small sails (2)

Disposition: Bermuda Government.

Bibliography: Bermuda Monetary Authority 1997, 31–42; Sportack 2005, 2882; Sportack 2006, 85–90.

52. Dorchester, Massachusetts, USA, July 1631.

Type of find: Hoard.

Date of deposit: 1617.

Contents: 2 BI.

Description: France, probably douzains, one dated 1596 (2)

"Mr. Ludlow, in digging the foundation of his house at Dorchester, found two pieces of French money: one was coined in 1596. They were in several places, and above a foot within the firm ground."

A note by James Savage suggests that the coins had been brought by the crew of a French ship that was wrecked on Cape Cod around 1617, of whom two of the crew were captives among the Indians until redeemed by Dormer; a third remained among the Indians until his death. The rest of the crew had perished.

Bibliography: Winthrop 1853, 71.
Sylvester Sage Crosby, "Correspondence," *American Journal of Numismatics* 5, no. 1 (July 1870): 16.

53. Off Wabasso, Florida, USA, 1966.

Type of find: Shipwreck.

Ship: The "Green Cabin Wreck," which is thought to be the *San Martin*, the lost *almiranta* of the 1618 Honduras fleet, which sank while on its way to Spain from Havana.

Sank: 1618.

Contents: 508 AR.

Description:
Spanish colonies, 8 reales, México
Spanish colonies, Philip II, 8 reales, Potosí, assayer B (Sebring)

Disposition: State of Florida (127).

Bibliography: Craig 2000b, 75, 78; Sebring 2004, lot 1551; Sedwick and Sedwick 2007, 153 (Sedwick 5); Smith 1988, 94–95.

54. Castle Harbor, Bermuda, 1966–67.

Type of find: Shipwreck.

Ship: Warwick.

Sank: 1619.

Contents: AR.

Description: Spanish colonies, 8 reales, México, in poor condition

Disposition: Bermuda government; however, a few cob 8 reales in poor condition entered the market from the estate of Mendel Peterson after his death in 2003.

Bibliography: Sedwick and Sedwick 2007, 154 (Sedwick 7).

55. Flowerdew Hundred Farm, south side of the James River, Prince George County, Virginia, USA, 1971–93.

Type of find: Archaeological excavation.

Date of site: 1619–30.

Contents: 1 B, 1 AR.

Description:
England, Elizabeth I, sixpence
Netherlands, Maurice of Orange brass medallion, 1617, with inscription: MAVRITIVS AVR[ANIAE] PRINC[EPS] COM[ES] NASS[AVIAE] ET MV[RSIAE] MAR[CHIO] VE[RAE] FL[ISSINGAEQUE] EQ[VES] OR[DINIS] PERISCELIDIS 'Maurice, Prince of Orange, Count of Nassau and Meurs, Margrave of Verre and Flushing, Knight of the Garter'
Deetz reads the date of the medallion as 1615. Van Loon, however, gives the date of the medallion as 1617. Van Loon's date has been substituted for that of Deetz.

Bibliography: Deetz 1993, 43–44; Van Loon 1726, 2: 87–88.

56. Near Bermuda Hundred, Virginia, USA, 2007.

Type of find: Single find.

Date of deposit: Ca. 1621.

Contents: 1 AR.

Description: England, Elizabeth I, sixpence, 1571, Tower mint, cut twice, weighs 1.4 grams.

Disposition: Thomas Kays.

Bibliography: Kays 2007, 11.

57. Bermuda, 1960.

Type of find: Shipwreck.

Ship: San Antonio.

Sank: September 12, 1621.

Contents: 50+ AR, small silver bars, gold chain.

Description: The coins included:
Spain, 8 reales, Philip III, Segovia, 1617
Spanish colonies, Philip III, 2 reales, probably Potosí
Spanish colonies, Philip III, 4 reales, probably Potosí
Spanish colonies, Philip III, 8 reales, Potosí, assayer Q
Spanish colonies, Philip III, 8 reales, Potosí, NDA
The excavation also turned up Indo-Pacific cowrie shells and small billets of copper, both used in the African slave trade. The bulk of the treasure, however, was salvaged by Bermudians in the seventeenth century after the ship sank.

Disposition: Bermuda government; some to Smithsonian Institution?

Bibliography: Lefroy 1877, 1:156–58; Marx 1971, 42, 47, 298, 302; Peterson 1961, 1975, 284–91; Pickford 1994, 127, 162; Potter 1972, 283–84; Sedwick and Sedwick 2007, 154; Smith 1988, 90–91; Tucker 1962, 66, 68.

58. Wolstenholme Town, Martin's Hundred, Virginia, USA, 1977–79.

Type of find: Archaeological excavation.

Date of site: 1620–March 22, 1622 (Fort and Company Compound).

Contents: 5 AE, 3 AR.

Description:
Spanish colonies, Charles and Johanna, México, reales, cut, third (3)*
German states, Nuremberg, jeton, obverse 3 open crowns and 3 lis, reverse: cross and orb within double tressure of 3 arcs and 3 angles, Hans Krauwinckel, [1580–1610] (2)
German states, Nuremberg, jeton, obverse: Apollo and Diana, reverse: "Meliager"
England, James I, farthing token, "Harington" type 1 [May 1613 to June 1614]
England, James I, farthing token, Lennox round [1613–25]

*Noël Hume's description of these coins is ambiguous, and no photograph or drawing has ever been published. Pittman lists only one Spanish colonies coin found at Martin's Hundred, which he attributes as a Philip II 2 reales of Lima, cut and broken into quarter of a full 2 reales. As an early style Lima piece it would have a similar pillar and waves design to the Charles and Johanna coinage.

Bibliography: Noël Hume 1984, 247–49; Noël Hume 1992, 189–90, 224–26, 317–18; Noël Hume and Noël Hume 2001.

William E. Pittman, personal communication, January 20, 2007.

59. Glen Cove, Long Island, New York, USA, August 1868.

Type of find: Single find.

Contents: 1 AR.

Description: Spanish colonies, Philip III, real, México, [1598–1621]

Bibliography: Charles E. Anthon, "Query and Reply," *American Journal of Numismatics* 3, no. 4 (August 1868): 32.

60. Marquesas Keys, off Florida, USA, 1973–1985.

Type of find: Shipwreck.

Ship: Nuestra Señora de Atocha.

Sank: September 6, 1622.

Contents: 5 AE, 185,000 AR, 120 AV.

Description: The compilation below comes from five sources:
 (1) the Christie's 1988 Auction
 (2) the catalog issued by Christie's known as the "Research Collection"
 (3) Neil Harris's 1986 article in the *Numismatist*
 (4) Corey Malcolm's article on the copper coins, and
 (5) the Coin Galleries 1994 Auction.

Spain, corroded maravedíes copper coin
Spain, 2 maravedíes, Segovia, 1611
Spain, Philip II, 2 maravedíes, Cuenca, with IIII/B counterstamp (revaluation at Burgos to 4 maravedíes)
Spain, 4 maravedíes, Burgos, 1619
Spain, 8 maravedíes, Segovia, 1607
Spain, Charles and Johanna, escudo, Burgos
Spain, real, Madrid, 1621V
Spain, 4 reales, Madrid, 1621V
Spain, 2 escudos, Madrid, assayer G [1615–20]
Spain, 8 reales, Segovia, assayer M?
Spain, 2 reales, Toledo, assayer C
Spain, 8 reales, Toledo, 1621P
Spain, 4 reales, Seville, assayer V
Spain, 8 reales, Seville, NDA
Spain, Charles and Johanna, escudo, Seville
Spain, 2 escudos, Seville (67): Philip II; assayer D (2); assayer G (6); NDA (58)
Spain, 8 escudos, Seville
Spain, 2 reales, Granada, assayer M
Spain, 4 reales, Granada, assayer D
Spanish colonies, 2 reales, México (6): Charles and Johanna, assayer L; Charles and Johanna, assayer O (2); Philip II, assayer O (2); Philip III, assayer A
Spanish colonies, 4 reales, México (4): assayer O; 1607; 1609A; 1612F
Spanish colonies, 8 reales, México (11): assayer O; assayer A; 1611F; assayer F (2); assayer D/F; 1620D; 1621/0D; 1621D (2); NDA
Spanish colonies, 2 reales, Panama, assayer Xo
Spanish colonies, 2 reales, Panama, assayer Bo (3)
Spanish colonies, 8 reales, Cartagena, 1622A (2)
Spanish colonies, 2 reales, Bogotá, 1622A (2)
Spanish colonies, 4 reales, Bogotá (3): assayer A; 1622A (2)
Spanish colonies, 8 reales, Bogotá (4): assayer A; 1622A (3)
Spanish colonies, 2 escudos, Bogotá, 1622 (3)
Spanish colonies, real, Lima, assayer Do
Spanish colonies, 2 reales, Lima (28): pillars and waves type, assayer R (2); shield type, assayer X (2); shield type, assayer Do (24)

Spanish colonies, 4 reales, Lima (9): pillars and waves type, assayer R; shield type, assayer Do (8)

Spanish colonies, 8 reales, Lima, assayer Do (8)

Spanish colonies, reales, Potosí (2): Philip II, assayer R; assayer A

Spanish colonies, 2 reales, Potosí (115): Philip II, assayer R (6); Philip II, assayer M (2); assayer L (13); assayer C below erasure; assayer A/B (3); assayer A (5); Philip III, assayer R (8); assayer B (41); assayer L/B; assayer B/L; assayer Q (2); 1617M (15); 1618PRAL (6); 1618T (2); 1619T (2); 1620T (4); NDA (2)

Spanish colonies, 4 reales, Potosí (54): Philip II, assayer R; Philip II, assayer M (2); assayer L (3); assayer C below erasure (2); assayer A/B; assayer A (2); Philip III, assayer R (5); assayer B (15); assaycr Q (4); Philip III, assayer M (2); 1617M; 1618PRAL; 1618T; 1619T (2); 161[-]; 1620T (2); 1621T; assayer T (2); 162[-]T; 1622T; NDA (3)

Spanish colonies, 8 reales, Potosí (383): Philip II, assayer M; assayer L; assayer C below erased B; assayer A/B; assayer A; Philip III, assayer R (41); assayer B (39); Philip III, assayer R/B; assayer D; assayer Q (66); Philip III, assayer M (31); 1617; 1617M (20); 1617M/Q; 1618 (2); 1618PRAL (5); 1618T/PRAL; 1618T (6); 1619 (2); 1619T (11); 161[-]; 161[-]Q; 161[-]T (2); 16[-] (2); 16[-]T (3); 1620 (2); 1620T (12); assayer T (55); 1621T (8); 1622T (2); NDA (17); contemporary counterfeits (5)

In January 2007, Heritage auctioned 2,622 silver coins from the *Atocha*. The mints, assayers, and dates were not provided. However, the denominations broke down as follows: reales (8); 2 reales (52); 4 reales (629); 8 reales (1,910); fragments (23).

The following listing comes from a database, http://www.historicshipwrecks.com, as of October 2007:

12,814 AR, 16 AV.

Spain, 2 escudos, Seville (16): 1597B; 1611; 162[-]; assayer P; assayer G (2); Philip II (2); Philip III (4); NDA (4)

Spanish colonies, 8 reales, México (167): assayer O (2); assayer F (161); assayer A (4)

Spanish colonies, 8 reales, Lima (712): assayer R (3); assayer D (709)

Spanish colonies, 8 reales, Cartagena, assayer A (2)

Spanish colonies, 8 reales, Bogotá, assayer A (40)

Spanish colonies, 8 reales, Potosí (11,893): assayer L (3); assayer R (215); assayer B/R (6); assayer B (2,226); assayer A (75); R/L (237); assayer C (6); assayer Q (8,985); assayer Q/M; assayer M/Q; assayer M (42); assayer PA (2); assayer RAL (13); assayer T (67); assayer T/RAL (7); TP (2); assayer P (5)

Disposition: In 1973, eleven gold coins minted in Seville, 6,240 silver coins from Lima, Potosí, Bogotá and México, gold chains, rings, and gold bars were recovered from an area the divers called "the Bank of Spain." The Atocha's cannons were recovered in the summer of 1975. The primary cultural deposit—the main treasure and the resting place of the hull—was not discovered until July 20, 1985. The broad wreckage field is explained by the theory that the Atocha sank on the site of the primary cultural deposit; then a subsequent hurricane swept the wreckage to the northwest.

Some of the more notable coins found were cataloged in the 1986 article by Neil Harris in the *Numismatist*. At least six of those coins were auctioned as part of "the Research Collection." Whether "the Research Collection" contained all of the silver coins in that article cannot be determined, since not all coins in "the Research Collection" were photographed. None of the gold coins in the *Numismatist* article formed part of "the Research Collection," nor were the gold coins in that article auctioned as part of the main Christie's auction.

The four better-preserved copper coins were found in 1985–86 near the lower hull structure. The corroded copper coin was found in summer 2000 at the northern extreme of the site, near what is believed to be the upper works of the ship.

Bibliography: Christie's 1988a, lots 78–113, 199–389; Christie's 1988b; Coin Galleries 1994; Daley 1977; Earle 2007, 15–18, 143–45; Harris 1986; Heritage 2007, lot 50,242 and lots 50,244–320; Lyon 1976, 1979; Proctor 2005, 137, 144–46; Sedwick and Sedwick 2007, 154–56 (Sedwick 8); Smith 1988, 92–94. Jon Nordheimer, "Archaeologists' Eyes Glittering Over Treasure," *New York Times,* July 24, 1985, A1 and B4 (includes a diagram reconstructing how the wreckage was strewn over the debris field).

Corey Malcolm, "An Early Lima Mint Coin from *Nuestra Señora de Atocha*," *Navigator,* June 1999, available at: http://www.melfisher.org/limamintcoin.htm.

Corey Malcolm, "The Forgotten Coins of the Atocha," *Navigator,* August 2000, available at: http://www.melfisher.org/forgottencoins.htm.

"Mel Fisher's Historic Shipwreck Research Database," http://www.historicshipwrecks.com.

61. Marquesa Keys, off Florida, USA, spring 1981.

Type of find: Shipwreck.

Ship: Santa Margarita.

Sank: September 6, 1622.

Contents: 4 AE, 15,000 AR, 56 AV.

Description: The following listing, except for the 15 2 escudos without a mint, comes from a database, http://www.historicshipwrecks.com, as of October 2007:

Spain, 4 maravedíes, Burgos, with Burgos counterstamp

Spain, 4 maravedíes

Spain, 8 maravedíes, Burgos

Spain, 8 maravedíes, Segovia, 1607

Spain, 2 reales, Seville

Spain, 4 reales, Seville, assayer D

Spain, 8 reales, Seville (2): 1621D; NDA

Spain, 2 escudos, Seville (10): Philip III, assayer G (2); assayer D; NDA (7)

Spain, 2 escudos (15)

Spanish colonies, reales, México (7): Philip III, assayer F; Philip III (5); NDA

Spanish colonies, 2 reales, México (22): Philip II F/D; Philip III, assayer F; Philip III, assayer D (4); Philip III (13); NDA (3)

Spanish colonies, 4 reales, México (43): Philip III, [-]9; Philip III, assayer F (2); Philip III, assayer D (4); Philip III (30); NDA (6)

Spanish colonies, 8 reales, México (72): Philip II, assayer F; Philip II, assayer D; Philip III, 1618D; Philip III, 162[-]D; Philip III, 16[-]F; Philip III, assayer F (6); Philip III, assayer D (16); Philip II; Philip III (36); Philip IV; NDA (7)

Spanish colonies, 4 reales, Bogotá, Philip III

Spanish colonies, 8 reales, Bogotá, assayer A

Spanish colonies, 2 reales, Lima (2): assayer D; Philip II

Spanish colonies, 4 reales, Lima, Philip II

Spanish colonies, 8 reales, Lima, Philip II, assayer D

Spanish colonies, reales, Potosí (17): Philip III (15); NDA (2)

Spanish colonies, 2 reales, Potosí (127): assayer B (15); assayer A; assayer M (5); assayer Q (2); assayer R (3); assayer T (3); 161[-]T; NDA (97)

Spanish colonies, 4 reales, Potosí (160): assayer B (3); assayer M (7); assayer R (3); assayer Q (6); assayer T (8); [1]6[1]8T; NDA (132)

Spanish colonies, 8 reales, Potosí (364): assayer A; assayer B (9); assayer M (22); assayer Q (45); assayer R (26); assayer T (30); 1618T; 1619T (3); 1620T (2); NDA (225)

Spanish colonies, no denomination, Potosí, assayer Q

Spanish colonies, real

Spanish colonies, 2 reales (50)

Spanish colonies, 4 reales (87)

Spanish colonies, 8 reales (98)

Spanish colonies, no denomination (132)

Gold chains, gold bars, and silver bars were also found; six of the gold bars appeared in the Christie's auction. Emeralds have been found as well.

The manifest listed 419 silver bars, 118,000 silver coins, and 1,488 ounces of gold bullion. The Spanish under Francisco Nuñez Melián salvaged over 33,000 silver coins and 387 silver bars in 1626–28.

Bibliography: Christie's 1988a, lots 158–66; Earle 2007, 15–18; Heritage 2007, lots 50, 321–324; Lyon 1982; Sebring 1986, 112; Sedwick and Sedwick 2007, 156–57 (Sedwick 9).

"Mel Fisher's Historic Shipwreck Research Database," http://www.historicshipwrecks.com.

62. Fort Orange, Albany, New York, USA 1971.

Type of find: Archaeological excavation.

Date of site: 1624–76.

Contents: 2 AR, 5 AE.

Description:

Netherlands, 2 stuivers, Holland, 1626

England, James I, farthing token, "Harington" type 1 [May 1613 to June 1614]

Great Britain, halfpence (2): George I; George II, 1736

France?, double tournois?, 1628, holed in center

USA, New Jersey, copper, 1786

Spanish colonies, ½ real, México, 1781

Disposition: New York State Bureau of Historic Sites Collection, Peebles Island, New York, USA.

Bibliography: Hoover 2007 (providing inventory of New York State Bureau of Historic Sites Collections, Peebles Island, New York, as of August 16, 2005).

63. Bay of All Saints, Brazil, 1981.

Type of find: Shipwreck.

Ship: Hollandia, the flagship of Piet Heyn.

Sank: March 1627.

Contents: AR.

Description:

Netherlands, lion daalders, mint not described

Netherlands, lion daalder, Overijssel, 1627 (2) (Thomas Sebring)

Disposition: Recovered by Robert Marx.

Bibliography: Sebring 1986, 74–119; Sebring 2004, lot 1602.

64. Three miles from Lucayan Beach, Grand Bahama Island, Bahamas, August 1964.

Type of find: Shipwreck.

Ship: Possibly the *Van Lynden*. Thought to be part of the Dutch fleet under Piet Heyn, carrying treasure captured from the Spanish. The coins possibly come from the *Van Lynden*, which sank in 1629; others say this is one of the Spanish treasure ships that Piet Heyn sank, and have proposed the *Santa Gertrudis* or the *Romario*. An alternative suggestion that this is *Nuestra Señora de los Remedios*, which sank in 1625, is improbable, given that at least ten coins have been auctioned that are dated later than 1625, and that most are dated 1628.

Sank: 1629.

Contents: 16,000 AR.

Description: This listing summarizes the coins auctioned by Schulman and by Sotheby's:

Spanish colonies, 2 reales, México (54): assayer F (2); 1614F; 1624D; assayer D; NDA (49)

Spanish colonies, 4 reales, México (364): 160[-]A; assayer F (2); assayer D/F; 1612 (2); 1613F; 1620D (2); 1622/0D; 1622D (3); 1624D (8); 1627 (2); 162[-]D (6); NDA (335)

Spanish colonies, 8 reales, México (5,283): assayer A; assayer F (5); 1612F (2); assayer D/F; 161[-]D/F; 1620D; 1622D (4); 1623D (2); 1624D (11); 1625D; 1626D; 1627D (4); 1629D; assayer D (5,000); NDA (248)

Spanish colonies, 4 reales, Potosí (3): assayer B; 1627 (2)

Spanish colonies, 8 reales, Potosí (8): assayer B (2); 1627 (2); assayer T; coin with positions of castles and lions on reverse inverted ["dyslexic mint worker"]; NDA (2)

The coins were chiefly 4 reales and 8 reales, México and Potosí, 1612–29. Many bore the date of 1628. (Oddly, no coin of 1628 appeared in the two public auctions held by Schulman and by Sotheby's.) A 2 reales of 1641 was also recovered, but this could be a later contamination of the 1629 shipwreck; the 1641 coin could have been dropped by one of the Bahamian or New England "wreck fishers" who recovered much silver from this area in the seventeenth century.

Disposition: Found by the divers Jack Slack, Gary Simmons, and Dick Tindall.

Bibliography: Lepera and Goodman 1974, 97–100, 147–48; Schulman 1969, lots 903–30; Sedwick and Sedwick 2007, 159 (Sedwick 13); Slack 1967; Sotheby's 1972, lots 1–114.

"The Big Find. Ancient Spanish Mint Ship Yields Richest Treasure to Date," *Look,* March 9, 1965, 102–6.

65. Portobelo, Panama, 1976–77.

Type of find: Hoard.

Date of deposit: 1629.

Contents: 4,500 AR.

Description:

Spanish colonies, 8 reales, México

Spanish colonies, 8 reales, Cartagena

Spanish colonies, 4 reales, Potosí (675)

Spanish colonies, 8 reales, Potosí (3,825)

Included all Potosí dates 1617–29. Included Potosí assayers B, R, Q, M, RAL, T, and P.

Bibliography: McLean 1995.

Charles E. Weber, "Reader Adds Observations to Informative Hoard Article," *Numismatist,* 109, no. 3 (March 1996): 256–57.

66. Martin's Hundred, Virginia, USA, 1970.

Type of find: Archaeological excavation.

Date of site: 1623–40 (Jackson/Ward Homestead).

Contents: 1 B.

Description: German states, Nuremberg, jeton, obverse: 3 open crowns and 3 lis, reverse: cross and orb within double tressure of 3 arcs and 3 angles, Hans Krauwinckel, [1580–1610]

Bibliography: Noël Hume 1984, 238; Noël Hume 1992, 17, 19; Noël Hume and Noël Hume 2001.

67. Church of San Bernardo, Awatovi, Arizona, USA, 1935–39.

Type of find: Funerary deposits.

Date of site: 1630–80.

Contents: 4 B.

Description:

Spain, oval Catholic religious medal, obverse Saint Christopher, reverse Saint Stephen

Spain, oval Catholic religious medal, obverse Saint Francis of Assisi, reverse Saint Anthony of Padua

Spain, rounded cruciform Catholic religious medal, obverse with Saints Theresa of Avila, Isidor the Farmer, and Ignatius Loyola;

reverse, 3 unidentified figures (the Three Magi?)

Spain, oval Catholic religious medal, fragment, obverse, unidentified figure of saint, reverse 2 unidentified figures (John the Baptist baptizing Jesus?)

Disposition: Peabody Museum West of the Pecos.

Bibliography: Smith and Fontana 1970.

68. Pemaquid, Maine, USA, 1999.

Type of find: Archaeological excavation.

Date of site: 1620–1770; date of earliest coin, 1631.

Contents: 78 AE, 5 AR.

Description:

England, Charles I, silver penny, 1631–32
Great Britain, George II, halfpence (33+): 1749 (5); 1753 (2+); ND (26)
Ireland, Wood's Hibernia farthing, 1723 (3)
Ireland, Charles II, halfpenny, 1680–81
Ireland, Wood's Hibernia halfpence (15): 1723 (11); 1724; ND (3)
Ireland, George II, halfpenny, young bust
Spain, real (½ pistareen), 1720
English colonies, Massachusetts, pine tree sixpence (Noe 33) [1667–74]
English colonies, Massachusetts, pine tree shilling (Noe 16) [1675–82]
Spanish colonies, 2 reales, México, 1766
The site is remarkable for the large numbers of Wood's Hibernia coinage. The explanation is that in 1729 a colony of fifty Irish families was established on the site. The Irish colony dissolved after 1733.

Bibliography: Mossman 1999, 1910–11.

69. Richmond Island, Maine, USA, May 11, 1855.

Type of find: Hoard.

Date of deposit: October 3, 1631.

Container: Rhenish salt-glazed stoneware from Frechen, possibly a Bartmannskrug.

Contents: 30 AR, 21 AV; gold signet ring.

Description:

Scotland, James VI, sword and scepter, 1602
England, Elizabeth I, threehalfpence (2): 1568; 156[-]
England, Elizabeth I, groat [1558–60]
England, Elizabeth I, sixpences (16): 1563; 1564; 1568; 1569; 1572; 1573; 1578; 1579; 1580; 1589; 1593; ND (5)
England, James I, sixpence, 1606
England, Charles I, sixpence, 1625
England, Elizabeth I, shillings (4): [1560–61]; [1582–84]; ND (2)
England, James I, shillings, [1604–5] (4)
England, Charles I, shilling, [1625–26]
England, James I, double crowns (3): [1618–19]; ND (2)
England, James I, laurels (8): [1621–23]; [1623–24] (3); ND (4)
England, James I, unites, [1606–7] (2)
England, Charles I, unites (7): [1625]; [1625–26]; [1626–27]; [1627–28]; ND (3)

Total value of the coinage: £18/10/7.

The gold ring weighs 12.7 grams, and has the inscription "United [hearts] Death only Partes," and the initials G.V.

In the jar the gold was arranged on one side, the silver on the other, and the ring in the middle. (Compare *NFA* 377.)

The coins are thought to have belonged to Walter Bagnall, who was killed by the Indians on October 3, 1631. Jordan proposes instead that the hoard might have been deposited by a subsequent trader, John Winter, who died in 1645. Since, however, the hoard closes with a coin of 1627–28 (the Charles I unite), given the large proportion of gold (Besly says that Civil War hoards from later years do not have much gold), and given that Bagnall's violent death provides a logical explanation for why the hoard was not recovered, the ascription of the deposit to Bagnall makes more sense.

Disposition: Found by a farmer, Hanscom, while plowing. Acquired by Dr. John M. Cummings, who owned Richmond Island. In 1857 he presented a gold unite of Charles I and a silver coin of Elizabeth I to the Massachusetts Historical Society. Cummings in 1873 presented two coins from this hoard to the Maine General Hospital Fair of Portland: a sixpence of Elizabeth I (dated 1573), and a Charles I gold unite. In 1921 Cummings's descendant, Mrs. Edward McClure Peters of Brooklyn, New York, announced her intention to sell the residue of the hoard. This had then been reduced to 18 silver coins and 11 gold coins. The Maine Historical Society raised the money to purchase it and acquired these coins, plus the ring, plus the fragments of the jug, in 1929; Maine Historical Society item numbers MHS collection 819, items 1 through 30. Jordan suggests that the eighteen coins that are currently untraced—the 10 silver coins and 8 gold coins—were given to Hanscom, the finder, in a split of the hoard between him and Cummings.

Bibliography: Breen 1952, 8–9 (Breen Hoards II); Brown and Dolley 1971, 59 (NS1); DeCosta 1871, 55–56; Jordan 2007; Moneydigging 1871, 32–33; Noe 1942, 34; Willis 1859, 127–51.

"Coins Found on Richmond Island, Maine," *American Journal of Numismatics* 5, no. 2 (October, 1870): 33–36.

"Coins Found at Richmond's Island, Me.," *American Journal of Numismatics* 8, no. 2 (October, 1873): 42.

70. Southern Peru, Early 2007.

Type of find: Hoard.

Date of deposit: 1632.

Contents: 500 AR.

Description:

Spanish colonies, reales, Potosí

Spanish colonies, 2 reales, Potosí

Spanish colonies, 4 reales, Potosí

Spanish colonies, 8 reales, Potosí: 1626, 1627, 1628, 1629, 1632

Mostly 8 reales, but also some 4 reales and a smattering of the smaller denominations. Most of the coins date to 1626–29; latest date in hoard 1632. Coins share a tell-tale patina (distractingly darkly toned with green spots). All the coins are in high grade.

Bibliography: Daniel Frank Sedwick, "Shipwreck (and Hoard) Histories: Early 1630s hoard in Southern Peru," http://www.sedwickcoins.com/Auction/DFS_TreasureAuction_Histories.htm.

71. Duxbury, Boston, Massachusetts, USA, January 1888.

Type of find: Single find.

Contents: 1 AR.

Description: German States, medal with the inscription "Gloria in Excelsis, 1633," with a winged figure in the circle, holding a sword and a torch.

Disposition: Found on the farm of Harrison Loring; donated to the Pilgrim Society, Plymouth, Massachusetts, USA.

Bibliography: "A Medal Exhumed," *American Journal of Numismatics* 22, no. 3 (January 1888): 75.

72. El Mesuno, six kilometers from San Bartolomeo de Honda, Colombia, August 22, 1935.

Type of find: Hoard.

Date of deposit: 1635.

Contents: 1,600 AV.

Description: Spanish colonies, Philip IV, 2 escudos, Bogotá (1,600)

Mostly assayer A; also included a few assayer P and possibly some assayer E. Dates known include 1628, 1633, and 1635.

The treasure also contained "ancient objects."

In the colonial period, gold was sent by mule from Santa Fé de Bogotá to Bartolomeo de Honda, and then by boat down to Cartagena for shipment to Spain. Nesmith suggests that one of the riverboats sank, concealing this hoard.

Found by the young fisherman José Ardila. His friend Manuel Valdés acquired many. Others who dug up the gold pieces included Aristobulo and Jorge Guzmán, and Segundo Ortiz.

Disposition: 500 to the Banco de la Republica, for the national collection, of which 375 to 400 remained in July 1959; about 40 came to the United States, of which one each was owned by well known Saint Louis and New York collectors; 19 were in the hands of a Toronto collector; and Wilcox had 19. Others were acquired by Victor Guillén and David Londoño. Spink's Numismatic Circular, March 1939, no. 78,714, offered a 2 escudos from the Mesuno Hoard. Several were in a Coin Galleries (Division of Stack's), New York, New York, USA, Fixed Price List, February-March 1959, lots G354 and G357.

Bibliography: Cancio 1978–79; Sedwick 1985, 1312–23; Sedwick and Sedwick 2007, 161–62 (Sedwick 16); Wilcox 1943.

"The Treasure of the Mesuno," *Coin Collector's Journal* 4, no. 3 (June 1937): 64.

James Risk, "Coins from the Mesuno Hoard," Coin Galleries (Division of Stack's), New York, New York, USA, *Fixed Price List*, February-March 1959, 1–4.

73. Harvard Yard, Cambridge, Massachusetts, USA, 1981 and summers 1984–87.

Type of find: Archaeological excavation.
Date of site: 1636–1987.
Contents: 14 AE, 1 NI, 2 AR.

Description:
Spain, real (½ pistareen), 1738
England, James I, Lennox farthing (item number 2003.1.425)
England, Charles I, Richmond farthing in excellent condition, suggesting that it was not long in circulation before it was lost (item number 992–9–10/74623) [note says: "Coin collected by Danny, one of the water line workmen when digging by hand near Wadsworth House. He carried this coin in his pocket for a few days"]
England, Charles I, Maltravers farthing, in excellent condition (item number 2003.1.425)
England, James I or Charles I, farthing, holed (item number 987–22–10/100153)
England, William III, farthing, ca. 1700
Great Britain, George II, farthing, 1739 (corrected from 1759)
England, William and Mary, halfpenny, 1694
Great Britain, halfpence (2): George I, 1724; George II, 1730
USA, 1¢ (5): 1820; 1827; 1828; 1831 (2)
USA, 5¢, 1882
USA, 10¢, 1884
Over 46 twentieth century coins were also found.

Disposition: Peabody Museum of Archaeology and Ethnology, Harvard University, Cambridge, Massachusetts, USA.

Bibliography: Drooker 1988; Stubbs 1992, 558–59.

Peabody Museum of Archaeology and Ethnology, Collections Online, http://www.peabody.harvard.edu.

Scott A. Templin, Curatorial Research Assistant, Peabody Museum of Archaeology and Ethnology, personal communication, May 11, 2007.

74. State Street, Portland, Maine, USA, June 1849.

Type of find: Single find.

Date of deposit: 1637–90.

Contents: 1 AR.

Description: England, Elizabeth I, sixpence, 1579

Disposition: Found by the gardener of William P. Fessenden in Fessenden's garden. Donated to the Maine Historical Society?

Bibliography: Willis 1859, 127–51.

75. Bermuda, 1959.

Type of find: Shipwreck.

Ship: Possibly the *Viga*, which was part of a 34-vessel fleet en route from Havana to Cadiz under the command of Don Geronimo Gomez de Sandoval. Lost with the patache *Galgo*.

Sank: May 1637 or 1639.

Contents: 50+ AR.

Description:

Spain, Philip IV, real, Seville (2)
Spain, Philip IV, 8 reales, Seville?
Spanish colonies, Philip IV, 8 reales, México
Spanish colonies, Philip IV, real, Potosí
Spanish colonies, Philip IV, 2 reales, Potosí
Spanish colonies, Philip IV, 4 reales, Potosí
Spanish colonies, Philip IV, 8 reales, Potosí (45)

Disposition: Excavated by Edward B. Tucker.

Bibliography: Marx 1971, 302; Potter 1972, 284–86. "Bermuda's New Treasure Trove Find," *Numismatic Circular* 67, no. 12 (December 1959): 226.

76. Ferryland, Newfoundland, Newfoundland and Labrador, Canada, 2001, 2005–6.

Type of find: Archaeological excavation.

Date of site: 1621–96; date of occupation of David Kirke house: 1638–51.

Contents: 4 PB, 30 AE, 1 B, 3 BI, 24 AR, 1 SN, 2 AV.

Description: There are three entries for this site, split into periods commencing in 1621, 1696, and 1865. This entry covers the period from the first settlement of the site until its destruction by French forces under the leadership of Pierre le Moyne d'Iberville in November 1696.

Netherlands, Friesland, bezemstuiver, 16[-]
Netherlands, Overijssel, 2 stuivers, 1619, twisted to make a love token or witch piece
Netherlands, Zeeland, 2 stuivers, 16[-]
Netherlands, 6 stuivers, 161[-], cut, quartered, worth about one penny
German states, Nuremberg, jetons (3): Hanns Krauwinckel II, rv. "HEIT ROTT MORGEN DOTT"; Hanns Krauwinckel II, rv. "GLVCK BESCHERT IST VNGWERT"; ND
England, lead piece worn smooth, possibly merchant's token of 17th century (or a David Kirke token?)
England, Charles II, farthing (3): 1673; 167[-] (2)
England, William and Mary, halfpenny (2): 1694; 169[-] tin
England, William III, halfpenny, [1695–98] (6)
England, James I, penny (2): bust and shield [1603–4]; rose and thistle [1604–19]
England, Charles I, penny [1630s]
England, Elizabeth I, threepence [1561–82] (2)
England, Elizabeth I, groat
England, Elizabeth I, sixpence (2): counterfeit with silver wash over copper core, 1574; genuine silver, 1579
England, Charles I, shilling [1642–48] (2)
England, James I, ¼ laurel, cut down to a fragment worth one shilling
Scotland, James VI (I), 20 pence, [1637–42]

Scotland, James VI (I), sword and scepter, [1601]
Ireland, James I, sixpence, [1603–4]
Ireland, James I, shilling, (2); [1604–5]; [1604–7] (both bent to make love tokens or witch pieces)
Ireland, James II, gun money, shilling, December 1689
France, Henry IV, double tournois, 1608
France, Louis XIII, doubles tournois (6): 1614A; [1642–43]; 1645E; ND (3)
France, provincial issue, Maximilian I of Bethune, ruler of Boisbelle and Henrichemont, double tournois (2): 163[-]; ND
France, provincial issue, Gaston, who had the usufruct of Dombes in Provence, double tournois, 1641
France, probably provincial issue, double tournois
France, Louis XIII, douzains (2): [1611–41], possibly a counterfeit; ND
France, Louis XIV, 4 sols, [1674–79], mint D (Vimy)
Spain, Philip III, 4 maravedíes, [1600–2]
Spain, Philip IV, 8 maravedíes, with numeral 8 counterstamp, 1652 (3)
Spain, Ferdinand and Isabella, ½ real, [1497–1504]
Portugal, John IV, ½ tostão counterstamped to be valued at 60 reis, 1642
Portugal, Philip II, 100 reis, 1598
Portugal, John IV, tostão of Sebastian counterstamped to be valued at 120 reis, 1642
English colonies, Newfoundland, DK (David Kirke) lead tokens (3)
Spanish colonies, Charles II, real, Potosí, 1672E
Spanish colonies, Philip IV, 8 reales, Potosí, before 1650
Unidentified copper coins (2)

Bibliography: Berry 2002, 1–71; Berry 2006; Jordan 2006.

77. Medford, Massachusetts, USA, spring 1787.

Type of find: Hoard.

Date of deposit: 1640.

Contents: 300? Bl.

Description: France, Louis XIII, douzains, counterstamped with fleur-de-lis (300?)

William Bentley described the find as follows in his diary on September 16, 1787:

"In removing a Stone wall in Mystic, or Medford, in 1783, there was found under it a large Collection of brass pieces nearly square, mixed with the smallest brass coins of Europe, the whole half a peck. A few round ones have a fleur-de-lis stamped on each side of them. The figures on the others were confused but representing no character. The Stone had lost all appearance of having ever been moved, & there is no recollection of the Currency of such pieces, which appear to have been of use."

These are probably counterstamped douzains of Louis XIII, raised to 15 deniers under the counterstamping order of 1640. Many of the counterstamps appear on coins of earlier kings, on squarish planchets.

Disposition: Found by workers widening the highway in Medford when they removed a stone wall.

Bibliography: Bentley 1905, 1:75.

Thaddeus Mason Harris, "Account of Copper Coins, Found in Medford, Massachusetts. In a letter to Hon. John Quincy Adams, Esq., Corresponding Secretary of the American Academy of Arts and Sciences," *Memoirs of the American Academy of Arts and Sciences* 3, no. 1 (1809): 195–96 (letter dated November 5, 1808).

D. G. B., *of West Chester, Pennsylvania, USA,* "Queries: Ancient Coins found in America,"

Historical Magazine 5 (October 1861): 314–15.

"Coins found in Medford, Mass.," *American Journal of Numismatics* 6, no. 4 (April 1872): 79–80.

"Extracts from the Diary of William Bentley, D. D. of Salem: Pub. Essex Institute, Salem, Mass., 1905," *Numismatist* 20, no. 1 (January 1907): 11.

78. Ambrosia Banks, North of Hispaniola, Dominican Republic, 1687, 1977–1978 and mid-1990s.

Type of find: Shipwreck.

Ship: Nuestra Señora de la Pura y Limpia Concepción.

Sank: November 2, 1641.

Contents: 40 AE, 63,000 AR. (These numbers comprise the modern salvage by Webber and Bowden, not the earlier salvage by Phips.)

Description:

Spain, 4 maravedíes (16)

Spain, 8 maravedíes (17)

Spain, 8 maravedíes, cast counterfeits (7)

Spain, silver coin, Cuenca

Spain, silver coin, Valladolid

Spain, silver coin, Madrid

Spain, silver coin, Seville

Spanish colonies, ½ real, México, assayer F

Spanish colonies, reales, México (4): [1580?]O; assayer F; 1634D; 1639P

Spanish colonies, 2 reales, México (17): [1580?]O; assayer F (2); [1608?]A; 1615/14F; [1616?]D/F; 1623D; 1626/5/4D; 1631/0D; 1632D (2); 1634/3; 1634D; 1637/6; 1639P; 1640P (2)

Spanish colonies, 4 reales, México (25): assayer F; 162[-]D; 1628D; 1631D; 1633/2D; 1635P; 1636P; 1637P (2); 1638P (2); 1639/8P (2); 1639P (5); 164[-]P; 1640/39P; 1640P (2); 1641/0P; 1641P; 16[-]P

Spanish colonies, 8 reales, México (57): 1623D; 1626D; 1627/6; 1628D (2); 1630D; 1631/0D; 1632/1/0D; 1632D (2); 1633D (2); 1634D (3); 1634P/D (2); 1634P (2); 1635P (2); 1636/5P; 1636P; 1637P (2); 1638P (3); 1639/8P (3); 1639P (3); counterfeit 1639P; 1640/39P (2); 1640P (3); 1641/40/39P (2); 1641/0P (3); 1641P (2); 1641/163P; 16[-]P; NDA (8)

Spanish colonies, 2 reales, Cartagena (8): 1626E (4); 1630E; 1634E (3)

Spanish colonies, 4 reales, Cartagena, 1628E

Spanish colonies, 8 reales, Cartagena, 1628E (2)

Spanish colonies, 2 reales, Bogotá (3): 1630P; 1635A; 1640A

Spanish colonies, 4 reales, Bogotá, 1627P

Spanish colonies, 8 reales, Bogotá (4): 1630P; 1633A; 1634A (2)

Spanish colonies, real, Potosí, assayer B

Spanish colonies, 2 reales, Potosí (43): assayer G (3); assayer A; assayer R; assayer R/B; assayer Q; assayer M; 1617M (2); 1618M; 1619T; 1620T (2); 1621T (2); 1621P; 1622P (2); [1622–23]P; [1624–26]Po (3); [1626]T (2); 1629T (2); 1630T (4); 1631T; 1632T; 1633T; 1634T; 1635T; 1636TR; 1637TR; 1638TR (4); 1639TR

Spanish colonies, 4 reales, Potosí (13): [1616]Q; assayer M; 1617M; [1622–23]P; 1627P; 1627T; 1628T; 1629T; 1633T; 1635TR (3); 1639TR

Spanish colonies, 8 reales, Potosí (38): assayer B; assayer R; assayer Q; assayer M/Q; assayer M; 1618RAL; 1619T; 1620T; 1621T (2); 1622P (2); [1624–26]Po (2); 1626Po; 1628T (2); 1629T (3); 1630T (2); 1631T; 1632T; 1633T; 1634T (2); 1635T (2); 1636TR (2); 1637TR (2); 1638TR; 1639TR (2); 1640TR (2)

£300,000 sterling in silver, including at least twenty-one silver ingots, was salvaged by William Phips in 1687 and taken to England. By weight, Phips is said to have recovered 37,538 8 reales, 27,556 pounds, 4 ounces of silver bars and cakes, and 25 pounds, 7 ounces of gold. Two medals commemorate this—Betts 66 and Betts 67. Nearly as much again was taken out of the ship in 1687, after Phips left, by salvagers from New York, New England, Barbados and other islands in the West Indies. In 1688, another 3,213 pounds, 10 ounces of silver was recovered by a less successful expedition under Sir John Narborough.

The 60,000 silver coins recovered in 1979 were dated 1600–41, of which 45,600 of the coins were dated 1639 and 1640. The coins split 55,800 México, 3,600 Potosí and Lima; the remaining 600 was spread among Bogotá, Cartagena, Cuenca, Madrid, Seville and Valladolid. The 40 bronze coins comprised 4 maravedíes, 8 maravedíes, and seven cast counterfeits. Only 1,800 coins bore dates. The most important discovery was dated coins from Cartagena and Bogotá of 1621 and 1622, since hitherto those mints were thought to have begun to coin in 1623.

Disposition of the 1979 salvage: 50% Sea Quest International, 50% to the Dominican Republic (who placed it on display in the Museo de las Casas Reales). The first marketing of the coins was through department stores: Harrod's in London, Neiman Marcus in Dallas and Wanamaker's in Philadelphia, who sold sets of cobs of 2 reales, 4 reales, and 8 reales in black walnut cases for $5,000. The more important coins were auctioned by Christensen in 1982 and are the basis for the enumeration above. Twelve coins from that sale are in the American Numismatic Society in New York, cataloged under item numbers 1987.63.1–12.

Disposition of the 1990s salvage: Tracy Bowden recovered another 3,000 silver coins; those coins were split 50% Bowden, 50% Dominican Republic.

Bibliography: Borrell 1983; Bowden 1996; Christensen 1982; Earle 1979; Earle 2007, 18–22, 55–75; Grissim 1980; Sedwick and Sedwick 2007, 162–63 (Sedwick 17).

Donn Pearlman, "Treasure Coins: The Conception still has many more to come," *Coinage,* July 1983, 17.

79. Chesapean Site, Virginia Beach, Virginia, USA, 1955.

Type of find: Archaeological excavation.

Date of site: 1645–55.

Contents: 4 AE.

Description:
England, James I, counterfeit Lennox round farthing
England, Charles I, Richmond farthing (2)
England, Charles I, Maltravers double ring farthing

Bibliography: Noël Hume 1984, 247.

80. New York, New York, USA, summer 1976–November 1984.

Type of find: Excavation. Series of finds made by William Asadorian, an amateur archaeologist.

Contents: 11 AE, 1 B, 2 AR.

Description: Found at Bowling Green, summer 1976:
Spain, 8 maravedíes, counterstamped twice with VIII in circle, [1649?]

Found in sewage sludge removed by contractors in Lower Manhattan and Midtown:
USA, 1¢ (6): 1828; 1847; large cents, ND (3); 1861
USA, counterfeit 50¢, 1918

Found at McDonald's site, by Water, Moore, and Pearl Streets, November 1984:
Brass nested coin weight, early 1700s

Found near Army Induction Center site, by Water, Moore, and Pearl Streets, November 1984:

France, Louis XVI, sol, 1790
Spain, Charles IV, 8 maravedíes, 1803
Findspot not recorded:
Great Britain, sixpence, 1865
Austria, kreuzer, 1885

Disposition: All the above except the counterstamped 8 maravedíes have been donated to the American Numismatic Society; accession number 2007.41/42.

Bibliography: Murray Schumach, "Dig He Must, and a 1600's Coin Turns Up at Bowling Green," *New York Times*, March 17, 1977, B1. Robert Wilson Hoge, personal communication, November 6, 2007.

81. Bay of All Saints, Brazil, 1981.

Type of find: Shipwreck.

Ship: Utrecht.

Sank: 1648.

Contents: 2+ AR, 2+ AV.

Description:
Netherlands, silver ducatons
Netherlands, gold florins

Disposition: Excavated by Robert Marx.

Bibliography: Sebring 1986, 121–22.

82. Papscanee Island, Castleton Island State Park, New York, USA 2001.

Type of find: Archaeological excavation.

Date of site: 1648–1929.

Contents: 1 AR. Archaeological excavations.

Description: Netherlands, 2 stuivers, Utrecht, 1624

Disposition: New York State Bureau of Historic Sites Collection, Peebles Island, New York, USA.

Bibliography: Hoover 2007 (providing inventory of New York State Bureau of Historic Sites Collections, Peebles Island, New York, as of August 16, 2005).

83. Stafford County, Virginia, USA, April 1991.

Type of find: Single find.

Date of deposit: 1650.

Contents: 1 AR.

Description: England, Elizabeth I, 4 pence (groat), cut quarter to make a penny

Disposition: Found by a metal detectorist.

Bibliography: Kays 2001, 2193.

84. Broad Financial Center, Whitehall and Pearl Streets, New York, New York, USA, winter of 1983–84.

Type of find: Archaeological excavation.

Date of site: Ca. 1650.

Contents: 1 AE.

Description:
Netherlands, jeton, 1590, with obverse inscription TVEMUR, Reverse NEC … 1590

As well as the jeton, a slate pencil, used to keep track of inventory, was also found. This site contained the warehouse of the merchant Augustine Heerman. The excavation was conducted by Joel Grossman of Greenhouse Associates.

Bibliography: Cantwell and DiZerega 2001, 154–55.

"Remains of New Amsterdam Unearthed," *Saint Louis Post-Dispatch*, September 8, 1984, C4 (UPI wire dispatch).

85. Bogotá, Colombia, 1959.

Type of find: Votive deposit.

Date of deposit: 1650.

Contents: 13 AR.

Description:
Spanish colonies, Philip IV, reales, México (2)
Spanish colonies, Philip IV, 2 reales, México
Spanish colonies, Philip IV, ½ real, Bogotá

Spanish colonies, Philip IV, reales, Potosí
Spanish colonies, Philip IV, 2 reales, Potosí, 1650O
Spanish colonies, Philip IV, 2 reales, Potosí (7)
Probably an "Arras," or wedding pledge.

Bibliography: Cancio 1979.

86. River Creek Site, York County, Virginia, USA, 1980.

Type of find: Archaeological excavation.

Date of site: 1650–80.

Contents: 1 AE.

Description: England, Charles I, rose farthing

Bibliography: Noël Hume 1984, 247.

87. Peninsula Point, Gaspé Bay, Québec, Canada, October 1911.

Type of find: Archaeological excavation.

Date of site: 1650–1770.

Contents: AE, BI, AR.

Description:

France, Louis XIV, double tournois, 1649 or earlier

France, Louis XIV, liard 1654–58, Saint Lo or Limoges

France, Louis XIV, douzain, counterstamped with a fleur de lis, overstruck as a sol of Navarre and Béarn, 1693 (Gadoury 94)

France, Louis XIV, 4 sols, 1675A

France, Louis XV, écu, 1721H

All coins found were French of Louis XIII, XIV, and XV.

Bibliography: Clarke 1911.

88. Munnsville, New York, USA, 1903.

Type of find: Hoard.

Date of deposit: 1654.

Contents: 2 AE.

Description:

France, Louis XIII, double tournois, 1639

France, Louis XIII, double tournois, 1640

Disposition: Theodore Stanford.

Bibliography: Beauchamp 1903, 50.

89. Indian Hill, Pompey, Onondaga County, New York, USA, 1880s.

Type of find: Hoard.

Date of site: 1654–82.

Contents: 5+ AE.

Description:

France, Louis XIV, liards, 165[-]A, holed for suspension (2)

France, Louis XIV, liards, mints B, D, and E

Found in an Indian site first visited by the French in 1654 and occupied by the Onondagas until 1682.

Bibliography: Beauchamp 1891, 45–46; 1903, 49.

90. Indian Castle, Pompey, New York, USA, 1903.

Type of find: Single find.

Date of site: 1600s.

Contents: 1 AR.

Description: Netherlands, 2 stuiver, Utrecht, 16[-], holed

Bibliography: Beauchamp 1903, 72.

91. East Hampton, New York, USA, February 1990.

Type of find: Single find.

Contents: 1 AR.

Description: English colonies, Massachusetts, New England sixpence, 1652

Disposition: Found in a frozen potato field with a metal detector by Lillian Rade. Auctioned by Sotheby's, November 21, 1991; bought by the Stack family for their personal collection.

Bibliography: Jed Stevenson, "Coins: Earliest Colonial Coinage," *New York Times*, July 7, 1991, Sec. 2, 34.

"Numismatic Narratives: ANA

Authentication Bureau identifies 300-Year-Old Coin," *Numismatist* 104, no. 9 (September 1991): 1385–86.

"Sotheby Auctions New England Sixpence," *Numismatist* 105, no. 2 (February 1992): 177.

92. Staten Island, New York, USA, 1872.

Type of find: Single find.

Contents: 1 AR.

Description: France, Louis XIV, ¼ ecu, 1653

Disposition: David Proskey.

Bibliography: Proskey 1873, 22.

93. Chanduy, Ecuador, November 1996–April 1997.

Type of find: Shipwreck.

Ship: Jesus Maria de la Limpia Concepción, also called *La Capitana*.

Sank: October 26–27, 1654.

Contents: 5,000 AR; 1 AV.

Description: This listing comprises the 1,945 silver coins, and the single gold coin, put up for auction by the salvors:

Spain, Philip II, 2 escudos, Seville

Non-counterstamped coins:

Spanish colonies, reales, Potosí (41): shield type, NDA (33); 1651O; 1652 (2); 1652E, transitional type (2); 1653 (3)

Spanish colonies, 2 reales, Potosí (159): shield type NDA (137); 1649Z; 1649Z/R; 1651E/O; 1651E; 1652E, shield type; 1652E, transitional type (3); pillar type, NDA (6); 1652 (2); 1653 (3) 1654 (3)

Spanish colonies, 4 reales, Potosí (133): 1652E, transitional type (8); 1652E (2); 1653/2E; 1653E (69); 1654E (53)

Spanish colonies, 8 reales, Potosí (1,019): shield type, NDA (70); 1649Z; 1649O; 1650O (3); 1651E/O; 1651E (7); 1652E, transitional type (21); 1652E (44); 1653E (454); 1654/3 (2); 1654E (414); 1653E royal

Counterstamped coins are listed by counterstamp, followed by the date and assayer of the host coins:

Spanish colonies, 4 reales, Potosí, with one counterstamp (87):

Crown (11): 1649O/Z; 1649O, 1651E; 1651O; assayer O (2); NDA (5)

Crowned L (24): 1649 (2); 1650O (2); 1651; assayer O; NDA (18)

Crowned F (7): 1650O; NDA (6)

Crowned Philip IV monogram: 1650O

Crowned J: NDA

Crowned S: NDA

Fleur de lis: NDA

Unidentified counterstamp: NDA (41)

Spanish colonies, 4 reales, Potosí, with multiple counterstamps (4):

Crown and crowned P: NDA

Crown and crowned A: assayer O

Crowned O and arms of Spain: 1651

Crown, crowned A, and crowned C: 1650O

Spanish colonies, 8 reales, Potosí, with one counterstamp (470):

Crown (82): 1649O (8); 1649Z (3); 1649 (3); 1650O; 1651E (6); 1651O; 1651E/O; assayer Z; NDA (58)

Crowned C (5): 1650O; 1651O; assayer O; NDA (2)

Crowned F (93): 1649O/Z; 1649O; 1650O (7); assayer O; 1651O (3); 1651E (9); 1652E (3); assayer Z; assayer E; NDA (66)

Crowned G (7): 1650O (4); 1651O; NDA (2)

Crowned L (175): 1649Z (7); 1649O/Z; 1649O (6); 1650O (19); 1651E (5); 1651O (6); 1651 (2); assayer Z; assayer O (3); assayer E (2); NDA (123)

Crowned backwards L (5): assayer O; NDA (4)

Crowned O (29): 1649Z; 1649O; 1649; 1650; 1650O (2); 1651O (2); 1651E/O; 1651E (4); NDA (16)

Crowned P (2): 1649O; 165[-]O

Crowned S (18): 1649O (4); NDA (14)

Crowned T (11): 165[-]O; 1651E; assayer E (3); NDA (6)

Crowned fancy Z: assayer E

Crowned 1652 (4): 1650O (3); assayer E/O

Fleur de lis (3): assayer O; NDA (2)

Crowned Philip IV monogram (8): 1650O/Z; 1650O (2); 1651O; 1651E (2); 165[-]O; assayer O

Crowned arms of Spain (12): assayer O (2); E/O; NDA (9)

Buenos Aires counterstamp: assayer O

Unidentified counterstamp (14): NDA (14)

Spanish colonies, 8 reales, Potosí, with two counterstamps (29):

Two different crown counterstamps (3): 1649O, 1650O; 165[-]O

Crown and crowned C (7): 1649O; 1650O; 1651E (3); assayer O (2)

Crown and crowned L (3): 1650O; 1651O; assayer E

Crown and crowned O (4): 1649O; assayer O (2); NDA

Crown and arms of Spain (2): 1650O; assayer E

Crowned L and arms of Spain (4): 1649Z; 1650O; 1651; assayer O

Crowned L and crowned C: assayer O

Crowned L and crowned G: 1651O

Crowned L and crowned T (2): 1651E; assayer O

Crowned O and arms of Spain: assayer O

Crowned P and crowned T: 1650O

Spanish colonies, 8 reales, Potosí, with three counterstamps (3):

Fleur de lis, crown and crowned C: 1650O

Crown, crowned A, and arms of Spain: assayer O

Crown, crowned C, and arms of Spain: assayer E

No attempt has been made to distinguish individual punches among the counterstamps listed above. Greater detail and further distinctions may be found in the Ponterio auction catalog.

The Spanish recovered 3.5 million pesos in 1654–62, which caused a scandal, since the registered treasure was only 3 million pesos. Some of what they recovered was put on the *Maravillas,* which sank in 1656. And some of what was salvaged from that was put on the *Madama do Brasil,* which sank in its turn off Gorda Cay in 1657.

Disposition: The recoveries in the 1990s of 5,000 coins were split 50% to the salvors, 50% to the Ecuadorean government.

Bibliography: Earle 2007, 82–84; Ponterio 1999; Sedwick and Sedwick 2007, 164–65 (Sedwick 19).

Diana Jean Schemo, "Search for a Galleon Off Ecuador Yields a Ship and a Dispute," *New York Times,* April 14, 1997, A10.

"Former Police Chief Finds Sunken Treasure," *Numismatist* 110, no. 7 (July 1997): 743.

94. Rio Cobre, where it runs past Villa de la Vega (Spanish Town), Jamaica, 1970s.

Type of find: Hoard.

Date of deposit: 1655.

Contents: 30 AE.

Description: Spanish colonies, 4 maravedíes, Santo Domingo (30)

Bibliography: Barker 1978, 308–10.

95. Whim's Estate, Saint Catherine, Jamaica, late 1976.

Type of find: Hoard.

Date of deposit: 1655.

Contents: 400 AE.

Description:

Spanish colonies, 4 maravedíes, Santo Domingo (400): not counterstamped (200); key counterstamp (11); anchor counterstamp

(99); anchor and key counterstamps (13); anchor and plain "S" counterstamps (4); long "S" counterstamp; plain "S" counterstamp (72)

Bibliography: Barker 1978, 308–10.

96. Seven's Estate, Clarendon, Jamaica, late 1976.

Type of find: Hoard.

Date of deposit: 1655.

Contents: 400 AE.

Description: Spanish colonies, 4 maravedíes, Santo Domingo

The following counterstamps were found in the hoard: key; wide "S"; anchor; plain "S"; serrated "S"; long "S"; retrograde "S"; V and X; and hand. All counterstamps but the first two are deemed to be Jamaican.

Bibliography: Barker 1978, 308–10.

97. Salta or Tucumán, northern Argentina, October 1968.

Type of find: Hoard.

Date of deposit: 1655.

Contents: 1,000 AR.

Description:

Spanish colonies, reales, Potosí (200)
Spanish colonies, 2 reales, Potosí (300)
Spanish colonies, 4 reales, Potosí (200)
Spanish colonies, 8 reales, Potosí (300): 1642R; 1644T; 1644TR; 1645T; 1646FR; 1647T (2); 164[7–9]Z; 1653E; 1654E; 1655E; NDA (290)

No coins were dated 1648–52. Cancio notes that it is odd that the hoard includes coins from before and after the transition of 1652.

Disposition: Dispersed through coin shops located on Corrientes, San Martín, and Reconquista streets in Buenos Aires. Cancio bought nine 8 reales.

Bibliography: Cancio 1981 (includes photographs of the 9 coins Cancio bought).

98. Middletown, Connecticut, USA, April 1880.

Type of find: Single find.

Contents: 1 AE.

Description: France, Louis XIV, liard, 1655B

Disposition: Found by Samuel Dutcher, a gardener for W. W. Wilcox, in Wilcox's garden.

Bibliography: "Numismatic Discoveries," *American Journal of Numismatics* 14, no. 4 (April 1880): 101.

99. Brackett and Vaughan Streets, Portland, Maine, USA, August 1849.

Type of find: Single find.

Contents: 1 AR.

Description: Netherlands, Province undetermined, lion daalder, 1655

Disposition: Maine Historical Society?

Bibliography: Willis 1859, 127–51.

100. Bahamas Bank, Bahamas, August 1950, 1972 and 1986.

Type of find: Shipwreck.

Ship: Nuestra Señora de las Maravillas.

Sank: January 4, 1656.

Contents: 830 AR, 282 AV.

Description:

Spanish colonies, 4 reales, México (108): 1654P; 1653–55 (107)
Spanish colonies, 8 reales, México (167): 1652P; 1654P (5); 1655P (3); 165[-]P (2); assayer P (3); 1651–55 (150); NDA (3)
Spanish colonies, 8 reales, Cartagena, 1655?
Spanish colonies, 8 reales, Bogotá (3): 1649; 1653, PoRAS (2)
Spanish colonies, 2 escudos, Bogotá (206): 164[-]R (2); 1654R (104); 1655R (4); assayer R (57); NDA (39)
Non-counterstamped coins:
Spanish colonies, reales, Potosí, NDA (17)
Spanish colonies, 2 reales, Potosí, NDA (17)

Spanish colonies, 4 reales, Potosí, 1653–54 (57): (39); NDA (18)

Spanish colonies, 8 reales, Potosí (268): assayer O (2); 1650O; assayer E; 1652E (5); 1653E (6); 1654E (6); 165[-]E; 1652–54 (228); NDA (18)

Counterstamped coins are listed by counterstamp, followed by the date and assayer of the host coins. All coins reported are single counterstamp coins.

Spanish colonies, 4 reales, Potosí (2):

Crowned L: 1649O

Indeterminate counterstamp: 1649

Spanish colonies, 8 reales, Potosí (182):

Crown (11): 1649O; assayer O; 1650O (2); 1651O (2); assayer E (3); 1651E (3); NDA

Crowned A: 1651E

Crowned L (31): 1649Z; assayer O (6); 1650O (7); 1651O (6); 1651E (6); 165[-]O (3); NDA (2)

Crowned F (18): 1649O; 1650O (2); 1651O; 1651E (11); assayer O (2); assayer E

Crowned O (2): 16[-]O; 1651E

Crowned T: assayer O (3)

Crowned Z: 1650O

Castles and lions: assayer E

Indeterminate counterstamp (122): shield type, 1649–51 (121); 1651E

The Spanish salvaged 480,000 pesos in coin together with 12 cannon in 13 days in June 1656. Further salvage efforts by the Spanish recovered about a quarter of the *Maravillas* treasure. Many English colonists from New England, New York, and the West Indies salvaged silver from this wreck in 1658–84, by which time most of the treasure that could be recovered using the techniques of that period had been salvaged. William Phips worked this wreck in 1684, but recovered little.

A silver bar and three coins recovered by Howard Lightburn and Roscoe Thompson in August 1950 probably came from the *Maravillas*. The three coins comprised 8 reales, México; 8 reales, Bogotá, 1649; and 8 reales, Potosí, with counterstamp. These coins are included in the listing above. The bar was presented to the Development Board of the Bahamas by Albert E. Worswick. One of the coins was acquired by Theodore Pyfrom of Nassau.

Some treasure was salvaged by Robert Marx and Willard Bascom in 1972 and auctioned by Schulman. Salvage was resumed by Herbert Humphreys, Jr., after 1986, and auctioned by Christie's.

Bibliography: Christie's 1992, lots 1–157 and 3225–31; Earle 1979, 93–94, 109–110, 151–152; Earle 2007, 22–25; Goldberg 2005, lots 2801–2932; Sebring 1986, 34–35; Sedwick and Sedwick 2007, 165–66 (Sedwick 20); Schulman 1974, lots 1–501I and A56–A63. "Silver Ingot Found in a Sunken Ship," *Sociedad Numismatica de México, Boletín* 1, no. 5 (March-December 1953): 21–28.

101. Indian site, Cayuga County, New York, USA, summer 1887.

Type of find: Hoard.

Date of deposit: 1656.

Container: Pewter mug.

Contents: 44 AE.

Description: France, Louis XIV, liards, 1656 (44)

Bibliography: Beauchamp 1891, 49; 1903, 49.

102. Southern Maryland, USA, October 1977.

Type of find: Single find.

Contents: 1 AE.

Description: English colonies, Maryland, Lord Baltimore, denarium, [1658]

Disposition: Found with a metal detector by a Maryland college student. Bowers & Ruddy, Auction (Johnson-Meyer), February 9, 1978:1 – Jerry Cohen – N.A.S.C.A. 1978

– John L. Roper, Jr. – Stack's, Auction, December 8–9, 1983:46.

Bibliography: Breen 1988, 20 (Breen 76); Stack's 2004, lot 274 (letter by John J. Ford, Jr. to Q. David Bowers, November 10, 1977, concerning the discovery of this piece).

103. Maryland, USA, ca. 1965.

Type of find: Single find.

Contents: 1 AE.

Description: English colonies, Maryland, Lord Baltimore denarium, [1658]

Disposition: Donated to the Smithsonian Institution by the Baltimore dealer Thomas Warfield with a note, "Found in Maryland in recent years." Weight, 50 grains.

Bibliography: Stack's 2007, lot 213.

104. Southern Maryland, USA, August 2007.

Type of find: Single find.

Contents: 1 AE.

Description: English colonies, Maryland, Lord Baltimore denarium, [1658]

Disposition: St. Mary's County Historical Society.

Bibliography: Stack's 2007, lot 213.

105. Jupiter Inlet, Florida, USA, July 13, 1987.

Type of find: Shipwreck.

Ship: San Miguel el Arcángel, an *aviso,* a rapid boat carrying messages back to Spain.

Sank: October 1659.

Contents: 800+ AR.

Description:
Spanish colonies, real, México, 1653
Spanish colonies, 4 reales, México (3): 1655 (2); 1657
Spanish colonies, 8 reales, México (15): 1653; 1654 (3); 1655 (3); 1656 (3); 1657 (5)
Spanish colonies 2 reales, Cartagena, 1655
Spanish colonies, 4 reales, Cartagena, 1655
Spanish colonies, 8 reales, Cartagena, 1655
Spanish colonies, 8 reales, Bogotá (2): 1652; 1655
Spanish colonies, 8 reales, Lima, 1659, star of Lima (10?)
Spanish colonies, reales, Potosí (7): 1652 (2); 1653; 1655 (2); 1656; 1657
Spanish colonies, 2 reales, Potosí (13): 1640; 1650; 1652 (2); 1653 (3); 1654 (3); 1657 (2); 1658
Spanish colonies, 4 reales, Potosí (31): 1652 (3); 1653 (4); 1654 (9); 1655 (3); 1656 (4); 1657 (3); 1658 (5)
Spanish colonies, 8 reales, Potosí (75): 1652 (11); 1653 (10); 1653E (Sebring); 1654 (14); 1655 (9); 1656 (6); 1657 (13); 1658 (11)

Carl J. Clausen, formerly the chief archaeologist for Florida, was working with the salvors in 1987 to develop an archaeological research design to document the artifacts recovered from the wrecksite.

Disposition: 198 to the State of Florida. The Sebring sale (American Numismatic Rarities, January 2004), lot 1564, had an 8 reales from Potosí, 1653E.

Bibliography: Craig 2000b, 78, 134, 165–66; Sebring 2004, lot 1564; Sedwick and Sedwick 2007, 167–68 (Sedwick 22).

Jupiter Wreck, Inc. v. Unidentified, Wrecked, and Abandoned Sailing Vessel, 691 F.Supp. 1377 (S. D. Fla. 1988).

106. Hingham, Massachusetts, USA, March 1862.

Type of find: Single find.

Contents: 1 AE.

Description: Spain, maravedí, 1659

Bibliography: "Boston Numismatic Society, Boston, March 6, 1862," *Historical Magazine* 6, no. 5 (May 1862): 152.

107. Near Williamsburg, Virginia, USA, April 1991.

Type of find: Single find.

Date of deposit: 1660.

Contents: 1 AR.

Description: England, Elizabeth I, sixpence, cut quarter to make three halfpence

Disposition: Found by a metal detectorist.

Bibliography: Kays 2001, 2193.

108. Charlestown, Rhode Island, USA, 1861.

Type of find: Funerary deposit. A native American grave, thought to be that of the daughter of the Sachem of the Niantic, who died around 1660.

Date of deposit: 1660.

Contents: 1 AE, 1 AR.

Description:
England, farthing
France, Louis XIV, ½ écu, 1650

Bibliography: Parsons 1863.

109. Rhode Island, USA, April 2006.

Type of find: Single find.

Contents: 1 AR.

Description: English colonies, Massachusetts, oak tree shilling, [1660–67]

Disposition: Found with a metal detector by John C. Bailey, a member of the Silver City Treasure Hunters Club of Taunton, Massachusetts.

Bibliography: Eric von Klinger, "Man's Oak Tree shilling offers 'bragging rights,'" *Coin World*, July 31, 2006, 3 (reference courtesy of Q. David Bowers).

110. Colombia, 1958.

Type of find: Hoard.

Date of deposit: 1662.

Contents: 46 AR.

Description:
Spanish colonies, reales, Cartagena (5): assayer S; assayer H (4)
Spanish colonies, ¼ real, Bogotá, pillar type?
Spanish colonies, ½ reales, Bogotá (8): 1652; 1657; 1658; 1662 (2); 16[-]; NDA (2)
Spanish colonies, reales, Bogotá, shield type (11): 1627P (3); 1628P; assayer P (5); assayer R; NDA
Spanish colonies, reales, Bogotá, pillar type (10): 1651; 1653 (2); 1655; 1662; 16[-]7; NDA (4)
Spanish colonies, 2 reales, Bogotá, shield type (5): 1627P (2); 1630P; 1647R; assayer R
Spanish colonies, 2 reales, Bogotá, pillar type, 1652
Spanish colonies, 4 reales, Bogotá, shield type, assayer T
Spanish colonies, 4 reales, Bogotá, pillar type (2): 1655; 1662PoR
Spanish colonies, 8 reales, Bogotá, shield type, 16[-]P
Spanish colonies, 8 reales, Bogotá, pillar type, 1657PoRS

Disposition: Clyde Hubbard.

Bibliography: Nesmith 1958b.

111. Brookline, Massachusetts, USA, September 1870.

Type of find: Single find.

Contents: 1 AR.

Description: English colonies, Massachusetts, oak tree twopence, 1662

Disposition: Found by a farmer on the old Harris farm in Brookline.

Bibliography: Augustine Shurtleff, "Cents of 1795, 1796, 1798, 1832," *American Journal of Numismatics* 6, no. 3 (January 1871): 63–64.

112. Yorktown, Virginia, USA, March 1997.

Type of find: Hoard.

Date of deposit: 1663.

Containers: Ceramic crocks.

Contents: 100 AE.

Description:
Scotland, twopence, 1663 (latest coin)
England, James I (James VI), Lennox style farthing, 1618–19 (earliest coin)

England, Richmond farthings
England, Rose farthings

Disposition: The pieces were recovered from farmers' fields in Yorktown, where they had been buried.

Bibliography: Mossman 1999, 1902.

113. Newtown, Queens, Long Island, New York, USA, April 1867.

Type of find: Single find.

Date of deposit: 1664.

Contents: 1 AR.

Description: Netherlands?, silver medal: obverse, figure of a man holding scepter and scroll, wearing chain and medal around neck, inscription: "Wahrhaftic conter[fey]," "Johann Van Leiden, een Koeninck der Wederdofer zo Monster," ['A true portrait of John of Leiden, a King of the Anabaptists in Münster'] Reverse: coat of arms, ball with band around surmounted by cross and crown over two crossed swords, "Gottes macht ist myn cracht. Anno MDXXXV" ['God's might is my power, Year 1535']

Silver medal found while tearing down a Dutch colonial house. The medal is commemorative of the Anabaptists of Münster, 1 6/8 inches in diameter, made of two sheets of silver put together.

Bibliography: "General City News: An Interesting Historical Relic," *New York Times*, April 9, 1867, 8.

"Tailor-Kings," *American Journal of Numismatics* 2, no. 2 (May 1867): 10–11.

114. Southern New Jersey, USA, July 1991.

Type of find: Single find.

Contents: 1 AE.

Description: England, Yorkshire, Guisburne, seventeenth century tradesman's token, 1666 (Boyne-Williamson Yorkshire 95)

Bibliography: Kleeberg 1992b, 37.

115. Philadelphia, Pennsylvania, USA, July 1991.

Type of find: Single find.

Contents: 1 AE.

Description: England, Surrey, Rotherhithe, seventeenth century tradesman's token, 1660s (Boyne-Williamson Surrey 274)

Bibliography: Kleeberg 1992b, 37.

116. Jamestown, Virginia, USA, 1958 and 1994–2002.

Type of find: Archaeological excavation.

Date of site: 1667–1700.

Contents: 2 AE, 1 SN.

Description:

England, Portsmouth, Henry Jenner, token, 1656

England, London, John Langston?, Globe Tavern, token, 1667 (found in context of 1667–1700)

English colonies, James II, 1/24 real for the American Plantations, 1688

Bibliography: Cotter 1958, 60, 191, 240, and plate 89; Kelso 2006, 207; Noël Hume 1995, 22 (mentions the James II 1/24 real).

117. Watson's Hill, Plymouth, Massachusetts, USA, July 1874.

Type of find: Single find.

Contents: 1 AR.

Description: English colonies, Massachusetts, pine tree threepence, 1652 [1667–74]

Disposition: It was picked up in the garden of Gideon Holbrook, on Watson's Hill, and acquired by Myles S. Weston.

Bibliography: "Notes and Queries," *American Journal of Numismatics* 9, no. 1 (July 1874): 22.

118. Saugus, Massachusetts, USA, October 1885.

Type of find: Single find.

Contents: 1 AR.

Description: English colonies, Massachusetts, pine tree threepence, 1652 [1667–74]
The coin was exhumed in a garden near the town.

Bibliography: Buried Treasures Found 1885, 42.

119. Abandoned farm field near the Merrimack River, New Hampshire, USA, April 1993.

Type of find: Single find.

Contents: 1 AR.

Description: English colonies, Massachusetts, pine tree threepence, Noe 36, 1652 [1667–74]

Disposition: Found with a metal detector by Thomas G. Brown.

Bibliography: "Colonial Threepence Found with Metal Detector," *Numismatist* 106, no. 4 (April 1993): 457–59.

120. Gray's Wharf, Boston, Massachusetts, USA, April 1862.

Type of find: Single find.

Contents: 1 AR.

Description: English colonies, Massachusetts, pine tree sixpence [1667–74]

Disposition: Found by a member of the Singleton family on Gray's Wharf, while picking over a cargo of gum from Africa.

Bibliography: "An Ancient Coin and a Curious Fact," *New England Historical and Genealogical Record* 16 (April 1862): 151.

121. Essex, Massachusetts, USA, October 1885.

Type of find: Single find.

Contents: 1 AR.

Description: English colonies, Massachusetts, pine tree sixpence, 1652 [1667–74]

Disposition: The coin was dug up by Frank W. Story.

Bibliography: Buried Treasures Found 1885, 42.

122. Wellingsley, near Plymouth, Massachusetts, USA, January 1889.

Type of find: Single find.

Contents: 1 AR.

Description: English colonies, Massachusetts, pine tree sixpence, 1652 [1667–74]

Bibliography: American Journal of Numismatics 23, no. 4 (April 1889): 77 (citing *Old Colony Memorial* [Plymouth, MA], January 17, 1889).

123. Samuels Farm, Windsor, Connecticut, USA, August 27, 1889.

Type of find: Single find.

Contents: 1 AR.

Description: English colonies, Massachusetts, pine tree sixpence, 1652 [1667–74]

Disposition: Found by a farmhand on the Samuels Farm, Edward Kennedy.

Bibliography: "An Ancient Coin Found," *New York Times*, August 28, 1889, 2.

124. Naval War College, Newport, Rhode Island, USA, April 1954.

Type of find: Single find.

Contents: 1 AR.

Description: English colonies, Massachusetts, pine tree sixpence, 1652 [1667–74]

Disposition: Found by Joseph Sylvia, groundskeeper at the Naval War College.

Bibliography: "'Dirty Penny' Revealed as Rare Coin," *Numismatic Scrapbook Magazine* 20, no. 4 (April 1954): 520.

125. Lowell Island, Massachusetts, USA, July 1852.

Type of find: Single find.

Contents: 1 AR.

Description: English colonies, Massachusetts, pine tree shilling, 1652 [1667–74]

139. Bacon's Castle, Surry County, Virginia, USA, 1995.

Type of find: Archaeological excavation.

Contents: 1 AE.

Description: England, Charles II, halfpenny, 1675

Bibliography: Noël Hume 1995, 21.

140. Québec, Québec, Canada, 1976–80.

Type of find: Archaeological excavation of the house of Champlain at Québec.

Date of French occupation of site: 1675–1700. The finds of a later, British, phase of occupation, perhaps 1760–1790, are listed under that date.

Contents: 10 AE, 7 BI, 1 AR. Archaeological excavations of the house of Champlain at Québec.

Description:

France, double tournois (8): feudal?; 1582; 1633; 1639; 1640; 1643H; 1643L or E; ND, probably mint H

France, Louis XIV, liard, 17[-]

France, Henry III, douzain, 1576H

France, Charles X (posthumous pretender issue), douzain, 1593, with 1640 fleur de lis counterstamp

France, Henry IV, douzain, 1595, with 1640 fleur de lis counterstamp

France, Louis XIII, douzain, 1622, with 1640 fleur de lis counterstamp

France, douzain fragment, with 1640 counterstamp

France, douzain fragments (2)

France, Louis XIV, denier tournois, 1648A

France, Louis XIV, 4 sols, 1675D

This above list is based on the report by Niellon and Moussette. Peter Moogk gives a general report on the coins found in the general Place Royale area, not only the Habitation site.

Disposition: Ministère des Affaires Culturelles (Secteur Place Royale), Québec, Québec, Canada.

Bibliography: Moogk 1989, 246–49; Niellon and Moussette 1981, 139–44.

141. Osbourne near Henricus, Virginia, USA, 2007.

Type of find: Single find.

Contents: 1 AR.

Description: Spanish colonies, real, Potosí, 1676E, weighs 1.3 grams

Disposition: Thomas Kays.

Bibliography: Kays 2007, 11.

142. Boston?, Massachusetts, USA, January 1874.

Type of find: Single find.

Contents: 1 AV.

Description: England, Charles II, guinea, 1676

Disposition: Found by the son of George L. Hart while playing in his father's garden.

Bibliography: Appleton 1874, 57.

143. Canada, 1889.

Type of find: Hoard.

Date of deposit: 1670s.

Container: Inkhorn.

Contents: 3 AR.

Description:

France, Louis XIV, ordinary silver coins (2)

French colonies, Louis XIV, 5 sols, "Gloriam Regni"

Three coins in an old inkhorn, which had been in Canada above 150 years. "This, along with the finding of the fifteen sols piece in Nova Scotia, serves to prove that this coinage circulated in Canada."

Disposition: Judge Georges Baby, president of the Numismatic and Antiquarian Society of Montreal.

Bibliography: Robert Wallace McLachlan, "Note," *Canadian Antiquarian and*

partially removing the old building at the corner of Washington and Warren Streets, Boston Highlands. The building had once been the residence of Governor Sumner.

Bibliography: "Notes and Queries," *American Journal of Numismatics* 8 no. 4 (April 1874): 94.

136. The Hamptons, New York, USA, 1980.

Type of find: Hoard.

Date of deposit: 1670.

Contents: 8 AE.

Description:
England, Maidstone, Kent, tokens (8): Boyne-Williamson Kent 380, 381 (2), 385, 392, 393, 396, 398.

One of the Hamptons originally was called Maidstone.

Disposition: Private collection. Color slides of the tokens were prepared at the ANS, courtesy of Henry Dittmer.

Bibliography: Kleeberg 1992b, 37.

137. Estancia Valley, near Moriarty, New Mexico, USA, winter 1957.

Type of find: Single find.

Date of deposit: 1674.

Contents: 1 B.

Description: Spain, Catholic religious medal; Obverse inscription reads SMA TERRESIA (Santísima Teresa, "Most Holy Teresa"), depicts Saint Teresa of Ávila in religious ecstasy with angel aiming arrow at her. Reverse, HONOFRIO, angel presents bread to the kneeling Theban hermit, Saint Onofrius.

The obverse depiction is modeled after Bernini's marble group for the Cornaro Chapel in the Church of Santa Maria della Vittoria in Rome, Italy.

Disposition: Found in a blow out at the end of the great drought of 1951–57. Owned by Mrs. Ann Spencer Dunning. On loan from her to the Museum of New Mexico.

Bibliography: Boyd 1970.

138. Roxbury, Massachusetts, USA, September 1863.

Type of find: Hoard.

Date of deposit: 1675.

Contents: 28 AR.

Description:
English colonies, Massachusetts, oak tree twopence (6): Noe 29–31 (3); Noe 32–34 (3)

English colonies, Massachusetts, oak tree threepence (2): Noe 23–27 (2)

English colonies, Massachusetts, oak tree sixpence (7): Noe 16; Noe 17?; Noe 20 (2); Noe 21; Noe 22

English colonies, Massachusetts, oak tree shilling, Noe 4

English colonies, Massachusetts, pine tree threepence (4): Noe 34–35 (2); Noe 36–37 (2)

English colonies, Massachusetts, pine tree sixpence (2): Noe 32; Noe 33

English colonies, Massachusetts, pine tree shilling (6): Noe 8?; Noe 11; Noe 15–28; Noe 29 (2); Noe 30

The identification of the die varieties is based upon adjectival descriptions in the second Woodward sale.

Disposition: Found by a nine year old boy, George Wilber Reed, the son of George P. Reed, in the cavity of a flat rock, in May's Woods, near Warren Street, on the road to Dorchester. Auctioned twice by William Elliot Woodward: May 17–21, 1864, when the pieces did not sell, and October 18–22, 1864.

Bibliography: Appleton 1874, 57; Breen 1952, 12–13 (Breen Hoards V); Noe 1952, 15–16; Woodward 1863a; Woodward 1864a; Woodward 1864b.

English colonies, Massachusetts, oak tree shillings, 1652 (15)

English colonies, Massachusetts, pine tree shillings, 1652 (15)

An "intelligent observer" noted at least four distinct die varieties among the coins.

The coins were found in sand that was being removed by a laborer while excavating a cellar under the extension of a store, not far from the railroad station. The remains of a wooden box, much decayed, were detected in the sand.

Disposition: A willow tree shilling in the Yale University Collection comes from this find (Noe 3-C). This is the piece in the Ferguson Haines sale, lot 1084, described there as "large well spread tree, Treasure Trove, Exeter, N. H., 1876."

Bibliography: Breen 1952, 15 (Breen Hoards X); Noe 1952, 16–17; Woodward 1880, lot 1084.

"Pine Tree Money Found," *American Journal of Numismatics* 11, no. 4 (April 1877): 92.

Charles Henry Bell, "The Exeter Bonanza," *American Journal of Numismatics* 12, no. 4 (April 1878): 105–6.

132. Boothbay Harbor, Maine, USA, 1865.

Type of find: Hoard.

Date of deposit: 1667–74.

Contents: 5 AR.

Description: English colonies, Massachusetts, oak tree and pine tree shillings (5)

The coins were found by Milton Ambrose of Boothbay, Maine in Wall's Cove, East Boothbay Harbor. "They have evidently been long in salt water, having lost about half of their original weight and thickness, and are destitute of ring, but arc of unquestionable genuineness, being of well-known varieties."

Disposition: One sold with William Elliot Woodward's personal collection in 1884, lot 354, described as: "Oak tree shilling, ex Boothbay, Me., piece broken from the edge, weight reduced by nearly one half." Others sold by Bangs & Co., New York, September 1–3, 1880, lots 429–32.

Bibliography: Breen 1952, 12–13 (Breen Hoards VII); Noe 1952, 18; Woodward 1880a; Woodward 1884, lot 354.

133. Salem, Massachusetts, USA, 1859.

Type of find: Hoard.

Date of deposit: 1667–74.

Contents: 1 AE, 4–5 AR.

Description:

England, Charles I, rose farthing [1635–44]

English colonies, Massachusetts, pine tree shillings (4–5) [1667–74]

Bibliography: Mossman 1999, 1902.

134. Bay of All Saints, Bahía, Brazil, September 1976.

Type of find: Shipwreck.

Ship: Santíssimo Sacramento.

Sank: May 5, 1668 at 11 pm, en route from Lisbon, Portugal to Bahia, Brazil.

Contents: 50 AR.

Description:

Portugal, John IV, silver coins, and Spain, Philip IV, silver coins, with the Brazilian counterstamp of 1642 (raising the value 20%) and the Brazilian counterstamp of 1663 (raising the value 25%) (50)

Bibliography: Pernambucano de Mello 1979; Pickford 1994, 165; Sedwick and Sedwick 2007, 169 (Sedwick 24); Smith 1988, 105–6.

135. Boston, Massachusetts, USA, April 1874.

Type of find: Single find.

Contents: 1 AE.

Description: England, Norwich, farthing token, 1668

It was found between the floors while

Disposition: Found by a worker in the old hulk of a vessel that lies upon the beach near the steamboat landing.

Bibliography: "Interesting," *Gleason's Pictorial Drawing Room Companion*, July 24, 1852, 61 (reference courtesy of Q. David Bowers).

126. West Springfield, Massachusetts, USA, July 1867.

Type of find: Single find.

Contents: 1 AR.

Description: English colonies, Massachusetts, pine tree shilling, 1652 [1667–74]

Disposition: Found by Orrin Loomis, aged 75, while walking in his fields.

Bibliography: "Scraps," *Historical Magazine*, 2nd series, 2 (July 1867): 63.

127. Farm near Bridgeport, Connecticut, USA, April 1921.

Type of find: Single find.

Contents: 1 AR.

Description: English colonies, Massachusetts, pine tree shilling, 1652 [1667–74]

Disposition: Dug up on a farm near the home of Leonard Kusterer (Kusterer lived in Bridgeport).

Disposition: acquired by Leonard Kusterer; exhibited by him at the April 8, 1921 meeting of the New York Numismatic Club.

Bibliography: "New York Numismatic Club Minutes, April 8, 1921," *Numismatist* 34, no. 7 (July 1921): 309.

128. Annapolis, Maryland, USA, January 1874.

Type of find: Single find.

Contents: 1 AR.

Description: English colonies, Massachusetts, shilling, probably a pine tree Noe 1, 1652 [1667–74]

Bibliography: Appleton 1874, 57 (citing the *Annapolis (MD) Republican*).

129. Williamstown, Massachusetts, USA, October 1910.

Type of find: Single find.

Contents: 1 AR.

Description: English colonies, Massachusetts, pine tree shilling, 1652 [1667–74]

Disposition: Found by Cassius D. Phelps.

Bibliography: William Theophilus Rogers Marvin, "A Curious Find in Williamstown, Mass.," *American Journal of Numismatics* 44, no. 4 (October 1910): 178–79.

130. Near the mouth of the Rappahannock River where it flows into Chesapeake Bay, Middlesex County, Virginia, USA, spring 2007.

Type of find: Hoard?

Date of deposit: 1667.

Contents: 1 AE, 2 AR.

Description:

England, Elizabeth I, shilling, 1567, cut

English colonies, Massachusetts, pine tree shilling, 1652, cut

English colonies, Maryland, Lord Baltimore denarium, [1658]

Disposition: Found by two metal detectorists. The denarium was sold by Stack's, August 5, 2007.

Bibliography: Stack's 2007, lot 213.

131. Exeter, New Hampshire, USA, October 1876.

Type of find: Hoard.

Date of deposit: 1667–74.

Container: Wooden box.

Contents: 30–40 AR.

Description:

English colonies, Massachusetts, willow tree shilling, 1652, Noe 3-C

Numismatic Journal, 2nd ser., 1, no. 1 (July 1889): 4.

144. George Washington Birthplace Monument, Wakefield, Virginia, USA, July 1935.

Type of find: Excavation.

Date of deposit: 1679.

Contents: 1 AE, 1 AR. Excavations.

Description:

    Ireland, Dublin, John Foxall, token, 1670s, Boyne-Williamson Ireland 326–27

    England, Charles II, sixpence, 1679

    The article in the *New York Times* does not specify the size of the silver coin; the sixpence denomination has been chosen as the likeliest casual loss. The original building burned down on Christmas day, 1780, but the finding of two coins of the 1670s suggests that they have an earlier date of deposit.

Bibliography: "Cavalier Tokens," *New York Times*, July 14, 1935, Sec. 10, 11.

145. Saint Ignace, Michigan, USA, fall 1966.

Type of find: Funerary deposit.

Date of site: 1679–98.

Contents: 3 AE.

Description:

    France, Catholic religious medallion, ovoid, obverse, Jesus, with obverse inscription IESV BONIT INFINIT MISERIR N ('Jesus, of infinite goodness, have mercy on us'), reverse, Virgin Mary, reverse inscription SANCTA MARIA MATER DEI ORA PR N. ('Holy Mary, Mother of God, pray for us')

    France, Catholic religious medallion, ovoid, obverse, Jesus, obverse inscription IESV BONITS INFINTA M.N. ('Jesus, of infinite goodness, have mercy on us'), reverse, Virgin Mary, reverse inscription MATER IESV. CHRISTI. ORA PRO.NOB. ('Mother of Jesus Christ, pray for us')

    (This medal may have been in the hand of the subject buried, with a rosary.)

    France, Catholic religious medallion, ovoid, obverse, bishop with crozier and child before him, obverse inscription, …CQV SAINCT MAR (probably Saint Ignatius of Antioch, bishop and martyr, and original inscription would have read IGNACE ANTIOQV SAINCT MAR; the "child" before him would then be a lion); reverse, triangle representing the Trinity.

Bibliography: Cleland 1971, 33–34.

146. Camden Tract, Caroline County, Virginia, USA, 1832.

Type of find: Single find.

Contents: 1 AR.

Description: English colonies, Virginia, Indian peace medal, "Ye King of Patomeck"

Disposition: Donated in 1834 to the Virginia Historical Society, Richmond.

Bibliography: MacCord 1969, 31, 38, 55; Stahl 1991, 161–62.

147. Camden Site, Caroline County, Virginia, USA, spring 1964–March 1965.

Type of find: Archaeological excavation.

Date of site: 1680.

Contents: 1 AE, 2 AR.

Description:

    England, "Carolus a Carolo," farthing, 1672

    English colonies, Virginia, Indian peace medal, "Ye King of Machotick"

    Spanish colonies, real, Potosí, 1662

Disposition: The real of Potosí was donated to the Virginia Historical Society, Richmond.

Bibliography: MacCord 1969.

148. Isla de Muerto, just off Santa Clara Island in the Bay of Guayaquil, Ecuador, 1998 to late summer 2001.

Type of find: Shipwreck.

Ship: Santa María de la Consolación.

Sank: June 28, 1681.

Contents: 8,000 AR.

Description:

Spanish colonies, 8 reales, star of Lima, 1659

Spanish colonies, ½ reales, Potosí (90): 1666E; 1675E; Philip IV; Philip IV or Charles II (39); Charles II (18); NDA (30)

Spanish colonies, reales, Potosí (1,810): assayer T (shield design); assayer O (2); assayer E (2); 1654E; 1655E; 1656E; 1657E (2); 1659E; 1660E; 1665E; 1668E; 1669E (2); 167[-]; 167[-]E; 1670E (2); 1671E (2); 1673E (3); 1674E (3); 1676E (2); 1677E (3); 1678E (3); 1678C; 1679V; Philip II – Philip IV (2); Philip III; Philip III or Philip IV (2); Philip IV (459); Philip IV or Charles II (206); Charles II (578); NDA (510); Philip IV or Charles II, heart shaped (7); NDA, heart shaped (7)

Spanish colonies, 2 reales, Potosí (699): assayer E (2); 1661E; 1664E; 1666E; 1669E; 16[-]7E; 167[-]E(2); 1670E; 1671E (2); 1672E; 1673E; 1674E; 1677E (2); 1678; 1679C; 1679V; Philip IV (195); Philip IV or Charles II (81); Charles II (207); NDA (192); Philip IV or Charles II, heart shaped (2); NDA, heart shaped (2)

Spanish colonies, 4 reales, Potosí (992): assayer E (2); 16[-]8E; 167[-]; 167[-]E; 1670E; 1678E (2); 1677E; 1678; assayer C (3); 1679C; assayer V (3); 1679V(2); Philip IV (227); Philip IV or Charles II (102); Charles II (337); NDA (300); Philip IV or Charles II, heart shaped (4); NDA, heart shaped (3)

Spanish colonies, 8 reales, Potosí (3,891): assayer E (15); 1665E; 1667E; 167[-] (4); 167[-]E (2); 1670E (2); 1675E; 1676E; 1677E; 1678E; assayer C/E (4); assayer C (19); 167[-]C; 1679C (5); 1679; assayer V (161); 1679V; 1680V (3); Philip II; Philip IV (1,051); Philip IV or Charles II (233); Charles II (1,145); NDA (1,228); Philip IV or Charles II, heart shaped (5); NDA, heart shaped (4)

Spanish colonies, fragments and unknown denomination (704)

The manifest of the ship gave the value of her registered cargo at 146,000 pesos.

Disposition: Auctioned by Spink America, New York, New York, USA, December 10–11, 2001.

Bibliography: Sedwick, 2007, 169–71 (Sedwick 26); Spink America 2001.

Paul Gilkes, "Dead Man's Island Yields Treasure, but from which Spanish Vessel?" *Coin World,* November 26, 2001.

149. Newton, New Jersey, USA, 1845.

Type of find: Single finds.

Date of deposit: 1683.

Contents: AE.

Description: Ireland, Saint Patrick halfpence

Coins found on the farm of Joseph B. Cooper, Esquire, which was the farm of Mark Newby.

Isaac Mickle wrote: "This Newby brought with him a good number of Irish half-penny pieces, which the Assembly in May, 1682, made a legal tender under the amount of five shillings—Leaming and Spicer, p. 415. They were called Patrick's half-pence. Newby lived on the farm now owned by that successful collector of coins, Joseph B. Copper, Esq., in Newton, where many of the Patrick halfpence have been ploughed up."

Bibliography: Mickle 1845, 144; Newman 1963, 621.

150. Laurel, Maryland, USA, 1987.

Type of find: Single find.

Contents: 1 AE.

Description: Ireland, Saint Patrick's farthing

Disposition: Found by a metal detectorist. Sold in the Colonial Coin Collectors Club Convention Auction, November 8, 1997, lot 309.

Bibliography: Mossman 1999, 1906–7.

151. Caleb Pusey House, Upland, outskirts of Chester, Pennsylvania, USA, 1962–67.

Type of find: Archaeological excavation.

Date of site: 1683–1951.

Contents: 2 AE, 1 SN, 1 AR.

Description:

England, halfpence (2): 1681; 1693

England, Maundy twopence

Spain, 4 reales, 1680, tin counterfeit

Coins from Peru, Mexico, France, and American colonies were also found, but are only described in those general terms in Cotter.

Bibliography: Cotter, Roberts, and Parrington 1992, 419–22 (citing Schiek 1974 in *Transactions of the Delaware Academy of Science* 5: 295–316).

152. Varina, Virginia, USA, 2007.

Type of find: Single find.

Date of deposit: ca. 1686.

Contents: 1 AR.

Description: England, Charles I, sixpence [1636–39], Tower mint, weighs 2.6 grams, clipped and bent

Bibliography: Kays 2007, 10.

153. Site of Indian Village, Scipioville, Cayuga County, New York, USA, 1889.

Type of find: Excavation.

Date of site: 1656–87

   Date of medal: 1687.

Contents: 4 B.

Description:

France, Catholic religious medal, oval medal of 1687 with obverse, female saint, right, with inscription SANTA ROSA DE LIMA ORD (Order of Saint Rosa of Lima); reverse, bust of male saint, left, holding crucifix, with inscription DE PAVL (probably Saint Vincent de Paul)

France, Catholic religious medal, oval medal with Saint Francis Xavier (a Jesuit saint)

France, Catholic religious medal, octagonal medal, with inscription S. Francis Ora. P. N. [Ora Pro Nobis ('pray for us')]

France, Catholic religious medal, octagonal medal, with two kneeling figures before altar, cross in halo of rays above

These are Catholic medals distributed to the Indians during the French period.

Bibliography: Beauchamp 1891, 46, 48; 1903, 72–73; Betts 1894, 32.

154. Connecticut River, Western Massachusetts, USA, 1980s.

Type of find: Single find.

Contents: 1 AR.

Description: Spanish colonies, 8 reales, Potosí, royal, 1687

Found on the site of a colonial settlers' fort near the Connecticut River.

Bibliography: Sedwick and Sedwick 2007, 198.

Daniel Sedwick, personal communication, February 26, 2007.

155. Lima, Peru, 1945.

Type of find: Hoard.

Date of deposit: 1689.

Contents: 1,500 AR.

Description: Contained 300–600 8 reales, plus coins of smaller denominations.

Nesmith saw 190 8 reales, dated 1654–89, which he enumerates as follows:

Spanish colonies, 8 reales, Lima (45): 1684V (2); 1685R; 1686R (7); 1687R (4); 1688R (29); 1689V (2)

Spanish colonies, 8 reales, Potosí (145): 1654E; 1656E; 1662E; 1663E; 1665E; 1666E; Philip IV, 1667E; Charles II, 1668E; 1672E; 167[-]E; 1675E (5); 1676E (2); 1677E (5); 1678E (12); 1679C (17); 1679V (7); 1680V (9); 1681V (12); 1682V (4); 1683V (7); 1684V (4); assayer V; 1685VR (16); 1686VR

(5); 1687VR (15); 1688VR (13); 1689VR
Disposition: Robert I. Nesmith (176); Arnold R. Perpall (14).
Bibliography: Nesmith 1946.

156. Williamsburg, Virginia, USA, 1960s.
Type of find: Single find.
Contents: 1 AE.
Description: Ireland, gun money, shilling?, 1689–90
Disposition: Found by a laborer digging a foundation for a motel.
Bibliography: Noël Hume 1970, 165.

157. Salem, Virginia, USA, 1981–88.
Type of find: Series of single finds.
  Date of earliest coin: 1690.
Contents: 1 AE, 1 B, 9 AR.
Description:
  Great Britain, halfpenny, 1730
  Ireland, gun money, shilling, 1690
  Spain, Charles IV, ½ real (¼ pistareen)
  Spain, 2 reales (cross pistareens) (quartered) (2): 1737; ND
  Spanish colonies, ½ real, 1781
  Spanish colonies, ½ reales, cut halves (2)
  Spanish colonies, 2 reales, 1773
  Spanish colonies, 2 reales, cut eighths (2)
Disposition: Found by a metal detectorist.
Bibliography: Lee Chambers, "Dan Johnson—Successful TH'er," *Treasure Found*, Summer 1988, 28–30, 32, 59.

158. Ligonier, Pennsylvania, USA, October 1894.
Type of find: Single find.
Contents: AR single find.
Description: England, William and Mary, silver medal, slightly larger than a silver dollar, with the motto "Pacem arrogat armis," dated 1690
Bibliography: "A Rare English Medal of 1690," *American Journal of Numismatics* 29, no. 2 (October 1894): 41.

159. Port Royal, in the harbor off Kingston, Jamaica, 1965–68.
Type of find: Archaeological excavation.
Date of site: June 7/17, 1692.
Container: Wooden chest with brass lock.
Contents: 1 B, 4,536 AR, 1 AV.
Description:
  China, cash, 1500s (found October 1966)
  3,000 silver coins were found in December 1966. The earliest coin found was 1653, the latest, 1690. Several hundred of the coins were in unusually good condition, having been preserved by a wooden chest. When the chest was lifted up, it crumbled to dust, leaving only a brass lock. This group included:
  Spanish colonies, 8 reales, México, NDA (2)
  Spanish colonies, 4 reales, Lima, 1688
  Spanish colonies, 8 reales, Lima (5): 1684 (2); 1686; 1687; 1688
  Spanish colonies, 4 reales, Potosí (2): 1688; NDA
  Spanish colonies, 8 reales, Potosí (7): 1686 (2); 1687; 1688 (2); NDA (3)
  Initial excavations were done in the 1950s by Edwin and Marion Link.
  In July 1967 Marx found one gold coin (4 escudos) and 1,536 silver coins. These were mostly 8 reales, but also included over 173 1 and 2 reales, and a few 4 reales. The date range was wide, beginning with the coins of Charles and Johanna from México (ca. 1552), and ending in 1690. Over 900 of the coins were dated in the 1680s. The mints split 20 México, 758 Lima, and 758 Potosí. Some of the artifacts recovered with the coins led Marx to conclude that he was excavating the site of a silversmith's shop. This may explain the very old coins, such as those of Charles

and Johanna: They were not a circulating medium, but were being used as bullion.

Disposition: Institute of Jamaica.

Bibliography: Link 1960; Marx 1967; 1973, 168, 186, 225–30, 234; Nesmith and Potter 1968, 142–49.

160. Charles City County, Virginia, USA, 1995.

Type of find: Archaeological excavation.

Contents: 1 AR.

Description: England, William and Mary, ½ crown, 1692

Found under the floor of a house under restoration; perhaps concealed there by a thief.

Bibliography: Noël Hume 1995, 22.

161. Morris Creek, near Elizabethport, New Jersey, USA, May 21, 1872.

Type of find: Hoard.

Date of deposit: 1694.

Contents: 80 AR.

Description:

Netherlands, lion daalder
Spanish colonies, 8 reales, Potosí (79): 1685; 1692 (76); 1694 (2)
Most of the coins were cobs from Potosí.

Disposition: Van Pelt found some silver coins in the oyster beds on May 19, 1872. This encouraged many others to go through the oyster beds. William, Alexander, and Harvey Dickson (also spelt Dixon) searched the oyster beds and were successful, with Alexander finding 62 coins, Harvey 13, and William 5. The few that had distinct dates were read as 1604 in the New-York Times, which has been corrected to 1694. Edmund J. Cleveland, a local numismatist (who later published contributions about medals, including Admiral Vernon pieces, in the *American Journal of Numismatics*), said that the coins were Peruvian cobs of 1692.

Bibliography: "Captain Kidd's Treasure Found," *American Journal of Numismatics* 7, no. 2 (October 1872): 31 (citing the *Elizabeth (NJ) Daily Monitor*, May 22, 1872).

"Great Excitement in Elizabethport— Dredging for Capt. Kidd's Treasure," *New-York Times*, May 23, 1872, 5.

162. Sailor's Snug Harbor, Staten Island, New York, USA, June 7, 1873.

Type of find: Single find.

Contents: 1 AV.

Description: France, Louis XIV, louis d'or, 1694

Disposition: Found while plowing by J. R. Clark of Sailor's Snug Harbor.

Bibliography: Proskey 1873, 22.

163. Boston, Massachusetts, USA, February 19, 1876.

Type of find: Single find.

Contents: 1 AR.

Description:

Italian states, Parma and Piacenza, Francis I, silver medal, depicting Francis on the obverse and on the reverse Justice and Religion, with the inscription "Junguntur ut imperent," 1694
The medal was reported as bearing the date 1604, but since Francis reigned 1694–1727, the date of the medal should be emended to read 1694.

It was found on Boston Common beneath the roots of an elm that blew down in a gale; the elm had 220 rings, which means it was planted in 1656. The date of the tree and the date of the medal may well be unconnected; medals often "wander" in the soil.

Disposition: Dr. Green exhibited the medal at the Boston Numismatic Society on March 3, 1876.

Bibliography: "Italian Medal found under 'the Old Elm,'" *American Journal of Numismatics*

10, No. 4 (April 1876): 93.

William Sumner Appleton, "Transactions of Societies: Boston Numismatic Society," *American Journal of Numismatics* 11, no. 1 (July 1876): 20.

164. Hunter Island, New York, USA, 1950–90.

Type of find: Single find.

Contents: 1 AE.

Description: England, William and Mary, halfpenny, 1694

Disposition: Found by Theodore Kazimiroff of the Bronx County Historical Society. Bequeathed by him to Kingsborough Community College, Brooklyn, New York.

Bibliography: Hecht 1993.

165. 121 Market Street, Philadelphia, Pennsylvania, USA, 1976.

Type of find: Archaeological excavation.

Date of site: 1685–1760. Entire site occupied 1685–1870. Excavations were from two privy pits, each in use for a narrower period of years. This is the first privy pit; the second privy pit is listed under 1829.

Date of coin: 1695.

Contents: 2 AE, 1 AR.

Description: England, William III, halfpenny, 1695–1701

Bibliography: Cotter, Roberts, and Parrington 1992, 240.

166. Schuyler Flatts, Colonie, New York, USA, 1971 and 1972.

Type of find: Archaeological excavation.

Date of site: 1660 onwards.

Date of earliest coin: 1695.

Contents: 8 AE.

Description:

England, William III, halfpenny
Great Britain George II, halfpence (3): 1738; 1749; 1749, burned
Ireland, Wood's Hibernia halfpence, 1723 (2)
USA, Connecticut, copper, 1787
French colonies, Louis XV, 9 deniers des colonies françoises, 1721H

Disposition: New York State Bureau of Historic Sites Collection, Peebles Island, New York, USA.

Bibliography: Hoover 2007 (providing inventory of New York State Bureau of Historic Sites Collections, Peebles Island, New York, as of August 16, 2005).

167. Pompey, New York, USA, 1813.

Type of find: Excavation.

Date of site: 1696.

Contents: B, AR.

Description:

France?, Catholic religious medal, "S. AGATHA ORA P. N.," (Sancta Agatha, ora pro nobis ['Saint Agatha, pray for us']), octagonal, brass
France?, Catholic religious medal, "S. LVCIA ORA P. N." ('Sancta Lucia, ora pro nobis [Saint Lucia, pray for us']), octagonal, silver
Catholic medals distributed to the Onondaga Indians during the French period. Found by Isaac Keeler.

Bibliography: Beauchamp 1891, 45–48, 1903, 72; Clark 1849, 2:279–80.

168. Ferryland, Newfoundand, Newfoundland and Labrador, Canada, 2001.

Type of find: Archaeological excavation.

Date of site: 1696–1865. There are three entries for this site, split into periods commencing in 1621, 1696, and 1865. This entry covers the period following the burning of the settlement by French forces under the leadership of Pierre le Moyne d'Iberville in November 1696 until the advent of provincial coinage in Newfoundland in 1865.

Contents: 20 AE, 4 AR.

Description:

Netherlands, Zeeland, duit, 1780
Great Britain, farthing, ND
Great Britain, George I, farthing, [1720–24]
Great Britain, George II, farthing, ND
England, William III, halfpence (3): [1695–1701]; [1699–1701] (2)
Great Britain, George II, halfpence (2): 1737; [1740–54]
Great Britain, George II or III, halfpenny, ND
Great Britain, George III, halfpenny, 1799
Great Britain, George III, penny, 1797
England, William III, sixpence, 1697
Great Britain, George IV, shilling, 1825
Great Britain, George IV, ½ crown, 1825
Ireland, George II, farthing, probably counterfeit
Ireland, George II, halfpenny, [1741–49]
France, Louis XIII, double tournois, 1632K
France, First Republic, sol, An 1 [1792–93]
France, Napoleon III, 5 centimes, 1854A
Portugal, John V, 10 reis, 1743
British colonies, Canada East, Montreal, Duncan & Co. Canada token, 1841
USA, uniface copper medallion with head of Liberty facing left and thirteen stars around
Spanish colonies, Philip V, ½ real, México, 1731JF

Bibliography: Berry 2002, 1–71.

169. Southern Haiti, ca. 1998.

Type of find: Hoard.

Date of deposit: 1697.

Contents: ca. 300 AR.

Description:

Spanish colonies, reales, Lima and Potosí (ca. 140)
Spanish colonies, 2 reales, Lima and Potosí (ca. 140)
Spanish colonies, 4 reales, Lima and Potosí (ca. 20)
Numbers of each denomination are estimates.
The coins were all dated before 1697. The hoard might have been linked to the booty taken back from the sack of Cartagena in 1697 by the very powerful buccaneer fleet that sailed from Saint-Domingue. There is thought to have been a major influx of circulating medium when the fleet returned.

Disposition: Taken to the United States and sold there.

Bibliography: F. Carl Braun, personal communication, January 27, 2008.

170. Northern tip of Grand Bahama, Bahamas, January 1961, and 1966.

Type of find: Shipwreck.

Ships: The "Memory Rocks Wrecks." Which ships these are it has not been possible to determine, because there are numerous shipwrecks, from many different years, all on top of each other.

Sank: 1697.

Contents: AR, possibly also AV.

Description:

Spanish colonies, 8 reales, minted at Potosí and Lima, with dates ranging 1693–97

Disposition: The salvage was done by Norman Scott's Explorations Unlimited, under contract to the government of the Bahamas.

Bibliography: Potter 1972, 277.

171. Manta, Ecuador, spring 1963.

Type of find: Single find.

Contents: 1 AV.

Description: Spanish colonies, Charles II, 2 escudos, Cuzco, 1698

Disposition: Found by two fishermen on a beach after an unusually hard storm.

Bibliography: "Rare Gold Washes Ashore," *Numismatist* 76, no. 7 (July 1963): 956.

172. Bay of All Saints, Brazil, 1981.
Type of find: Shipwreck.
Ship: Santo Ecclesiastico, also known as the "Standing Cannon Wreck."
Sank: 1699, after colliding with a whale.
Contents: 81 AR.
Description:
  Netherlands, schellings, corroded (5)
  Portugal, John IV, 100 reis (5)
  Portugal, John IV, 200 reis (5)
  Portugal, John IV, 400 reis (5)
  Portugal, John IV, tostão
  Portugal, John IV, ½ cruzados (22): Oporto (8); Lisbon (14)
  Portugal, John IV, cruzados (17): Oporto (5); Lisbon (12)
  Portuguese colonies, Brazil, Peter II, 640 reis (4): 1695 (2); 1696 (2)
  Spanish colonies, 8 reales, México (6): 1652P; 1653P; 1654P (2); 1655P (2)
  Spanish colonies, 4 reales, Potosí (3): 1653; 1654 (2)
  Spanish colonies, 8 reales, Potosí (5): 1651, counterstamped crown; 1652; 1653 (2); NDA
  Spanish colonies, 8 reales, corroded (8)
Bibliography: Christie's 1983, lots 485–513; Sebring 1986, 121; Sebring 2004, lot 1678.

173. Kaneenda, Onondaga Lake, New York, USA, 1880s.
Type of find: Single find.
Date of site: 1700.
Contents: 1 B.
Description: France, Catholic oval religious medal with Saint John Capistrano on one side and Saint Paschal Boiron on the other
  Found at a small Onondaga Indian site near the entrance of Onondaga Creek into the lake.

Disposition: Major T. H. Poole of Syracuse, New York.
Bibliography: Beauchamp 1891, 42, 1903, 73.

174. Northern side of the stockade, Albany, New York, USA, August 2001.
Type of find: Archaeological excavation.
Date of site: 1700–49.
Contents: 10 AE.
Description:
  Netherlands, ½ duit, 16[-]
  Great Britain, George II, farthing, 1749
  Great Britain, George II, halfpence (5)
  Ireland, Wood's Hibernia halfpenny, 1723?
Bibliography: Danforth 2001, 2224.

175. Shinnecock, near Sag Harbor, Long Island, New York, USA, August 1876.
Type of find: Funerary deposit. An Indian grave of the Shinnecock tribe.
Date of deposit: 1700.
Container: Small copper box with a sliding cover, the top and sides of the box were engraved with various designs, in which figured the sun, moon, and stars.
Contents: 32 AR.
Description: Spanish colonies, 8 reales, Potosí, 1665–1700 (32)
Disposition: The box and other relics were found in an Indian grave, and claimed by the Shinnecock tribe, which retained them.
Bibliography: New York Observer and Chronicle 54, no. 33 (August 17, 1876): 261.
  "Coins in Indian Graves," *American Journal of Numismatics* 11, no. 2 (October 1876): 41–42.
  William W. Tooker, "Indian Relics," *American Journal of Numismatics* 11, no. 3 (January 1877): 71 (citing the *Sag Harbor (NY) Express*).

176. Salem, Massachusetts, USA, July 1737.

Type of find: Hoard.
Date of deposit: Ca. 1700.
Containers: 6 earthenware jars.
Contents: 6,093 AR.
Description:

English colonies, Massachusetts, shillings, 1652 (6,000)
Spanish colonies, 8 reales (93)
"BOSTON
We hear from Salem that on Friday last a Servant of *William Brown* Esq; youngest surviving Son of the Hon. Col. *Brown*, deceased, in freeing a cellar of his from Water and Rubbish, struck his Spade against an Earthen Jarr of Silver buried in a Hole wherein was five Jarrs more, containing together one thousand ninety three Ounces of Silver of several Species, among which was about six thousand *New England Shillings*, scarcely discolour'd."
Boston (MA) Gazette, July 11, 1737, 2.

"We hear from Salem, that on Friday last William Brown, Esq., the youngest surviving Son of Hon. Col. Brown, deceased, having had Information of some Money conceal'd in a Place which he owned, caused search to be made for the same, where was found five or six Jarrs full of Silver, containing about one thousand ninety-three Ounces of Silver of several Species, among which was about six thousand New-England Shillings, scarcely discolor'd."
Boston (MA) Weekly News-Letter, July 14, 1737, 2.

"*Boston, July 19.* [Same as *News-Letter* entry, plus the following]; and as Mr. Brown suppos'd the same was conceal'd by his Ancestors, we hear he has in point of Honor and Justice, shar'd the same with his elder and only Brother, Samuel Brown Esq;"
Philadelphia American Weekly Mercury, July 28, 1737, 3.

Bibliography: Noe 1952, 18 (Noe doubts the details of the find).
Boston Gazette, July 11, 1737, 2.
Boston Weekly News-Letter, July 14, 1737, 2.
Philadelphia American Weekly Mercury, July 28, 1737, 3.
American Journal of Numismatics 16, no. 2 (October 1881): 46.
"An Old 'Find,' of New England Shillings," *American Journal of Numismatics* 25, no. 1 (July 1890): 31.

177. Staten Island, New York, USA, 1893.

Type of find: Hoard.
Date of deposit: 1701.
Contents: 2 AE.
Description:

England, William and Mary, counterfeit halfpenny, 1694
England, William III, counterfeit halfpenny
Slip of paper in coin box reads: "Dug up on Staten Id., N.Y. many years ago. I think I have had them at least 50 years. GHC"

Disposition: George H. Clapp; 1943 to the American Numismatic Society in New York (item numbers 1943.70.1 and 1943.70.2).

178. Castine, Maine, USA, November 1840–April 1841.

Type of find: Hoard.
Date of deposit: May 1704.
(Kays argues that the hoard was actually deposited in 1779. This, however, is not possible because of the écus. Hoards of écus from the eighteenth century almost invariably commence with the date 1726.)
Contents: 2,000 AR.
Description:

Netherlands, lion daalder, Gelderland, 1641
Netherlands, lion daalder, dated before 1620
Netherlands, 3 gulden, Westfriesland, 1682
England, Charles I, shilling, Tower mint,

mintmark triangle in circle [1641–43]
France, Louis XIV, 4 sols "des traitants," 1676D
France, Louis XIII, 1/4 écu, 1642A, second Warin die, two stops
France, Louis XIV, ½ écu, 1655L
France, Louis XIV, ½ écu, 1690K
France, Louis XIV, écu, 1652A
France, Louis XIII and Louis XIV, écus (1,000) (écus mostly mint A, Paris)
Portugal, John IV, tostão, Oporto
English colonies, Massachusetts, pine tree sixpence (30–75) (included variety Noe 33)
English colonies, Massachusetts, pine tree shilling (30–75) (included varieties Noe 2, 12, 26.2, and 29)
Spanish colonies, 2 reales, México
Spanish colonies, 8 reales, México (3): assayer P; assayer G; NDA
Spanish colonies, 8 reales, Bogotá, 1657PoR
Spanish colonies, 8 reales, star of Lima, 1659
Spanish colonies, 2 reales, Potosí, 1683V
Spanish colonies, 8 reales, Potosí, 1678E
Spanish colonies, 8 reales (60–150)
Portuguese colonies, Brazil, 4 reales, Segovia, 1659, with 300 reis counterstamp of 1663 (raising value 25%)

Disposition: Found by Captain Stephen Grindle. 17 to Dr. Joseph L. Stevens; later donated by him to the Maine Historical Society. 5 to Joseph Williamson; later donated by him to the Maine Historical Society. One piece, the unique Noe 12, reading MASASTHUSETS, which in 1863 was in the collection of Charles E. Payson of Portland, Maine, is now in the collection of the Eric P. Newman Numismatic Education Society, Washington University, St. Louis, Missouri, USA.

The following was published in the *Worcester (MA) Palladium,* June 30, 1841: "*Money Digging*—a farmer in the vicinity of Castine, in Maine, the present season, preparing his land for tillage, had occasion to excavate the top of a ledge, and on removing the earth, found lying loose, on the top of a rock, a quantity of ancient coin, of pure silver. Many of these coins are a curiosity, being of all possible shapes and forms. It would seem they were cut down to an exact weight. They have all upon them a coinage, but most of them very uncouth and without date, and clearly show the great improvements made since the days of our fathers, in the coinage of money."

Bibliography: Breen 1952, 8 (Breen Hoards I); DeCosta 1871, 55–56; Kays 2005, 2837–68; Money-digging 1871, 32–33 (reprints the passage from DeCosta); Nesmith 1958a, 26–27; Noe 1942; Noe 1952, 15–16; Williamson 1859, 105–26; Woodward 1863b.

"Money Digging," *Worcester (MA) Palladium,* June 30, 1841 (reference courtesy of Q. David Bowers).

179. Longmeadow, Massachusetts, USA, April 1877.

Type of find: Single find.

Date of deposit: 1675–1705.

Contents: AR single find.

Description: English colonies, Massachusetts, small planchet size pine tree shilling, 1652 [1675–82]

Disposition: The coin was found by Oliver Field in his field near the river, where it had probably been deposited before 1705, when the village was moved from the long meadow to the brow of the hill.

Bibliography: "Pine Tree Money Found," *American Journal of Numismatics* 11, no. 4 (April 1877): 92.

180. Barnegat, New Jersey, USA, November 1922.

Type of find: Hoard.

Date of deposit: 1706.

Container: Iron pot.

Contents: AV.

Description: Spanish colonies, 4 and 8 escudos, 1600s to 1706

Disposition: Found on the farm of Walter Thompson. Split fifty-fifty by the laborers Walter Ridgeway and Paul Mills.

Bibliography: "Pot of Spanish Gold Found on New Jersey Coast," *Numismatist* 35, no. 11 (November 1922): 568.

181. Stafford County, Virginia, USA, April 2001.

Type of find: Single find.

Contents: 1 AR.

Description: Spain, Charles III, pretender, [1707–14], 2 reales (pistareen), Barcelona, cut quarter

The coin is coin turn rather than the normal medal turn (i.e., 6 o'clock die axis rather than 12 o'clock die axis).

Disposition: Found by a metal detectorist.

Bibliography: Kays 2001, 2193.

182. Haverhill, New Hampshire, USA, 1951.

Type of find: Single find.

Contents: 1 AR.

Description: Spain, Charles III, pretender, 2 reales, (pistareen), [1707–14], Barcelona

Bibliography: Historical New Hampshire 7 (April 1951): 2.

183. New York, New York, USA, 1961.

Type of find: Hoard.

Date of deposit: 1709.

Container: Leather tobacco pouch.

Contents: 60 BI.

Description: German states, Trier, Dreipetermännchen (3 petermenger), of the following dates:

1689	2	1693, type 4	1	1706	5
1691	5	1694	12	1707	5
1692	9	1695	4	1708	1
1693, type 3	9	1705	6	1709	1

In 1711 the weight of the 3 petermenger was reduced, so a hoarder might reject all coins dated later than 1709. The hoard may thus have a slightly later date of deposit.

Found during the demolition of an old building. Possibly related to the expulsion of the Palatine Protestants from the Rhineland and their emigration to New York State.

Bibliography: Cibis 1975.

184. Havana, Cuba, 1924.

Type of find: Foundation deposit.

Date of deposit: 1709.

Contents: 6 AE.

Description:

Spain, Charles III, pretender, ardite, Barcelona, 1709 (4)

Spain, Charles III, pretender, dinero, Barcelona, 1709 (2)

Disposition: Found in the foundation of a convent in Havana. Given to the American Numismatic Society in New York by W. H. Cox, 1924 (1924.160.1-6).

185. Scatarie Island, off Cape Breton, Nova Scotia, Canada, September 1968, August 1985–February 1989.

Type of find: Shipwreck.

Ship: HMS *Feversham*.

Sank: October 7, 1711.

Contents: 1 AE, 1,384 AR, 17 AV.

Drew £569/12/5 sterling for provisions in New York on September 4, 1711.

Description:

Copper coin fragment

Netherlands, ½ lion daalders, Gelderland (2): 1632; 1641

Netherlands, ½ lion daalders, Holland (3): 1617; ND (2)
Netherlands, ½ lion daalders, Utrecht (3): 1616; 1640; 1647
Netherlands, ½ lion daalder, Zeeland, 1642
Netherlands, lion daalders, Campen (4): 1649; 16[-] (2); 1667
Netherlands, lion daalder, Friesland, 1610
Netherlands, lion daalders, Gelderland (2): 1644; 1652
Netherlands, lion daalders, Holland (2): 1576; 1589
Netherlands, lion daalder, Utrecht, 1663
Netherlands, lion daalders, West Friesland (3): 161[-]; 1640; 1641
Netherlands, lion daalder, Zeeland, ND
England, Charles I, twopence
England, shillings (5): Charles II; 1696B, 1696; 1697; 1697B
England, ½ crowns (8): 1645, Herford?; Charles II, 4th bust; 1689; 1696; 1697; 1697 Norwich; 1697E; 1699
France, Louis XIV, 1/12 ecu
Spain, real, 1500s
Portugal, 400 reis, 1687
English colonies, Massachusetts, New England shilling, Noe 3-C
English colonies, Massachusetts, willow tree shillings (6): Noe 1-A (2); Noe 3-D; Noe 3-E (2); unattributed
English colonies, Massachusetts, oak tree sixpence, Noe 22
English colonies, Massachusetts, oak tree shillings (45): Noe 1 (2); Noe 3; Noe 4 (2); Noe 5 (10); Noe 6 (2); Noe 8; Noe 9 (5); Noe 10 (5); Noe 11 (2); Noe 10–14; Noe 12 (3); Noe 13 (6); Noe 14 (4); unattributed
English colonies, Massachusetts, oak tree shillings, cut (3): Noe 2; Noe 13; Noe 14
English colonies, Massachusetts, pine tree sixpence, Noe 33
English colonies, Massachusetts, pine tree shillings (106): Noe 1 (6); Noe 2 (3); Noe 3; Noe 5 (4); Noe 6 (6); Noe 7 (3); Noe 8 (7); Noe 9; Noe 10 (6); Noe 11 (3); Noe 15 (6); Noe 16 (10); Noe 17 (2); Noe 19; Noe 20 (3); Noe 21; Noe 23 (2); Noe 25 (7); Noe 26; Noe 27; Noe 28; Noe 29 (21); Noe 30 (7); Noe 33; unattributed (2)
English colonies, Massachusetts, pine tree shillings, cut (17): Noe 1 (2); Noe 5 (2); Noe 6; Noe 8; Noe 10 (4); Noe 11; Noe 26; Noe unknown (5)
Spanish colonies, ½ reales, México (31): Philip IV, assayer P (12); Charles II (18); assayer L
Spanish colonies, reales, México (54): Philip III (4); Philip IV (35); Philip IV, assayer P; 1666G (2); Charles II (6); Philip V, assayer L (2); Philip V (5)
Spanish colonies, 2 reales, México (25): 1656P; Philip IV (12); Charles II, assayer L; Charles II (5); Philip V (6)
Spanish colonies, 4 reales, México (24): Philip IV, assayer P (2); Philip IV (9); Philip IV, plugged; Charles II (5); Philip V, assayer J; Philip V (4); NDA, plugged (2)
Spanish colonies, 8 reales, México (41): Philip III, plugged; Philip III, assayer D, plugged; Philip III (2); Philip IV, plugged (6); Philip IV, assayer P, plugged (3); Philip IV, assayer P; Philip IV (14); Charles II, plugged (2); Philip V, plugged; Philip V (3); Philip V, assayer J (2); assayer L (2); assayer L, holed; NDA, clipped; NDA, plugged; NDA, cut to the size of a 4 reales
Spanish colonies, 2 reales, Bogotá, 1653
Spanish colonies, 4 reales, Bogotá, 1693VA
Spanish colonies, 2 escudos, Bogotá (16): 1692; 1699?; 16[-]; 1701 or 1704; 1708?; 1709 (3); assayer A; NDA (7)
Spanish colonies, 2 escudos, Cuzco, 1698CM
Spanish colonies, ½ reales, Lima (2)
Spanish colonies, reales, Lima (94): 1662V;

1684V (2); 1685; 1685R (2); 1686R (5); 168[-]R (3); 1687; 1687R (2); 1688R (3); 1689R (4); 1689V (5); 1690R (6); 1690V (7); 1691R; 1692V (6); 1693V; 1694M (5); 1696 (2); 1696H(6); 1697R; 1698H (2); 1699; 1699R (7); 1700H (5); 1701H (3); 1706R (3); 1709M (2); Philip V, NDA (3); unattributed, Lima, shield type; assayer M; assayer R; assayer V; no date or assayer

Spanish colonies, 2 reales, Lima (19): 1659V; 1686R; 1692V; 1693V; 1697H (3); 1698R; 1699R (5); 1700H (3); 1702H; 1704H (2)

Spanish colonies, 4 reales, Lima (4): 1692V; 1692V, plugged; 1700H; 1700 or 1701H

Spanish colonies, 8 reales, Lima (17): 1686R, plugged; 1688R; 1692V (2); 1694M; 1697H; 1699R (4); 1702H (2); 1702H, plugged; 1704H; NDA (2); NDA, plugged

Spanish colonies, ½ reales, Potosí (11)

Spanish colonies, reales, Potosí (343): Philip III (19); Philip IV, shield type (16); 1652E (2); 1653E (4); 1654E (2); Philip IV, ND (2); 1655E (4); 1656E (3); 1657E (3); 1658E (10); 1659E (9); 166[-]E; 1660E (6); 1661E (2); 1662E (4); 1663E (7); 1664E (5); 1665E (10); Philip IV, assayer E (4); Charles II, assayer E (7); 1666E (3); 1667E (5); 1668E (2); 1669E (5); 167[-]E (5); 1670E (3); 1671E (4); 1672E (6); 1673 (2); 1674E (2); 1675E (5); 1676E (8); 1677E (6); 1678 (2); 1678E (4); 1679, assayer not visible; 1679C; 168[-]V (3); 168[-]VR; 1680V (2); 1681V (9); 1682V (5); 1683V (4); 1684V; 1684VR (3); 1685VR (5); 1686VR (5); 1687VR (4); 1688VR (6); 1689VR (8); 1690VR (9); 1691VR (5); 1692VR (6); 1693VR (6); 1694VR (3); 1695VR (2); 1696VR (4); 1697F (2); 1698F (4); 1699F (2); assayer V (2); assayer VR (16); Charles II, NDA (11); 1700Y; 1702Y (2); 1708Y; 1709Y; NDA (32)

Spanish colonies, 2 reales, Potosí (127): Philip II or III, assayer B; Philip IV, assayer T; Philip IV, shield type (5); 1653E (3); 1658E;

1663E (2); 1664E (2); 1668E (2); 1671E (2); 1672E (2); 1673E (3); 1675E; 1676E; 167[-]E (2); 1677E (4); 1678E (4); assayer E (2); 1679C (2); 1679V; 1679, assayer not visible; 168[-]V (2); 1681V (2); 1682V (2); 1682 V or VR; 1683V (5); 1684V (2); 1684 V or VR; assayer V; 1685VR (2); 1686VR (2); 1687VR (2); 1688VR (4); 1689VR (5); 169[-]; 169[-]VR (2); 1690VR (2); 1691VR (4); 1692VR (2); 1693VR (4); 1694VR, 1695VR (4); 1696VR (3); 1697VR; assayer VR (6); 1697F; 1698F (2); 1699F (6); 1700F; 1701F; assayer Y (2); 16[-]5; NDA (7); NDA, holed; NDA, with large crown counterstamp (2)

Spanish colonies, 4 reales, Potosí (3): 1687VR, plugged; 1699VR; NDA

Spanish colonies, 8 reales, Potosí (28): shield type, plugged (2); assayer E, plugged; 1677E; 1681V; 1682V, plugged; 1684V; 1689VR; 1690VR (2); 1691VR (3); 1692VR (3); 1693VR (2); 1694VR, plugged; assayer VR (2); 1697F; 1697; 1698F; 1699F; 1703Y (2); 1711?

Spanish colonies, 8 reales, with Portuguese colonies (Brazil) counterstamp and North American plug

Spanish colonies, ½ reales, NDA (30)

Spanish colonies, reales (209): NDA (208); NDA, holed and plugged

Spanish colonies, 2 reales, NDA (14)

Spanish colonies, 4 reales (7): NDA (5); NDA, holed and plugged (2)

Spanish colonies, 8 reales (21): NDA (14); NDA, holed; NDA, holed and plugged (5); NDA, clipped

Silver coin fragments (11)

Disposition:

(1) Some fishermen may have recovered some of the Colombian 2 escudo cobs in November 1873, when twenty such coins were sold to a jeweler in Saint John's, New Brunswick.

(2) Alex Storm found the *Feversham* in 1968;

his recoveries were sold to a "highly reputable Canadian institution" in 1972.

(3) Auctioned by Christie's, February 7, 1989; 8 coins from that sale are now in the American Numismatic Society in New York (item numbers 1990.49.1–8). More coins from the *Feversham* were auctioned by Jeffrey Hoare, February 26–27, 1993, by Coin Galleries on July 13, 1994 and April 15, 1998, and by Stack's, January 12–13, 1999.

Bibliography: Christie's 1989; Coin Galleries 1994, lots 2965–97; Coin Galleries 1998, lots 1750–85; Hoare 1993; Lasser 1989; Sedwick and Sedwick 2007, 175–76 (Sedwick 33); Stack's 1999, lots 1–48 and 1146–90; Storm 2002, 78–121.

"Kidd's Treasure Found Once More," *New York Times,* November 15, 1873, 2.

186. New Bern, North Carolina, USA, 1996.

Type of find: Single find.

Date of deposit: The community of New Bern was not founded until 1711, which provides a terminus post quem for the date of deposit.

Contents: 1 AE.

Description: Ireland, Saint Patrick's farthing

Disposition: sold by Will Georges Civil War Antiques, New Bern, North Carolina, Winter Catalogue 1 (Winter 1996): 6. Original catalog not consulted; citation from Mossman.

Bibliography: Mossman 1999, 1906–7.

187. Fort Hunter, Florida, New York, USA, 1987.

Type of find: Archaeological excavation.

Date of site: 1711 onwards.

Contents: 3 AE.

Description:
England, William III, halfpenny (2): 1697?; ND
Great Britain, George II, halfpenny, 1730

Disposition: New York State Bureau of Historic Sites Collection, Peebles Island, New York, USA.

Bibliography: Hoover 2007 (providing inventory of New York State Bureau of Historic Sites Collections, Peebles Island, New York, as of August 16, 2005).

188. Fort Crailo State Historic Site, Rensselaer, New York, USA, 1988.

Type of find: Archaeological excavation.

Date of site: 1712–1924.

Contents: 3 AE, 1 AR.

Description:
Great Britain, halfpenny, 1774
English colonies, Massachusetts, pine tree shilling, 1652
USA, 1¢, 1831
USA, token, Mark Valentine, 19th century

Disposition: New York State Bureau of Historic Sites Collection, Peebles Island, New York, USA.

Bibliography: Hoover 2007 (providing inventory of New York State Bureau of Historic Sites Collections, Peebles Island, New York, as of August 16, 2005).

189. Louisbourg, Nova Scotia, Canada, 1962–75.

Type of find: Archaeological excavation.

Date of site: 1713–60.

Contents: 1 PB, 1,003 AE, 2 B, 199 BI, 94 AR, 2 AV, 44 metal not indicated.

Description: Three articles discuss the coins found at Louisbourg, and an artifacts database is available on the web; the coin finds will be enumerated in three sub-entries. The sub-entries to some extent duplicate each other.

(1) This listing is based on the articles from 1976 and 1987 by Peter Moogk, which discuss the coins found on the site as a whole: 551 AE, 177 BI, 50 AR.

Great Britain, farthing (10)
Great Britain, George II, halfpence (172): 1746 (20); 1740s (70); other dates (82)
Great Britain, sixpence
France, double tournois (6)
France, liards (299): 1650s (mostly mint B, some E and L) (239); other dates (60)
France, 6 deniers, "dardennes," 1710–12, mostly mint & (43)
France, ½ sol, 1720s (2)
France, sol, 1719–21 (5)
France, sol de Béarn
France, miscellaneous copper coins (5)
France, douzains, bearing counterstamp of 1640 (27)
France, sols de 15 deniers, overstrikes, 1693–97, chiefly mints Λ, B, and E (89)
France, 30 deniers "mousquetaires" 1709–13 (12)
France, sols, 1738 series (5)
France, 2 sols, 1738 series (40)
France, miscellaneous billon coins (4)
France, 1/20 écu (2)
France, 1/10 écu (4)
France, ¼ écu
France, ½ écu (6)
France, écus (5): 1655T; 1724K; 1725H; ND (2)
France, jeton, late seventeenth century
Spain, 2 maravedíes
Spain, 8 or 12 maravedíes
Spain, miscellaneous copper
Spain, reales (½ pistareens) (2)
Spain, 2 reales (pistareens), 1717–24 (8)
Spain, miscellaneous silver coins (2)
Portugal, 10 reis, 1720
French colonies, 9 deniers des colonies françoises, 1721–22 (5)
British colonies, Rosa Americana twopence, 1720s
Spanish colonies, ½ real cob (2)
Spanish colonies, real cob (5)
Spanish colonies, 2 reales cob (2)
Spanish colonies, 2 reales milled (5)
Spanish colonies, 4 reales cob
Spanish colonies, 8 reales, México, 1738
Spanish colonies, 8 reales milled (2)
Crude copper piece with "xii T/.c.III" on one side (coin weight?)

(2) In a 1968 article, Sansoucy Walker gives an account of some 20 coins, found in a find spot with a much narrower term of occupation:

16 AE, 4 BI. The coins all came from Layer 2, which is dated to 1755–60, except for the 9 deniers des colonies françoises, which came from Layer 6/7/8, which is dated to 1749–55.

France, liard, 1655
France, liard, date not visible but mintmark B
France, worn copper coins thought to be liards, 1655 (10)
France, douzain with fleur de lis counterstamp of 1640
France, sol de 15 deniers, 1697E, overstruck on coin bearing 1640 counterstamp
France, billon coin worn smooth (possibly another sol de 15 deniers)
30 deniers aux 2L couronnés ("mousquetaires") [1709–13]
Great Britain, George II, halfpenny, 1730
Great Britain, halfpence (2)
French colonies, 9 deniers des colonies françoises, 1722H

(3) The following listing is based on a search for "coin" in October 2007 in the Louisbourg database of archaeological artifacts, available at http://fortress.uccb.ns.ca/archaeology/welcomenew.htm:

1 PB, 1,003 AE, 2 B, 199 BI, 94 AR, 2 AV, 44 metal not indicated
Netherlands, duit, 1741
German states, Nuremberg, jeton

England, William III, farthing
England, William III, sixpence, 1690s
England, William and Mary, jeton, brass
Great Britain, farthings (6): 1749; ND (5)
Great Britain, halfpence (211): 1720 (2); 1723; 1724 (2); 172[-]; 1731; 1733; 1734 (2); 1735; 1735 or 1739; 1737; 1738; 1739 (2); 1740 (6); 1742; 1743 or 1745; 1744 (3); 1744 or 1746; 1745 or 1746; 1746 (22); 1747; 1748 (7); 1749 (2); 174[-] (7); 17[-]2; 1750 (2); 1752(2); 1755 (2); 1753 (3); 1754; 175[-]; George II (9); counterfeit 1760; counterfeit 1763; counterfeit 1777; counterfeit 1779; George III, 177[-]; 1861; ND (116)
Ireland, halfpenny (5): George II (2); 1760; George III; ND
Ireland, Wood's Hibernia, halfpenny, 1722 or 1723
Ireland, pence (2): ND; counterfeit?, 1811
France, deniers tournois (2): Louis XIII; ND
France, doubles tournois (5): 1613; Louis XIII; ND (3)
France, liards (334): 1655 (5); 1655B; 1655E; 1656 (2); 1656D; 1657 (3); 1657D; 1657K; 1655–58 (11); young Louis XIV, mint D; pre-1693, mint C or G; 1689 mint 9 (Rennes); 1695; 1698; 1698L; 169[-]; mature Louis XIV; mature Louis XIV, mint K; mint A (2); mint B (16); mint C; mint D (4); mint G (2); mint E (7); mint I; mint L (2); mint O; mint R; mint S; mint X; ND (258); counterfeits (2)
France, 6 deniers, "dardennes" (41): 1710; 1710H; 1712; 1712H; 1712&; mint H (5); mint N (4); mint & (4); ND (23)
France, douzains, bearing counterstamp of 1640 (25): 1500s; 1594H; mint H (3); mint cow (Pau); ND (18); ND, holed
France, sols de 15 deniers, overstrikes and new flans, 1693–97 (49): 1693; mint A; mint A or AA; mint B (2); mint E; ND (43)
France, sols de 15 denier, overstrikes on counterstamped douzains, 1693–97 (4): 1692H; ND (3)
France, sol des mines, Pau, 1723
France, 30 deniers, "mousquetaires" (18): 1710D; 1710H; 1711 (2); ND (14)
France, ½ sols (2): 1721; 1721S or 9 (Rennes)
France, sol, copper (4): 1719; 1720, mint 9 (Rennes); 1721S; ND
France, sol, 1738 series (2)
France, 2 sols, 1738 series (43): 1739 (3); 1740B; 1740E; 1741; 1742A; 1743 or 1746; 1743E; mint M; mint 9 (Rennes); ND (32)
France, Louis XIV, mature head, 1/20 écu, 1690s
France, 1/10 écus (5): 1711; 1715H; 1726–40; ND (2)
France, 1/5 écu, 1726
France, ½ écus (5): 1727D; 1727T; 1728T; 1729D; 1729M
France, écus (13): 1724K; 1725H; 1726H; 1726S; 1728D; 1730 cow (2); 1740B (2); 1742K; 1743 T or P; mint T; ND
France, louis d'or (2): 1723K, short fronds; 1724K, long fronds
France, Louis XIV, jeton, 1660s-70s
France, copper jeton
French states, Navarre/Béarn, Louis XIV, sol, 1695
French states, Navarre, Henry III/IV, copper 2 sol, 1603
French states, Dukes of Burgundy, douzain, 167[-]
Spain, 4 maravedíes (2): 1636–55; ND
Spain, 8 maravedíes, counterstamped
Spain, ½ real (¼ pistareen), 1725
Spain, reales (½ pistareens) (4): 1718; 1720; 1740; ND
Spain, 2 reales (pistareen) (10): 1708; Madrid, 1717; 1717; Segovia, 1718J; Seville, 1723; 1723J; Seville, 1724J; 1725, cut in half; Seville, 1737; Philip V, Seville, assayer J, 1/16 cut
Spain, 4 reales (2): 1718; cut in half

Portugal, 5 reis

French colonies, 9 deniers des colonies françoises (6): 1722H; mint H; ND (4)

British colonies, Nova Scotia, halfpenny token, 1823

British colonies, Nova Scotia, cent

British colonies, New Brunswick, cent, 1861

British colonies, Canada, cent, 1861

Canada, cents (5): 1907; 1919; 1968; 1972; ND

Canada, 50¢, 1910

British colonies, Rosa Americana halfpenny, 1722 or 1723

British colonies, Rosa Americana

USA, Connecticut, copper

USA, ½ cent, 1804

Spanish colonies, ½ real, México

Spanish colonies, 2 reales, México (3): 1743; ND (2)

Spanish colonies, 8 reales, México (3): 1738 (2); 1743

Spanish colonies, real, Guatemala, holed

Spanish colonies, 4 reales, Potosí, 1705

Spanish colonies, 8 reales, Potosí, 1710Y

Spanish colonies, cob ½ real, Lima or Potosí

Spanish colonies, cob ½ real

Spanish colonies, cob real, holed

Spanish colonies, 2 reales

Copper coins (360)

Billon coins (57)

Silver coins (37)

Coins of indeterminate metal (44)

Lead seal made by impressing a pistareen

Disposition: Fortress of Louisbourg, Parks Canada.

Bibliography: Moogk 1976b, 1987; Walker 1968.

Fortress of Louisbourg, artifacts database, http://fortress.uccb.ns.ca/archaeology/welcomenew.htm (accessed October 27, 2007).

190. Off the East Coast of Florida, near the mouth of the San Sebastian River, about 25 miles north of Fort Pierce, USA, 1960–70.

Type of find: Shipwreck.

Ships: The 1715 plate fleet. The original fleet totaled twelve, of which only one, the French escort vessel *El Grifon*, escaped shipwreck. The following attributions of the sites come from the third edition of the *Practical Book of Cobs* by the Sedwicks. The fourth edition, however, does not have these attributions, and points out that the separate wrecksites may represent different parts of the same ship. The fourth edition also mentions two additional wrecksites: the "Pines Wreck" off Sebastian, Florida, and the "Cannon Wreck," off Wabasso, Florida.

"Cabin Wreck" is thought to be *Nuestra Señora de la Regla*, the *Capitana de Flota*.

"Wedge Wreck" is thought to be the *Urca de Lima*.

"Corrigan's Wreck" is thought to be *Santo Cristo de San Roman*.

"Rio Mar Wreck" is thought to be the *Carmen*, the *Capitana de Tierra Firma*.

"Sandy Point Wreck" is thought to be the *Nuestra Señora del Rosario*, the *Almiranta*.

"Douglass Beach Wreck" is thought to be *Nuestra Señora de las Nieves*. This wreck, also called the "Gold Wreck," was originally called the "Colored Beach Wreck," a term from the period of racial segregation in Florida. The beach has since been renamed, in honor of Frederick Douglass, "Douglass Beach."

Sank: July 31, 1715.

Contents: 11,727 AR; 2,610 AV.

Description: Most catalogs of the coins do not indicate which wreck the coins come from, so this treasure fleet will be listed in an omnibus entry. It appears, however, that most of the silver coins came from the "Cabin Wreck," and most of the gold coins came from the

"Douglass Beach Wreck."
Spain, Philip II?, 2 escudos, Seville, NDA
Spain, 8 escudos, Seville (3): Philip IV; Charles II; 1701M
Spanish colonies, ½ reales, México (137): 1692; 1702L; 1705; 1710J; 1711J; 1712J; 1713J; 1714J (3); 1715J; 171[-]J; NDA (125)
Spanish colonies, reales, México (4,270): 1705; 1706J; 1707J; 1708J; 1709J (2); 1710J (3); 1711J (6); 1712J (4); 1713J (2); 1714J (4); 1715J; 171[-]J (7); NDA (4,234)
Spanish colonies, 2 reales, México (1,173): 1707J; 1708J; 1709J (2); 1711J; 1712J (5); 1713J; 1714J (4); 1715J (2); 171[-]J; NDA (1,155)
Spanish colonies, 4 reales, México (1,273): 1704L; 1706J; 1707J (3); 1708J (2); 1709J (2); 170[-]; 1710J (4); 1711J (5); 1712J (12); 1713J (56); 1714J (124); 1715J (30); 171[-]J (54); 17[-] (2); assayer J (10); NDA (966)
Spanish colonies, 8 reales, México (3,252): 1680; ca. 1690; 1695 (2); 1697; 1699; 1700; 1702L (2); 1703L (4); 1704L (4); 1705 (3); 1706J (2); 1707J (2); 1708J (80: 1709J (6); 170[-]; 1710J (7); 1711J (40); 1712J (41); 1713J (117); 1714J (459); 1715J (152); 171[-]J (97); 17[-] (15); assayer J (71); NDA (2,314)
Spanish colonies, escudos, México (814): assayer L (8); 1694L (2); 1698L (4); 1700L; 1701L; 1702L (4); 1703L (5); 1704L (3); assayer J (12); 1707J; 1708J; 1709J (2); 1710J (4); 170[-]; 1711J (45); 1712J (50); 1713J (27); 1714J (122); 1715J; NDA (520)
Spanish colonies, 2 escudos, México (519): assayer L (3); 1704L (2); assayer J (7); 1708J; Philip V, assayer L (2); 1711J (2); 1712J (9); 1713J (26); 1714J (261); 1715J (3); NDA (203)
Spanish colonies, 4 escudos, México (439): assayer L; 1693L; 1694L; 1698L; 1699/8L; 1705J; 1706J; 1710J; 1711J (5); 1712J (19); 1713J (181); 1714J (72); 1715J (3); NDA (151)

Spanish colonies, 8 escudos, México (361): assayer L (2); 169[-]L; 1697/6L; 1702L (12); 1708J; 1709J; 1711J; 1712J (7); 1713J (85); 1714J (139); 1715J (22); NDA (87)
Spanish colonies, escudos, Bogotá (23): Charles II; Philip V (20); 1710 (2)
Spanish colonies, 2 escudos, Bogotá (349): Philip IV (4); 1649R; 1654R (2); 1672; 1683; 1687; 1689; 1690; 1694 (2); 1697; 1698 (2); 1699 (2); 169[-] (4); 1701 (12); 1703 (4); 1704 (7); 1705 (24); 1706 (5); 1707 (4); 1708 (5); 1709 (7); 170[-] (2); 1710; 1711 (2); 1712 (5); 1713 (2); 1714; 1715; Philip V, NDA (244)
Spanish colonies, escudos, Cuzco, 1698M (2)
Spanish colonies, 2 escudos, Cuzco, 1698M (9)
Spanish colonies, ½ reales, Lima (3): 17[-]; 1705H; 1710H
Spanish colonies, reales, Lima (72): 1684 (2); 1685; 1686R (3); 1688R (2); 1690R (2); 1692V (3); 1693V (2); 1694M (5); 1695R (3); 1696H (5); 1697H (9) 1698H (4); 1699R (11); 1700H (5); 170[-] (2); 1701H (2); 1702H (5); 1703H (3); 1704H; 1707H (2)
Spanish colonies, 2 reales, Lima (29): 1687R; 1691R; 1692V (3); 1693V; 1695R; 1697H (3); 1698H (2); 1699R (3); 1700H (2); 1701H; 1702H (2); 1703H; 1704H (3); 1705H; 1709H (2); 1710H
Spanish colonies, 4 reales, Lima (47): 1684 (2); 1686R; 1691R; 1692V (3); 1693V; 1695R; 1697H (2); 1698H (4); 1699R (3); 1700H (3); 1701H; 1703H (7); 1704H (2); 1705H (3); 1710H (2); 1711M; NDA (2)
Spanish colonies, 8 reales, Lima (611): 1684; 1685; 1687R (2); 1688R (4); 1689V; 169[-]; 1691R (4); 1693V (10); 1694M; 1695R (9); 1696H (9); 1697H (9); 1698H (16); 1699H; 1699R (23); 1700H (4); 1701H (11); 1702H (5); 1703H (21); 1704H (2); 1705H (2); 1707H; 1708H (3); 1709H (6); 1710H (6);

1711M (9); 1712M (2); NDA (2)

Spanish colonies, escudos, Lima (14): 1697H (2); 1799R; 1701H; 1703H; 1704H; 1709M (2); 1710H; 1711M (2); 1713M; NDA

Spanish colonies, 2 escudos, Lima (62): 1696H; 1697H (2); 1698H; 1701H; 1702H; 1703H (4); 1704H (3); 1705H (4); 1707H; 1708H (6); 1709M (15); 1710H (7); 1711M (11); 1712M (4); NDA

Spanish colonies, 4 escudos, Lima (11): 1697H (2); 1699R; 1707H (2); 1709M (2); 1710H (2); 1711M (2)

Spanish colonies, 8 escudos, Lima (103): 1697H; 1698H; 1699R (3); 1701H; 1704H (2); 1705H (2); 1707H (3); 1708H (6); 1709M (4); 1710H (8); 1711M (10); 1712M (55); 1713M (4); 1714M (3)

Spanish colonies, reales, Potosí (84): 1654E; 1661E; 1671; 1676E; 1678V; 1682V; 1685VR; 1686VR (5); 1687VR (3); 1688VR (3); 1689VR (4); 169[-] (2); 1690VR (6); 1691VR (3); 1692VR (5); 1693VR (9); 1694VR (2); 1695VR (3); 1696VR (3); 1697VR; 1698F (5); 1699F (3); 1700F; 1701Y (2); 1703Y; 1707Y; 1710Y; 1712Y; NDA (13)

Spanish colonies, 2 reales, Potosí (37): 1659E; 1661E; 1662E; 1666E; 1685VR (2);1686VR (2); 1687VR; 1688VR (2); 1689VR; 1690VR (2); 1691VR (2); 1693VR; 1695VR (4); 1696VR (2); 1697VR; 1698F; 1699F (2); 1700F; 1701Y (2); 1702Y; 1703Y (2); 1704Y; 1706Y; 1709Y (2)

Spanish colonies, 4 reales, Potosí (80): 1679C; 1684V; 1685VR; 1687VR (2); 1688VR (4); 1689VR; 1690VR (7); 1691VR (4); 1692VR (2); 1693VR (4); 1694VR (2); 1695VR (3); 1696VR (2); 1697VR (4); 1698F; 1699F (3); 1700F (8); 17[-]; 170[-]; 1701Y (4); 1702Y (8); 1703Y (4); 1705Y; 1706Y (3); 1708Y (2); 1709Y (3); 1710Y; 1711Y; 1714Y

Spanish colonies, 8 reales, Potosí (206): assayer E; 1675E; 1680V; 1683V; 1684V; 1686VR (5); 1687VR (3); 1688VR (4);

1689VR (2); 169[-] (3); 1690VR (9); 1691VR (7); 1692VR (7); 1693VR (11); 1694VR (8); 1695VR (9); 1696VR (11); 1697VR (12); 1698F (14); 1699F (12); 1700F (13); 17[-] (2); 170[-]; 1701Y (14); 1702Y (12); 1703Y (8); 1704Y; 1705Y; 1706Y; 1707Y (5); 1708Y (7); 1709Y (7); 1710Y (2); 1711Y; NDA (9)

Spanish colonies, 4 reales, no mint (8)

Spanish colonies, 8 reales, no mint (445)

Brass nested coin weights were also found (see Schulman Auction Catalog, November 27–29, 1972, lot 24).

Disposition: The fleet's registered treasure was fourteen million pesos. The Spanish salvaged 4–6 million pesos at the time. Captain Henry Jennings, a privateer, robbed the Spanish salvors of 350,000 pesos. The 1960s recoveries were split 75% Real Eight; 25% State of Florida. Some of Florida's share is now at the Museum of Florida History in Tallahassee. A 1714 "royal" 8 escudos of México was donated to the Museo Arqueologico Nacional in Madrid by Real 8 in November 1972.

Bibliography: Allen 1967; Bowers and Ruddy 1977; Burgess and Clausen 1976; Christie's 1988a, lots 175–92D, 311; Craig 2000a, 2000b, 75, 78, 134–35; Ponterio 1993, lots 550, 553–554, 721–722, 724, 809, 811, 812; Schulman 1972; Sedwick 1985, 1312–23; Sedwick and Sedwick 2007, 177–81 (Sedwick 35); Smith 1988, 94–95; Wagner and Taylor 1966.

191. Wrightsville, York County, Pennsylvania, USA, 1835.

Type of find: Funerary deposit?

Date of deposit: 1716.

Contents: 3 B.

Description: British colonies, George I, brass Indian peace medals (Indian and Deer) (Betts 165) (3)

Found with a brass kettle; a string of white beads, 1½ yards long; red paint; and 25 rings, one of which was dated 1716, which provides the date of deposit.

Disposition: One of these medals formed part of the coin collection of Harmon A. Chambers, which was bought en bloc and presented to the Wyoming Historical and Geological Society in 1858. The provenance to Chambers is based on the fact that Chambers dated his specimen 1716, and it is difficult to imagine where he got this date unless it was from the ring found with these medals. This specimen is still in the collection of what is now the Luzerne County Historical Society as of 2007, item number 91.68.1.

Bibliography: Hayden 1886, 225–26, 228–29 (citing the *Columbia Spy* for 1835).

Jesse Teitelbaum, executive director, Luzerne County Historical Society, letter to John M. Kleeberg, June 12, 2007.

192. Natrona, Pennsylvania, USA, 1912.

Type of find: Funerary deposit.

Date of deposit: Ca. 1716.

Contents: 9 B.

Description:

British colonies, George I, brass Indian peace medals (Indian and Deer) (Betts 165) (7)

British colonies George I, brass Indian peace medals (Indian and Deer) (Betts 164) (2)

It has been suggested that these medals were found in the grave of a British Indian agent who died before he could distribute them.

The medals were found when the Penn Salt Manufacturing Company was digging a ditch for a water line that ran across Dr. Bungarner's property at 51 Federal Street, Natrona, which is about twenty miles north of Pittsburgh. From 1714 to 1734 Natrona was called "Chartier's Town," and there was an Indian settlement there.

Bibliography: Bowers 1997, 31–33; Bowers and Merena 1987, lots 1131–39.

193. Jacob's Plains, also known as the Upper Flats, Wilkes Barre, Pennsylvania, USA, 1814.

Type of find: Single find.

Contents: 1 AE.

Description: British colonies, George I, laureate, facing right, Indian and deer Indian peace medal

Disposition: Found by Chief Justice Gibson, Charles Miner, and Jacob Cist, Esq. The men gave it to Cist as the individual among them who was most curious and careful in such matters. Cist deposited it with the Historical Society of Pennsylvania, Philadelphia; Miner in his 1845 book proposes that the medal be placed with the Indian relics in a museum in Wilkes Barre. Horace Edwin Hayden in an 1886 paper echoed this proposal, but says that the popular assumption that the medal in the collection of the Wyoming Historical and Geological Society is this specimen is incorrect. The medal in the collection of that society is therefore deemed to be one of three found at Wrightsville in 1835.

Bibliography: Beauchamp 1903, 57; Hayden 1886, 217–38; Miner 1845, 27 (with an engraving illustrating the medal).

Edmund J. Cleveland, "The King George I. Indian Medal," *American Journal of Numismatics* 26, no. 4 (April 1892): 83.

194. Banks of the Susquehanna River, Sunbury, Pennsylvania, USA, 1886.

Type of find: Single find.

Contents: 1 B.

Description: British colonies, George I, Indian and deer Indian Peace medal

Disposition: Found by J. H. Jenkins, who was deceased as of 1886. It was then owned by his son, Steuben Jenkins, of Wyoming, Pennsylvania. Date of finding not indicated by Hayden, so date of recording of the find used instead.

Bibliography: Hayden 1886, 227.

195. Virginia, USA, 1903.
Type of find: Single find.
Contents: 1 AE.
Description: British colonies, George I, Indian and deer Indian Peace medal, with George I, laureate facing left rather than right
Bibliography: Beauchamp 1903, 57.

196. Tunkhannock, Pennsylvania, USA, 1903.
Type of find: Single find.
Contents: 1 AE.
Description: British colonies, George I, Indian and deer Indian Peace medal, with large Indian throwing spear at deer at left
Bibliography: Beauchamp 1903, 57.

197. Long Clove Road, Rockland County, New York, USA, August 2004.
Type of find: Single find.
Contents: 1 AE.
Description: British colonies, George I, uniface Indian peace medal (Indian and deer medal but without the deer reverse)
Disposition: Found by a metal detectorist.
Bibliography: Sebring 2004 (auctioned in the Sebring sale, although not part of the Sebring collection).
Eric von Klinger, "George I medal second of its type. Metal detectorist finds Indian peace medal on surface," *Coin World,* December 6, 2004, 3, 30.

198. Wellfleet, Massachusetts, USA, July 1984.
Type of find: Shipwreck.
Ship: Whydah. A slaveship hijacked by the pirate Samuel Bellamy, and turned into a pirate ship.
Sank: April 26, 1717.
Contents: 1 PB, 10 AE, 8,379 AR, 9 AV.

Description:
Scotland, bawbee
Great Britain, sixpence
Great Britain, ½ crown
Great Britain, crown
France, 15 sou (2)
France, 20 sou (3)
France, 30 sou (2)
France, ½ ecu (2)
France, écu
Spain, 8 escudo royal, 1642
Spanish or Spanish colonies, escudo (2)
Spanish colonies, 2 escudo, probably Bogotá
Spanish or Spanish colonies, 2 escudo (4)
Spanish colonies, 8 escudos, Lima (2): 1708H; 1712M
Spanish colonies, 8 reales, Potosí (5): 1684; 1687 (heart); 1688; 1698; 1713
Spanish colonies, ½ reales (751)
Spanish colonies, reales (1,613)
Spanish colonies, 2 reales (2,257)
Spanish colonies, 4 reales (935)
Spanish colonies, 8 reales (2,790)
Spanish colonies, denomination undetermined (6)
Miscellaneous copper coins (9)
Unidentified coins in a cluster (8)
Indeterminate lead token
Also found were:
Brass coin weights (19, including nested set of 7)
Before the shipwreck was recovered, coins would wash up on the beach. In the 1950s a pair of honeymooners found a coin, which Robert Nesmith identified as an 8 reales struck in Peru in the 1660s.
Disposition: All to the salvors, after litigation with the state of Massachusetts.
Bibliography: Clifford and Turchi 1993; Kiesling 1994; Nesmith 1958a, 19–20; Sedwick and Sedwick 2007, 181–82 (Sedwick 36).

David Fairbank White, "How the Sea Gave up a $400 Million Pirate Treasure," *Parade Magazine* (*New York Daily News* edition), January 27, 1985, 6–9.

199. Halifax Road, Portsmouth, Virginia, USA, 1985–95.
Type of find: Single find.
Contents: 1 AR.
Description: Spain, real (½ pistareen), cut half, 1718
Disposition: Found by a metal detectorist. Acquired by Thomas A. Kays.
Bibliography: Kays 1996, 1637–45; 2001, 2175.

200. New Kent County, Virginia, USA, April 2001.
Type of find: Single find.
Contents: 1 AR.
Description: Spain, 2 reales (pistareen), probably Segovia, 1718, eighth cut with a square nail hole in center
Disposition: Found by a metal detectorist.
Bibliography: Kays 2001, 2186.

201. Rosewell Plantation, Virginia, USA, 1962.
Type of find: Archaeological excavation.
Contents: 1 AR.
Description: France, Louis XV, ½ écu, 1719H
Bibliography: Noël Hume 1995, 17, 20.

202. Coleraine, Massachusetts, USA, April 1877.
Type of find: Single find.
Contents: 1 AR.
Description: Spain, Philip V, 2 reales (pistareen)
Disposition: Found among the ruins of the L part of his hotel by O. M. Gaines, which he has recently torn down.
Bibliography: "Notes and Queries," *American Journal of Numismatics* 11, no. 4 (April 1877): 99.

203. Mexico, December 1974.
Type of find: Hoard.
Date of deposit: 1720.
Contents: 18 AR.
Description: Spanish colonies, Philip V, 8 reales, México, assayer J (18)
Disposition: Auctioned by Schulman Coin & Mint, Inc., December 2–4, 1974, lots 540–544.
Bibliography: Schulman 1974, lots 540–44.

204. Louisbourg, Nova Scotia, Canada, August 21, 1962.
Type of find: Foundation deposit.
Date of deposit: November 1720.
Container: Wood and lead casket.
Contents: 2 AE, 1 AR.
Description:
France, Louis XV, Louisbourg medals (Betts 145), bronze (2)
France, Louis XV, Louisbourg medal (Betts 145), silver
Bibliography: Moogk 1976a, 434–40.

205. Louisbourg, Nova Scotia, Canada, 1923.
Type of find: Foundation deposit.
Date of deposit: 1720?
Contents: 1 AE.
Description: France, Louis XV, Louisbourg medal (Betts 145) bronze
Found in the foundations of the French lighthouse at Louisbourg.
Bibliography: Moogk 1976a, 437.

206. Cahokia Wedge, Cahokia (East Saint Louis), Illinois, USA, spring–fall 1986.
Type of find: Archaeological excavation.
Date of site: 1699–1841
Date of earliest coin: 1721.
Contents: 1 AE, 1 AR.

Description:
French colonies, 9 deniers des colonies françoises, 1721H
Spanish colonies, Charles III, 8 reales, probably México

Bibliography: Gums 1987.

207. Culpeper, Virginia, USA, 1985–95.

Type of find: Single find.

Contents: 1 AR.

Description: Spain, real, (½ pistareen), Seville, 1721IJ

Disposition: Found by a metal detectorist. Acquired by Thomas A. Kays.

Bibliography: Kays 1996, 1637–45.

208. Washington, Pennsylvania, (near the border of what is now West Virginia), USA, April 1835.

Type of find: Single find.

Contents: 1 AE.

Description: British colonies, Rosa Americana, 1722

Bibliography: Mease 1838, 282–83; Newman 1992, 9.

209. Charleston, South Carolina, USA, 1835.

Type of find: Single find.

Contents: 1 AE.

Description: British colonies, Rosa Americana, 1722
Found while digging the foundation of Saint Philip's Church.

Bibliography: Mease 1838, 282–83; Newman 1992, 9.

210. Bennington, Vermont, USA, August 2001.

Type of find: Single find.

Contents: 1 AE.

Description: Ireland, Wood's Hibernia halfpenny, 1722

Disposition: Found by a metal detectorist.

Bibliography: Danforth 2001, 2226.

211. Bergen (now Hudson County), New Jersey, USA, 1821.

Type of find: Single find.

Contents: 1 AE.

Description: French colonies, 9 deniers des colonies françoises, 1722
The coin was plowed up.

Bibliography: State Senator (later Judge) Gabriel Furman, Albany, New York, "Letter to Vice-Chancellor Frederick Whittlesey, November 25, 1841," *Historical Magazine*, new series, 9, no. 2 (February 1871): 88.

212. North Anna River, below Richmond, Virginia, USA, April 2001.

Type of find: Single find.

Contents: 1 AR.

Description: Spain, 2 reales, (pistareen), Cuenca, ca. 1722, cut in half and heavily scored to cut again so that it is nearly ready to come apart

Bibliography: Kays 2001, 2186.

213. Mobile, Alabama, USA, 1992.

Type of find: Archaeological excavation of the center of French Mobile.

Date of site: 1720s.

Contents: 1 B, 3 AE.

Description:
French colonies, 9 deniers des colonies françoises, 1721
French colonies, 9 deniers des colonies françoises, 1722
French colonies, 12 deniers des colonies françoises, 1717Q
France, Louis XIV, jeton

Disposition: Rescue dig conducted by the archaeologist Greg Spies.

Bibliography: Hodder 1992, 24, 34.

214. Somerset, Rhode Island, USA, January 1874.

Type of find: Foundation deposit.

Contents: 1 AE.

Description: British colonies, Rosa Americana, twopence, 1723
Embedded underneath the foundation stone of an old stonewall on the farm of David Buffinton.

Bibliography: Appleton 1874, 57–58.

215. Fort Shantok, west bank of the Thames River, three miles south of Norwich, New London County, Connecticut, USA, summer 1962.

Type of find: Archaeological excavation.

Date of site: 1600–1750.

Date of layer in which coin was found: 1710–50.

Date of earliest coin: 1723.

Contents: 1 AE.

Description: Ireland, George I, farthing, eleven string harp, 1723 (reference Seaby Irish coins 235)

Bibliography: Salwen 1966.

216. New Rochelle, New York, USA, 1950–90.

Type of find: Hoard.

Date of deposit: 1723.

Contents: 2 AE.

Description: Ireland, Wood's Hibernia halfpence, 1723 (2)

Disposition: Found by Theodore Kazimiroff of the Bronx County Historical Society. Bequeathed to Kingsborough Community College, Brooklyn, New York.

Bibliography: Hecht 1993; Mossman 1999, 1912.

217. East Moriches, Long Island, New York, USA, April 1898.

Type of find: Single find.

Contents: 1 AE.

Description: Ireland, Wood's Hibernia halfpenny, 1723

Disposition: Found by Captain Herbert Benjamin.

Bibliography: "Old Coins Unearthed," *Brooklyn Daily Eagle*, April 25, 1898, 4.

218. Upper New York State, USA, 1999.

Type of find: Single find.

Contents: 1 AE.

Description: Ireland, Wood's Hibernia halfpenny, 1723

Bibliography: Mossman 1999, 1912.

219. Gloucester, Massachusetts, USA, October 1979.

Type of find: Single find.

Contents: 1 AE.

Description: Ireland, Wood's Hibernia halfpenny, 1723

Disposition: Found by a metal detectorist.

Bibliography: Mossman 1999, 1912.

220. Shenandoah Valley, Virginia, USA, March 1997.

Type of find: Single find.

Contents: 1 AE.

Description: Ireland, Wood's Hibernia halfpenny, 1723
As of April 1999, this find had been reported but not confirmed.

Disposition: Found by a metal detectorist.

Bibliography: Mossman 1999, 1912.

221. New Hampshire, USA, September 1998.

Type of find: Single find.

Contents: 1 AE.

Description: Ireland, Wood's Hibernia halfpenny, 1723

Disposition: Found by a metal detectorist. Sold on eBay, September 2, 1998, item #27724544.

Bibliography: Mossman 1999, 1912.

222. Hopewell, Virginia, USA, April 2001.

Type of find: Single find.

Contents: 1 AE.

Description: Spain, counterfeit 2 reales (pistareen), 1723

Disposition: Found by a metal detectorist.

Bibliography: Kays 2001, 2185.

223. New Kent County, Virginia, USA, April 2001.

Type of find: Single find.

Contents: 1 AR.

Description: Spain, 2 reales (pistareen), cut quarter, gilded to pass as a half escudo

Disposition: Found by a metal detectorist.

Bibliography: Kays 2001, 2185.

224. Douw's Point, Rensselaer, New York, USA, 1971.

Type of find: Archaeological excavation.

Date of site: 1724 onwards.

Contents: 3 AE.

Description:
Great Britain, George II, halfpenny, 1720
Ireland, Wood's Hibernia halfpenny, 1723
USA, Connecticut, copper, 1787, draped bust left

Disposition: New York State Bureau of Historic Sites Collection, Peebles Island, New York, USA.

Bibliography: Hoover 2007 (providing inventory of New York State Bureau of Historic Sites Collections, Peebles Island, New York, as of August 16, 2005).

225. Congress Street, Boston, Massachusetts, USA, 1854 and October 1895.

Type of find: Hoard.

Date of deposit: 1724?

Contents: 300? AE.

Description:
Ireland, Wood's Hibernia halfpence (300?)
Ireland, Wood's Hibernia pence
Number of halfpence in the 1854 find an estimate; the exact number was not given; Colburn merely referred to a "large hoard."

Disposition: Found while excavating for a block of warehouses in Congress Street, Boston.
The Wood's Hibernia penny, also found while excavating in Congress Street, but in October 1895, was probably scatter from the initial hoard.

Bibliography: Jeremiah Colburn, "English Coins Struck for the American Colonies, Coins issued by the Several States and by the Federal Government Previous to the Establishment of the Mint in 1792," *Historical Magazine* 1, no. 10 (October 1857): 300 note.
"Workmen Find an Interesting Coin," *Journal of the American-Irish Historical Society* 6 (1906): 59 (citing the *Boston (MA) Transcript*, October 12, 1895).

226. Head of Frenchman Bay, Sullivan, Maine, USA, 1844.

Type of find: Hoard.

Date of deposit: 1724.

Contents: 600+ AR.

Description:
France, ½ écus, 1724 (400)
France, écus, 1724 (200)
$400 worth was found. The numbers are estimates based on this dollar amount. The hoard was found by a farmer plowing land in front of where "Ocean House" stood in 1859.
Probably the écu aux 8 L type, given the narrow range of dates—the écu aux 8 L type was minted in only 1724 and 1725.

Disposition: Most melted, but some specimens were obtained by William G. Stearns of Harvard College.

Bibliography: DeCosta 1871, 55; Williamson 1859, 126 note 3 (citing the *Machias (ME) Union,* July 8, 1856).

227. Fredericksburg area, Virginia, USA, 1995.
Type of find: Single find.
Contents: 1 AR.
Description: Spain, 2 reales (pistareen), Seville, 1724J
Disposition: Found by a metal detectorist.
Bibliography: Kays 1996, 1637–45.

228. Fredericksburg area, Virginia, USA, 1995.
Type of find: Single find.
Contents: 1 AR.
Description: Spain, 2 reales (pistareen), Seville, 1724J
Disposition: Found by a metal detectorist.
Bibliography: Kays 1996, 1637–45.

229. Dumfries, Virginia, USA, 1995.
Type of find: Single finds.
Contents: 13 AR.
Description:
  Spain, Philip V, 2 reales (pistareen), cut quarters (12)
  Spain, Philip V, 2 reales (pistareen) cut eighth
Disposition: Found by metal detectorists. Recovered from colonial sites that have since been bulldozed around Dumfries.
Bibliography: Kays 1996, 1637–45.

230. Vault Hill, Van Cortlandt Park, Bronx, New York, USA, 1950–90.
Type of find: Hoard.
Date of deposit: 1724.
Contents: 2 AE.
Description: Great Britain, George I, halfpence, 1724 (2)
Disposition: Found by Theodore Kazimiroff of the Bronx County Historical Society. Bequeathed to Kingsborough Community College, Brooklyn, New York.
Bibliography: Hecht 1993.

231. Southern New Jersey, USA, 1990s.
Type of find: Single finds.
Contents: 3 AE.
Description: Ireland, Wood's Hibernia halfpence, 1720s (3)
Disposition: Found by metal detectorists.
Bibliography: Gredesky 2000, 2063–64.

232. Frederick, Maryland, USA, January 1999.
Type of find: Single find.
Contents: 1 AE.
Description: Ireland, Wood's Hibernia farthing, basal state
Bibliography: Mossman 1999, 1911.

233. Williamsburg, Virginia, USA, October 1997.
Type of find: Archaeological excavation.
Contents: 2 AE.
Description: Ireland, Wood's Hibernia halfpence, ND (2)
Bibliography: Mossman 1999, 1912.

234. Prince Edward County, Virginia, USA, October 1997.
Type of find: Single find.
Contents: 1 AE.
Description: Ireland, Wood's Hibernia halfpenny
Bibliography: Mossman 1999, 1912.

235. Alexandria, Virginia, USA, June 1997.
Type of find: Single find.
Contents: 1 AE.
Description: Ireland, Wood's Hibernia halfpenny, 1724
Disposition: Found by a metal detectorist.
Bibliography: Mossman 1999, 1912.

236. Falls Church, Virginia, USA, March 1997.

Type of find: Single find.

Contents: 1 AE.

Description: Ireland, Wood's Hibernia halfpenny, ND
As of April 1999, this find had been reported but not confirmed.

Disposition: Found by a metal detectorist.

Bibliography: Mossman 1999, 1912.

237. Albany, New York, USA, 1999.

Type of find: Single find.

Contents: 1 AE.

Description: Ireland, Wood's Hibernia halfpenny, ND

Bibliography: Gredesky 2000, 2063–64.

238. Brown's Mills, New Jersey, USA, fall 1986.

Type of find: Single find.

Contents: 1 AR.

Description: Spain, Louis I, 2 reales (pistareen), Segovia, 1724F
Found at a place called "Princes Mansion."

Disposition: Found with a metal detector by W. J. Carr.

Bibliography: "Uncommon Common Coin," *Treasure Found*, Fall 1986, 28–29.

239. Samaná Bay, Dominican Republic, 1976.

Type of find: Shipwreck.

Ship: Nuestra Señora de Guadalupe. Westbound mercury transport from Cadiz.

Sank: August 25, 1724.

Contents: 400 AR, 3 AV.

Description: 400+ Spanish coins of the reign of Philip V, including:
Spanish Netherlands, Philip V, ducatoon, 1709
Spain, Philip V, 8 escudos (3)
Spanish colonies, 8 escudos, México (4)
Spanish colonies, 8 escudos, Bogotá (3)
Spanish colonies, 8 escudos, Lima (3)
Spanish colonies, 2 escudos, Cuzco (3)

Disposition: Museo de las Casas Reales, Dominican Republic.

Bibliography: Peterson 1979; Pickford 1994, 60–61, 129, 164; Sedwick and Sedwick 2007, 183–84 (Sedwick 39); Smith 1988, 103.

240. Samaná Bay, Dominican Republic, 1977.

Type of find: Shipwreck.

Ship: Conde de Tolosa. Westbound mercury transport from Cadiz.

Sank: August 25, 1724.

Contents: 400 B, AE; AV.

Description:
Spain, brass and bronze Catholic religious medals (400+)
Spain, Gold decoration with the cross of the order of Santiago, framed by 24 diamonds

Disposition: Museo de las Casas Reales, Dominican Republic.

Bibliography: Peterson 1979; Pickford 1994, 60–61, 129, 164; Sedwick and Sedwick 2007, 183–84 (Sedwick 39); Smith 1988, 104.

241. Flint River, Dougherty County, Georgia, USA, June 1894.

Type of find: Single find.

Contents: 1 AR.

Description: Spain, 2 reales (pistareen), 1725

Disposition: Found by Captain William Jennings, of Dawson, Georgia.

Bibliography: "Probably Worth Fifteen Cents," *Numismatist* 7, no. 6 (June 1894): 114.

242. Chameau Rock, Kelpy Cove, off Cape Breton, Nova Scotia, Canada, September–October 1965.

Type of find: Shipwreck.

Ship: Le Chameau.

Sank: August 26, 1725.

Contents: 7,861 AR, 878 AV.

Description: All coins are French coins of Louis XV.

Mint	Écus aux 8 L		Louis		
	1724	1725	1723	1724	1725
A		2	21	8	1
B			3	5	
C			3	6	1
D		1	12	9	1
E	1		4	8	1
G	5	33	2	34	2
H	21	2166	20	48	38
I		46	2	14	3
K	21	146	20	86	24
L			11	29	1
M			6	33	
N	1	2	5	10	1
O		36	2	4	1
P			1	2	
Q			2	3	
R	1		3	3	1
S			2	2	1
T	20	123	2	14	
V			2	2	1
W			2	4	1
X			2	2	1
Y			2	4	1
Z			2	3	1
AA			2	1	1
BB			1	1	
CC			1	1	
&			6	6	
9			7	6	
Cow		1	1	7	15
Mint illegible	31	64			

France, Louis XV, 1/6 écu (6): 1719A; 1719K; 1720A; 1720H; 1721E; 1722G

France, Louis XV, 1/3 écu (6): 1720T; 1721G; 1721H; 1721 Rennes; 1723H; ND, mint G, flip over double strike

France, Louis XV, ½ écu, 1725H (10)

France, Louis XV, écu, 1721K

France, écu de France, 1724H

France, écu aux 8 L, ND (3,742)

France, 2 louis, 1724A

George Sobin says that the écu aux 8 L, 1725H date/mintmark combination accounted for about 80% of the silver coins in the *Chameau* treasure.

Disposition: The salvage was done by Alex Storm. The litigation concerning the find was tried in the Supreme Court of Nova Scotia. The gold coins were divided up approximately as follows. 341 were sold to a local dealer and onwards to a New York City dealer (possibly John Ford) in early 1971; these coins were mostly sold in Europe. 43 coins went to the Province of Nova Scotia under the Treasure Trove Act; 3 coins were sold other ways, leaving 493 gold louis that were auctioned by Parke-Bernet in 1971. This adds up to 880 coins, which is fairly close to the 878 listed above. The Parke-Bernet auction did not include examples of all the date and mintmark varieties recovered. Many silver coins were auctioned by Stack's in 1999. The Stack's auction had only three gold coins, but one of them was the only double louis so far known to come from *Le Chameau*. The Stack's auction of Ford's collection in 2006 included 73 gold louis from *Le Chameau*, which are said to have been given to Ford in exchange for his numismatic advisory services to the treasure recovery venture. Presumably these 73 coins were part of the 341 coins that went to the New York City dealer.

Bibliography: Breen 1988, 44–45, 49–51, 703 (Breen 299–389); Charlton 1976; Parke-Bernet 1971; Sobin 1974; Stack's 1999, lots 1191–1304; Stack's 2006a, lots 384–456; Storm 2002, 19–77.

243. Virginia, USA, 1985–95.

Type of find: Single find.

Contents: 1 AR.

Description: Spain, real (½ pistareen), Seville, 172[-]J

Disposition: Found by a metal detectorist. Acquired by Thomas A. Kays.

Bibliography: Kays 1996, 1637–45.

244. Meseta Central, Mexico City, Mexico, 1995.

Type of find: Hoard.

Date of deposit: Late 1720s.

Container: Ceramic jar.

Contents: Ca. 100 AR.

Description:
Spanish colonies, Charles II, Philip V, and Louis I, ½ reales, México
Spanish colonies, Philip V, reales, México
The coins were all cobs, so the hoard closes before 1732; the hoard includes coins of Louis I, so it closes after 1724. The coins were found stashed below the floor of a colonial era building in Mexico City in a ceramic jar.

Bibliography: Paul A. Brombal, Advertisement, *World Coin News*, August 28, 1995, 13.
Paul A. Brombal Coins and Jewelry, "The Meseta Central Hoard," http://www.pbrombal.com#Meseta.

245. Staten Island, New York, USA, 1820.

Type of find: Single find.

Contents: 1 AV.

Description: Portuguese colonies, Brazil, 12,800 reis, [1727–33]

Disposition: Unearthed near the remains of the old Lovelace or Duxbury homestead

Bibliography: Antiquities 1869, 74.

246. Gorriti Island, near Punta del Este, Uruguay, 1990.

Type of find: Shipwreck.

Ship: Seahorse, a South Seas Company slave ship, which had just unloaded its human cargo and had been paid in silver cobs before it sank.

Sank: September 29, 1728.

Contents: 50 AR.

Description: Spanish colonies, 8 reales, Potosí

Disposition: Found by local fishers; the coins entered the numismatic market through a dealer in Key West, Florida.

Bibliography: Sedwick and Sedwick 2007, 184–85 (Sedwick 41).

247. Clermont State Historic Site, Clermont/Germantown, New York, USA, 1976, 1979, 1988.

Type of find: Archaeological excavation.

Date of site: 1728–1850.

Contents: 4 AE.

Description:
Great Britain, halfpence (3): 1724; 1733; 1740
Ireland, George III, halfpenny, 1760

Disposition: New York State Bureau of Historic Sites Collection, Peebles Island, New York, USA.

Bibliography: Hoover 2007 (providing inventory of New York State Bureau of Historic Sites Collections, Peebles Island, New York, as of August 16, 2005).

248. Pennsylvania, USA, 1903.

Type of find: Single find.

Contents: 1 AE.

Contents: British colonies, George II, Indian and deer Indian peace medal
The medal depicts George II, laureate, facing left, in armor.

Bibliography: Beauchamp 1903, 57.

249. Dunkirk, near Richmond along the Pamunkey River, Virginia, USA, 1985–95.

Type of find: Single find.

Contents: 1 AR.

Description: Spanish colonies, real, Potosí, 1729Y

Disposition: Found by a metal detectorist. Acquired by Thomas A. Kays.

Bibliography: Kays 1996, 1637–45.

250. Fairmount, Philadelphia, Pennsylvania, USA, 1846.

Type of find: Single find.

Contents: 1 AV.

Description: Spanish colonies, 2 escudo
"The quarter cob-doubloon, No. 5, an old piece, was lately picked up by a schoolboy, on a heap of rubbish near Fairmount; and from its appearance at the time, was taken for a bit of iron. It may have lain there half a century."

Disposition: U.S. Mint collection.

Bibliography: Dubois 1846, 133.

251. Near Statesville, Iredell County, North Carolina, USA, 1861.

Type of find: Single find.

Contents: 1 AV.

Description: Spanish colonies, Philip V, 8 escudos, México, ca. 1730

Disposition: Found in a cornfield upon land owned by the descendants of Mr. Gay by a woman hoeing corn. Sold for $16.

Bibliography: E. F. R., of Statesville, North Carolina, USA, "Query: A Question for the Curious," *Historical Magazine*, 2nd series, 6 (August 1869): 103–4.
E. F. R., *of Statesville, North Carolina, USA,* "Flotsam: A Fossil Tooth of an Extinct Horse in Iredell County, N.C.," *Historical Magazine,* 2nd series, 8 (October 1870): 249.

252. 8 or 10 miles northeast of Statesville, Iredell County, North Carolina, USA, July 1869.

Type of find: Single find.

Contents: 1 AV.

Description: Spanish colonies, Philip V, 4 escudos, México, ca. 1730

Disposition: Plowed up in a field by a man named Tanner. Assayed by Frederic Eckfeldt at the Charlotte Mint, who said that it dated from around 1740, weighed half an ounce, and assayed at .895 fine. This fineness is lower than genuine México pieces of 1730 (which assay at .917), so the piece may have been a U.S. contemporary counterfeit of the 1784–1834 period, part of the series of "regulated gold."

Bibliography: E. F. R., of Statesville, North Carolina, USA, "Query: A Question for the Curious," *Historical Magazine*, 2nd series, 6 (August 1869): 103–4.

253. Along the James River, Virginia, USA, April 2001.

Type of find: Single find.

Date of deposit: Ca. 1730.

Contents: 1 AR.

Description: English colonies, Massachusetts, oak tree shilling, 1652 [1660–67], cut quarter, variety Noe 11 or 12

Disposition: Found by a metal detectorist.

Bibliography: Kays 2001, 2193–94.

254. Grounds of the Bartow-Pell Mansion, Bronx, New York, USA, 1950–90.

Type of find: Single find.

Contents: 1 AE.

Description: Great Britain, George II, halfpenny, 1730

Disposition: Found by Theodore Kazimiroff of the Bronx County Historical Society.

Bequeathed to Kingsborough Community College, Brooklyn, New York.

Bibliography: Hecht 1993.

255. Fort Michilimackinac, south shores of the Straits of Mackinac, Michigan, USA, 1958–79.

Type of find: Archaeological excavation.

Date of the French occupation: 1730–1761.

Contents: 9 BI.

Description:

France, Louis XIV, sol de 15 deniers overstruck on an old flan, 1694
France, Louis XIV, sol de 15 deniers overstruck on an old flan, mint O
France, Louis XIV, sol de 15 deniers overstruck on an old counterstamped douzain
France, Louis XIV, sol de 15 deniers
France, Louis XV, 2 sol (5): 1740M; 1740; 1751H; ND (2)

Heldman could not identify the sols de 15 deniers that were recovered at the site. His descriptions have been corrected. His misidentification of his figure 3A as a crowned C counterstamp may have led him to date the coins too late, and thus assume that they came from the period of British occupation. On the contrary, all the French coins found are consistent with the period of French occupation. The coins from the period of British occupation are listed in a separate entry.

Bibliography: Heldman 1980.

256. Site of colonial settlement of Dogtown Commons, Cape Ann, Massachusetts, USA, December 2006.

Type of find: Single finds.

Date of deposit: 1730–50.

Contents: 2 AE, 1 AR.

Description:

Great Britain, George I, halfpence, 1720s (2)
Spain, Philip V, 2 reales (pistareen), [1708–39], cut quarter

The copper coins are only described as "two copper coins dated in the 1720s." The attribution is based on what would be the most likely two copper coins of the 1720s to be found in this context.

Disposition: Found by a metal detectorist.

Bibliography: Leonard 2006, 44.

257. John's Island, South Carolina, USA, 1985–95.

Type of find: Single find.

Contents: 1 AR.

Description: Spain, real (½ pistareen), Madrid, 1732IF

Disposition: Found by a metal detectorist. Acquired by Thomas A. Kays.

Bibliography: Kays 1996, 637–45.

258. Farm of William Campbell, lot number 3, La Fayette, New York, USA, 1840.

Type of find: Single find.

Contents: 1 AR.

Description: German states, Protestant religious medal with inscription, GEHE AUS DEINEM VATTERLAND (Get thee out of thy country) 1 b[uch]. M[oses]. XII, v. 1, (Genesis 12:1) and in exergue, LASST HIER DIE GVTER (Leave the goods here). On reverse, VND DV SOLLT EIN SEEGEN SEYN (And thou shalt be a blessing) 1 b. Mos. XII v. 2 (Genesis 12:2), and in exergue, GOTT GIBT SIE WIEDER (God will give them [the goods] back again).

This is a medal of 1732 referring to the expulsion of the Protestants from the Archbishopric of Salzburg. Its discovery in upstate New York may be connected with the settlement of German Protestant refugees in upper New York, such as at New Paltz.

Disposition: Found on the farm of William Campbell by his son.

Bibliography: Beauchamp 1891, 49; 1903, 70–71; Clark 1849, 2:274–76.

259. Between Crocker and Davis Reefs, off Treasure Harbor, Florida Keys, Florida, USA, 1930 and 1948.

Type of find: Shipwreck.

Ship: El Rubi Segundo. Part of the 1733 plate fleet. This ship was the *Capitana*.

Sank: July 15, 1733.

Contents: 3+ AV, 1,000+ AR. Shipwreck.

Description:
  Spanish colonies, 8 reales, México? (1,000+)
  Spanish colonies, escudos, Lima? (2): 1721; 1733
  Spanish colonies, 2 escudo, 1728, Lima
  Spanish colonies, 8 reales, Potosí, 1651, counterstamped with crowned F (2)
  Silver bars (3)
  The Spanish salvaged 5,258,035 pesos in minted, worked, and bar silver, plus gold, of private interests, and 727,733 pesos 7½ reales of His Majesty's silver in July-August 1733.

Disposition: Excavated by Art McKee, who established a museum of sunken treasure in 1949, which was subsequently closed. Excavated by Tim Watkins and Martin Meylach after 1960.

Bibliography: Meylach 1971, 46–49, 103–36; Nesmith 1958a, 30–34, 36–39, 42–46; Peterson 1975, 376–86; Sedwick and Sedwick 2007, 185–86 (Sedwick 42); Smith 1988, 99. Arnold R. Perpall, "Un Interesante Hallazgo," *Boletín Ibero-Americano de Numismática* 1, no. 14 (January-February 1951): 1.

260. Little Conch Reef, Florida Keys, Florida, USA, 1955.

Type of find: Shipwreck.

Ship: Nuestra Señora de Balvaneda (alias *El Infante*), part of the 1733 plate fleet.

Sank: July 15, 1733.

Contents: 25 AR.

Description:
  Spanish colonies, 8 reales, pillar dollars, México, 1732 (6)
  Spanish colonies, 8 reales, pillar dollars, México, 1733 (6)
  Spanish colonies, 8 reales, cobs (12)
  The Spanish recovered 567,384 pesos, 4 reales, in minted and worked silver in July-August 1733.

Bibliography: Marx 1971, 48–49, 74, 192, 209–15; Peterson 1975, 376–86; Potter 1972, 227–28; Smith 1988, 99.

261. Hawk Channel, off Indian Key, southeast of the upper tip of Lower Matecumbe, Florida Keys, USA, 1971.

Type of find: Shipwreck.

Ship: San Pedro, part of 1733 plate fleet.

Sank: July 15, 1733.

Contents: 3,000 AR.

Description:
  Spanish colonies, ½ reales (100)
  Spanish colonies, reales, 1731 (1,000)
  Spanish colonies, reales, 1732 (1,000)
  Spanish colonies, reales 1733 (1,000)
  The Spanish did not recover any silver from this shipwreck in July-August 1733; only wet anil and wet cochineal. The modern recovery is thought to be the contents of one or two Spanish moneybags.

Bibliography: Marx 1971, 48–49, 74, 192, 209–15; Meylach 1971, 69–72, 75–76; Peterson 1975, 376–86; Potter 1972, 230; Smith 1988, 99, 102.

262. South of Conch Key, Florida Keys, Florida, USA, 1960s.

Type of find: Shipwreck.

Ship: El Sueco de Arizón, part of 1733 plate fleet.

Sank: July 15, 1733.

Contents: 700+ AR.

Description:

Spanish colonies, 4 reales, México, 1720–33 (100+)

Spanish colonies, 8 reales, México, 1720–33 (100+)

Spanish colonies, 8 reales, México, 1733, pillar dollars (12)

Disposition: 25% to the State of Florida.

Bibliography: Daley 1977, 63–64; Marx 1971, 48–49, 74, 192, 209–15; Peterson 1975, 376–86; Potter 1972, 228–29; Smith 1988, 102.

263. Between Davis and Little Conch Reefs, off Plantation Key, Florida Keys, Florida, USA, 1968.

Type of find: Shipwreck.

Ship: San José de las Animas. Part of the 1733 plate fleet.

Sank: July 15, 1733.

Contents: 1 AE, 950 AR, 12 AV.

Description: These coins were listed in the American Auction Association catalog of February 1974:

Spanish colonies, 4 reales, México (3): 1731F; 1732F cob; 1732 pattern without date or assayer on obverse

Spanish colonies, 8 reales, México (11): 1731F; 1732F (cob) (2); 1733F (cob); 1733F (recortado) (3); 1732F (pillar) (2); 1733F; 1733F MX mintmark

Spanish colonies, escudos, México (5): assayer L (2); assayer J (2); NDA

Spanish colonies, 2 escudos, México, 1714J (3)

Spanish colonies, 8 escudos, México, 1714J (2)

Spanish colonies, 2 escudos, Bogotá (2): 1705; NDA

Spanish colonies, 8 reales, Lima (2): 1704H; 1708H

Spanish colonies, 8 reales, Potosí, 1719Y

Disposition: The Spanish recovered 227,084 pesos in worked silver from this wreck in July-August 1733, and also wet cochineal and balm. Modern recovery was by Tom Gurr. Mendel Peterson and George Fisher also worked on the wreck. Tom Gurr entered into a dispute with the State of Florida over the disposition of the artifacts and dumped some into a canal behind his home. The coins were consigned to Bowers and Ruddy Galleries, who put them in their American Auction Association Catalog of February 1974, but the State of Florida obtained an injunction preventing the sale. After further litigation, the coins went to the State of Florida.

Bibliography: American Auction Association 1974, lots 1595–1623; Bowers 1997, 201–4; Peterson 1975, 376–86 (includes photographs of the site on page 383); Potter 1972, 224–27.

264. Florida Keys, USA, 1972.

Type of find: Shipwreck.

Ship: Nuestra Señora de las Angustias y San Rafael, also known as *El Charanguero Grande.* Part of the 1733 plate fleet.

Sank: July 15, 1733.

Contents: 2 AV.

Description:

Spanish colonies, Philip V, 2 escudos, [1724–27]

Spanish colonies, 4 escudos royal

Bibliography: Marx 1971, 48–49, 74, 192, 209–15; Peterson 1975, 376–86; Potter 1972, 224–27; Smith 1988, 102.

265. Albany, New York, USA, August 2001.

Type of find: Archaeological excavation.

Date of site: 1733–45.

Contents: 5 AE.

Contents: Ireland, Wood's Hibernia halfpenny, 1723?

Great Britain, halfpence, 1735–45 (5)
Bibliography: Danforth 2001, 2224.

266. Oriskany, New York, USA, 1849.
Type of find: Funerary deposits.
Date of deposit: 1735.
Contents: 4+ AE.
Description:
British colonies, George I, Indian and deer peace medal
British colonies, George II, Indian and deer peace medal, 1731
British colonies, Indian and deer peace medal, 1731–35 (2+)
When the Erie Canal was enlarged at Oriskany in 1849, the excavations turned up ten to twelve Indian graves, including medals.
Bibliography: Beauchamp 1903, 56.

267. Newton, Norfolk, Virginia, USA, September 14–November 30, 1978.
Type of find: Archaeological excavation.
Date of site: 1735–90.
Contents: 1 AR.
Description: Spain, real (½ pistareen), Madrid, 1735JF
Bibliography: Wittkofski, McCartney, and Bogley 1980.

268. State Street and James Street, Albany, New York, USA, 1972.
Type of find: Archaeological excavation.
Date of site: 1700–50.
Date of coin: 1736.
Contents: 1 AE.
Description: Portuguese colonies, Brazil, 10 reis, 1736, holed twice
Bibliography: Huey 2004.

269. Saint Augustine, Florida, USA, 1976.
Type of find: Archaeological excavation.
Date of site: 1736–63.
Contents: 1 B, 1 AR.
Description:
German states, Nuremberg, jeton with Louis XV crowned left on obverse, Ex Pace Vbertas (abundance from peace) on reverse, in exergue I I D R P
Spanish colonies, Philip V, cob real, México
Bibliography: Shepard 1983.

270. Off the coast of the Carolinas, USA, during the Civil War.
Type of find: Shipwreck.
Ship: Unknown wreck of a boat.
Date of deposit: 1737.
Contents: 1 AE.
Description: British colonies, Connecticut, Higley, 3 pence, with VALUE ME AS YOU PLEASE/J CUT MY WAY THROUGH
Disposition: Found by Luther B. Newell of Hanover, New Hampshire, while serving in the Federal Navy. In 1883 he sold it to Perley R. Bugbee, who still owned it in 1927.
Bibliography: Bugbee 1927.

271. North shore of Boston Harbor, near Grover's Cliff, Beachmont, Boston, Massachusetts, USA, 1884.
Type of find: Hoard.
Date of deposit: 1737.
Contents: 6+ AV.
Description:
Great Britain, guineas (2): 1737; ND
Spanish colonies, 8 escudos
Portuguese colonies, Brazil, John V, 4,000 reis, Bahia, 1720
Portuguese colonies, Brazil, 12,800 reis (2)
Bibliography: Brown and Dolley 1971, 59 (NT2); Nesmith 1958a, 20–21; Nesmith and Potter 1968, 53.
"Finding Treasure Near Boston," *American*

Journal of Numismatics 18, no. 4 (April 1884): 95.

272. Canton, Massachusetts, USA, October 1876.

Type of find: Hoard.

Date of deposit: 1737.

Contents: 3+ AE.

Description:

England, William III, halfpence (2): 1697; 1700

Great Britain, George II, halfpenny, 1737

Copper coins dug up in front of Lawer Ames's office on Washington Street in Canton. The coins were nearly as bright when found as when they came from the mint.

Bibliography: "Relics of the Past," *American Journal of Numismatics* 11, no. 2 (October 1876): 33.

273. Somerset County, Maryland, USA, April 2001.

Type of find: Single find.

Contents: 1 AR.

Description: Spain, real (½ pistareen), Seville, 1738PJ

Disposition: Found by a metal detectorist.

Bibliography: Kays 2001, 2193–94.

274. Shanklin site, five kilometers west southwest of Hungerford, Wharton County, Texas, USA, 1969.

Type of find: Archaeological excavation from plowed surface.

Date of site: 1700–1900.

Date of coin: 1738.

Contents: 1 AR.

Description: Spanish colonies, 8 reales, México, 1738MF (grades AU55)

Bibliography: Hudgins 1984–86.

275. Virginia, USA, 1985–95.

Type of find: Hoard.

Contents: 2 AR.

Description:

Spanish colonies, ½ real, México, 1739MF

Spanish colonies, 2 reales, México, 1739MF

Kays assigns both coins the same grade: VF. Judging by his photograph, this is a gross undergrading by today's standards. These may be from a small hoard of uncirculated Mexican pillar fractions—a lost purse, perhaps.

Disposition: Found by a metal detectorist. Acquired by Thomas A. Kays.

Bibliography: Kays 1996, 1637–45.

276. Lake Eustes, near Tampa, Florida, USA, November 1955.

Type of find: Single find.

Contents: 1 AR.

Description: Spanish colonies, 8 reales, México, 1739

Bibliography: Numismatic Scrapbook Magazine 21, no. 11 (November 1955): 1700.

277. Harrison Avenue and Bennett Street, Boston, Massachusetts, USA, October 1899.

Type of find: Single find.

Contents: 1 B.

Description: Great Britain, Admiral Vernon medal, oval, in brass:

Obv: THE BRITISH GLORY REVIV'D BY HON. EDWARD VERNON ESQ: VICE. ADMIRAL OF THE BLEW/A VIEW OF FORT CHAGRE

Rev: PORTO.BELLO.TAKEN.BY.THE. COURAGE. AND CONDUCT. OF ADMIRAL VERNON.WITH SIX MEN OF WAR.ONLY.NOV 22.ANNO DOM 1739+

This variety is unlisted in *Medallic Illustrations* and in Milford Haven's collection of naval medals; nor was an example of this variety in the John J. Ford, Jr., collection. It mules two dies known in other combinations.

Disposition: Lent to the cabinet of the Boston Numismatic Society.

Bibliography: Edmund J. Cleveland, "Newly Discovered Vernons," *American Journal of Numismatics* 34, no. 3 (October 1899): 46.

278. Elmsford, near White Plains, New York, USA, September 1895.

Type of find: Hoard.

Date of deposit: 1740.

Contents: 50+ AE, AR.

Description:
Great Britain, farthings, 1702–40 (40)
Great Britain, shilling, ca. 1740 (10)
Most of the coins were British farthings dated 1702–1740, although a few shillings of the same date in very poor condition were also found.

Bibliography: "A Queer Coin Find," *Numismatist* 8, no. 9 (September, 1895): 242.

279. Along the James River, Virginia, USA, fall 1985.

Type of find: Single finds.

Date of site: 1740–1910.

Contents: 1 AE, 1 AR.
Great Britain, halfpenny, 1730
Spain, 2 reales (cross pistareen), cut quarter, probably Seville mint

Disposition: Found with a metal detector by Dan Johnson, Roanoke, Virginia, USA.

Bibliography: "Adding to a Mystery," *Treasure Found*, Fall 1985, 39–40.

280. Pajatambo, on the coast between the Moche and Viru Valleys, Peru, 1974.

Type of find: Archaeological excavation.

Date of site: 1740–60.

Contents: 4 AR.

Description:
Spanish colonies, Philip V, reales, Potosí, assayer P (2)
Spanish colonies, Philip V, 2 reales, Potosí, assayer Y (2)

Bibliography: Beck 1983.

281. Burlington County, New Jersey, USA, October 1986–2005.

Type of find: Single finds.

Date of site: 1740–1876. Although Burlington County was settled quite early, with some towns founded as early as 1677, the artifact assemblages seem most consistent with mid to late eighteenth century dates.

Contents: 869 AE, 1 SN, 1 B, 128 AR, 1 AV, 116 metal not indicated.

Description:
Series of metal detecting finds made on sixty-three different sites in Burlington County, plus finds from three sites in Mercer County, two sites in Middlesex County, and one site in Ocean County.

England, farthings (19): Charles II ND (13); William and Mary ND; William III ND (5)

Great Britain, farthings (17): George I ND (3); 1723 (2); George II, ND (10); 1749; 1821

England, Charles II, counterfeit farthing, ND

Great Britain, George II, counterfeit farthing, ND

England, halfpence (51): William and Mary, ND (4); William and Mary, tin; William III, ND (36); 1694 (2); 1698 (3); 1699; 1700 (2); 1701; 1701 cut in half

Great Britain, halfpence (130): George I, ND (21); 1717 (2); 1718; 1721; 1722; 1723 (7); 1724; George II, ND (47); 1730; 1731; 1732; 1733 (2); 1734 (4); 1735 (5); 1735 cut in half; 1736 (2); 1737 (5); 1738 (2); 1739 (2); 1740(4); 1745 (5); 1752; 1753; George III,

ND; 1799 (3); ND (8)

Great Britain, counterfeit halfpence (39): George II, ND (3); George III, ND (25); George III, ND, cut in half; 1771; 1772; 1773; 1774 (2); 1775 (3); 177[-]; ND

Great Britain, penny, 1797 (3)

Great Britain, eighteenth century ("Conder") token, 1791

Great Britain, counterfeit guinea, cut half, 1779

Ireland, Wood's Hibernia farthing, 1723

Ireland, farthing, 1806

Ireland, halfpence (32): William and Mary, ND (3); 1693; George II, ND (11); 1737; 1744; 1751; 1753; George III, ND (8); 1760; 1781 (3); 1782

Ireland, Wood's Hibernia halfpence (21): 1723 (6); 1724; ND (14)

Ireland, James II, gun money, crown, 1690

Ireland, seventeenth century town tokens (3): 1659 (2); ND

Russia, Alexander I, 2 kopeks (2): 1812; ND

Sweden, Gustaf IV, ½ skilling, 1801

Denmark, counterfeit 2 skillings, late 1700s

German states, Soest, 3 pfennigs, mid-1700s

Netherlands, duit, 1753

Spanish Netherlands, liard, 1710

France, Louis XIV, liard, young bust [1655–58]: 2

France, Louis XV, ½ sol

France, Louis XVI, ½ sol

France, Louis XVI, sol (3): 1790; ND (2)

France, 2 sols, bronze, 1792

France, 30 sous, 179[-], cut in half

France, écu, 1778, cut two thirds

Rome, Constantine era coin

Spain, Charles III or IV, 2 maravedíes

Spain, Philip IV, 4 maravedíes, revaluation counterstamp of 1655

Spain, Charles III or IV, 4 maravedíes

Spain, real (½ pistareen), Madrid, 1742

Spain, real (½ pistareen), Seville, 1774

Spain, 2 reales (pistareen), Seville, 1725

Spain, 2 reales (pistareen), Madrid, 1727

Portugal, 5 reis (2): 1752; 1755

Portugal, 10 reis (4): 1755 cut two thirds; ND (3)

Portugal, 40 reis, 1814

British colonies, Lower Canada, tokens (4): 1812; ND (3)

English colonies, Massachusetts, cut quarter of silver pine tree shilling, Noe 2 or 3

British colonies, William Pitt halfpenny token, 1766 (2)

British colonies, Virginia, halfpence (5)

USA, Connecticut, coppers (11): Miller varieties 1.2C; 5.3-N; 13-D; 33.6-KK; cut half, unattributed; unattributed (6)

USA, Georgius Triumpho token, 1783

USA, New York, Machin's Mills halfpence (2): Vlack 12-78B; unattributed

USA, New Jersey, coppers (43): Maris varieties 14-J; 15-T; 17-b; 21-N; 32-T; 34-J; 37-f; 38-c; 43-d (3); 46-e (3); 48-g; 50-f; 54-k (2); 59-o; 64-t; 66-v; 73-aa; 75-bb; 77-dd; unattributed (19)

USA, Nova Constellatio coppers (5): 1783 (2); 1785; ND (2)

USA, Vermont, coppers (2): Ryder 2; Ryder 27; unattributed

USA, Fugio 1¢ (2)

USA, ½¢ (100): Liberty cap ND; 1794; 1795 (2); 1797 (4); draped bust ND (19); 1800 (2); 1803 (6); 1804 (8); 1805 (2); 1806; 1807 (5); 1808 (5); classic head ND (19); 1809 (7); 1810 (4); 1814; 1825 (2); 1826 (2); 1828 (2); 1829; 1834 (4); coronet ND; 1851

USA, 1¢ (293): 1793 chain; Liberty cap ND (6); 1793 Liberty cap; 1794 (12); draped bust ND (28); draped bust ND cut half (2); 1796 (5); 1797 (4); 1798 (3); 1799; 1800 (5); 1801 (9); 1802 (2); 1803 (2); 1804; 1807 (3); classic head ND; classic head ND cut half; 1808 (2);

1810 (6); 1811 (3); 1812 (8); 1813 (5); 1814 (6); coronet ND (77); coronet ND cut in half; 1816 (7); 1817 (6); 1818 (10); 1819 (6); 1820 (3); 1821; 1822 (4); 1823 (2); 1825 (6); 1826 (6); 1827 (6); 1828 (4); 1829 (3); 1830 (2); 1831; 1832; 1836; 1837 (2); 1838 (7); 1839; 1842; 1843 (2); 1845 (3); 1847 (3); 1849; 1850 (2); 1851 (3); 1852 (2); 1856; 1857

USA, silver 3¢ (6): 1852 (2); 1852 cut in half; 1853 (2); ND

USA, silver 5¢ (18): 1803; 1829; 1832 (3); 1835; 1841; 1843; 1845; 1847; 1853 (5); 1858; capped bust ND (2)

USA, 10¢ (10): 1805; 1814; 1833; 1834; 1835; 1841; 1843; 1853; 1854; capped bust ND

USA, 50¢, 1808

USA, silver $1, 1799

USA, hard times tokens (4): 1837 (2); General Harrison, 1840; ND

USA, other tokens (3)

French colonies, sol tampé, crowned C counterstamp on blank planchet [1779]

Danish colonies, Danish West Indies, 12 skillings, 1767

Danish colonies, Danish West Indies, 24 skillings

Spanish colonies, ½ reales, México (35): 1744; 1772 (2); 1774 (5); 1776; 1778 (2); 1779; 1780; 1781 (6); 1782 (2); 1783; 1784 (2); 1786; 1788; 1791; 1792; 1797; 1807 (2); 1814; 1815; 1816; 1817

Spanish colonies, reales, México (6): 1753; 1775; 1781; 1782; 1803 (2)

Spanish colonies, 2 reales, México (6): 1768; 1771; 1781; 1784; 1785; 1804

Spanish colonies, counterfeit 8 reales, México, cut halves (5): 1787, 1790, 1792, 1793, 1796

Spanish colonies, counterfeit 8 reales, México, 1806, holed

Spanish colonies, ½ reales, Guatemala (2): 1783; 1802

Spanish colonies, 2 reales, Guatemala (2): 1772; 1787

Spanish colonies, ½ real, Lima, 1757

Spanish colonies, real, Potosí, cob, cut in half

Spanish colonies, real, Potosí, 1773

Spanish colonies, ½ reales, mint not legible (5): 1773; 1776; 1781; 1788; 1814

Spanish colonies, ½ reales, date and mint not legible (22)

Spanish colonies, reales, mint not given, cobs (3) (including one cut in half)

Spanish colonies, real, cob, counterfeit

Spanish colonies, reales, mint not legible (2): 1779; 1782

Spanish colonies, 2 reales, mint not legible, 1795

Spanish colonies, 2 reales, mint and date not legible

Spanish colonies, 2 reales, Charles III or Charles IV, counterfeit

Spanish colonies, counterfeit 8 reales, cut half, mint not given

Spanish colonies, counterfeit 8 reales, cut thirds (2)

Portuguese colonies, Brazil, Maria and Peter III, 5 reis

Portuguese colonies, Brazil, 10 reis, 1784

Portuguese colonies, Brazil, 20 reis, 1825

Unattributed (141)

Disposition: Wayne H. Shelby.

Bibliography: Shelby 2003, 2005.

282. Philadelphia, Pennsylvania, USA, November 1974 through February 1975.

Type of find: Hoard. Called the "Philadelphia Highway Find."

Date of deposit: 1741.

Contents: 362 AE.

Description: England, William III, counterfeit halfpence, 1699 (362) (BMC Type 2)

A detailed listing of the other coins found,

which date from 1681 through 1907, is provided separately below, in *NFA* 371 and 686. This was found in dirt dug up to build a highway that was moved and deposited elsewhere, which explains why the stratigraphy was disturbed.

Disposition: Private collections of original finders; Philadelphia Maritime Museum; specimens have been given to the British Museum, the Royal Mint Museum, and the American Numismatic Society in New York (item number 1976.195.1); also in the collections of Peter Gaspar and Eric P. Newman. Many of the artifacts found by the William R. Paull family of Audubon Park, New Jersey, are on permanent display in the Philadelphia Maritime Museum, 321 Chestnut Street, Philadelphia, Pennsylvania, USA.

Bibliography: Gaspar and Newman 1978; Newman and Gaspar 1978; Reiter 1978.

283. Off Havana, Cuba, July 2002.

Type of find: Shipwreck.

Ship: Probably the *Invencible*.

Sank: June 20, 1741.

Contents: AR.

Description: Spain, real (½ pistareen), 1726J, Seville (Thomas Sebring)

Bibliography: Sebring 2004, lot 1587.

284. Along the Chickahominy River, Richmond, Virginia, USA, 1985–95.

Type of find: Single find.

Contents: 1 AR.

Description: Spanish colonies, real, Potosí, 1742

Disposition: Found by a metal detectorist. Acquired by Thomas A. Kays.

Bibliography: Kays 1996, 1637–45.

285. Near Massey, a town near Espanola, Ontario, Canada, 1986.

Type of find: Hoard.

Date of deposit: 1742.

Contents: 2 AR.

Description: Spanish colonies, 8 reales, México, 1742 (2)

Bibliography: Willey 1986, 293.

286. Battery Park, New York, New York, USA, December 2005.

Type of find: Excavations to dig a subway tunnel under Battery Park.

Contents: 1 AE.

Description: Great Britain, halfpenny, 1744 Found next to the base of a wall at the Battery in Manhattan, and thought to date the wall to the 1740s.

Bibliography: Patrick McGeehan, "Found: Old Wall in New York, and It's Blocking the Subway," *New York Times*, December 8, 2005.

287. Point Michaud, Cape Breton Island, Nova Scotia, Canada, 1899–1901.

Type of find: Shipwreck.

Ship: Possibly the *Saint Michel*, which left France (Rochefort?), en route to Louisbourg.

Sank: July 1745.

Contents: 76 AV.

Description: France, Louis XV, louis, 1726, 1727, 1728, 1729, 1730, 1742; mints included A, B, H, Q, and BB (76)

13 gold coins were found on a beach by a young girl in April 1900. The gold coins were in "fine, almost uncirculated condition." She also found one copper and one silver coin, but they were too worn to identify.

Droulers suggests a date of deposit of 1730, but this is not possible if there was indeed a 1742 coin, as noted by Storm. Storm also mentions a louis of 1724, however this cannot be reconciled with Droulers's account, which states that all coins were the "aux lunettes" type, which was only struck from 1726 onwards. This entry follows Droulers in omitting the 1724 gold louis, as being more consistent with what we know of French gold louis hoards (*viz.*, hoards deposited after 1726 do not have any coins earlier than 1726).

Bibliography: Bissett 1902; Droulers 1980; Storm 2002, 155–58.

Joseph Hooper, "Hooper's Restrikes: Found on Cape Breton Shore," *Numismatist* 13, no. 11 (November 1900): 295.

288. Saratoga Springs, New York, USA, September 1936.

Type of find: Single find.

Contents: 1 AE.

Description: Great Britain, George II, halfpenny, 1745

Disposition: Found by Private Aubrey B. Ackley of Maine while on duty at Saratoga. His commanding officer obtained permission for him to keep it as a souvenir.

Bibliography: "Finds 1745 Penny at Saratoga," *New York Times*, September 4, 1936, 21.

289. Beatty, near Springfield, Ohio, USA, July 1904.

Type of find: Hoard.

Date of deposit: 1745.

Contents: 300 AV.

Description: Portuguese colonies, Brazil, 6,400 reis? (300)

Gold coins with a value to collectors of $1,500 unearthed by John Stonebrunner. The *Numismatist* said the coins all bore dates of the eighteenth century and that they would be exhibited at the Ohio building at the Saint Louis exhibition. The coins are supposed to have been buried by the French in 1745. The coins are not described; the description is an educated guess based on common gold coins in circulation in the Americas in the 1740s.

Bibliography: *Numismatist* 17, no. 7 (July 1904): 214.

290. Salmedina Reef, Portobelo, Panama, summer 1975.

Type of find: Shipwreck.

Ship: Possibly the Spanish privateer *Golgoa*, which was driven ashore near Portobelo by two English warships after a short battle and quickly went to pieces.

Sank: 1746.

Contents: 43+ AR.

Description:

Spanish colonies, 8 reales, México, [1732ff.] (2+)

Spanish colonies, 4 reales, Potosí (21): 1740; ND (20)

Disposition: National Museum, Panama City, Panama.

Bibliography: Marx 1971, 425; Wignall 1982, 212–15 and photograph facing page 167.

291. Found in the Onondaga Valley, between the Onondaga Fort of 1756 and the Reservation, Onondaga County, New York, USA, 1893.

Type of find: Single find.

Contents: B single find.

Description: Great Britain, medal of the Duke of Cumberland, with WILL: DUKE: CUMB: BRITISH HERO BORN 15 APR 1721 on obverse and REBELION JUSTLY REWARDED/AT CARLILE ANNO 1745 on reverse.

Disposition: Found by George Slocum, still owned by him in 1903.

Bibliography: Beauchamp 1903, 58, 1908, 1: 67.

292. Powhatan Courthouse, Virginia, USA, April 1881.

Type of find: Foundation deposit.

Contents: 1 B.

Description: Great Britain, medal of the Duke of Cumberland, reading on the reverse, "Rebellion is justly rewarded/Culloden, 16 Ap., 1746."

Disposition: Found imbedded in the mortar while tearing down a chimney. Acquired by A. M. Howard, Powhatan Courthouse.

Bibliography: "Medals Discovered," *Coin Collector's Journal* 6 (whole no. 65) (April 1881): 56–57.

American Journal of Numismatics 15, no. 4 (April 1881): 78.

293. Brownsville, Tennessee, USA, 1861–65.

Type of find: Single find.

Contents: 1 B.

Description: Great Britain, medal of the Duke of Cumberland, with Will. Duke of Cumberland on obverse and Rebellion justly rewarded on reverse; about the size of a Spanish dollar.

Bibliography: "Medal of the Duke of Cumberland," *American Journal of Numismatics* 11, no. 2 (October 1876): 31 (citing the *Blue Ridge Blade*).

294. Pittsfield, Massachusetts, USA, July 1938.

Type of find: Single find.

Contents: 1 AR.

Description: Spain, Philip V, 2 reales (pistareen), 1746

Disposition: Found by George E. Herie while working in his garden.

Bibliography: "Finds Spanish coin of 1746," *New York Times*, July 2, 1938, 15.

295. "The Castle," near David Williams's place, Pompey, New York, USA, 1815.

Type of find: Single find.

Contents: 1 B.

Description: Netherlands, medal of William, Prince of Orange, with an equestrian with drawn sword on one side and "William, Prince of Orange" and coat of arms on the other. Probably Van Loon 235, although that has its inscription in Dutch, not English; the date of the medal would then be 1747.

Bibliography: Beauchamp 1891, 48; Clark 1849, 2:258; Van Loon 1:235.

296. Site of old Fort Harden, Schuylerville, near Troy, New York, USA, July 1883.

Type of find: Single find.

Contents: 1 AR.

Description: Spain, Ferdinand VI, probably a 2 reales (pistareen)

Bibliography: "An Old Coin Found," *New York Times*, July 19, 1883, 2.

297. Hartland, Connecticut, USA, July 1876.

Type of find: Single find.

Contents: 1 AR.

Description: France, Louis XV, écu, 1748

Disposition: It was found while tearing down an old residence belonging to Dwight Beman.

Bibliography: "Buried Treasure," *American Journal of Numismatics* 11, no. 1 (July 1876): 13.

298. Independence Hall, Philadelphia, Pennsylvania, USA, August 29, 1996.

Type of find: Archaeological excavation.

Date of site: 1750s. Believed to have been dropped when workers were building the Independence Hall tower.

Contents: 1 AE.

Description: Ireland, Wood's Hibernia halfpenny, ND

Disposition: Found beneath the grand staircase leading up to the tower.

Bibliography: Mossman 1999, 1912.

"A routine dig turns up an 18th-century

British coin. Found, at Independence Hall: A bit of long-ago real life," *Philadelphia Inquirer,* August 31, 1996, A1 and A10.

299. Pensacola, Florida, USA, 1982–94.
Type of find: Archaeological excavation.
Date of site: 1750–1821.
Contents: 2 B, 21 AR.
Description:
  Spanish colonies, Charles IV, ½ real, México
  Spanish colonies, Philip V, real, México
  Spanish colonies, Philip V, real, México, cut third
  Spanish colonies, Ferdinand VI, real, México, cut third
  Spanish colonies, Charles III, real, México, cut third
  Spanish colonies, Ferdinand VI, real, Lima, cut quarter
  Spanish colonies, cob, ½ real or real, Potosí
  Spanish colonies, ½ real
  Spanish colonies, Philip V, real, cut quarter
  Spanish colonies, Ferdinand VI, real, cut third
  Spanish colonies, Ferdinand VII, real (2)
  Spanish colonies, Charles III, 2 reales, cut eighth
  Spanish colonies, Charles III, 2 reales, cut quarter
  Spanish colonies, Charles III or IV, 2 reales, cut sixth (3)
  Spanish colonies, Charles III or IV, 4 reales, cut sixth
  Spanish colonies, indeterminate silver coins (3)
  Brass tokens (2)
Bibliography: Bense 1999, 138–39.

300. Surry, Virginia, USA, 1859.
Type of find: Hoard.
Date of deposit: 1750.
Container: Jar.
Contents: 500+ AR.
Description: Included:
  Spain, ½ reales? (¼ pistareens?)
  Spanish colonies, 8 reales, cob
  Spanish colonies, 8 reales, cut
A jar plowed up that contained $500 of old silver coins, including "cob dollars, cut dollars, and half bits." The identity of the half bits is difficult to determine. Normally a half bit would be a Spanish *medio*—a quarter pistareen. On page 277, however, Mordecai says that half bits are cut money, made by dividing a Spanish colonies real into sixths, or a Spanish pistareen into fifths.
Bibliography: Kays 2001, 2182; Mordecai 1860, 278, note ⋆.

301. Orangeburg, South Carolina, USA, October 1876.
Type of find: Single find.
Date of deposit: 1750.
Contents: 1 AE.
Description: France, Henry II, medal, on the reverse two women in a chariot and the inscription RES IN ITAL GERM ET GAL FORTITER AC FOELIC. GESTAS ('military campaigns forcefully and fortunately executed in Italy, Germany, and France').
The medal commemorates events of around the year 1559; however, Scher states that the earliest date that can be assigned to these Valois medals is 1745–49.
Bibliography: Scher 1994, 318.
  "Relics of the Past," *American Journal of Numismatics* 11, no. 2 (October 1876): 33–34 (citing the *Charleston (S.C.) News and Courier).*

302. Seneca River, Baldwinsville, New York, USA, 1887.
Type of find: Single find.
Date of deposit: 1750?

Contents: 1 B.

Description: German states, Catholic religious medal in brass: on obverse, Virgin Mary with halo and palm branches. Inscription: "GEHE PAGEN … NDE EMPFANGEN. RITT.FUR. UNS. ('Go … and receive," plus possible misreading of Bett fur uns, i.e., "Pray for us.') On reverse: the emblem of Mary, an M surmounted by a cross with fifteen stars around; below a flaming heart (the sacred heart of Jesus) and another heart pierced by a sword. Inscription: D: W: ZU: D: UNSRE: ZU: FURCHT.NEHMEN (these we will take up for our worship).

Disposition: By the time Beauchamp wrote in 1903, this medal had disappeared.

Bibliography: Beauchamp 1891, 42; 1903, 71.

303. Salem, Massachusetts, USA, 1850.

Type of find: Hoard.

Date of deposit: 1750.

Contents: AE.

Description:

Great Britain, George II, farthing, 1749
Great Britain, George II, farthing, 1750
Great Britain, George II, halfpence, 1749
Great Britain, George II, halfpence, 1750

John Robinson wrote in a note in the box with the ANS specimen: "These halfpence were sent to Boston in 1750 to pay for the Louisbourg expedition. Some of these halfpence went to Salem to pay Colonel Benjamin Pickman. They were kept in the bag till 1850 when young Benjamin Pickman and Frank Lee divided it." The halfpence are red uncirculated.

Disposition: Francis Henry Lee, whose collection passed to the Essex Institute; Benjamin Pickman; Alfred Walcott; John Robinson; and probably also Thomas V. Hall, of 1744 Broadway, New York.

American Numismatic Society item number 1921.20.2 is certainly from this hoard (gift of John Robinson) and 1885.17.4 probably is (gift of Thomas V. Hall).

Bibliography: Robinson 1917, 330.

Card in box with the American Numismatic Society specimen, written by John Robinson (quoted above) (item number 1921.20.2).

304. Jamestown, Virginia, USA, 1962.

Type of find: Archaeological excavation.

Date of deposit: 1750–76.

Contents: 2 AR.

Description:

Spain, Philip V, 2 reales (pistareen), Seville, dated 17[-], cut half (found near the foundations of Structure 6)

Spain, 2 reales (pistareen), cut half, badly worn (found near the foundation of Structure 15)

Disposition: United States Park Service.

Bibliography: Leonard 2006, 44; Peterson 1962, 582–85.

305. Yorktown, Virginia, USA, 1962.

Type of find: Archaeological excavation.

Date of deposit: 1750–76.

Contents: 2 AR.

Description: Spain, Philip V, 2 reales (pistareens), cut quarters, Seville mint (found near Redoubt 10) (2)

Disposition: United States Park Service.

Bibliography: Leonard 2006, 44; Peterson 1962, 582–85.

306. Washington's Headquarters State Historic Site, Liberty and Washington Streets, Newburgh, New York, USA, 1974.

Type of find: Archaeological excavation.

Date of site: 1750–1850.

Contents: 1 AE.

Description: Great Britain, George II, halfpenny, 1735

Disposition: New York State Bureau of Historic Sites Collection, Peebles Island, New York, USA.

Bibliography: Hoover 2007 (providing inventory of New York State Bureau of Historic Sites Collections, Peebles Island, New York, as of August 16, 2005).

307. Pompey, New York, USA, 1840s.

Type of find: Single find.

Contents: 1 AR.

Description: France?, Catholic religious medal inscribed "B. virg. Sin. P. origi. Con." [Beata virgo sine peccato originali concepto] ('Blessed Virgin, conceived without original sin') on obverse, serpent and two naked figures (Adam & Eve?) on reverse.

A Catholic medal distributed to the Onondaga Indians during the French period.

Disposition: "Recently" (thus Clark) found on the farm of David Hinsdale.

Bibliography: Beauchamp 1903, 72; Clark 1849, 2:273–74.

308. Munnsville, New York, USA, 1903.

Type of find: Single find.

Contents: 1 B.

Description: France?, oval Catholic religious medal with bust of Jesus on obverse, inscription IESVS FILIVS DEI (Jesus, the Son of God), Mary on reverse with inscription MATER DEI (the Mother of God).

Disposition: Theodore Stanford.

Bibliography: Beauchamp 1903, 73.

309. Union Springs, New York, USA, fall 1902.

Type of find: Single find.

Contents: 1 B.

Description: France?, oval Catholic religious medal with head of Jesus on obverse, inscription SALVATOR MUNDI ('the Savior of the World'), Mary on reverse with inscription MATER CHRISTI ('the Mother of Christ').

Disposition: Rev. W. H. Casey.

Bibliography: Beauchamp 1903, 73.

310. Grand Army Plaza, west of Flatbush Avenue, Brooklyn, New York, USA, June 1934.

Type of find: Hoard.

Container: Bag.

Contents: 78 AE, 2 AR.

Description:

Great Britain, halfpenny, 1749

Great Britain?, copper medallion two inches in diameter in deep relief with the date 1721

USA, 1¢, 1819–76

Spanish colonies, ½ real, 177[-], probably México

Spanish colonies, 8 reales, 1776, probably México

Disposition: Found by workers resodding the embankments of Grand Army Plaza. The 8 reales of 1776 was taken by Savio Ferrara; Stanley Richards got forty copper coins that had been in a rotted bag; William Viola got ten coins; Larry Maggio got sixteen coins.

Bibliography: "80 Old Coins Dug Up in Brooklyn Plaza. Workers, Sodding Area by Flatbush Av., Find American, British and Spanish Pieces," *New York Times*, June 13, 1934, 25.

311. Broadway and 14th Street, New York, New York, USA, April 1892.

Type of find: Single find.

Contents: 1 AE.

Description: German states, Hanover, medal by Morikofer struck by the Royal Academy of Sciences of Göttingen in 1751 for one of the annual prizes

Bibliography: Lyman Haynes Low?, "Found in Broadway, N. Y.," *American Journal of Numismatics* 26, no. 4 (April 1892): 89.

312. Fort Beauséjour (Fort Cumberland), Chignecto Isthmus, Nova Scotia, Canada, 1971.

Type of find: Archaeological excavation.

Date of French occupation: 1751–55.

Date of British occupation: 1755–61 and 1776–83.

Contents: 28 AE, 2 BI, 51 AR. Archaeological excavations.

Description: Coins from the French period:
France, Louis XIII, douzain, with 1640s fleur de lis counterstamp
France, Louis XIV, sol de 15 deniers, 1695–1705
Spain, 2 reales (pistareens) (3): 1721, 1723, 1727
Spanish colonies, cob real, México
Spanish colonies, reales, Lima or Potosí, about half from the 1740s (45)
Spanish colonies, cob ½ real, 1745
The Spanish and Spanish colonies coins were found together, suggesting an emergency hoard hidden during the siege of the fort in 1755.

Description: Coins from the British period:
Great Britain, halfpence (23): George II, young head [1729–39], ND (9); 1748; 1752, 1749; 1753; George II, old head [1746–54], ND (4); 1773; counterfeit 1775; George III, ND (4)
Ireland, halfpence (4): 1747 (3); George III, ND
Coin from later trade relations of 1787 onwards:
USA, Massachusetts, 1¢, 178[-]

Bibliography: Mossman 2003.

313. Fort Gaspereau (Fort Monckton), Chignecto Isthmus, Nova Scotia, Canada, 1971.

Type of find: Archaeological excavation.

Date of French occupation: 1751–55.

Date of British occupation: 1756.

Contents: 5 AE, 3 BI.

Description: Coins from the French period:
German states, Nuremberg, pfennig, 1714–77
France, liard de France, Rouen mint
France, mousquetaire of 30 deniers, 1711, Lyons mint
France, 2 sol, 1738, Pau
Coins from the British period:
Great Britain, halfpence(4): 1749 (2); 1752 (2)

Bibliography: Mossman 2003.

314. River Plate, off Montevideo, Uruguay, 1992.

Type of find: Shipwreck.

Ship: Nuestra Señora de la Luz.

Sank: July 2, 1752.

Contents: 320 AR; 1,658 AV.

Description:
Spain, reales (½ pistareens) (6)
Spain, 2 reales (pistareen), 1737
Spain, 2 reales (pistareens), Seville, assayer J (2)
Spain, 2 reales (pistareens) (11)
Spanish colonies, 2 reales, México (9): 1746MF (2); 1747MF (2); 1749MF (2); NDA (3)
Spanish colonies, 8 reales, México, 1743–49 (10)
Spanish colonies, 8 escudos, México (9): 1738MF; 1742MF; 1744MF; 1745MF; 1747MF; 1749MF; 1750MF (3)
Spanish colonies, 2 reales, Guatemala
Spanish colonies, 2 escudos, Bogotá (21): 1735M; 1738M; 1740; 1741M (2); 174[-] (6); 1750M (3); assayer S; 1750–51 (3); NDA (3)
Spanish colonies, 8 reales, Lima
Spanish colonies, 4 escudos, Lima, 1750R (53)
Spanish colonies, 8 escudos, Lima (22):

1743V; 1748R (2); 1749R (13); 1750R (6)
Spanish colonies, ½ reales, Potosí (19)
Spanish colonies, 4 reales, Potosí (49): 1750q(7); 1750E (7); 1751q (17); 1751E (18)
Spanish colonies, 8 reales, Potosí (72): 1736E (14); 1743; 1748q (3); 1749q (4); 1750q (12); 1750E (9); 1751q (13); 1751E (16)
Spanish colonies, 4 escudos, Santiago (282): 1749J (138); 1750J (144)
Spanish colonies, 8 escudos, Santiago (1,316): 1750J (233); 1751J (1,083)
Spain and Spanish colonies, ½ reales, México, Seville, Madrid, and Segovia, 1716–45 (22) (the Spanish mints, namely 1/4 pistareens, predominated)
Spain and Spanish colonies, reales, México, Seville, Madrid, and Segovia, 1716–45 (23) (the Spanish mints, namely ½ pistareens, predominated)
Spain and Spanish colonies, 2 reales, México, Seville, Madrid, and Segovia, dates 1716–45 (58) (the Spanish mints, namely pistareens, predominated)
Spain and Spanish colonies, fragments, México, Seville, Madrid, and Segovia, dates 1716–45 (4)
Portuguese colonies, Brazil, John V, 6,400 reis, Rio (8): 1747; 1748; 1749 (2); 1750 (4)

Disposition: Auctions at Sotheby's, New York, NY, USA, March 24–25, 1993 and Castells & Castells, Montevideo, Uruguay, November 6, 1997.

Bibliography: Apolant 1992; Castells & Castells 1997; López 2001; Sotheby's 1993; Sedwick and Sedwick 2007, 191–92 (Sedwick 50).

315. Terence Bay, near Halifax, Nova Scotia, Canada, 1980 and 1983.

Type of find: Shipwreck.
Ship: New England fishing schooner.
Sank: 1752.
Contents: 3 AE.
Description: Great Britain, halfpence (3): George I; 1749; 1752
The 1749 and 1752 halfpence had little evidence of wear. All the coins were found in the forecastle.
Bibliography: Carter and Kenchington 1985.

316. Arlington Avenue and West 231st Street, Spuyten Duyvil Hill, Riverdale, the Bronx, New York, New York, USA, 1920.

Type of find: Archaeological excavation.
Date of site: 1752–76.
Contents: 4+ AE, 1 AR.
Description:
England, halfpenny, William III
Great Britain, halfpence (3): 1752; 1753; counterfeit ND
Spanish colonies, ½ real, México, 1757
Bibliography: Bolton 1921, 14, 18.

317. On an old Indian trail near Hamilton Inlet, Labrador, Newfoundland and Labrador, Canada, 1900.

Type of find: Single find.
Contents: 1 AR.
Description: British colonies, George II Indian Peace Medal, [1753], Betts 396, Stahl-Scully 12
Described as being found in "Hamilton Cove"; however, there appears to be no such geographical feature in Labrador. This has accordingly been emended to "Hamilton Inlet."
Disposition: P. B. Murphy of Québec; John Sanford Saltus; 1917 to the American Numismatic Society in New York, item number 1917.137.3.
Bibliography: Stahl 1991, 164; Stahl and Scully 1991, 218.
"Correspondence," *Numismatist* 21, no. 1 (January 1908): 50–51.

318. Baldwinsville, New York, USA, 1880s.

Type of find: Single find.

Contents: 1 AR.

Description: British colonies, George II Indian Peace Medal, [1753], Betts 396, Stahl-Scully 12

Disposition: Property of a farmer, John Jones, near Baldwinsville, who was dead by 1887. It had been a family heirloom.

Bibliography: Beauchamp 1891, 44; Beauchamp 1903, 55; Stahl 1991, 164; Stahl and Scully 1991, 218.

319. New Rochelle, New York, USA, March 1927.

Type of find: Single find.

Contents: 1 AR.

Description: France, Louis XV, écu, 1754AA

Disposition: The coin was found by A. Nardozzi while digging in his cellar. He was building an extension to his house, 79 Charles Street, New Rochelle. He dug further, thinking it might be part of a hoard, but only found the one coin.

Bibliography: "French Coin of 1754 Unearthed in Cellar. Silver Piece Bearing Ancient Date found by Digger on New Rochelle Property," *New York Times*, March 27, 1927, Sec. 2, 22.

320. Along the Chickahominy River, Richmond, Virginia, USA, 1985–95.

Type of find: Single find.

Contents: 1 AR.

Description: Spanish colonies, ½ real, México, 1754M

Disposition: Found by a metal detectorist. Acquired by Thomas A. Kays.

Bibliography: Kays 1996, 1637–45.

321. Fort Halifax, Kennebec River, Maine, USA, August 1998.

Type of find: Archaeological excavation.

Date of site: 1754–81. (A military outpost manned by the Massachusetts militia until 1766, and thereafter an Indian trading post through the revolution.)

Contents: 4+ AE.

Description:

Great Britain, George II, halfpence: 2+

Great Britain, George III, counterfeit halfpence: 2+

Great Britain, George II, cast counterfeit halfpenny

British colonies, Rosa Americana, penny

Bibliography: Mossman 1998, 1827.

322. Fort Edward and Roger's Island, New York, USA, July 29, 1848, July 1875, 1991–95, 1997–98, and 2001–5.

Type of find: Single finds in 1848, 1875; archaeological excavations in the 1990s and 2000s.

Date of site: 1755–59, with some lesser occupation 1759–66 and 1775–77.

Contents: 42 AE, 38 AR.

Description:

The following 2 coins were obtained by Benson John Lossing in July 1848:

Spanish colonies, ½ real, Lima or Potosí, 1741

Spanish colonies, 2 reales, Lima, 1743

The following 2 coins were found in 1875:

German states, Saxony, Elector Christian II, thaler, 1604, depicting Christian and on the reverse John George and Augustus (Dav.7566)

Italian states, Tuscany, Grand Duke Cosmo III, tollero, 1692 (Dav.4215)

The following coins were found during archaeological excavations in the 1990s:

Great Britain, halfpence (21)

Spanish colonies, real, México, 1751

Spanish colonies, 4 reales, probably México

Spanish colonies, 8 reales, probably México (2)
Spanish colonies, cob ½ real
Spanish colonies, real, unidentified mint and date
Spanish colonies, cobs, denomination unidentified (5)
The following coins were found during excavation of the sutler's house in the seasons 2001–5:
Great Britain, farthing, 1743
England, William III, halfpenny
Great Britain, halfpence (18): 1723, 1734, 1738 1739, 1742, 1748, 1749, ND (11)
Ireland, halfpenny
France, liard, mint D (Lyons), ND
English colonies, Massachusetts, oak tree shilling, Noe 14, holed
Spanish colonies, ½ reales, cob (9)
Spanish colonies, reales, cob, Potosí (3): 1658; ND (2)
Spanish colonies, 4 reales, cob
Spanish colonies, ½ reales, milled, México, 1738 (2)
Spanish colonies, reales, México (3)
Spanish colonies, 2 reales, cob
Spanish colonies, cut eighths from 8 reales, Ferdinand VI, México (2)
Unidentified silver coin

Bibliography: Lossing 1851, 1: 103; Starbuck 2004; Starbuck 2007.

Benson John Lossing, *The Pictorial Field Book of the Revolution, or, Illustrations, by Pen and Pencil, of the History, Biography, Scenery, Relics, and Traditions of the War for Independence* (New York: Harper & Brothers, 1851), 1:103.

"Notes and Queries," *American Journal of Numismatics* 10, no. 1 (July 1875): 23.

Oliver Hoover, personal communication, January 10, 2008.

323. James Fresh's Farm, old Braddock Road, near Keyser's, Allegany County, Maryland, USA, July 1877.

Type of find: Hoard.

Date of deposit: July 1755.

Contents: ca. 30 AR.

Description:
 Spanish colonies, cob 8 reales, México (ca. 20)
 Spanish colonies, pillar 8 reales, México (ca. 10)
 Number of coins and mint are educated guesses.

Bibliography: "Old Coins Found," *New York Times*, July 11, 1877, 2 (citing the *Baltimore Sun*).

324. Fort Ontario State Historic Site, Oswego, New York, USA, 1984.

Type of find: Archaeological excavation.

Date of site: 1755–1946.

Contents: 5 AE, 1 AR.

Description:
 Great Britain, halfpence (2): George II, 1735; George III, 1770?
 USA, Vermont, coppers (2): 1786; 1788
 Spanish colonies, ½ real, 1775

Disposition: New York State Bureau of Historic Sites Collection, Peebles Island, New York, USA.

Bibliography: Hoover 2007 (providing inventory of New York State Bureau of Historic Sites Collections, Peebles Island, New York, as of August 16, 2005).

325. Fort Augusta, Sunbury, Pennsylvania, USA, 2005.

Type of find: Archaeological excavation.

Date of site: 1756–94.

Contents: 2 AE.

Description: Great Britain, George II, halfpence (2)

Bibliography: Hoover 2007 (providing inventory of as of November 23, 2005).

326. Fort Loudoun, Monroe County, Tennessee, USA, 2005.

Type of find: Archaeological excavation.

Date of site: 1756–60.

Contents: 14 AE, 1 AR.

Description:

England, William III, halfpenny

Great Britain, George II, young bust farthing

Great Britain, halfpence (11): George I (2); George II (5); George III (2); ND; counterstamped H&F

Ireland, George III, halfpenny

Spanish colonies, Ferdinand VI, 8 reales

Bibliography: Hoover 2007 (providing inventory as of November 23, 2005).

327. Between St. Esprit and Fourchu (Fuchett), near Louisbourg, Nova Scotia, Canada, bow section found 1969, midsection found July 14, 1986, salvaged summers 1986 and 1987.

Type of find: Shipwreck.

Ship: HMS *Tilbury*.

Sank: September 25, 1757. Sailed from Cork, Ireland in May 1757; at Halifax, Nova Scotia, joined the troops that Lord Loudon had brought from New York; anchored at Chebucto Head, September 9, 1757; anchored at Louisbourg, between St. Esprit and Fourchu (Fuchett), September 24, 1757.

Contents: 430 AR, 16 AV.

Description:

Great Britain, guinea, 1713

Portugal, 4 escudos (6,400 reis), 1755

Spain, 2 reales (pistareen), Barcelona 1711R

Spain, 2 reales (pistareen), Madrid, 1721A

Spanish colonies, 2 reales, México (2): 1737MF; 1738MF

Spanish colonies, 8 reales, México, 1733MF (recortado)

Spanish colonies, 8 reales, México (pillars) (72): 1734MF (holed); 1736MF; 1737MF; 1739MF (4); 1740MF; 1741MF (4); 1742MF (3); 1743MF (2); 1744MF; 1745MF (2); 1746MF (3); 1747MF (9); 1748MF; 1749MF (5); 1750MF (3); 1751MF (2); 1752MF (5); 1753MF (4); 1754MF (6) (royal crowns); 1754MF (4) (imperial and royal crowns); 1754MM (imperial and royal crowns); 1755MM (9)

Spanish colonies, 8 reales, Guatemala (2): 1751J; 1752J

Spanish colonies, 8 reales, Lima (cob), 1748V

Spanish colonies, 8 reales, Lima (3): 1753J (2); 1754JD

Spanish colonies, 8 reales, Potosí (cobs) (9): 1753q (2); 1754q (2); 1754C; 1755q (4)

Portuguese colonies, Brazil, 6,400 reis, 1755R

May have also included a Spanish colonies, 2 escudos from Bogotá. Sebring had an 8 reales, Potosí, 1755q.

Disposition: Auctioned at the Canadian Numismatic Association convention in Québec, July 1989. One of the pillar dollars in 2002 was in the Alex Storm collection, ex Pierre Leclerc. A portion of the treasure was acquired by the government of the Province of Nova Scotia.

The wreck was salvaged in 1986 by the Canadian divers Giles Brisebois and Pierre Leclerc of Montreal. John Major, the Federal Receiver of Wreck in Dartmouth, Nova Scotia, seized coins from the divers, but then returned the coins to them when it turned out that the Canadian Federal government had no interest in acquiring any of the coins recovered. However, the 1989 auction catalog says that the government of the Province of Nova Scotia acquired a portion of the treasure.

Bibliography: Laramée 1989; Sebring 1991, 1215–17; Sebring 1995, 15; Sebring 2004, lot 1635; Sedwick and Sedwick 2007, 194–95 (Sedwick 53); Storm 2002, 141–51.
"Treasure Hunt in the Deep," *Maclean's*, August 10, 1987, 40–41.

328. Ninth Street and Christian Street, Philadelphia, Pennsylvania, USA, January 1880.

Type of find: Building excavation.

Date of deposit: 1757.

Contents: 2 AR.

Description:
British colonies, Pennsylvania, Kittaning destroyed medal, 1756
British colonies, Pennsylvania, Quaker Indian Peace Medal, 1757

Disposition: Purchased by Major Skiles from the laborer who found the medals.

Bibliography: "Old Medals Found in Philadelphia," *New York Times*, January 18, 1880, 5 (citing the *Philadelphia Ledger*).
"Old Medals Found in Philadelphia," *American Journal of Numismatics* 14, no. 4 (April 1880): 92.

329. Lempster, New Hampshire, USA, January 1883.

Type of find: Single find.

Contents: 1 AR.

Description: France, Louis XV, écu, 1757

Disposition: The coin was plowed up by A. F. Bailey.

Bibliography: "Notes and Queries," *American Journal of Numismatics* 17, no. 3 (January 1883): 72.

330. Fort Stanwix, Rome, New York, USA, 1965, July 1970–75.

Type of find: Archaeological excavation.

Date of site: 1758–81.

Contents: 44 AE, 1 BI, 8 AR.

Description:
Great Britain, halfpence (44): 1700; 1722; 1723 (2); 1730 (2); 1732 (2); 1734; 1735; 1737; 1740 (2); 1743; 1745; 1752; 1753; ND (28)
France, sol, 1740
Spain, coin, 1699
Spain, 2 reales (pistareen), cut half
Spanish colonies, reales (2): 1741, 1768
Spanish colonies, 2 reales (3): 1755, 1766, 1779
Spanish colonies, 8 reales, cut fragment of a sixteenth, counterstamped with a broad arrow

Bibliography: Hanson and Hsu 1975, 147–49.

331. Franklin, Pennsylvania, USA, January 1883.

Type of find: Hoard.

Date of deposit: 1759.

Container: Chest.

Contents: 2,700 AR.

Description: France, écus?
French coins found in a chest. The chest is thought to have been buried in 1759, when Fort Magnault was evacuated.

Bibliography: "Coin Finds," *American Journal of Numismatics* 17, no. 3 (January 1883): 60.

332. Hanover Street, Portsmouth, New Hampshire, USA, June 27, 1874.

Type of find: Hoard.

Date of deposit: 1759.

Contents: 2 AV.

Description: Portugal or Portuguese colonies (Brazil), 6,400 reis (2): 1750; 1759

Disposition: Unearthed by George Hersey while digging for a gas pipe near the residence of James F. Jenness.

Bibliography: Portsmouth (NH) Journal, June 27, 1874 (reference courtesy of Q. David Bowers and Richard E. Winslow III).

333. Staten Island, New York, USA, summer 1868.

Type of find: Single find.

Contents: 1 B.

Description: Great Britain, George II medal, 1759, commemorating British victories in the Seven Years War (Betts 416)

Disposition: Found by a laborer repairing the public road at the northwest corner of the old Quarantine wall in Staten Island.

Bibliography: Antiquities 1869, 74.

334. Fort Crown Point, Crown Point, New York, USA, 1968.

Type of find: Archaeological excavation.

Date of site: 1759–1780.

Contents: 3 AE.

Description: England, William III, halfpenny

Great Britain, halfpence (2): 1740; 1752

Disposition: New York State Bureau of Historic Sites Collection, Peebles Island, New York, USA.

Bibliography: Hoover 2007 (providing inventory of New York State Bureau of Historic Sites Collections, Peebles Island, New York, as of August 16, 2005).

335. Eagle Village, Manlius, Onondaga County, New York, USA, 1840s.

Type of find: Single find.

Contents: 1 AR.

Description: British colonies, New York, Daniel Christian Fueter Montreal Indian Peace Medal of 1760, engraved to Caneiya of the "Onondagos"

Disposition: Seen by Beauchamp at L. W. Ledyard's in Cazenovia, New York, and in Ledyard's possession for many years.

Bibliography: Beauchamp 1891, 42–44; Beauchamp 1903, 61; Clark 1849, 2:274.

336. Kelly Place, near the bank of the Mourning Kill and the old Canadian trail, Ballston Spa, New York, USA, 1875.

Type of find: Single find.

Contents: 1 AR.

Description: British colonies, New York, Daniel Christian Fueter Montreal Indian Peace Medal of 1760, engraved to Songose of the "Mohigrans"

Disposition: Found by Kelly of Ballston Spa; sold to Joseph E. Westcot; sold 1902 to E. Hallenbeck, 749 Liberty Street, Schenectady, New York. Seen and drawn by Beauchamp. Then to Robert Brule and C. A. Laframboise; sold to John J. Ford, Jr., on June 8, 1961. Auctioned by Stack's in the John J. Ford, Jr. Sale, Part XVI, October 17, 2006, lot 47.

Bibliography: Beauchamp 1903, 63; Stack's 2006b, lot 47.

337. Western Massachusetts, USA, September 2003.

Type of find: Single finds.

Date of deposit: 1760 (found in a French and Indian War context [1754–63]).

Contents: 3 AE.

Description:

Great Britain, George II medal of ca. 1760, uniface, holed (*Medallic Illustrations* no. 1760)

Great Britain, George II, halfpence (2)

The medal is thought to have been used as an Indian Peace Medal.

Disposition: Found by a metal detectorist. Consigned to American Numismatic Rarities for auction.

Bibliography: Sebring 2004, lot 1728 (Sebring sale, but not from the Sebring collection). Eric von Klinger, "Detectorist finds George

II medal in Massachusetts hillside," *Coin World,* February 2, 2004, 72.

338. Chignecto Isthmus, Nova Scotia, Canada, and Prince Edward Island, Canada, December 2003.
Type of find: Series of single finds.
Date of site: 1760 onwards.
Contents: 73 AE, 2 BI, 15 AR.
Description:
French coins:
France, Louis XIV, liards (4): 16[-]D; 1697; 1703; 1708
France, liards de France (7)
France, dardennes de 6 deniers (2): 1711H; 1711N
France, Louis XIV, 30 deniers mousquetaire, 1709
France, Louis XV, 2 sols de 24 deniers, 1738
France, Louis XV, 1/20 écu, 1732T
France, Louis XV, 1/5 écu, 1726K
France, Louis XV, 1/3 écu, 1722Q
French colonies, Louis XV, 9 deniers des colonies françoises, 1721H
Spanish coins:
Spain, Charles IV, 8 maravedíes
Spain, Philip V, real (½ pistareen), 1738
Spain, Philip V, 2 reales (pistareens) (3): 1717 Madrid (2); 1731
Spanish colonies, Charles III, 8 reales, México, 1788FM
Spanish colonies, real, Lima, 1748R (emended from reported 1746R)
Spanish colonies, cob reales, Potosí, 1771 (2)
Spanish colonies, cob ½ reales (2)
Spanish colonies, 2 reales, 1751
British coins:
Great Britain, George III, farthing
Great Britain, halfpence (53): George I ND; George II ND (36+); 1752; George III ND (12+); counterfeit George III ND

Ireland, Wood's Hibernia, halfpence? 1723 (4)
USA, New Jersey, copper
British colonies, Rosa Americana, twopence
The Rosa Americana twopence was found on Prince Edward Island.
Disposition: Found by metal detectorists.
Bibliography: Mossman 2003.

339. Fort Ticonderoga, New York, USA, November 1861.
Type of find: Single find.
Contents: 1 AE.
Description: France, probably a liard
Disposition: Exhibited by William Sumner Appleton at the meeting of the Boston Numismatic Society.
Bibliography: "Boston Numismatic Society," *Historical Magazine* 5 (November 1861): 340.

340. Rensselaer or Saratoga Counties, New York, USA, January 1999.
Type of find: Single find.
Contents: 1 AE.
Description: Ireland, Voce Populi halfpenny, Nelson 7
Bibliography: Mossman 1999, 1914.

341. Port Deposit, Maryland, USA, August 1998.
Type of find: Single find.
Contents: 1 AE.
Description: Ireland, Voce Populi halfpenny
Disposition: Sold on ebay, August 10, 1998, item #24016948.
Bibliography: Mossman 1999, 1914.

342. Place Royale, Québec, Québec, Canada, 1976–80.
Type of find: Archaeological excavation (the house of Champlain at Québec).

Date of the British phase of occupation: 1760–90.

Contents: 6 AE.

Description:

   Great Britain, George II, halfpenny

   Great Britain, George III, halfpence (3)

   Ireland, George III, halfpenny

   USA, Connecticut, copper, 1785?

   The above list is based on the report by Niellon and Moussette. Peter Moogk gives a general report on the coins found in the general Place Royale area, not only the Habitation site.

Disposition: Ministère des Affaires Culturelles (Secteur Place Royale), Québec, Québec, Canada.

Bibliography: Moogk 1989, 246–49; Niellon and Moussette 1981, 139–44.

343. Aspy Bay, Breton Island, Nova Scotia, Canada, 1977 and 2001–4.

Type of find: Shipwreck.

Ship: L'Auguste de Bordeaux.

Sank: November 15, 1761, after leaving the port of Montréal. The ship was taking 121 French aristocrats and officers into exile after the British capture of Canada. Only 7 survived the shipwreck.

Contents: 2,022 AR, 33 AV.

Description:

   England, ½ guinea, 1695

   Great Britain, ½ guinea, 1759

   Great Britain, guineas (2): 1756; 1759

   France, 2 sols (2)

   France, 1/6 écu, [1720–23], mint H (2)

   France, 1/5 écu, 1727A

   France, 1/3 écu (4): 1720H (petit louis d'argent); 1720H (de France); 1721H; 1721O

   France, ½ écus (92): 1726A; 1726C; 1726D (2); 1729V; 1729 9 (Rennes); 1731O; ND (85)

   France, écus (524): 1726A; 1726C; 1726E; 1726R; 1726T; 1726 9 (Rennes); 1726 (2); 1728L; 1729L; 1729 cow (Pau); 1731M; 1731 9(Rennes) (2); 1732Z; 1733A; 1733Q; 1735O; 1736I; 1740K (Sebring); 1741 cow (Pau); 1742H; 1743BB; 1744J; 1748H; 1749V; 1754 cow (Pau); 1755T; mint D; mint J; mint M; mint &; 1726–30 (492)

   France, silver coins (6)

   France, louis (25): 1726A; 1726O; 1726V; 1726&; 1727L; 1727N; 1728C; 1729I; 1729K; 1729T; 1730Z; 1731O; 1735P; 1736 9 (Rennes); 1738Q; 1745W; 1745Q; 1747A; 1747W; 1749W; 1753A (2); 1754A; 1755A; 1757 cow

   France, double louis (2): 1748T; 1752L

   French states, Dauphiné, Grenoble, douzain, with 1640 fleur-de-lis counterstamp

   Spanish colonies, 8 reales, México (1,015): 1732MF (cobs) (3); 1735MF; 1736MF (3); 1737MF; 1738/7MF; 1738MF (2); 1739/8MF; 1739MF (4); 1740MF (5); 1741MF (14); 1742MF (7); 1743MF (8); 1744MF (12); 1745MF (14); 1746MF (14); 1747MF (Philip) (13); 1747/6 (Ferdinand); 1747MF (Ferdinand) (6); 1747MF (16); 1748/7MF (4); 1748MF (16); 1749MF (21); 1750MF (19); 1751MF (18); 1752MF (26); 1753/2MF; 1753MF (19); 1754/3 (4); 1754MF (8); 1754MM (2); 1754 (9); 1754MF royal crowns (2); 1754 royal crowns (6); 1754MF imperial and royal crown; 1754MM imperial and royal crown (3); 1754 imperial and royal crown (6); 1755MM (57); 1756/5MM; 1756MM (68); 1757/6MM; 1757MM (98); 1754–58 (13); 1757–58 (400); 1758MM (71); 1759MM (6); pillar dollars, ND (9)

   Spanish colonies, 8 reales, Guatemala (8): 1751J; 1752J (5); 175[-]J (2)

   Spanish colonies, 8 reales, Lima (98): 1742 (3); 1752; ND, cob; 1753J; 1754JD (8); 1754; 1755JD; 1755JM (8); 1756/5JM (2); 1756JM (17); 1757JM (11); ND (44)

Spanish colonies, 8 reales, Potosí (21): 1684V; 1705; 1737; 1742; 1748q; 1751; 1752q; 1753; 1753q; 1754; 1754q (5); 1755q (4); 1756q (2)

Portugal, 4 escudos, 1753

Disposition: Excavated in 1977. Excavated again in 2001–4 by Auguste Expedition LLC.

Bibliography: Canadian Numismatic Company 2008, lots 2273–2687; Coin Galleries 1998, lots 1786–87.

344. Fort Michilimackinac, south shores of the Straits of Mackinac, Michigan, USA, 1958–79.

Type of find: Archaeological excavation.

Date of British occupation: 1761–81.

Contents: 24 AE, 3 AR.

Description:

Great Britain, George II, farthing, 1747
Great Britain, farthing (6)
England, William III, halfpence (3)
Great Britain, halfpence (13): George I, 1720 (3); George II, 1736; George II, young head (2); George II, old head; ND (6)
Ireland, George II, halfpenny, young head
Spain, Philip V, ½ real (¼ pistareen), Madrid, 1731JF
Spanish colonies, 8 reales, pillar type, cut quarter, counterstamped "2" three times and with a broad arrow
Spanish colonies 8 reales, cut eighth, counterstamped "1" three times and with a broad arrow
Heldman misattributed the 1731 Spanish coin to México; it is from Madrid. This has been corrected.
The three Spanish coins were all recovered from a latrine that can be dated to the very last period of British occupation of Fort Michilimackinac, namely 1774–81.

Bibliography: Heldman 1980.

345. Fulton and Water Streets, New York, New York, USA, 1982.

Type of find: Excavations at a construction site, partly by Robert Apuzzo.

Date of site: 1760s.

Contents: 7 AE, 1 PB.

Description:

Great Britain, halfpence (6): 1722; 1725; 1732; 1740; 1742; 1752
Ireland, Wood's Hibernia halfpenny, date not given
Spanish colonies, 8 reales, México, 1776FM, lead counterfeit, bent to cancel it
The copper coins appear to come from a site of the 1760s, because no George III halfpence were found, and a pewter spoon with the maker's mark FB was found, which is the mark of Frederick Bassett, who was active in New York City in 1761–80. The lead counterfeit 8 reales of 1776 is a later intrusion, probably bent and then discarded.

Disposition: the coins were sold through Harmer Rooke in the 1980s.

Bibliography: Apuzzo 1992, 74–77.

346. Saint John River Valley, Nova Scotia, Canada, December 2003.

Type of find: Series of finds.

Date of site: 1762 onwards.

Contents: 41 AE, 7 AR.

Description:

Great Britain, halfpence (12): 1721; George II ND (3); George II [1729–39 rat on leg]; 1742; 1744; 1770; counterfeit 1772; counterfeit 1773; counterfeit 1775 (2)
Great Britain, evasive halfpence (4): Atkins 204, 275, 284, 323
Ireland, halfpence (4): counterfeit 1769; 178[-]; counterfeit 1781; counterfeit 1783
Ireland, Dalton and Hamer Dublin 83, George Calvert token

France, Louis XVI, sols (2): 1780H; 1791A

British colonies, Lower and Upper Canada, blacksmith copper, Wood 33

USA, Connecticut, coppers (11): 1785 Miller 3.1-L; 1786 Miller 5.2-H1; 1786 Miller 5.11-R; 1786 Miller 29.2-o; 1786 not attributed; 1787 Miller 33.29-Gg.1; 1787 Miller 13-D; 1787 Miller 33.19 var; 1787 not attributed (2); 1788 Miller 17-Q

USA, Vermont, copper, Ryder 20

USA, New Jersey, coppers (2): 1786 14-J; 1787 63-S

USA, Massachusetts, 1¢, 1787

British colonies, Bermuda, penny, 1793

Spanish colonies, reales, México (2): 1749; 1750

Spanish colonies, 2 reales, México (2): 1779, holed; 1782

Spanish colonies, 8 reales, México (2): 1806 TH; 1810HI, holed

Spanish colonies, 2 reales, Lima, 1793

Disposition: Found by metal detectorists.

Bibliography: Mossman 2003.

347. Lake Champlain, Vermont, near Fort Ticonderoga, USA, 1983–85.

Type of find: Shipwreck.

Ship: The sloop *Boscawen*.

Abandoned: 1763.

Contents: 2 AE, 2 BI.

Description:

German states, Bayreuth, heller, 1752 (holed)

Great Britain, George I, farthing, 1718

France, Louis XV, 2 sous, 1738A, holed

France, Louis XV, 2 sous, 1753A, half a coin

Bibliography: Crisman 1988, 142–47.

348. Johnson Hall State Historic Site, Johnstown, New York, USA, 1959, 1986, and 1987.

Type of find: Archaeological excavation.

Date of site: February 1763–1906.

Contents: 3 AE.

Description: Great Britain, George II, halfpence (3): 1740; 1747; 1749

Disposition: New York State Bureau of Historic Sites Collection, Peebles Island, New York, USA.

Bibliography: Hoover 2007 (providing inventory of New York State Bureau of Historic Sites Collections, Peebles Island, New York, as of August 16, 2005).

349. Franklin Court, Philadelphia, Pennsylvania, USA, 1966.

Type of find: Archaeological excavation.

Date of site: 1763–1812.

Contents: 1 AE.

Description: Great Britain, halfpenny, 1720
Described as an "English penny of 1720"; the description has been emended accordingly.

Bibliography: Cotter, Roberts, and Parrington 1992, 96, 143.

350. Loudon, Tennessee, USA, October 12, 1875.

Type of find: Single find; funerary deposit.

Contents: 1 AR.

Description: British colonies, New York, Happy While United Indian Peace Medal, 1764
24 silver buttons and a gold chain were also found with the skeleton.

Disposition: Found in an Indian grave near the site of old Fort Loudon, on the Tellico River, just above its junction with the Little Tennessee, while J. J. Snider was excavating for a barn.

Bibliography: "Historical Relics of Olden Times," *American Journal of Numismatics* 10, no. 3 (January 1876): 54 (citing the *Loudon (TN) Times* of October 16, 1875).

351. Berlin (now Kitchener), Ontario, Canada, 1896.

Type of find: Single find.

Contents: 1 AR.

Description: British colonies, New York, Happy While United Indian Peace Medal, 1764, counterstamped DCF

Disposition: Found by Henry Stuebing while plowing; in 1899 in the cabinet of his son, M. C. Steubing. Further provenance: Hunter Collection – S. H. Chapman 12/1920:71 – W. Phillips – Glendining's 6/1925 – British Museum.

Bibliography: Adams 1999, 71; McLachlan 1899, 14.

"British Indian Medals," *American Journal of Numismatics* 31, no. 1 (July 1896): 9.

352. St. Martin, New Brunswick, Canada, December 15, 1887.

Type of find: Hoard.

Date of deposit: 1765.

Contents: 300 AV.

Description: Great Britain, guineas, 1765 (300)

Source for the data regarding the coins is Bank Cashier Givan.

Bibliography: Worcester (MA) *Aegis & Gazette*, December 17, 1887 (reference courtesy of Q. David Bowers).

353. Fort Niagara, New York, USA, 1840.

Type of find: Single find.

Contents: 1 AR.

Description: British colonies, New York, Happy While United Indian Peace Medal, 1766

Disposition: found by Ezekial Jewett, a post trader, near the fort in 1840. Gift of William H. Perkins, Robert W. DeForest and James B. Ford to the American Numismatic Society, 1925; item number 1925.173.1.

Bibliography: Stahl and Scully 1991, 221.

354. Bakersfield, Vermont, USA, November 1930.

Type of find: Single find.

Contents: 1 AE.

Description: Russia, 5 kopek, Siberia, 1766

Disposition: Dr. Edwin A. Hayatt.

Bibliography: "Siberian Coin Dug up in Vermont," *Numismatist* 43, no. 11 (November 1930): 770.

355. Haymarket, Virginia, USA, 1995.

Type of find: Single find.

Contents: 1 AR.

Description: Spain, 2 reales (pistareen), Madrid, 1767PJ

Disposition: Found by a metal detectorist.

Bibliography: Kays 1996, 1637–45.

356. Chesapeake Bay dredge?, Virginia, USA, 1985–95.

Type of find: Single find.

Contents: 1 AR.

Description: Spanish colonies, 4 reales, México, 1767MF

Disposition: Found by a metal detectorist: Acquired by Thomas A. Kays.

Bibliography: Kays 1996, 1637–45.

357. Beach near Highlands, New Jersey, USA, April 1948.

Type of find: Hoard.

Date of deposit: 1770.

Contents: 35 AV.

Description:

France, louis, 1770

Portuguese colonies, Brazil, 6,400 reis, 1730–68 (34)

The dates of the 6,400 reis found included 1730, 1748, 1749, 1751, and 1768.

The hoard may have included one or two 12,800 reis as well.

Disposition: 7 coins to William Cottrell, a lobsterman, then aged 75, of 73 Fourth Street, Highlands, and his son Lloyd Cottrell.

The coins were apparently thrown up on shore by a dredge while clearing a channel in the Shrewsbury River. The first coin was found on the top of the bank of the Navesink River.

Bibliography: Nesmith 1958a, 21; Nesmith and Potter 1968, 53; Potter 1972, 481.

"Coins of 1770 Start Gold Rush in Jersey," *New York Times*, April 10, 1948, 1.

"N. J. Fishermen Find Rare Gold Coins in River. 400 Join in Treasure Hunt; 15 Pieces Dating From 1730 Dug Out of Sand," *New York Herald Tribune*, April 10, 1948, 13.

"Owner of Beach Trying to Stop N.J. Gold Rush. Doubloon Diggers Ignore Highlands Police Chief; State Troopers Move In," *New York Herald Tribune*, April 11, 1948, 3.

Norman Katkov, "Jersey Gold Rush Looks Like a Doubloon-Cross," *New York World-Telegram*, April 12, 1948, 5.

"Jersey Gold Hunt Turns to Comedy as Beach Owners Battle Diggers. All-Day War is Waged, with Bungalow Colony and the Police Making Sallies on Invaders—No Booty Found," *New York Times*, April 12, 1948, 23.

358. Prymus, Delaware County, Pennsylvania, USA, November 1895.

Type of find: Hoard.

Date of deposit: 1770.

Container: Outer casing of a smoothing iron.

Contents: 33 AR.

Description: Spanish colonies, Ferdinand VI and Charles III, 8 reales, México (33)

The dates found were 1748, 1754, 1755, 1756, 1758, 1760, 1764, 1765, 1766, 1767, 1768, 1769, 1770.

Disposition: One sold to the owner of the premises; 32 sold to S. H. & H. Chapman. George Heath, of Monroe, Michigan, bought 12 of these dollars, and then offered them on at $1.25 apiece.

Bibliography: "With the Editor," *Numismatist* 8, no. 11 (November, 1895): 286.

"A Find," *Numismatist* 8, no. 11 (November, 1895): 288.

359. Knowlwood, Westchester County, New York, USA, March 1895.

Type of find: Hoard.

Date of deposit: 1770.

Contents: 250 AE, AR, AV.

Description: Great Britain, halfpence?

Spanish colonies, 8 reales?

Portuguese colonies, 6,400 reis?

The coins ranged in date from 1735 to 1770. Countries and denominations not given; those listed above are an educated guess.

Found by men grading on the estate of August T. Gillender, a real estate broker of New York.

Bibliography: "The World of Fad," *Numismatist* 8, no. 3 (March, 1895): 75.

360. Silver City, New Mexico, USA, August 1919.

Type of find: Single find.

Contents: 1 AR.

Description: Spanish colonies, Charles III, probably ½ real, probably México, 1770, holed

Denomination and mint not specified; those given above are an educated guess.

Disposition: Found by C. B. Morrill while grading the road on the northern edge of Silver City. Photograph sent to *El Palacio* by C. B. Cosgrove of Silver City.

Bibliography: "Finds at Silver City," *El Palacio* 7, no. 4 (August 31, 1919): 73.

361. Monticello, Charlottesville, Virginia, USA, 1979–91.
Type of find: Archaeological excavation.
Date of site: 1770–1923.
Contents: 23 AE, 5 NI, 15 AR.
Description:
  Ireland, halfpenny, 1783
  Spain, 2 reales (pistareen), cut (5): 1716; 1733; 1746; 1764; ND (2)
  British colonies, Virginia, halfpence, 1773 (2)
  USA, ½¢, 1809 (2)
  USA, 1¢ (17): 1793; 1806 (2); 1808; 1816; 1817 (2); 1818; 1863; 1870 (2); 1875; 1882; 1884; 1888; 1914; large 1¢, ND
  USA, 2¢, 1868
  USA, nickel 3¢, 1868
  USA, nickel 5¢ (4): 1866; 1867; 1891; 1916
  USA, silver 5¢ (2): 1797; 1858
  USA, 10¢, 1920
  USA, 25¢ (2): 1877; 1916
  Spanish colonies, ½ real, México?, 1772
  Spanish colonies, ½ real, México?, 1772, cut
  Spanish colonies, ½ real, México?, 1777
  Spanish colonies, real, México?, 1781
Disposition: Thomas Jefferson Memorial Foundation.
Bibliography: Kelso 1997; Whitley 1991.

362. Fort Saint Joseph, Michigan, USA, May-July 1990.
Type of find: Single finds.
Date of deposit: 1771.
Contents: 3 AE.
Description:
  Great Britain, George I, farthing, 1720
  Great Britain, halfpence (3): 1737; 1740; 1771 (or possibly 1774)
  Two coins are shown in photographs; they both appear to be genuine halfpence rather than counterfeits.
Disposition: Found by a metal detectorist at an Indian encampment near the site of Fort Saint Joseph; donated to the Fort Saint Joseph Museum.
Bibliography: Danny Mangold, "Thrilled by Georgian Coppers? It depends on where you find them! An Etching of Michigan's Colonial Past," *Searcher* 6, no. 8 (April 1991): 34–35.

363. Fauquier County, Virginia, USA, 1861.
Type of find: Hoard.
Date of deposit: 1772.
Container: Earthenware jar.
Contents: 800 AR.
Description:
  Spanish colonies, 8 reales, México (799)
  Spanish colonies, 8 reales, México, 1772FM
  The 1772FM coin was the only coin specifically described; the remainder of the hoard is an educated guess. This was a hoard of $800 in foreign coin plowed up by a man in Fauquier County just before the Civil War.
Bibliography: Kays 2005, 2843 (citing the *Fairfax (VA) Herald*, May 20, 1887).

364. John and Water Streets, New York, New York, USA, 1982.
Type of find: Excavation by Robert Apuzzo.
Date of site: Eighteenth century.
Contents: 1 AR.
Description: Spanish colonies, real, México, 1772FM
Bibliography: Apuzzo 1992, 76–77.

365. Long Beach, Stratford, Connecticut, USA, October 1889.
Type of find: Hoard.
Date of deposit: 1770s.
Contents: ca. 20 AR, AV.

Description:
England, shillings, ca. 1700 (ca. 10)
England, guineas, ca. 1700 (ca. 10)
Described as "English gold and silver coins of ca. 1700." Amounts and denominations are an educated guess.

Bibliography: "Captain Kidd's Treasure," *American Journal of Numismatics* 24, no. 2 (October 1889): 41–42 (citing the *Hartford (CT) Times*).

366. Under water at a colonial landing near Yorktown, Virginia, USA, April 2001.

Type of find: Single find.

Contents: 1 AR.

Description: Spanish colonies, Charles III, 8 reales [1772–89]

Disposition: Found by a metal detectorist.

Bibliography: Kays 2001, 2196.

367. Banks of the Ohio River, Point Pleasant, West Virginia, USA, 1858.

Type of find: Funerary deposit?

Date of deposit: October 10, 1774 (the date of a battle between Indians and American settlers at Point Pleasant).

Contents: 2 AE.

Description: British colonies, George I, Indian and deer Indian Peace Medal
British colonies, George II, small size Indian and deer Peace Medal (this is the description in the 1874 publication; in the 1886 publication Hayden describes it as a George I medal)

Disposition: Found by Dr. Samuel G. Shaw of Point Pleasant, a collector of Indian relics; presented to Horace Edwin Hayden of Brownsville, Pennsylvania. Shaw was deceased by 1886.

Bibliography: Beauchamp 1903, 57; Hayden 1874; Hayden 1886, 217–38.

368. On the banks of King's Creek, York County, not far from Columbia, South Carolina, USA, October 1900.

Type of find: Hoard.

Date of deposit: 1775.

Container: Big iron pot.

Contents: ca. 30. AV.

Description: Great Britain, guineas (ca. 15)
Great Britain, 5 guineas (ca. 15)
All dates were prior to 1775. Numbers of coins are an educated guess.

Disposition: The pot was rooted up by pigs in a pigsty belonging to a tenant of R. L. Wallace. Wallace and the tenant divided the gold between them.

Bibliography: "British Gold Found: Believed to have been buried before the Revolutionary War," *Numismatist* 13, no. 11 (November 1900): 300–1.

369. Stafford Court House, Virginia, USA, April 2001.

Type of find: Single find.

Date of deposit: Ca. 1775.

Contents: 1 AR.

Description: England, William III, shilling [1694–1704], cut quarter

Disposition: Found by a metal detectorist.

Bibliography: Kays 2001, 2194.

370. John Bridge's Tavern Site, Ligonier, Pennsylvania, USA, 1967.

Type of find: Archaeological excavation.

Date of site: 1775–95.

Contents: 29 AE, 10 AR.

Description:
Great Britain, George II, farthing, 1730
Great Britain, halfpence (3): George II, ND; George III, ND; George III, ND, cut
Great Britain, counterfeit halfpence (12): George II, ND (3); George III, 1774; George

III, 1775; George III, ND (7)
Copper disks, probably British halfpence (4)
France, ½ sol, 1774
France, sol, [1768–74]
Spain, 2 reales, (cross pistareens), [1708–37] (3): cut quarter; cut eighths (2)
British colonies, Virginia, halfpenny, 1773
USA, New York, Atlee halfpence (2): 1771, Vlack 2-71A; 1774, Vlack 8-74A
USA, New Jersey, copper, 1787, Maris 6-C
USA, Connecticut, copper, 1787, Miller 33.36-T2
USA, Connecticut, copper, 1787, Miller 38-I.2
USA, Nova Constellatio copper, 1785, Crosby 5-E
Spanish colonies, ½ reales (7): 1738; 1744; 1748; 1775; 1785; 1787; 1788
Excluded from this list are one shield nickel 5¢ and two Lincoln 1¢, which are modern intrusions after the site was abandoned.

Disposition: Fort Ligonier Museum, Ligonier, Pennsylvania, USA, except for the George II farthing, which is in a private collection.

Bibliography: Trudgen 1995.

371. Philadelphia, Pennsylvania, USA, November 1974 and February 1975.

Type of find: Hoard?

Date of deposit: 1770s.

Contents: 2 PB or SN.

Description: Great Britain, George II and George III counterfeit halfpence (2)
Possibly associated with the main Philadelphia highway hoard. For the other finds, see *NFA* 282 and 686.

Bibliography: Gaspar and Newman 1978; Reiter 1978.

372. Mount Independence, Vermont, USA, 1990–93.

Type of find: Archaeological excavation.

Date of site: 1775–77.

Contents: 1 AR.

Description: Spanish colonies, ½ real, México, minted before 1760
The identification of the coin as a ½ real of México is not certain from the article, but an educated guess based on what would be the likeliest Spanish coin of the period to be found in an archaeological excavation.

Bibliography: Starbuck 1993.

373. Santa Cruz de Terrenate, Arizona, USA, 1951–53.

Type of find: Archaeological excavation.

Date of site: 1775–79.

Contents: 1 B.

Description: Poland, Catholic religious medal with Saint Casimir, reading: S. CASIMIRVS PAT REG POL ET M D L ('Saint Casimir, Patron of the Kingdom of Poland and of the Grand Duchy of Lithuania').
The medal of Saint Casimir may indicate the presence of a Polish individual at the site.

Bibliography: Di Peso 1976.

374. Gouldsborough, North Carolina, USA, 1884.

Type of find: Votive deposit (found underneath the front door; it was an old custom to place one or more coins under the doorpost for good luck).

Date of deposit: 1775.

Contents: 3 AE.

Description: Great Britain, George III, halfpence, date illegible
Great Britain, George III, halfpence, 1775 (2)
The coins were probably counterfeit, judging by the date; 1775 is a common date for counterfeit halfpence.

Bibliography: Various 1884, 96.

375. Fort Montgomery State Historic Site, Popolopen Creek and Hudson River, Orange County, New York, USA, 1958 and 1967.

Type of find: Archaeological excavation.

Date of site: March 1776 to October 6, 1777.

Contents: 7 AE, 3 AR.

Description:

   Great Britain, halfpence (7): 1720; 1732 (2); 1737; 1740; 1745 (2)

   Spain, real (½ pistareen), 1768

   Spanish colonies, ½ real, México, 1773

   Spanish colonies, 8 reales, 1757

Disposition: New York State Bureau of Historic Sites Collection, Peebles Island, New York, USA.

Bibliography: Hoover 2007 (providing inventory of New York State Bureau of Historic Sites Collections, Peebles Island, New York, as of August 16, 2005).

376. Setaucket, Long Island, New York, USA, 1894.

Type of find: Hoard.

Date of deposit: 1776. Probably buried shortly before the British captured Setaucket. During the Revolution, Reverend Mr. Brewster, pastor of the old Presbyterian Church on the green, lived in the house.

Contents: 100 AR.

Description: Spanish colonies, 8 reales, México?, 1770–74 (100)

Disposition: The coins were found by the schoolteacher George W. Hawkins. He still had most of them in 1924, although he had sold some over the intervening thirty years.

Bibliography: "Buried Treasure Stirs Setaucket, L. I. Unearthed by Teacher-Gardener Thirty Years Ago, Neighbors Just Learn of Discovery," *New York Times*, September 12, 1924, 22.

   "Buried Treasure Stirs Setaucket, L. I.," *Numismatist* 37, no. 10 (October 1924): 657.

377. Abraham Schuyler Farm, Dutch Kills, Queens County, Long Island, New York, USA, 1842.

Type of find: Hoard.

Date of deposit: 1776.

Container: earthenware pot.

Contents: ca. 1,000 AR; ca. 2,000 AV.

Description:

   Great Britain, guineas (ca. 1,000)

   Spain, 2 reales (pistareens) (ca. 1,000)

   Spanish colonies, 8 escudos (ca. 1,000)

   Amounts are estimates based on the dollar amount of the hoard ($40,000). The coins were placed in the pot with the gold in the center and the silver around it (compare *NFA* 69).

Disposition: It was first turned up by a sow rooting with her nose. Charles Conklin, the lessee of the Abraham Schuyler Farm, was also the finder. Abraham Schuyler sued to recover the coins, but was non-suited.

Bibliography: Henry Lloyd, "Curious Old Hymn Book and Golden Buried Treasure at Huntington," *Brooklyn Daily Eagle*, September 16, 1888, 2.

378. Fort George, New York, New York, USA, June 1790.

Type of find: Excavation.

Date of deposit: 1776.

Contents: AE, AR.

Description: German states, Göttingen, 1/24 thaler (Reichsgroschen), 1605 (Schrock 101–2)

   1605 and 1606 are common dates for Göttingen groschen; for this date Schrock has distinguished seven varieties of obverse legend and seven of reverse legend, indicating that there were at least seven obverse dies and at least seven reverse dies, an indication of a large production.

Disposition: "During the course of the operations in leveling the works at Fort-George, several articles have been discovered.... Besides the above, a few pieces of coin have been found; the most curious is a silver piece about the size and value of a pistareen coined at Göttingen in 1605." *New York Journal,* June 18, 1790.

Bibliography: Schrock 1987; Stokes 1926, 5:1268.

379. Portsmouth, New Hampshire, USA, June 1870.

Type of find: Excavation.

Date of deposit: 1776.

Contents: 2+ AE.

Description: USA, New Hampshire pine tree copper, 1776 (Breen 706)

Several coppers were found by workers while digging up the foundation of the old Portsmouth Savings Bank; the only one fully described was the WM 1776 copper. Exhibited at the June 2, 1870 meeting of the Boston Numismatic Society by Henry Dearborn Fowle.

Disposition: Henry Dearborn Fowle. When Crosby wrote, it was still in the possession of the finder, by whom he presumably means Henry Dearborn Fowle. The engraving in Crosby resembles the Garrett specimen, which would make the pedigree thenceforward Waldo Newcomer, then John W. Garrett, auctioned October 1, 1980, lot 1324. This piece was donated to the American Numismatic Society, bequest of Herbert Oechsner: item number 1988.75.1.

Bibliography: Appleton 1874, 57–58; Crosby 1875, 176.

William Sumner Appleton, "Transactions of Societies: Boston Numismatic Society," *American Journal of Numismatics* 5, no. 1 (July 1870): 13.

380. Stamford, Connecticut, USA, November 1868.

Type of find: Excavation.

Date of deposit: 1776.

Contents: 56 AE, 9 AR, 1 P.

Description:
England, Elizabeth, probably a sixpence, 1573
England/Great Britain, Anne, George I-III, halfpence (19)
British colonies, New Jersey, shilling note, March 2, 1776

Disposition: Found while tearing down the old Washington House.

Bibliography: "Notes and Queries: The Old Washington House, at Stamford, Ct.," *New England Historical and Genealogical Record* 23, no. 3 (July 1869): 351.

381. Fort No. 8, University Heights, Fordham, the Bronx, New York, New York, USA, 1950–90.

Type of find: Excavation.

Date of site: 1776–83.

Contents: 2 AE.

Description:
England, William and Mary, halfpenny, 169[-]
Great Britain, George II, halfpenny, 1730

Disposition: Found by Theodore Kazimiroff of the Bronx County Historical Society; bequeathed to Kingsborough Community College, Brooklyn, New York.

Bibliography: Hecht 1993.

382. Pell's Point, New York, New York, USA, 1950–90.

Type of find: Excavation.

Date of deposit: Thought to be relics of the battle fought by Sir William Howe, 1776.

Contents: 2 AR.

Description:

Spanish colonies, Charles III, ½ real, probably México, 1772

Spanish colonies, Charles III, real, México, 1772

Disposition: Found by Theodore Kazimiroff of the Bronx County Historical Society; bequeathed to Kingsborough Community College, Brooklyn, New York.

Bibliography: Hecht 1993.

383. Site of British Military Hut-Camp, Dyckman Farm, from Academy Street to 204th Street, between Prescott Avenue and Seaman Avenue, Inwood, New York, New York, USA, 1912–18.

Type of find: Archaeological excavation.

Date of site: 1776–79. 3 AE, 1 PB.

Description:

German states, small copper coin, holed
Great Britain, counterfeit halfpenny, 1776
USA, bar copper
Spanish colonies, 8 reales, México, assayers FM, counterfeit in lead
Exact find spot of bar copper not described; possibly a later intrusion.

Disposition: In 1927 displayed in the Dyckman House collection, Broadway and 204th Street, New York, New York, USA.

Bibliography: Bolton 1918–19, 131, 17–18; Calver 1928, 120–21.

384. Fort, Coteau du Lac, Québec, Canada, 1965–66.

Type of find: Archaeological excavation.

Date of site: 1776–1856.

Contents: 80 AE.

Description: Coins found included:

Denmark, skilling KM, 1771
Great Britain, George III, counterfeit halfpenny
British colonies, Lower Canada, Wellington halfpenny token
British colonies, Lower Canada, token with laureate and draped bust of George III and 1820 below

Bibliography: Falan and Ingram 1973.

385. New Windsor, New York, USA, 1869.

Type of find: Hoard.

Date of deposit: 1777.

Container: An egg-shaped, brown earthenware jar (looks like a Spanish olive jar).

Contents: 652 AR; 1 AV.

Description:

Spain, gold medal, "struck in honor of some Spaniard, dated 1654"
France, écu, 1734
Spanish colonies, 8 reales, 1621–1773 (649)
Spanish colonies, 8 reales, 1770
Spanish colonies, 8 reales, 1768
Mostly Spanish dollars; the earliest date was 1621. The latest date in the hoard was 1773.

The treasure is thought to have belonged to someone who fled from the locality on the approach of the American troops, and buried the coins before their arrival.

Disposition: Found on the estate of Thomas Ellison by Silas Corwin. The mansion was once the headquarters of General Washington. The jar was found four feet below the surface. Its open end was downward, and it rested on a flat stone.

The Corwin family sold most of the coins for large prices, but retained some as curiosities. Some are supposed to have gone to the State Museum of Newburgh, New York. One coin went to Dr. Goodrich, the State Treasurer of Connecticut, according to the *Hartford (CT) Times*.

Bibliography: Bolton 1931, 112, 117 (includes photograph of the jar); Breen 1952, 9 (Breen Hoards III); Brown and Dolley 1971, 59

(NT1); Noe 1942, 34–34.

American Journal of Numismatics 18, no. 4 (April 1884): 79.

"A Revolutionary Relic," *American Journal of Numismatics* 20, no. 4 (April 1886): 92.

386. Arch Street, Philadelphia, Pennsylvania, USA, 1860.

Type of find: Funerary deposit.

Contents: 1 AR.

Description: British colonies, Hungry Wolf Indian Peace Medal

Disposition: Cabinet of the United States Mint, Philadelphia, Pennsylvania, USA.

Bibliography: Snowden 1861, 118.

387. Near the Saint Joe's River in Michigan, USA, 1889.

Type of find: Funerary deposit.

Date of deposit: 1777.

Contents: 2 AR.

Description: British colonies, Hungry Wolf Indian Peace Medal, with two different dies (2)

Bibliography: McLachlan 1899, 14.

388. Presque Isle, at the mouth of the Shawnee River, Michigan, USA, 1894.

Type of find: Funerary deposit (found in the grave of Otussa, the son of Pontiac).

Contents: 1 AR.

Description: British colonies, Hungry Wolf Indian Peace Medal

Disposition: Cabinet of the United States Mint, Philadelphia, Pennsylvania, USA.

Bibliography: Betts 1894, 238–39 notes; McLachlan 1899, 14.

"Rare Medal in Pawnshop. Numismatist Finds Indian Relic worth $250 for sale at $2," *New York Times*, June 24, 1914, 7.

389. Wisconsin, USA, August 1926.

Type of find: Funerary deposit.

Contents: 1 AR.

Description: British colonies, Hungry Wolf Indian Peace Medal

Disposition: The find was announced by Dr. Alphonse Gerend, of the Wisconsin Archaeological Society.

Bibliography: "Indian Peace Medal Found in Wisconsin," *Numismatist* 39, no. 8 (August 1926): 425.

390. 70th Street and the East River, New York, New York, USA, August 1905.

Type of find: Hoard.

Date of deposit: 1777.

Containers: 4 pots.

Contents: 300 AE, 20 AV.

Description:
Great Britain, George I and George II, halfpence (300)
Great Britain, George II and George III, guineas, 1758–77 (20)

Disposition: Three pots containing 300 George I and II halfpence were found by workers at the site of an old colonial mansion, at 70th street and the East River. A fourth pot, containing guineas, was found by Italian laborers, who absconded with it; the guineas were sold by an Italian contractor to a coin dealer with a store at Broadway and 14th Street; the dealer paid $5.10 for each guinea. Mrs. William Lowe, the wife of the owner of the property, put some of the copper coins aside and may have strung them into a necklace.

Bibliography: "Ancient Guineas Found. Italian Would Not Tell Where—Dates Between 1758 and 1777," *New York Tribune*, August 19, 1905, 7.

"Ha'pennies of the Georges: Pot of them found on the East Side Worth Only Their Metal Weight," *Numismatist* 18, no. 9 (September 1905): 286–87.

391. Red Bank Shoal, just downstream from Fort Mercer, Delaware River, Pennsylvania, USA, 1867.

Type of find: Shipwreck.
Ship: Augusta.
Sank: October 1777.
Contents: 2+ AR, 7 AV.
Description:
  Great Britain, George III, guineas, 1760–70 (7)
  Spanish colonies, 8 reales, probably México
Bibliography: Cotter, Roberts, and Parrington 1992, 464.

392. Carver's Falls, Vermont, USA, December 1901.

Type of find: Shipwreck.
Ship: Unknown.
Sank: 1777.
Container: Old iron chest.
Contents: 10,000 AV.
Description: Great Britain, guineas (10,000)
  The guineas had been sent from Canada and were intended to pay Burgoyne's troops, when this supply ship was attacked by the Americans. The British defenders were all killed, but they scuttled the ship.
Disposition: Found by the engineer George West; deposited in the Allen National Bank, Fairhaven, Vermont.
Bibliography: Brown and Dolley 1971, 59 (NT3).
  "Find Treasure Lost by British in 1777," *Numismatist* 14, no. 12 (December 1901): 337.

393. Stony Point State Historic Site, New York, USA, 1915 and 1936.

Type of find: Archaeological excavation.
Date of site: 1777?
Contents: 5 AE, 1 AR.
Description:
  Great Britain, halfpence (4): 1731? 1737; 1773; 17[-]
  Ireland, halfpenny, 1766, burned
  Spanish colonies, ½ real, México, 1788
Disposition: New York State Bureau of Historic Sites Collection, Peebles Island, New York, USA.
Bibliography: Hoover 2007 (providing inventory of New York State Bureau of Historic Sites Collections, Peebles Island, New York, as of August 16, 2005).

394. Valley Forge, Pennsylvania, USA, 1962.

Type of find: Archaeological excavation.
Date of site: 1777–78.
Contents: 1 AE.
Description: Great Britain, halfpenny, 1773
Bibliography: Cotter, Roberts, and Parrington 1992, 439.

395. Alburgh, Vermont, USA, 1884.

Type of find: Hoard.
Date of deposit: 1770s.
Contents: 7+ AR, 1 AV.
Description:
  Spain, Philip V, 2 reales (pistareens) (2)
  Spanish colonies, Charles III, 8 reales, México, assayers FF [1777–84]
  Spanish colonies, Charles III, 8 reales, México
  Portuguese colonies, Brazil, John VI, 1,600 reis, 1726 (impossible date; error for 1729?)
Disposition: Found by a farmer while plowing.
Bibliography: Various 1884, 95–96.

396. Oak Bluffs, Massachusetts, USA, May 1926.

Type of find: Hoard.
Date of deposit: 1777.
Contents: 5 BI.

Description: German states, Frankfurt/Main, kreuzers, 1738–77 (5)

Dates not wholly certain; the 1738 kreuzer could be 1788.

Bibliography: "Can this be 'buried treasure'?," *Numismatist* 39, no. 5 (May 1926): 247.

397. Otsego County, New York, USA, October 1885.

Type of find: Hoard.
Date of deposit: 1777.
Contents: 9 P.
Description:
  USA, Continental currency, $ 1/8
  USA, Continental currency, 50¢
  USA, Continental currency, $2/3
  USA, Continental currency, $7
  USA, Continental currency, $8
  USA, Continental currency, $20 (2)
  USA, Continental currency, $40
  The notes were found while demolishing a chimney.

Bibliography: Buried Treasures Found 1885, 42.

398. Fort Frontenac, Kingston, Ontario, Canada, 1993.

Type of find: Archaeological excavation.
Contents: 1 AV.
Description: Spanish colonies, escudo, 1777
Bibliography: Spittal 1993, 250.

399. Watchogue House, East Moriches, Long Island, New York, USA, April 1898.

Type of find: Single find.
Contents: 1 AR.
Description: Spanish colonies, 8 reales, 1777, probably México
Disposition: Found by William E. Reeve while plowing in the garden of the Watchogue House.
Bibliography: "Old Coins Unearthed," *Brooklyn Daily Eagle*, April 25, 1898, 4.

400. Old Garratt farm, Garrattsville, near New Lisbon, New York, USA, July 18, 1903.

Type of find: Hoard.
Date of deposit: Autumn 1778.
Container: Jar.
Contents: 8 AE; 37 AR; 34 AV.
Description:
  Great Britain, George III, halfpence (8)
  Great Britain, George II, ½ crowns or crowns (37)
  Great Britain, George III, guineas, 1761–69 (34)

The American Revolution in this part of upstate New York was more a civil war than a struggle against the British, and the settlers in Butternut Valley were Tory sympathizers, including the Garratts. Some Butternut Valley menfolk participated with Chief Joseph Brant in the British and Iroquois burning of Springfield prior to the raid on Cherry Valley in November 1778. The hoard is thought to have been concealed when this civil war broke out in upstate New York in the autumn of 1778. The Garratts are known to have concealed their silverware under their pigpen and found it when they returned to the Valley after the war.

Disposition: Found by John Rockwell, who owned the farm, and his worker Nathan Smith. They found all but two of the guineas. One of the guineas was found by John Rockwell some years previously, and another guinea was found by Hube Gregory of Norwich, New York, while visiting in 1898, and he wore the coin on his watch chain. The denomination of the silver coins is not given, but they are described as "about the size of a half-dollar."

Bibliography: "Another Revolutionary Find," *Morris (NY) Chronicle*, July 22, 1903 (transcribed and sent to John M. Kleeberg by Leigh C. Eckmair, historian of the Town of Butternuts, New York). A similar article appeared in the *Gilbertsville (NY) Otsego Journal*, July 30, 1903, but this account is the first and most detailed.

"Dug up a Pot of Gold," *Numismatist* 16, no. 8 (August 1903): 248.

Leigh C. Eckmair, telephone conversation with John M. Kleeberg, May 6, 2007.

401. Newton or Monroe, New Jersey, USA, July 1922.

Type of find: Single find.

Contents: 1 AR.

Description: Spanish colonies, Charles III, 8 reales, probably México, 1778

Disposition: Found by Mrs. Fred Mabee where a road was being rebuilt.

Bibliography: "Finds Old Spanish Coin," *New York Times*, July 9, 1922, 14.

"Thinks Portrait of Charles III that of a Woman," *Numismatist* 35, no. 11 (November 1922): 568.

402. Opelousas, Louisiana, USA, July 1882.

Type of find: Hoard.

Date of deposit: 1779.

Container: 10-Gallon jar.

Contents: 8,000–10,000 AR.

Description: Spanish colonies, Charles III, 8 reales, México, 1779 (8,000–10,000)

Disposition: Lewis Lowry found the coins while plowing; some were brought to New Orleans for examination.

Bibliography: "Spanish Silver by the Gallon," *American Journal of Numismatics* 17, no. 1 (July 1882): 23.

403. The Phinney Site, along the Penobscot River, Maine, USA, September 2003.

Type of find: Archaeological excavation; votive deposit.

Date of site: August 16, 1779.

Contents: 1 AR.

Description: Spain, Philip V, 2 reales (pistareen), Segovia, 1708

Archaeological excavation of shipwrecks scuttled after the Americans suffered a naval defeat at the hands of the British. The coin was recovered from the base of a burned vessel's mainmast step mortise. It is a custom to place a coin or two for luck when stepping a mast.

Bibliography: Kays 2005, 2853 (citing Naval Historical Center, Underwater Archaeology Branch Website, The Phinney Site, September 10, 2003).

404. British Fort, Richmond, Staten Island, New York, USA, 1920.

Type of find: Archaeological excavation.

Date of deposit: 1780; *date of site:* 1776–83.

Contents: 11 AE, 1 AR.

Description:

England, William III, halfpenny with scalloped edges plus two holes to make it into a humdinger or buzzer

Great Britain, halfpence (10): George II; George III; George II or III (8)

Spanish colonies, Charles III, ½ real, probably México, 1774

Bibliography: Bolton 1919, 82–88; Calver 1920, 71; Calver 1921, 101–2.

405. Near Fort Brewerton, New York, USA, 1903.

Type of find: Single finds.

Date of deposit: 1780–1801.

Contents: 1 AE, 1 AV.

Description:

German states, Brunswick-Wolfenbüttel, ducat, [1780–1801]

Copper medal, 37.6 millimeters in diameter, with erect woman with shield and cornucopia on obverse, and with the legend, "Honor obtain'd through virtue" on the reverse

The ducat is the most probable attribution of an item described as a "Fine gold piece bearing the arms of the Duke of Brunswick."

Bibliography: Beauchamp 1903, 69.

406. 1½ miles east of Cold Spring Village, New York, USA, spring 1920.

Type of find: Archaeological excavation.

Date of site: 1780–1810 ("Connecticut Village," a winter camp of the Continental Army in the latter part of the Revolutionary War).

Contents: 5 AE.

Description:

Great Britain, halfpence (2): George II; George III
USA, New York, Machin's Mills counterfeit halfpenny, 1787
USA, Connecticut, copper, 1788
USA, 1¢, 1802

This documented findspot of a Machin's Mills counterfeit is the closest one to the mint (at Newburgh).

Bibliography: Calver 1920, 73.

407. Harriton, Lower Merion Township, Pennsylvania, USA, 1976.

Type of find: Archaeological excavation.

Date of site: 1704–1926; date of Charles Thomson's residence: 1729–1824; date of earliest coin: 1781.

Contents: 1 AE.

Description: Ireland, halfpenny, 1781

Bibliography: Cotter, Roberts, and Parrington 1992, 381.

408. Hancockville, Union District, now Cherokee County, South Carolina, USA, August 1822.

Type of find: Hoard.

Date of deposit: January 1781.

Container: Pot.

Contents: ca. 1,000 AR, ca. 100 AV.

Description:

Spanish colonies, 8 reales, México (ca. 1,000)
Spanish colonies, 8 escudos, México (ca. 100)
Denominations and mints given here are educated guesses; hoard described only as several thousand dollars in silver and gold coin. Thought to be buried during the Revolutionary War; if so, the likeliest time is January 1781, when armies moved through what would become Cherokee County on the way to the Battle of Cowpens. Hancockville is a historical town, no longer in existence.

Bibliography: "Treasure Trove," *Hartford (CT) American Mercury*, August 26, 1822, 3.
"Treasure Trove," *Cooperstown (NY) Watch-Tower*, August 26, 1822, 2.
"Treasure Trove," *Newburyport (MA) Herald*, August 27, 1822, 3.
"Treasure Trove," *Ithaca (NY) Republican Chronicle*, August 28, 1822, 2.

409. Currituck County, North Carolina, USA, May 1857.

Type of find: Hoard.

Date of deposit: 1781.

Contents: ca. 1,000 AR, ca. 250 AV.

Description:

Spanish colonies, 8 reales, México (ca. 1,000)
Spanish colonies, 8 escudos, México (ca. 250)
Described as Spanish gold and silver to the amount of $6,000. Denominations and mint are educated guesses. Supposed to have been buried during the American Revolution. If so, the hoard probably was buried in 1781, when Cornwallis and Tarleton moved their forces out of the Carolinas and north into Virginia, culminating in the Yorktown campaign.

Disposition: Found by Benjamin S. Day.

Bibliography: "Treasure Trove," *Pittsfield (MA) Sun*, May 14, 1857, 2 (citing the *Norfolk (VA) Herald*, May 7, 1857).

410. Charlotte Court House, Virginia, USA, May 1827.

Type of find: Hoard.

Date of deposit: 1781.

Contents: ca. 20 AV.

Description:

Portuguese colonies, Brazil, 3,200 reis (ca. 5)
Portuguese colonies, Brazil, 6,400 reis (ca. 15)
½ joes and joes totaling $370. Total number of coins and number of each denomination are educated guesses.

Disposition: Rooted up by hogs in a thick growth of underwood in an uncultivated spot.

Bibliography: Providence (RI) Patriot, May 23, 1827, 1, citing a Lynchburg (VA) paper.
Amherst (NH) Farmer's Cabinet, May 26, 1827, 3.
Cooperstown (NY) Watch-Tower, May 28, 1827, 2.
Easton (MD) Republican Star, May 29, 1827, 3.
Dedham (MA) Village Register, May 31, 1827, 2.

411. Yorktown, Virginia, USA, 1995.

Type of find: Archaeological excavation.

Date of site: 1781.

Contents: 1 AR.

Description: German states, Schwarzenberg, Ferdinand and Maria, thaler, 1696 (Dav.7701)

The coin was found in a context of the siege of Yorktown. Noël Hume suggests that the coin was lost by one of the German auxiliaries (the "Hessians"), who were encamped at Yorktown. The British recruited German auxiliaries from Hanover, Brunswick, Hesse-Cassel, and Ansbach-Bayreuth; the French recruited German auxiliaries from Palatinate-Zweibrücken. Schwarzenberg is in Franconia, so the piece might have been lost by a soldier from that area, i.e. Ansbach-Bayreuth.

Bibliography: Noël Hume 1995, 19–20.

412. Freehold Township, New Jersey, USA, 2001.

Type of find: Hoard. Called "the George Hoard," after a pseudonym of the finder, "George."

Date of deposit: 1781.

Contents: 55 P.

Description:

British colonies, New Jersey, bill of credit, issue of June 14, 1757, # 6
British colonies, New Jersey, bill of credit, issue of November 20, 1757, # 6
British colonies, New Jersey, bill of credit, issue of May 1, 1758, # 6
British colonies, New Jersey, bill of credit, issue of April 10, 1759, # 3
British colonies, New Jersey, bill of credit, issue of April 23, 1761, # 6
British colonies, New Jersey, bill of credit, issue of December 31, 1763 (2): 3 shillings; 12 shillings
British colonies, New Jersey, bill of credit, issue of March 25, 1776 (27): 3 shillings; 6 shillings (4); 12 shillings (21); 15 shillings
USA, New Jersey, bill of credit, issue of January 9, 1781, 1 shilling
USA, New Jersey, bills of credit, not identified (17)
USA, New York, bill of credit
USA, Continental currency (2)

The hoard suddenly fell out of the ceiling of an eighteenth century farmhouse one night in 2001. An unusual feature of the hoard is that most of the bills had technically expired by 1781. Gladfelter, however, points out that deadlines for redeeming paper money were often not strictly enforced and the colonies would redeem currency turned in after the deadline.

Disposition: Sold by Elliot P. Durann, who owned a coin shop in Freehold Borough, New Jersey; photocopies of thirty-five of the New Jersey bills of credit were made by David Gladfelter.

Bibliography: Gladfelter 2002.

413. Santa Clara, California, USA, June 8, 1911.

Type of find: Foundation deposit.
Date of deposit: November 19, 1781.
Contents: 2 AE, 7 AR.
Description:
Spain, bronze medal of Saint Francis of Assisi with Saint Anthony of Padua on the reverse
Spain, bronze medal of Our Lady of Soledad with Saint Joseph and Child on the reverse
Spanish colonies, Philip V, ½ real, México, assayers MF
Spanish colonies, Charles III, ½ real, México, 1769
Spanish colonies, Charles III, reales, México, 1778 (2)
Spanish colonies, Charles III, 2 reales, México, 1778 (3)
Contents of the cornerstone of the Second Santa Clara Mission Church, which was laid by fray Junipero Serra, fray Juan Crespi, fray Thomas de la Pena, fray Antonio Murguia, and Don José Laso de la Vega.
Disposition: Galtes Museum of the University of Santa Clara.
Bibliography: Spearman 1948.

414. Pierre Part, Louisiana, USA, 1929.

Type of find: Single find.
Contents: 1 AR.
Description: Spanish colonies, Charles III, real, México, 1781
Disposition: Earl J. Gaudet.
Bibliography: "The Found Photo Album," *Treasure Found* (Summer 1989): 27.

415. Near Indian Hill, Pompey, New York, USA, 1821.

Type of find: Single find.
Contents: 1 B.
Description: French colonies, 3 sous, 1781A
Described as having the inscription "Nalf, Lanfar & Co." This appears to have been a misreading of "Colonies Françaises."
Disposition: Found by John Watson. Given to Samuel L. Mitchell to grace his collection of curious relics and coins.
Bibliography: Beauchamp 1891, 48; Beauchamp 1903, 69; Clark 1849, 2: 255.

416. Prairie du Chien, Wisconsin, USA, 1864.

Type of find: Funerary deposit.
Contents: 1 AR.
Description: Spanish colonies, Charles III, silver AL MERITO Indian Peace Medal (Vives 67)
The medal is 2 1/8 inches in diameter, and has a hole drilled for suspension.
Described in the Wisconsin Historical Museum records as reading "POR MERITO"; however, the medal is very worn and better preserved examples read "AL MERITO."
J. D. Butler suggested that these medals were presented on November 20, 1781 by Don Francisco Cruzat, the Spanish governor. The medal is supposed to have belonged to Huisconsin, a Mitasse chief of Sacs and Foxes.
Disposition: The medal was donated by the Honorable Horace Beach to the Wisconsin Historical Society. As of 2007, the medal was in the collection of the Wisconsin Historical Museum (item number 1955.1280/N3899, item number formerly was H3639).
Bibliography: Butler 1882a; Butler 1882b.
Jennifer L. Kolb, Deputy Director, Wisconsin Historical Museum, letter to John M. Kleeberg, March 26, 2007.

417. Tupelo, Mississippi, USA, October 1885.

Type of find: Funerary deposit.

Contents: 1 AR.

Description: Spanish colonies, Charles III or Charles IV, AL MERITO Indian Peace Medal (Vives 67)
Description is the likeliest attribution of "silver medal bearing a Spanish inscription."

Bibliography: Buried Treasures Found 1885, 42.

418. Beside the Shenandoah River, Clarke County, Virginia, USA, April 2007.

Type of find: Single find.

Contents: 1 AE.

Description: Great Britain, George III, counterfeit halfpenny, 1781, Newman 41–81B

Disposition: Found by Kevin Jackson with a metal detector.

Bibliography: Jackson and Moore 2007.

419. Corner of Henry and Pierrepoint Street, Brooklyn, New York, USA, August 1921.

Type of find: Single find.

Contents: 1 AE.

Description: Ireland, halfpenny, 1782
Found on what had been the site of the British Fort Sterling during the Revolutionary War.

Bibliography: O. Nash Morton, "Relics of Fort Sterling. An interesting Coin Found in Brooklyn Excavation," *New York Times*, August 31, 1921, 12.

420. 120 Wall Street, New York, New York, USA, 1929.

Type of find: Excavation.

Contents: 2 AE. *Date of deposit:* 1780s.

Description: Great Britain, George III, halfpence (2)
Description is the likeliest attribution of "bronze coins of the British period."

Disposition: Found by workers excavating 120 Wall Street.

Bibliography: Bolton 1931, 111.

421. Williamsburg, Virginia, USA, 1932–2002.

Type of find: Archaeological excavation.

Contents: 2 PB, 160 AE, 1 B, 2 BI, 78 AR.

Description: This listing enumerates only the seventeenth, eighteenth, and early nineteenth century coins found (except for the Chinese cash, which dates from after 1875).
China, Guangxu, cash, Fujian province
Denmark, Christian VII, 2 skilling, 1785
Russia, Alexander I, 2 kopek, 1812
Hungary, Maria Theresa, poltura, 1763 (this coin reported by Newman, 1956)
German states, Electoral Palatinate, Charles Philip, 20 kreuzers, 17Z1[1721]IGW
German states, Nuremberg, jeton, Louis XV, rv. "MICHAEL LEICHKAUM"
Netherlands, 6 stuivers, quartered, cut
England, James I, farthing
England, Charles I, rose farthing
England, Charles II, farthings (2): 1672; 1673
Great Britain, George II, farthing, 1736
England, Charles II, halfpenny
England, William III, halfpenny
Great Britain, George I, halfpence (3): 1721; 1722; ND
Great Britain, George II, halfpence (11): 1738; 1740; 1740, lead counterfeits (2); 1741; 1748; ND (5)
Great Britain, George III, halfpence, 1774
Great Britain, evasive halfpenny, "George Rules/North Wales," 1781
England, Elizabeth I, sixpence (2): [1582], cut in a third; ND, halved
England, Charles I, shilling, triangle mintmark [1639–40]
England, William III, shilling, [1694–1702]
Scotland, Charles II, bawbee sixpence
Ireland, Wood's Hibernia, halfpenny, 1723

Ireland, George II, halfpence (2)
France, Louis XV, liard
France, Louis XV, ½ sol, [1720–23]
Spain, Charles III (the pretender), ½ real (¼ pistareen), Barcelona, 1707–14
Spain, real (½ pistareen), Segovia, 1721, assayer F
Spain, reales (½ pistareens), Seville (5): 1721J; assayer P [1728–29], cut, quartered; 1734PA; assayer PA [1731–36], cut, halved; [1737–45], cut, quartered
Spain, real (½ pistareen), no mint, cut, quartered
Spain, 2 reales (pistareen), Cuenca, cut, quartered
Spain, 2 reales (pistareens), Madrid (4): 1717–19, cut, halved; assayer A, [1721–25], cut, halved; ND, cut, quartered (2)
Spain, 2 reales (pistareens), Segovia (8): 1719, cut, quartered; 1724, cut, quartered; [1719–29], assayer FJ, cut, quartered (4); ND, cut, quartered (2)
Spain, 2 reales (pistareens), Seville (10): 1721J; 1736AP; [1731–45], cut, quartered; ND, cut, quartered (6); ND, cut, eighth
Spain, 2 reales (pistareens), no mint (9): [1718–29], cut, quartered; ND (8)
British colonies, George I, Rosa Americana halfpence, 1722 (2)
British colonies, George I, Rosa Americana pence (3): 1722 (2); ND
British colonies, George I, Rosa Americana, twopence
British colonies, Virginia, halfpence, 1773 (97): Newman 6-X; 7-D; 8-H; unattributed (94)
USA, ½¢ (5): 1793; Liberty cap; 1809; 1826; 1833
USA, 1¢ (21): Liberty cap, 1795 (3); 1798; 1800 (2); 1801; draped bust (3); 1810; 1811; 1817; 1818; 1819; matron head (3); 1834; 1838; large 1¢, ND

British colonies, Bermuda, halfpenny, 1793
British colonies, Tobago, 2¼ pence, TB/o counterstamp of 1798 on French colonies 2 sols with French crowned C counterstamp of 1763 (2): 1749; 1759 (dates of the French host coins)
French colonies, Windward Islands, 12 sols, 1731H
Spanish colonies, ¼ real, broken in half, probably México
Spanish colonies, ½ reales, México (6): 1777; 1778; 1783; 1787; [1780–88]; [1785–86]
Spanish colonies, reales, México (5): 1739; [1758–59]; 1783; cob, ND; ND
Spanish colonies, 2 reales, México (3): 1715–16, cut, quartered; 1756, holed; 1787FM, holed
Spanish colonies, 8 reales, México (2): [1770–89], cut, eighth; ND, cut, eighth
Spanish colonies, reales, Lima (2): 1698H; 1717
Spanish colonies, 2 reales, Lima, 1728
Spanish colonies, ½ real, Potosí, 1695VR
Spanish colonies, 2 reales, Potosí (3): [1627–29]; 1673; ND
Spanish colonies, ½ real, no mint, ND
Spanish colonies, reales, no mint (2): 1728; 1772

The above listing is based on the letter of William Pittman to John M. Kleeberg, 2007, except for the listing of the Spanish colonies silver, which comes from the Lasser exhibition catalog, and the Hungarian poltura, which comes from Newman.

Bibliography: Kays 2001, 2170; Lasser 1997; Newman 1956, 33–34; Noël Hume 1971, 11; Noël Hume 1974; Walsh 1997.

William E. Pittman, letter, January 20, 2007 to John M. Kleeberg (includes data for a forthcoming article on the finds by Pittman).

422. Ramseur, North Carolina, USA, August 1938.

Type of find: Hoard.

Date of deposit: 1783.

Contents: 63 AV.

Description: Great Britain, guineas
France, louis, 1651
Spanish colonies, 8 escudos
Portuguese colonies, Brazil, 6,400 reis
British, French, Brazilian and Spanish colonies gold coins. Denominations not given; description based on the commonest denomination of each issuer. Earliest dated piece 1651 (and must be a French louis), latest 1783. Found in a chimney by laborers. This report was sent in by A. B. Andrews of Raleigh, North Carolina.

Disposition: The coins were sold to an Asheboro jeweler for their bullion value.

Bibliography: Kleeberg 2008, 3245.
"Small Hoard of Gold Coins Found in North Carolina," *Numismatist* 51, no. 10 (October 1938): 886.
A note in the ANS copy of the *Numismatist* says, "See pamphlet file 1064;" but it has not been possible to track down this reference.

423. Manheim Township, Pennsylvania, USA, February 1926.

Type of find: Hoard.

Date of deposit: 1780s.

Contents: AE.

Description:
Great Britain, George II and George III, halfpence, most likely counterfeit
Ireland, George II and George III, halfpence, most likely counterfeit
Found in large numbers on the farm of L. B. Huber between Landis Valley and Eden in Manheim Township.

Bibliography: Martin 1927, 5.

424. Hart's Corners, Westchester County, New York, USA, October 1864.

Type of find: Hoard.

Date of deposit: 1783.

Contents: AE, AR.

Description: Only coin known from this deposit is:
USA, Nova Constellatio copper, 1783

Bibliography: "An Old Coin," *Banker's Magazine*, n.s. 14, no. 4 (October 1864): 306.

425. New York, New York, USA, March 1924.

Type of find: Excavation.

Date of deposit: 1783.

Contents: 9 AE.

Description:
Ireland, counterfeit halfpenny, 1780 (only described as copper coin of 1780; attribution is likeliest coin of that date)
USA, Nova Constellatio copper, 1783
No two coins were alike.

Disposition: Found 80 feet underground while digging the foundations of the New York Telephone building. 50 feet below ground the men found the wreck of a boat. This is not unusual in New York City, where superannuated ships were filled with rubble and sunk to make crib hulks to create wharves or landfill—an example is the Ronson ship, discovered in 1981 (compare *NFA* 653).

Bibliography: "Coins Found Fifty Feet Under Ground," *Numismatist* 37, no. 3 (March 1924): 243.

426. New York, New York, USA, 1891.

Type of find: Single find.

Contents: 1 AE.

Description: USA, Nova Constellatio copper, 1783, Crosby 3-C

Disposition: Found while tearing down a colonial house. The condition was "bright and unused." Sold to Ebenezer Gilbert for 75¢. In the sale of Gilbert's collection by Thomas Elder in 1910, there was the following Nova Constellatio (lot 82): "1783. Nova Constellatio. Blocked U.S. Clubbed rays. Similar to Crosby 75, p. 331. About uncirculated, light olive. A gem."

Bibliography: Elder 1910, lot 82.

"Coin Collecting Reminiscences," *Numismatist* 14, no. 11 (November 1901): 301–5.

"Collecting Curious Coins," *New York Times: Magazine Supplement,* October 20, 1901, 17.

427. 10 Cornhill Street, Annapolis, Maryland, USA, September-October 2003.

Type of find: Archaeological excavation.

Date of site: 1780s.

Contents: 29 AE, 2 AR.

Description:

Great Britain, George III, farthing
England, William III, halfpenny, 1698
Great Britain, halfpence (14): George I, 1721; George II (5); George III (7); ND
Ireland, George III, halfpence (3)
Portugal, 10 reis, 1752
British colonies, Virginia, halfpence, 1773 (2)
USA, Nova Constellatio copper, 1783
USA, Connecticut, copper, 1785
USA, Maryland, John Chalmers, threepence
USA, 1¢, 1838
Spanish colonies, 8 reales, cut piece
Unidentified coins (4)

It is disputed as to whether 10 or 14 Cornhill Street was the site of Chalmers's mint; after further excavations, Mumford contended that 10 Cornhill Street was the site of the mint. Mumford also believes that the numerous base metal coins found were used for smithing, probably to make buttons.

Disposition: Excavations in the basement by Will Mumford. Mumford said he wanted the Chalmers threepence to go to the Historic Annapolis Foundation.

Bibliography: Mumford 2005.

Eric von Klinger, "Impeccable timing: Collector digs up Chalmers coin hour before lecture on subject," *Coin World,* December 8, 2003, C1, 88.

428. Sparta Township, Sussex County, New Jersey, USA, November 1926.

Type of find: Single find.

Contents: 1 AR.

Description: USA, Maryland, Annapolis, John Chalmers, sixpence, 1783

Disposition: Found by the schoolgirl Alice Padgett of Sparta Township. The *New York Times* said that the coin was in fair condition.

Bibliography: "Lucky Dime Found by Girl is Rare 1783 Coin Worth $300," *New York Times,* November 15, 1926, 3.

"Is this an Annapolis Sixpence?" *Numismatist* 40, no. 1 (January 1927): 29.

429. Northern Virginia, USA, summer 1994.

Type of find: Single find.

Contents: 1 AR.

Description: USA, Maryland, Annapolis, John Chalmers, long worm shilling, 1783

Disposition: Found by a metal detectorist.

Bibliography: Kays 1995, 1488.

430. Norfolk, Virginia, USA, March 1998.

Type of find: Archaeological excavation.

Contents: 1 B.

Description: German states, Nuremberg, jeton figure of Minerva, issued by Ernst Ludwig Sigmund Lauffer, 1783–93.

Bibliography: Gerry Scharfenberger, letter to John M. Kleeberg, March 1998.

431. Site of former tavern, Fort Vengeance Monument Site, Pittsford, Vermont, USA, 2000.

Type of find: Archaeological excavation.

Date of site: 1783–1808.

Contents: 3 AE, 2 AR.

Description: Great Britain, George III, counterfeit halfpenny, 1772

USA, Vermont, copper, 1786, Ryder 7, with unusual broad planchet clip of about one third cut off

USA, 1¢, 1797, S-132

Spanish colonies, ½ real, México, 1786FM

Spanish colonies, real, México, 1746M

Bibliography: Hoge 2002.

432. 50 miles south of the Mississippi Delta, Louisiana, USA, August 2, 1993.

Type of find: Shipwreck.

Ship: El Cazador.

Sank: The ship left Veracruz for Nueva Madrid (i.e., New Orleans, Louisiana) on January 11, 1784, and was declared lost in June of that year.

Contents: 12,000 AR, 3 AV.

Description:

Spain, ½ escudo, Madrid, 1754JB

Spanish colonies, ½ reales, México (21): 1732F; 1733; 1734MF; 1735MF; 1736MF; 1737MF; 1738MF; 1739MF; 1740MF; 1741MF; 1742M; 1743M; 1744M; 1745M; 1746M; 1747M; 1748M; 1749M; 1783FF; ND, holed coin; partial date

Spanish colonies, reales, México (37): 1732F; 1734MF; 1735MF; 1736MF; 1737MF; 1738MF; 1739MF; 1740MF; 1741MF; 1742M; 1744M; 1745M; 1746M; 1747M; 1748M; 1749M; Charles III (21)

Spanish colonies, 2 reales, México (356): 1734MF; 1735MF; 1736MF; 1737MF; 1738MF; 1739MF; 1740MF; 1741MF; 1742M; 1743M; 1744M; 1745M; 1746M; 1747M (6); 1748M; 1749M; Philip V and Ferdinand VI, pillars (52); 1783FF (154); Charles III, bust type (129)

Spanish colonies, 4 reales, México (5): 1783FF; Charles III (4)

Spanish colonies, 8 reales, México (11,579): 1774FF; 1778FF; 1779FF (2); 1780FF (5); 1781FF (5); 1782FF (3); 1872FF (transposition for 1782); 1783FF (11,262); Charles III, bust type (300)

Spanish colonies, 8 escudos, Bogotá (2): 1779JJ; 1780JJ

Spanish colonies, 4 reales, Potosí, 1779PR

The ship's manifesto listed 400,000 8 reales and 50,000 pesos in fractions.

Disposition: Found by a commercial fishing boat, the *Mistake*, captained by Jerry Murphy and owned by Jim Reahard, of Grand Bay, Alabama. Reahard hired the admiralty lawyer David Paul Horan of Key West, Florida, to file a claim. The investors behind it were known as the Grumpy Partnership. The *New York Times* story is based partly upon a press conference held in New Orleans on December 6, 1993. In 1994 Reahard hired instead Oceaneering International Inc., of Houston, who expected to recover 20 tons of coins in two weeks at a cost of $250,000 to $500,000. The *New York Times* said in October 1994 that "less than a third" of the treasure had been recovered in the autumn of 1993. In November 1994 Oceaneering reported that they had recovered three tons of coins so far. The coins were in stacks 3 to 4 inches high. Further excavation was done by Herbert Humphreys's firm, Marex International Inc., of Memphis, Tennessee; Marex has also been involved in the re-salvaging of *Nuestra Señora de las Maravillas* and of HMS *Thunderer*. The treasure was sold to the Franklin Mint in 2007, who planned to market it further; some of the highlights were auctioned by R. M. Smythe in October 2007.

Bibliography: Sebring 2004, lots 1594–95; Smythe 2007, lots 1575–1617.

William J. Broad, "1784 Spanish Ship is Found in Gulf. Finders Say Vessel 50 Miles off Louisiana Holds Treasure from Mexico," *New York Times,* December 19, 1993, 38.

Allen R. Myerson, "High Seas Delaying Recovery of Sunken Treasure," *New York Times,* October 31, 1994, A12.

"Sunken Spanish Brig Yields Mementos of the Past," *New York Times,* November 21, 1994, A11.

Marex Int'l, Inc., v. the Unidentified, Wrecked and Abandoned Vessel, 952 F.Supp. 825, 826 (S.D. Ga. 1997).

"Coins are Back at the Franklin Mint," *Numismatist* 170, no. 5 (May 2007): 38.

433. Asbury Park, New Jersey, USA, March 1956.

Type of find: Hoard.

Date of deposit: 1784.

Contents: 6 AR.

Description: Spain, Charles III, 2 reales (pistareens), 1780–84 (6)

Since all the coins are described as bearing a male bust, the date "1760" in the news article has been corrected to 1780.

Disposition: Found by Charles Holland, a worker, while raking the beach at Asbury Park, New Jersey.

Bibliography: "Coin Hunt is Hatched By Easter Egg Affair," *New York Times,* March 30, 1956, 8.

434. Addison, New York, USA, May 1934.

Type of find: Single find.

Contents: 1 AV.

Description: Portugal, 400 reis, 1784

Described as a gold dollar of 1784; the coin in the description above is the gold coin of 1784 that could most probably be mistaken for a gold dollar.

Disposition: Found by New York State Temporary Emergency Relief Administration (TERA) workers excavating Main Street on a grading project.

Bibliography: "Gold Dollar of 1784 Found," *New York Times,* May 17, 1934, 3.

435. New Haven, Missouri, USA, August 1938.

Type of find: Single find.

Contents: 1 AR.

Description: Spanish colonies, 8 reales, México?, 1784

Disposition: Found by a farmer while plowing.

Bibliography: Numismatic Scrapbook Magazine 4, no. 8 (August 1938): 314.

436. Convento, Missión de Nuestra Señora de los Angeles de Porcinuncula, Pecos, New Mexico, USA, summer 1966.

Type of find: Archaeological excavation. Found in an adobe brick.

Date of site: 1784–92.

Contents: 1 AR.

Description: Spanish colonies, real, México, 1784FM

Bibliography: Vina Windes, "Probing for New Clues in Old Ruins," *New Mexico Magazine* 45, no. 9 (September 1967): 3–5.

"Real Dates New Mexico Mission," *Numismatic Scrapbook Magazine* 36, no. 12 (December 1970): 1566.

437. New Market East, Philadelphia, Pennsylvania, USA, 1973.

Type of find: Archaeological excavation.

Date of site: 1755–85.

Contents: 1 AE.

Description: Great Britain, halfpenny, ND

Bibliography: Cotter, Roberts, and Parrington 1992, 160.

438. One mile north of Rehoboth, Delaware, USA, 1930.

Type of find: Shipwreck.

Ship: Faithful Steward.

Sank: September 2, 1785, en route from Londonderry, Ireland, to Philadelphia, Pennsylvania, USA.

Contents: 1,000 AE, 2 AR, 17 AV.

Description:

   Great Britain, George II, halfpence, 1749 (2)
   Great Britain, George III, halfpence, 1774
   Great Britain, George III, halfpence, 1775 (100)
   Great Britain, guineas, 1766–82 (17)
   Ireland, George III, halfpence (500)
   Ireland, George III, halfpence, 1782 (100)
   France, écu, 1756
   Spain, reales (½ pistareens) (2)
   All the halfpence seen so far have been counterfeits.

Disposition: After a dredging operation in 1930, children found so many British and Irish halfpennies on the beach they could fill buckets with them. Major Lindsley D. Beach, U.S.A., retired, found nearly 100 copper coins in the winter of 1936–37. In winter 1938 George Marsh found a French écu of 1756; he found 300 other coins in two months. In August 1939, after six days of a northeasterly blow and pounding seas, a Baltimore visitor found two gold coins (probably guineas). In that same month, Mrs. Henry Fehr of Whitemarsh, near Philadelphia, found thirty-nine copper coins; and her sister, Mrs. John W. Watson of Chestnut Hill, near Philadelphia, found forty-four copper coins. Douglas Keefe of Atlantic City, New Jersey, found gold guineas and Spanish reales (possibly 1/2 pistareens), plus more British and Irish coppers, some with holes drilled through King George's nose.

Some of the finds of the 1930s went to the Zwaanandael Museum in Lewes, Delaware. Julius Reiver found four coins, and donated three to the American Numismatic Society. D. J. Ogden gave a talk about the *Faithful Steward* on October 17, 1949 to the Kanawha Valley Coin Club, which met in Charleston, West Virginia. He also displayed coins that had washed ashore from the wreck and been picked up. Another display of Irish halfpence from the *Faithful Steward* was made before the Philadelphia Coin Club in 1951.

Bibliography: Kleeberg 1996; Sebring 1991, 1216–20.

"Maryland Beach Yields Old Coins," *New York Times,* December 28, 1936, 12.

"Find George III Coins. CCC Boys Gather Hundreds of Coppers on Delaware Beach," *New York Times,* February 24, 1937, 25.

"Find Cache of Coins," *Numismatic Scrapbook Magazine* 3, no. 3 (March 1937): 52.

"Coins of 1749, 1775 Tossed up on Beach. More Old Coppers are Found at Lewes, Del.—Ancient Sea Chest is Buried in Sand," *New York Times,* March 14, 1937, 21.

"Ocean Washes Up Old Coins," *Numismatic Scrapbook Magazine* 4, no. 2 (February 1938): 69.

"French Coin of 1756 Found in Delaware," *Numismatic Scrapbook Magazine* 4, no 10 (October 1938): 410.

"Storm Reveals Old Coins. Summer Visitors Dig Colonial Pennies in Delaware," *New York Times,* September 1, 1939, 17.

"Kanawha Valley Coin Club, Minutes, October 17, 1949," *Numismatist* 67, no. 1 (January 1950): 57.

"Philadelphia Coin Club, Minutes," *Numismatist* 68, no. 5 (May 1951): 543.

439. Washington, New Jersey, USA, October 1925.

Type of find: Hoard.

Date of deposit: 1785.

Container: Pot.

Contents: 4 AE.

Description:
  Great Britain, George II, halfpenny, 1754
  Great Britain, George III, counterfeit halfpenny, 1776
  Ireland, George III halfpenny, ND
  USA, Connecticut, copper

Disposition: The pot was plowed up by the farmer George Golier.

Bibliography: "Jersey Farmer Plows Up Pot of 18th Century English Coins," *New York Times*, October 2, 1925, 25.

440. Wasaga Beach, Ontario, Canada, early 1970s.

Type of find: Archaeological excavation by the Ontario Provincial Government at the Naval Establishments at Wasaga Beach.

Contents: 1 AV.

Description: Great Britain, guinea, 1785

Bibliography: Spittal 1993, 250.

441. Trojan Site, Columbia River, near Rainier, Oregon, USA, 1970.

Type of find: Archaeological excavation.

Date of site: 1785–1830.

Contents: 3 B.

Description:
  China, Kangxi, cash (2): Board of Revenue, Beijing; Taiyuan, Shanxi province
  China, Qianlong, cash, Yunnan province

Bibliography: Beals 1980, 62, 70.

442. Decker Site, on Scappoose Bay, off the Columbia River, near Warren, Oregon, USA, 1960, 1962, and 1963.

Type of find: Archaeological excavation by the Oregon Archaeological Society; funerary deposit.

Date of site: 1785–1830.

Contents: 4 B.

Description:
  China, Kangxi, cash
  China, Qianlong, cash, Suzhou, Jiangsu province
  China, cash, illegible (2)
  3 of the coins had been burned in a cremation.

Bibliography: Beals 1980, 62, 64, 70.

443. Northern Bank of Clackamas River, Gladstone, Oregon, USA, 1980.

Type of find: Archaeological excavation; funerary deposit.

Date of site: 1785–1830.

Contents: 7 B.

Description:
  China, Qianlong, cash (6): Board of Revenue, Beijing; Yunnan provincial mints (3); Guilin, Guangxi province; illegible mint
  China, cash, illegible

Disposition: Clackamas County Historical Society Museum, Oregon City, Oregon, USA.

Bibliography: Beals 1980, 64, 70.

444. Charleston, South Carolina, USA, July 1883.

Type of find: Hoard.

Date of deposit: 1786.

Contents: 3 B.

Description: USA, New Jersey, copper, 1786, struck in brass
  Date given as 1785; impossible date, emended to read 1786.
  The coin was found "with several other pieces."

Bibliography: William Sumner Appleton, "Notes and Queries: Newspaper Numismatics," *American Journal of Numismatics* 18, no. 1 (July 1883): 22.

445. Roxbury, Massachusetts, USA, July 1939.

Type of find: Hoard.

Date of deposit: 1786.

Contents: 40 P.

Description: USA, Massachusetts, paper money, $2, May 5, 1780 (40) (all cancelled)

Bibliography: Benjamin C. Lowenstam, "A Package of Colonial Notes," *Numismatist* 52, no. 7 (July 1939): 547.

446. Berlin, Connecticut, USA, 1861.

Type of find: Single find.

Contents: 1 AE.

Description: USA, Inimica Tyrannis America/ Confederatio, copper, 1785

Disposition: Found by workers digging up an old drain.

Bibliography: Sigler 1946, 111.

447. Cambridge, Massachusetts, USA, May 1894.

Type of find: Hoard.

Date of deposit: 1787.

Contents: 63 AE.

Description: USA, Connecticut, coppers (63) One known: 1787 Miller 32.8-8aa.

Disposition: The coins were found in a barn. Provenance thereafter of the one coin known, Dr. Thomas Hall-Hillyer Ryder-Frederick C. C. Boyd-John J. Ford, Jr.- sold by Stack's, June 8, 1994, lot 84.

Bibliography: Stack's 1994, lot 84.

448. Duxbury, Massachusetts, USA, July 1874.

Type of find: Single find.

Contents: 1 AE.

Description: USA, Fugio 1¢, 1787

Disposition: It was found in the wall of the house of Captain Maglathlin of Duxbury, while attaching a bay window.

Bibliography: "Notes and Queries," *American Journal of Numismatics* 9, no. 1 (July 1874): 21.

449. Searsport, Maine, USA, 1890.

Type of find: Single find.

Contents: 1 AE.

Description: USA, Fugio 1¢, 1787

Disposition: Turned up by a plow in a cornfield. Presented in 1893 by a grateful client to Fahie Berkeley, a lawyer of Remson Street, Brooklyn, in commemoration of a successful lawsuit.

Bibliography: "A Rare Old Coin. Mr. Berkeley Carries a Fugio Cent as a Pocket Piece," *Brooklyn Daily Eagle*, October 9, 1893, 7.

450. Western Massachusetts, USA, September 2003.

Type of find: Single find.

Contents: 1 AE.

Description: USA, Massachusetts, 1¢, Ryder 3-G

Disposition: Found by a metal detectorist. This metal detectorist, active in Western Massachusetts, has also found Connecticut and New Jersey coppers, and Fugio 1¢.

Bibliography: Eric von Klinger, "Detectorist finds George II medal in Massachusetts hillside," *Coin World*, February 2, 2004, 72.

451. Hunt's Point, the Bronx, New York, USA, 1950–90.

Type of find: Excavation.

Date of deposit: 1787.

Contents: 2 AE.

Description: USA, Connecticut, coppers, 1787 (2)

Disposition: Found by Theodore Kazimiroff of the Bronx County Historical Society. Bequeathed by him to Kingsborough Community College, Brooklyn, New York, USA.

Bibliography: Hecht 1993.

452. On the site of the old Forbes Road Tavern, between Bedford and Ligonier, Pennsylvania, USA, April 2001.

Type of find: Hoard.

Date of deposit: 1787.

Contents: 12 AE, 1 AR.

Description: Spain, Charles III, 8 maravedíes, Segovia [1772–88]

Great Britain, George I, halfpenny, 1724, counterstamped NI

Great Britain, George II, counterfeit halfpence (3): 17[-] (2); 1733

Great Britain, George III, counterfeit halfpence (2): 17[-]2; 1775

USA, New York, Atlee counterfeit halfpenny, 1787, Vlack 17–87B

USA, Connecticut, copper, 1787, Miller 33.19-Z.1

USA, New Jersey, copper, Maris 39-A

Spanish colonies, real, México, 1746M

Copper disks (2)

A silver thimble was also found.

Thought to be the contents of a lost purse.

Disposition: Found by a metal detectorist.

Bibliography: Ference and Trudgen 2001.

453. Knox Headquarters State Historic Site, New Windsor, Orange County, New York, USA, 1975 and 1988.

Type of find: Archaeological excavation.

Date of site: 1754–1900, date of earliest coin: 1787.

Contents: 2 AE.

Description: USA, New York Machin's Mills, halfpence (2): 1778; 1787

Disposition: New York State Bureau of Historic Sites Collection, Peebles Island, New York, USA.

Bibliography: Hoover 2007 (providing inventory of New York State Bureau of Historic Sites Collections, Peebles Island, New York, as of August 16, 2005).

454. Gallows Hill, Salem, Massachusetts, USA, August 1874.

Type of find: Single find.

Contents: 1 AR.

Description: Spanish colonies, Charles III, 8 reales, [1772–1788]

The reverse of the coin had been filed smooth, and a ship under full sail very handsomely engraved upon the smooth surface, with an English flag at the stern, and at the bottom the name *Galatea*.

Bibliography: "Notes and Queries," *American Journal of Numismatics* 9, no. 2 (October 1874): 47 (citing the *Boston Advertiser* of August 8, 1874).

455. Irvin Village Site, west side of U.S. Highway 25W and north side of Cove Creek, just outside Caryville, Tennessee, USA, January–July 1934.

Type of find: Archaeological excavation of a Cherokee township site.

Date of deposit: 1788.

Contents: 1 AE.

Description: USA, New Jersey, copper, 1787

Disposition: Smithsonian Institution?

Bibliography: Dunn 1939; Webb 1938, 56–57.

456. Stepney, Fairfield County, Connecticut, USA, 1950.

Type of find: Hoard.

Date of deposit: early 1788.

Container: iron kettle of eighteenth century manufacture.

Contents: 209 AE.

Description: Hoard included (Breen saw 181):

Great Britain and Ireland, counterfeit halfpence (60) (not Machin's Mills)

USA, Vermont, head types (8) (Ryder 16 from this lot was sold to Mrs. Norweb in 1959)

USA, Vermont-Britannia mulings (3): Ryder 13 (2); Ryder 27

USA, New York, Nova Eborac

USA, New York, Machin's Mills counterfeit halfpence (12–16)

Three of the 1787s had Ryder 13 reverses (also known as Vlack 87C) and one was the same variety as on Richardson's copper coins of Vermont, page 4. The six pieces that went to Eric P. Newman were the Vlack varieties 6-72A (114.75 grains), 9-76B (116.5 grains), 11-78A (110.5 grains), 17-87A (118.75 grains), 19-87C (119.25 grains) and 23-88A (97 grains). Newman's pieces are in extraordinary condition—MS-60 and up.

USA, Connecticut, coppers, 1785–88 (ca. 125), with 75 different die varieties represented; here are Breen's attributions (his misattribution of a 4.1-G as a 4.2-G has been corrected) of the die varieties of 105 of the Connecticut coppers:

USA, Connecticut, coppers, 1785 (8): Miller 3.3-F.3 (2); 3.4-F.2 (2); 3.5-B; 4.4-C (2); 6.3-G.1

USA, Connecticut, coppers, 1786 (19): Miller 3-D.1; 4.1-G (3); 4.2-G; 5.2-H.1; 5.2-I; 5.2-L; 5.4-O.1; 5.5-M; 5.8-F (3); 5.9-B; 5.10-L (2); 5.11-R; 5.14-S (2)

USA, Connecticut, coppers, 1787 (74): Miller 2-B (3); 8-O; 9-D; 9-E; 9-R; 11.1-E; 11.2-K; 14-H; 20-a.2; 26-a.1; 31.1-gg.1; 31.4-k.1 (2); 32.2-r.3; 32.3-X.4; 32.5-aa; 33.1-Z.13; 33.2-Z.12 (3); 33.2-Z.17; 33.6-KK; 33.7-r.2; 33.7-r.4; 33.9-s.2; 33.10-Z.7; 33.10-Z.8; 33.12-Z.16; 33.12-Z.24; 33.13-Z.1; 33.13-Z.7; 33.14-Z.14; 33.15-r.1 (2); 33.16-Z.15; 33.17-r.1; 33.17-gg.2; 33.19-Z.1 (2); 33.28-Z.11; 33.28-Z.16 (4); 33.32-Z.13 (3); 33.36-T.2; 33.40-Z.2; 37.1-cc.1; 37.2-K.5; 37.3-i (3); 37.8-HH; 37.8-LL (2); 37.9-E (2); 37.11-ff.2 (2); 37.12-LL; 38-l.2; 38-GG (2); 41-ii; 44-W.4; 46-BB; 53-FF (3)

USA, Connecticut, coppers, 1788 (4): Miller 9-E; 12.1-F.1 (2); 12.2-E

Found in an iron kettle, of 18th century manufacture, in a barn built about 1760.

Some of the coins were in mint state, or nearly so, especially the later issues. There were no Vermont landscapes, Fugios, Massachusetts, Nova Constellatios, or New Jerseys. Perhaps the assembler of this hoard was picking out all the "head type" coins in circulation, believing that they would hold their value better, should confidence in the copper medium collapse. In August 1789, however, all coppers (except New Jerseys) lost their value, and so the hoarder chose not to recover the deposit.

Disposition: Sold to Stack's, where studied by Breen. Six Machin's Mills halfpence were bought by Eric P. Newman. Emery May Norweb bought a Vermont copper, a Ryder 16, via Richard Picker (provenance in lot 1282 of the Norweb auction). The bulk of the Connecticuts were bought by Norman Bryant via Henry Fortier. Q. David Bowers is thought to have bought the Connecticut collections of Norman Bryant, Ted Craige, and Norman Shultz, consolidated the collections and sold many of the Connecticuts through fixed price offerings in *Rare Coin Review* numbers 12 and 14. Bowers also consigned many of this group of Connecticuts to the 1975 Early American Coppers sale, where Breen's catalog description identified some as Stepney pieces (but see Bowers's comments below). For a careful identification of the Stepney pieces, based on the provenance research of Robert Martin, see the 1998 Mossman article cited below. The weights of the Newman coins come from a letter of Eric P. Newman to John M. Kleeberg.

In an e-mail message of January 27, 2008, to the author, in reponse to an inquiry about the provenance of the coins from the Stepney hoard, Q. David Bowers wrote as follows: "I don't know anything about the Stepney

Hoard. Any of Breen's attributions of MY coins to that source were his guesswork. He never consulted me when writing the catalogue. He fell out with Stanley Apfelbaum, who would not let him read the printer's proofs. I don't recall Norman Shultz having any Connecticut coppers that specifically passed to me; however, I did buy all of the Bryant and Craige collections, and if some other source says these included Shultz coins, then it must be. I started collecting Connecticuts in 1955 and bought many here and there, including cherrypicking the stocks of Stack's and Hollinbeck."

Bibliography: Barnsley 1993; Breen 1952, 20–24 (Breen XVII); Breen 1988, 97 (Breen 992); Kleeberg 2005; Lloyd 1998; Mossman 1998; Newman 1958.

Q. David Bowers, e-mail message to John M. Kleeberg, January 27, 2008.

457. New York, New York, USA, 1859.

Type of find: Hoard.

Date of deposit: 1788.

Container: Keg, later: 3 bags.

Contents: 5,000 AE.

Description: USA, Fugio 1¢, 1787 (5,000)

This is the keg of Fugios that was found at the office of the Bank of New York, 48 Wall Street. After the Bank moved the number was reduced to three bags, rather than a keg. By the late nineteen-eighties the amount left was one bag (712 coins), about half of which were uncirculated, about half damaged by water. Anthony Terranova, who saw the hoard then, said that there were about a dozen interesting errors in the hoard.

William Cowper Prime wrote in March 1860: "Only a year ago a keg of these coppers was found in the vault of a New York City bank, in fresh proof condition. This statement has been doubted; but we are indebted to the cashier of the bank for fine specimens of the contents of the keg, which abundantly prove the truth of the story."

In 1948 Damon G. Douglas and Richard D. Kenney at the American Numismatic Society counted, weighed, and measured these Fugios. There were 1,641. Douglas also weighed and measured any Fugios he could find elsewhere that were traceable to the hoard. They broke down as follows (varieties in the hoard listed first, varieties traced elsewhere listed after "plus"):

Newman 8-B (246 plus 11, total 257)
Newman 8-X (189 plus 5, total 194)
Newman 9-P (12 plus 4, total 16)
Newman 9-S (1 plus 1, total 2)
Newman 11-A (10 plus 2, total 12)
Newman 11-B (60 plus 3, total 63)
Newman 11-X (132 plus 4, total 136)
Newman 12-X (264 plus 0, total 264)
Newman 13-X (726 plus 18, total 744)
Newman X-X (brockage)

Total: (1,641 in hoard in 1948, plus 48 from hoard but outside the Bank of New York, total 1,689)

Disposition: 14 donated by the Bank of New York in 1949 to the American Numismatic Society in New York. 712 still at the Bank of New York in the 1990s, according to Anthony Terranova.

A list of the varieties donated by the Bank of New York in 1949 to the ANS follows:

Newman X-X (brockage), 1949.136.1
Newman 9-P (2), 1949.136.2 and 1949.136.3
Newman 8-B (2), 1949.136.4 and 1949.136.5
Newman 8-X (2), 1949.136.6 and 1949.136.7
Newman 9-S, 1949.136.8
Newman 11-B (2), 1949.136.9 and 1949.136.10
Newman 11-X, 1949.136.11

Newman 12-X (2), 1949.136.12 and 1949.136.13

Newman 13-X, 1949.136.14

Bibliography: Breen 1952, 14–15 (Breen IX); Breen 1988, 147–49 (Breen 1306, 1310); Kessler 1976; Prime 1860, 476; Prime 1861; Terranova 1997.

Damon G. Douglas Papers, Box 2, folders 1 and 2: Charts and Data Sheets, in the Library of the American Numismatic Society.

458. "Solitude" or "Old Wheatsheaf Farm," Morristown, New Jersey, USA, 1925.

Type of find: Excavation.

Date of deposit: 1788.

Contents: 30 AE.

Description: USA, New Jersey, coppers, 1787–88, large planchet varieties (Maris 59-o to 67-v) (30)

Disposition: Most of the coppers were found hidden behind an old mantelpiece. At least one, a PLURIBS variety (Maris 60-p or 61-p) was discovered in the garden while landscaping. The varieties are not precisely known, but Sipsey in 1964 said that one could be certain that they were large planchet varieties and that these therefore could be attributed to the Morristown mint. This find was important in enabling researchers in the series to attribute these coins to Mould at Morristown and not to Rahway.

Bibliography: Bowers 1997, 34–35; Sipsey 1964.

459. San Juan Harbor, Puerto Rico, USA, July 1939.

Type of find: Shipwreck?

Ship: Unidentified.

Sank: 1788?

Contents: AV.

Description: Spanish colonies, Charles III, 8 escudos, 1780s

Spanish gold coins, some of them 150 years old, found by a dredge while deepening the harbor. Denomination is an educated guess.

Bibliography: Edwin Brooks, "Dredge Spanish Coins in Harbor," *Numismatic Scrapbook Magazine* 5, no. 7 (July 1939): 354.

460. Peebles Island State Park, New York, USA, 1982.

Type of find: Archaeological excavation.

Date of earliest coin: 1788.

Contents: 2 AE.

Description:
USA, New York, Machin's Mills counterfeit halfpenny, 1788
USA, 1¢, 1797

Disposition: New York State Bureau of Historic Sites Collection, Peebles Island, New York, USA.

Bibliography: Hoover 2007 (providing inventory of New York State Bureau of Historic Sites Collections, Peebles Island, New York, as of August 16, 2005).

461. Washington, Pennsylvania, USA, August 1834.

Type of find: Single find.

Contents: 1 AE.

Description: British colonies, Virginia, halfpenny, 1773

Bibliography: Mease 1838, 282–83; Newman 1992, 9.

"Items," *Niles Weekly Register*, August 2, 1834, 384–85.

462. Richmond, Virginia, USA, 1803.

Type of find: Hoard.

Date of deposit: 1789.

Contents: 2,500 AE.

Description: British colonies, Virginia, halfpence, 1773 (2,500)

Known to have included the following

Newman varieties: 2-E; 3-F; 4-G; 4-O; 4-P; 5-B; 5-Z; 6-X; 7-D; 8-O; 9-B; 20-N; 20-X; 21-N; 22-S; 23-Q; 23-R; 24-K; 25-M; 26-Y; 27-J. The variety that is most notably absent from this hoard (so far as we know) is 8-H.

Disposition: The hoard was acquired by Israel I. Cohen between 1784 and 1803 in Richmond—possibly 1789, when the copper panic would have led someone holding these halfpence to default and surrender them to a creditor. The hoard was slowly released by his son, Colonel Mendes I. Cohen and his family; 2,200 sold in one lot in an auction in 1929. In October 1871 Colonel Cohen donated a halfpenny from this hoard to the Boston Numismatic Society. The auction of Colonel Cohen's collection in 1875 had five lots of Virginia halfpence. Two were described as "large planchet, uncirculated"; two were described as "small planchet, uncirculated"; and one was described as "large planchet, bronze proof."

In his auction of January 21, 1880, John W. Haseltine wrote under lot 713: "Many persons think that these Virginia ½ d are restrikes, but that is not so; they were the property of the late Mr. Cohen, of Baltimore, and descended to him from his father; I purchased quite a number from him and found 12 different varieties among them, all from different dies."

Bibliography: Breen 1952, 16–17 (Breen Hoards XIII); Breen 1988, 30; Cogan 1875, lots 2261–65; Haseltine 1880, lot 713; Newman 1956, 34; Newman 1962.

William Sumner Appleton, "Transactions of Societies: Boston Numismatic Society," *American Journal of Numismatics* 5, no. 3 (January, 1871): 66.

463. Knoxville, Tennessee, USA, 1859.

Type of find: Hoard.
Date of deposit: 1789.
Contents: 10? AE.
Description: British colonies, Virginia, halfpence, 1773 (10?)
"Some few years since a quantity dug up from the summit of the hill, on which the college now stands at Knoxville, Tennessee" (Dickeson).
Bibliography: Dickeson 1865, 84; Newman 1956, 34.

464. Easton, Pennsylvania, USA, 1859.

Type of find: Hoard.
Date of deposit: 1789.
Contents: 10? AE.
Description: British colonies, Virginia, halfpence, 1773 (10?)
"quite a number were exhumed from a locality near Easton, Pennsylvania" (Dickeson).
Bibliography: Dickeson 1865, 84; Newman 1956, 34.

465. Kingsmill Plantations, near Williamsburg, Virginia, USA, 1972–76.

Type of find: Archaeological excavation of Kingsmill Tenement/Quarter Site.
Date of deposit: 1789.
Contents: 23 AE, 5 AR.
Description:
Spain, 2 reales (pistareens), cut quarters (2)
Spain, 2 reales (pistareen), cut half
English colonies, Massachusetts, pine tree? shilling, Noe 3?
British colonies, Virginia, halfpence (23)
Spanish colonies, pillar dollar, México, cut quarter
Quarters occupied by African-Americans held as slaves. The Virginia halfpence appear to have been abandoned because of the Copper Panic of 1789.
Disposition: Virginia Historic Landmarks Commission.
Bibliography: Kelso 1979; Kelso 1984.

466. Rancocas, New Jersey, USA, January 1898.

Type of find: Hoard.

Date of deposit: 1789.

Container: Chamois bag inside a blanched coconut shell.

Contents: 50 AE.

Description: USA, New Jersey, coppers (50)

Disposition: Found by William H. Reineck of 3517 Filbert Street, West Philadelphia, while doing some brickwork.

Bibliography: "Buried Coins Discovered," *Brooklyn Daily Eagle*, January 9, 1898, 20 (citing the *Philadelphia Record*).

467. Northwestern Connecticut, USA, 1998.

Type of find: Hoard.

Date of deposit: 1789.

Contents: 27 AE.

Description:
Great Britain, halfpence (7): 1749 (2); 1771 (3); 1772 (2)
USA, Vermont, copper, Ryder 2 (2)
USA, Connecticut, coppers (18)

Bibliography: Carlotto 1998, 6.

468. Southwestern Massachusetts, USA, 1998.

Type of find: Single finds.

Contents: 100+ AE single finds

Description: Single finds made by a metal detecting family of over 100 coins of the Confederation period. Included:
USA, Vermont, coppers (3): Ryder 2; Ryder 16; Ryder 22

Bibliography: Carlotto 1998, 6

469. Southern USA, 1861–65.

Type of find: Single find.

Contents: 1 AR.

Description: USA, George Washington Indian Peace Medal, 1789, with Indian and armed female on obverse, heraldic eagle on reverse

Disposition: Said to have been found by a Union soldier in the South during the Civil War; sold in the John F. Noegel sale, 1915, to Mrs. L. A. Bland. Purchased by the American Numismatic Society, 1916; item number 1916.999.197.

Bibliography: Stahl and Scully 1991, 218.

470. Confederate Army Campsite, Guinea Station, Northern Virginia, USA, April 2001.

Type of find: Single find.

Date of deposit: 1789–90 (the date of the introduction of these side cuts to Barbados).

Contents: 1 AR.

Description: Barbados, side cut of Spain, 2 reales (pistareen), ca. 1718

Bibliography: Kays 2001, 2185.

471. Along the James River below Richmond, USA, April 2001.

Type of find: Single find.

Date of deposit: 1789–90 (the date of the introduction of these side cuts to Barbados).

Contents: 1 AR.

Description: Barbados, side one third cut of 2 reales (pistareen), probably Madrid, ca. 1721

Bibliography: Kays 2001, 2184.

472. Warm Springs, Bath County, Virginia, USA, July 1877.

Type of find: Single find.

Contents: 1 B.

Description: Great Britain, jeton, George III, 1789, "in memory of the good old days"

Bibliography: E. W. H., "Notes and Queries," *American Journal of Numismatics* 12, no. 2 (October 1877): 52.
David Proskey and Charles Porter Nichols, "Notes and Queries," *American Journal of Numismatics* 12 no. 3 (January 1878): 79.

473. Southern USA, 1989.

Type of find: Single find.

Contents: 1 AV.

Description: Great Britain, guinea, 1766, with Ephraim Brasher's EB counterstamp

Bibliography: Coin World, January 9, 1991.

474. Near White Post, Virginia, USA, May 1830.

Type of find: Hoard.

Date of deposit: 1790.

Contents: ca. 45 AV.

Description:
Portuguese colonies, Brazil, 1,600 reis (ca. 10)
Portuguese colonies, Brazil, 3,200 reis (ca. 15)
Portuguese colonies, Brazil, 6,400 reis (ca. 20)
Described as $240 in ¼ joes, ½ joes, and joes. Many were clipped and plugged (i.e., regulated). Total number of coins and amounts of individual denominations are educated guesses.

Disposition: Found by the slaves of Rev. Thomas Kennerly while blowing rocks. After exchanging for bills, divided among the slaves by Kennerly. The farm was formerly the residence of Lord Fairfax.

Bibliography: Baltimore (MD) Patriot, May 24, 1830, 2 (citing the *Winchester (VA) Republican,* May 21, 1830).
Easton (MD) Republican Star, June 1, 1830, 3.
Keene New Hampshire Sentinel, June 4, 1830, 3.

475. Santo Domingo, Dominican Republic, 1958.

Type of find: Hoard.

Date of deposit: 1790.

Contents: AR.

Container: Iron chest hidden in the wall of an adobe house in Santo Domingo.

Description: Only one coin known:
Spanish colonies, Charles IV, 8 reales, México, 1789 or 1790
The coins were covered with rust from the iron chest.

Disposition: Robert I. Nesmith.

Bibliography: Nesmith 1958a, plate G, coin number 43.

476. Site of Washington's Headquarters, Montclair, New Jersey, USA, July 1922.

Type of find: Hoard.

Date of deposit: 1790s.

Contents: 39 AE.

Description:
British colonies, Rosa Americana, penny, 1722, holed
Cast counterfeits:
Great Britain, George II, halfpenny, 1729 (2) (item numbers 1975.117.13, 1975.117.14)
Great Britain, George II, halfpenny, 1749 (item number 1975.117.15)
Bungtowns:
USA, Massachusetts, North Swansea, halfpenny, 1784, Vlack 14-84A, Breen 974 (item number 1975.117.18)
Great Britain, counterfeit of George II British halfpenny, 1752 (item number 1975.117.16)
Great Britain, very crude counterfeit of George III Irish halfpenny, ND (item number 1975.117.40)
Ireland, counterfeit of George III halfpenny, date illegible, overstruck on double-struck British counterfeit halfpenny, dated 1775 (item number 1975.117.45)
Counterfeit British and Irish halfpence:
Group I (Mould and Atlee):
USA, New York, halfpence, Vlack 24-72C, Breen 1004 (2) (item number 1975.117.33 and 1975.117.34)
USA, New York, halfpenny, Vlack 6-76A, Breen 1008 (item number 1975.117.36)

Group II (Brasher and Bailey):
USA, New York, halfpence, Vlack 17-87B, Breen 996 (4) (item number 1975.117.35, 1975.117.41, 1975.117.42, 1975.117.44)
USA, New York, halfpenny, Vlack 17-87A, Breen 996 (item number 1975.117.27)
Group III (Machin's Mills):
USA, New York, halfpence, Vlack 12-78B (2) (item numbers 1975.117.22 and 1975.117.43)
USA, New York, halfpence, Vlack 13–78B (4) (item numbers 1975.117.19, 1975.117.20, 1975.117.21, and 1975.117.38)
USA, New York, halfpenny, Vlack 13-88CT (item number 1975.117.31)
USA, New York, halfpenny, Vlack 18-87C (item number 1975.117.37)
USA, New York, halfpence, Vlack 19-87C (5) (item numbers 1975.117.23, 1975.117.24, 1975.117.25, 1975.117.26, and 1975.117.39)
USA, New York, halfpenny, Vlack 23-87C, Breen 995(item number 1975.117.17)
USA, New York, halfpence, Vlack 23-88A, Breen 997 (4) (item numbers 1975.117.28, 1975.117.29, 1975.117.30, and 1975.117.32)
USA, New Jersey, copper, 1786, Maris 17-K (item number 1945.42.661)
USA, New Jersey, coppers, 1787, Maris 31-L (2) (item numbers 1945.42.682 and 1945.42.683)
USA, New Jersey, copper, 1787, Maris 38-Z (item number 1945.42.699)
USA, New Jersey, copper, 1787, Maris 73-Λa (item number 1945.42.760)

Disposition: H. Prescott Clark Beach; on his death the collection was sold to Henry Grünthal, who in 1975 donated the counterfeits to the American Numismatic Society; accession number 1975.117. The hoard also contained at least five New Jersey coppers; these coins are found under the accession number 1945.42.

Bibliography: Kleeberg 1995–96.

477. Ten Mile River Scout Reservation, fifty miles west of Newburgh, New York, USA, 1970–2000.
Type of find: Single finds.
Date of site: 1790–1820.
Contents: 34 AE, 2 AR.
Description:
Parcel I: British and Irish halfpence, Spanish colonies silver, and USA state coppers:
Great Britain, farthing, possibly George III
Great Britain, George I, halfpenny, 1722
Great Britain, George II, halfpence (2): 1733; cast counterfeit, ND
Great Britain, George III, counterfeit halfpence (7): 1774; 1775 (2); ND (4)
Ireland, counterfeit halfpence (2): George II; George III
USA, Vermont, coppers (2): Ryder 13; Ryder 19
USA, New Jersey, coppers (3): Maris 16-L; Maris 61-p; Maris 67-v
USA, Connecticut, coppers (4): 1787 Miller 16.1-M; 1787 Miller 14-H; 1787 draped bust left; ND
Spanish colonies, reales, México (2): 1783; 1801
Parcel II: USA federal coins:
USA, ½¢ (2): 1807; ND
USA, 1¢ (10): 1794; Liberty cap 1¢, ND; 1¢ with reverse of 1796–98; 1798, S-179; 1798; 1802, S-237; 1807, S-271; classic head 1¢, ND; coronet 1¢, ND (2)
The pre-federal coins were all found in one distinct area; the federal coins in another. These areas are distinguished above as "Parcel I" and "Parcel II."
The area was used for hauling heavy timber, as indicated by the finding of oxshoes but no horseshoes. The site was abandoned around 1820 after all the good timber had been

harvested. The stratigraphy was extensively disturbed by earth moved by the Civilization Conservation Corps in the 1930s when they made it into a Boy Scout camping site.

Disposition: Series of finds made by the metal detectorists Russell Hannah and his family. Donated to the Ten Mile River Boy Scout Museum. Six coins (not included in the number above) were given to other people over the years.

Bibliography: Lorenzo 2001.

478. Ijamsville, Maryland, USA, late 1930s.

Type of find: Single find.

Contents: 1 AE.

Description: USA, "Washington the Great" or "Ugly Head" copper

Disposition: Found by a teenage boy underneath a porch.

Bibliography: Breen 1988, 124 (Breen 1185).

479. Durango, Mexico, March 21, 1893.

Type of find: Hoard.

Date of deposit: Before 1790.

Container: Large earthen box.

Contents: 5,000 AV.

Description: Spanish colonies, 8 escudos (5,000)

Disposition: A large earthen box found while workers were excavating for a new building to be erected on the property of Francisco Ortise, near the Palace Hotel. Upon being opened the box was found to be filled with old Spanish coins, here assumed to be Spanish colonies 8 escudos. The value of the treasure was given at $100,000.

Bibliography: "Buried Treasure Found," *Numismatist* 6, no. 4 (April 1893): 53.

480. 417 Arch Street, Camden, New Jersey, USA, October 1876.

Type of find: Foundation deposit.

Date of deposit: 1792.

Contents: 1 AE.

Description: USA, Washington President/Large Eagle copper, 1791 (Baker 15, Breen 1206)

Bibliography: "Relics of the Past," *American Journal of Numismatics* 11, no. 2 (October 1876): 33.

481. 7th and Filbert Streets, Philadelphia, Pennsylvania, USA, 1907 and August 1911.

Type of find: Excavation of the First United States Mint by Frank H. Stewart.

Date of site: 1792–1833.

Contents: 20 AE, 1 AR.

Description:

USA, ½¢ (2): draped bust ½ cent; 1826

USA, ½¢ planchets (3)

USA, silver center 1¢ planchets without the silver center (2)

USA, 1¢ (6): 1816; 1826; 1832; 1834; matron head; ND

USA, 1¢ planchet with edge lettered ONE HUNDRED FOR A DOLLAR, weighing 9 pennyweights

USA, 1¢ planchets (3)

USA, 1¢ scissel

USA, copper counterfeit of silver 5¢, 1795

USA, 50¢ planchet

USA, copper counterfeit of $5, 1804

Disposition: the 1907 finds (the 6 copper cents) were given to the Congress Hall Collection, Philadelphia, Pennsylvania, USA.

Bibliography: Cotter, Roberts, and Parrington 1992, 194; Stewart 1924, 118, 119, 158, 160, 162.

482. Amherst Island, Ontario, Canada, May 1898.

Type of find: Single find.

Contents: 1 AE.

Description: Ireland, token, "Associated Irish miners arms," on one side; picture of Saint

Patrick on the other, 1792

Disposition: Found while plowing on the farm of C. Morrow.

Bibliography: Joseph Hooper, "Hooper's Restrikes," *Numismatist* 11, no. 5 (May 1898): 132.

483. Site of an old Creek town in Alabama, USA, 1929.

Type of find: Single find.

Contents: 1 AR.

Description: USA, George Washington Indian Peace Medal showing only an eagle on globe, made of silver backed by wood

Disposition: State of Alabama Department of Archives and History.

Bibliography: Prucha 1971, 88.

484. Nutley, New Jersey, USA, January 1898.

Type of find: Hoard.

Date of deposit: 1792.

Container: Leather pouch.

Contents: 164 AR.

Description: Spanish colonies, 8 reales
German states, Hesse-Cassel, thalers?
The coins were contained in a leather pouch found beneath a tree stump. The leather pouch fell apart into dust when handled. The coins were described as "coins of Spanish and Hessian type."

Disposition: Found by Emil Schneider, an aged German who then managed the Hotel du Feurbach, better known as the "Fire Box," at the terminal of Washington Avenue in Nutley.

Bibliography: "With the Editor: Coins in a Tree Stump," *Numismatist* 11, no. 2 (February 1898): 53 (citing the *New York Journal.*)

485. Fernanda, Florida, USA, April 1929.

Type of find: Hoard.

Date of deposit: 1793.

Contents: 512 AE, AR.

Description: Great Britain, halfpence
Spanish colonies, 8 reales
Dates ranged from 1683 to 1793.

Disposition: Found in the backyard of W. H. Schreck.

Bibliography: "Schreck has Prolific Back Yard," *Numismatist* 42, no. 4 (April 1929): 251.

486. Flower Hill, Long Island, New York, USA, November 1939.

Type of find: Single find.

Contents: 1 AR.

Description: Spanish colonies, Charles IV, 8 reales, México, 1793FM
Dug up in the ruins of the old village of Flower Hill, Long Island. The area had been the site of the Flower Hill Post Office, David Davis's general store, and David Ireland's tavern. The coin is thought to have been lost by one of the customers of David Ireland's tavern.

Disposition: Found by a laborer, Knut Jorgensen, while collecting the granite stones that originally formed a collar of an old well. Walter Uhl, the developer and builder, said that he would present the coin to the Public Library at Port Washington, Long Island. Uhl may have changed his mind or the coin may have subsequently been lost, for the coin could not be located at the Public Library in 2007.

Bibliography: "Digs up 1793 'Piece of 8.' Worker on Flower Hill Development Unearths Spanish Coin," *New York Times*, November 5, 1939, Sec. 11, 1.

"Ancient Coin Found By Laborer Is To Be Donated To Library," *Port Washington (NY) News,* November 10, 1939, 4–5 (courtesy of Francesca Pitaro).

Numismatic Scrapbook Magazine 5, no. 12 (December 1939): 576.

"Digs Up Piece-of-Eight," *Numismatist* 52, no. 12 (December 1939): 1012.

Francesca Pitaro, Consulting Archivist, Port Washington Public Library, letter to John M. Kleeberg, March 19, 2007.

487. Tupelo, Mississippi, USA, 1956.

Type of find: Funerary deposit.

Contents: 1 AR.

Description: USA, George Washington Indian Peace Medal, 1793, hallmarked JL

Bibliography: Prucha 1971, 85.

488. Near Greenville, Augusta County, Virginia, USA, spring 1974–77.

Type of find: Archaeological excavation of Liberty Hall Academy, which grew into Washington and Lee University.

Date of site: 1793–1803.

Contents: 1 AE, 3 AR.

Description:
Spain, 2 reales (cross pistareen), eighth cut
USA, 1¢, 1793, basal state
USA, 50¢, 1801
Spanish colonies, real, post-1772 type

Bibliography: McDaniel 1977, 145, 153.

489. Fort York, Toronto, Ontario, Canada, 1987–93.

Type of find: Archaeological excavation.

Date of use of the site as a fortress: 1793–1871.

Date of first period (establishment of fort through War of 1812): 1793–1815.

Contents: 15 AE, 2 AR.

Description:
Great Britain, George III, farthing, 1806–7
Great Britain, George III, farthing, 1806 (2)
Great Britain, farthing size coin, possibly a British eighteenth century token
Great Britain, George II, halfpenny, 1750
Great Britain, George II, halfpence (2)
Great Britain, George III, halfpence (2)
Ireland, George III, halfpenny, 1781
Ireland, Camac, Kyan and Camac token, 1791
France, sol, 1792
USA, Connecticut, copper, 1785–88 (2) (see comment below)
USA, New Jersey, copper, 1786–88
Spanish colonies, Charles III, ½ real, mint unknown
Spanish colonies, Charles III, ½ real, México
One of the Connecticut coppers was found in the destruction layer from the Battle of York of 1813.

Bibliography: Spittal 1993, 244–53.

490. Waltham, Massachusetts, USA, January 1894.

Type of find: Hoard.

Date of deposit: 1794.

Container: Bag.

Contents: 400 AR.

Description: Spanish colonies, 8 reales (400)

"Two ancient watches, a pearl necklace, a diamond pin, several gold rings besides other jewelry of the best material and workmanship, several old letters and documents and a bag of Spanish coins valued at $400. The whole find aggregated in value $3,000 at least and to all appearances had been secreted fully one hundred years."

Reported by O. W. Page, Secretary of the American Numismatic Association, who lived in Waltham, Massachusetts.

Bibliography: "Personal and Local," *Numismatist* 7, no. 1 (January 1894): 54.

491. Asbury Park, New Jersey, USA, May 1950.

Type of find: Hoard.

Date of deposit: 1794.

Container: Leather pouch.

Contents: 35 AR and AV.

Description:
  Great Britain, guineas
  France, écus
  Spanish colonies, 8 reales
  Spanish, French, and English coins, dated 1702 to 1794. Denominations are an educated guess. The coins were in a leather pouch, which was badly decayed.

Disposition: Discovered when a steam shovel excavating a new outdoor swimming pool next to the Berkeley-Carteret Hotel brought the coins to the surface. Found by Joseph Barr, the municipal superintendant of maintenance for the city of Asbury Park. He said the coins would be sent to the American Museum of Natural History (did he mean the American Numismatic Society?) to determine the value.

Bibliography: "Cache of Old Coins Found. Discovery Revives Legends of Pirate Treasure in Jersey," *New York Times*, May 17, 1950, 31.

492. Upper Sackville, Halifax County, Nova Scotia, Canada, June 1959.

Type of find: Hoard.
Date of deposit: 1794.
Contents: 200+ AR.
Description:
  Spanish colonies, 2 reales (30)
  Spanish colonies, 4 reales (20)
  Spanish colonies, 8 reales (150)
  Spanish colonies, mostly 8 reales, although 4 reales and 2 reales were also found, from the mints of México, Lima, and Potosí, dated 1752–94.

Disposition: Found on a lot on which is built one of the district's earliest houses, dating from about 1780. George Huskins was preparing to build a new house when the bulldozer turned them up. Held by the Royal Canadian Mounted Police for six months, and then returned to the finders.

Bibliography: Morris 1960.
  Edward Morris, "The Upper Sackville Hoard," *Canadian Numismatic Journal* 5, no. 5 (May 1960): 229.

493. New Kent County, Virginia, USA, April 2001.

Type of find: Single find.
Contents: 1 AR.
Description: USA, silver 5¢, 1794
Bibliography: Kays 2001, 2179.

494. Harrison Township, Gloucester County, New Jersey, USA, July 1866.

Type of find: Single find.
Contents: 1 AE.
Description: Great Britain, gilt copper medal dated 1792, commemorating Lord Cornwallis's defeat of Tippu Sultan in the Third Anglo-Mysore War, concluded by the Treaty of Sriranjapattana. Obverse inscription: Car. Marchio Cornwallis Strategus Accerimus [Charles, Marquis Cornwallis, Most Brilliant General]; Reverse inscription: Fas sit parcere hosti [It is proper to be merciful to the enemy] / Sultano Tippoo Devicto Obsides Recipit MDCCXCII [After defeating Tippu Sultan, he took hostages for good behavior, 1792]
  The medal, although dated 1792, would have been issued in 1794 or later, when Cornwallis was created a Marquis.

Bibliography: "An Interesting Relic," *American Journal of Numismatics* 1, no. 4 (July 1866): 28 (citing the *Philadelphia Inquirer*).

495. Fredericksburg, Virginia, USA, December 1862.

Type of find: Single find.
Contents: 1 AR.
Description: Spanish colonies, Charles IV, 2 reales, México, 1795FM, holed
Disposition: Found by Isaac Bradley while

on duty at Fredericksburg. Acquired by Theodore Venn Buttrey, Jr.; donated by him to the American Numismatic Society in New York, item number 1967.221.29.

Bibliography: small label attached to edge hole of the coin, with a string.

496. Fredericksburg, Virginia, USA, 1985–1995.

Type of find: Single finds from colonial contexts.

Contents: 1 PB, 12 AR.

Description:

Spain, Philip V, real (½ pistareen), Segovia, cut half

Spain, 2 reales (pistareen), 1737, cut quarter

Spain, 2 reales (pistareen), Seville, 1722J

Spanish colonies, ½ real, México, 1782FF

Spanish colonies, ½ real, México, 1785FF, holed

Spanish colonies, 2 reales, México, 1780FF

Spanish colonies, 8 reales, México, 1772FF, high quality lead counterfeit

Spanish colonies, real, Lima, 1787MJ

Spanish colonies, 2 reales, Lima, 1775MJ

Spanish colonies, 2 reales, Lima, 1789IJ

Spanish colonies, real, Potosí, 1780PR

Spanish colonies, 2 reales, Potosí, 1769JR

Spanish colonies, Charles III, pillar 2 reales, cut quarter

Disposition: Found by metal detectorists. Acquired by Thomas A. Kays.

Bibliography: Kays 1996, 1637–45.

497. Civil War site near Fredericksburg, Virginia, USA, May 1993.

Type of find: Single finds.

Date of deposit: 1795.

Contents: 3 AE, 6 AR.

Description:

Spain, 2 reales (pistareens), 5 quarter cuts, minimum of 4 different coins out of the five, the one seen was Seville, 1737P

British colonies, Virginia, halfpence

USA, 1¢, 1850s

USA, silver 5¢, 1794 or 1795, weighed 0.4 grams, third cut

Disposition: Found by a metal detectorist. The coins were sold by Claude Murphy of Winston-Salem, North Carolina. 1 purchased by Robert D. Leonard, Jr.

Bibliography: Robert D. Leonard, Jr., conversation with John M. Kleeberg, May 1993.

498. West Brattleboro, Vermont, USA, fall 1985.

Type of find: Single find.

Contents: 1 AE.

Description: USA, 1¢, 1795, probably variety S-77

Disposition: Found by a metal detectorist, Francis A. Nokes.

Bibliography: Treasure Found (Fall 1985): 38–39.

499. Sackets Harbor, New York, USA, 1960.

Type of find: Archaeological excavation.

Date of site: 1790s?

Contents: 1 AR.

Description: Spain, 2 reales (pistareen), cut quarter

Disposition: Found by Lieutenant J. Duncan Campbell.

Bibliography: Peterson 1962, 582–85.

500. Leedstown, Virginia, USA, 1936.

Type of find: Single find.

Contents: 1 AR.

Description: Spanish colonies, 8 reales, cut quarter

Disposition: Found by J. Paul Hudson.

Bibliography: Peterson 1962, 582–85.

501. 139 Cedar Street, New York, New York, USA, April 1894.

Type of find: Hoard.
Date of deposit: 1792.
Container: Three-legged iron pot.
Contents: 3+ AE, 2+ AR.
Description:
  Rome, Nero, with reverse figure of Securitas
  Great Britain, halfpence
  Spanish colonies, Charles IV, 2 reales
  Spanish colonies, 8 reales (called "a silver coin the size of a United States dollar")
  The Roman coin had the inscription IMP NERO CAESAR P MAX TR P P P; reverse, figure of justice, SC, SECUR. It was about the size of a 2¢ piece (i.e., 23 millimeters in diameter), but thicker. The reverse type was a woman reclining on a stone couch, holding a staff in her right hand, and surrounded by hieroglyphics.
Disposition: An iron pot containing coins was found by workmers excavating the foundations for the extension to the electrical exchange, 139 Cedar Street. It mostly contained American coins of the revolutionary period; the workers retained most of it for themselves, and refused to give the hoard to the owner of the property, John Petit. Petit was only able to obtain 3 coins, including one of the Roman coins.
Bibliography: "Treasure-Trove in Cedar-St. Italians unearth an iron pot containing ancient and valuable coins," *New York Tribune*, May 1, 1894, 4.
"Coin of Nero in Cedar Street. Workmen Find a Pot of Old Money and Carry Away All Except Three Pieces," *New York Times*, May 1, 1894, 8.

502. Port Chester, New York, USA, December 1926.

Type of find: Single find.
Contents: 1 AE.
Description: USA, 1¢, 1796
Bibliography: "Digs Up 1796 Penny in Port Chester," *New York Times*, December 5, 1926, 20.

503. Lawrence, Kansas, USA, March 1870.

Type of find: Funerary deposit.
Date of deposit: 1796.
Contents: 2 AR.
Description:
  British colonies, George III, Indian Peace Medal (king on obverse, coat of arms on reverse)
  USA, George Washington, Indian Peace Medal (Second Presidency, 1796—Seasons' Medal)
  The two medals were connected by a gold chain; found by a farmer while building a fence.
Bibliography: Quid Nunc, "A Numismatic 'What is it?'" *American Journal of Numismatics* 4, no. 11 (March 1870): 86.

504. Holgate, southernmost tip of Long Beach Island, New Jersey, USA, 1956–76.

Type of find: Shipwreck.
Ship: Unidentified.
Sank: 1797.
Contents: AR.
Description:
  Spain, 2 reales (cross pistareens), including one from Segovia
  Spanish colonies, 8 reales
Disposition: Jack Irwin.
  Dr. Jack Irwin of North Beach, New Jersey, found Spanish silver coins on the beach after winter storms for over twenty years. He may have also found copper coins. His best year was 1962. The dates ran from 1710 to 1797. The photograph accompanying the article shows that he found many cross pistareens.

Bibliography: Edward Brown, "Long Beach Island: Monetary Dividends," *New York Times*, August 29, 1976, Sec. 11 (New Jersey), 14.

505. Salem, Massachusetts, USA, 1863.

Type of find: Hoard.

Date of deposit: December 1797.

Container: Bag.

Contents: 1,000 AE.

Description: USA, 1¢, 1796 and 1797 (1,000)

Included varieties S-104 (rusted dies only), S-118, S-119, S-123, S-135, S-136, and S-137.

The mint at the time distributed cents in bags of 1,000.

Commonly called the "Goodhue-Nichols Find."

Obtained from the mint by Benjamin Goodhue in December 1797, who gave them to his daughters. They and their descendants preserved them, and then the hoard went to David Nichols of Gallows Hill, near Salem, Massachusetts, who married into the Goodhue family. Nichols passed out many at face value. Nichols also began selling them to coin dealers around 1863.

The following appeared in the *American Journal of Numismatics* of July 1875: "About 1856–7 Mr. A. F. Walcott of Salem, Mass., a young collector of coins, was presented with a bag of 'bright cents,' by a relative, Mr. William Pickman of that city. They had been laid away for very many years—quite forgotten—and when found were as bright as the day they were coined. Of the Mint series there were those of 1795, 1796, 1797, and 1798, and 1803, also a few Massachusetts *Indian* cents. Mr. Walcott exchanged them with various collectors and at the Mint, where they were looked upon with suspicion and inquiries made as to where they came from, &c., &c. We remember that several collectors looked upon them doubtingly, thinking that some expert had been making them. The prices paid for some of these pieces at the present time would astonish our friend if he were in this part of the world." Note that Walcott and Pickman were also associated with the distribution of the mint-red 1749 halfpence (*NFA* 303).

Frossard commented in January 1882: "January 23 and 24....Catalogue by Mr. W. E. Woodward (44th sale). We note No. 972 and '73, the former a Jefferson head cent, now extremely rare, said to be in nearly fine condition, the latter a '96 Draped bust cent from the Nichols hoard."

John Robinson of Salem said in 1917: "David Nichols, living near Gallows Hill, would occasionally open the bag of mint-bright cents of 1796 and 1797 and give us one of each. The lot came, it was said, from the Hon. Benjamin Goodhue, who received them in part pay for his services in the U. S. Senate. As I remember them at the time [*viz.*, the 1860s] there were about 50 or 60 of each date in the bag."

Bibliography: Breen 1952, 9–12 (Breen Hoards IV); Robinson 1917, 329.

"Editorial," *American Journal of Numismatics* 10, no. 1 (July 1875): 24.

Edouard Frossard, "Coin Sales," *Numisma* 6, no. 2 (March 1882): [5].

506. In the mountains, near Powers, Oregon, USA, June 1994.

Type of find: Single finds.

Date of deposit: 1790s.

Contents: 2 B.

Description:

China, Kangxi, cash, mint illegible [1662–1723]

China, Qianlong, cash, Board of works, Beijing [1763–96]

Bibliography: Correspondence to American Numismatic Society Curator Dr. Michael L. Bates, June 15, 1994.

507. Off Cape Henlopen, Delaware, USA, summers 1984, 1985, 1986.

Type of find: Shipwreck.

Ship: HMS *De Braak*.

Sank: May 25, 1798. Departed Plymouth, England, May 1, 1798, and subsequently stopped at Falmouth, England, and Cork, Ireland.

Contents: ca. 500 AR, ca. 250 AV.

Description:

Great Britain, guineas (34)

Spanish colonies, 8 reales, pillar and bust dollars (500)

Spanish colonies, Charles IV, 8 escudos, México (90): 1792 (10); 1793 (10); 1794 (10); 1795 (10); 1796 (10); ND (40)

Spanish colonies, Charles IV, 8 escudos, Lima (90): 1792 (10); 1793 (10); 1794 (10); 1795 (10); 1796 (10); ND (40)

Portuguese colonies, Brazil, 6,400 reis (30): 1794; ND (29)

The numbers of each denomination are educated guesses.

Disposition: 650 of the coins recovered were seen and appraised by James Lamb of Christie's. The coins are now owned by the State of Delaware.

Bibliography: Shomette 1993, 131, 212, 222, 223, 225, 255, 262, 282.

508. New Bedford, Massachusetts, USA, January 1914.

Type of find: Hoard.

Date of deposit: 1798.

Contents: 11 AE.

Description: Included:

Great Britain, halfpenny, 1774

USA, Fugio 1¢, 1787

USA, 1¢, 1797

USA, 1¢, 1798

Bibliography: Bowers 1997, 95.

509. Lewis's Tavern, Albany, New York, USA, 1972.

Type of find: Archaeological excavation.

Date of site: 1784–1810;

Date of earliest coin: 1798.

Contents: 1 AE.

Description: USA, 1¢, 1798

Disposition: New York State Bureau of Historic Sites Collection, Peebles Island, New York, USA.

Bibliography: Hoover 2007 (providing inventory of New York State Bureau of Historic Sites Collections, Peebles Island, New York, as of August 16, 2005).

510. Mission San Luis Rey, next to San Diego, California, USA, 1955–60.

Type of find: Archaeological excavation.

Date of site: 1798–1846.

Contents: 1 B, 5 AR.

Description:

Spain, Catholic religious medal

Spanish colonies, ½ reales, México (4): 1772; 1817–18 (3)

Bolivia, ½ sol, 1830

Denominations and mint are educated guesses, as is the material; the article only provides dates of coins and refers to type of coins in general terms ("Spain, Bolivia").

Bibliography: Soto 1961, 34, 36.

511. West Indies, December 1887.

Type of find: Hoard.

Date of deposit: 1799.

Contents: 8,500 AV.

Description: Spanish colonies, 8 escudos, all dated before 1800 (8,500)

Disposition: The coins were received at the Assay Office on Wall Street to be melted. The Assay Office did not reveal the name of the depositor, although the shipment is known to have come from the West Indies. The coins were worth $17.16 apiece.

Bibliography: "Numismatic Notes," *Coin Collector's Journal* 13 (whole no. 147) (February 1888): 31.

512. Magdalena, Jalisco, Mexico, July 1930.

Type of find: Hoard.
Date of deposit: 1800?
Container: Pot.
Contents: 3,000 AV.
Description: Spanish colonies, probably 8 escudos (3,000)
Disposition: Plowed up by a farmer, Cresencio Avila, in Magdalena.
Bibliography: "Mexican Receives Farm Grant, Plows Up $50,000 Pot of Gold," *New York Times*, July 15, 1930, 7.
"Mexican Plows up Pot of Gold," *Numismatist* 43, no. 9 (September 1930): 569.

513. South side of Martha's Vineyard, Massachusetts, USA, May 1833.

Type of find: Hoard.
Date of deposit: 1800?
Container: Bag.
Contents: 2,000–3,000 AR.
Description: Spanish colonies, 8 reales (2,000–3,000)
$2,000–$3,000 worth of silver coin (probably Spanish colonies 8 reales, although not described in detail) found by two persons plowing a field; the coins seemed to have been tied up in a bag.
Bibliography: "Brief Notices," *Niles' National Register* (Baltimore, MD), May 25, 1833, 199.

514. Germantown, Pennsylvania, USA, June 1833.

Type of find: Hoard.
Date of deposit: 1800?
Container: Pot.
Contents: AR.
Description: Spanish colonies, 8 reales, probably México
"A long concealed pot of Spanish dollars has been discovered in digging a cellar for a house."
Bibliography: "Brief Notices," *Niles Weekly Register* (Baltimore, MD), June 8, 1833, 235.

515. Northborough, Massachusetts, USA, September 1839.

Type of find: Hoard.
Date of deposit: 1800?
Container: Metal kettle.
Contents: 400 AR, 200 AV.
Description:
Great Britain, guineas (200)
Spanish colonies, 8 reales (400)
Three pecks of old coin: one third gold, two thirds silver. Amounts, coins, and denominations are educated guesses. The coins were found by Lewis Brigham while digging for woodchucks.
Bibliography: "Chronicle: Hidden Treasure," *Niles' National Register* (Baltimore, MD), October 5, 1839, 96.
"Hidden Treasure," *Worcester (MA) Palladium*, October 9, 1839 (reference courtesy of Q. David Bowers).

516. Coney Island, Brooklyn, New York, USA, January 1840.

Type of find: Hoard.
Date of deposit: 1800?
Contents: 1,000+ AR.

Description: Spanish colonies, 8 reales (1,000) $1,000 in silver found buried on the beach. Probably Spanish colonies, 8 reales, although not described in detail.

Bibliography: "Chronicle: Hidden Treasure," Niles' *National Register* (Baltimore, MD), June 11, 1840, 320.

517. Gloucester and Salem Counties, New Jersey, USA, 1999.

Type of find: Single finds.

Contents: 43 AE.

Description:

Sweden, ½ skilling, 1802–9
England, Charles II, farthing
England, William III, farthing
Great Britain, George II, farthing
Great Britain, unidentifiable farthings (2)
England, William and Mary, halfpenny, 1694
England, William III type 3 halfpenny [1699–1701]
Great Britain, George I, halfpenny
Great Britain, George II, halfpence, young head (2)
Great Britain, George II, halfpenny, [1740–45]
Great Britain, George II, halfpenny, 1750
Great Britain, George II, old head, halfpenny [1740–54]
Great Britain, George III, counterfeit halfpence, including one with M counterstamp (3)
Great Britain, George III, halfpence, 1799 (3)
Great Britain, George III, halfpence, 1806–7 (7)
Great Britain, unidentifiable halfpence (8)
Great Britain, George III, twopence, 1797 (2)
Ireland, Wood's Hibernia farthing, holed
Ireland, George III, halfpenny
Ireland, George III, halfpenny, 1766 or 1769
Ireland, George III, halfpence, 1805 (2)
France, ½ sol

Disposition: Found by a metal detectorist in southern New Jersey.

Bibliography: Gredesky 2000, 2063–64.

518. New Brunswick, New Jersey, USA, January 1899.

Type of find: Hoard.

Date of deposit: 1800.

Contents: 75 AR, 25 AV.

Description:

Spanish colonies, 8 reales, in very fine condition (75)
Spanish colonies, 2 and 4 escudos (25)
Found while digging a foundation where the old post office stood. Reported by Jacob Weigel.

Bibliography: "With the Editor and Advertisers," *Numismatist* 12, no. 1 (January 1899): 17.

519. Lafayette, South Christian, Kentucky, USA, July 1900.

Type of find: Hoard.

Date of deposit: 1800?

Container: Old stone pitcher.

Contents: 1,000 AV.

Description: Great Britain, guineas (1,000)
The gold amounted to $3,700.

Disposition: A buggy house had covered the coins. The coins were plowed up by Thomas Johnson, a prominent planter.

Bibliography: Joseph Hooper, "Hooper's Restrikes," *Numismatist* 13, no. 7 (July 1900): 184.

520. Mantoloking, New Jersey, USA, September 1949.

Type of find: Shipwreck.

Ship: Unidentified.

Sank: Ca. 1800.

Contents: 100+ B.

Description:
Great Britain, George III, jeton modeled after a ½ guinea in brass, 1789 (11)
Great Britain, George III, jeton modeled after a guinea in brass, 1789 (7)

Disposition: Found by Gay Crampton and her family on the beach in a blob of resin. One person from Philadelphia claimed the recovery of 93 ½ guinea and guinea jetons.
"Mrs. D. Crampton of Montclair, New Jersey, gave a very interesting talk concerning the 'treasure and gold coins' recently found by her daughter on the beach at Mantoloking, New Jersey." Exhibits included: "Mrs. D. Crampton: Treasure trove found at Mantoloking, New Jersey." (minutes of the New York Numismatic Club, October 14, 1949, written up by Vernon L. Brown)

Bibliography: Nesmith 1958a, 21–23; Nesmith and Potter 1968, 53–54 (p. 54 has a photograph of the finds).
"Treasure Seekers. Booty From Old Wrecks Found on Jersey Shore," *New York Times,* October 9, 1949, 18.
Vernon L. Brown, "Treasure (?) Chest Found," *Numismatic Scrapbook Magazine* 15, no. 10 (October 1949): 930.
"New York Numismatic Club, Minutes, October 14, 1949," *Numismatist* 66, no. 12 (December 1949): 745.

521. South of Punta Santa Elena, Ecuador, June 1872, and Guayaquil, Ecuador, May 1936.

Type of find: Shipwreck.

Ship: The Spanish frigate *Santa Leocadia,* departed Paita, Peru, bound for Panamá.

Sank: November 16, 1800.

Contents: AR.

Description:
Spanish colonies, 8 reales, 1799 (2)
Spanish colonies, 8 reales, Lima, 1800IJ (Thomas Sebring)
Spanish colonies, cob ½ reales, Potosí
Spanish colonies, cob reales, Potosí
Spanish colonies, cob 2 reales, Potosí
The ship was traveling from Peru to Panama, and carrying 2 million pesos in silver when she went down.

Disposition: Pickford says the ship was largely salvaged. Sedwick believes the modern salvage to be the contents of a small private purse and not part of the 2 million pesos in registered cargo.
In June 1872 the Wrecking Company, based in San Francisco, sent an expedition to the coast of Ecuador to raise the treasure from this shipwreck. The expedition reported back that they had located the treasure and had begun raising it.
In the spring of 1936, after a hard storm, 8 reales dated 1799 washed up onto the beach at Guayaquil.

Bibliography: Pickford 1994, 166; Sebring 2004, lot 1596; Sedwick and Sedwick 2007, 196 (Sedwick 55).
"The Treasure on the Sunken Spanish Frigate Leocadia," *New York Times,* 8 June 1872, 5.
"Lost Gold Tossed up by Tides," *New York Times Magazine,* May 17, 1936, Sec. 6, 22.

522. Alexandria, Virginia, USA, 1985–95.

Type of find: Single find.

Contents: 1 AR.

Description: Spanish colonies, 2 reales, México, 1799FM

Disposition: Found by a metal detectorist. Acquired by Thomas A. Kays.

Bibliography: Kays 1996, 1637–45.

523. Philadelphia, Pennsylvania, USA, November 1861.

Type of find: Single find.

Contents: 1 AE.

Description: USA, "Confederatio Americana Juvenus" [sic] medal (Betts 540)

Date of this medal unknown; might have been struck ca. 1800.

Bibliography: Betts 1894, 243–44. "Boston Numismatic Society," *Historical Magazine* 5 (November 1861): 340.

524. Greenwich, Connecticut, USA, July 1876.

Type of find: Hoard.

Date of deposit: 1800.

Container: Tin box.

Contents: 10 AR.

Description: Spanish colonies, 8 reales (10)

A tin box containing about ten dollars in silver coins (probably Spanish colonies 8 reales, although not so described), some of them dating back more than one hundred years.

Bibliography: "Buried Treasure," *American Journal of Numismatics* 11, no. 1 (July 1876), 15.

525. Trenton, New Jersey, USA, June 18, 1881.

Type of find: Single find.

Contents: 1 AV.

Description: USA, $10, 1800

Disposition: Found by workers while tearing down the old Van Sant mansion on Broad Street, Trenton.

Bibliography: "Items," *Coin Collector's Journal* 6 (whole no. 69) (August 1881): 126.

526. Near Les Cayes, Haiti, 2006.

Type of find: Hoard.

Date of deposit: 1800?

Contents: 500 AR.

Description: Spanish colonies, 8 reales (500)

Disposition: Carlos Jara M. bought 250 in two parcels; the dealer John Albright of Coral Gables, Florida, also purchased a few. As of 2008 pieces from this hoard are still being sold in Haiti from time to time.

Date of deposit is an educated guess.

Bibliography: Jara 2008.

527. Market Steet Bridge, Philadelphia, Pennsylvania, USA, April 1887.

Type of find: Foundation deposit.

Date of deposit: 1801.

Contents: 2 SN.

Description:

USA, George Washington medal by Manly (Baker 61)

Great Britain, George Washington medal by Westwood (Baker 80)

Also contained some coins, but they are not described.

Disposition: Frederick J. Amweg, C. E.; from him to the Numismatic and Antiquarian Society's exhibit in Memorial Hall, Fairmount Park.

Bibliography: "Two Washington Medals Taken from Bridge Pier," *Numismatist* 45, no. 1 (January 1932): 21–23.

528. Montserrat, August 1939.

Type of find: Hoard.

Date of deposit: 1785–1801.

Contents: 18–23 AR.

Description: 3 coins are known:

Spanish colonies, 8 reales, México, 1776, with three couped cross counterstamps for Montserrat

Spanish colonies, 8 reales, México, 1773, with inverted assayer's initals "FM"

Spanish colonies, 8 reales, México, 1777

Disposition: 3 coins (those listed above) bought by the American Numismatic Society; item numbers 1939.121.1–3.

Bibliography: American Numismatic Society accession records, coin records, and notes on the undersides of coin boxes.

529. 300 block, South Lee Street, Alexandria, Virginia, USA, 1985–95.
Type of find: Single find.
Contents: 1 AR.
Description: Spanish colonies, 2 reales, Lima, 1801IJ
Disposition: Found by a metal detectorist. Acquired by Thomas A. Kays.
Bibliography: Kays 1996, 1637–45.

530. Plaza de Mayo – San José, Buenos Aires, Argentina, June 1958.
Type of find: Hoard.
Date of deposit: 1801.
Contents: 174 AR.
Description: Spanish colonies, 8 reales, Potosí, 1801PP (174)
Bibliography: "Información General: Hallazgo de un 'Tesoro,'" *Boletín del Instituto Bonaerense de Numismática y Antigüedades* 7 (1959): 173–74.

531. 310 Cypress Street, Philadelphia, Pennsylvania, USA, 1976.
Type of find: Archaeological excavation.
Date of site: 1801–25.
Contents: 1 AE.
Description: USA, 1¢, 1801, with edge clip
Bibliography: Cotter, Roberts, and Parrington 1992, 182–83.

532. Independence Square, Philadelphia, Pennsylvania, USA, April 1876.
Type of find: Excavations.
Date of deposit: 1803?
Contents: 5+ AE, 1 AR, 2 AV.
Description:
  Russia, 5 roubles, 1796
  German states, Prussia, Frederick William, frederic d'or, date illegible
  Great Britain, halfpence, 1770s (2+)
  USA, 1¢ (3): 1796; 1798; 1803
  Spanish colonies, ½ real, 1778
Disposition: Found by workers breaking the ground when Independence Square was being improved in anticipation of the centennial celebrations. The relics were handed over to Commissioner Dixey by Jacob Jacoby, the superintendant of the work of improvement, and they were deposited in Dixey's office, Fifth and Walnut Streets. Cotter says that nearly 100 coins have been recovered from around Independence Square. They range from 1723 (presumably these are Wood's issues) to the 1900s and were minted by England, Ireland, Spain, France, the Netherlands and the United States, plus the state issues of the Confederation period.
Bibliography: Cotter, Roberts, and Parrington 1992, 116.
"Relics Dug Up in Independence Square," *American Journal of Numismatics* 10, no. 4 (April 1876): 77 (citing the *Philadelphia Press*).

533. Three Mile Run, near Somerville, New Jersey, USA, October 1923.
Type of find: Single find.
Contents: 1 AE.
Description: USA, 1¢, 1803
Disposition: Found by a lady digging potatoes.
Bibliography: "Coins found in odd Places," *Numismatist* 36, no. 10 (October 1923): 497.

534. Washington, DC, USA, January 1876.
Type of find: Single find.
Contents: 1 AE.
Description: Great Britain, George Washington medal by Eccleston in copper, 1805 (Baker 85)
Disposition: Dug up by street workers.
Bibliography: "Eccleston Medal Exhumed," *American Journal of Numismatics* 10, no. 3 (January 1876): 62.

535. Bunkie, Avoyelles Parish, Louisiana, USA, March 4, 1930.

Type of find: Hoard.

Date of deposit: 1805.

Container: Iron pot.

Contents: 3,000 AR.

Description:

Spain, 2 reales (pistareens)

Spanish colonies, 8 reales

The coins were dated from 1763 to 1805; presumably the 1763 coin is a coin of lower denomination than 8 reales, possibly a pistareen, since the pillar dollars quickly dropped out of circulation after 1772. Fractional coins, especially pistareens, continued to circulate into the nineteenth century. The newspaper report said that the hoard included a silver dollar bearing the date 1804 with the likeness of George Washington, but this is probably an error for a Spanish colonies 8 reales of 1804 with Charles IV, who does have a distant resemblance to George Washington.

Disposition: Plowed up by Forest Normand of Avoyelles Parish.

Bibliography: Bowers 1997, 405; Saxon 1930, 296.

"What Others Say," *Numismatic Scrapbook Magazine* 24, no. 3 (March 1958): 475.

536. Bell's Jetty, Dominica, 1923.

Type of find: Hoard.

Date of deposit: 1805.

Contents: 3 AV.

Description:

Portuguese colonies, Brazil, Joseph I, 6,400 reis, Rio de Janeiro, 1772, counterfeit, counterstamped with 20 over eagle counterstamp of Martinique

Portuguese colonies, Brazil, Joseph I, 6,400 reis, Rio de Janeiro, 1775, regulated by the North American jeweler IH and by West Indies script B, endowed with a plug, plug removed by Guadeloupe, finally given a 20 over eagle counterstamp of Martinique

Portuguese colonies, Brazil, Joseph I, 6,400 reis, Rio de Janeiro, counterstamped by the jewelers G (eye) once and by WB three times

Disposition: American Numismatic Society; item numbers 1923.40.2, 1923.40.3, and 1927.143.1.

Bibliography: Gordon 1987, 101, 108.

537. Confluence of Potlatch Creek and Clearwater River, Idaho, near Arrow, Idaho, USA, 1899.

Type of find: Single find.

Contents: 1 AR.

Description: USA, Thomas Jefferson Indian Peace Medal, 1801, 55 millimeters

Disposition: Found when a rail line was constructed through nearby Kendrick. Given to the American Museum of Natural History, New York, New York by Edward H. Adams, catalog number 5012865; for many years believed lost because the medal was erroneously described as being in the American Numismatic Society, but it was relocated in 2002.

Bibliography: Gunselman and Sprague 2003 (includes information about 2002 location of the medal); Loeffelbein 2003, 29 (erroneously states that the medal is lost).

538. Goat Island, Columbia River, Washington, USA, 1891.

Type of find: Single find.

Contents: 1 AR.

Description: USA, Thomas Jefferson Indian Peace Medal, 1801, 55 millimeters

Disposition: Oregon Historical Society, Portland, Oregon.

Bibliography: Gunselman and Sprague 2003.

539. Nebraska, USA, 1971.
Type of find: Single find.
Contents: 1 AR.
Description: USA, Thomas Jefferson Indian Peace Medal, 1801, 55 millimeters
Disposition: Huntington Library, Pasadena, California, USA.
Bibliography: Gunselman and Sprague 2003.

540. Fort Clatsop, Oregon, USA, October 1834.
Type of find: Single find.
Contents: 1 AR.
Description: USA, Thomas Jefferson Indian Peace Medal, 1801
Disposition: This medal can no longer be located today.
Bibliography: Gunselman and Sprague 2003.

541. Minnesota, USA, 1965.
Type of find: Single find.
Contents: 1 AR.
Description: USA, Thomas Jefferson Indian Peace Medal, 1801, 105 millimeters
Disposition: Jefferson National Expansion Memorial Museum, Saint Louis, Missouri.
Bibliography: Gunselman and Sprague 2003.

542. Saint Louis, Missouri, USA, 1965.
Type of find: Single find.
Contents: 1 AR.
Description: USA, Thomas Jefferson Indian Peace Medal, 1801, 77 millimeters
Disposition: State of Idaho Historical Society, Boise, Idaho.
Bibliography: Gunselman and Sprague 2003.

543. Along the Milk River, Montana, USA, 1890s.
Type of find: Single find.
Contents: 1 AR.
Description: USA, Thomas Jefferson Indian Peace Medal, 1801
Disposition: Found by a sheepherder who called it "the biggest silver dollar he had ever seen," and traded it for a plug of tobacco to a cowhand; the cowhand then transferred it to his boss, the rancher R. C. Sinclair. Sinclair moved to Kendrick, Idaho, in the mid-1890s. In 1905 he displayed his medal at the Lewis and Clark Centennial and American Pacific Exposition and Oriental Fair in Portland, Oregon. The medal has not been traced since.
Bibliography: Loeffelbein 2003, 29.

544. Hillsboro, Ohio, USA, October 1962.
Type of find: Hoard.
Date of deposit: 1805.
Contents: 15 AV.
Description: USA, probably $5, 1795–1805 (15) Denomination not given, but $5 is the most likely one for a U.S. gold coin of this period.
Bibliography: Numismatic Scrapbook Magazine 28, no. 10 (October 1962): 2791.

545. Mandan Territory, South Dakota, USA, 1971.
Type of find: Single find.
Date of deposit: 1806.
Contents: 1 AR.
Description: USA, Thomas Jefferson Indian Peace Medal, 1801, 105 millimeters
Thought to be the medal given to Chief Sheheke, "Big White," who traveled to Washington, DC, where he died in 1806.
Disposition: Last known owner Kenneth O. Leonard, Garrison, North Dakota.
Bibliography: Gunselman and Sprague 2003.

546. Hastings, Nebraska, USA, March 1926.
Type of find: Funerary deposits.
Date of deposit: 1806.
Contents: 4 AR.

Description:
Indian Peace Medals found in Pawnee graves:
Spanish colonies, Indian Peace Medal, 1797, made by placing a Spanish colonies 8 reales of 1797 in the center of a chased silver plate
Spanish colonies, Indian Peace Medal, dated 1778
British colonies, Indian Peace Medal, young bust of George III on obverse, arms on reverse, dated 1762
USA, Thomas Jefferson, Indian Peace Medal, large size
USA, Thomas Jefferson, Indian Peace Medal, small size
Found by A. T. Hill on his farm, which was formerly a gravesite of the Pawnees.

Disposition: Nebraska Historical Society.

Bibliography: Gunselman and Sprague 2003; Prucha 1971, 12.
"Medals found in Pawnee Indian Graves," *Numismatist* 39, no. 3 (March 1926): 139–40.

547. Schuyler Mansion, 32 Catherine Street, Albany, New York, USA, 1969.

Type of find: Archaeological excavation.

Date of site: 1761–1804

Date of earliest coin: 1807.

Contents: 1 AE.

Description: USA, 1¢, 1807

Disposition: New York State Bureau of Historic Sites Collection, Peebles Island, New York, USA.

Bibliography: Hoover 2007 (providing inventory of New York State Bureau of Historic Sites Collections, Peebles Island, New York, as of August 16, 2005).

548. Old Mill Site, Northern Virginia, USA, summer 1994.

Type of find: Hoard.

Date of deposit: 1808.

Contents: 21 AR.

Description: Spanish colonies, 8 reales, México, 1774–1800 (21)

Bibliography: Kays 1995, 1488; Kays 1996, 1637–45.

549. Cameron Street, Alexandria, Virginia, USA, 1985–95.

Type of find: Single find.

Contents: 1 AR.

Description: Spanish colonies, 2 reales, México, 1808TH

Disposition: Found by a metal detectorist. Acquired by Thomas A. Kays.

Bibliography: Kays 1996, 1637–45.

550. Lima, Michigan, USA, August 1897.

Type of find: Single find.

Contents: 1 AE.

Description: USA, ½¢, 1809

Disposition: Found by Art Gurrin.

Bibliography: "With the Editor," *Numismatist* 10, no. 8 (August 1897): 139.

551. Mansion House, Philadelphia, Pennsylvania, USA, 1859.

Type of find: Foundation deposit.

Date of deposit: 1809.

Contents: AE.

Description: USA, 1¢, 1809
"The most perfect specimens known, taken from the cornerstone of the Mansion House in Philadelphia by Mr. Hoxie when it was demolished."

Disposition: Mr. Hoxie.

Bibliography: Dickeson 1865, 209.

552. Westhampton Beach, Long Island, New York, USA, June 23, 1898.

Type of find: Hoard.

Date of deposit: 1809.

Contents: 5 AE, 1 AR.

Description:
England, Edward II, silver penny
USA, Connecticut?, copper, 1786
USA, Fugio 1¢, 1787
USA, ½¢ (2): 1806; 1809
Unidentified copper coin

Bibliography: "A Find of Old Coins," *Brooklyn Daily Eagle*, June 24, 1898, 4.

553. Clifton Plantation, western end of the Island of New Providence, Bahamas, 1998–99.

Type of find: Foundation deposit.

Date of site: 1809–23.

Contents: 2 AE.

Description: British colonies, Bahamas, penny, 1806, with EXPULSIS PIRATIS RESTITUTA COMMERCIA (once the pirates had been expelled, commerce was restored) (2)

Disposition: Pompey Museum of Slavery, downtown Nassau, Bahamas.

Bibliography: Wilkie and Farnsworth 2005.

554. Fort Adams, Mississippi, USA, summer 1960.

Type of find: Archaeological excavation.

Date of site: 1799–1810.

Contents: 1 AR.

Description: Spanish colonies, 2 reales, 1773, transverse quarter cut

Disposition: Unearthed by Colonel J. Duncan Campbell and Edgar M. Howell.

Bibliography: Peterson 1962, 582–85.

555. East of Jamaica, 2001.

Type of find: Shipwreck.

Ship: Unidentified. Called the "Coconut Wreck," because the site is strewn with coconuts.

Sank: 1809–10.

Container: Wrapped in a newspaper printed in Jamaica on August 6, 1809 and placed in a French gold box.

Contents: 1,500 AR, 13 AV. Shipwreck.

Description:
France, louis, 1788A
France, double louis, 1789K
Portugal, 4 escudos, 1779, clipped
Portugal or Portuguese colonies, 4 escudos or 6,400 reis (retained by the salvors)
Spanish colonies, 8 reales, México, through 1809 (a guess at the identity of the 1,500 silver coins)
Spanish colonies, 2 escudos, 1761JV, Bogotá
Portuguese colonies, Brazil, 6,400 reis, 1754 Bahia, regulated by F&G (Fletcher and Gardiner)
Portuguese colonies, Brazil, 6,400 reis, 1766 Rio, regulated by script B (John Burger), F&G (Fletcher & Gardiner), G (eye) (West Indies regulator Guy?), and 22/Eagle (Martinique 1805)
Portuguese colonies, Brazil, 6,400 reis (6): 1747 Bahia (clipped around); contemporary counterfeit 1762 Rio; 1765 Rio (clipped); 1766 Rio (not clipped); 1771 Rio (clipped); 1776 Rio (clipped twice)

Disposition: Stack's auction, January 15–16, 2008.

Bibliography: Stack's 2008a, lots 7006–17.

556. Vero Beach, Florida, USA, 1977 and 1990–91.

Type of find: Shipwreck.

Ship: The *Roberts*, called the "Holden Wreck," also known as the "Frank Gordon I Site" after an early major investor who later died.

Sank: 1810.

Contents: 400+ AR.

Description: A catalogue of 94 coins in the Florida State Collection follows, plus Sebring's Mexican coin of 1809:

Spanish colonies, ½ reales, México (5): 1773; 1779; 1788; 1792; 1798

Spanish colonies, reales, México (3): 1782; 1793; 1802

Spanish colonies, 2 reales, México (25): 1745; 1752; 1765; 1772; 1773 (2); 1775; 1776; 1778; 1779; 1781 (2); 1782 (2); 1783; 1788; 1789; 1794; 1797; 1798; 1799; 1804; 1805; 1806; 1807

Spanish colonies, 4 reales, México (3): 1783; 179[-]; 1793

Spanish colonies, 8 reales, México (40): 1773; 1779; 1780; 1783; 1784; 1785; 1786; 1787; 1788; 1789; 1791; 1792; 1793; 1795; 1796; 1797; 1798; 1799; 18[-]; 1800; 1801 (2); 1802; 1803 (3); 1804; 1805; 1806; 1807 (2); 1808 (3); 1809 (4); 1810 (2)

Spanish colonies, reales, Guatemala (2): 1790; 1796

Spanish colonies, 2 reales, Guatemala (3): 1780; 1790; 1804

Spanish colonies, 8 reales, Guatemala (6): 1779; 1796; 1805; 1806; 1807; 1808

Spanish colonies, real, Lima, 1788

Spanish colonies, 8 reales, Lima (11): 1776; 1782; 1794; 1797; 1800; 1801; 1804; 1805; 1806; 1807; 1808

Spanish colonies, ½ real, Potosí, 1775

Spanish colonies, 2 reales, Potosí, 1776 (2)

Spanish colonies, 4 reales, Potosí, 1786

Spanish colonies, 8 reales, Potosí (6): 177[-]; 1788; 179[-]; 1794; 1798; 1805

Disposition: Most of the few hundred coins known are beach finds, although excavations were carried out on the wreck in 1990–91.

100+ AR to the State of Florida. The site was excavated in 1990–91 by Salvors, Inc., as subcontractors. Sebring owned a Spanish colonies, 8 reales, México, 1809, assayers TH, provenanced to this wreck.

Bibliography: Craig 2000b, 22, 75, 79, 135, 166, 168; Sebring 2004, lot 1623.

Florida Master Site File, File on Roberts Wreck.

557. Matildaville, Virginia, USA, 1986.

Type of find: Archaeological excavation.

Date of deposit: 1810.

Contents: 2 AE, 1 AR.

Description:
  USA, 1¢, 1802?
  USA, 1¢, date illegible but draped bust type (1796–1807)
  USA, 10¢, 1809

Disposition: The coins were found during excavations on the site of the Superintendant's House of the Patowmack Canal. The canal was active 1788–1830. George Washington was one of the stockholders.

Bibliography: Garrett 1987 (see photograph on p. 745).

558. Bermuda, April 1938.

Type of find: Hoard.

Date of deposit: 1810.

Container: Mahogany desk.

Contents: 151 AV.

Description:
  Spanish colonies, Ferdinand VII, 4 escudos
  Spanish colonies, Charles III, 8 escudos
  Spanish colonies, Charles IV, 8 escudos
  Portuguese colonies, Brazil, 6,400 reis

Disposition: Found by R. L. Pearman, a cabinetmaker, while knocking apart an old mahogany desk owned by his family for generations. An American numismatist visiting Bermuda told Pearman that the find was worth between $10,000 and $11,000.

Bibliography: "Bermuda Cabinet-Maker Finds Valuable Old Coins," *New York Times*, February 24, 1938, 9.

"Old Desk Yields a Lot of Gold Coins," *Numismatist* 51, no. 4 (April 1938): 361.

Numismatic Scrapbook Magazine 4, no. 8 (August 1938): 306.

"Cached Coins Worth $10,000," *New York Times*, May 5, 1938, 25.

559. Mahanoy City, Schuylkill County, Pennsylvania, USA, August 1880.

Type of find: Hoard.

Date of deposit: 1810.

Contents: ca. 400 AR.

Description: Spanish colonies, 8 reales, México (ca. 400)

Denomination, metal, and mint are educated guesses.

The coins are believed to have been buried by Bailey, a hunter from New Jersey, after Bailey murdered Foulhover, a Jewish pedlar, for the money in his saddlebags. Foulhover used to travel on horseback with his wares between Reading and Sunbury. This is supposed to be the first instance of one white man murdering another in cold blood in what subsequently became Schuylkill County.

Disposition: The coins were found in a field that had recently been plowed and the coins turned to the surface had been cleaned by rains, so they could be spotted fairly easily. The five boys who found the coins were Clinton C. Winters, Herbert Noakes, Henry and Philip Kline, and Herbert Enterhister.

Bibliography: "Old Coins Found in a Field. The Luck of Five Mahanoy City Boys—the Treasure the Proceeds of a Murder Committed 70 Years Ago," *New York Times*, August 11, 1880, 5.

560. Danielson, Connecticut, USA, late spring 1999.

Type of find: Hoard.

Date of deposit: ca. 1810.

Container: Wrapped in leather.

Contents: 14 AE.

Description:

Great Britain, counterfeit halfpence, 1775 (2)
Great Britain, Washington Liberty and security penny, 1795
Ireland, Wood's Hibernia halfpenny, 1723
USA, Vermont, copper, 1787, Ryder 13
USA, Connecticut, copper, 1785, Miller 4.4-D
USA, Connecticut, copper, 1785, Miller 6.4-I
USA, Connecticut, copper, 1786, Miller 4.2-S
USA, Connecticut, copper, 1787, Miller 32.1-X.3
USA, Connecticut, copper, 1787, Miller 32.2.-X.1
USA, Connecticut, copper, 1787, Miller 37.8-LL
USA, Connecticut, copper, 1787, Miller 43.2-X.4
USA, Connecticut, copper, 1788, Miller 11-G
USA, Nova Constellatio copper, 1785

The coins were found wrapped in leather inside a barn. Many of the coins were well worn, suggesting that they had been in circulation for some time.

Disposition: Sold over eBay over a period of several weeks.

Bibliography: Trudgen 2000.

561. Morgantown, West Virginia, USA, May 1927.

Type of find: Hoard.

Date of deposit: 1811.

Contents: 7 AR.

Description:

Spanish colonies, 2 reales, 1700s and 1800s
USA, 50¢, 1811

Disposition: Found by workers excavating in front of the new chemistry building of the State University.

Bibliography: "More Buried 'Treasure' Unearthed," *Numismatist* 40, no. 5 (May 1927): 299.

562. Between Port-au-Prince and St. Marc, mid-region of Haiti, 1997.

Type of find: Hoard.

Date of deposit: 1812?

Contents: ca. 600 AR.

Description:
   Spanish colonies, 8 reales, México (ca. 500)
   Spanish colonies, 8 reales, Mexican War of Independence mint
   Spanish colonies, Charles III, 8 reales, 1772, Guatemala
   Spanish colonies, 8 reales, Lima (ca. 49)
   Spanish colonies, 8 reales, Potosí (ca. 49)
   Amounts from each mint and date of deposit are educated guesses.

Disposition: Purchased by the elder Carlos Jara.

Bibliography: Jara 2008.

563. Fairfield, Ontario, Canada, 1941.

Type of find: Archaeological excavation of the Indian settlement of Fairfield.

Date of site: October 7, 1812.

Contents: 4 AE, 1 AR.

Description: The coins found included:
   Russia, 2 kopek, 1757
   Great Britain, halfpenny, 1775
   Great Britain, penny, 1797 (emended from impossible date of 1794)
   USA, ½¢, 1807
   Spanish colonies, Charles III, bust type, 8 reales, cut quarter piece, probably from México

Bibliography: Brown and Dolley 1971, 59 (NU3); Buttrey 1967.

564. Waterville, Maine, USA, June 1880.

Type of find: Single find.

Contents: 1 AE.

Description: Great Britain, Glastonbury, token of 1812, Batty 365, holed

Disposition: A. A. Plaisted of Waterville, Maine.

Bibliography: Appleton 1883; Appleton 1886; McLachlan 1884; McLachlan 1885b; Richardson 1883; Richardson 1886.

565. 226 Spring Street, Spring Street and Clarke Street, New York, New York, USA, July 1877.

Type of find: Hoard.

Date of deposit: 1814.

Container: Pot.

Contents: 1,500+ AR.

Description:
   Spain, 2 reales (pistareens), 1702
   USA, 50¢, 1812
   USA, 50¢, date unknown
   Spanish colonies, reales
   Spanish colonies, 2 reales, 1760
   Spanish colonies, 2 reales, 1781
   Spanish colonies, 2 reales, 1790
   Spanish colonies, 2 reales, 1781, with counterstamp "M. Fry"
   Spanish colonies, 2 reales, date unknown
   Spanish colonies, 2 reales, Guatemala, 1800M
   The Spanish and Spanish colonies coins were dated mostly 1760–90, but a few dated as old as 1702. They are described as being the size of late nineteenth century USA quarter and half dollars—probably referring to reales and 2 reales.

This hoard was found when Schutt, Kelsey & Co. were excavating for a root beer cellar at 226 Spring Street. The hoard was in dirt that was excavated and dumped in the street, and then found by small boys searching through the dirt. The hoard was originally in a pot, which was broken during the digging. It is thought to have been buried by a previous property owner, Warren Swayze. The building dated from 1764.

Disposition: John Kelsey and Schutt. Most of the treasure was found by small boys and pocketed by them.

Bibliography: "Schutt's Silver Mine. Buried Treasure in the Eighth Ward. Several Hundred Dollars in Old Spanish Coin taken from a Cellar in Spring Street," *New York Times,* July 7, 1877, 5.

"A Gold Mine in a Cellar. Spanish Coin Found at No. 226 Spring St.," *New York Tribune,* July 7, 1877, 2.

566. Near Tlacochahuaya, Oaxaca, Mexico, August 1885.

Type of find: Hoard.

Date of deposit: 1813.

Container: Straw pouch or bag.

Contents: 428 AE.

Description:

Mexico, Morelos, reales, 1812 (2)

Mexico, Morelos, 2 reales (336): 1811 (4); 1812 (258); 1813 (74)

Mexico, Morelos, 8 reales (90): 1812 (31); 1813 (59)

Disposition: The coins were found by a young American archaeologist excavating a small tumulus.

9 coins from this hoard were auctioned by Lyman Haynes Low, September 20, 1886, and were there more closely described (KM numbers are references to the Krause-Mishler catalog)

Mexico, 2 reales, 1812 (2) (KM 226.1)

Mexico, 2 reales, 1813, TC SUD (KM 245)

Mexico, Morelos, 8 reales, 1812 (KM 233.2)

Mexico, Morelos, 8 reales, 1813 (KM 233.3 or 233.4)

Mexico, Morelos, 8 reales, 1813 (KM 233.3)

Mexico, Morelos, 8 reales, 1813 (KM 234) (Low says that 4 of this variety were discovered in the hoard)

Mexico, Morelos, 8 reales, 1813, TC SUD (KM 248) (according to Low, when he wrote only 5 examples were known of this variety)

Mexico, Morelos, 8 reales, 1812, with Morelos counterstamp *Mo* (KM 265.4)

Mexico, Morelos, 8 reales, 1813, with Morelos counterstamp *Mo* (KM 265.4)

Bibliography: Low 1886a; Low 1886b, lots 93–102; Low 1893 (additional varieties identified by Low in the subsequent eight years—more a variety study than a hoard study).

Low 1886a has also appeared as two separate printings with line drawings—first in English, and later in Spanish. However, the line drawings do not depict the actual coins in the hoard. The line drawings were printed from cuts borrowed by Low from Benjamin Betts of Brooklyn, New York, USA. Betts had bought the cuts used to illustrate the Jules Fonrobert Collection, auctioned by Adolph Weyl in Berlin, Germany, in 1878, after the sale. The illustrations thus show Fonrobert coins, not the coins of the Tlacochahuaya hoard.

567. Addison, New York, USA, May 1934.

Type of find: Single find.

Contents: 1 AR.

Description: Spanish colonies, Ferdinand VII, ½ real, México, 1813

Disposition: Found by New York State Temporary Emergency Relief Administration (TERA) workers excavating Main Street on a grading project. The identification of the coin is based on the silver coin of 1813 that would be the likeliest casual loss.

Bibliography: "Gold Dollar of 1784 Found," *New York Times,* May 17, 1934, 3.

568. Scio, Harrison County, Ohio, USA, July 1896.

Type of find: Single find.

Contents: 1 AR.

Description: Spanish colonies, ½ real, probably

México, 1813

Disposition: James B. Wooster of Buffalo, New York.

Bibliography: "Old Coin Found in an Ohio Rock. It Bears Date 1243, and a Curious Story is Told of It," *New York Times*, July 27, 1896, 5.

569. 125 North Second Street, Philadelphia, Pennsylvania, USA, January 1872 and South Broad Street, Philadelphia, Pennsylvania, USA, end of June, beginning of July 1897.

Type of find: Hoard.

Date of deposit: August 1814.

Contents: 50 AV.

Description:

France, louis (6): 1660; 1687K; 1693A; 1696A; 1705K; 1747

France, 2 louis

USA, New York, Ephraim Brasher, Lima style doubloon, 1742

USA, New York, Ephraim Brasher, New York style doubloon, 1787

USA, New York?, Spanish colonies, 8 escudos, with IB counterstamp

Spanish colonies, 8 escudos, cob

Spanish colonies, 8 escudos, milled

Portuguese colonies, Brazil, John V, 4,000 reis, 1720

Portuguese colonies, Brazil, 4,000 reis

Portuguese colonies, Brazil, 6,400 reis

Dates seen by William Ewing Dubois ranged from 1660 to 1749. Dubois saw about a dozen. Dubois was surprised that he did not see any British guineas. Some of the coins had been clipped. One coin, "of very ancient pattern," had the letters IB. The clipping and the letters IB indicate that these are "regulated" gold coins of the type that circulated in the United States from 1784 onwards.

The date of deposit is based upon what we know about the resident of 125 North Second Street, namely Peter Kurtz.

Disposition: Found by workers excavating a cellar under the foundation of an old house in Philadelphia. The dirt excavated from this cellar was used for fill and redeposited on South Broad Street.

In 1897 a second parcel of this hoard was discovered there, namely Brasher's New York style doubloon. Its discovery was thus described in the Jackman auction catalog, lot 140: "Found by laborers digging a cellar for a building on South Broad Street, Philadelphia; with it was a 5 cents nickel of either 1866 or 1867 with rays (but date of which was eaten off by corrosion); on making inquiry in the neighborhood a man about eighty years of age stated that he well remembered the filling in of this section with city refuse about 1866 or 1867 and it is more than likely this coin owes its being there to some such act, as it was more than six feet below the surface." The laborers tried to sell it at a bar, but the barman said he knew enough not to take old brass buttons. It was hawked around the city for about two weeks, but refused by all, including by the coin dealer Mason & Co., until it was bought by S. H. & H. Chapman, who sold it to Alison W. Jackman on July 15, 1897.

Disposition of the Brasher New York style doubloon: Bought by S. H. & H. Chapman; sold to Alison W. Jackman; auctioned in the Jackman sale, June 28–29, 1918, by Henry Chapman; after intermediate owners, acquired by Frederick C. C. Boyd; bought from him by New Netherlands (John Jay Ford, Jr.) and sold to Mr. and Mrs. R. Henry Norweb; donated by them to the American Numismatic Society, New York, 1969; item number 1969.62.1.

Bibliography: Breen 1958, 141; Breen 1988, 92–93 (Breen 981); Chapman 1918, lot 140; Kleeberg 2008.

"A Strange Discovery. Hidden Treasure Unearthed – a Large Quantity of Ancient Gold Coin Found in a Cellar on Second Street – Lively Time among the Diggers – Regular California Claim Scene – Coins Over Two Hundred Years Old – Strange Mystery Brought out by a Laborer's Spade," *Philadelphia Inquirer,* January 23, 1872, 3.

"Treasure Trove. Strange Discovery of Ancient Coin in Philadelphia," *New York Times,* January 27, 1872, 4.

"Discovery of Ancient Coin," *American Journal of Numismatics* 6, no. 4 (April 1872): 86–87.

570. Saint John, Virgin Islands, USA, 1989.

Type of find: Single find.

Contents: 1 BI.

Description: British colonies, Saint Vincent, black dog, retrograde S counterstamp, 1814, on French colonies, Cayenne, 2 sous, 1782A

Disposition: Found with a metal detector by Captain David Decuir.

Bibliography: "Detector Signals… Coast to Coast: Coin Struck," *Treasure Found* (Spring 1989): 15.

571. Phillipsburg, Québec, Canada, December 1938.

Type of find: Hoard.

Date of deposit: 1815.

Contents: ca. 500 AE.

Description: British colonies, Lower Canada, halfpenny tokens, 1815 (Breton 994)
Number of coins recovered is uncertain; amount is only described as a "large hoard."

Bibliography: Atchison 2007, 235 (citing *Money Talk* 1, no. 3 [December 1938], 13).

572. Raridon, Ohio, USA, July 14, 1904.

Type of find: Hoard.

Date of deposit: 1815.

Container: Old vessel.

Contents: 312 AV.

Description: Spanish colonies, 8 escudos (312)
$5,000 in gold in an old vessel unearthed by the farmer Randal Marcum; some of the coins were as old as 1773. The coins are not described, but were almost certainly Spanish colonies 8 escudos, given that the oldest date was 1773 (in 1772 there was a fineness reduction in the Spanish gold coinage). Supposed to have been buried by John Oglethorpe, whom Indians killed in 1815.

Bibliography: Numismatist 17, no. 7 (July 1904): 207.

573. Five miles south of the western tip of Isla Coche, near Margarita Island and Cumana Bay, off Venezuela, February 1844, 1849, and January 1872.

Type of find: Shipwreck.

Ship: San Pedro de Alcantara.

Sank: April 24, 1815.

Contents: 289,600 AR, AV.

Description:
Spanish colonies, Ferdinand VII, 8 reales
Spanish colonies, 8 escudos, Lima, 1807JP (Thomas Sebring)
The ship is said to have been carrying 800,000 pesos when she blew up.

Disposition: The Spanish salvaged much at the time of the wreck. In 1816 Captain Goodrich of Newburyport, Massachusetts, recovered $30,000. In 1845 there were salvage operations by the "San Pedro Company" of Baltimore, which recovered $200,000. In 1845 $18,500 worth was sent to the U.S. Mint for recoinage; an encrusted cluster was sent to the U.S. Mint Cabinet. Another attempt was made in 1849, when only a few thousand dollars were recovered. An attempt was made by a group from Gardiner, Maine, in 1853 who used diving bells. In 1856 Nicholas Town recovered $28,000. In 1858 Captain

Whipple recovered $30,000. In 1871–72 another attempt at salvage was made by the American Submarine Company, which recovered $1,600 in silver coin. Its manager was George W. Fuller; in January 1872 he exhibited Spanish milled dollars (some black, some pristine) and other artifacts that had been recovered from the wreck at Lee & Osgood on Main Street in Norwich, Connecticut. Captain L. H. Folingsby undertook another attempt in 1877.

Bibliography: Coffman 1957, 102, 118, 219, 247; Dubois 1846, 134–35; Dubois 1884, 90; Pickford 1994, 53, 129, 164; Potter 1972, 116, 141–44; Sebring 2004, lot 1597 (from Bowers & Merena, Auction Catalog ("Treasures of the World"), June 2002, lot 1090); Snowden 1861, 157.

"Stated Meeting, October 17, 1845," *Proceedings of the American Philosophical Society* 4, no. 34 (September 1845): 200–1 (incorporates the text of a letter of William Ewing Dubois).

"Recovery of Lost Treasures," *Illustrated News,* August, 27, 1853 (citing the *Kennebec (ME) Journal*) (reference courtesy of Q. David Bowers).

"The Treasure of the San Pedro—Further Accounts from the Expedition," *New York Times,* December 26, 1871, 5.

"The Cumana Bay Treasure. Partial Disappointment of the Wrecking Expedition—A New Enterprise to be Entered Upon," *New York Times*, January 27, 1872, 8.

"A Message from the Sea," *American Journal of Numismatics* 9, no. 1 (July 1874): 21.

"Treasure from the Deep," *American Journal of Numismatics* 9, no. 2 (October 1874): 37.

"Seeking Sunken Millions. The lost San Pedro Alcantara. The Eventful Last Voyage of a Man-of-War. Battle and Pillage. Over $6,000,000 on Board. Horrible End of a Revel. Diving for Lost Riches. An American Expedition now Setting Out," *New York Times,* October 29, 1877, 1.

"After Six Million Dollars. The Folingsby Expedition Ready for the Spanish Main. Appliances for the recovery of the Treasure of the *San Pedro Alcantara.* Refitting of the Canadian Gun-boat *Peter Mitchell.* Powerful and Novel Dredges. An Eye in the Ocean's Depths. President Alcantara and Venezuela," *New York Times,* December 16, 1877, 1.

"Diving for Dollars," *Coin Collector's Journal* 12 (whole no. 136) (March 1887): 47–48.

574. Fort York, Toronto, Ontario, Canada, 1987–93.

Type of find: Archaeological excavation.

Date of site: 1793–1871.

Date of second period (end of War of 1812 through introduction of decimal coinage): 1815–58.

Contents: 39+ AE, 3 AR.

Description:

Great Britain, sixpence (2): 1818; 1844

Ireland, medallion, "Friendly Visit of George IV to Ireland," 1821

British colonies, Prince Edward Island, ships colonies and commerce token (2)

British colonies, Lower Canada, ships colonies and commerce token with large bust on obverse (Breton 1002)

British colonies, Lower Canada, Montreal 1816 halfpenny token

British colonies, Lower Canada, bouquet sous (3+)

British colonies, Lower Canada, spread eagle halfpenny token, 1814

British colonies, Lower Canada, spread eagle halfpenny token, 1815

British colonies, Lower Canada, The Illustrious Wellington/Waterloo, 1816, token, in both 8 and 10 string varieties (4+)

British colonies, Lower Canada, Field

Marshal Wellington/Britannia token (2+)

British colonies, Lower Canada, Wellington halfpenny token with oak leaves, Britannia, and 1814

British colonies, Lower Canada, Habitant tokens, Québec Bank (2)

British colonies, Lower Canada, Tiffin halfpenny (2)

British colonies, Lower Canada, Bank of Montreal front view token, 1842

British colonies, Lower Canada, Canada, worn halfpenny, "rejuvenated" by striking with a Halliday or Tiffin token, resulting in a faint backward bust

British colonies, Upper Canada, Lesslie and sons token, 1824

British colonies, Upper Canada, Speed the plough/No labour no bread token

British colonies, Upper Canada, Sir Isaac Brook [sic]/Hero of Upper Canada token, 1812

British colonies, Upper Canada, Brock token, 1816

British colonies, Upper Canada, sloop halfpenny, 1833, with "to facilitate trade"

British colonies, Canada West, Bank of Upper Canada Saint George token, halfpenny (2+)

British colonies, Canada West, Bank of Upper Canada Saint George token, penny (2+)

British colonies, Lower and Upper Canada, blacksmith coppers (3+)

British colonies, Lower and Upper Canada, North American token, 1781 (minted in Dublin, Ireland, 1825)

USA, 1¢, 1816–57 (2+)

USA 1¢, 1843

USA, silver 5¢, 1849

Bibliography: Spittal 1993, 244–53.

575. Penetanguishene, Simcoe County, Ontario, Canada, summer 1991.

Type of find: Archaeological excavation.

Date of site: 1817–34.

Contents: 1 AV.

Description: Great Britain, guinea, 1793

Disposition: Excavation by Wilfred Laurier University (Dr. J. Trigg) of the Naval and Military Establishments at Penetanguishene.

Bibliography: Spittal 1993, 250.

576. Near Concepción, Chile, ca. 1993.

Type of find: Hoard.

Date of deposit: 1817.

Contents: 100 AR.

Description:

Spanish colonies, Ferdinand VII, ¼ reales, Santiago (25)

Spanish colonies, Ferdinand VII, reales, Santiago (75): 1813 (40); 1817 (35)

Specific numbers of each denomination are educated guesses.

Disposition: Most were purchased by Christian Jeff, a Chilean living in Puerto Rico. Paul Karon handled many of the pieces afterwards.

Bibliography: Jara 2008.

577. Upstate New York, USA, summer 2005.

Type of find: Single find.

Contents: 1 AR.

Description: USA, 50¢, 1817/4 (Overton 102a) Graded EF40, in 2005–6 this coin ranked as the second finest known of the variety.

Disposition: Found by a mason, George Williams, while raking over fill dirt. Sold at auction by Heritage Numismatic Auctions on January 5, 2006, at the Florida United Numismatists Convention in Orlando, Florida, USA.

Bibliography: Eric von Klinger, "Worker discovers eighth 1817/4 Capped Bust 50¢. Finds rarity while raking through dirt," *Coin World*, October 24, 2005, C1.

Eric von Klinger, "Contractor's 2005 dirt

pile find realizes $253,000 at FUN sale," *Coin World,* January 23, 2006, C1.

578. Portland, Maine, USA, July 1846.

Type of find: Hoard.

Date of deposit: August 1818.

Container: Chest, keg, or box.

Contents: ca. 1,000 AR; ca. 500 AV.

Description:

Spanish colonies, 8 reales, México (ca. 1,000)

Spanish colonies, 8 escudos, México (ca. 500)

Amounts, mints and denominations are an educated guess; coins were only described as $11,000 in gold and silver. Thought to be the money stolen from the Cumberland Bank in Portland and buried in August 1818.

The Cumberland Bank theft was perpetrated by a leading shipowner and citizen of Portland, Daniel Manly, and the captain of one of his ships, Captain Rolf (or Roth). They used false keys to enter the bank on Saturday night, August 1, 1818. When the theft was discovered, Manly came down to the bank and said, "Upon my word, that was a *manly* trick." Part of the stolen money was discovered when some boys, playing under a fire engine house, fell over a bag of silver dollars. When his identity as one of the perpetrators was discovered, Captain Rolf blew his brains out. Manly was later discovered by something he had said, and was arrested, convicted and imprisoned. A year or two after his release from prison he died of smallpox, being the only person in the area to suffer from that disease. It is thought he caught the smallpox while burying his stolen money, because he buried it near the hospital, where bodies of smallpox victims had been buried.

The directors of the bank sent notices to the newspapers at the time stating that all the money had been recovered, but this does not seem to have been true.

According to Haxby's catalog of obsolete banknotes, the Cumberland Bank was founded in 1812 as a Massachusetts bank. It transferred its charter to Maine upon statehood in 1820. In 1831 it became the Maine Bank. In 1843 it closed.

Bibliography: "Particulars of the late Robbery at the Cumberland Bank," *Worcester (MA) National Aegis,* August 12, 1818, 2.

"A Treasure Trove," *Barre (MA) Gazette,* July 3, 1846, 3.

"Stolen Money Found," *Worcester (MA) Palladium,* July 8, 1846 (citing the *New Haven (CT) Courier*) (reference courtesy of Q. David Bowers).

579. Riverside Golf Course, near the San José Mission, on the banks of the San Antonio River, San Antonio, Texas, USA, early 1959.

Type of find: Hoard.

Date of deposit: 1818.

Contents: 58–60 AE.

Description: Spanish colonies, Texas, San Antonio, José Antonio de la Garza, jola (token), 1818 (58–60)

Disposition: Found by James J. Zotz, Sr., and his sons James and Richard. One coin donated to the Witte Memorial Museum, December 17, 1959 by James Zotz; item number 59-177-42.

Bibliography: Breen 1988, 108; Brown 1966, 1467; Brown 1972, 517.

[George W. Vogt], "Texas golf washout turns up remarkable find," *Coin World*, April 23, 1980, 90.

Bob Medlar Papers.

580. Near Leon Creek on the old Castroville Road, San Antonio, Texas, USA, 1939.

Type of find: Single find.

Contents: 1 AE.

Description: Spanish colonies, Texas, San Antonio, José Antonio de la Garza, jola (token), 1818

Disposition: Found by a woman in San Antonio in 1939.

Bibliography: Brown 1972, 517.
Clarence J. LaRoche, "Coins Struck in 1817. S. A. Spanish Mint made change, history," *San Antonio News*, October 20, 1965, 8-E.

581. San Antonio, Texas, USA, 1972.

Type of find: Single find.

Contents: 1 AE.

Description: Spanish colonies, Texas, San Antonio, José Antonio de la Garza, jola (token), 1818

Disposition: Found during restoration work on one of the nearby Spanish missions and placed on display there.

Bibliography: Brown 1972, 517.

582. Fort Crawford, Prairie du Chien, Wisconsin, USA, September 1938.

Type of find: Archaeological excavation.

Date of site: 1818–60.

Contents: 4 AR, 1 AV.

Description:
USA, California, fractional gold, 50¢, 1856, inscribed "California Gold," probably Breen-Gillio 434
Spanish colonies, ½ reales? (4): 1781; 1784; 1794; 1803

Disposition: Found by WPA workers.

Bibliography: "Fort Ruins Yields Old Coins," *Numismatic Scrapbook Magazine* 4, no. 9 (September 1938): 342.

583. One mile west of French Lick Springs, Indiana, USA, February 1904.

Type of find: Single find.

Contents: 1 AR.

Date of deposit: After 1818.

Description: USA, silver medal voted by Congress to William Henry Harrison after the Battle of the Thames, October 5, 1813

Disposition: Found by Lieutenant W. M. Kendal of Jasper, Indiana.

Bibliography: Numismatist 17, no. 2 (February 1904): 58.

584. Montréal, Québec, Canada, January 1892.

Type of find: Hoard.

Date of deposit: December 29, 1818.

Contents: 7+ P.

Description:
British colonies, Lower Canada, Dobie & Badgley, note, 15 sols, May 1, 1790
British colonies, Lower Canada, Dobie & Badgley, note, 30 sols, May 1, 1790
British colonies, Lower Canada, Dobie & Badgley, note, 3 livres, May 1, 1790
British colonies, Lower Canada, Dobie & Badgley, note, 6 livres, May 1, 1790
British colonies, Lower Canada, Manufacturers and Mechanics Bank, $50 check, December 29, 1818
British colonies, Lower Canada, Bank of Canada, checks

Bibliography: "Treasure Trove," *Canadian Antiquarian and Numismatic Journal*, 2nd series, 2, no. 1 (January 1892): 29.

585. Fall River, Massachusetts, USA, 1881.

Type of find: Hoard.

Date of deposit: ca. 1820.

Container: Small calico bag.

Contents: 12 AE, 1 AR.

Description:
USA, 1¢ (12)
USA, 10¢, 1807

Disposition: Contents of a small calico bag that was the property of Charles Sewell, who had been given it by a maiden sister; she had been given it by her mother. Nicholas Hathaway bought the bag.

Bibliography: Édouard Frossard, *Numisma* 6, no. 1 (January 1882): [5].

586. Alexandria, Virginia, USA, 1929.

Type of find: Foundation deposit.

Date of deposit: ca. 1820.

Contents: 2 AR.

Description:
Spanish colonies, 8 reales, México, 1791FM, with small size Chinese chopmarks
Spanish colonies, 8 reales, México, 1803FF

Disposition: Found by a boy in the foundation of an old building in Alexandria; the boy kept them as good luck items, selling them onwards to Thomas A. Kays in 1994.

Bibliography: Kays 1996, 1637–45.

587. Arkansas Post, Arkansas, USA, 1971.

Type of find: Archaeological excavation.

Date of site: 1752-January 1863, however the coins have nineteenth century dates, so placed here ca. 1820.

Contents: 3 AR.

Description:
Spanish colonies, cut wedge from 2 reales, México, with inscription ATIA (i.e., 1772–1808)
USA, silver 5¢, 1851O
USA, 10¢, 1858O

Bibliography: Martin 1977, 56–57.

588. Cambridgeport, Massachusetts, USA, April 1874.

Type of find: Excavation.

Date of deposit: ca. 1820?

Contents: 1 AE, 1 AR, 10+ P.

Description:
USA, 1¢, 1798
USA, paper money (10+)
Spanish colonies, 8 reales, 1811

The paper money was "bills of various denominations to the nominal value of five hundred dollars."

This hoard was found on taking down an old chimney in the Broadway House in Cambridgeport.

Bibliography: "Editorial," *American Journal of Numismatics* 8, no. 4 (April 1874): 96.

589. Near Elma, Washington, USA, November 1894.

Type of find: Single find.

Contents: 1 B.

Description: British colonies, Hudson's Bay Company Territories, North West Company, brass token, 1820

Disposition: Found by Joseph Anderson.

Bibliography: Joseph Hooper, "Hooper's Restrikes," *Numismatist* 7, no. 11 (November 1894): 250 (citing the *Portland Morning Oregonian*).

590. Vancouver, Washington, USA, October 1954.

Type of find: Excavation.

Date of deposit: 1820.

Contents: 3 B.

Description: British colonies, Hudson's Bay Company Territories, North West Company, brass token, 1820 (3)

Disposition: Found among the ruins of Fort Vancouver. Exhibited by Steve Bibler at the October 28, 1954 meeting of the Seattle Coin Club.

Bibliography: "Seattle Coin Club, Minutes, October 28, 1954," *Numismatist* 67, no. 12 (December 1954): 1340.

591. Stevenson, Washington, USA, 1951.

Type of find: Hoard.

Date of deposit: 1820.

Contents: B, AR.

Description:
British colonies, Hudson's Bay Company Territories, North West Company, brass token, 1820
USA and other countries' coins (all holed)
Trade beads were found as well.

Disposition: Found while digging in a backyard along the Columbia River. The North West token was sold to J. G. Eberle of Stevenson, Washington. Despite the title of the article, the pieces were not found in a grave.

Bibliography: J. G. Eberle, "Canadian Rarities Found in Grave," *Numismatic Scrapbook Magazine* 27, no. 4 (April 1961): 1155–56.

592. Umpqua River Valley, Oregon, USA, 1950s.

Type of find: Funerary deposit.

Date of deposit: 1820.

Container: Copper kettle.

Contents: 26 B.

Description: British colonies, Hudson's Bay Company Territories, North West Company, brass token, 1820 (26)

Disposition: Found in an Indian burial mound by the banks of the river. The pieces were in a copper kettle. 22 were sold through Bowers & Ruddy via a listing in their *Rare Coin Review* 31 (1978): 11. One was donated to a museum, and the three remaining were too corroded to market.

Bibliography: Bowers 1979, 391; Bowers 1997, 39.
Bowers and Ruddy Galleries, *Rare Coin Review* 31 (1978): 11.

593. Oregon, USA, 1970s?

Type of find: Hoard.

Date of deposit: 1820.

Contents: 14 B.

Description: British colonies, Hudson's Bay Company Territories, North West Company, brass token, 1820 (14)

Disposition: Given to a western museum.

Bibliography: Bowers 1997, 39.

594. Georgia, USA, 1869.

Type of find: Hoard. Called "the Randall Hoard."

Date of deposit: 1820.

Contents: 14,000 AE.

Description:
USA, 1¢, 1817 (85) (Newcomb 14)
USA, 1¢, 1818 (1,464) (Newcomb 10)
USA, 1¢, 1819 (68) (Newcomb 8)
USA, 1¢, 1820 (Newcomb 13 and Newcomb 15)
The cents are usually spotty red or partly red mint state with many bag marks. The 1820 Newcomb 13 is the best struck, the 1818 Newcomb 10 is by far the commonest.

Disposition: Acquired by a New York merchant from a Georgia merchant in exchange for a debt. Then acquired by a grocer, John Chapman, of Norwich, New York, who could not distribute them because the people called them "Chapman's counterfeits." John Swan Randall bought the lot at a little below face value. Randall gave four cents, one of each date to American Numismatic Society in 1870 (1870.2.1-4), one of them (1870.2.4) sold off in a New Netherlands sale with American Numismatic Society duplicates, 1950. Randall sold cents in the W. Elliot Woodward Sale of February 23, 1874, lots 1016 and 1017; and in the Edward Cogan sale of May 6–9, 1878, lots 1813–23 and 2414–24.

Frossard wrote in 1877: "The dates 1817, 1818, 1819, 1820 and from 1845 up to 1857, are frequently found in uncirculated and even bright condition, and as such sell at from 10c to $1.00 each."

Bibliography: Breen 1952, 8–9 (Breen Hoards VIII); Cohen 1985.

Édouard Frossard, *Numisma* 1, no. 2 (March 1877): [6].

595. Dartmouth, Nova Scotia, Canada, October 1886.

Type of find: Hoard.

Date of deposit: 1820s?

Contents: Ca. 30 AE.

Description:

British colonies, Nova Scotia, White's farthings (ca. 3)

British colonies, Nova Scotia, Halifax Steamboat Company/Ferry Token (25) (Breton 900)

The tokens were found while demolishing the old Toll House of the Halifax Dartmouth Ferriage Co.

All were in "beautiful bright red condition."

Disposition: Consigned to Édouard Frossard for sale.

Bibliography: Breton 1894, 172 (Breton 900); MacDonald 1965; MacDonald 1969.

"Halifax Penny Tokens," *American Journal of Numismatics* 21, no. 2 (October 1886): 39.

Henry Hechler, "Halifax Ferry Tokens," *American Journal of Numismatics* 21, no. 4 (April 1887): 90.

596. South Mountain, Bucks County, Pennsylvania, USA, January 1857.

Type of find: Hoard.

Date of deposit: 1820s?

Contents: 145 AR, AV.

Description:

France, écus (100)

Spanish colonies, 8 escudos (45)

"One thousand dollars in old Spanish and American gold coins and French silver." Probably Spanish colonies 8 escudos and French écus. Found by a servant woman in the smokehouse of Peter Texter.

Bibliography: Bowers 1997, 130.

"Wayside Gatherings," *Ballou's Pictorial Drawing Room Companion,* January 31, 1857, 79.

597. Old Town, Fernandina, Florida, USA, February 1926.

Type of find: Hoard.

Date of deposit: 1820s.

Contents: 3+ AR.

Description:

Spanish colonies, Charles IV, 8 reales, 1796

Spanish colonies, Ferdinand VII, 8 reales

Disposition: Found by Robert Cribb, a fisher from the shrimpboat Republic. The coins were found near Old Town and not far from Fort Clinch.

Bibliography: "Florida Fisherman Finds Spanish Coins," *Numismatist* 39, no. 2 (February 1926): 92.

598. Downtown México City, Mexico, 1950s or 1960s.

Type of find: Hoard.

Date of deposit: 1820?

Contents: 300 AV.

Description: Spanish colonies, 8 escudos, México (300)

Denomination is an educated guess.

Disposition: Found by construction workers doing work in the house of an Arab lady. First they found 150 pieces; then they began to rip the house apart, looking for more; they found another 150 pieces, and began to really tear the house down. The lady complained to the authorities that the construction workers were destroying her house. All to Casa Baron, an exchange dealer in Mexico City who handled most of the hoards found in Mexico at this period.

Bibliography: Hubbard 1993.

599. Nantucket, Massachusetts, USA, April 1880.

Type of find: Single find.

Contents: 1 AE.

Description: USA, Massachusetts, Nantucket, Tristram Coffin medal (Betts 533)

Bibliography: "Numismatic Discoveries," *American Journal of Numismatics* 14, no. 4 (April 1880): 101.

600. Broward County, Florida, USA, 1966.

Type of find: Shipwreck.

Ship: Unknown, but called the "Sunrise Wreck."

Sank: 1823.

Contents: 48+ AR.

Description: Spanish colonies, 8 reales, 1773, 1821, 1823

Disposition: Excavated by General Exploration, Inc. under a contract concluded in 1967 with the State of Florida. 12 coins went to the State of Florida.

Bibliography: Craig 2000b, 22.
Florida Master Site File, File on Sunrise Wreck.

601. Boston, Massachusetts, USA, 1912.

Type of find: Foundation deposit. Cornerstone of the Boston branch of the Second Bank of the United States.

Date of deposit: July 4, 1824.

Contents: 1 AV.

Description: USA, gold medallion of James Otis, weighing 11.9 grams

Disposition: Sold by R. P. Durkin & Co. on April 24, 1990.

Bibliography: Bowers 1997, 51–52.

602. West Hampton, six miles from Bangor, Maine, USA, October 1885.

Type of find: Hoard.

Date of deposit: 1825.

Container: Copper pot.

Contents: 197 AR.

Description:
France, écu
Spain, pesetas
Spain, 8 reales
Mexico, 8 reales
Bolivia, 8 soles
The oldest coins dated to ca. 1760; the most recent coins were dated 1825.

Disposition: Found by Thomas Patten, underneath a rock pile on his farm.

Bibliography: Buried Treasures Found 1885, 42.

603. Haiti, May 1966.

Type of find: Hoard.

Date of deposit: 1825.

Contents: ca. 4,000 AR.

Description:
The hoard was mostly 8 reales, with 2 reales being a significant part. Over 674 of the finer coins were offered by Dan Engelberg in a series of advertisements:
Spain, Philip V, ½ reales (¼ pistareen), Seville, 1732A
Spain, Charles III, ½ reales (¼ pistareen), Seville, 1788C
Spain, Philip V, reales (½ pistareens), Seville (5): 1721J; 1726J; 1728P; 1734PA; 1738PJ
Spain, Ferdinand VI, real (½ pistareen), Madrid, 1755JP
Spain, Charles III, real (½ pistareen), Madrid, 1764JP
Spain, Charles IIII, real (½ pistareen), Seville, 1796CN
Spain, Charles III, pretender, 2 reales (pistareen), Barcelona, 1708
Spain, Philip V, 2 reales (pistareen), Barcelona, 1711
Spain, Philip V, 2 reales (pistareen), Cuenca,

1721JJ

Spain, Philip V, 2 reales (pistareens), Madrid (3): 1723A (2); 1725A

Spain, Philip V, 2 reales (pistareens), Segovia (4): 1719J; 1721F; 1722F; 1723F

Spain, Philip V, 2 reales (pistareens), Seville (5): 1722J (2); 1724J; 1725J; 1735

Spain, Ferdinand VI, 2 reales (pistareen), Seville, 1758JV

Spain, Charles III, 2 reales (pistareens), Madrid (4): 1770PJ; 1775PJ; 1779PJ; 1781PJ

Spain, Charles IIII, 2 reales (pistareens), Madrid (3): 1799MF; 1801FA; 1807FA

Spain, Joseph Napoleon, 4 reales de vellon, Madrid (2): 1809AI; 1810AI

Spain, Philip V, 8 reales, Seville, 1736AP

Spain, Charles III, 8 reales, Madrid, 1772PJ

Spain, Charles III, 8 reales, Seville, 1788C

Spain, Ferdinand VII, 8 reales, Madrid, 1816GJ

Spanish colonies, Philip V, ½ reales, México (11): 1736MF; 1738MF; 1742M; 1744M (2); 1745M; 1746M (4); 1748M

Spanish colonies, Ferdinand VI, ½ reales, México (28): 1748M; 1749M; 1759M (2); 1751M (3); 1753M (3); 1754M (4); 1755M; 1756M (4); 1757M (4); 1758M; 1759M; 1760M (3)

Spanish colonies, Charles III, ½ reales, México (39): 1762M (3); 1763M; 1764M; 1768M (3); 1769M (2); 1772MF (2); 1773MF (2); 1773FM (3); 1774MF; 1778FF; 1779FF; 1780FF; 1781FF* (5); 1783FF; 1784FF (2); 1785FM (3); 1786FM; 1788FM (2)

Spanish colonies, Charles IV, ½ reales, México (2): 1789FM; 1790FM

Spanish colonies, Charles IIII, ½ reales, México (32): 1793FM; 1794FM (2); 1797FM (3); 1798FM (2); 1799FM (3); 1800FM (3); 1801FT (2); 1801FF; 1802FT (2); 1803FT; 1804 TH (2); 1805 TH (2); 1806 TH (3); 1807 TH (3); 1808 TH (2)

Spanish colonies, Ferdinand VII, ½ reales, México (12): 1809 TH (2); 1810 TH; 1810HJ; 1811HJ (2); 1812HJ (2); 1814JJ; 1816JJ; 1819JJ; 1821JJ

Spanish colonies, Philip V, reales, México (4): 1738MF; 1744M; 1745M (2)

Spanish colonies, Ferdinand VI, reales, México (3): 1751M; 1753M; 1756M

Spanish colonies, Charles III, reales, México (7): 1764M; 1770M; 1775FM; 1781FF (2); 1782FF (2)

Spanish colonies, Charles IIII, reales, México (14): 1797FM; 1798FM; 1799FM; 1800FM; 1801FT; 1801FM (2); 1801FT; 1802FT; 1803FT (2); 1807 TH; 1808 TH (2)

Spanish colonies, Ferdinand VII, reales, México (3): 1809 TH; 1816JJ; 1821JJ

Spanish colonies, Philip V, 2 reales, México, 1746M (2)

Spanish colonies, Ferdinand VI, 2 reales, México (3): 1750M; 1752M; 1754M

Spanish colonies, Charles III, 2 reales, México (47): 1760M; 1764M; 1766M; 1767M; 1771F; 1772MF (2); 1773MF; 1773FM (3); 1774FM (3); 1775FM (2); 1776FM (3); 1777FM (2); 1778FF (2); 1779FF (2); 1780FF (3); 1781FF (4); 1782FF (4); 1783FF (2); 1784FF (3); 1785FM (3); 1786FM (2); 1787FM; 1788FM

Spanish colonies, Charles IV, 2 reales, México, 1789FM

Spanish colonies, Charles IIII, 2 reales, México, 1790FM

Spanish colonies, Ferdinand VII, 2 reales, México, 1820JJ

Spanish colonies, Ferdinand VI, 8 reales, México (23): 1747MF; 1748MF (3); 1749MF; 1750MF (2); 1751MF (2); 1752MF; 1753 MF (2); 1754MF; 1755MM (2); 1756MM (2); 1757MM; 1758MM; 1759MM (2); 1760MM

Spanish colonies, Charles III, 8 reales, México (105): 1761MM (3); 1762MM (3); 1763MF; 1764MF (2); 1765MF; 1766MF (3); 1767MF (2); 1768MF (2); 1769MF; 1770FM

(2); 1770FM, chopmarked (2); 1770MF (2); 1771FM (3); 1771FM, chopmarked; 1772MF* (4); 1773MF; 1773FM (2); 1774FM* (4); 1775FM* (3); 1776FM* (3); 1777FM* (4); 1777FF* (3); 1778FF* (4); 1779FF* (4); 1780FF* (3); 1781FF* (4); 1782FF* (5); 1783FF* (4); 1784FM* (5); 1785FM* (4); 1786FM* (4); 1787/6FM; 1787FM* (6); 1788FM* (4); 1789FM* (5)

Spanish colonies, Charles IV, 8 reales, México (11): 1789FM* (5); 1790FM* (5); 1791FM (contemporary counterfeit with impossible date)

Spanish colonies, Charles IIII, 8 reales, México (56): 1790FM* (4); 1791FM* (4); 1792FM* (4); 1793FM* (3); 1794FM* (4); 1795FM* (5); 1796FM* (4); 1797FM* (4); 1798FM* (4); 1799FM* (3); 1800FM* (4); 1801FM; 1801FT* (3); 1802FT; 1803FT; 1804 TH; 1805 TH (2); 1806 TH (2); 1807 TH; 1808 TH

Spanish colonies, Ferdinand VII, 8 reales, México (13): 1809 TH; 1810 HJ (3); 1813JJ; 1817JJ; 1818JJ; 1819JJ (4); 1820JJ; 1821JJ

Spanish colonies, Ferdinand VII, 8 reales, Zacatecas, 1821RG (3)

Spanish colonies, Ferdinand VII, 8 reales, Durango, 1821CG

Spanish colonies, Ferdinand VII, ¼ real, Guatemala, 1821

Spanish colonies, Ferdinand VII, real, Guatemala, 1819M

Spanish colonies, Philip V, cut cob 2 reales, Guatemala, 1739

Spanish colonies, Charles III, 2 reales, Guatemala (4): 1791M; 1793M; 1795M; 1797M

Spanish colonies, Charles III, 8 reales, Guatemala (5): 1776P; 1777P; 1781P; 1787M* (2)

Spanish colonies, Charles IIII, 8 reales, Guatemala, 1804M

Spanish colonies, Ferdinand VII, 8 reales, Guatemala (10): 1810M; 1813M; 1816M; 1817M (2); 1818M (2); 1821M (3)

Spanish colonies, Charles IIII, real, Bogotá, 1800JJ

Spanish colonies, Ferdinand VII, 2 reales, Popayan, 1820FM

Spanish colonies, Charles III, ½ real, Lima, 1776MI

Spanish colonies, Charles IIII, ½ real, Lima (2): 1800IJ; 1804JP

Spanish colonies, Ferdinand VII, ½ real, Lima (3): 1817JP; 1818JP; 1819JP

Spanish colonies, Charles III, reales, Lima (2): 1780MJ; 1782MI

Spanish colonies, Ferdinand VII, reales, Lima (7): 1816JP; 1817JP; 1818JP (2); 1819JP (2); 1820JP

Spanish colonies, Philip V, cob 2 reales, Lima, 1735N

Spanish colonies, Charles III, 2 reales, Lima (2): 1778MJ; 1780MJ

Spanish colonies, Charles IIII, 2 reales, Lima (4): 1792IJ; 1802IJ; 1803IJ; 1807JP

Spanish colonies, Ferdinand VII, 2 reales, Lima (4): 1817JP (2); 1819JP; 1820JP

Spanish colonies, Ferdinand VII, 4 reales, Lima (2): 1812JP; 1819JP

Spanish colonies, Ferdinand VI, 8 reales, Lima (2): 1753J; 1754JD

Spanish colonies, Charles III, 8 reales, Lima (55): 1761JM; 1769JM; 1770JM; 1771JM; 1772JM (2); 1773JM (2); 1773MJ; 1774MJ* (3); 1775MJ* (2); 1776MJ; 1777MJ; 1778MJ; 1779MJ* (3); 1780MJ; 1780MI* (3); 1781MI* (4); 1782MI* (2); 1783MI* (3); 1784MI* (2); 1785MI* (4); 1786MI* (4); 1787MI* (4); 1787IJ*; 1788IJ* (4); 1789IJ* (3)

Spanish colonies, Charles IV, 8 reales, Lima (8): 1789IJ* (3); 1790IJ* (3); 1791IJ* (2)

Spanish colonies, Charles IIII, 8 reales, Lima (14): 1791IJ*; 1792IJ* (3); 1793IJ* (4); 1802IJ; 1804JR; 1807JP; 1808JP (3)

Spanish colonies, Ferdinand VII, 8 reales, Lima (6): 1813JP; 1814JP* (3); 1820JP; 1821JP

Spanish colonies, Ferdinand VII, 8 reales, Cuzco, 1824T

Spanish colonies, Ferdinand VII, ½ real, Potosí, 1821PJ

Spanish colonies, Charles III, real, Potosí, 1774JR

Spanish colonies, Ferdinand VII, real, Potosí, 1819PJ

Spanish colonies, Philip II or Philip III, cob 2 reales, Potosí, assayer B

Spanish colonies, Philip IV, cob 2 reales, Potosí, 1629T

Spanish colonies, Charles II, cob 2 reales, Potosí, 1699F

Spanish colonies, Philip V, cob 2 reales, Potosí (2): 1730M; 1744q

Spanish colonies, Charles III, cob 2 reales, Potosí (3): 1748q; 1761V; 1767V

Spanish colonies, Charles III, 2 reales, Potosí (3): 1774JR; 1778PR; 1786PR

Spanish colonies, Charles III, 4 reales, Potosí (2): 1774JR; 1775JR

Spanish colonies, Charles IIII, 4 reales, Potosí (11): 1793PR (2); 1797PP (2); 1798PP; 1802PP; 1807PJ; 1808PJ (3); 1809PJ

Spanish colonies, Charles III, 8 reales, Potosí (37): 1775JR* (3); 1776PR* (3); 1777PR* (3); 1778PR (3); 1779PR; 1780PR (3); 1781PR; 1782PR (2); 1783PR* (2); 1785PR* (3); 1786PR* (4); 1787PR (2); 1788PR* (4); 1789PR (3)

Spanish colonies, Charles IV, 8 reales, Potosí (5): 1789PR* (3); 1790PR (2)

Spanish colonies, Charles IIII, 8 reales, Potosí (14): 1792PR; 1794PR (2); 1796PP (2); 1798PP (2); 1801PP; 1805PJ; 1806PJ; 1808PJ (4)

Spanish colonies, Ferdinand VII, 8 reales, Potosí (22): 1814PJ (2); 1815PJ; 1817PJ (2); 1818PJ (2); 1819PJ (3); 1820PJ (3); 1821PJ (3); 1824PJ (2); 1825JL (3)

Spanish colonies, Charles IIII, 2 reales, Santiago, 1798DA

Spanish colonies, Charles IV, 8 reales, Santiago, 1789DA

Spanish colonies, Charles IIII, 8 reales, Santiago, 1799DA

Engelberg did not indicate the total number of coins in the hoard, nor the amount of each date. The numbers following the dates are where Engelberg has offered coins in more than one grade; thus if he offers coins in three different grades, the hoard must have contained at least three coins of that date. The asterisks indicate dates where there is at least one uncirculated coin.

An unusual characteristic of the hoard is that there are no uncirculated coins dated later than 1801, even though the hoard does not close until 1825. The ample numbers of uncirculated coins before 1801, and the lack of them thereafter probably reflect the wealth of Haiti in the late eighteenth century, and the subsequent disruption of commerce.

Engelberg lists four Central American ¼ reales dated 1837–43 and five Colombian ¼ reales dated 1863–67 with his listings of the rest of the hoard; however, these coins are dated so much later than the rest of the hoard that they were probably thrown in with the rest of the parcel to make up the lot, and not part of the original hoard. They have been excluded from this listing.

Disposition: The hoard was originally acquired by Ken Fischer for "face" value (US $1 per 8 reales, 25¢ per 2 reales). Sold through Dan Engelberg advertisements in *Numismatic Scrapbook Magazine*, 1966–67.

Bibliography: Jara 2008.

Dan Engelberg, Advertisements, *Numismatic Scrapbook Magazine* 32, no. 5 (May 1966): 1166–69; 32, no. 6 (June 1966): 1396–99; 32, no. 12 (December 1996): 2738–39; 33, no. 7 (July 1967): 1324–27.

604. Levis, ten miles from Neillsville, Clark County, Wisconsin, USA, October 1885.

Type of find: Funerary deposit.

Contents: 1 AR.

Description: USA, John Quincy Adams Indian Peace Medal, 1825

Disposition: The medal was exhumed on the farm of Austin Buttery.

Bibliography: "Adams Indian Peace Medal," *American Journal of Numismatics* 20, no. 2 (October 1885): 41.

605. Burton, Ohio, USA, November 1933.

Type of find: Single find.

Contents: 1 AE.

Description: USA, ½¢, 1825

Bibliography: "We Wonder if George would Consider this a Compliment," *Numismatist* 46, no. 11 (November 1933): 696.

606. Mount Vernon, New York, USA, December 14, 1897.

Type of find: Hoard.

Date of deposit: 1825.

Container: Secret drawers of an old desk.

Contents: 30+ P.

Description: USA, New Jersey, Monmouth Bank, "small notes" (i.e., denominated $1, $2, or $3), 1825, totaling $64

Disposition: L. I. Townley of Mount Vernon, New York, sent an old fashioned desk to James C. Ogden, a furniture dealer of Elizabeth, New Jersey, which Ogden was to overhaul and to send to John P. Feeney of Jersey City, the former Chief of State Police. Ogden discovered two secret drawers in the desk, one of which contained a package with the bills. The bills are said to have been sent to the bank for redemption, which is puzzling, since Haxby reference says that the bank closed down in the 1820s.

Bibliography: "Treasure Trove in an Old Desk," *New York Times*, December 16, 1897, 1.

607. Middletown, New York, USA, December 1926.

Type of find: Hoard.

Date of deposit: Ca. 1826.

Contents: 30 AR.

Description:
France, écus
Spanish colonies, 8 reales
"Century-old coins of French and Spanish mintage"—presumably écus and Spanish colonies 8 reales.

Disposition: Found on the land of Leslie H. Prince.

Bibliography: "Workmen Find Old Coins—Dig Up French and Spanish Pieces at Middletown, N.Y.," *New York Times*, December 18, 1926, 10.

608. Boston, Massachusetts, USA, January 1896.

Type of find: Foundation deposit.

Date of deposit: 1826.

Contents: 10 AE, 3 AR.

Description:
Great Britain, counterfeit halfpence (2): 1802; 1815 (both are impossible dates)
France, sol, 1780
British colonies, Nova Scotia, 1814 (probably a Broke token, Breton 798)
USA, 1¢ (3): 1822; 1823; 1826
USA, 10¢, 1823
Spanish colonies, probably reales, probably México, 1810 (2)
Not described (3)

Disposition: Found under the fluted stone pillars that stood at the entrance to the Tremont House, a hotel in Boston.

Bibliography: "Coins under the Tremont House Pillars," *American Journal of Numismatics* 30, no. 3 (January 1896): 83.

Joseph Hooper, "Hooper's Restrikes," *Numismatist* 10, no. 9–10 (September-October 1897): 164.

609. Washington Street and Second Street, Hoboken, New Jersey, USA, May 1868.

Type of find: Foundation deposit.
Date of deposit: 1826.
Contents: 1 AE, 1 AR.
Description:
  USA, 1¢, 1826
  USA, 50¢
Disposition: Discovered by a laborer while altering a building at the Southwest corner of Washington and Second streets, Hoboken. The building belonged to Theophilus Butts, and was built in 1826.
Bibliography: "A Cruel Hoax," *American Journal of Numismatics* 3, no. 2 (June 1868): 12.

610. Near Spotsylvania Courthouse, Virginia, USA, fall 1925.

Type of find: Hoard.
Date of deposit: 1826.
Container: Box.
Contents: 2,000 AR.
Description:
  USA, 50¢, 1812 (1,000)
  USA, 50¢, 1826 (1,000)
Disposition: Found in a box, containing other silver, by a farmer during the fall plowing near Spotsylvania Courthouse. He intended holding the coins for a premium, but the exigencies of winter compelled him to spend them. The coins ended up in circulation in Fredericksburg.
Bibliography: "Hundred-Year-Old Coins Circulating in Virginia," *Numismatist* 39, no. 3 (March 1926): 129 (citing the *Baltimore Sun*).

611. 6019 Germantown Avenue, Germantown, Pennsylvania, USA, October 4, 1930.

Type of find: Hoard.
Date of deposit: 1826.
Contents: 7 AE, 13 AR.
Description:
  Great Britain, George II, halfpenny, 1738 (7)
  USA, 50¢ (7): 1826; date not specified (6)
  The coins were bright and shiny. The number of coins found is an estimate, based on an interpretation of the adjective "several."
Disposition: The coins were found by the construction workers Vincent Mercaldo and W. A. Lowrie. The coins were found in a wall of the Daniel Mackinett house in Germantown, where Washington and Lafayette had been entertained. In colonial times it was known as the "Green Tree Inn." It was built in 1748. Some of the coins were found between loose stones, others were buried in the plaster.
Bibliography: "Germantown Home Yields Rare Coins. Hoard Found Imbedded in Mortar of Walls in Mackinett Mansion. Pre-Revolution House Being Removed to Make Way for Church Building," *Philadelphia Inquirer*, October 5, 1930, 6.

"Mansion Walls Hide Coins. Hoard Dating from 1738 Found in Moving Germantown Rooftree," *New York Times*, October 5, 1930, 20.

612. Willemansett, Massachusetts, USA, September 1956.

Type of find: Hoard.
Date of deposit: 1826.
Contents: 2+ AR, 1+ AV.
Description:
  USA, 50¢, 1826

USA, silver $1, 1797
USA, $5, 1823

Bibliography: "Buried Treasures Found," *Numismatic Scrapbook Magazine* 22, no. 9 (September 1956): 1486.

613. Washington, DC, USA, December 1938.

Type of find: Foundation deposit in a Masonic cornerstone.

Date of deposit: 1826.

Contents: 1 AE, 3 AR.

Description:
USA, 1¢, 1826
USA, 10¢, 1821
USA, 25¢, 1824
USA, 50¢, 1824

Bibliography: Harry X Boosel, "Capital Comments," *Numismatic Scrapbook Magazine* 5, no. 1 (January 1939): 29.

614. Hamilton, Ontario, Canada, 1978.

Type of find: Foundation deposit in the cornerstone of the Hamilton Court House.

Date of deposit: 1827.

Contents: 1+ AE.

Description: British colonies, Upper Canada, Lesslie token, 1822

An important find for re-dating the Lesslie token, which McLachlan thought had been struck after 1834.

Bibliography: Banning 1986, 476; Willey 1982, 320.

615. Feeding Hills, West Springfield, Massachusetts, USA, November 19, 1845.

Type of find: Hoard.

Date of deposit: 1827.

Container: Wrapped in sheet lead and secured with wire. The notes were arranged in three separate divisions.

Contents: 27 P.

Description: USA, Connecticut, Hartford, Phoenix Bank, $10, 1827 (27)

Genuine notes of this date are rare. This hoard may well have consisted of counterfeits (Haxby CT-195, C148a).

Bibliography: "Money Found," *Worcester (MA) Palladium,* November 19, 1845 (citing the *Springfield (MA) Republican*) (reference courtesy of Q. David Bowers).

616. Alexandria, Virginia, USA, 1884.

Type of find: Hoard.

Date of deposit: 1828.

Contents: 1,000 AE.

Description:
USA, ½¢, 1811
USA, ½¢, 1828, 13 stars (999)

Disposition: Frederic Charles Cogswell Boyd had several hundred half cents from this hoard, acquired from David Proskey. In the early 1950s, he sold 200 to 300 to New Netherlands.

Bibliography: Bowers 1997, 49–50; Breen 1952, 17–18 (Breen XIV); Breen 1988, 169, 171 (Breen 1566).

617. Skyring Island, Tierra del Fuego, Chile, 1981.

Type of find: Foundation deposit in a memorial cairn established after an ascent of Skyring Island by the crew of the Beagle.

Date of deposit: May 16, 1829.

Contents: 14 AE.

Description:
Great Britain, George IV, HBMS Adventure and Beagle medals, 1828 (4)
Great Britain, coin
Italy, coin
Brazil, coin
Argentina, coin
Other coins corroded beyond recognition

Disposition: Found by Eduardo Barison and Lieutenant Eugenio Arellano of the Chilean Navy in 1981. Given to a Chilean museum.

Bibliography: Allen 1982, 69–73; Hanscom 1998.

618. Second United States Mint, Chestnut and Juniper Streets, Philadelphia, Pennsylvania, USA, 1902.

Type of find: Foundation deposit.

Date of deposit: July 4, 1829.

Contents: 3 AR.

Description:
USA, silver 5¢, 1829
USA, 10¢, 1829
Coins from the cornerstone of the Second United States Mint, Chestnut and Juniper Streets. The identity of the third coin is not listed.

Bibliography: Breen 1988, 281 (Breen 2982). "Mint Cornerstone Found," *Numismatist* 16, no. 5 (May 1903): 148–49.

619. 121 Market Street, Philadelphia, Pennsylvania, USA, 1976.

Type of find: Archaeological excavation from two privy pits.

Date of site: 1685–1870.

Date of use of second privy pit: 1810–70.

Date of coin: 1829.

Contents: 1 AR.

Description: Mexico, 8 reales, 1829

Bibliography: Cotter, Roberts, and Parrington 1992, 240.

620. Near Stockton, Kansas, USA, November 1925.

Type of find: Single find.

Contents: 1 AR.

Description: USA, Andrew Jackson Indian Peace Medal, 1829.

Disposition: Found by George Hammond in an alfalfa field.

Bibliography: "Indian Medal of Andrew Jackson Dug Up," *Numismatist* 38, no. 11 (November 1925): 597.

621. Burford, Ontario, Canada, USA, fall 1980.

Type of find: Archaeological excavation of the John Yeigh Pottery.

Date of site: 1802–29.

Contents: 1 AE.

Description: Great Britain, Thomas Seymour evasive halfpenny, Atkins 493–43

Bibliography: Michael 1982.

622. Bay Minette, Baldwin County, Alabama, USA, April 1924.

Type of find: Hoard.

Date of deposit: 1830?

Contents: AV.

Description:
Spanish colonies, 8 escudos
Mexico, 8 escudos

Disposition: Plowed up by C. C. Coleman, a prosperous farmer and turpentine operator.

Bibliography: "Hunt Buried Treasure. Plowing Up of Gold Coins Excites Alabama County," *New York Times*, April 7, 1924, 17. "Old Spanish Coins Found in Alabama," *Numismatist* 37, no. 6 (June 1924): 420.

623. Springport, Indiana, USA, March 1933.

Type of find: Hoard.

Date of deposit: 1830?

Contents: 6 B.

Description: Coin weights for gold coins. The weights read:
US Dollars/3
US Dollars/4
US Dollars/5
US Dollars/10

FS Dollars/3
FS Dollars/5
Found in a hundred-year-old well.
Since the weights are for United States old tenor gold, they must pre-date 1834.

Bibliography: McDonald 2000.
"Are these Coin Weights?" *Numismatist* 46, no. 3 (March 1933): 181.

624. Harrisburg, Ontario, Canada, August 1899.

Type of find: Hoard.

Date of deposit: 1830.

Contents: 40–50 AR.

Description:
USA, 50¢, 1830
Mexico, 8 reales, 1830

Bibliography: Joseph Hooper, "Hooper's Restrikes," *Numismatist* 12, no. 8 (August 1899): 190.

625. Dubuque, Iowa, USA, June 1947.

Type of find: Hoard.

Date of deposit: 1830.

Contents: 900+ AR, AV.

Description:
Spanish colonies, 8 reales
Spanish colonies, 8 escudos

Disposition: Silver and gold coins, some minted in 1822, total face value $9,000, found by John Berens in the cellar of house he had bought. The face value totalled $9,000. He turned the coins over to Allan T. Daykin, the county auditor, to inventory and advertise. If the rightful owner can prove ownership within a year, the owner gets it less 10% to the finder; otherwise, all goes to the finder. Coins not described in detail; description in entry is an educated guess of what the coins would most likely be.

Bibliography: Weikert 1954, 123.

"Notes and Queries: Old Gold and Silver Coins Found," *Numismatist* 60, no. 8 (August 1947): 591–92.

626. La Herradura, Cordoba Province, Argentina, April 1961.

Type of find: Foundation deposit in the destroyed cornerstone of a house being torn down.

Date of deposit: Ca. 1830.

Contents: ca. 400 AR.

Description:
Spanish colonies, Charles IV, 8 reales
Spanish colonies, Ferdinand VII, 8 reales
Bolivia, 8 soles
Amount, denominations and date of deposit are educated guesses. Described as "10 kilos of silver coins from the time of Charles IV, Ferdinand VII, and Simon Bolivar."

Bibliography: "Neue Münzfunde," *Numismatisches Nachrichtenblatt* 10, no. 5 (May 1961): 86 (citing *Argentinisches Tageblatt*, April 6, 1961).

627. Mostul Village, Clackamas River, 9 miles upstream from Gladstone, Oregon, USA, 1971–73.

Type of find: Funerary deposit.

Date of deposit: 1830?

Contents: 3 B.

Description:
China, Kangxi, cash, Beijing, either Board of Works or Board of Revenue
China, Kangxi, cash, Beijing, Board of Revenue
China, cash, illegible

Disposition: Archaeological excavation by Mount Hood Community College archaeology classes under the direction of John Woodward.

Bibliography: Beals 1980, 64–65, 70.

628. Mobile, Alabama, USA, 1868.

Type of find: Single find.

Contents: 1 AR.

Description: USA, Catholic religious silver medal, dated 1830, depicting the Virgin Mary and twelve stars around her, with the inscription: "O Mary, conceived without sin, Pray for us who have recourse to you."

Bibliography: Beauchamp 1891, 42; Beauchamp 1903, 49.

629. Biddeford, Maine, USA, October 1931.

Type of find: Hoard.

Date of deposit: 1831.

Contents: 60 AR, AV.

Description:
Spanish colonies, 8 reales
Spanish colonies, 8 escudos

Disposition: Spanish coins more than a century old unearthed by Ralph Labbe and Ovila Bouthot while digging in their garden.

Bibliography: "Spanish Coins Found in Maine," *Numismatist* 44, no. 10 (October 1931): 675.

630. Milan, Michigan, USA, August 1898.

Type of find: Hoard.

Date of deposit: 1831.

Contents: 28 AV.

Description:
Great Britain, George III, ½ sovereigns, 1817 (2)
Great Britain, William IV, sovereigns, 1831 (26)
Note: the sovereigns are described as being from the reign of George IV, but dated 1831. This has been corrected to William IV, on the rationale that an observer not educated in Latin might misread GULIELMUS as meaning George.

Disposition: Found by John Pilbeam, a prominent farmer living about three miles north of Milan, Michigan.

Bibliography: "With the Editor," *Numismatist* 11, no. 8 (August 1898): 210.

631. Two miles south of Bloomington, Indiana, USA, August 17, 1891.

Type of find: Hoard.

Date of deposit: 1831.

Contents: Ca. 300 AR.

Description:
France, 5 francs, Year 8 (1800)
USA, 50¢: 1830; 1831
Spanish colonies, Charles IV, 8 reales, México, 1795FM
Spanish colonies, Ferdinand VII, 8 reales, probably México, 1814
Mexico (Republic), 8 reales (largest number of pieces in the hoard, so 200?)
Number of coins in the hoard is an educated guess, but two full sacks were recovered. The coins were very well preserved, but no container was found.

Disposition: Found by Henry C. Rhorer, Edgar Rhorer, Kent Cooper and James Sneddy. Kent Cooper was the son of George W. Cooper, the local congressional representative, and was visiting his uncle, Henry C. Rhorer. Divided among the four finders.

Bibliography: "Old Coins Dug Up. Treasure Reported Found Near Bloomington, Ind.," *New York Times*, August 25, 1891, 3 (citing the *Louisville (KY) Courier-Journal* of August 21, 1891) (reference courtesy of Q. David Bowers). The *Courier-Journal* published illustrations depicting some of the coins in the hoard.

632. Scatarie Island, Louisbourg, Nova Scotia, Canada, September 17, 1968.

Type of find: Shipwreck.

Ship: Leonidas.

Sank: August 12, 1832.

Contents: 600 AE.

Description:
   Great Britain, William IV, farthings
   Great Britain, William IV, halfpence
   Great Britain, William IV, pence
   600 coins found; distribution among the three denominations not specified, assumed to be roughly even.
Bibliography: Storm 2002, 109–13.

633. Island in the Susquehanna River, near Danville, Pennsylvania, USA, 1885.

Type of find: Hoard.
Date of deposit: 1832.
Container: Iron box.
Contents: 20,000 AR, 150 AV.
Description:
   Spanish colonies, ½ reales, México
   Spanish colonies, reales, México
   Spanish colonies, 2 reales, México
   Spanish colonies, 8 reales, México
   Spanish colonies, 8 escudos, México
   Mexico, 8 reales
   Earliest date of the coins before 1800, latest date 1832. Found by George Stoit and Henry Alder.
Bibliography: Thomas L. Elder, "Recollections of an Old Collector: A Big Pennsylvania Treasure Trove," *Hobbies—the Magazine for Collectors*, September 1939, 87 (reference courtesy of Q. David Bowers).

634. Civil War camp, Texas, USA, 1985–95.

Type of find: Hoard.
Date of deposit: 1832.
Contents: 9 AR.
Description:
   USA, 50¢, 1830, uncirculated
   USA, 50¢, 1831, uncirculated (2)
   USA, 50¢, 1803–31 (5)
   Spanish colonies, Charles IV, 4 reales, Potosí
   The hoard included an 1830 and two 1831 half dollars in uncirculated condition.
Bibliography: Kays 1996, 1637–45.

635. Philadelphia, Pennsylvania, USA, May 2007.

Type of find: Foundation deposit.
Date of deposit: 1833.
Contents: 1 AE.
Description: USA, 1¢, 1833
   This is a foundation deposit on the cornerstone of a commercial building built above the "President's House." The "President's House" was torn down in 1832, and the construction of the building above began in 1833.
Bibliography: Stephan Salisbury, "Dig yields some unexpected finds," *Philadelphia Inquirer*, May 4, 2007, A1.

636. Castle Island, Bermuda, early 1900s.

Type of find: Hoard.
Date of deposit: 1833.
Contents: 1,000 AR.
Description:
   Spanish colonies, Ferdinand VI, 2 reales, cut quarter
   Spanish colonies, Charles III, 2 reales, cut quarter
   Spanish colonies, cob real, Potosí, 1741, cut half
   Half section of a cob real of Potosí dated 1741
   Spanish colonies, silver coins, 1711–33
Bibliography: Peterson 1962, 582–85.

637. Jericho Beach, Scituate, Massachusetts, USA, October 1886.

Type of find: Single find.
Contents: 1 AE.
Description: Great Britain, William IV, medal commemorating abolition of slavery in the

British Empire, 1833

Described thus: "In commemoration of the extinction of colonial slavery throughout the British dominions in the reign of William IV," (so the medal would date from 1833); "This is the Lord's doings, 1784."

Bibliography: "Notes and Queries: Lost and Found," *American Journal of Numismatics* 21, no. 2 (October 1886): 44.

638. On the prairie, south of Dickinson, North Dakota, USA, summer 1882.

Type of find: Funerary deposit.

Date of deposit: 1833.

Contents: 1 AR.

Description: USA, New York, John Jacob Astor, American Fur Company, Indian Peace Medal, 1832–33

Disposition: Found by the photographer Frank Jay Haynes on the prairie near a skull with a bullet hole in it and an old flintlock rifle. Auctioned by S. H. Chapman, December 9, 1920 (Hunter Collection), lot 115; bought by the American Numismatic Society, New York, New York, USA; item number 1920.210.1.

Bibliography: Belden 1927, 41; Stack's 2006b, lot 182 (mentioned).

639. Warner, New Hampshire, USA, 1884.

Type of find: Hoard.

Date of deposit: 1834.

Container: Iron box.

Contents: 1,000? AR.

Description: Great Britain, shillings (1,000?)

Disposition: "Iron box filled with English shillings found in the well of Reuben Clough of Warner, while it was being cleaned recently. The well, which is thirty feet deep, had not been cleaned for half a century."

Bibliography: Brown and Dolley 1971, 59 (NU2); Various 1884, 96.

640. Place Royale, Québec, Québec, Canada, 1976–80.

Type of find: Archaeological excavations of the Place Royale area.

Date of Lower Canada/Canada East Phase of Occupation: 1791–1867, placed at 1835 since that year was a peak year for colonial copper token circulation in Canada.

Contents: 21 AE, 2 AR.

Description:

Great Britain, halfpence with young head of Victoria (3)

Great Britain, light halfpenny tokens of the early nineteenth century (3)

Ireland, George III, halfpence, 1805 (3)

France, ½ franc, 1810

British colonies, Canadian colonial copper halfpenny tokens (10) (including one blacksmith, and Breton Nos. 522, 527, 692/4, 716, 720, 888, 971?, 997, 1012)

British colonies, Province of Canada, 1¢, 1859 (2)

USA, silver 5¢, 1853

The above list is based upon the article by Peter Moogk.

Disposition: Ministère des Affaires Culturelles (Secteur Place Royale).

Bibliography: Moogk 1989, 246–49; Niellon and Moussette 1981, 139–44.

641. East Main Street, next to Saint Frances de Sales Roman Catholic Church, Patchogue, Long Island, New York, USA, March 30, 1897.

Type of find: Hoard.

Date of deposit: 1835.

Contents: 10 AE, 100 AR.

Description:

Spain, probably 2 reales (pistareens), 1739 to 1821, one dated 1801 (corrected from 1601)

USA, 10¢, 1832 (corrected from 1732) to 1835

USA, 25¢

The dime dated 1835 was as bright as when it left the Mint.

Disposition: Found in a grove formerly owned by the Conklin family and bought by Peter Waters. Peter Waters found it while digging.

Bibliography: "Mr. Waters' Lucky Find. He Unearths a Quantity of Ancient Coins on his Patchogue Property and is Looking for More," *Brooklyn Daily Eagle*, March 31, 1897, 5.

642. Old Mission, near Clarksville, Texas, USA, January 1846.

Type of find: Hoard.

Date of deposit: 1835?

Container: Old oaken box.

Contents: 2,500 AR.

Description: Spanish colonies, 8 reales, México (2,500)

The mint is an educated guess. The date of deposit was chosen on the grounds that Santa Anna's attempt to reconquer Texas during the Alamo campaign would be the period when people would be most likely to bury money and flee.

Bibliography: "Treasure-trove!," *Barre (MA) Patriot*, January 16, 1846, 3 (citing the *New Orleans Delta*).

643. Sag Harbor, New York, USA, October 1880.

Type of find: Hoard.

Date of deposit: 1836.

Contents: 1,500 AR.

Description: USA, 50¢, 1836 (1,500)

Property of a doctor of Sag Harbor, who obtained them at issue and hoarded them at the time of the financial pressure in 1836 that culminated in the Panic of 1837.

Bibliography: Bowers 1997, 44–45; Breen 1988, 389 (Breen 4719).

Canadian Antiquarian and Numismatic Journal (October 1880): 96.

"Half Dollars of 1836," *American Journal of Numismatics* 15, no. 2 (October 1880): 43.

644. Québec City, Québec, Canada, 1889.

Type of find: Hoard.

Date of deposit: 1837.

Containers: Boxes.

Contents: 12,000 AE.

Description:

British colonies, Prince Edward Island, "Ships Colonies & Commerce," (McLachlan 602–6, Leroux 793) (600 to 700)

British colonies, Lower Canada, Tiffin copper, 1815 (McLachlan 552–57, Leroux 771–73) (3,000)

British colonies, Lower Canada, Harp copper, 1820 (McLachlan 597, Leroux 786) (800)

British colonies, Lower Canada, George III, 1820 copper (McLachlan 594, Leroux 785) (50)

British colonies, Lower Canada, eagle copper, 1814 (McLachlan 560) (2) (both very poor)

British colonies, Lower Canada, George Orde's token, 1834, from very worn dies (25)

British colonies, Lower and Upper Canada, Vexator Canadensis (McLachlan 21–22, Leroux 500–1) (4)

British colonies, Lower and Upper Canada, Canida copper (60)

British colonies, Lower and Upper Canada, Blacksmith imitations ("George II") (McLachlan 612–13) (500)

British colonies, Lower and Upper Canada, GLORIUVS III VIS (McLachlan 616, Wood 33)

British colonies, Lower and Upper Canada?, Imitations of Irish halfpennies (McLachlan.610–11) (25) (six different varieties)

Three boxes containing 12,000 old coppers refused by the banks in the late 1830s in the Bank of Montreal branch. McLachlan saw 5,000, which included Tiffins, Bust & Harp tokens, blacksmiths, and Ships Colonies & Commerce (including varieties Lees 1, 2 and 3).

Disposition: To the hands of collectors, including over 5,000 to W. G. L. Paxman, who picked out some for his own collection and forwarded the balance to McLachlan. McLachlan must have sold them onward after examining them, for the hoard was not preserved as part of his collection. Most, quite possibly all, examples of the Canida copper come from this hoard.

Bibliography: McLachlan 1889.

645. Chambly, Québec, Canada, January 1885.

Type of find: Hoard.

Date of deposit: 1837.

Contents: 6+ AE.

Description:
British colonies, Lower Canada, 1812 halfpenny tokens, McLachlan 557 (4+)
British colonies, Lower Canada, Bank halfpennies, 1837
British colonies, Lower Canada, Bank pennies, 1837

Disposition: A hoard of old coppers found when repairing the canteen in the old barracks at Chambly after it was sold. The barracks had been untenanted since the rebellion in 1837.

Bibliography: McLachlan 1885a, 58; McLachlan 1886.

646. Along the Saint Lawrence River, near Massena, New York, USA, July 1954.

Type of find: Hoard.

Date of deposit: 1837.

Contents: 500 AE.

Description:
Great Britain, halfpence
British colonies, Lower Canada, Bank of Montreal, token
USA, 1¢
Included USA and British copper coins, plus a token of the Bank of Montreal. The account of the hoard says that it was "more than 125 years old," which would make the date of deposit 1829, but given its composition and its find spot it fits best with the other copper hoards known to be associated with the Lower and Upper Canada rebellions of 1837, namely the Bank of Montreal hoard and the find at Chambly Barracks.

Bibliography: "Coin Hoard Found Along the St. Lawrence," *Numismatic Scrapbook Magazine* 20, no. 7 (July 1954): 893.

647. Canada? January 1979.

Type of find: Hoard.

Date of deposit: 1837?

Contents: 56 AE.

Description: British colonies, Lower and Upper Canada, blacksmith coppers of the following Wood varieties:

W-1	2	W-13	4	W-18	4
W-2	2	W-14	6	W-23	7
W-3	2	W-15	1	W-33	13
W-4	4	W-16	1		
W-11	9	W-17	1		

Disposition: Offered for sale by a coin dealer at a U.S. coin show; bought by L. B. Fauver.

Bibliography: Fauver 1980.

648. Napanee River, Ontario, Canada, November 1995.

Type of find: Hoard.

Date of deposit: 1837?

Contents: 5+ AE, 1 AR.

Description:
Spain, real (½ pistareen), 1723

British colonies, Upper Canada, Brock tokens

British colonies, Upper Canada, Wellington tokens

The Spanish real was the oldest coin.

Disposition: To the Lennox and Addington Historical Society, and installed in their display case.

Bibliography: Irwin 1995.

649. Tipton, Indiana, USA, June 4, 1900.

Type of find: Single find.

Contents: 1 AE.

Description: USA, hard times token, Low 54, "Am I not a Woman and a Sister?, 1838"

Disposition: Found by the youth Garrett Todd while spading in his father's garden.

Bibliography: "Talisman of Slavery Found. A Copper Token Used on the Undergound Railway Dug Up in an Indiana Garden. How It Assisted in the Escape of Negroes to Canada and Carried with It the Obligation to Protect the Fugitive. Only About Twenty of the Tokens Made," *Boston Evening Transcript*, June 9, 1900, 5 (citing the *New York Tribune*).

"Old Copper Tokens. Their Frequency Fifty Years Ago—Their Insignificance Exaggerated," *New York Tribune*, July 2, 1900, 11.

"The 'Talisman of Slavery,'" *American Journal of Numismatics* 35, no. 1 (July 1900): 22.

650. Mexico.

Type of find: Single find.

Contents: 1 AV.

Description: Mexico, 8 escudos, 1839, Durango

Disposition: Found in an adobe wall. Acquired by Clyde Hubbard.

Bibliography: Clyde Hubbard, face-to-face conversation with John M. Kleeberg, July 29, 1993.

651. 18 nautical miles east of Myrtle Beach, South Carolina, USA, August 1996.

Type of find: Shipwreck.

Ship: SS *North Carolina*.

Sank: July 26, 1840.

Contents: 10 AR, 18 AV.

Description:
USA, 50¢, 1834–40 (10)
USA, $2.50 (18)

Disposition: Recovered by Herbert Humphreys's operation, MAREX ("Marine Archaeology Exploration") International, Inc. Number of 50¢ recovered is an estimate.

Bibliography: Marex Int'l, Inc., v. the Unidentified, Wrecked and Abandoned Vessel, 952 F.Supp. 825 (S.D. Ga. 1997).

652. Pennsylvania, USA, February 1935.

Type of find: Hoard.

Date of deposit: 1840.

Contents: 100 AR.

Description:
USA, 50¢, 1810–39 (49)
USA, 50¢, 1840
USA, 50¢, type unknown (50)

Disposition: Money saved up by an old lady for her burial in a sealed can and given to the undertaker, which he later split between his two sons.

Bibliography: Botsford 1935.

653. Delancey and Mangin Streets, New York, New York, USA, March 1898.

Type of find: Excavation.

Date of latest coin: Ca. 1840.

Contents: 5 AE.

Description: Great Britain, evasive halfpenny, Isaac Newton
Ireland, George IV, halfpenny, 1823
USA, 1¢, 1798
USA, hard times token, Low 51–53

Found by Italian laborers while excavating the foundations for the Williamsburg Bridge. The coins were among the oaken timbers of a shipwreck; the ship was probably sunk as a crib hulk to make landfill for a pier (compare *NFA* 425).

Disposition: 2 to E. Shanley of the firm of Shanley and Ryan; 3 to A. MacC. Parker.

Bibliography: "Old Schooner Unearthed. Bridge Builders' Queer Find Under Delancey Street. Ancient Coins Discovered," *Brooklyn Daily Eagle*, March 27, 1898, 36.

654. Silas Crossing, Georgia, USA, November 1942.

Type of find: Hoard.

Date of deposit: 1840.

Contents: 200+ AR.

Description:

Spanish colonies, 8 reales, México

Spanish colonies, 8 reales, Potosí

Mexico, 8 reales, 1840

The oldest coins were Spanish dollars with the date 1772 and the likeness of Charles III (note that this shows the effect of the 1772 debasement). The most recent coin was a Mexican coin of 1840.

Bibliography: "Accident Reveals Hoard of Silver Coins," *Numismatist* 55, no. 11 (November 1942): 833.

655. Independence Hall, Philadelphia, Pennsylvania, USA, 1968.

Type of find: Archaeological excavation of two cisterns.

Date of site: 1840–80.

Contents: 1 NI, 2 AV.

Description: Cistern 3 contained:

USA, shield nickel 5¢ [1866–83]

German states, Brunswick-Lüneburg, 5 thaler, 1815

Cistern 3A contained:

USA, $5, 1834 (new tenor; no motto)

Bibliography: Cotter, Roberts, and Parrington 1992, 118, 146–47.

656. New Vineyard, Maine, USA, September 29, 1906.

Type of find: Hoard.

Date of deposit: 1840s.

Containers: 3 cans (a small cylindrical can, a milk can, and a large watering can). The watering can is identical to one produced by Gustin & Blake of Chelsea, Vermont, in 1835.

Contents: 1,300 AR.

Description:

USA, 50¢

Spanish colonies, 8 reales

Disposition: The coins were found while excavating on the site of Old Porter Mill, which had burned down on September 25, 1906. The land belonged to Leonard J. Hackett. The hoard was found on a Saturday afternoon, and deposited in a national bank on the Monday following. The aggregate face value was $1,284.67. The coins are described as USA and non-USA silver coins in the case report; the description above is an educated guess of what would be the likeliest contents. After litigation the value was divided among the three finders, Orlando Weeks, Edwin E. Morton, and Fessenden E. Hackett. The money may have been buried by Porter, a former owner of the premises.

Bibliography: Weeks v. Hackett, 71 A. 858 (Me. 1908).

Q. David Bowers, "Looking back: Nostalgia has way of making time stand still," *Coin World*, May 30, 2005, 58 (postcard with photograph of the hoard).

657. Fifth Street, Huntingdon, Pennsylvania, USA, June 15, 1886.

Type of find: Hoard.

Date of deposit: 1840s?

Container: Earthenware pot.

Contents: 200+ AR, AV.

Description:
    USA, 50¢
    Spanish colonies, 8 reales, México
    Spanish colonies, 8 escudos, México
    Described as Mexican and U.S. silver and gold coins "of ancient date"; this has been assumed to mean U.S. half dollars and Spanish colonies 8 reales and 8 escudos, worth several thousand dollars. It was found while excavating for a new water reservoir at the head of Fifth-street.

Disposition: In litigation among J. D. McClain, the finder; Peter Herdic, also known as "the Williamsport Lumber King," the owner of the land; and Mrs. Christian Colestock, whose late husband owned the land before Herdic and who, she said, buried the money on the land.

Bibliography: "A Quarrel over Buried Treasure," *New York Times*, June 17, 1886, 1.

658. Abandoned fort site along the Mohawk River on private property near Albany, New York, USA, December 2001.

Type of find: Hoard. Called "the Mohawk Valley Hoard."

Date of deposit: 1842.

Contents: 650–700 AR.

Description:
    USA, 25¢ (112+): 1805, B2 (2); 1805, B3; 1805, B5; 1806/5, B1 (3); 1806, B2; 1806, B3 (3); 1806, B5 (2); 1806, B9 (5); 1806, B9A (2); 1807, B1 (2); 1807, B2 (4); 1818/5, B1 (2); 1818, B4; 1818, B5; 1818, B9; 1818, B10; 1819, B2 (2); 1819, B3; 1821, B4 (2); 1822, B1; 1831, B3 (2); 1834, B1 (2); ND (70+)
    USA, 50¢ (337+): 1794, O101A; 1806/5, O101; 1795, O131; 1806, O109; 1806, O116 (2); 1806, O118A; 1806, O119 (2); 1806, O120; 1807, O101; 1807, O102 (2); 1807, O103; 1807, O103A; 1807, O104; 1807, O105A; 1807, O108; 1807, O109A; 1807, O112 (3); 1807, O113A; 1807, O115; 1808/7, O101; 1808, O103; 1808, O104 (3); 1808, O106; 1808, O107A; 1809, O103 (3); 1809, O105(2); 1809, O109A; 1809, O111 (2); 1809, O114; 1810, O101A; 1810, O105; 1811/10, O101 (2); 1811, O105A; 1811, O106; 1811, O108; 1811, O110A; 1812/1, O102; 1812, O103; 1812, O104; 1812, O104A; 1812, O107; 1812, O109A; 1813, O103 (2); 1813, O104; 1813, O105 (2); 1813, O106A; 1813, O107A (4); 1813, O109 (2); 1813, O110 (4); 1814, O103; 1814, O104A; 1814, O107; 1814, O109 (2); 1815/2, O101; 1817/13, O101; 1817, O107; 1817, O110 (2); 1818/7, O101; 1818, O108; 1819, O107A (2); 1819, O110; 1819, O113; 1820, O108; 1821, O106; 1822, O104; 1822, O113; 1823, O106A; 1824/var, O103; 1824, O115; 1825, O105; 1825, O107; 1826, O101; 1826, O102; 1826, O106; 1826, O107; 1826, O113; 1826, O113A; 1826, O117; 1827, O104; 1827, O106; 1827, O141; 1828, O108; 1829, O112A; 1830, O101; 1830, O107A; 1830, O108 (2); 1831, O104; 1831, O108; 1831, O111; 1832, O122; 1833, O106; 1833, O109 (2); 1833, O111 (2); 1834, O101; 1834, O104; 1834, O106; 1834, O107; 1834, O109; 1834, O113; 1834, O114; 1834, O115; 1834, O116; 1834, O117; 1834, O120; 1835, O106 (2); 1835, O107; 1835, O108; 1835, O110; 1836, O106; 1836, O110; 1836, O112; 1836, O116A; 1837; ND (200+)

    Spanish colonies, reales (20)

    Spanish colonies, 2 reales (80): 1775; 1776; 1778; 1780; 1781; 1782; 1784; 1785; 1786; 1787; 1788; 1795

    Spanish colonies, 8 reales (only one found in the hoard)

    Mexico, 2 reales, 1842

    Die variety references: B, for 25¢, is Browning; O, for 50¢, is Overton.

The hoard comprises 550 to nearly 600 U.S. silver coins, dating from 1794 until 1838, mostly 50¢, and over 100 Spanish colonies (and Mexican) silver coins, dating from 1775 until 1842, the latter mostly 2 reales. All the coins had chisel marks at 12 o'clock on the obverse, half marked with a slash, half with a dot.

Disposition: The coins were found buried in a series of eighteen discrete caches by a metal detecting club. One cache was below a rotted tree trunk and produced 30–40 USA 50¢. The finders have photographs showing how the coins were unearthed. 209 to Keshequa Coins, who had them encapsulated in special holders from Numismatic Conservation Services marked with "Mohawk Valley Hoard."

Bibliography: Paul Gilkes, "Metal detectorists uncover rare half dollar die variety. Find third example of O-115 variety of 1807 50¢," *Coin World*, May 2, 2005, 2.

Paul Gilkes, "Mohawk River site yields coinage. Finds include O-115 variety, other 1807 half dollars," *Coin World*, May 2, 2005, 2.

Paul Gilkes, "Dealer marketing hoard coins. NCS authenticates, slabs 180 of silver pieces," *Coin World*, May 2, 2005, 2.

Beth Deisher, "Secrecy Showcases Treasure Greed," *Coin World*, May 2, 2005 (reference courtesy of Q. David Bowers).

Peter M. Rexford, "Stamps & Coins: Digging up the Goods on Old Money," *Sacramento Bee*, June 11, 2005.

Paul Gilkes, "Hoard site yields more rare varieties. Early half dollars appear among coin found near fort site," *Coin World*, June 13, 2005 (reference courtesy of Q. David Bowers).

Keshequa Coins, "The Mohawk Valley Hoard: Bust Quarters from the Mohawk Valley Hoard," http://www.keshequacoins.com/MohawkValleyHoardQuarters.html.

Keshequa Coins, "The Mohawk Valley Hoard: Bust Quarters from the Mohawk Valley Hoard," http://www.kesequacoins.com/MohawkValleyHoardHalves.html.

Marilyn Capawan, "Keshequa Coins announces the recently discovered Mohawk Valley Hoard of bust quarters and halves," http://www.kesequacoins.com/MVHStory.html.

659. New Orleans, Louisiana, USA, October 29, 1982.

Type of find: Hoard.

Date of deposit: 1842.

Containers: 2 boxes of cypress or cedar wood, each measuring ten by twelve by eight inches, each packed with 2 bags, and each bag packed with $1,000 worth of coins.

Contents: 13,000 AR.

Description: 4,000 coins were from the USA, and of those, 3,200 were 25¢ pieces:

USA, 25¢, 1805–1838

USA, 25¢, 1840O, no drapery (15)

USA, 25¢, 1840O, with drapery (7)

USA, 25¢, 1841 (including discovery example of doubled die reverse) (3)

USA, 25¢, 1841O (2,000) (over 200 examples of just one die variety of 1841O come from this hoard)

USA, 25¢, 1842O

USA, 50¢, 1811–37

USA, silver $1, 1798

The hoard included approximately 9,000 non-U.S. coins:

France, écus

Spain, 2 reales (pistareen), 1726

Spanish colonies, 8 reales, México, 1777

Spanish colonies, 2 reales and 8 reales (5,000)

Mexico, 2 reales

Mexico, 8 reales

Mexico, 8 reales, 1826

Mexico, 8 reales, 1837
Mexico, 8 reales, 1838
Peru, 2 reales
Peru, 8 reales
Peru, North Peru, 8 reales, 1838
Bolivia, 2 soles
Bolivia, 8 soles

Breen says that the coins are in the upper grades short of mint state. Many show chalky discoloration and matte surfaces, or have been cleaned to minimize evidence of flood damage, but otherwise show little or no evidence of wear.

Disposition: A backhoe excavating a construction site in New Orleans broke open the two boxes. An unemployed young man got twenty-five New Orleans quarters of the 1840s, Spanish coins of the mid 1700s, and a Mexican coin of 1826. Frances Kline, an employee of the Whitney National Bank, got four quarters from the 1840s and one Spanish coin. Jack Serio, who owned a building next to the construction site, got a dozen coins. The backhoe operator got most. There is a story of a third box, which two people took away in a pickup truck, but this is probably not true.

Bibliography: Bowers 1997, 63–65; Breen 1988, 346–47 (Breen 3938, 3939, 3942, 3945, 3946).

David Leser, "Coins turned up, so did well-heeled fortune hunters," *New Orleans Times-Picayune*, October 29, 1982, 1, 4.

"Diggers' Discovery Sets Off Gold Rush," *Saint Louis Post-Dispatch*, October 29, 1982, 2 (Associated Press dispatch).

Ed Anderson, "Bank on it: Coins are for Keeps," *New Orleans Times-Picayune*, October 30, 1982, 19, 20.

"Workers Unearth Old Coins," *New York Times*, October 31, 1982, Sec. 1, 64.

James H. Cohen, "New Orleans Hoard Yields O-Mint Treasures," *Coin World*, November 24, 1982, 1, 3.

660. Centralia, Illinois, USA, July 1937.

Type of find: Hoard.

Date of deposit: 1842.

Contents: ca. 75 AR.

Description:
USA, 50¢ (ca. 50)
Mexico, 8 reales (ca. 25)
"$50 in dollars and half dollars, dated from 1803 to 1842." The numbers found, and the assumption that the dollars are Mexican 8 reales, are educated guesses.

Disposition: Dr. G. W. Baldwin and S. Bradshaw.

Bibliography: "Treasure Trove Found. Illinois Doctor Will Dig Deeper at Marked Site of Old Coins," *New York Times*, July 18, 1937, 23. "Treasure Trove Found," *Numismatic Scrapbook Magazine* 3, no. 11 (November 1937): 260.

661. Between Bloxom and Hallwood on the Eastern Shore, Virginia, USA, June 1953.

Type of find: Hoard.

Date of deposit: 1842.

Contents: 5+ AR.

Description:
Spain, 2 reales (pistareen), 1739
USA, 10¢
USA, 25¢
USA, 50¢
USA, silver $1, 1803

Dates are known to have ranged from 1739 to 1842. The pistareen is an educated guess based on the most probable silver coin dated 1739 to be found. Gold was also reported to have been found, but that is questionable.

Bibliography: "'Gold Rush' Hits Virginia," *Numismatic Scrapbook Magazine* 19, no. 7 (July 1953): 628.

662. Site of Fort Harrison, Clearwater, Florida, USA, 1955–57.

Type of find: Hoard.
Date of deposit: 1843.
Contents: 52–60 AR.
Description:
  USA, 50¢, 1841O (40)
  USA, 50¢, 1843O (12–20)
Disposition: Some sold by Grover C. and Clarence Criswell in the mid-1950s; one 50¢ 1841O sold in the Coin Galleries Mail Bid Sale, November 9, 1988, lot 2166, there described as BU, full mint frost, "from the 'Clearwater Hoard' of 40 pieces found in Florida on the site of former Fort Harrison and presumably buried by a soldier on duty there at about the time of issue."
Bibliography: Bowers 1997, 56–57; Coin Galleries 1988, lot 2166.

663. Saint John's Church, York Mills, Ontario, Canada, 1968.

Type of find: Foundation deposit.
Date of deposit: 1843.
Contents: 2 AE, 3 AR.
Description:
  Great Britain, halfpence
  USA, 50¢
  The source notes only that the copper coins were British, and the silver coins were not. Description above based on what would be the most common copper and silver coins in circulation at the time.
Bibliography: Brown and Dolley 1971, 59 (NU4).

664. Worcester, Massachusetts, USA, July 30, 1899.

Type of find: Foundation deposit (cornerstone of the old stone courthouse).
Date of deposit: October 3, 1843.
Contents: 1 AE, 4 AR.
Description:
  USA, 1¢, 1843
  USA, silver 5¢, 1843
  USA, silver 10¢, 1843
  USA, silver 25¢, 1843
  USA, silver 50¢, 1843
  Described as coins of the United States with a specimen of every denomination in copper, nickel, and silver. No nickel coins were struck by the United States in 1843. The coins listed above are the common coins of 1843. It is unlikely, but not impossible, that the set also included an 1843 ½¢ (only struck in proof) and an 1843 silver $1 (not in general circulation).
Disposition: A proposal was made to turn over the contents to the American Antiquarian Society. It is not clear if this proposal was acted upon.
Bibliography: "Interesting Find. Workmen at Court House Unearth Old Corner Stone," *Worcester (MA) Daily Spy*, August 1, 1899 (reference courtesy of Q. David Bowers).

665. Near Saint Joseph, Missouri, USA, 1927.

Type of find: Single find.
Contents: 1 SN.
Description: USA, Indian Peace Medal made for the Pierre Chouteau Company, with Washington on the obverse, 1843
Disposition: Western Reserve Historical Society, Cleveland.
Bibliography: Belden 1927, 42–43.

666. Mineral Point, Wisconsin, USA, 1923.

Type of find: Single find.
Contents: 1 SN.
Description: USA, Indian Peace Medal made for the Pierre Chouteau Company, with Washington on the obverse, 1843
Disposition: W. C. Wyman Collection; purchased from the Wyman Collection by

the American Numismatic Society, New York, New York, USA; item number 1923.52.9.

Bibliography: Belden 1927, 43.

667. Near Missoula, Montana, USA, 1939.

Type of find: Funerary deposit.

Contents: 1 SN.

Description: USA, Indian Peace Medal made for the Pierre Chouteau Company, with Washington on the obverse, 1843

Disposition: Found in a grave. In 2006 in the Crane Collection in Denver.

Bibliography: Stack's 2006b, lot 184.

668. Norwalk, Huron County, Ohio, USA, August 1901.

Type of find: Hoard.

Date of deposit: 1844.

Contents: 33+ P.

Description: USA, New York, Elmira, Chemung Canal Bank, $10, February 1, 1844 (31)

All but one of the notes were on New York State banks, and had dates ranging from 1832 to 1844. Of the New York State banknotes, 31 were $10 bills issued by the Chemung Canal Bank of Elmira, NY, dated February 1, 1844 (Haxby NY-820 G46). The total face value of the notes found was $425.

Disposition: It was found by Theo Sanders, the son of James Sanders, while helping to tear down an old barn three miles south of Norwalk on the Fairfield Road. The farm was owned in 1901 by A. W. Niles, of Garrett, Indiana. Prior owners had been A. J. Andrews, of Norwood avenue; W. W. Sweet; and Clinton Jones, who owned the farm until 1850. The money would have been hidden during the time when the barn was owned by Clinton Jones. To find out who would redeem the notes, Mr. Pitt Curtiss, the vice-president of the Huron County Bank, wrote to the superintendent of banks at Albany.

Bibliography: "The Chemung Canal Bank of Elmira, N.Y.: Redeems its Notes after Fifty-seven years," *Numismatist* 14, no. 9 (September 1901): 247–49.

669. San Salvador, El Salvador, 1974.

Type of find: Hoard.

Date of deposit: 1845.

Contents: 61 AR.

Description:

Spanish colonies, Philip III, real, México

Spanish colonies, Charles and Johanna, 2 reales, México, assayer G

Spanish colonies, 4 reales, cob, México

Spanish colonies, Philip V, 4 reales, cob, México

Spanish colonies, 8 reales, cob, México (2)

Spanish colonies, Philip V, 8 reales, cob, México

Spanish colonies, 8 reales, counterfeit cob, México

Spanish colonies, Ferdinand VI, ½ real, Guatemala, holed

Spanish colonies, reales, Guatemala (2): 1748, holed; Ferdinand VI

Spanish colonies, 2 reales, Guatemala, 1752, holed

Spanish colonies, 8 reales, Guatemala, 1749

Spanish colonies, 8 reales, Guatemala, 1747, with Central America sun and volcanoes counterstamp, holed (2)

Spanish colonies, 8 reales, Guatemala, 1752, holed and plugged with Central America sun and volcanoes counterstamp

Spanish colonies, real, Lima (2): 1693; Philip V, holed

Spanish colonies, reales, Potosí (16): 1688; 1716Y; 1726; 1729Y; 1741; 1748Q; 1750; 1757; 1759; 1765; 1766; 1768; 1770; Charles III (3)

Spanish colonies, real, Potosí, 1739, counterstamped with Costa Rica arms

Spanish colonies, 2 reales, Potosí (11): assayer T; 1689; 1689VR; 1716Y; 1733; 1737; 1743 (3); 174[-]; Charles III

Spanish colonies, 4 reales, Potosí, 1772Y, with crown counterstamp

Spanish colonies, 8 reales, Potosí, assayer T (2) (1 holed and plugged)

Spanish colonies, 8 reales, Potosí, 1757

Spanish colonies, 8 reales, Potosí, 1738M, with Central America sun and volcanoes counterstamp

Spanish colonies, real, 17[-]

Spanish colonies, real, counterstamped with Costa Rica arms (4) (2 holed)

Spanish colonies, Philip II, real with Central America sun and volcanoes counterstamp, holed (2)

Spanish colonies, 8 reales, 1753, holed

Spanish colonies, 8 reales, 1756, with Central America sun and volcanoes counterstamp, holed

Disposition: Found while demolishing an old house that had burnt down in San Salvador. Auctioned by Schulman Coin and Mint, December 2–4, 1974.

Bibliography: Schulman 1974, lots 503–39.

670. Economy, Pennsylvania, USA, latter half of 1878.

Type of find: Hoard. Commonly known as "the Economite Hoard."

Date of deposit: 1846.

Contents: 510,000+ AR, of which 4,000+ AR was left in 1878.

Description:

USA, 25¢, 1818–28 (400)

USA, 50¢ (117,184): 1794 (150 [1 in Haseltine sale]); 1795 (650); 1796 (2); 1797; 1801 (300); 1802 (200); 1803 (300); 1805/4 (25); 1805 (600); 1806 (1,500); 1807 (2,000); 1815 (100); common dates, 1808–36 (111,356)

USA, silver $1 (3,707): 1794; 1795 (800 [60 in Haseltine sale]); 1796 (125); 1797 (80); 1798, large eagle (560); 1798, small eagle (30 [50 1798 dollars total in Haseltine sale]); 1799, five stars facing (12); 1799 (1,250 [66 1799 dollars in Haseltine sale]); 1800 (250); 1801–3 (600)

French, Spanish, and Spanish colonies silver coins (12,600+)

17 U.S. half dollars from the hoard are in the Old Economy Museum, given by Christiana Knodeler in 1975; their dates and varieties are:

USA, 50¢ (17): 1817, O110; 1818, O107; 1819, O109; 1821, O104; 1823, O111; 1826, O120; 1826, O107; 1827, O120; 1827, O104; 1828, O109; 1833, O103; 1834, O116; 1834, O103; 1835, O108; 1836, O102; 1836, O119

Die variety reference: O = Overton.

Disposition: The coins, originally totaling $510,000, were sealed in special vaults around 1846. Half was withdrawn from the vaults in 1876 to invest in the Pittsburgh and Lake Erie Railroad. The rest came to light in 1878, when Harmony Society members began to use the money, spending at face value a 1796 and a 1797 50¢ pieces before they realized that the coins had a higher numismatic and bullion value. The residue was sold to John Haseltine in 1878 for $6,500. The Economite 50¢ pieces continued to circulate in the Old Economy, Pennsylvania, Youngstown, Ohio, and Salem, Ohio areas into the 1930s.

Frossard wrote in 1882:

"Not long ago a well known coin dealer, by dint of hard scraping, gathered some $4,000, with which he bought, at a nominal premium, and in the rural districts of Pennsylvania, a large sum of silver coins, the accumulated savings for many years, of a religious society. There were, we are told, 1 1794 dollar, a large number of dollars up to 1803, about 75 1794 halves, 300 '95, etc., etc."

Frossard listed the sale in the *Numisma* of March 1885:

"January 30, 31. Coins and Medals, including a large number of U.S. Dollars and half Dollars from the Economites hoard at Beaver Falls, Pa....Catalogue by John W. Haseltine; sold by Bangs & Co."

Frossard commented further on the matter in the *Numisma* of May 1885:

"The sudden suspension of Mr. John W. Haseltine, one of the leading and best informed coin dealers of the country, has stirred quite a ripple of surprise and regret among his many friends and correspondents. Hard times, strong competition from every side for the smallest business and disappointment in several ventures, are generally ascribed as the causes of the suspension. Mr. Haseltine has been in the coin business at Philadelphia for the last 18 years, and during that time held 85 public auction sales of coins and medals, the last one taking place at Bangs & Co., N.Y., on January 30 and 31, when he disposed of a large part of his stock, especially American dollars, etc., from the Economite's Hoard, purchased by him some years ago. Whatever Mr. Haseltine may undertake in the future, he carries with him the hearty good wishes of a host of collectors and friends."

The *Coin Collector's Journal* for March 1881 says that Haseltine bought $4,000 face value worth of the scarce dates for $6,500, except the 1794 dollar, for which he paid $22.

Bibliography: Bowers 1997, 103–17; Breen 1952, 8–9 (Breen Hoards XI); Breen 1988, 380; Kovach 1993; Noe 1920, 41–44, 46.

"The Economite Treasure," *Coin Collector's Journal* 6 (whole no. 64) (March 1881): 47–48. This article was based on information from Joseph M. Lippincott, who obtained it from Mr. Morrison, the Cashier of the Economy Savings Institution.

Édouard Frossard, *Numisma* 6, no. 1 (January 1882): [5].

Édouard Frossard, "Coin Sales," *Numisma* 9, no. 2 (March 1885): [7].

Édouard Frossard, *Numisma* 9, no. 3 (May 1885): [6].

Coin Collector's Journal 8, no. 10 (October 1941): 145.

671. Guatemala, near the border with Mexico, first half of 2003.

Type of find: Hoard.

Date of deposit: 1846.

Container: Tinaja (earthenware jar).

Contents: Ca. 3,000 AR.

Description:

Spanish colonies, coins, México
Mexico, Iturbide, 8 reales (2+): 1821; 1822
Mexico, 8 reales, hooknecks (2+): 1823; 1824
Mexico, 8 reales, mule with reverse of 8 escudos
Spanish colonies, cobs, Guatemala ("lots," i.e. ca. 2,000)
Spanish colonies, Ferdinand VII, 8 reales, Guatemala
Central American Republic (Guatemala), 8 reales (2+): 1826; 1842
Central American Republic (Honduras), coins
Central American Republic (Costa Rica), 8 reales, 1831 (2+, in both F and AU)
Spanish colonies, Charles and Johanna, real, México, with Costa Rica counterstamp of 1846
Spanish colonies, real, Potosí, with Costa Rica counterstamp

Disposition: Found by workers of Roy Villagran when working on a foundation in a tinaja, an earthenware jar. None of the coins was dated later than 1846.

Bibliography: Paul M. Green, "Central America used to borderless markets," *World Coin*

News (Iola, WI), September 2003, 50.

Paul M. Green, letter to John M. Kleeberg.

672. Fruitland, Wicomico County, Maryland, USA, January 1906.

Type of find: Hoard.

Date of deposit: 1846.

Container: Shot bag.

Contents: 120 AR.

Description:

Great Britain, shillings

USA, silver 5¢

USA, 10¢

USA, 25¢

USA, 50¢

USA, silver $1

Spanish colonies, 8 reales

Mexico, 8 reales

Dates ranged 1700–1846, nearly all was new; dates 1836, 1837, 1838, 1839 were also present.

Disposition: The coins were in a shot bag found by James H. Cathell in the Forktown Tavern, which was being torn down. The tavern was kept by William Smith until his death in 1858.

Bibliography: "Bag of Money Found in Old Hotel," *Numismatist* 19, no. 1 (January 1906): 28–29 (citing the *Baltimore Sun*).

673. Off the coast of Texas and Louisiana, USA, 1990–2007.

Type of find: Shipwreck.

Ship: S.S. *New York*.

Sank: September 7, 1846.

Contents: 1 AE, 2,000+ AR, 400+ AV.

Description:

Denmark, Frederick VI, frederiks d'or, Altona, 1831FF

Denmark, Frederick VI, 2 frederiks d'or, Altona (4): 1831FF; 1835FF; 1837FF; 1838FF

Denmark, Christian VIII, 2 christians d'or, Altona, 1844F

German states, Prussia, Frederick II, 2 frederick d'or, 1776A

German states, Prussia, Frederick William III, 2 frederick d'or, Berlin (3): 1801A; 1806A; 1813A

German states, Prussia, Frederick William IV, 2 frederick d'or, Berlin, 1841A

German states, Hanover, George IV, 5 thalers, Hannover, 1828B

German states, Hanover, George IV, 10 thalers, Hannover (3): 1822B; 1825B; 1827B

German states, Hanover, William IV, 10 thalers (3): 1835B (HANNOV); 1835B (HANNOVER); 1836B

German states, Hanover, Ernest Augustus, 10 thalers (4): 1838B; 1839S; 1844B; 1844S

German states, Brunswick-Lüneburg, Charles II, 10 thalers, 1824

German states, Brunswick-Lüneburg, William, 10 thalers (3): 1832; 1833; 1834

German states, Saxony, Frederick Augustus III, 10 thalers, 1795IEC

Netherlands, William I, 5 gulden, Brussels, 1827

Netherlands, William I, 10 gulden (3): 1825, Brussels; 1833, Utrecht; 1840, Utrecht

Great Britain, George III, sovereigns (3): 1817 (2); 1820

Great Britain, George IV, sovereigns (29): 1821 (8); 1822 (3); 1824 (2); 1825 (2); 1826 (7); 1827 (3); 1829; 1830 (3)

Great Britain, William IV, sovereigns (7): 1832 (2); 1833; 1835; 1836; 1837 (2)

Great Britain, Victoria, sovereigns (10): 1838; 1839; 1842 (4); 1843 (4)

France, Louis XVI, louis, 1786BB

France, Napoleon, 20 francs (8): Year 12A [1804]; 1807A; 1808A (2); 1809A; 1811A; 1813A; 1813W

France, Louis XVIII, 20 francs (8): 1814A;

1815A; 1818A (2); 1819A; 1824A (3)
France, Charles X, 20 francs, 1830A
France, Louis Philippe, 5 francs, 1841BB
France, Louis Philippe, 20 francs (13): 1831A (3); 1834A (2); 1836A; 1838A; 1839A (2); 1840A (2); 1841A; 1844A
France, Louis Philippe, 40 francs, 1834A
Italian states, Napoleonic Kingdom of Italy, 20 lire, Milan, 1809
Italian States, Sardinia, Charles Felix, 20 lire, 1825L
Spain, Philip IV, 2 reales (pistareen), Madrid, 1721A
Spain, Charles IV, 2 escudos, Madrid (2): 1801FA; 1806FA
USA, 1¢, 1843
USA, 10¢ (3): 1838O; 1839O; 1841O
USA, 25¢ (2): 1834; 1842O
USA, 50¢ (29): 1795, O130; 1802, O101; 1803, O103; 1806, O115; 1806, O116; 1807, O108; 1807; 1808/7, O101; 1808, O107; 1815/2, O101 (holed); 1817, O113 (2); 1822, O104; 1824, O110; 1826, O108a; 1832, O103; 1834, O109; 1839 capped bust; 1839O; 1839 seated liberty; 1841O; 1842O; 1843; 1843O; 1844O (3); 1845O; 1846O
USA, $1, 1795
USA, $2.50 (32): 1836 (6); 1839O (2); 1843; 1843C; 1843O (18); 1844D (2); 1845D; 1846
USA, $5 (128): 1834 (17); 1835 (2); 1836 (10); 1837 (2); 1838 (6); 1839; 1839D (2); 1840 (3); 1840D; 1840O; 1841C; 1841D; 1842D (2); 1842O; 1843 (15); 1843C (2); 1843D (3); 1843O (6); 1844 (4); 1844C; 1844D (3); 1844O (19); 1845 (7); 1845D (5); 1845O (10); 1846 (3)
USA, $10 (23): 1842 (3); 1842O (3); 1843 (2); 1843O (2); 1844O (6); 1845O (7)
USA, North Carolina, Christopher Bechtler, $5, 140G
Spanish colonies, Charles IV, 8 reales, México (2): 1796FM; 1797FM
Spanish colonies, Ferdinand VII, 8 reales, Zacatecas, 1821RG
Mexico, 8 reales, Durango, 1839/1RM
Mexico, 8 reales, Guanajuato, 1845PM
Mexico, 8 reales, Zacatecas (2): 1834OM; 1846OM
Mexico, 8 escudos, México, 1827JM
Spanish colonies, Ferdinand VII, 8 reales, Guatemala, 1816
Central American Republic, 8 reales, Guatemala, 1825M
Spanish colonies, 8 escudos, Popayan, 1816FR
Colombia, 2 escudos, Bogotá, 1824JF
Peru, North Peru, 8 reales, Lima, 1837M
Peru, 8 reales, Lima, 1843MB
Chile, 8 escudos, Santiago, 1824I
Die variety reference for half dollars: O = Overton.

Disposition: Recovered by Avery Munson, Craig DeRouen, Gary Hebert, and Renée Hebert. Encapsulated by Numismatic Guaranty Corporation and Numismatic Conservation Services. Auctioned by Stack's, July 27, 2008.

Bibliography: Stack's 2008b. Q. David Bowers is currently writing a book about this shipwreck.
Numismatic Guaranty Corporation, Inventory, available at http://www.collectorssociety.com/images/article_images/SSNY_Gold_Census.pdf.

674. Pilgrim's Beach, Plymouth, Massachusetts, USA, August 1942.

Type of find: Hoard.

Date of deposit: 1846–47.

Container: Box. Inside the box, the coins were wrapped up in an old Boston newspaper.

Contents: 438+ AR, 5+ AV.

Description:
USA, 50¢ (400)
USA, silver $1 (38)

The hoard also contained $50 in gold coins and 46 non-U.S. coins. The oldest gold coin was dated 1834 and the oldest silver coin 1795.

Disposition: The hoard was found on Pilgrim's Beach by Ben Lay of Colebrook, New Hampshire, and his son Fred.

Bibliography: "Find Treasure Chest in Sand at Plymouth. New Hampshire Man and Son Dig Up Century-Old Coins," *New York Times*, August 16, 1942, 44.

"Century-old Treasure Box found at Plymouth Beach," *Numismatist* 55, no. 10 (October 1942): 731.

675. Donner Lake, California, USA, May 1891.

Type of find: Hoard.

Date of deposit: March 3, 1847.

Contents: 196 AR.

Description:

German states, Saxony, thaler, 1835

France, 5 francs (55): An VIII [1800]; An XI [1803]; An XIII [1805]; 1806; 1808 (3); 1809; 1811; 1812 (10); 1814 (2); 1816; 1818; 1819; 1820; 1822 (2); 1823; 1824; 1825; 1827 (2); 1828; 1829 (2); 1831 (3); 1832 (2); 1833 (3); 1834 (2); 1837; 1838 (2); 1839; 1840; 1841 (2); 1844; Louis Philippe [1830–48]

USA, 50¢ (72): 1810; 1813; 1815; 1817; 1818 (3); 1822 (2); 1823 (2); 1824 (2); 1825 (2); 1826 (3); 1827 (2); 1828; 1829 (6); 1830 (6); 1831; 1832 (6); 1833 (3); 1834 (2); 1835 (3); 1836 (4); 1837 (4); 1838 (2); 1839 (3); 1840; 1841 (3); 1842 (3); 1843 (4)

Spanish colonies, 4 reales (from México?) (2): 1800; 1805

Spanish colonies, 8 reales, México (5): 1805; 1810 (2); 1812; 1821

Mexico, 8 reales (49): 1826; 1827; 1828 (2); 1830; 1831 (2); 1832 (3); 1833; 1834 (4); 1835 (3); 1836 (4); 1837 (3); 1838 (3); 1839 (3); 183[-]; 1840 (3); 1841 (5); 1842 (4); 1843 (2); 1844; 1845 (2)

Bolivia, 8 reales, 1836

Argentina, La Plata, 8 reales, 1835

Other dollar sized coins, not otherwise identified (9)

Buried by Mrs. Elizabeth Graves, née Cooper, prior to her departure with the Second Relief Expedition on March 3, 1847. She was too weak to carry the money. She died on or about March 7, 1847.

There is supposed to be a photograph of these coins at the Emigrant Trail Museum at Truckee, California, in the Donner State Park.

For a photograph of the discovery of this cache, in 1891, see Daniel M. Rosen, "Log Entries for March, 1847," http://www.donnerpartydiary.com/mar47.htm.

Disposition: Half to the finders, half to the Graves family.

Bibliography: Bowers 1997, 45–49; Kleeberg 1995, 97–98; Whitely 1963.

"The Donner Treasure. Claim Made that the Money has been Found," *Sacramento Record-Union*, May 16, 1891.

"Found the Coin. Relics of a Rocky Mountain Tragedy Unearthed," *Brooklyn Daily Eagle*, May 16, 1891, 6.

Daniel M. Rosen, "The Donner Party," http://www.donnerpartydiary.com.

Daniel M. Rosen, "Log Entries for March, 1847," http://www.donnerpartydiary.com/mar47.htm.

676. Four miles south of Victory Point, King William Island, Nunavut Territory, Canada, 1879.

Type of find: Funerary deposit.

Date of deposit: Spring 1848.

Contents: 1 AR.

Description: Great Britain, medal, GEORGIUS IIII DG BRITTANNIARUM REX 1820 on reverse, SECOND MATHEMATICAL PRIZE ROYAL NAVAL COLLEGE, awarded to JOHN IRVING MIDSUMMER 1830.

From the grave of Lieutenant John Irving, the third officer of the Terror, and a member of Sir John Franklin's search for the Northwest passage.

Disposition: Found by the Inuit; given by them to Lieutenant Schwatka's exploring party; then to the American Geographical Society.

Bibliography: Frossard 1880.

677. Starvation Cove, west of Point Richardson on the Adelaide Peninsula (Utjulik), Nunavut Territory, Canada, 1879.

Type of find: Funerary deposit.

Date of deposit: Spring 1848.

Contents: 1 SN.

Description: Great Britain, medalet commemorating the launching of the steamship Great Britain by Prince Albert, July 1843

The finding of this medalet confirmed that Schwatka had found the remains of Europeans, and probably those of the Franklin expedition.

Disposition: Found by the Inuit; given by them to Lieutenant Schwatka's exploring party, who donated it to the American Geographical Society.

Bibliography: Frossard 1880.

678. Saint Clair River, off Marine City, Michigan, USA, August 1896.

Type of find: Single find.

Contents: 1 AR.

Description: Great Britain, 1848 war decoration, with Queen Victoria on the obverse and the date 1848; on the reverse is the Queen crowning the Duke of Wellington, and the inscription, "To the British Army." Underneath are the dates "1793–1814." The medal has the crossbar "Fort Detroit." On the edge of the medal is the inscription, "J. Coakley, Forty-First foot." J. Coakley was a British army pensioner, who was known to have lived in Marine City, Michigan.

Disposition: Found in the bed of the Saint Clair River. Acquired by Mr. Farman, of Marine City.

Bibliography: "A War Medal Find," *Numismatist* 9, no. 8 (August, 1896): 169–70 (citing the *Detroit Free Press*).

679. Norwich, Ontario, Canada, August 1940.

Type of find: Hoard.

Date of deposit: 1849.

Contents: 55 P.

Description:
British colonies, Canada West, Farmer's Joint Stock Bank of Toronto, 25 shillings, February 1, 1849
British colonies, Canada West, Farmer's Joint Stock Bank of Toronto, $1, February 1, 1849
British colonies, Canada West, Farmer's Joint Stock Bank of Toronto, $2, February 1, 1849
British colonies, Canada West, Farmer's Joint Stock Bank of Toronto, $3, February 1, 1849
British colonies, Canada West, Farmer's Joint Stock Bank of Toronto, $5, February 1, 1849

Bibliography: J. Douglas Ferguson, "Canadian Coin Notes," *Coin Collector's Journal* 7, no. 8 (August 1940): 243.

680. Springfield, Ohio, USA, June 1960.

Type of find: Foundation deposit in a cornerstone of the Independent Order of Odd Fellows Building.

Date of deposit: 1849.

Container: Iron box.

Contents: 4 AR.

Description:
USA, 10¢, 1849
USA, 25¢, 1848
USA, 50¢, 1849

USA, silver $1, 1847
Reported by Mrs. Heding H. Sondergelt of the Clark County Coin Club.
Bibliography: "Cornerstone Yields Silver Coins," *Numismatist* 73, no. 6 (June 1960): 736.

681. Near Waynesboro, Virginia, USA, June 1929.

Type of find: Hoard.
Date of deposit: 1849.
Container: Earthenware pot.
Contents: 200+ AV.
Description:
USA, $2.50
USA, $5
Gold coins of several denominations, found in an earthenware pot, with dates ranging from 1795 to 1849. Denominations not specifically described; $2.50 and $5 listed here, since they were the commonest denominations in this period.
Bibliography: "Virginia Soil Yields Many Gold Coins," *Numismatist* 42, no. 6 (June 1929): 392.

682. New Bethlehem, Pennsylvania, USA, June 1999.

Type of find: Single find.
Contents: 1 AV.
Description: USA, California, Pacific Company, $1, 1849
Disposition: Found with a metal detector by Jerald Reinford. Sold at auction by Bowers and Merena, June 23, 2000, lot 1014.
Bibliography: Bowers & Merena 2000, lot 1014. "Metal Detector Locates Coin Valued at $57,500," *Numismatist* 113, no. 9 (September 2000): 1009.
Coinfacts.com, "Pacific Company 1849 $1 Gold," http://www.coinfacts.com/pioneer_gold/pacific_company/pacific_company_1849_1_gold.htm.

683. Ventura, California, USA, August 1924.

Type of find: Hoard.
Date of deposit: 1850.
Contents: Ca. 50 P.
Description: USA, obsolete banknotes?, all dated 1841, mostly denominated $1
Disposition: Found in a tree by F. W. Barron, an ex-Canadian soldier.
Bibliography: "War Veteran Finds $50 in Old Tree," *Numismatist* 37, no. 8 (August 1924): 498.

684. Alajulea, Costa Rica, 2005.

Type of find: Hoard.
Date of deposit: 1850.
Contents: 3+ AV.
Description:
Costa Rica, escudo, 1850
Costa Rica, 2 escudos, 1850
Costa Rica, ½ onza, 1850
Bibliography: Paul M. Green, letter to John M. Kleeberg.

685. Placerville, California, USA, early 1985.

Type of find: Single find.
Contents: 1 AV.
Description: USA, California, Dubosq & Co., $10, 1850
Disposition: Found in a creek bed with a metal detector by Allan Pankey. At the American Numismatic Association convention held in Milwaukee in 1986 it was sold to Ron Gillio.
Bibliography: Breen 1988, 639 (Breen 7815). "Bay Area Yields Dubosq & Co. Slug," *Numismatist* 99, no. 10 (October 1986): 2014.

686. Philadelphia, Pennsylvania, USA, November 1974 through February 1975.

Type of find: Excavations of a site occupied from the early eighteenth century through the early twentieth century. This was also the site where the Philadelphia Highway Hoard of counterfeit halfpence was found. For the other finds, see finds numbers 282 and 371.

Contents: 4 PB, 65 AE, 7 SN, 1 NI, 1 AV.

Description:

India, 1809–17, unidentified copper coin

England, William III farthing, 169[-], tin with copper plug

Great Britain, George III, farthing, 1774

England, William III halfpenny, 1700, *BMC* type 3 (2)

Great Britain, halfpence (31): 1719 (2); 1722; 1723 (3); 1724; 1730 (2); 1731; 1734, cast lead counterfeit; 1735; 1737 (2); 1737, cast pewter counterfeit made into a humdinger; 1738 cast pewter counterfeit with wood grain striations (2); George II (young head), 17[-], copper plated tin counterfeit; George II 17[-], pewter counterfeit; 1746; 1748; 1750; 1755; 1757 (2); old head, 17[-], counterfeit; 1771; 1772; 1773, lead counterfeit; George II, 177[-], broken lead counterfeit; 1775

Great Britain, Henry Kettle counter made to look like ½ eagle, 1803

Great Britain, Parys Mines, Anglesey token, 1787

Great Britain, lead William, Duke of Cumberland medal, 1746

Ireland, halfpence (7): 1681; 1737; 1750; 1752; 1776; 1781; 1804

Ireland, Wood's Hibernia halfpenny, 1723 (3)

France, Louis XV, écu, 1733, Pau mint, counterfeit in tin

France, Louis XV, écu, 1735, Paris mint

France, Louis XV, écu, 1735, mint unidentified

France, Louis XV, écu, 17[-], 40% of white metal counterfeit

France, Louis XV, louis d'or, 1726, Paris mint

USA, Immune Columbia/Nova Constellatio copper, 1785

USA, New Jersey, copper, 1787

USA, ½¢ (2): 1800; 1805

USA, 1¢ (22): 1794 (5); 1795; 1796; 1797 (2); 1798 (2); 1803; 1808; 1810; 1812; 1816 (2); 1831; 1832; 1862; 1890; 1907

USA, silver 5¢, 1850

USA, nickel 5¢, 1867

USA, 10¢, 1882

USA, 25¢, 1876

USA, 50¢ (3): 1809; 1827; 1834

USA, silver $1, 1802/1

USA, Pennsylvania, Philadelphia, token, COMPLIMENTS OF J.E.W. - FRONT & DOCK, holed

Spanish colonies, ½ real, 1781, México

Spanish colonies, reales, México (5): 1740; 1763; 1779; 1781 (2)

Spanish colonies, 2 reales, México (2): 1780; 1783

Spanish colonies, 8 reales, México (2): 1753; 1755

Disposition: Many of the artifacts found by the William R. Paull family are on permanent display in the Philadelphia Maritime Museum, 321 Chestnut Street.

Bibliography: Gaspar and Newman 1978; Newman and Gaspar 1978; Reiter 1978.

687. Flagstaff, Arizona, USA, November 1924.

Type of find: Hoard.

Date of deposit: 1850.

Contents: 80 AE.

Description:

Great Britain, George I halfpenny, 1723 (oldest coin)

USA, hard times tokens

Disposition: Found by a Mexican laborer under a rock. Acquired by Ted Spencer of the First National Bank of Flagstaff.

Bibliography: "Old Coins Found at Flagstaff, Ariz.," *Numismatist* 37, no. 11 (November 1924): 709.

688. College Bluff, near Red Wing, Minnesota, USA, May 1868.

Type of find: Single find.
Date of deposit: 1850.
Contents: 1 AR.
Description: USA, James Madison Indian Peace Medal, 1809
    Supposed to have belonged to a Lakota warrior named Tam-a-ha, who lived at Fort Snelling until about 1850.
Disposition: Found by a boy, who sold it for $50.
Bibliography: "Varia," *American Journal of Numismatics* 3, no. 3 (July 1868): 23 (citing the *New York Times*, May 10, 1868).

689. Quathiaski Cove, Cuadra Island, British Columbia, Canada, 1986.

Type of find: Single find.
Date of deposit: 1850s?
Contents: 1 AR.
Description: France, Anglo-Gallic issues, Henry V, gros
Disposition: Found three feet below the surface on a hilltop overlooking the cave.
Bibliography: Willey 1986, 293.

690. Vancouver's Island, British Columbia, Canada, July 1887.

Type of find: Hoard.
Date of deposit: 1850s.
Contents: 2 B.
Description:
    China, Qianlong, cash
    China, Xianfeng, cash
Disposition: Presented to the Numismatic and Antiquarian Society of Philadelphia.
Bibliography: Gates P. Thruston, "Archaeological: The Ancient Peoples of North America," *American Journal of Numismatics* 22, no. 1 (July 1887): 14.

691. Staten Island, New York, New York, USA, 1896.

Type of find: Hoard.
Date of deposit: 1850s.
Container: Pot.
Contents: AV.
Description: USA, $10, 1845
Disposition: Found in a pot by Daniel Wandell; gold coins thought to have been buried by his father in the 1850s.
Bibliography: "A Pot of Money," *Brooklyn Daily Eagle*, July 20, 1896, 6.

692. Smartsville, California, USA, July 1925.

Type of find: Hoard.
Date of deposit: 1850.
Container: Rusted can.
Contents: AR, AV.
Description:
    France, 20 franc, dated prior to 1851
    France, other coins dated prior to 1851
Disposition: The coins were found in an abandoned mine ("an old hydraulic property") by a rancher miner, Edward Poor. A bank offered $4.90 for the 20 franc coin.
Bibliography: "Abandoned Mine Gives up Old Coins," *Numismatist* 38, no. 7 (July 1925): 359.

693. Rincon Point, San Francisco, California, USA, 1987.

Type of find: Archaeological excavation.
Date of site: 1850–65.
Contents: 4 B.
Description: China, cash (4)
Bibliography: Pastron 1989.

694. Carmel, California, USA, December 25, 1982.

Type of find: Single find.

Contents: 1 AV.

Description: USA, California, Shultz & Co. $5, 1851

Disposition: Found on the beach with a metal detector. Sold at auction by Butterfield & Butterfield, San Francisco, May 26, 1983.

Bibliography: "Schultz and Co. Coin Auctioned," *Numismatist* 96, no. 8 (August 1983): 1595.

695. Bidwell's Bar, California, USA, April 1932.

Type of find: Hoard.

Date of deposit: 1851.

Contents: 2 AV.

Description:
USA, $2.50, 1847
USA, $2.50, 1851

Disposition: Found by a miner panning for gold.

Bibliography: "Miner Finds Gold Already Minted," *Numismatist* 45, no. 4 (April 1932): 226.

696. Yorkville, South Carolina, USA, February 1932.

Type of find: Single find.

Contents: 1 AV.

Description: USA, North Carolina, Bechtler, gold $1

Disposition: W. Gist Finley, attorney.

Bibliography: "Bechtler Gold Dollar Dug Up in South Carolina," *Numismatist* 45, no. 3 (March 1932): 148.

697. Beach south of Morro Bay, San Luis Obispo, California, USA, May 1955.

Type of find: Hoard.

Date of deposit: 1852.

Contents: 17 AV.

Description: USA, Humbert/USAOG, $50 slugs (17)

Disposition: Found by George Biddle. Placed in the custody of the sheriff until the ownership is determined.

Bibliography: "Report of 17 Gold Slugs Found on California Beach," *Numismatic Scrapbook Magazine* 21, no. 5 (May 1955): 767.

698. North side of Anacapa Island, about 30 miles off Santa Barbara, California, USA, 1963–1976.

Type of find: Shipwreck.

Ship: SS *Winfield Scott*.

Sank: December 2, 1853, en route from San Francisco to Panama.

Contents: 1 AR, 92–93+ AV.

Description:
USA, gold $1 (14) (unattributed, so some may actually be California private gold)
USA, $2.50 (5)
USA, $5 (3)
USA, California, Humbert, $10, 1852
USA, California, Moffat, $5, 1849
USA, California, Moffat, $5, 1850
USA, California, Frontier & Deviercy, octagonal 25¢, 1853 (Breen-Gillio 101) (5)
USA, California, Frontier & Deviercy, round 25¢ (Breen-Gillio 205)
USA, California, Frontier & Deviercy, round 25¢ (Breen-Gillio 206)
USA, California, Frontier & Deviercy, round 25¢, 1853 (Breen-Gillio 209) (2)
USA, California, Joseph Bros., 25¢, 1853 (Breen-Gillio 101) (5)
USA, California, Joseph Bros., 25¢, [1853] (Breen-Gillio 204)
USA, California, Joseph Bros., 25¢, [1853] (Breen-Gillio 205)
USA, California, Joseph Bros., 25¢, [1853] (Breen-Gillio 206)
USA, California, A. L. Nouizillet, round 25¢, [1853] (Breen-Gillio 222) (2)
USA, California, A. L. Nouizillet, round 25¢, [1853–54] (Breen-Gillio 223) (10)

USA, California, Frontier & Deviercy, octagonal 50¢, 1853 (Breen-Gillio 302) (3)

USA, California, Frontier & Deviercy, octagonal 50¢, 1853 (Breen-Gillio 301–4)

USA, California, Frontier & Deviercy, round 50¢, 1853 (Breen-Gillio 401)

USA, California, Gaime, Guillemot & Co. round 50¢, 1853 (Breen-Gillio 414)

USA, California, Joseph Bros., 50¢, 1852 (Breen-Gillio 401)

USA, California, M. Deriberpie, round 50¢, 1853 (Breen-Gillio 421)

USA, California, A. L. Nouizillet, round 50¢, 1853 (Breen-Gillio 428)

USA, California, A. L. Nouizillet, round 50¢, 1853 (Breen-Gillio 430) (3)

USA, California, round 50¢, date and variety unknown

USA, California, M. Deriberpie, octagonal dollar, 1853 (Breen-Gillio 514)

USA, California, M. Deriberpie, octagonal dollar, 1853 (Breen Gillio 519) (2)

USA, California, M. Deriberpie, octagonal dollar, 1853 (Breen-Gillio 525)

USA, California, M. Deriberpie, octagonal dollar, 1853 (Breen-Gillio 526) (2)

USA, California, A. L. Nouizillet, octagonal dollar, 1853 (Breen-Gillio 530) (15–16)

USA, California, A. L. Nouizillet, octagonal dollar, 1853 (Breen-Gillio 531) (2)

USA, California, octagonal 50¢, date and variety unknown

USA, California, round 50¢, 1853, variety unknown

Peru, 8 reales, 1833

This shipwreck is important because it established that many California fractional gold pieces were actually contemporary issues and not later souvenirs.

Disposition: The wreck was salvaged by the scuba divers Glenn E. Miller, Pete Greenwood, Dick Anderson, and Mark Williams. Many of the coins were sold to Kenneth W. Lee, but he did not keep track of the provenance.

Bibliography: Bowers 1997, 224–30; Breen 1988, 641–43, 645, 649–50 (Breen 7820, 7836, 7838, 7854, 7856, 7898, 7901, 7905); Breen and Gillio 2003; Potter 1972, 467–68.

699. Springfield Township, Illinois, USA, March 1896.

Type of find: Hoard.

Date of deposit: 1853.

Container: Rusty old tin can.

Contents: 25 AR, AV.

Description: USA, Humbert/United States Assay Office of Gold, $50 (5)

A rusty old tin can, filled with U.S. coins. Included "five of the old-fashioned octagonal $50 gold pieces." Total value given at $480.

Disposition: Plowed up by John H. Riardon on the farm of farmer Hughes. Riardon was allowed to keep the find.

Bibliography: "Plowed up a Can of Gold," *Numismatist* 9, no. 3 (March 1896): 59–60 (citing the *Cincinnati Enquirer*).

700. Iowa City, Iowa, USA, July 1907.

Type of find: Hoard.

Date of deposit: early 1850s.

Contents: 3 AV.

Description:
USA, $5 (2)
USA, $20

Disposition: Plowed up by the farmer John Curry. The land had been entered by Byron Dennis in the 1840s.

Bibliography: Bowers 1997, 133 (citing the *Granite State News* of June 20, 1907).

701. Off Point Arguello, California, USA, 1968.

Type of find: Shipwreck.

Ship: Yankee Blade.

Sank: October 1, 1854.

Contents: 100+ AV.

Description: USA, $20, 1854 S (100+)

Disposition: According to Nesmith and Potter, the *Yankee Blade* was relocated by 1968 by a salvage team consisting of Lawrence Thomas, Ernest Porter and Dean Tyler, who operated from the *Hornet*. By the 1970s divers were selling 1854S $20s into the southern California numismatic trade.

Bibliography: Bowers 1997, 165–66, 230–36; Breen 1988, 564 (Breen 7171); Nesmith and Potter 1968, 134; Stack's 1993 (ex Paramount section of Auction '80, lot 966); Superior 1982, lots 1446–48.

"Loss of the *Yankee Blade*," New York Daily Times, November 10, 1854, 1.

Ira Goldberg, President, Superior Stamp & Coin Co., Inc., letter to John M. Kleeberg, December 24, 1992.

702. In the cellar of 132 South Eden Street, Baltimore, Maryland, USA, August 31, 1934.

Type of find: Hoard.

Date of deposit: September 1857.

Container: Copper receptacle.

Contents: 3,558 AV.

Description:

USA, gold $1 (3,931): 1849 (95); 1850 (78); 1851 (452); 1852 (322); 1853 (976); 1854 (316); 1855 (215); 1856 (296); ND (1,181)

USA, $2.50 (83): 1834 (3); 1835 (3); 1836 (7); 1837; 1839D; 1843 (5); 1843C; 1843O (4); 1845 (3); 1847O; 1848D; 1850 (3); 1851 (5); 1852 (11); 1853 (14); 1854 (7); 1855 (3); 1856 (4)

USA, $5 (394): 1834 (25); 1835 (6); 1836 (22); 1837 (5); 1838 (11); 1838C; 1839 (5); 1840 (11); 1841 (3); 1842 (3); 1842D; 1843 (19); 1843C (2); 1843D; 1843O (5); 1844 (15); 1844C (2); 1844O (6); 1845 (22); 1845O (3); 1846 (16); 1846C (4); 1846D; 1847 (29); 1847C; 1847D; 1847O; 1848 (14); 1848C (5); 1848D; 1849 (12); 1849C; 1849D; 1850 (12); 1850D (2); 1851 (18); 1852 (24); 1852C (5); 1852D (2); 1853 (21); 1853C (3); 1853D (3); 1854 (18); 1854D (6); 1854O; 1855 (22); 1855C (3); 1855D; 1856 (4)

USA, $10 (118): 1839 (3); 1840 (2); 1841 (4); 1842 (6); 1842O; 1843 (3); 1844 (2); 1845 (2); 1845O; 1846; 1847 (17); 1847O (7); 1848 (5); 1848O (2); 1849 (13); 1849O; 1850 (14); 1850O (2); 1851 (3); 1851O (3); 1852 (3); 1853 (4); 1853O (3); 1854; 1854S; 1855 (7); 1856 (3)

USA, $20 (332): 1850 (94); 1850O (5); 1851 (83); 1851O (10); 1852 (51); 1852O (2); 1853 (30); 1854 (14); 1855 (8); 1855S (12); 1856; 1856O; 1856S (23)

Disposition: The main dispersal of the hoard was at the Perry Fuller auction held on May 2, 1935. The $20 1856O sold for the highest price, $105, at the auction, and was bought by the collector Samuel Glenn of Boydton, Virginia. At the May 10, 1935 meeting of the New York Numismatic Club, the dealer John Zug of Maryland displayed the following seven $20s acquired from the auction: 1850, 1851, 1852, 1853, 1854, 1855 and 1856. A further parcel from the hoard was sold to anonymous old gold dealers and to Eli and Yale Merrill in the summer of 1935. Augsburger discovered an inventory of the dates of the Merrill parcel in the court records; the inventory records the dates, but not the mintmarks. These numbers have been added to the inventory above, included in the numbers for Philadelphia pieces.

The find was made on premises owned by Elizabeth H. French and Mary P. B. Findley. Bessie Jones, the widowed mother of Theodore Jones, was one of the tenants of the building. Suit was brought by the owners of the premises, and also by other claimants who stated that the coins had been buried by one Andrew J. Saulsbury and that they had succeeded to his ownership of the coins. The case, Gaither v. Jones, was decided in favor of the finders on February 16, 1935 by the Circuit Court No. 2 of Baltimore City, Eugene O'Dunne, J. On appeal, the Court of Appeals of Maryland divided 4 to 4 and so the decree below was affirmed; the affirmance was per curiam, and it is not known what was the point that caused the 4-4 division. Further litigation ensued regarding the "second" parcel, concluded in favor of the finders on December 28, 1937. One of the finders, Henry Grob, died on August 25, 1937.

Bibliography: Augsburger 2008; Bowers 1997, 141–42; Breen 1952, 18–20 (Breen XVI); Breen 1988, 562–63 (Breen 7139, 7143, 7145, 7147, 7149, 7154, 7155, 7165, 7174, 7181, 7182); Fuller 1935; Warren 1938, 129–31.

"A Large Quantity of Gold U.S. Coins Unearthed," *Numismatist* 47, no. 10 (October 1934): 677–78.

"Court Gives Boys $27,800 Gold They Found, Poor Youths Will Buy Homes for Mothers," *New York Times*, February 17, 1935, 1.

"Baltimore Hoard of Gold Coins to be Sold at Auction," *Numismatist* 48, no. 4 (April 1935): 237.

Perry W. Fuller, Advertisement, *Numismatist* 48, no. 4 (April 1935): 261.

"Boys' $11,425 in Gold is Bought for $22,500. *New Yorkers* Are Among Bidders at Baltimore Auction—$20 Coin is Sold for $105," *New York Times*, May 3, 1935, 3.

"New York Numismatic Club, May 10, 1935 Meeting," *Numismatist* 48, no. 6 (June 1935): 383.

Foster v. McNabb, 179 A.928 (Md. 1935) (per curiam) (4–4 split). (Reuben Foster was the administrator de bonis non of the estate of Andrew Saulsbury; Charles A. McNabb was a court clerk who was the guardian ad litem for Jones and Grob.)

"Boys Get Treasure Trove," *New York Times*, April 16, 1936, 8.

Lee F. Hewitt, "As I See It…," *Numismatic Scrapbook Magazine* 3, no. 10 (October 1937): 220.

703. Golspie, Ontario, Canada, August 1929.

Type of find: Single find.

Contents: 1 AR.

Description: USA, 50¢, 1856

Disposition: Found by James Collins while splitting an old apple tree at the home of George Lindsay.

Bibliography: "We'll Bet Somebody Put It There," *Numismatist* 42, no. 8 (August 1929): 503.

704. North Fork of the American River, California, USA, 1979.

Type of find: Hoard.

Date of deposit: Late 1850s.

Contents: 10 AV.

Description:
USA, $5, 185[-]S (2)
USA, $20, 185[-]S (5)
USA, California, Kellogg, $20 (3)

Disposition: Found by Joe Soule when looking for gold nuggets with a dredge on the North Fork of the American River.

Bibliography: Bowers 1997, 149.

705. Ballaja Barracks, San Juan, Puerto Rico, USA, September 22, 1943.

Type of find: Foundation deposit in cornerstone of the barracks.

Date of deposit: 1857.

Contents: 2 AR.

Description: Spain, Isabella II, 20 reales (2): 1853; 1854

Bibliography: Sigler 1948.

Phares O. Sigler, "Spanish Coins Found at San Juan, Puerto Rico," *Coin Collector's*

Journal 15, no. 5 (September-October, 1948): 108–9.

706. Pepper Park, on the site of the old Indian River Inlet, between Vero Beach and Fort Pierce, Florida, USA, spring 1963 and July–September 1964.

Type of find: Shipwreck.

Ship: Ship's boat from the *William and Mary*.

Sank: May 1, 1857.

Contents: 147+ AR, 3,264 AV.

Description: The coins are known in the trade as "seawater" or "saltwater uncs." The following denominations were recovered; the gold coins are the full total, the silver coins comprise only those reported to the State of Florida in 1964:

USA, silver 5¢ (28)
USA, 25¢ (83)
USA, 50¢ (26)
USA, gold $1, 1849–56 (508) (159 reported to the State)
USA, $2.50, 1834–56 (787) (137 reported to the State)
USA, $5, 1834–56 (929) (125 reported to the State)
USA, $10, 1840–52 (490) (48 reported to the State)
USA, $20, 1850–56 (550) (113 reported to the State)

The finders falsely told the State of Florida in 1964 that only 582 gold coins had been recovered. Of these coins, the number of each date is known for the $1 pieces from Philadelphia, plus the total number of $1 pieces from New Orleans:

USA, $1 (155): 1849 (5); 1850 (6); 1851 (25); 1852 (20); 1853 (72); 1854 (15); 1855 (5); 1856 (7)
USA, $1, 1849O-53O, 1855O (4)

As of June 30, 1972, the following 195 coins remained from the find to be divided among the State of Florida, Albert N. Ashley, and James R. Gordy:

USA, $1 (2): 1850O; 1855
USA, $2.50 (7): 1843O; 1851O; 1852C; 1854 (2); 1855; 1856
USA, $5 (21): 1834; 1838 (2); 1841 (2); 1843C; 1844O; 1846 (2); 1846D (2); 1850C (2); 1850D; 1853D; 1854C (2); 1855D (2); 1856C; 1856D
USA, $10 (7): 1839; 1845; 1847 (2); 1849 (2); 1850
USA, $20 (158): 1850 (7); 1850O (6); 1851 (10); 1851O (4); 1852 (17); 1852O (3); 1853 (23); 1853O (5); 1854 (15); 1854S (3); 1855 (26); 1855S (7); 1856 (11); 1856S (20); 1857S

The following date and mintmark combinations have turned up in the numismatic trade as "seawater uncs"; this data is based upon the books by Akers, Breen, and Winter, plus the auctions of the Harry Bass Collection:

USA, $2.50: 1846C; 1846D; 1846O; 1856C
USA, $5: 1834; 1835; 1836; 1840D; 1840O; 1842; 1843C; 1843O; 1844O; 1845; 1846; 1846C; 1846D; 1847C; 1848C; 1848D; 1850C; 1852C; 1852D; 1853D; 1854D; 1855C; 1855D; 1856C; 1856D; 1856S
USA, $10: 1842, small date; 1842O; 1843; 1844O; 1845O; 1846/5O; 1847; 1847O; 1848
USA, $20: 1855S; 1856; 1856S

In 1857 $23,000 in coin was withdrawn from the subtreasury in Charleston, South Carolina to pay federal troops fighting in the Third Seminole War. It was given to an army paymaster, Major Jeremiah Yellot Dashiell, who was carrying it to Fort Capron when his boat capsized and the payroll bag was lost, the coins sinking beneath the soft sand so that they were irretrievable.

Disposition: Found by James Robert Gordy, aged 16, and Albert N. Ashley while skin-diving and fishing for crawfish off Fort

Pierce in the spring of 1963. Gordy's father, Ken F. Gordy, applied to the Florida Internal Improvement Fund for a concession to raise the coins, and the State of Florida agreed in exchange for one quarter of the coins. From July through September 1964 the finders raised 225 silver coins and 477 gold coins. In September 1964 the finders turned over to the State of Florida 105 gold coins. The State of Florida eventually obtained 160 silver coins plus 146 gold coins. The finders did not reveal, however, that they had recovered 2,682 gold coins in 1963, for a total of 3,264 gold coins over the two seasons. These coins were dispersed through the numismatic trade and are known as "seawater uncs" (because they have no true wear from circulation). Study of the circumstances of the find indicates that the abrasion was not caused by saltwater, but rather by the fine sand on the bottom of the inlet in which the coins fell. In 1968 the finders fell out and sued each other in the Circuit Court of Saint Lucie County, and their concealment of the true extent of the find was revealed. The State of Florida intervened in the litigation. A stipulation among the litigants concluded on April 12, 1972 ended the litigation by agreeing to split the coins held at the Saint Lucie County Bank as follows: First the indebtedness of Ashley and Gordy to the Saint Lucie County Bank would be settled; then 55% of the value of the rest would go to the State of Florida; 22.5% would go to James R. Gordy; 22.5% would go to Albert N. Ashley; Ken F. Gordy would get nothing. As of June 6, 1972 the indebtedness to the Saint Lucie County Bank was $11,408.28. 114 coins were sold off at a rate of $101 apiece to WorldWide Coins in Atlanta, Georgia, USA, on or about June 23, 1972. From an account in Bowers' book on American hoards, it becomes clear that a few dozen of these coins were sold onward to Q. David Bowers, with a final group of eighteen sold by Bowers through an advertisment in *Coin World* in 1973. 195 coins, comprising $1 (2), $2.50 (7), $5 (21), $10 (7), $20 (158), remained, and were presumably divided among the parties in accordance with the stipulation of April 12, 1972.

Bibliography: Akers 1975; Akers 1979; Akers 1980; Akers 1982; Bowers 1997, 163–65 (note especially discussion of transaction with WorldWide Coin Investments on pages 164–65); Bowers and Merena 1999–2000; Breen 1988, 529, 532–34, 565 (Breen 6545, 6548, 6549, 6587, 6599, 6600, 6604, 6605, 6607, 6608, 6616, 6617, 6622, 7180); Clausen 1968; Craig 2000b, 68; Potter 1972, 208–9; Winter 1997; Winter 1998.

Don Wharton, "What actually happened in those Florida treasure hunts," *Empire Magazine*, May 12, 1968, 47 (Sunday color supplement of the *Denver Post*). Partially reprinted in: Don Wharton, "Those Florida Treasure Hunts," *Reader's Digest*, June 1968, 206.

State of Florida Master Site File, File on Gordy gold.

State of Florida, Underwater Archaeology Program Files.

707. Off the coast of North Carolina, USA, salvaged October 1988, August-October 1989, June-September 1990, June-September 1991.

Type of find: Shipwreck.

Ship: Central America.

Sank: September 12, 1857, en route from Aspinwall, Panama, and Havana, Cuba, to New York City.

Containers: Photographs of the recovery process show that some coins and bars were recovered from wooden chests.

Contents: 33 AR; 7,708 AV.

Description:

German states, Hanover, 10 thalers, 1825
Great Britain, sovereign, 1851

France, 20 francs, 1831
USA, silver 5¢, 1854, with arrows
USA, 25¢ (9): 1853 with arrows; ND (8)
USA, 50¢ (21): bust type; 1826, with small size Chinese chopmarks; 1830; 1848; 1855–57S (2); 1857S; ND (14)
USA, gold $1, 1854
USA, $2.50 (36): 1834; 1843O; 1845; 1846; 1846O; 1847O; 1850 (2); 1851 (11); 1852 (2); 1853 (3); 1854; 1855; 1856S (9); 1857S
USA, $3, 1856S (3)
USA, $5 (118): 1834 (5); 1835; 1836; 1838 (2); 1840 (3); 1840C; 1842D; 1843 (4); 1844D; 1844O (2); 1845D; 1846 (2); 1847 (8); 1848 (3); 1848C; 1849; 1849C; 1850D; 1851 (2); 1852 (4); 1852C; 1852D; 1854 (2); 1854O; 1855 (3); 1855C; 1855S (12); 1856; 1856S (32); 1857S (19)
USA, $10 (109): 1841; 1843 (2); 1843O (2); 1844O (2); 1845O (3); 1846O (3); 1847 (7); 1847O (6); 1848; 1848O (2); 1849 (6); 1850 (2); 1851O (2); 1852 (2); 1852O (2); 1853; 1853O; 1854; 1854O (2); 1854S (13); 1855 (2); 1855S (6); 1856S (28); 1857S (12)
USA, $20 (7,090): 1850 (29); 1850O; 1851 (33); 1851O (8); 1852 (32); 1852O (4); 1853 (28); 1853O (2); 1854 (20); 1854S (25); 1855 (7); 1855S (338) (including one counterstamped J. L Polhemus); 1856 (6); 1856S (1,153); 1857 (2); 1857S (5,402)
USA, California, Humbert, $10, 1852, 884 fine (79)
USA, California, Humbert, $50, lettered edge, 880 fine (3)
USA, California, Humbert, $50, reeded edge, 880 fine (4)
USA, California, Humbert, $50, 1851, reeded edge, 887 fine (2)
USA, California, Humbert, $50, 1852, reeded edge, 887 fine (2)
USA, California, USAOG, $10, 1852, 884 fine (92)
USA, California, USAOG, $10, 1853, 884 fine (3)
USA, California, USAOG, $10, 1853, 900 fine (9)
USA, California, USAOG, $50, 1852, 887 fine (3)
USA, California, USAOG, $50, 1852, 900 fine
USA, California, Moffat, $5, 1850
USA, California, Moffat, $10 (37): 1849 (25); 1852 (12)
USA, California, Baldwin, $10, 1851 (2)
USA, California, Wass, Molitor, $10, 1852 (73) (including one counterstamped W. W. Light)
USA, California, Wass, Molitor, $10, 1855 (24)
USA, California, Wass, Molitor, $50, 1855
USA, California, Kellogg, $20, 1854 (4)
USA, California, Kellogg, $20, 1855 (5)
USA, California, A. L. Nouizillet, 25¢ (4)
Chile, 50 centavos: 1853; 1856
Gold bars:
USA, California, Blake & Co. (34)
USA, California, Harris, Marchand & Co. (37)
USA, California, Henry Hentsch & Co. (33)
USA, California, Justh & Hunter (85)
USA, California, Kellogg & Humbert (343)

Disposition: Auctioned by Sotheby's, June 2000, and Christie's, December 2000; also sold at retail by the California Gold Marketing Group.

Bibliography: Bowers 2002; Breen 1990; Christie's 2000; Evans 2000; Kinder 1998; Sotheby's 1999 (original date cancelled and actually held in June 2000); Thompson 1998.

708. Centre and Franklin Streets, New York, New York, USA, September 1948.

Type of find: Hoard.

Date of deposit: October 1, 1857.

Contents: 50 P.

Description:

USA, Maine, Fairmont, New England Bank, $10, October 1, 1857 (50)

USA, Maine, Fairmont, New England Bank, $20, October, 1, 1857 (50)

Fifty sheets of $1,500 in $10 and $20 notes of the New England Bank of Fairmont, Maine, dated October 1, 1857. The notes were proofs, unsigned and with heavy crosses on each side. This bank was never incorporated and the notes were issued fraudulently. Since the hoard was found by wreckers while tearing down the old Criminal Courts building, it seems likely that the notes were part of the evidence in a prosecution against the perpetrators of the New England Bank fraud.

Disposition: Henry Drachman, secretary of the D.E.H. Demolition Company.

Bibliography: "'Fortune' Mere Paper. Banknotes Found by Wreckers Turn Out to be Proofs," *New York Times*, September 21, 1948, 20.

709. Eastern Pennsylvania, USA, April 1996.

Type of find: Hoard. Called "the Butternut Hoard."

Date of deposit: 1857.

Contents: 4,700 AE.

Description:

USA, 1¢ (4,700): 1794 (9); 1795 (14); 1796 (8); 1797 (16); 1798 (64); 1799 (2); 1800 (47); 1801 (57); 1802 (97); 1803 (49); 1805 (6); 1806 (24); 1807 (45); 1808 (24); 1809 (4); 1810 (89); 1811 (11); 1812 (43); 1813 (10); 1814 (20); 1816 (106); 1817 (97); 1818 (157); 1819 (165); 1820 (137); 1821 (70); 1822 (259); 1823 (56); 1824 (61); 1825 (48); 1826 (110); 1827 (224); 1828 (163); 1829 (56); 1830 (54); 1831 (196); 1832 (73); 1833 (145); 1834 (87); 1835 (136); 1836 (72); 1837 (492); 1838 (373); 1839 (222); 1840 (5); 1841 (3); 1842 (6); 1843 (94); 1844 (65); 1845 (3); 1846 (5); 1847 (8); 1848 (6); 1849 (5); 1850 (6); 1851 (17); 1852 (10); 1853 (10); 1854 (3); 1855 (8); 1856 (26); 1857 (2); not yet attributed by date (220)

Disposition: Bought from a family in Eastern Pennsylvania by Bob Miller of New Jersey. Sold by Bob Miller to Steven K. Ellsworth in late April 1996.

Bibliography: Ellsworth and Schwerdt 1996.

710. Fort York, Toronto, Ontario, Canada, 1987–93.

Type of find: Archaeological excavation.

Date of site: 1793–1871.

Date of third period (decimal coinage): 1858–71.

Contents: 5 AE, 5 AR.

Description:

Great Britain, penny, 1860

Canada, 1¢ (2)

Canada, 5¢ (2)

Canada, 10¢ (2)

Canada, 10¢, 1872

USA, 1¢, 1863

USA, 2¢, 1865

Bibliography: Spittal 1993, 244–53.

711. Spring Creek, western Nance County, Nebraska, USA, spring 1883 (or 1884).

Type of find: Funerary deposit.

Date of deposit: Ca. 1858.

Contents: AR single find.

Description: USA, Indian Peace Medal, 1821, privately engraved by the young women of Miss White's Seminary of Washington, DC, to commemorate the action of Petalesharo (ca. 1797–ca. 1858) of the Pawnees in rescuing a Comanche woman from a Ski'-di human sacrifice ceremony to the morning star.

Disposition: Plowed up and extracted from Petalesharo's grave in spring 1883 (ANS records say 1884) by Orlando Thompson, accompanied by his niece Mary Thompson, to whom he presented the medal. Miss Mary Thompson later became Mrs. G. W. Ellsworth of 645 North 30th Street, Lincoln, Nebraska. Lent to the Nebraska Historical Society by Mary Thompson; the medal was recalled from the Nebraska Historical Society in May 1922 and purchased by John Sanford Saltus, who presented it to the American Numismatic Society in New York; item number 1922.89.1.

Bibliography: Blackman 1919; May 1999; Stahl 1990.

M. Sorenson, "Medals: Items from the Press," *Numismatist* 35, no. 9 (September 1922): 415–16.

712. Jackson, Tennessee, USA, September 13, 1985.

Type of find: Hoard.
Date of deposit: 1858.
Container: Jar.
Contents: 1,000 AV.
Description:
  USA, $2.50, 1853
  USA, $5, 1840
  USA, $5, 1847
  USA, $20, 1858
  USA, $20, 1858O

There were said to be two $50 slugs as well.

Disposition: Found when a backhoe ripped up an asphalt parking lot. Grabbed by more than 20 people.

Bibliography: Banning 1987, 5–6 (citing *Numismatic News*, October 15, 1985, 1, 6).

Bowers and Merena, Wolfeboro, New Hampshire, USA, Auction Catalog (Harry Bass III), May 2000, commentary in lot 640.

713. Near the railroad station, Panama City, Panama, April 1884.

Type of find: Hoard.
Date of deposit: 1860?
Contents: 38 AV.
Description: USA, $20 (38)
Disposition: Found by men digging on the works near the railroad station.

"Gold Coin Found at Panama," *New York Times*, May 5, 1884, 5 (citing the *Panama Star and Herald*, April 23, 1884).

714. Pyramid Lake Indian Reservation, near Reno, Nevada, USA, July 1967.

Type of find: Hoard.
Date of deposit: 1860.
Contents: 175+ AV.
Description: USA, $5?, 1834? onwards

Gold coins said to date back to 1814; 1814 is almost certainly a misprint for 1834. Thought to have been left from a military encampment in the area during the Second Pyramid Lake Indian War; the date of deposit was arrived at by this assumption. Denominations not described, but probably included $5, the commonest U.S. gold coin denomination.

Disposition: Found by members of the Nicon Tribal Council, Pyramid Lake Indian Reservation.

Bibliography: Bowers 1997, 147–48 (citing "Indians Locate Gold Coin Hoard," *Coin World*, July 19, 1967).

715. Stewart County, Tennessee, not far from Hopkinsville, Kentucky, USA, June 1926.

Type of find: Hoard.
Date of deposit: 1861.
Container: Glass jar.
Contents: 36+ AV.
Description:
  USA, $5, of which "several" were dated 1834

USA, $20

The coins were all dated before the Civil War. A broken glass jar was nearby.

Bibliography: Bowers 1997, 137 (erroneously gives the number of 1834 coins as seven; original newspaper has the adjective "several," exact number not specified).

"Find $675 in Buried Gold. Tennessee Boys Planting Tobacco Unearth Coins Antedating Civil War," *New York Times*, June 15, 1926, 12.

716. Fredericksburg, Virginia, USA, 1985–95.

Type of find: Single finds recovered from Civil War sites.

Contents: 10 AR.

Description: Kays says that ½ reales (*medios*) are commonly found on Civil War campsites such as Fredericksburg, alongside Federal half dimes. In his collection Kays has nine *medios*, plus one quarter pistareen, from Civil War sites. These coins (called, in New Orleans, picayunes), continued to circulate into the 1860s:

Spain, Philip V ½ real (¼ pistareen), Madrid, ND

Spanish colonies, ½ reales, México (9): Charles III, ND (2); 1780 (2); 1781; 1782; 1784; 1785 (2)

Disposition: Found by metal detectorists. Acquired by Thomas A. Kays.

Bibliography: Kays 1996, 1637–45.

717. Bedford County, Tennessee, USA, 1983.

Type of find: Hoard.

Date of deposit: 1861.

Container: Iron pot.

Contents: 250 AV.

Description: USA, $5, 1834–61 (250)

The coins were in an iron pot that had decomposed, buried eight to twenty inches below the surface. None was dated later than 1861. The Numismatist says that the coins were dated after 1830, but it is virtually certain that the oldest coin in the hoard would have been 1834.

Disposition: The coins were found on a farm by Max Wiser and Ed McClarty, who were using a metal detector and trespassing at the time. Awarded by the court to Clyde E. and Helen Morgan, who owned the farm.

Bibliography: "Discovery of Hoard Leads to Law Suit," *Numismatist* 97, no. 6 (June 1984): 1135–36.

Morgan v. Wiser, 711 S.W. 2d 220 (Tenn. App. 1985).

718. Near Prairie Town, Illinois, USA, 1969.

Type of find: Hoard.

Date of deposit: 1861.

Contents: 93 AR, 68 AV.

Description:

USA, 25¢ and 50¢ (93)

USA, $2.50 (9)

USA, $5 (40): 1838C; 1838D; other dates (38)

USA, $10 (7): 1856; 1856S; 1858S; 1860 (2); other dates (2)

USA, $20 (12): 1861 (5); other dates (7)

Disposition: Found when a basement in a farmhouse was excavated. The man who found the hoard offered it to Kenneth V. Voss in the early 1970s for $7,500, but Voss declined. It was later sold to one of Voss's friends and co-workers for about $12,500.

The 1861 $20s were in choice condition; one gem example of these was sold for $11,000 at the 1979 ANA Convention in Saint Louis. The silver coins had little wear but were damaged from moisture.

Bibliography: Bowers 1997, 285 (citing information from Kenneth V. Voss and Bennie Hutchins).

719. Ottawa, Iowa, USA, May 1964.
Type of find: Hoard.
Date of deposit: 1861.
Contents: P.
Description: USA, demand notes, 1861
   $1,500 in old bills, dating back to the first U.S. issues of the Civil War period.
Disposition: Found by Wallace McClure while remodeling an old house.
Bibliography: Numismatic Scrapbook Magazine 30, no. 5 (May 1964): 1247.

720. Florence, Alabama, USA, April 1942.
Type of find: Hoard.
Date of deposit: 1860s?
Container: Pot.
Contents: 273 AV.
Description:
   USA, $5
   USA, $20?
Disposition: $5,885 in gold coins found in a pot by four youngsters. Two of the children were the sons of Lynn Scandlin, a taxicab driver. Ownership disputed with someone who claimed the coins were found on his property.
Bibliography: "Children Find $5,885 in Pot," *New York Times*, April 3, 1942, 40.

721. Corpus Christi, Texas, USA, February 1956.
Type of find: Hoard.
Date of deposit: 1861.
Contents: 33 AR.
Description:
   USA, 50¢
   Spanish colonies, 8 reales
   Mexico, 8 reales
   The coins were dated 1810–61.
Disposition: Found in a load of sandy loam delivered for P. H. Curran's lawn.
Bibliography: "Quick Silver," *New York Times*, February 13, 1956, 47.

722. Scary Creek, Kanawha County, West Virginia, USA, June 1990 and April 1991.
Type of find: Single finds.
Date of site: July 1861.
Contents: 3 AE, 7 AR, 1 AV.
Description:
   USA, 1¢ (2): 1830; 1848
   USA, silver 3¢, 1853
   USA, 10¢ (2): 1853 with arrows; 1861
   USA, 50¢ (2): 1830 (holed at top); 1833
   USA, $2.50, 1861
   USA, uniface merchant's token, $2.50
   Spanish colonies, Charles III, 2 reales, México, 1774
   Spanish colonies, Charles IV, 8 reales, 1807, holed at top
Disposition: Found with a metal detector by Jesse W. McComas.
Bibliography: Jesse W. McComas, "My Field of Dreams," *Treasure Found* (Fall 1992): 22–25.

723. Tennessee, USA, April 2001.
Type of find: Single find.
Date of site: 1861–65 (Civil War troop site).
Contents: 1 AR.
Description: Spanish colonies, Charles III or IV, 8 reales [1772–1808], cut quarter
Disposition: Found by a metal detectorist.
Bibliography: Kays 2001, 2196.

724. Deep Creek, Norfolk County, Virginia, USA, April 1880.
Type of find: Hoard.
Date of deposit: 1861.
Container: Iron chest.
Contents: 200+ AV.
Description: USA, gold coins, 1834 onwards (200+)

The coins were in an iron chest, and are thought to have been buried during the Civil War. The total value was several thousand dollars. *The American Journal of Numismatics* says that the dates went as far back as 1830, but this is almost certainly an error for 1834.

Bibliography: "Numismatic Discoveries," *American Journal of Numismatics* 14, no. 4 (April 1880): 101.

725. Gordonsville, Orange County, Texas, USA, 1985–95.

Type of find: Single find.

Date of deposit: 1861–65.

Container: Leather coin purse.

Contents: 1 AR.

Description: Spanish colonies, 4 reales, Potosí, 1807PJ

Found at a Texas Civil War camp.

Disposition: Thomas A. Kays.

Bibliography: Kays 1996, 1637–45.

726. Sullivan's Island, Columbia River, Oregon, USA, 1934.

Type of find: Archaeological excavation by Herbert Krieger of the Smithsonian Institution.

Date of deposit: 1862.

Contents: 82 Æ.

Description:

China, Kangxi, cash (13): Linqing, Shandong province; Shandong province; Hangzhou, Zhejiang province; mint illegible (10)

China, Yongzheng, cash, Board of Works, Beijing

China, Qianlong, cash (38): Yunnan province (30); Board of Revenue, Beijing (5); Guilin, Guangxi province (2); Zhili (Hebei) province

China, Jiaqing, cash, Yunnan province (5)

China, Daoguang, cash, Board of Works, Beijing

China, Tongzhi, cash, Kung-chang, Gansu province

China, cash, illegible (23)

Disposition: Smithsonian Institution?

Bibliography: Beals 1980, 65–66, 70.

727. Fort Fillmore, New Mexico, USA, October 1874.

Type of find: Hoard.

Date of deposit: 1862.

Container: Small wooden box.

Contents: 184 AV.

Description: USA, gold $1 (184)

Disposition: A boy found a gold dollar on an anthill in the old commissary building at Fort Fillmore, New Mexico. The following day three dollars were found in the same place, evidently brought up by the ants. A search was made, and a small wooden box, badly decayed, containing 180 gold dollars was found about a foot below the surface.

Bibliography: "Notes and Queries," *American Journal of Numismatics* 9, no. 2 (October 1874): 47.

728. Sayville, Long Island, New York, USA, March 1909.

Type of find: Single finds.

Date of deposit: 1862–65.

Contents: Æ.

Description: USA, Civil War tokens

Disposition: Found under an old letter drop box on the site of what had been a Post Office during the Civil War.

Bibliography: "Civil War Coins Unearthed," *New York Times*, March 31, 1909, 5.

729. Hudson, Wisconsin, USA, September 1936.

Type of find: Hoard.

Date of deposit: Summer 1862.

Contents: 6 AV.

Description: USA, gold coins, 1834–50s (6)

Disposition: Gold coins plowed up by Hans Peterson, many more than 70 years old, and some more than a century. This description suggests that the coins ranged in date from 1834 to the 1850s. Total value $100.

Bibliography: "Gold Coin Finds Reported in Press," *Numismatist* 49, no. 9 (September 1936): 705.

730. Crawfordsville, Indiana, USA, January 1902.

Type of find: Hoard.

Date of deposit: Summer 1862.

Container: Tin canister.

Contents: AV, P.

Description:
Mexico, gold coins, 1850s
USA, shinplaster money, 10¢ to 50¢
Estate of America Stipe. Gold and banknotes totalling nearly $2,000.

Bibliography: Joseph Hooper, "Hooper's Restrikes," *Numismatist* 15, no. 2 (February 1902): 47.

731. Muskegon, Michigan, USA, December 31, 1894.

Type of find: Hoard.

Date of deposit: Summer 1862.

Contents: 32+ AV.

Description: USA, gold coins (32+)

Disposition: $606 of lawful gold coin, found by two boys, Willie Peterson and Wecko Carlson, in an old stump; last date 1861.

Bibliography: George F. Heath, "With the Editor," *Numismatist* 8, no. 1 (January, 1895): 25.

732. Biddeford, Maine, USA, January 1926.

Type of find: Hoard.

Date of deposit: Summer 1862.

Container: Large iron kettle.

Contents: 300 B.

Description: USA, Louis Kossuth medal, obverse: "Nothing is impossible to him that wills"; reverse: "United States, The Birthplace of Freedom"

Disposition: Found by the farmer Philip Perreault.

Bibliography: "Phil Now Believes in Dreams," *Numismatist* 39, no. 2 (February 1926): 63.

733. New Boston, Illinois, USA, summer 1956.

Type of find: Hoard.

Date of deposit: Summer 1862.

Contents: AR, AV.

Description:
USA, silver coins
USA, $2.50
USA, $20
Silver and gold coins, dating 1808 to 1860. Included $2.50 and $20 coins.

Disposition: Found by workers digging a trench for a new building. A local lawyer held the coins, pending determination of the rightful owner. A livery stable was once located on the spot.

Bibliography: "Coins Found During Construction," *Numismatist* 69, no. 10 (October 1956): 1124.

734. Falls of Schuylkill, Pennsylvania, USA, March 1896.

Type of find: Hoard.

Date of deposit: 1862.

Contents: 200+ P.

Description: USA, obsolete banknotes (200+) $15,000 in wildcat banknotes snugly wrapped up in tinfoil and a stout piece of paper. Supposed to have been hidden early in the Civil War by the brewer John Stein.

Disposition: Found by John Shannon. Upon being told that the banks were mostly broken, he sent them to a broker in Philadelphia in the hope he could get some of them redeemed.

Bibliography: "The Money was Out of Date," *Numismatist* 9, no. 3 (March 1896): 60–61 (citing the *Philadelphia Record*).

735. Delton, Michigan, USA, February 1899.

Type of find: Hoard.

Date of deposit: Summer 1862.

Contents: 119 AE.

Description:
China, cash
Sweden, 2 öre 1861
Denmark, ½ skilling, 1847
Netherlands, cent?
German states, pfenning (2)
German states, 2 pfenning (2)
Great Britain, farthing, 1822
British colonies, Canada East and West, coppers, 1844–1862 (92)
British colonies, Prince Edward Island, token? 1857
USA, 1¢, 1803
USA, 1¢, 1819–1854 (14)
Unidentifiable (2)

Disposition: Found by George Norwood beneath a woodpile adjacent to the Chicago, Kalamazoo, & Saginaw Railway. Q. David Bowers suggests that the hoard was put together in Canada because it has many U.S. large cents, but no U.S. small cents.

Bibliography: Bowers 1997, 50–51; Kleeberg 1994, ix–x.
George F. Heath, "Editorial," *Numismatist* 13, no. 2 (February 1900): 62.
George W. Rice, "Editorial," *Numismatist* 13, no. 3 (March 1900): 89.

736. Quincy, Illinois, USA, April 1939.

Type of find: Hoard.

Date of deposit: Summer 1862.

Container: Clay pot.

Contents: 7 AV.

Description: USA, $20, 1852–60

Disposition: Uncovered by 4 WPA workers.

Bibliography: Ted Hammer, "Here and There," *Numismatic Scrapbook Magazine* 5, no. 4 (April 1939): 177.

737. Superior, California, USA, January 1916.

Type of find: Hoard.

Date of deposit: 1862.

Container: Rusty tin can.

Contents: 30+ AV.

Description: USA, $20, 1862S (30)
Gold coins and nuggets in a rusty tin can. $600 was in double eagles dated 1862.

Disposition: Found by the nine-year-old son of Judge A. B. Mackenzie.

Bibliography: "Miscellaneous Numismatic News and Comment," *Numismatist* 29, no. 1 (January 1916): 36.

738. Twelfth and Poplar Streets, Saint Louis, Missouri, USA, May 16, 1928.

Type of find: Hoard.

Date of deposit: 1862.

Contents: 300+ AR.

Description:
Great Britain, silver coins (shillings?)
USA, silver 3¢
USA, silver 5¢ (90+)
USA, 10¢
USA, 25¢
USA, 50¢
Mexico, small silver coins
Central America, small silver coins
Dates ranged from 1805 to 1862.

Disposition: Found by workers excavating at Twelfth and Poplar Streets in Saint Louis. One worker found 90 silver 5¢, with at least 20 different dates represented.

Bibliography: John H. Snow, "Many Silver Coins Unearthed in St. Louis," *Numismatist* 41, no. 6 (June 1928): 337.

739. Hagerstown, Maryland, USA, March 1919.

Type of find: Hoard.
Date of deposit: September 1862.
Container: Earthen crock of antique design.
Contents: 20? AV.
Description: USA, gold coins, 1834–55 (20?)
An earthen crock of antique design, which contained gold coins dated between "1830," (almost certainly an error for 1834) and 1855, which probably had been hidden during the Civil War.
Disposition: It was found by Emanuel Lorshbaugh, a carpenter, while repairing a building on a farm belonging to Charles Custis of Hagerstown, several miles from Hagerstown on the Williamsport pike.
Possibly buried during Robert E. Lee's invasion of Maryland, shortly before the battle of Antietam.
Bibliography: "Numismatic Notes of Interest to Collectors," *Numismatist* 32, no. 3 (March 1919): 140.

740. Boonsboro, Maryland, USA, July 1919.

Type of find: Single find.
Date of deposit: September 17, 1862.
Contents: 1 SN.
Description: USA, Washington medal by Merriam, made into a dog tag (Baker 122T) with inscription on the reverse: [first name illegible] Murphy/Company K, Twenty-first Regiment, O. C.-V. P. G. C. B., Boonton, N. J. The dogtag of one of the 6,000 men who fell in the battle of Antietam. The date of deposit was arrived at using this assumption.
Bibliography: "Token 'dated 1732,' Unearthed," *Numismatist* 32, no. 7 (July 1919): 290.

741. New Boston, Connecticut, USA, July 1888.

Type of find: Hoard.
Date of deposit: 1862?
Contents: 95,250 AE, 60,000 NI, 300 AR, 350 AV.
Description: Mostly copper coins hoarded by Aaron White, a lawyer of Connecticut who distrusted government paper money. The hoard included:
Great Britain, COLONEL PERCIE KIRK/ BRITON'S OWN HAPPY ISLE 1686, proof (Atkins 65) (191)
Ireland, Wood's Hibernia halfpence, 1723 (47)
British colonies, Lower and Upper Canada, North American token (7)
British colonies, Rosa Americana, worn
USA, Nova Constellatio copper, worn (7)
USA, Fugio 1¢, worn (41)
USA, Vermont, coppers, 1788 (5)
USA, Massachusetts, 1¢ (42)
USA, Connecticut, coppers (56)
USA, New York, Nova Eborac copper
USA, New Jersey, coppers (29)
USA, ½¢, 1800–55 (945)
USA, 1¢ (120,068): 1795, plain edge (19); 1795, lettered edge (2); 1796, Liberty cap (2); 1797 (26); 1800 (14); 1802 (34); 1803 (42); 1804 altered date; 1805 (23); 1806 (16); 1807 (34); 1808 (24); 1809; 1810 (29); 1811/0; 1811 (6); 1812 (65); 1813 (18); 1795–1813, worn, holed, counterstamped (471); 1816–56 (3,902); large 1¢, ND (55,000); nickel 1¢ (60,338)
USA, 2¢ (5,000)
USA, 50¢ (200)
USA, silver $1 (100)
USA, gold $1 (350)
USA, hard times tokens, including Low 55 (Loco Foco) and the "balky mule" type (172)

USA, Belleville Mint, T. DUSEAMAN BUTCHER token (2)

USA, Civil War tokens (534)

USA, brass token, CONTRAHENDO ET SOLVENDO (559)

USA, Aaron White's token, SUSPENDENS (253+): copper (105); brass (147); white metal

USA, Aaron White, brass calendar medal (16)

Non-USA copper coins (20,000 to 30,000)

Disposition: 18,000 copper and nickel pieces from the hoard were auctioned by Édouard Frossard on July 20, 1888.

Bibliography: Breen 1952, 1007–9 (Breen Hoards XXI); Jones 1938.

742. Genoa, Nebraska, USA, 1913.

Type of find: Funerary deposit.

Date of deposit: 1862–68.

Contents: 1 AR.

Description: USA, Indian Peace Medal, Abraham Lincoln, 1862

Disposition: Dug up by John Vaught from a Pawnee burial ground while repairing the water works reservoir on a hill back of town. Dented on a side by the shovel. Bought by the American Numismatic Society, New York, New York, USA; item number 1915.25.1.

Bibliography: Parker 1913.

743. Wurtsboro, Sullivan County, New York, USA, October 1922.

Type of find: Single find.

Contents: 1 AE.

Description: USA, Civil War token, 1863, Fuld 173–76

Described as a medal with on a man on the horse and the words, "First in war, first in peace," and the date "1775" (probable misreading for 1863). The reverse had a shield and a wreath around the outer edge.

Disposition: Found by workers while excavating for a new water main. Acquired by C. B. Newkirk, Wurtsboro.

Bibliography: "Rare Coin Dug Up at Wurtsboro," *New York Times*, October 11, 1922, 20.

744. Pearl River Swamp, east of Jackson Missisippi, USA, November 7, 1899.

Type of find: Hoard.

Date of deposit: May 14, 1863.

Container: Iron case.

Contents: 2,500+ AV.

Description: USA, $20, 1850 (ca. 2,500)

The coins were all said to be dated prior to 1850, but this cannot be reconciled with the statement that nearly all of them were $20s. The treasure is thought to have been buried during the Civil War, so the date of deposit is the date of the capture of Jackson, Mississippi.

Disposition: Found by the hunter Johnson while hunting in the Pearl River swamp.

Bibliography: "Buried War Treasure Found," *Brooklyn Daily Eagle*, November 7, 1899, 7.

745. Natchez, Mississippi, USA, 1957.

Type of find: Hoard.

Date of deposit: July 1863.

Contents: 400? AR.

Description:

USA, silver 5¢, 1816–57 (200?)

USA, 10¢, 1816–57 (200?)

Disposition: Found by Larry Bolyer, then aged 7, between bricks in a brick wall, the remains of an old house, possibly its chimney, on the bank of the Mississippi River. Despite the caption to the photograph in the Nesmith and Potter book, the coins were not in a chest. The other boy in the picture in the Nesmith and Potter book, Don Hunter, was not a co-finder, but Bolyer's friend who had just come down to see the *Delta Queen* arrive. Enough was found to fill two or three of the #3 washtubs of Bolyer's mother. Hunter told his family and many people turned up, and finally the law took the coins away from Bolyer and his mother, claiming that because the coins had been found on government land they belonged to the City of Natchez. Dates included 1816 and 1817; the coins were as bright and shiny as if they had just been coined.

Bibliography: Nesmith and Potter 1968, 71.

Larry Bolyer, telephone conversation with John M. Kleeberg, March 26, 2007.

746. Oconowomoc, Wisconsin, USA, July 1931.

Type of find: Hoard.

Date of deposit: 1863.

Contents: 1 AR, 50 AV.

Description:
  USA, silver $1
  USA, $10
  USA, $20
  One coin bore the date 1847; another 1863 (presumably this is the range of dates of the hoard).

Disposition: Found by Martin A. Born; deposited by him into the National Bank of Commerce of Milwaukee.

Bibliography: "Gold Coins Dug Up in Wisconsin," *Numismatist* 44, no. 7 (July 1931): 527.

747. Old plantation site near Vicksburg, Mississippi, USA, 1973.

Type of find: Hoard.

Date of deposit: April-July 1863.

Contents: 14 AV.

Description:
  USA, $5 (7): 1834, 1835*, 1844O (2)*, 1846C*, 1849C*, 1860C*
  USA, $10 (6): 1843O, 1847O*, 1853, 1854O*, 1855, 1858O
  USA, $20, 1859O*
  This hoard is remarkable for the predominance of Southern branch mints—10 out of 14; this can partly be accounted for by the proximity of New Orleans.

Supposedly one of three caches—two containing gold coins, the third containing jewels, silverplate, and other family treasures—buried by the plantation owner when Grant's army was advancing towards Vicksburg. The plantation house was burned, the site looted, and the owner killed.

Disposition: Treasure hunters found one cache in 1973, but did not locate the two others. 9 coins were sold by American Auction Association, February 7, 1974, lots 1–9 (the coins marked with an asterisk); the other 5 coins were retained by the finders.

Bibliography: American Auction Association 1974, lots 1–9; Bowers 1997, 285–86.

748. Ohio, USA, January 1911.

Type of find: Hoard.

Date of deposit: July 1863.

Containers: Fruit jars.

Contents: 3,000 AV.

Description:
  USA, gold $1 (651)
  USA, $2.50, of which only 4 were dated before 1834
  USA, gold $5 (1,100), of which only 2 dated prior to 1834
  USA $20 (1,000)
  All coins were in a fine state of preservation; latest date 1861.

Disposition: Gold coins in fruit jars, unearthed by an Ohio contractor.

Bibliography: Edgar H. Adams, "Live American Numismatic Items," *Numismatist* 24, no. 1 (January 1911): 2.

749. Near Little Rock, Arkansas, USA, March 1955.

Type of find: Hoard.

Date of deposit: September 10, 1863.

Contents: 30 AV.

Description: USA, $20, 1850–63

Found on an Arkansas River plantation by two tenant farmers. Thought hidden to guard against capture by Union troops; the plantation was used as a Union hospital, and has the graves of the 70th Ohio Infantry. The 70th Ohio Infantry was stationed at Little Rock, Arkansas, June-August 1865; however, the hoard was probably buried immediately before the Union capture of Little Rock (September 10, 1863).

Disposition: Sold to a Chicago dealer.

Bibliography: "Arkansas Gold Find," *Numismatic Scrapbook Magazine* 21, no. 4 (April 1955): 488.

750. Shoshone Wells, Nevada, USA, 1981–83.

Type of find: Archaeological excavation.

Date of site: 1863–1902.

Contents: 2 B, 2 AR.

Description:
China, Kangxi, cash
China, Qianlong, cash
USA, 10¢ (2): 1871; 1900S
The site was occupied by Chinese miners.

Disposition: University of Nevada-Reno.

Bibliography: Hardesty 1988.

751. Pasadena, California, USA, 1989.

Type of find: Single finds.

Date of deposit: 1864.

Contents: 1 AR, 1 AV.

Description:
USA, 50¢, 1864S
USA, $3, 1856S

Disposition: Found with a metal detector by Arthur Passanado.

Bibliography: "Detector Signals… Coast to Coast: Nickel Size Gold," *Treasure Found* (Spring 1989): 15.

752. Natural Bridge, Rockbridge County, Virginia, USA, February 1959.

Type of find: Hoard.

Date of deposit: June 1864.

Container: Earthenware crock.

Contents: 2 AE, 1,299 AR, 3 AV.

Description:
USA, large 1¢
USA, small 1¢
USA, silver 3¢ (43)
USA, silver 5¢ (195)
USA, 10¢ (285)
USA, 25¢ (534)
USA, 50¢ (112)
USA, silver $1, 1798
USA, gold $1 (3)
Spanish colonies, small silver coins (129)
The dates of the U.S. coins ranged from 1798 to 1859; the Spanish colonies coins were older. The coins are supposed to have been buried just before the Union general David Hunter's raid during the Civil War.

Disposition: Found by Tom Reid while operating a bulldozer on the farm of Dr. A. A. Houser. The coins were counted by Emmett W. Tardy, ANA L.M. 196 of Lexington, Virginia, who said that about 90% of the coins were in extra fine condition.

Bibliography: Emmett W. Tardy, "A Buried Treasure Unearthed," *Numismatic Scrapbook Magazine* 25, no. 4 (April 1959): 1066.
"Treasure Unearthed," *Numismatist* 72, no. 5 (May 1959): 543.

753. Roubidoux River bed, Fort Leonard Wood, four miles south of Waynesville, Pulaski County, Missouri, USA, November 30, 1962.

Type of find: Hoard.

Date of deposit: September 1864.

Container: Walnut box held together by wooden dowels.

Contents: 5,000+ AR.

Description:

USA, seated Liberty 25¢

USA, seated Liberty 50¢: 1844; 1853, arrows and rays; 1853O, arrows and rays; 1854 with arrows (2); 1855 with arrows; 1856 (2); 1857 (3); 1858; 1859 (3); 1862

Those coins with dates listed above are in the collection of Maurice Vaughan.

All coins seen were dated between 1840 and 1862. They were in excellent condition: "bright, shiny money and really glistened." There is also said to have been a second box that contained silver 5¢ and 25¢ dated between 1840 and 1861. The fate of the second box is unknown and may be just a rumor. The grades of the coins vary according to the dates: one of the oldest coins, 1844, grades VF-30; the most recent coin, 1862, grades AU-55.

This is believed to be the treasure of Wilson M. Tilley, who made much money selling mules to the Union Army during the Civil War. Tilley was killed, probably by bushwhackers, on or about September 10, 1864. This would have been part of an advance terror attack by bushwhackers, immediately preceding the Confederate invasion of Missouri that began on September 19, 1864.

Disposition: Found by J. W. "Jap" Mace of Roby, Missouri, while operating a bulldozer. As soon as the coins spilled out, the bulldozer operator jumped in and began gathering up the coins, followed by the other construction workers; one filled an entire lunchbox with coins. Other soldiers jumped in and began gathering up coins too, until the MPs intervened and drove everyone away, saying that the coins all belonged to the federal government. 47+ of the 50¢ were acquired by Maurice Vaughan of Waynesville, Missouri.

Bibliography: Bowers 1997, 282, 284–85; King 1984, 3–4, 87, 99–103.

Numismatic Scrapbook Magazine 29, no. 1 (January 1963): 276.

Leo Mullen, "Civil War Treasure," PD. *Saint Louis Post-Dispatch*, April 15, 1984, 6–7.

Robert Hall of Anchorage, Alaska, conversation with John M. Kleeberg, Baltimore, Maryland, July 29, 1993 (Robert Hall was an eyewitness to the discovery of the hoard).

754. Roanoke, Virginia, USA, February 1957.

Type of find: Hoard.

Date of deposit: October 1864 (The period of Sheridan's victory in the Shenandoah Valley has been chosen as the likeliest date of deposit).

Contents: 315+ P.

Description: Confederate States of America, Virginia, $3 (18+) (hitherto unknown varieties)

$31,272 in face value of Confederate States of America and Virginia banknotes. Last date 1862.

Disposition: Found in a secret vault in an inner false wall in a bank. Written up in the *Roanoke Times*, February 17, 1957. Traded to George O. Walton.

Bibliography: "Secret Vault Uncovers Hoard of Southern Currency," *Numismatic Scrapbook Magazine* 23, no. 3 (March 1957): 451.

755. Wilmington, North Carolina, USA, December 1924.

Type of find: Hoard.

Date of deposit: February 1865.

Container: Hard rubber match case.

Contents: 4 P.

Description: USA, compound interest notes (4)
The bills are thought to have been lost by a Union soldier who fell in a battle at the site.

Disposition: Dug up by building workers.

Bibliography: "Compound Interest Notes Dug Up by Workmen," *Numismatist* 38, no. 2 (February 1925): 110–11.

756. Four and a half miles from Columbia, South Carolina, USA, April 1956.

Type of find: Hoard.

Date of deposit: February 17, 1865, shortly before the burning of Columbia, South Carolina.

Container: Jar.

Contents: 100 AR.

Description:
USA, silver 3¢
USA, silver 5¢
USA, 10¢
USA, 25¢
USA, 50¢

The coins were dated 1801 through 1857, and well preserved.

Silver spoons, with the monogram DEV (8)
The estate on which the coins were found at one time belonged to the Deveraux family.

Disposition: The coins were found by three prison guards and twenty convicts while excavating the foundation for a church with a bulldozer.

Bibliography: "Civil War Treasure Found," *Numismatic Scrapbook Magazine* 22, no. 4 (April 1956): 740.
"Convicts Find Old Coins," *Numismatist* 69, no. 5 (May 1956): 538.

757. Shady Grove Farm, fifteen miles from Demopolis, Alabama, USA, May 1926.

Type of find: Hoard.

Date of deposit: March 1865.

Contents: 1,000 AV.

Description: USA, $20, 1850 (1,000)

Disposition: Found by Gayus Whitfield of Middleboro, Kentucky. Buried by his father, C. Boaz Whitfield, during the Civil War.

Bibliography: "$200,000 in Gold, Buried in Civil War, Found; Is Traced by Old Papers to Alabama Farm," *New York Times*, June 1, 1926, 1.
"Why Did He Wait So Long?" *New York Times*, June 2, 1926, 24.
"Finds $200,000 in Gold Coin Buried by Father," *Numismatist* 39, no. 7 (July 1926): 397.

758. Tuskegee, Alabama, USA, July 1935.

Type of find: Hoard.

Date of deposit: March 1865 (possibly cached at the time of Wilson's Raid).

Contents: 10+ AV.

Description: USA, gold coins, dated 1834–54 (10+)
The coins totaled $185 in face value.

Disposition: Found while razing an old hotel when the workers pried a mantle from the wall.

Bibliography: "Possibly Some Rarities Here," *Numismatist* 48, no. 7 (July 1935): 420.

759. Clay County, Alabama, USA, 1890.

Type of find: Hoard.

Date of deposit: March 27, 1865.

Contents: 30 AV.

Description: USA, $20, 1850–65 (including three $20s dated 1865)
Consisted only of double eagles; dates are said to run from 1848–65, which however, could not be the case if the hoard only consisted of $20s. Dates have accordingly been corrected to 1850.

Disposition: Found while plowing by Robert A. Wilson. He was sued by a relative, John L. Wilson, who claimed that the hoard had been cached by Wilson L. Harkins, of whose estate John Wilson was the administrator, and who owned the farm in 1865. John Wilson produced a former slave of Harkins, who testified that Harkins had cached the hoard at the time of Wilson's Raid, on March 27, 1865. Robert Wilson defended by noting that the hoard contained three $20s dated 1865, and since the Union blockade was so tight, $20s of that date could not have made their way from the Philadelphia Mint to Alabama by March 27, 1865. The Circuit Court of Clay County found for the defendant. The date of deposit has been chosen on the grounds that the plaintiff's case is more convincing—there was much contraband trade across the lines during the Civil War.

Bibliography: "Awarded to the Finder. A Lawsuit over Treasure Plowed up on a Farm," *New York Times*, April 1, 1893, 10 (with dateline from Carrollton, Georgia).

760. Rockville, Alabama, USA, March 1937.

Type of find: Hoard.
Date of deposit: March 1865?
Container: Porcelain urn.
Contents: 200 AR, 130 AV.
Description:
  USA, 50¢ (200)
  USA, $20 (130)
  A hoard deposited at the time of the Civil War, known to total $2,700 in face value, made up of hundreds of silver and gold coins. One coin known to be a 50¢ piece. Other details are educated guesses.

Bibliography: "Civil War Coin Cache Found," *Numismatic Scrapbook Magazine* 3, no. 3 (March 1937): 60.

761. Clinton, Connecticut, USA, December 1935.

Type of find: Hoard.
Date of deposit: 1865.
Containers: 2 bags.
Contents: 1,000 AR.
Description:
  France, 5 francs?
  Spanish colonies, 8 reales?
  The coins were dated between 1817 and 1865 and included many Spanish and French issues. Denominations are educated guesses. The money was in an old flue in the home of Albert Marquard. The home was built before 1835.

Bibliography: "$1,000 in Old Coins Found in Flue," *New York Times*, December 11, 1935, 29.

762. Raleigh, North Carolina, USA, beginning of 1961.

Type of find: Hoard.
Date of deposit: April 12, 1865.
Contents: 5,145 P.
Description:
  Confederate States of America, 50¢ (535): 1863 (419); 1864 (116) (many notes in series)
  Confederate States of America, $1 (166): 1862 (73); 1863 (59); 1864 (34)
  Confederate States of America, $2 (821): 1861 (9); 1862 (351); 1863 (165); 1864 (296) (many notes in series)
  Confederate States of America, $5 (282): 1863 (28); 1864 (254)
  Confederate States of America, $10, 1864 (1,093)
  Confederate States of America, $20, 1864 (158)
  Confederate States of America, $50, 1864 (2)

Confederate States of America, $100, 1864 (4)
Confederate States of America, $500, 1864
Confederate States of America, Virginia Treasury Note, $5, 1861 (2)
Confederate States of America, Virginia Treasury Note, $1, 1862 (102)
Confederate States of America, Virginia Treasury Note, $5, 1862 (16)
Confederate States of America, Virginia Treasury Note, $10, 1862
Confederate States of America, Virginia Treasury Note, $50, 1862
Confederate States of America, Virginia, Richmond, 25¢, 1862
Confederate States of America, Virginia, Richmond, 75¢, 1862
Confederate States of America, Virginia, Danville, 25¢, 1862
Confederate States of America, Virginia, Danville, 50¢, 1862 (2)
Confederate States of America, Virginia, Danville, 75¢, 1861
Confederate States of America, North Carolina, 5¢, 1863 (30)
Confederate States of America, North Carolina, 10¢ (480): 1861 (380) (in cut sheets); 1862 (97); 1863 (3)
Confederate States of America, North Carolina, 25¢ (522): 1861 (75) (in uncut sheets); 1862 (369); 1863 (64); 1864 (14)
Confederate States of America, North Carolina, 50¢ (222): 1861 (86) (in uncut sheets); 1862 (63); 1863 (35); 1864 (38)
Confederate States of America, North Carolina, 75¢, 1863 (14)
Confederate States of America, North Carolina, $1 (287): 1861 (218); 1862 (31); 1863 (38)
Confederate States of America, North Carolina, $2 (95): 1861 (69); 1863 (26)
Confederate States of America, North Carolina, $3, 1863 (6)
Confederate States of America, North Carolina, $5 (15): 1862 (9); 1863 (6)
Confederate States of America, North Carolina, $10, 1862
Confederate States of America, North Carolina, $20, 1862 (2)
Confederate States of America, North Carolina, $5, 1863 (6)
Confederate States of America, North Carolina, Greensboro Mutual Life Insurance Trust Company, 25¢ (6): 1861; 1862 (5)
Confederate States of America, North Carolina, Greensboro Mutual Life Insurance Trust Company, 50¢ (6): 1862 (2); 1863; uncertain date (3)
Confederate States of America, South Carolina, Charleston, Bank of the State of South Carolina, 15¢ (2): 1862; 1863
Confederate States of America, South Carolina, Charleston, Bank of the State of South Carolina, 25¢ (10): 1861 (5); 1862 (3); 1863 (2)
Confederate States of America, South Carolina, Charleston, Bank of the State of South Carolina, 50¢ (27): 1861; 1862 (11); 1863 (15)
Confederate States of America, South Carolina, Charleston, Bank of the State of South Carolina, 75¢, 1863 (8)
Confederate States of America, South Carolina, Charleston, 50¢, 1862
Confederate States of America, South Carolina, Charleston, $3, 1862
Confederate States of America, Georgia, 50¢, 1863 (8)
Confederate States of America, Georgia, Augusta Savings Bank, 25¢, 1861 (5)
Confederate States of America, Georgia, Augusta Savings Bank, 50¢, 1861 (4)
Confederate States of America, Georgia, Augusta Savings Bank, 75¢, 1861

Confederate States of America, Georgia, Augusta Savings Bank, $2, 1861

Confederate States of America, Georgia, Augusta Savings Bank, $3, 1861

Confederate States of America, Georgia, Bank of Augusta, 50¢, 1863

Confederate States of America, Georgia, Augusta, Union Bank, 50¢, 1862

Confederate States of America, Georgia, Savannah, Bank of the State of Georgia, 50¢, 1862

Confederate States of America, Georgia, Savannah, Mechanics Savings & Loan Association, 50¢, 1864

Confederate States of America, Georgia, Macon Savings Bank, 25¢, 1863

Confederate States of America, Alabama, 10¢, 1863

Confederate States of America, Alabama, 25¢, 1863 (3)

Confederate States of America, Alabama, 50¢, 1863 (3)

Confederate States of America, Mississippi, $20, 1862

Confederate States of America, Louisiana, $5, 1863

Confederate States of America, bond, Act of February 17, 1864, $500

Confederate States of America, bond, Act of February 17, 1864, $1,000 (12)

Confederate States of America, bond, Act of February 17, 1864, $5,000 (6)

Confederate States of America, bond, Act of February 17, 1864, $10,000

Confederate States of America, bond coupons, due on January 1, 1865, $15 (53)

Confederate States of America, bond coupons, due on January 1, 1865, $30 (96)

Confederate States of America, bond coupons, due on January 1, 1865, $40 (17)

Disposition: North Carolina Museum of History, Raleigh, North Carolina, on loan from the North Carolina Railroad.

Bibliography: Doty 1984.

763. Montgomery, near Middletown, New York, USA, February 1924.

Type of find: Hoard.

Date of deposit: 1865.

Container: Pitcher.

Contents: 50+ P.

Description: Confederate States of America, paper money (50+)

$5,000 in Confederate bills of various denominations.

The bills were found by carpenters in a pitcher in a chimney, while repairing a house in Montgomery, New York.

Bibliography: "Find $5,000 in Confederate Bills," *New York Times*, February 3, 1924, Sec. 1, 9.

764. Off Crescent City, California, USA, August-September 1996, August 1997, and intervening summers through September 2000.

Type of find: Shipwreck.

Ship: Brother Jonathan.

Sank: August 1865.

Contents: 1,259 AV.

Description:

USA, $5 (60): 1834; 1835; 1836 (2); 1837; 1838 (2); 1839D; 1840 (2); 1842D: 1842O; 1843; 1843O; 1844; 1844O; 1845 (3); 1845O; 1846; 1846D; 1847 (2); 1847C; 1848; 1848C; 1851 (3); 1852 (5); 1852D; 1853D; 1855S; 1856 (3); 1857S (2); 1858S (2); 1859S; 1860S (3); 1861 (2); 1861S; 1862S; 1863S (2); 1865S (2)

USA, $10 (5): 1847; 1849; 1856S; 1861S; 1865S

USA, $20 (1,138): 1850; 1852 (3); 1853; 1855S (4); 1856S (5); 1857; 1857S (8); 1858S (12); 1859S (20); 1860S (25); 1861 (5); 1861S

(55); 1862S (88); 1863S (139); 1864S (149); 1865 (2); 1865S (620)

Disposition: Deep Sea Research, auctioned by Bowers and Merena, May 29, 1999 (1,006); State of California (200); Del Norte County Museum (1). California plans to place its share in local museums in Crescent City and elsewhere.

A subsequent dive by Deep Sea Research in September 2000 recovered 52 coins; 38 coins were put up for sale, all $20s ranging in date from 1859S to 1865S.

Bibliography: Bowers 1998; Bowers and Merena 1999.

"Shipwreck coins in holders. NGC certifies coins from last salvage operation," *Coin World*, December 1, 2003, 82.

765. 100 miles southeast of Savannah, Georgia, USA, August 2003–March 2005.

Type of find: Shipwreck.

Ship: Republic.

Sank: October 25, 1865.

Contents: 46,994 AR, 4,166 AV, with a face value of $100,000, 25% of the $400,000 loss.

Description:

USA, 25¢ (5,188)

USA, 50¢ (41,806), including these dates: 1853O arrows and rays; 1854O; 1856O; 1858O; 1859O; 1860O; 1861O; included 1858O with WAR/1861 etched into the obverse

USA, $10 (1,442): 1838 (4); 1839 (9); 1840 (11); 1841 (20); 1841O; 1842 (17); 1843 (20); 1843O (35); 1844O (32); 1845 (2); 1845O (19); 1846 (6); 1846/5O (13); 1846O; 1847 (221); 1847 (123); 1848 (39); 1848O (9); 1849 (167); 1849O (8); 1850 (72); 1850O (16); 1851 (33); 1851O (99); 1852 (59); 1852O (3); 1853/2 (6); 1853 (59); 1853O (13); 1854 (22); 1854O (17); 1854S (41); 1855 (44); 1855O (7); 1856 (22); 1856O (5); 1856S (27); 1857 (9); 1857O (3); 1857S (11); 1858; 1858O (4); 1858S (4); 1859 (9); 1859O (2); 1860 (9); 1860O (4); 1860S (4); 1861 (60); 1861S (2); 1862 (9); 1862S; 1863; 1863S (3); 1864 (2); 1865; 1865S

USA, $20 (2,674): 1850 (55); 1850O (10); 1851 (52); 1851O (15); 1852 (104); 1852O (20); 1853/2 (9); 1853 (58); 1853O (7); 1854 (43); 1854O; 1854S (8); 1855 (18); 1855O (3); 1855S (57); 1856 (17); 1856S (65); 1857 (26); 1857O (4); 1857S (86); 1858 (9); 1858O (8); 1858S (68); 1859 (3); 1859O (2); 1859S (67); 1860 (96); 1860O; 1860S (70); 1861 (458); 1861O; 1861S (Paquet reverse); 1861S (98); 1862 (9); 1862S (127); 1863 (35); 1863S (180); 1864 (42); 1864S (168); 1865 (320); 1865S (253)

Bibliography: William J. Broad, "Far Beneath the Waves, Salvagers Find History That's Laden With Gold," *New York Times*, August 17, 2003, Sec. 1, 14.

William T. Gibbs, "Shipwreck may carry gold fortune. Firm says ship may carry $150 million in double eagles," *Coin World*, September 1, 2003, C1, 8.

William T. Gibbs, "Odyssey official uncertain of details of *Republic* gold. Firm hopes to begin search in September," *Coin World*, September 8, 2003, C1, 24, 26.

Dan Owens, "The Final Voyage of SS *Republic*. Atlantic hurricane sinks steamship and its gold," *Coin World*, September 8, 2003, 96, 98.

Al Doyle, "U.S. gold market makers await shipwreck reports. Some worry about lower prices for $20 coins," *Coin World*, September 15, 2003, C1, 40.

"Ship leaves to explore gold shipwreck," *Coin World*, October 13, 2003, 8.

William T. Gibbs, "Salvors find gold at ship site. SS *Republic* site reportedly yields 80 coins, two chests," *Coin World*, November 24, 2003, 3, 36.

William T. Gibbs, "NCS to conserve *Republic* coinage—Odyssey Marine Explorations names NGC as coins' grader," *Coin World*, January 12, 2004, C1, 32.

"*Republic* coin recovery accelerating. Salvors recover 17,000 silver, gold coins from shipwreck," *Coin World*, February 16, 2004, C1, 26.

"SS *Republic* $20 tied for finest known. NGC grades 1854O Coronet double eagle from wreck AU-55," *Coin World*, May 3, 2004, 3.

"Treasure Trove: A Moment in Time. National Geographic documentary takes viewers on a deep-sea adventure in history and gold," *Numismatist* 118, no. 1 (January 2005): 33.

Numismatic Guaranty Corporation, "SS *Republic* Coins: Gold Coin Population Report as of March 27, 2005," http://shipwreck.net/popreport3-27-05r.pdf.

"Odyssey ends SS *Republic* recovery; on to Mediterranean," *Coin World*, April 4, 2005, 48.

766. Guatemala, about 1956.

Type of find: Hoard.

Date of deposit: 1865 or early 1866.

Contents: 13,000 AR.

Description:

USA, 50¢ (13,000): 1859 (500); 1859S (500); 1860 (500); 1860S (500); 1861 (2,000); 1861S (2,000); 1862 (2,000); 1862S (2,000); 1863 (500); 1863S (500); 1864 (500); 1864S (500); 1865 (500); 1865S (500)

The coins were all cleaned with baking soda or some other abrasive. Breen saw them at the New Netherlands Coin Company in 1956.

Bibliography: Bowers 1997, 124–25, 127; Breen 1988, 401–3 (Breen 4892, 4896, 4900, 4902, 4907, 4908, 4909, 4910, 4911, 4913, 4915, 4917, 4919, 4922, 4926, 4927).

767. Boston Saloon, Virginia City, Nevada, USA, summer 2000.

Type of find: Archaeological excavation by Kelly Dixon.

Date of site: 1856–76.

Contents: 1 AV.

Description: USA, $2.50

Bibliography: "Black Saloon," *Archaeology* 53, no. 6 (November/December 2000): 23.

768. Ferryland, Newfoundland, Newfoundland and Labrador, Canada, 2001.

Type of find: Archaeological excavation.

Date of site: 1865–1950. There are three entries for this site, split into periods commencing in 1621, 1696, and 1865. This entry covers the period from the introduction of provincial coinage into Newfoundland until the latest coin found.

Contents: 6 AE, 1 AR.

Description:

British colonies, Newfoundland, Victoria, 1¢ (4): 1872H; 1873; 1876H; 1880 or 1890

British colonies, Newfoundland, George VI, 5¢, 1943c

Canada, George V, 1¢, 1903

Canada, George VI, 1¢, [1937–47]

Bibliography: Berry 2002, 1–71.

769. Port Richmond, Staten Island, New York, USA, June 1901.

Type of find: Hoard.

Date of deposit: 1866.

Containers: 2 copper kettles.

Contents: 2,000+ AV.

Description:

USA, $5

USA, $10

USA, $20

Disposition: Found by Melville E. Wygant while tearing down an old-fashioned chimney on the old Hatfield homestead, Richmond Avenue.

Bibliography: "Buried Gold," *Brooklyn Daily Eagle*, June 9, 1901, section 2, 4.

Joseph Hooper, "Hooper's Restrikes," *Numismatist* 14, no. 9 (September 1901): 246.

770. Kerens, Texas, USA, 1947.

Type of find: Hoard.

Date of deposit: 1866.

Contents: 166 AV.

Description:

USA, $2.50 (2): 1861; 1866

USA, $5 (88): 1834 (4); 1835; 1836 (5); 1838 (2); 1840; 1841; 1842D; 1842O; 1843 (5); 1843D; 1844 (2); 1844O (6); 1845; 1846 (2); 1846D (2); 1846O (2); 1847 (7); 1848 (2); 1849 (2); 1850 (2); 1851 (3); 1851O; 1852 (5); 1852D; 1853 (5); 1853C (2); 1853D; 1854; 1854O; 1855D; 1855S; 1856 (2); 1856D; 1856S; 1858C; 1858D; 1861 (10)

USA, $10 (19): 1842; 1843 (2); 1847 (3); 1847O (4); 1849 (2); 1850; 1852; 1852O; 1853; 1854S; 1856; 1857

USA, $20 (57): 1850 (2); 1851 (2); 1851O; 1852; 1852O; 1853 (4); 1854 (3); 1855S (2); 1856; 1856S; 1857 (2); 1857S (2); 1858 (3); 1858S (2); 1859S; 1860 (3); 1861 (8); 1861S (4); 1862S; 1863; 1863S (3); 1864 (2); 1864S (2); 1865 (2); 1865S (2); 1866S

Disposition: Discovered on a farm owned by A. L. Bain. 75 years previously the land had been owned by the Ingram family. It was found by his tenant, Jack Glasgow, and the employees Clifton Glasgow, Henry Crook, Fred Burton, Wilmer Ely, and Fred Rhynes. Bain undertook the negotiations with the Secret Service and emphasized that he wanted his tenant and the employees to realize as much as possible out of their find.

The coins were examined by W. A. Philipot, Jr., the Secretary of the Texas Bankers Association and a collector of rare coins. The Curator of History at the Smithsonian Institution informed the Secret Service that the coins were "of recognized special value to collectors of rare and unusual coin," and the Secret Service accordingly allowed the finders to keep the hoard. Bain said he was going to try to get a bid from American Numismatic Association President L. W. Hoffecker of El Paso, Texas, and other coin dealers and collectors.

Bibliography: "Gold Coins Valued at $1830 Ploughed Up on A. L. Bain Farm Twelve Miles South of Kerens," *Corsicana (TX) Daily Sun*, April 16, 1947.

Secret Service Files, 1947.

Dave Ginsburg, "Kerens, Texas Gold Hoard Information Sought," *E-Sylum* 9, no. 21 (May 21, 2006); http://www.coinbooks.org/club_nbs_esylum_v09n21.html.

Dave Ginsburg, e-mail message to John M. Kleeberg, May 11, 2007 (supplied image of the *Corsicana (TX) Daily Sun* and of the Secret Service files concerning the discovery of the hoard).

Leonard Augsburger, e-mail message to John M. Kleeberg, May 11, 2007.

771. Sedalia, Benton County, Missouri, USA, January 1894.

Type of find: Single find.

Contents: 1 PB.

Description: USA, New York, Medal of John Wesley, with "Founder of Methodism/The World is My Parish," and "Wesley Chapel and Parsonage/Dedicated by Philip Embury 1768"

Cast in type metal. The American Numismatic Society has an example of this medal, item number 1967.225.24. The example in their collection is dated 1866, issued in connection with the Methodist centennial.

Disposition: Found by a German farmer, Charles C. Fritzinger.

Bibliography: "An Old New York Medal," *American Journal of Numismatics* 28, no. 3 (January 1894): 69–70.

772. Little Blue River, two and a half miles west of Gilead, Thayer County, Nebraska, USA, August 1908.

Type of find: Hoard.

Date of deposit: August 1867, when William Abernathy, the owner of the gold, was killed by Indians.

Contents: 58 AV.

Description: USA, California, Kellogg & Co., double eagles, 1854–55 (58)

Disposition: Found by James McFarland and John May. Three pieces were confiscated from May by a man named Spaulding. The remaining pieces were paid into a bank in Geneva, Nebraska.

Bibliography: Bowers 1997, 133–36; Breen 1952, 1005–6 (Breen Hoards XVIII); Breen 1988, 651–52.

"Find of $1,160 in Kellogg & Co. Double Eagles," *Numismatist* 28, no. 1 (January 1915): 27.

773. Mobile, Alabama, USA, September 1960.

Type of find: Hoard.

Date of deposit: 1867.

Contents: 15+ AV.

Description:
USA, $5
USA, $10
USA, $20, 1851–67 (most of the hoard)

Disposition: Found when a bulldozer was clearing a site.

Bibliography: "Bulldozed Coins Start Alabama Gold Rush," *Numismatic Scrapbook Magazine* 26, no. 9 (September 1960): 2526.

774. Winfield Scott Memorial, Glenwood Cemetery, Philadelphia, Pennsylvania, USA, June 1927.

Type of find: Foundation deposit.

Date of deposit: 1868.

Contents: 4 AE, 1 B, 1 AR, 1 AV.

Description:
USA, ½¢, 1835
USA, silver $1, 1868
USA, hard times token, Millions for Defence, not one cent for tribute, 1837
USA, Civil War token, Army and Navy/ The Federal Union, It Must and Shall Be Preserved
USA, Civil War token, The Flag of our Union, 1863/If Anybody Attempts to Tear it Down, Shoot him on the Spot
USA, medal, Winfield Scott, with scenes of Mexican cities of his campaign; medal measured 3 inches in diameter
USA, brass decoration in the shape of a star
USA, gold marksman's medal shaped like a Maltese cross
Coins, tokens, and medals placed in the cornerstone of the Winfield Scott Memorial to Veterans of the Mexican War in Glenwood Cemetery.

Bibliography: "Coins from Cornerstone of Winfield Scott Monument," *Numismatist* 40, no. 6 (June 1927): 323 (citing the *Philadelphia Ledger*).

775. Bridgeport, Washington, USA, 1955.

Type of find: Hoard.

Date of deposit: 1860s-70s.

Contents: 3 B.

Description:
China, Qianlong, cash, Yunnan province
China, Qianlong, cash, Chengdu, Sichuan province
China, Baoding, cash, Zhili (Hebei) province

Bibliography: Beals 1980, 66, 70.

776. Under a house at George and John Streets, Cincinnati, Ohio, USA, late April 1940.

Type of find: Hoard.

Date of deposit: 1870.

Contents: 13 AR, 170 AV.

Description:
  France, 5 francs?
  Mexico, 8 reales?
  USA, 50¢ (including 1843O, Beistle 4G)
  USA, silver $1
  USA, gold $1
  USA, gold $3
  USA, $5 (20)
  USA, $10 (20)
  USA, $20 (100)
  Silver and gold coins of the USA, France, and Mexico, dated 1813 to 1870. Included all denominations of U.S. coins from 50¢ to $20. Total face value about $2,500.

Disposition: Dug up by a relief worker while employed on a street project. The coins flew into the air and just as quickly disappeared into hats, pockets, and lunch pails. Fifteen of the finders turned their coins over to the city solicitor, pending decision as to who gets the money.
  Dr. Charles E. Weber, who subsequently moved to Tulsa, Oklahoma, was able to purchase at the time one of the coins from the hoard: 50¢, 1843O, Beistle 4G.

Bibliography: "Relief Worker Digs Up $250," *New York Times*, April 24, 1940, 11.
  Joseph Coffin, "Items in Brief," *Numismatic Scrapbook Magazine* 6, no. 5 (May 1940): 305 (citing two clippings from the *Cincinnati Post* sent in by L. G. Butler).
  Dr. Charles E. Weber, letter to Q. David Bowers (reference courtesy of Q. David Bowers).

777. Kingston, Missouri, USA, Fall of 1966.

Type of find: Hoard. Called "the Oat Bin Hoard."

Date of deposit: 1870s.

Containers: Large glass jar (three to five gallon size) inside a large crock with the lid still on it, plus a leather money belt.

Contents: 1,000 P.

Description:
  USA, United States Note, $500 (depicting Gallatin), 1862
  USA, United States Note, $1,000, (depicting Morris), 1862
  USA, national banknotes, mostly from Booneville, Missouri, plus Kansas towns, including Saint Mary's, Wamego, and Topeka; also included a Dakota Territory note.
  USA, City National Bank of Selma, Alabama, $100
  A photograph of an array of the backs of 22 notes from the Oat Bin Hoard shows, besides the Selma, Alabama, note, first charter national banknotes from the following states:
  USA, Colorado, $50
  USA, Kentucky, $10 (6)
  USA, Kentucky, $20 (3)
  USA, Missouri, $10 (2)
  USA, Ohio, $5
  USA, Ohio, $10 (4)
  USA, Ohio, $20
  USA, Rhode Island, $20
  USA, Texas, $20
  USA, West Virginia, $20
  This hoard totaled $40,000 face value (some sources say more than $28,000). It was brought to the Midwest from Virginia shortly after the Civil War. Other notes probably were added at a later date, given the predominance of Missouri and Kansas notes. It was found in an oat bin that had not been

emptied for many years while cleaning up the farmstead of an estate that was being settled. One of the notes, that on the City National Bank of Selma, Alabama, is on a bank that was not chartered until November 1870, so the hoard could not have closed before that date. Given the late date for a bank from so far to the east of the find spot, it is possible that the owner moved from Virginia to Missouri or Kansas at a date in the 1870s, rather than immediately after the Civil War; possibly a Republican leaving the South after the end of Reconstruction.

Disposition: Bought by Dr. Howard Carter of Leawood, Kansas, in 1966 from the estate; Carter lived in a suburb of Kansas City, but had a medical practice in Hamilton, Missouri, and had bought a small bank in Kingston, Missouri. Sold that year to Dean Oakes and Don Jensen, with Oakes and Jensen holding the Nationals as partners and the "type" currency being bought by Oakes alone. In 1968, 50 of the choicest notes were stolen in Chicago. Two notes were recovered shortly after the theft. The remaining 48 notes were recovered through the efforts of Dennis Forgue in 1979. The notes were subsequently auctioned by Hickman & Oakes on November 24, 1979.

Bibliography: Bowers 1997, 345–47 (citing "Storied 'Oat Bin' Nationals Go To Auction," *Bank Note Reporter*, November 1979, 1).

Joanne C. Dauer and Edward C. Dauer, "The Oat Bin Hoard as told by Dean Oakes," *Bank Note Reporter*, January 2006 (reference courtesy of Q. David Bowers).

778. Allegheny County, Pennsylvania, USA, December 1887.

Type of find: Hoard.

Date of deposit: 1870s.

Contents: 4+P.

Description: USA, $320 in bills, all dated before 1879, which the finder sold in exchange for $50 in gold.

Disposition: While cleaning out an outhouse, a man named Dennis found the bills, and sold them for $50 in gold to John Caldwell. Caldwell left the bills for safekeeping with John Ulrich, the man who owned the premises. John Warren, son of George Warren, sued for the money. Warren had owned the tavern where the bills were found and had peculiar habits about hiding money. All the bills were dated before Warren's death in 1879.

Bibliography: Warren v. Ulrich, 18 A. 618 (Pa. 1889).

779. Geneva, Nebraska, USA, June 1922.

Type of find: Hoard.

Date of deposit: 1872.

Container: Rusty pot.

Contents: 50 AV.

Description: USA, $20 (50): 1872; ND (49)

Disposition: Double eagles in a rusty pot plowed up by Alvin Oberkotter. Latest date was 1872.

Bibliography: "Plows up $1,000 in Garden," *Numismatist* 35, no. 6 (June 1922): 303.

780. Carson City, Nevada, USA, 1973.

Type of find: Foundation deposit.

Date of deposit: 1873.

Contents: 3 AR.

Description: USA, silver $1, 1873CC (3)

Three uncirculated 1873CC dollars found in a Carson City cornerstone. One of these three may have been Auction 81:1598.

Bibliography: Breen 1988, 443 (Breen 5495).

781. 443 North Fifth Street, corner of Noble Street, Philadelphia, Pennsylvania, USA, August-September 1927.

Type of find: Hoard.

Date of deposit: October 1873.

Container: Bag.

Contents: 100–200 AV.

Description: The following denominations and dates were reported as being found:
USA, gold $1
USA, $2.50: 1834; 1851 (2); 1853
USA, $5: 1834; 1846; 1847
USA, $10: 1838; 1839 (2); 1843
USA, $20: 1854; 1873

Many of the coins were dated before 1850, and some were as old as 1834; the *Philadelphia Inquirer* says that this was particularly the case "of the $20s" (perhaps an error for $2.50s). According to the *Philadelphia Inquirer*, the total amount found was said to amount to $2,000; the *New York Times* said $3,000.

The coins were found in rubble dumped as fill at 26th and Spring Garden Streets, on the site of what would be the new art museum. The rubble had been brought from 443 North Fifth Street (this is the address in the *Philadelphia Inquirer*; the *New York Times* says 440 North Fifth Street), at the corner of Noble Street; the building had been owned by the German Independence Congregation. In the 1870s the neighborhood was a row of brickhouses with white steps inhabited by thrifty Quakers. An old lady in the neighborhood said that the house had been owned by a French doctor who tended many of the Quakers, and died about 1880; she believed that he buried the coins. The coins were probably withdrawn from the bank and buried in connection with the Panic of October 1873.

Disposition: The *Philadelphia Inquirer* published the names and addresses of the following children who found coins:
John Boyzgonia, 2236 Wood Street, $10
Anna Hykowitz, 2452 Perot Street, $10, 1839
Stanley Connor, 2424 Perot Street, $5, 1834
Eugene Duge, 3212 Summer Street, $2.50, 1853
John Suplicky, 2209 Wood Street, $5, 1847
John Vincent, 717 North 25th Street, $20, 1854
Ludwig Kijewski, 2215 Summer Street, $10, 1838
Robert Thomas, 329 North 24th Street, several gold $1s; $2.50, 1851 (2); $5, 1846; $10, 1839 (erroneously described as $20)

Bibliography: "Dump Yields Hoard of Old Gold Coins. $1500 in Precious Metal Taken from Mudhills Near Art Museum; Boys, Girls and Men Dig Feverishly With Fingers Despite Heavy Rain," *Philadelphia Inquirer*, August 29, 1927, 2.

"Philadelphia Mud Yields $1,000 More - Hundreds Join Gold 'Prospectors,' in Soil Dug Up from Foundations of Old Building," *New York Times*, August 29, 1927, 4.

"Museum Gold Rush Continues Unabated. Men, Women and Children Dig in Dirt as 'White Collar' Gallery Cheers. Day's Work Yields About $500, one 'Find' Proves to Be Brass Sovereigns," *Philadelphia Inquirer*, August 30, 1927, 2.

"Diggers Find More Gold—Prizes in Philadelphia's Mud-Bank Klondike Reach $2,000," *New York Times* August 30, 1927, 9.

"Law Fails to Stem Parkway Gold Rush. Diggers at Art Museum Dump, Ousted by Police, Return to Labors; Contractors, Hampered in Work of Filling in, Protest 'Prospecting,'" *Philadelphia Inquirer*, August 31, 1927, 2.

"Gold Diggers Continue Philadelphia Hunt. 500 Dodge Police, but Find Only One Coin—Turn to Demolished House," *New York Times*, August 31, 1927, 3.

"Philadelphia Has a Gold Rush. But City Dumping Hinders Mad Hunt—Rich Study in

Human Nature," *New York Times*, September 4, 1927, Sec. 8, 4.

"Philadelphians Find Gold Coins Among Debris," *Numismatist* 40, no. 10 (October 1927): 626.

782. Lane County, Oregon, USA, 1886.

Type of find: Hoard.

Date of deposit: 1870s?

Containers: 2 cans.

Contents: 100+ AR, AV.

Description:

    USA, silver coins (30+)

    USA, gold coins (70+)

    The boys Hugh Gray and Darwin E. Yoran lifted a plank in a barn and found two cans of money, one with gold and silver coins totaling $925.85, and another with gold totaling $1,000. The money had been buried by Johanna Goodchild, by then deceased.

Disposition: half of the value to Yoran and Gray, half to the county. The find was advertised in the *Oregon State Journal*.

Bibliography: Sovern v. Yoran, 20 P. 100 (Ore. May 7, 1886).

783. Lynn, Massachusetts, USA, 1972.

Type of find: Foundation deposit in the cornerstone of the First Methodist Church.

Date of deposit: 1877.

Container: Cornerstone box.

Contents: 1 AE, 2 NI, 4 AR.

Description:

    USA, 1¢, 1877

    USA, nickel 3¢, 1877, proof

    USA, nickel 5¢, 1877, proof

    USA, 10¢, 1877S

    USA, 25¢, 1877S

    USA, 50¢, 1877CC

    USA, silver trade $1, 1877

Disposition: Sold by American Auction Association, February 7, 1974, lots 10–16.

Bibliography: American Auction Association 1974, lots 10–16; Bowers 1997, 60.

784. New Brunswick, New Jersey, USA, August 1901.

Type of find: Hoard.

Date of deposit: 1877.

Contents: 10,250+ P.

Description:

    USA, New Jersey, State Bank at New Brunswick, sheets of four banknotes each with two $50 bills, one $100 and one $500 bill (Haxby NJ-350 G76a, 80a, 84a) (250)

    USA, New Jersey, State Bank at New Brunswick, sheets with four $1 bills apiece (Haxby NJ-350 G16a) (10,000)

    $50,000 in sheets of bills of other denominations

Disposition: On the failure of the bank in 1877, the sheets and plates passed to the receiver, Colonel John W. Newell. On Newell's death in 1897, the plates and the paper sheets were sold as junk to Adam Ludwig. Ludwig kept the plates and a few dozen sheets, but sold most of the sheets to Jacob Weigel. In 1901 the sheets were seized by the Secret Service.

Bibliography: "Sold Notes as Curios: Jacob Weigel Innocent of Any Crime," *Numismatist* 14, no. 10 (October 1901): 278–81 (reprinted from the *New Brunswick (NJ) Daily Times* of August 21, 1901).

Basil G. Hamilton, "A Commercial Traveler," *Numismatist* 17, no. 2 (February 1904): 55 (the notes have green backs and resemble U.S. Federal currency; this case involved someone passing them off as genuine U.S. money in Canada).

785. Canyon City (not far from Redding), Trinity County, California USA, October 1906.

Type of find: Hoard.

Date of deposit: Ca. 1874.

Container: Cigar box.

Contents: 220+ AV.

Description: USA, USAOG, $50, 1852–53 (17)

Cigar box containing $5,000 in gold, including seventeen $50 slugs. Thought to belong to Jacob Killenger, who was killed in a mine cave-in. Found by a number of Chinese miners operating as the Jin Que Company. By 1906 Canyon City was abandoned.

Bibliography: Joseph Hooper, "Hooper's Restrikes: A California Find," *Numismatist* 19, no. 10 (October 1906): 342.

786. Philadelphia, Pennsylvania, USA, 1966.

Type of find: Archaeological excavation of the "Man Full of Trouble" Tavern.

Date of site: Ca. 1875.

Contents: 1 AE, 1 AR.

Description:
USA, 2¢
USA, Liberty seated silver 5¢

Bibliography: Cotter, Roberts and Parrington, 1992, 169.

787. Chico, California, USA, November 1984.

Type of find: Hoard.

Date of deposit: 1876.

Container: Iron post.

Contents: 44 AV.

Description:
USA, $5, ND (3?)
USA, $10 (6): 1839; ND (5?)
USA, $20 (35): 1875CC; 1876; ND (33)

Bibliography: Bowers 1997, 151 (citing Bob Grant, "Treasure Hunter Hits Gold Coin Bonanza," *Treasure Magazine* [November 1984]).

788. Off Kitty Hawk, North Carolina, USA, July 1881.

Type of find: Shipwreck.

Ship: USS *Huron*.

Sank: November 1877.

Contents: 1 AR, 6 AV.

Description:
Great Britain, sovereigns (6)
USA?, silver coin

A small safe containing six English sovereigns; an old silver coin; a wedding ring; and two U.S. Navy decorations, Maltese cross shaped, reading FIDELITY ZEAL OBEDIENCE, in center U.S.N. On the reverse of one is engraved Henry F. Emerson, on the other James Couch.

Bibliography: "Relics from the U.S.S. Huron," *Coin Collector's Journal* 6 (whole no. 68) (July 1881): 103.

789. Hull, Liberty County, Texas, USA, 1936.

Type of find: Hoard.

Date of deposit: 1878.

Contents: 9 AV.

Description:
USA, $20 (9): 1851, 1855, 1857S, 1858O, 1861S (Paquet reverse), 1866, 1866S, 1867S, 1876

Disposition: Sold January 31, 1937 to Arthur J. Fecht; bequeathed by Fecht to the American Numismatic Society in New York, 1946, but to be held in trust for Fecht's sister, Neoma Fecht, until her decease; coins transferred, 1948, to the American Numismatic Society; upon the decease of Neoma Fecht in 1980, full legal and equitable ownership vested in the American Numismatic Society, item numbers 1980.109.2109, 2293, 2295, 2297, 2298, 2302, 2304, 2306, 2308.

Bibliography: Kleeberg 1999.

790. Mayagüez, Puerto Rico, USA, July 1990.

Type of find: Hoard.

Date of deposit: 1878.

Contents: 4 AE.

Description: Dominican Republic, ¼ reales,

counterstamped MONA (4)
Although latest coin is dated 1848, guano mining operations on Mona Island, Puerto Rico, did not commence until 1878—hence the date of deposit.

Bibliography: Archilla-Diez 1990, 1089.

791. Milwaukee, Wisconsin, USA, October 1928.

Type of find: Single find.

Contents: 1 AR.

Description: USA, silver $1, 1878

Disposition: Found 20 feet below the surface by Martin Matson in a sewer trench.

Bibliography: "Finds Silver Dollar Twenty Feet Below Surface," *Numismatist* 41, no. 10 (October 1928): 627.

792. New Castle, Indiana, USA, May 19, 1920.

Type of find: Hoard.

Date of deposit: 1878.

Container: Stone jar.

Contents: 68+ AV.

Description:
USA, $5
USA, $10
USA, $20
A stone jar containing $1,325 in gold. One of the coins was dated 1878, thought to be the date of deposit. Possibly buried by Rachel Charlesworth, who resided on the farm from 1870 until her death in 1888.

Disposition: Awarded by the court to Leo Todd, the finder.

Bibliography: Vickery v. Hardin, 133 N.E. 922 (Ind. 1922).

793. Washington Square, San Francisco, California, USA, April 1979.

Type of find: Foundation deposit in the base of a drinking fountain, with a statue of Benjamin Franklin, set up by Henry D. Cogswell.

Date of deposit: June 1879.

Contents: AE 6, AR 30, AV 2, P 1.

Description:
Japan, 100 mon [1835–70], Craig 7
Egypt, 5 qirsh, accession date 1255, year 11
France, 5 centimes (2): 1854D; 1855BB
Spain, 2 reales (pistareen), 1774
Spain, 2 reales (pistareen), Seville, 1778CF
USA, silver 3¢, 1851
USA, silver 5¢, 1873S (9)
USA, 10¢, 1877S (9)
USA, 25¢ (3): 1877S (2); 1878S
USA, 50¢ (3): 1875S; 1877S (2)
USA, silver $1, 1879S (2)
USA, gold $1, 1873
USA, paper 5¢, fractional currency, 1863, Friedberg 1233 or 1234
USA, Mechanics Institute Fair, 1875, souvenir medalet
USA, 1876 Centennial, souvenir medalet

Disposition: California Historical Society.

Bibliography: Lange 1984.

794. Buffalo, Illinois, USA, July 1931.

Type of find: Hoard.

Date of deposit: 1880.

Containers: 2 jugs.

Contents: 912+ AV.

Description:
USA, gold $1 (228)
USA, $2.50
USA, $3
USA, $5
USA, $20 (159)
The oldest coin in the hoard was dated 1812. The total face value was $6,028.50. The coins were thought to have belonged to Dr. Peter Leeds.

Bibliography: Bowers 1997, 140.
"Many Gold Coins Unearthed at Buffalo, Ill.," *Numismatist* 44, no. 9 (September 1931): 642.

795. 310 West Commerce Street, San Antonio, Texas, USA, August 20, 2007.

Type of find: Hoard.

Date of deposit: 1880.

Contents: 200 AR, 1 AV.

Description:
USA, 25¢
USA, 50¢
USA, Morgan silver $1 (100)
USA, silver $1, 1880
USA, gold coin
The coins dated from 1852 until 1880.

Disposition: Found by a construction crew while digging up dirt to lay a foundation for a new Mexican arts and crafts store for the tourist trade. Jack Suneson, the owner of the land, obtained the hoard. Harry Shafer, a retired professor of archaeology from Texas A&M University, is assisting Suneson with the study of the hoard.

Bibliography: John Tedesco, "Coin cache unearthed," *San Antonio Express-News*, August 21, 2007, available at http://www.mysanantonio.com/news/metro/stories/MYSA082207.1B.coin.discovery.3329726.html (includes photograph of a Liberty seated quarter from the hoard).

796. Moose Jaw, Saskatchewan, Canada, 1985.

Type of find: Single find.

Date of deposit: 1880?

Contents: 1 AR.

Description: Italian states, Fosdinovo, Maria Maddalena Centurioni, wife of Pasquale Malaspina (reigned 1663–69), luigino, 1667 (reference: Cammarano 070-071 variety)

The luigino is dated 1667, and has the obverse inscription: Haec est Virtus Imago [this is the image of virtue]; on the reverse: Dns Adivtor et Redem Mevs [the Lord is my aid and my redeemer].

Disposition: Found in a load of fill.

Bibliography: Cammarano 1998, 133; Willey 1986, 293.

R. C. Willey, "From the Editor," *Canadian Numismatic Journal* 30, no. 8 (September 1985): 336.

797. Last Mountain House, north of Regina, Saskatchewan, Canada, 1986.

Type of find: Archaeological excavation.

Date of deposit: 1880?

Contents: 1 AE.

Description: British colonies, Nova Scotia, penny, 1824

Bibliography: Willey 1986, 293.

798. Amity, Arkansas, USA, January 1965.

Type of find: Hoard.

Date of deposit: 1880s?

Contents: 30+ AV.

Description:
USA, gold $1
USA, $5
USA, $10
USA, $20
Gold coins totaling $538.

Disposition: Found when the construction worker J. C. Bean was clearing a site with a bulldozer to build a new house. Two observers made off with $100 worth, so Bean only got $438.

Bibliography: Bowers 1997, 147.

"Arkansas Worker Finds Gold Hoard," *Coin World*, January 27, 1965, 41.

799. Jackson County, Oregon, USA, March 1894.

Type of find: Hoard.

Date of deposit: 1880s?

Container: Can.

Contents: 350+ AV.

Description: USA, $20?

Disposition: W. O. Danielson, aged 10, and C.

P. Danielson, aged 8, were cleaning out an old henhouse owned by W. B. "Dee" Roberts when they found a can with over $7,000 in U.S. gold coins. The can had been buried for a long time. They turned the can over to Mary Roberts and O'Neill. Dee Roberts gave them a nickel as a reward and told them to keep their mouths shut.

When brought up on appeal, the court said that the finders were entitled to the treasure trove, if the coins truly had not been buried by Dee and Mary Roberts, as Dee and Mary Roberts claimed.

Bibliography: Danielson v. Roberts, 74 P. 913 (Ore. 1904).

800. Oregon, USA, March 1907.

Type of find: Hoard.

Date of deposit: 1880s?

Contents: 22 AV.

Description: USA, $10 (22)

Disposition: Found by R. H. Roberson while removing rubbish. Judgment for the finder, Roberson.

Bibliography: Roberson v. Ellis, 114 P. 100 (Ore. 1911).

801. New Milford, Connecticut, USA, December 1907.

Type of find: Hoard.

Date of deposit: 1880s?

Container: Teakettle.

Contents: 150 AV.

Description: USA, $20 (150)

Disposition: Gold in a teakettle found by T. T. Jones on his farm in the Merryall district while digging a trench. Jones had acquired the farm of Edgar Peet a year previously.

Bibliography: Bowers 1997, 136–37.

802. Elizabeth, New Jersey, USA, August 1886.

Type of find: Hoard.

Date of deposit: 1880s.

Container: Stocking.

Contents: 10+ P.

Description: USA, paper money
$775 in bills found in a stocking besides the railroad tracks of the Central Railroad of New Jersey in the western part of Elizabeth.

Disposition: Divided equally among the five boys who found it: Crawford, Cashman and the three others.

Bibliography: "A Treasure Trove. Litigation over Money found in a Ball of Rags," *New York Times,* February 2, 1890, 17.

Keron v. Cashman, 33 A. 1055 (N.J. Chancery 1896).

803. Chester, South Carolina, USA, March 1937.

Type of find: Hoard.

Date of deposit: 1881.

Container: Pot.

Contents: 695 AV.

Description:
  USA, gold $1 (37)
  USA, $2.50 (44)
  USA, $3 (4)
  USA, $5 (307)
  USA, $10 (113)
  USA, $20 (190)
  Dates ranged from 1834 (correcting it from 1830 in the original report) to 1881, with many coins dated 1856.

Disposition: Found on property once owned by Littleton Land, who died in 1885. Taken to the Federal Reserve Bank in Charlotte, North Carolina, where the coins were exchanged for paper money.

Bibliography: Weikert 1954, 123.

"A Hoard of Gold Coins Unearthed in South Carolina," *Numismatist* 50, no. 5 (May 1937): 397.

804. Guatemala City, Guatemala, February 4, 1976.

Type of find: Hoard.
Date of deposit: 1882.
Container: Box.
Contents: 30 AR, 1,000 AV.
  Spanish colonies, 8 escudos, México
  Mexico, 8 escudos, Oaxaca
  Mexico, 10 pesos, Alamos, 1874DL
  Guatemala, 16 pesos, 1863R

"Boxes and boxes of gold coins"; also some silver coins. Contained gold from all over Latin America. The colonial issues were nothing much to speak of. Mexican issues predominated, especially Republican 8 escudos. There was a tremendous number of Guatemalan pieces. There were choice 8 escudos from Oaxaca. Clyde Hubbard's example of the 1874 Alamos 10 peso with assayer DL comes from this hoard. The story behind it is that a man had bought a house in Guatemala City because it was associated with the story of a buried treasure, and when the earthquake hit, he had a treasure in his bedroom. The hoard appeared at the time of the Texas Numismatists Association show in Amarillo, Texas, and went through the Houston dealer Pat Johnson.

Note in the Krause-Mishler catalog says: "A few AU-Unc specimens of the 1863R were found in a box shook loose from its hiding place during the 1977 [sic] earthquake."

Disposition: Clyde Hubbard obtained some; the rest is said to have gone to investors in Florida.
Bibliography: Hubbard 1993; Krause and Mishler 2000, 540.

805. New York, New York, USA, June 19, 1957.

Type of find: Foundation deposit in the cornerstone of the New York Produce Exchange Building.
Date of deposit: 1882.
Contents: 1 AE, 2 NI, 1 SN, 4 AR, 6 AV.
Description:
  USA, 1¢, 1882
  USA, nickel 3¢, 1882
  USA, nickel 5¢, 1882
  USA, 10¢, 1882
  USA, 25¢, 1882
  USA, 50¢, 1882
  USA, silver $1, 1882
  USA, gold $1, 1882
  USA, $2.50, 1882
  USA, $3, 1882
  USA, $5, 1882
  USA, $10, 1882
  USA, $20, 1882
  USA, New York, American Numismatic Society, Egyptian Obelisk Medal

Bibliography: "Set of 1882 Coins In Cornerstone," *Numismatic Scrapbook Magazine* 23, no. 7 (July 1957): 1439.

806. Lot 10, con VI, Garafraxa Township, Belwood, Ontario, Canada, April 1932.

Type of find: Hoard.
Date of deposit: 1883.
Container: Earthenware crock.
Contents: 3,915 AE + AR.
Description:
  Great Britain, shilling, 1816 (oldest coin)
  British colonies, Canada West, Bank of Upper Canada, tokens
  British colonies, Province of Canada, 10¢, 1858
  USA, silver 5¢ (295)
  USA, 10¢ (56)
  USA, 25¢, dating from 1838 onwards (386)
  USA, 50¢, dating from 1838 onwards (579)

Face value totaled $1,070.50. Another source says that the hoard had $1,585.00 in old coins. Buried by John Alpaugh, who was of Pennsylvania Dutch origin and came to Ontario in 1816 and who died insane on April 5, 1883. He did not believe in banks. Found by the son of the current owner of the farm, Jim Broadfoot.

Disposition: Fergus lawyer J. A. Wilson got a ruling from the Attorney General of the Province of Ontario on finder's rights; Broadfoot was allowed to keep it. 5 coins from the hoard were donated to the Wellington County Museum and Archives.

Bibliography: "Treasure," *Transactions of the Canadian Numismatic Research Society* 24 (1988): 88.

"Treasure Trove discovered: 3,915 nineteenth century silver coins unearthed in Belwood," *Transactions of the Canadian Numismatic Research Society* 32 (1996): 49.

807. Nogales, Sonora, Mexico, January 1965.

Type of find: Hoard.
Date of deposit: 1884.
Contents: 400+ AR.
Description: Mexico, 8 reales, Guanajuato, 1884 (400+)
Disposition: Found when a house belonging to Lieutenant Antonio Frias Cortes was being demolished. Many of the coins vanished into the pockets of onlookers. Only 400 were secured for Frias.
Bibliography: "Coin Hoard Discovered in Mexico," *Coin World*, January 6, 1965, 20.

808. Wildwood Gables, New Jersey, USA, February 1930.

Type of find: Hoard.
Date of deposit: 1885.
Container: Stout canvas bag.
Contents: AR; 1 AV.
Description:
  USA, minor silver coins, dated 1880–85
  USA, $10

Coins washed up onto a beach.
Bibliography: "Coins Washed up by Tide at Wildwood, N.J.," *Numismatist* 43, no. 2 (February 1930): 74.

809. Yreka, California, USA, winter 1969.

Type of find: Archaeological excavation.
Date of site: 1886–1925.
Contents: 25 AE, 72 B, 18 NI, 2 ZN, 17 AR.
Description:
  China, Shunzhi, cash (3): Board of Revenue, Beijing (2); illegible mint
  China, Kangxi, cash (17): Board of Revenue, Beijing (7); Board of Works, Beijing (5); Wuchang, Hubei province (2); Ch'ang; Zhejiang; illegible mint
  China, Yongzheng, cash, illegible mint
  China, Qianlong, cash (31): Board of Revenue, Beijing (19); Board of Works, Beijing (7); Zhihli (Hebei) province; Yunnan province; illegible mint (3)
  China, Jiaqing, cash (4): Board of Revenue, Beijing (2); Fujian province; illegible mint
  China, Daoguang, cash (2): Board of Works, Beijing; Zhangzhou, Fujian province
  China, Xianfeng, cash, Guangxi province
  China, cash, illegible (11)
  China, Hong Kong, cents (2)
  Vietnam, Annam, dong (2)
  USA, 1¢ (23)
  USA, nickel 5¢ (18)
  USA, 10¢ (14)
  USA, 25¢ (2)
  USA, 50¢
  USA, California, Yreka, local tokens (3): the Clarendon Bar; unidentified (2)
Bibliography: Farris 1982.

810. Newfoundland, Newfoundland and Labrador, Canada, 1894.

Type of find: Hoard.
Date of deposit: 1887.

Contents: 8 AE, 14 AR, 10 AV.

Description:

Germany, mark, 1876
Germany, 10 marks, 1872 (2)
Great Britain, halfpence, 1861 (3)
Great Britain, crown, 1875
France, 10 centimes, 1868
France, 20 centimes, 1867
France, 20 centimes, 1878 (4)
France, ½ franc, 1887 (3)
France, franc, 1871
Spain, 2 reales (pistareen), 1778 (5)
Italy, lira, 1871
Greece, drachma, 1822 (2)
British colonies, Newfoundland, $2, 1870
USA, $2.50, 1851
Spanish colonies, 2 reales, 1801
Spanish colonies, 2 escudos, 1788 (3)
Spanish colonies, 4 escudos, 1780
Spanish colonies, 8 escudos, 1788
Bolivia or Chile or Mexico, escudo, 1841 (called "1/8 doubloon, 1841;" all three of those countries are Spanish American countries that issued escudos dated 1841)

Disposition: Used to pay a premium to Mutual Life of New York.

Bibliography: Graham 1986.

811. Philadelphia, Pennsylvania, USA, September 1965.

Type of find: Foundation deposit in the cornerstone of the Methodist Hospital.

Date of deposit: June 21, 1888.

Contents: 1 AE, 2 NI, 4 AR, 6 AV.

Description:

USA, 1¢, 1888
USA, nickel 3¢, 1888
USA, nickel 5¢, 1888
USA, 10¢, 1888
USA, 25¢, 1888
USA, 50¢, 1888
USA, silver $1, 1888
USA, gold $1, 1888
USA, $2.50, 1888
USA, $3, 1888
USA, $5, 1888
USA, $10, 1888
USA, $20, 1888

Disposition: Building razed in 1965 and the coins sold for $3,500.

Bibliography: "Cornerstone Coins Sold for $3,500," *Numismatic Scrapbook Magazine* 31, no. 9 (September 1965): 2461.

812. Cleveland, Ohio, USA, March 1956.

Type of find: Foundation deposit in the cornerstone of a police station.

Date of deposit: 1889.

Contents: 3+ AR.

Description: USA, silver $1, 1889

Disposition: Found when the police station was being torn down.

Bibliography: Numismatic Scrapbook Magazine 22, no. 3 (March 1956): 401.

813. Tortola, British Virgin Islands, 1889, and London, England, UK, October 1983.

Type of find: Hoard.

Date of deposit: 1889.

Contents: 338 AE, 2 BI.

Description:

British colonies, Tortola, black dogs (340): official counterstamp T (2); counterfeit counterstamp T (118); official counterstamp H (22); counterfeit counterstamp H (192); genuine counterstamp T over genuine counterstamp H (2); counterfeit counterstamp H over counterfeit counterstamp T; counterstamp H and counterstamp T

Bibliography: Lyall 1983.

814. Bloomsburg, Pennsylvania, USA, April 1938.

Type of find: Hoard.

Date of deposit: 1890.

Contents: 149 AV.

Description: USA, $20 (149)

Disposition: Found by John Johnson and other workers deepening a cellar. Litigated among the finders, the owner of the land and F. Harold Kline, who claimed that it had been hidden by his father, Frank P. Kline. A three column story was written about it by Robert K. Botsford in the *Berwick (PA) Enterprise.*

Bibliography: Weikert 1953, 1186.
"Hoard of Gold Coins Found in Bloomsburg, Pa.," *Numismatist* 51, no. 4 (April 1938): 333.
"Newspaper Numismatics: Another Treasure Trove," *Numismatic Scrapbook Magazine* 4, no. 4 (April 1938): 141.

815. Saratoga Springs, New York, USA, July 1932.

Type of find: Hoard.

Date of deposit: 1890.

Containers: Cans, preserve jars, and milk bottles.

Contents: 50+ AR, AV.

Description:
USA, silver 3¢
USA, $20
Coins ranged from silver 3¢ pieces up through $20 pieces.

Disposition: $1,000 to $3,000 found when workers excavating for the foundation of a new drink hall on the Saratoga Springs State Reservation. The coins were found in cans, preserve jars, and milk bottles. One man recovered a milk bottle with $300 in gold. The latest date was 1890. The rush for the coins was ultimately stopped by the New York State Police on the orders of Attorney General Bennett.

Bibliography: "Halt Saratoga Gold Rush. Troopers Act After Diggers Find $1,000 to $3,000 in Coins," *New York Times,* July 27, 1932, 19.
"Rush For Buried Coins at Saratoga Springs, N.Y.," *Numismatist* 45, no. 9 (September 1932): 583.

816. Corner of White and Centre Streets, New York, New York, USA, September 1948.

Type of find: Foundation deposit in the cornerstone of the old Criminal Courts Building.

Date of deposit: October 25, 1890.

Contents: 9 AV.

Description:
USA, $2.50
USA, $5
USA, $10
USA, $20
Contained 9 gold coins, ranging from $2.50 to $20.

Disposition: Turned over to Frederick H. Zurmuhlen, the Commissioner of Public Works of New York City.

Bibliography: "Cornerstone Box Yields Gold Coins. Records, Newspapers Found by Wreckers of the Old Criminal Courts Building," *New York Times,* September 17, 1948, 27.

817. Marshall, Michigan, USA, May 1930.

Type of find: Hoard.

Date of deposit: 1890.

Container: Jug.

Contents: 100+ AR, AV.

Description:
USA, silver coins
USA, $20, 1850–90

Disposition: Found by William Caffery, a laborer, when tearing down an old building on the farm of Charles Budlong. Until 1892 the farm was owned by a man named Lee.

Bibliography: "Finds Coins in a Jug," *Numismatist* 43, no. 5 (May 1930): 283. "Treasures in Tin Cans," *Literary Digest*, May 6, 1933, 30.

818. Deadwood, South Dakota, USA, April 1906.

Type of find: Hoard.

Date of deposit: Ca. 1890.

Contents: 4 AR, 2 AV.

Description:
  USA, 25¢
  USA, $1 (3)
  USA, $20 (2)
  Also found were three forks, three dessert spoons, and six teaspoons.

Disposition: Found by laborers while excavating under the old French hotel to lay the foundations for the new courthouse.

Bibliography: *Lincoln Nebraska State Journal*, April 25, 1906, 4 (reference courtesy of Q. David Bowers).

819. Main Street, Ventura, California, USA, 1974–76.

Type of find: Archaeological excavation of the Chinatown of Ventura, California.

Date of site: 1890–1907.

Contents: 77 AE.

Description:
  China, cash (62)
  China, counterfeit cash (10)
  Vietnam, Annam, cash (3)
  USA, 1¢ (2): 1898; 1907
  The Chinese cash was mostly from Guangdong province. One cash piece was as old as 1644 (i.e., from the Ming Dynasty).

Bibliography: Greenwood 1978.

820. Genoa, Nevada, USA, October 1949.

Type of find: Hoard.

Date of deposit: 1892.

Container: Rusted metal box bearing the stamp "San Francisco—Carson City."

Contents: 3+ AV.

Description: USA, $20, 1855–92

Bibliography: Peter Frankus, "Gold Hoard Discovered," *Numismatic Scrapbook Magazine* 15, no. 11 (November 1949): 942.

821. Urbana, Illinois, USA, December 1965.

Type of find: Foundation deposit in the cornerstone of the City Hall.

Date of deposit: 1893.

Contents: 1+ AR.

Description: USA, silver $1, 1893S

Disposition: Found when the City Hall was demolished.

Bibliography: "1893-S Found in Cornerstone," *Numismatic Scrapbook Magazine* 31, no. 12 (December 1965): 3313.

822. Helena, Montana, USA, February 1942.

Type of find: Hoard.

Date of deposit: 1893.

Contents: 40 AR.

Description: USA or Spanish colonies, $1, cut (40)
  The coins were wedge-shaped, apparently cut USA silver dollars or Spanish colonies 8 reales.

Bibliography: "Curious Wedge Shaped Half Dollars Located," *Numismatist* 55, no. 2 (February 1942): 112.

823. South of Slocomb, Geneva County, Alabama, USA, May 1942.

Type of find: Hoard.

Date of deposit: 1894.

Contents: 127 AV.

Description: USA, $20, 1850–94 (127)

Disposition: Found by Pearlie Knight; divided between Pearlie Knight, tenant farmer, and

Ellen Blount, his landlady.

Bibliography: "Double Eagles Again on the Wing," *Numismatist* 56, no. 6 (June 1943): 460.

824. LaCrosse, Wisconsin, USA, April 1984.

Type of find: Hoard.

Date of deposit: 1897.

Container: Iron pot.

Contents: AV.

Description: USA, $5, $10, $20, 1870–97

Disposition: The coins were found by four teenagers when remodeling the home of Robert Poehling. The coins were in an iron pot concealed in the basement beneath the kitchen. They are thought to have been concealed by a local merchant, Mons Anderson, who died in 1905.

Bibliography: Bowers 1997, 151 (citing "Wisconsin Hoard Yields 19th Century U.S. Gold," *Coin World* April 11, 1984, 57).

825. Topton, Pennsylvania, USA, July 1996.

Type of find: Foundation deposit in the cornerstone of Old Main, which in the 1890s had been a Lutheran Home.

Date of deposit: 1897.

Contents: 1 AE, 3 AR.

Description:
USA, 1¢, 1897
USA, silver $1, 1799
USA, silver $1, 1800
USA, silver $1, 1897

Bibliography: Bowers 1997, 68.

826. Boston Common, Boston, Massachusetts, USA, October 1910.

Type of find: Excavations.

Date of site: 1779–1897.

Last dated coin: 1897.

Contents: 75+ AE.

Description: Coins found by workers while resodding Boston Common, thus a series of single finds, not a hoard. The coins were dated between 1779 and 1897. Many were U.S. large cents, dated 1800–52. Many non-U.S. coins were found as well.

Bibliography: Howland Wood, "Buried Coins," *American Journal of Numismatics* 44, no. 4 (October 1910): 156–57.

827. Santiago Bay, Cuba, July 30, 1898.

Type of find: Shipwrecks.

Ships: Infanta Maria Theresa and *Cristobal Colon*.

Sank: July 3, 1898 (Battle of Santiago Bay).

Contents: AR.

Description:
Spain, Isabella II, 40 centimos, 1866
Spain, Alphonse XII, 2 pesetas, 1882
Spain, Alphonse XII, 5 pesetas, 1875
Spain, Alphonse XIII, 5 pesetas, 1891

The 1875 coin came from the *Cristobal Colon*; all other coins came from the *Infanta Maria Theresa*. The wrecks were salvaged by Lieutenant Richard Pearson Hobson on July 30, 1898.

Disposition: Sold off by the United States government and then sold onwards as souvenirs by stockbrokers and coin dealers such as Bolognesi, Hartfield & Co. and E. S. Minor. The 1875 and 1866 coins were owned by Thomas Sebring and sold off in the sale of his collection in January 2004; the 1882 and 1891 coins were donated to the American Numismatic Society by Edward T. Newell, item nos. 0000.999.43753 and 000.999.43750.

Bibliography: Sebring 1989; Sebring 2004, lots 1600–1.

828. Oakland, California, USA, June 1923.

Type of find: Hoard.

Date of deposit: 1898.

Contents: AV.

Description: Spain, gold coins (25 pesetas?) Spanish gold coins, stashed by the crew of USS *Yorktown* in drain pipes, bilge tanks, etc., during the Spanish-American War.

Disposition: Found by the wreckers of the vessel at the Crowley Shipyards when the USS *Yorktown* was scrapped.

Bibliography: "Gold Coins found in old U. S. Cruiser," *Numismatist* 36, no. 6 (June 1923): 255.

829. Philadelphia, Pennsylvania, USA, late 1960s.

Type of find: Hoard.

Date of deposit: 1898.

Container: Sack.

Contents: 1,250 B.

Description: USA, Philadelphia, Pennsylvania, Polish American Republican Club, tokens

Disposition: Found by two construction workers inside a wall while working on an old building that had been home of the Polish American Republican Club. Sold to David E. Schenkman.

Bibliography: David E. Schenkman, "Tokens & Medals: Be Careful What You Ask For. What do you do when your supply suddenly far outnumbers the potential demand?" *Numismatist* 117, no. 9 (September 2004): 66.

830. Cleveland, Ohio, USA, October 1962.

Type of find: Hoard.

Date of deposit: Ca. 1900.

Container: Coffee can.

Contents: 150+ AR, AV.

Description:
USA, silver coins
USA, gold coins
$3,000 in nineteenth century gold and silver coins.

Disposition: Found by a retired mechanic in a coffee can in a gulley; the find was reported to the police, and no one claimed the coins, so the coins went to the finder.

Bibliography: Robert Obojski, "Discoveries of Hoards Keep Interest High in Fields of Ancient, Classic Coins," *Numismatic Scrapbook Magazine* 28, no. 11 (November 1962): 3364.

831. Heppner, Oregon, USA, 1958 and 1968.

Type of find: Hoard.

Date of deposit: Ca. 1900.

Contents: 37 AV.

Description:
USA, $5 (4)
USA, $20, 1891CC
USA, other gold coins (32)

Disposition: $375 found in May 1968 in gold coins, including a $20 1891CC, cached on the Don Greenup Ranch by the original homesteader. In 1958 three boys found four $5 gold pieces while fishing in the pond.

Bibliography: "Heppner Gold Cache Gives Up 33 Coins," *Numismatic Scrapbook Magazine* 34, no. 5 (May 1968): 757.

832. Jamestown, Colorado, USA, March 1967.

Type of find: Hoard.

Date of deposit: Ca. 1900.

Contents: 175 AV.

Description: USA, $20 (175)

Disposition: Found by Tom McKinney, aged 16, while climbing in the mountains; he turned them over to the Secret Service, but was allowed to keep them after nobody else claimed to be the owner.

Bibliography: "Keeps Gold Find," *Numismatic Scrapbook Magazine* 33, no. 3 (March 1967): 456.

833. Mayhew, Lake Benton County, Minnesota, USA, November 1920.

Type of find: Hoard.

Date of deposit: 1900.

Container: Old baking power tin.

Contents: 65 AV.

Description: USA, $20 (65)

Disposition: Found three feet deep in the ground, under a rock, an old baking powder tin, containing $1,300 in gold. It was all in $20 gold pieces. Found by Michael Busch on land recently purchased by William Busch of Sauk Rapids.

Bibliography: "A Find of Gold Coins," *Numismatist* 33, no. 11 (November 1920): 529.

834. San Juan Island, Washington, USA, September 1970.

Type of find: Hoard.

Date of deposit: 1900.

Contents: 95+ AR, AV, P.

Description: USA, $20 (45)

45 $20 gold pieces, other gold and silver coins, and $365 in hand signed bills. The coins had a face value of $1,395, and none was dated after 1900; some were as old as 1853. Found by Mrs. Rhoda Anderson, aged 91, when the abandoned British army barracks was destroyed. San Juan Island was awarded to the United States in an arbitration by Kaiser Wilhelm I in 1872; the barracks thus dates from before 1872.

Bibliography: "Rhoda's Pot of Gold," *Numismatic Scrapbook Magazine* 36, no. 9 (September 1970): 1122.

"Hidden Treasure," *Canadian Numismatic Journal* 15, no. 11 (November 1970): 319.

835. Seattle, Washington, USA, February 1929.

Type of find: Hoard.

Date of deposit: 1900.

Contents: AV, P.

Description:
USA, gold coins
South America, currency
Gold nuggets, gold chains, U.S. gold coins, South American currency (Chilean paper money?), rings, lockets, necklaces and brooches.

Disposition: Found by workers repairing a street at Washington Street and First Avenue South, Seattle, found on the site of the M. & N. saloon. Thought to have been lost by the patrons of the saloon.

Bibliography: Bowers 1997, 138–39.

"Workmen Dug Up Coins and Jewelry," *Numismatist* 42, no. 2 (February 1929): 68.

836. Virginia, USA, April 1959.

Type of find: Single find.

Contents: 1 AV.

Description: USA, $20, 1900S

Bibliography: Earl G. Snyder, "Digs His Own Gold," *Numismatic Scrapbook Magazine* 26, no. 3 (March 1960): 913.

837. Confluence of the Snake and Palouse Rivers, west of Lewiston, Idaho, USA, July 8–11, 1964.

Type of find: Funerary deposit in a canoe.

Date of deposit: 1900–15.

Contents: 1 AR.

Description: USA, Thomas Jefferson Indian Peace Medal, 55 millimeters

Disposition: The medal was discovered when Palus Indian graves were moved as Little Goose Dam was under construction. It was unearthed at Burial Site 95, and was around the neck of an Indian ancestor who had been buried inside a canoe. Owned by the Nez Perce tribe; on display at the Nez Perce National Historical Park in Spalding, Idaho.

Bibliography: Gunselman and Sprague 2003; Loeffelbein 2003, 29.

838. Tucson, Arizona, USA, 1967–73.

Type of find: Archaeological excavation by the Arizona State Museum as part of the Tucson Urban Renewal Project.

Date of site: 1900–50?

Contents: 2 AE, 85 B, 2 NB, 1 ZN.

Description:

Japan, Kanei Tsuho, mon (2)

Japan, 4 mon [1863–1867]

China, Kangxi, cash (21): Board of Revenue, Beijing (6); Board of Works, Beijing (3); Linqing, Shandong province; Hangzhou, Zhejiang province?; Ningbo, Zhejiang province; Chengdu, Sichuan?; unidentified mint (8)

China, Qianlong, cash (14): Board of Revenue, Beijing (6); Guangzhou, Guangdong province; Kungming, Yunnan province (2); unidentified mint (5)

China, Jiaqing, cash (15): Board of Revenue, Beijing (2); Board of Works, Beijing (2); Baoding, Zhili (Hebei) province; Xian, Shaanxi province; Hangzhou, Zhejiang province (3); unidentified mint (6)

China, Daoguang, cash (6): Board of Revenue, Beijing (2); Guangzhou, Guangdong province; Kunming, Yunnan province; Dongchuan, Yunnan province; unidentified mint

China, Xianfeng, cash (2): Kunming, Yunnan province; unidentified mint

China, Guangxu, cash (11): Board of Works, Beijing; Guangzhou, Guandong province (9); unidentified mint

China, cash, unidentified (14)

China, Republic, 10 cash [1920s]

China, Hong Kong, George VI, 10¢ (2): 1948; 1949

Vietnam, United Dai Viet, Tu Duc, zinc dong

Bibliography: Olsen 1983.

839. Coldwater or Bronson, Michigan, USA, July 1939.

Type of find: Hoard.

Date of deposit: 1902.

Container: Foot long tile and old metal cylinder.

Contents: 150 AV.

Description:

USA, $5

USA, $10

USA, $20

Dates ranged from 1880 to 1902.

Disposition: Found in two separate caches. The first cache, totalling $1,800, was unearthed from a tile. The second cache, totaling $1,120, was found in an old metal cylinder under the porch of the farmhouse, so totaled $2,920. Michigan law, according to the reports at the time, gave finds of money, after advertising, half to the county and half to the finder. Subject to litigation between Frank Belote, tenant and father of the three brothers who found the hoard, and Laddie Kregger, Belote's landlord. Kregger also forbade the Belotes from doing any more digging.

Bibliography: Weikert 1954, 123.

Edwin Brooks, "Three Boys Dig Up $1,800," *Numismatic Scrapbook Magazine* 5, no. 9 (September 1939): 422.

Frank C. Ross, "Collected Notes," *Hobbies: the Magazine for Collectors*, September 1939, 89.

840. Staffordville Area, Ontario, Canada, September 1976.

Type of find: Hoard. Called "the Otterville Hoard."

Date of deposit: 1903.

Contents: 110 AR, 3 P.

Description:

British colonies, Newfoundland, 20¢, 1888

Canada, 5¢ (17): 1885; 1887; 1888 (2);

1891 (5); 1892; 1893 (3); 1894; 1896; 1902; 1903H

Canada, 10¢ (28): 1880H; 1885; 1886; 1887 (2); 1888 (5); 1890 (3); 1891 (4); 1892 (6); 1894 (4); 1903H

Canada, 25¢ (43): 1871H (3); 1872H (10); 1874; 1874H (15); 1875H (2); 1881H (2); 1882H (2); 1883H (2); 1886 (3); 1888 (3)

Canada, 50¢ (22): 1870 (10); 1871 (2); 1871H; 1872H (9)

Canada, Dominion of Canada note, $1, June 1, 1878, T. D. Harrington

Canada, Dominion of Canada note, $2, July 2, 1887, J. M. Courtney

Canada, Dominion of Canada note, $1, March 31, 1898, J. M. Courtney

Disposition: Auctioned by Robert Carney of Otter Valley Auctions, Ltd. on September 25, 1976.

Bibliography: Esler 1977.

841. Victor, New York, USA, October 1954.

Type of find: Hoard.

Date of deposit: 1904.

Container: Rusty can concealed in a stovepipe in a ceiling.

Contents: 35+ AR.

Description: USA, gold coins, probably $20s (35+)

Disposition: Found by Michael Barry, age 12.

Bibliography: "Lost and Found," *Numismatic Scrapbook Magazine* 20, no. 10 (October 1954): 1271.

842. Monterey, California, USA, January 1948.

Type of find: Hoard.

Date of deposit: 1904.

Container: Rusty tinplate can.

Contents: 250–400+ AV.

Description:
  USA, $20 (150): 1900; 1904S; ND (148)

Disposition: The coins had been buried around 1900 by Will H. Martin, who had little faith in banks. They were discovered when excavation began for building a school. A young boy, Michael Maiorana, found 37 coins in a rusty tinplate can; treasure hunters tried to take it away from him, but the construction workers protected him until the police arrived. In gratitude, Maiorana gave away all but 14 coins to his police escort and the construction workers.

"A feature of the evening was Mrs. Gibbons displaying a 1904S twenty dollar gold piece from the hoard recently discovered in California. Mr. and Mrs. Gibbons had seen the 'diggings' and purchased one of the coins with a few grains of Monterey soil still clinging to it." (Mentioned in the minutes of the Oregon Numismatic Society for February 9, 1948.)

"Mr. Wise: Double eagle 1900 unc.; Double eagle 1900 proof—the unc. double eagle being one of 150 dug up in Monterey, California in 1948." (Mentioned in the minutes of the Brooklyn Coin Club for September 7, 1949.)

Bibliography: Nesmith 1958a, 24–25; Nesmith and Potter 1968, 72–73.

"1948 Brings Another Gold Rush to California," *New York Times*, January 14, 1948, 2.

"Oregon Numismatic Society, Minutes, February 9, 1948," *Numismatist* 65, no. 5 (May 1948): 364.

"Brooklyn Coin Club, Minutes, September 7, 1949," *Numismatist* 66, no. 11 (November 1949): 687.

843. Philadelphia, Pennsylvania, USA, December 1935.

Type of find: Hoard.

Date of deposit: 1905.

Contents: 260+ AR.

Description:
   USA, 10 ¢ (130+)
   USA, 25 ¢ (130+)
   Value $65.

Disposition: Found by workers digging in a backyard. Allegedly buried by gamblers a generation ago when escaping from a police raid.

Bibliography: "'Tainted' Money Dug Up in Philadelphia," *Numismatist* 48, no. 12 (December 1935): 889.

844. Colorado Springs, Colorado, USA, December 1955.

Type of find: Hoard.

Date of deposit: 1906.

Contents: 4,000 AE.

Description: USA, Zebulon Pike medals, struck by the U.S. Mint in Philadelphia (4,000)

Disposition: Found while razing a bank building.

Bibliography: C. S. Yeowell, "Raze Bank Building; Discover Hoard of Medals," *Numismatic Scrapbook Magazine* 21, no. 12 (December 1955): 1722.

845. New York, New York, USA, March 1931–March 1932.

Type of find: Hoard.

Date of deposit: October 1907.

Contents: 93+ P.

Description:
   USA, probably gold certificate, $100
   USA, gold certificate, $500, 1882
   USA, gold certificate, $1,000
   USA, gold certificate, $5,000
   USA, gold certificate, $10,000, 1882 (50)
   The total value of the paper money was $747,000.
   Union Pacific, first mortgage land grant bonds, total value apparently $155,000
   Union Pacific, preferred stock, certificates for 1,020 shares
   Diamond and emerald necklace, which was later sold for $37,000
   Diamond bar pin with three pendants and twenty-nine diamonds
   2 pairs of gold and diamond earrings, one with two 12 carat diamonds, the other with two 3.50 carat diamonds
   Solitaire diamond ring with a 5 carat diamond
   Gold and diamond necklace, with thirty-five graduated diamonds, with aggregate weight of 118.50 carats

Disposition: USA paper money, Union Pacific bonds, and jewelry hoarded by Mrs. Ida E. Wood in the Herald Square Hotel, ever since she withdrew her money from the Morton Trust Company shortly before the Panic of October 1907. From 1907 to 1913 she had kept it in the Safe Deposit Company of New York. From 1913 to 1928 she had kept it in the Lincoln Safe Deposit Company, on Third Avenue. From 1928 onwards she kept it in the hotel, including $500,000 in $10,000 bills in a cloth bag concealed on her person. Ida E. Wood was born Ellen Walsh, in Oldham, Lancashire, England. She first lived with, and in 1867 married, Benjamin Wood, owner and editor of the *New York Daily News*. The *New York Daily News*, which has no connection with the twentieth century tabloid, was a sleazy publication that concentrated on sex and crime; it was extremely successful. Benjamin Wood was the brother of Fernando Wood, twice mayor of New York. Fernando and Benjamin Wood were outspoken in their pro-Southern sympathies, and the *New York Daily News* was a leading Copperhead propaganda organ. To conceal her humble origins, Ida Wood changed her name from Ellen Walsh, and gave out that she was Ida Mayfield, the daughter of Henry Mayfield, the owner of a Louisiana cane sugar plantation. This was all fictitious.

Bibliography: Cox 1964.
"No Premium on Wood Currency," *Numismatist* 44, no. 12 (December 1931): 865.

846. Corner of Graham and Prospect Avenues, Hempstead, Long Island, New York, USA, January 1935.
Type of find: Hoard.
Date of deposit: November 1907.
Container: Glass jar.
Contents: 20+ P.
Description:
   USA, silver certificate
   USA, gold certificate
   Glass jar containing $1,960 in gold and silver certificates; found with a 35 year old bottle of brandy, when Malinowski and Ransewski dug up his cellar.
Disposition: $200 to Cypmunt Ransewski, the digger; $1,250 was used to pay household bills; the owner's wife, Mrs. Agnes Malinowski, absconded with the remaining $510.
Bibliography: "$1,960 in Treasure Dug Up in Cellar. Hempstead Discovery of Last January Revealed as Digger Demands Larger Share," *New York Times*, March 20, 1935, 23.

847. Cleary City, Alaska, USA, summer 1990.
Type of find: Hoard.
Date of deposit: November 1907.
Contents: 83 B.
Description:
   Canada, Yukon, Dawson, Kilgore & Landahl, token
   USA, Alaska, Eddie Willis, tokens (31)
   USA, Alaska, Fritz, token (20)
   USA, Alaska, Fairbanks, Palace Cigar Store, tokens (18)
   USA, Alaska, Dyea, W. A. & H., tokens (11)
   USA, location unknown, Wm. Lind, 526 Union Ave. N, token
   Unidentifiable token
Bibliography: Hanscom 1995.

848. Olnes, Alaska, USA, ca. 1990.
Type of find: Hoard.
Date of deposit: 1907.
Contents: 10? B.
Description: USA, Alaska, tokens reading TOTEM/GOOD FOR 12½ Cents in TRADE (10?)
Bibliography: Hanscom 1995.

849. Rawhide, Nevada, USA, summer 1966.
Type of find: Hoard.
Date of deposit: 1908.
Contents: 100 P.
Description:
   USA, Nevada, Northern saloon cardboard token, 12½¢ (20)
   USA, Nevada, Northern saloon cardboard token, 25¢ (40)
   USA, Nevada, Northern saloon cardboard token, 50¢ (40)
Bibliography: McDonald 1988.

850. Tara, ten miles southwest of Owen Sound, Ontario, Canada, late 1957.
Type of find: Hoard.
Date of deposit: 1909.
Container: A roll covered in the lead wrapper from an old tea package.
Contents: 32 P.
Description:
   Canadian chartered banknotes of 1906–1909:
   Canada, Bank of Hamilton, $5
   Canada, Bank of Toronto, $5
   Canada, Merchants Bank, $5
   Canada, Merchants Bank, $10
   Canada, Molsons Bank, $5
   Canada, Molsons Bank, $10
   Canada, Standard Bank, 1891, reddish, $5

Canada, Traders Bank, $5

Disposition: Found when removing a siding from a frame house. Bought by Walter Holmes.

Bibliography: Holmes 1959.

851. Lovelock, Nevada, USA, spring 1977.

Type of find: Hoard.

Date of deposit: 1910.

Container: Crockery pot snuff container.

Contents: 90 AV.

Description: USA, gold coins (90)

Gold coins with a total face value of $1,800, dating from the late nineteenth century to 1910.

Disposition: Found in the basement of an abandoned home. To the Nevada State Museum.

Bibliography: Bowers 1997, 148–49 (citing Mark Richards, "Found: $26,000 Coin Hoard," *Treasure Found Magazine*, Summer 1978).

852. Royston, Georgia, USA, 1978.

Type of find: Hoard.

Date of deposit: 1910.

Contents: 111 AV.

Description: USA, gold coins

The coins were valued by coin dealers at $30–40,000. They were found concealed in a chimney hearth in the Old Adams Homeplace; the chimney had been built in 1910 or 1911.

Disposition: To the family who had owned the Adams Homeplace at the time the chimney was constructed.

Bibliography: Davison v. Strickland, 243 S.E. 2d 705 (Ga. Ct. App. 1978).

853. Du Quoin, Illinois, USA, October 1952.

Type of find: Hoard.

Date of deposit: 1910?

Container: Colored glass, wide-mouthed jar of the drugstore pill variety.

Contents: 28 AV.

Description:

Spain, 25 pesetas (9)

USA, $5

USA, $10

USA, $20 (17)

Disposition: Found in a public dump. The U.S. gold was turned into the Federal Reserve Bank of Chicago; the Spanish coins were returned to the finder.

Bibliography: D. A. Purdy, "What Others Say," *Numismatic Scrapbook Magazine* 18, no. 10 (October 1952): 860.

854. Hodgenville, Kentucky, USA, May 1942.

Type of find: Hoard.

Date of deposit: 1911.

Contents: 50+ AV.

Description: USA, $10 and $20, 1850–1911

Disposition: Gold hoard found underneath a chicken house, which at one point belonged to Mr. William H. Cooper. The coins were taken to the Lincoln National Bank. Judge Handley sued to recover the money for the heirs, and was awarded it by the court.

Bibliography: Bowers 1997, 143–44; Handley 1943.

855. Pasco, Florida, USA, February 1958.

Type of find: Hoard.

Date of deposit: 1912.

Containers: Fruit jars.

Contents: AR.

Description: USA, silver coins, 1893–1912

Disposition: Found in a freshly plowed field by two boys.

Bibliography: "Boys Find Treasure," *Numismatic Scrapbook Magazine* 24, no. 2 (February 1958): 237.

856. Heber, Utah, USA, May 1962.

Type of find: Hoard.

Date of deposit: 1912.

Contents: 150+ AV.

Description: USA, gold coins (150+)
$2,300 in U.S. gold coins buried by the thrifty wife of a rancher.

Disposition: Uncovered by a bulldozer.

Bibliography: "Bulldozer Uncovers Hoard," *Numismatic Scrapbook Magazine* 28, no. 5 (May 1962): 1554.

857. Duluth, Minnesota, USA, August 1937.

Type of find: Hoard.

Date of deposit: January 1914.

Container: Bag in the bottom of a can.

Contents: 50+ AV.

Description: USA, $5, 10 and $20, 1875–1900
The oldest date of the coins is given as 1815. This has been corrected to 1875. With the coins was found a piece of a Duluth newspaper dated January 14, 1914.

Bibliography: "Cache of Gold Unearthed in Duluth," *Numismatist* 50, no. 8 (August 1937): 756.

858. Sun Valley, Blaine County, Idaho, USA, November 4, 1996.

Type of find: Hoard.

Date of deposit: 1914.

Container: Wrapped in rolls of paper placed in a mason jar. The mason jar was subsequently discarded and not retained.

Contents: 96 AV.

Description:
USA, $5 (36): 1857O; 1882S; 1886S (2); 1895; 1897S; 1898S (2); 1899; 1899S (6); 1900S; 1901S (8); 1902S (3); 1903S (2); 1905S (3); 1906S (2); 1909; 1909S

USA, $10 (22): 1882; 1891CC; 1896S; 1897; 1898S; 1899; 1899S; 1901S (2); 1902S; 1903; 1905S (2); 1906D (2); 1906S (3); 1909D; 1909S (2); 1910S

USA, $20 (38): 1870S; 1876S; 1880S; 1881S; 1882S; 1884S; 1887S; 1888S (2); 1890S (3); 1891S; 1894S; 1897S; 1898S; 1899S (2); 1900S (2); 1901S; 1902S (5); 1903S; 1904S (4); 1905S (3); 1906S; 1907S Liberty; 1910D; 1914

Disposition: The coins were found by two construction workers, Gregory Corliss and Larry Anderson, while excavating for a driveway. Previous residents of the land were the Peterlins, reclusive brothers who lived in Broadford Farms, which is now the ranch of Jann Wenner. Broadford Townsite was a silver mining town. Awarded by the court to Jann Wenner, the landowner.

Bibliography: Tad Friend, "Letter from Sun Valley: The Gold Diggers," *New Yorker*, May 31, 1999, 80–87.

Richard B. Cunningham, "The Slow Death of Treasure Trove," *Archaeology*, February 7, 2000, http://www.archaeology.org/online/features/trove/index.html.

Corliss v. Wenner, 34 P.3d 1100 (Idaho App. 2001).

Ally McClure (on behalf of Jann Wenner), e-mail messages to John M. Kleeberg, December 14 and December 20, 2006 (attaching photographs of the hoard).

859. Albuquerque, New Mexico, USA, August 1960.

Type of find: Hoard.

Date of deposit: 1916.

Contents: 431 AV.

Description:
USA, $5 (100)
USA, $10 (202)
USA, $20 (129)
Dates ran from 1847 to 1916.

Disposition: Bequeathed by a 92-year-old relative to an Albuquerque couple; auctioned by the Albuquerque Federal Savings Association; sold to H. H. Trickey.

Bibliography: "Buried Treasure Auctioned," *Numismatic Scrapbook Magazine* 26, no. 8 (August 1960): 2457.

860. Valmy, Wisconsin, USA, July 1996.

Type of find: Hoard.
Date of deposit: 1916.
Contents: 29 AR, 21 AV.
Description: USA, silver and gold coins, some dated to 1854, valued at $7,000.
Disposition: Found by Betty Brauer, the landowner, while pulling weeds around a pen she was preparing for her beagles. A few years before her sons had found some old silver dollars while digging for night crawlers for fishbait.
Bibliography: Bowers 1997, 68.
Jesse Garza, "Woman discovers some buried booty. Lucky find while pulling weeds adds up to more than a $7,000 strike," *Milwaukee Journal Sentinel*, August 11, 1996, 5.

861. Nebraska, USA, 1974.

Type of find: Hoard.
Date of deposit: 1916.
Container: Can.
Contents: 236 P.
Description:
USA, Nebraska, First National Bank of Wood River, $10 (177)
USA, Nebraska, First National Bank of Wood River, $20 (59)
The notes are 1902–8 plain backs. If the photograph in Bowers's book shows a note from the hoard, the note is one of the type issued in 1916–24 (1908 face, plain back, with geographic letter). The notes had been tightly rolled up and stored in dry circumstances, perhaps in one or more cans, but did have some rust stains or other areas of discoloration. Since there are three tens for every twenty, the notes would have been printed in the 10–10–10–20 format.
Disposition: Bought by Dean Oakes and John Hickman from a Nebraska dealer, Marvin Luke; sold through Hickman & Oakes 60th Price List, 1974.
Bibliography: Bowers 1997, 350.
Robert Hepworth Lloyd, "The Unfortunate Series: 1902–1908," *Paper Money* 26, no. 3 (May/June 1987): 88 (explains how to date the notes of this complex series).

862. Marshalltown, Iowa, USA, June 1933.

Type of find: Hoard.
Date of deposit: 1921.
Containers: 3 glass jars in a granite bucket.
Contents: 192 AR, 89 AV, 26 P.
Description:
USA, 25¢ (19)
USA, 50¢ (33)
USA, silver $1 (140)
USA, $5 (33)
USA, $10 (34)
USA, $20 (22)
USA, $1 bill (13)
USA, $2 bill (2)
USA, $5 bill (10)
USA, $10 bill, dated 1921, signed Fawcett Nevada
The hoard was in three glass jars in a granite bucket concealed beneath the floor of a closet.
Disposition: The value of the hoard was given to Ida Mae Zornes, the eleven-year-old girl who found it.
Bibliography: Zornes v. Bowen, 274 N.W. 877 (Iowa 1937).

863. San Salvador, El Salvador, summer 1983.

Type of find: Hoard.
Date of deposit: 1922.
Contents: 47,000 AV.

Description:
USA, $20 (47,000): 1901S (2,000); 1902S (2,000); 1905S (2,000); 1907D (2,000); 1907S (2,000); 1908D no motto (1,000); 1908D with motto (1,000); 1909D (2,000); 1909S (2,000); 1910S (6,000); 1911S (6,000); 1914S (6,000); 1915S (6,000); 1916S (6,500); 1922S (500)

Thought to be part of the gold reserves of El Salvador. Paid over by the United States to El Salvador in return for coconut or banana exports. Sold in the early 1980s to finance the Salvadorean civil war.

Disposition: Sold through Manfra, Tordella, and Brooks in New York City. A bag of 460 1909S $20s, which provenances to this hoard, was sold by Heritage Numismatic Auctions, Inc., June 15–18, 1989, lots 2346–425.

Bibliography: Breen 1988, 543, 572, 577–78 (Breen 6827, 7335, 7370, 7374, 7378, 7386, 7389, 7392, 7393, 7397, 7398, 7403, 7408); Bowers 1997, 341–42 (citing "Heritage Schedules Sale for June 15–18 in Dallas," *Coin World*, June 7, 1989, 20); Heritage 1989, lots 2346–425.

864. Warwick, Orange County, New York, USA, July 1936.

Type of find: Hoard.

Date of deposit: 1924.

Contents: 6+ AV.

Description:
USA, $5
USA, $10
USA, $20

The coins are thought to have been hidden by Mrs. Sarah McConnell, who died around 1924.

Disposition: Found by Everett Doty, who opened an account and deposited the money into the Warwick National Bank.

Bibliography: "Cucumber Patch Yields Gold Hoard. Printer in Park Row Days of The Times, Scenting a 'Story,' Finds Warwick 'Prospector.' They Sift Dirt Together. Homestead Ruins Give Up 3 Pieces, $20, $10 and $5, and Reporter at 80 gets a 'Beat,'" *New York Times*, August 3, 1936, 17.

865. Lincoln, Nebraska, USA, November 1984.

Type of find: Hoard.

Date of deposit: 1920s.

Contents: 80+ P.

Description: USA, national banknotes, 1920s (80+)

$8,000 in national banknotes from the 1920s.

Disposition: Found by two Lincoln, Nebraska hikers near a stream east of town. Most were wet and mildewed. Exchanged by the United States Treasury for currency of equal face value.

Bibliography: "Hikers Stumble Upon $8,000," *Numismatist* 97, no. 11 (November 1984): 2269.

866. 422 Lock Street, Cincinnati, Ohio, USA, May 1940.

Type of find: Hoard.

Date of deposit: 1928.

Contents: 310+ P.

Description:
USA, $5, paper money, large size
USA, $10, paper money, large size
USA, $20, paper money, large size
USA, gold certificates

$6,190 in face value, comprising old large type bills including $5s, $10s, and $20s and some gold certificates. Did not include any $1 bills. Found by a mentally disabled person, David Mitchell, who had trespassed into 422 Lock Street.

Disposition: To Charles Schaub who owned

the Lock Street home and stated that he had hidden the money.

Bibliography: Niederlehner v. Weatherly, 54 N.E.2d 312 (Ohio Ct. App. 1943). Niederlehner v. Weatherly, 69 N.E.2d 787 (Ohio Ct. App. 1946).

867. Milford, near Cincinnati, Ohio, USA, March 1953.

Type of find: Hoard.
Date of deposit: 1933.
Contents: 60 AV, 36+ P.
Description:
USA, $20 (60)
USA, paper money, large size (36+)
$1,200 in USA $20, $3,600 in large size bills.
Disposition: Found by two boys aged 9 and 10, in an abandoned house in Milford, a small town near Cincinnati.
Bibliography: "Hoard Found by Two Children," *Numismatic Scrapbook Magazine* 19, no. 3 (March 1953): 228.

868. South Dakota, USA, August 1960.

Type of find: Hoard.
Date of deposit: 1933.
Container: Can.
Contents: 47+ P.
Description:
USA, $5, paper money, large size
USA, $10, paper money, large size
USA, $20, paper money, large size
$900 in large size $5, $10, and $20 bills.
Disposition: Found in a can by a farmer excavating for a basement.
Bibliography: *Numismatic Scrapbook Magazine* 26, no. 8 (August 1960): 2474.

869. Selma, Iowa, USA, 1987–89.

Type of find: Hoard.
Date of deposit: 1933.
Contents: AE, AR, P.
Description:
USA, 50¢, 1890s
USA, $10, gold certificate, 1928
USA, $20, gold certificate, 1928
$24,547.74 face value buried in the ground in tin cans and glass jars on his property by Charles Nelson, who died in 1945. Included half dollars dated before 1900 and $10 and $20 gold certificates dated 1928.
Disposition: to Charles Nelson's heirs.
Bibliography: Ritz v. Selma United Methodist Church, 467 N.W.2d 266 (Iowa 1991).

870. Green Isle Township, Minnesota, USA, 1946.

Type of find: Hoard.
Date of deposit: 1933.
Contents: 300 AR; 1,171 AV; P.
Description:
USA, $5 (413): 1843; 1845; 1851; 1852; 1853D; 1857C; 1861 (2); 1865S; 1871S (2); 1874; 1874S; 1876CC; 1878 (2); 1878S (4); 1879 (2); 1879CC; 1879S (2); 1880 (25); 1880S (14); 1881 (28); 1881CC; 1881S (7); 1882 (16); 1882CC; 1882S (8); 1883S; 1884 (2); 1884S (2); 1885 (4); 1885S (8); 1886 (2); 1886S (30); 1887S (16); 1888S (8); 1890CC; 1892; 1892CC (3); 1894; 1894S; 1895S (2); 1897 (5); 1897S (11); 1898 (6); 1899 (2); 1899S (22); 1900 (4); 1900S (6); 1901 (3); 1901S (45)
USA, $10 (292): 1843O; 1844O; 1846; 1847O; 1849 (2); 1851O; 1874S; 1879 (4); 1880 (15); 1880CC; 1880S (7); 1881 (32); 1881CC; 1881O; 1881S (6); 1882 (14); 1882O; 1882S; 1883S (2); 1885 (2); 1885S; 1886S (12); 1887; 1887S (15); 1888S (6); 1889S (7); 1891CC; 1892 (3); 1892CC; 1893 (4); 1893S (5); 1894 (3); 1894O; 1894S (2); 1895 (2); 1895S; 1896S (4); 1897; 1897S; 1898 (5); 1898S (6); 1899 (7); 1899S (13); 1900S; 1901; 1901S

(29); 1902S (4); 1903S (9); 1905S (6); 1906; 1906D (4); 1906S (10); 1907 Liberty (3); 1907 Saint Gaudens (2); 1907S (2); 1908; 1908D; 1909D; 1909S; 1910D; 1910S (12); 1911; 1912 (2); 1914

USA, $20 (466): 1851; 1851O; 1852 (3); 1852O; 1853 (2); 1856S; 1857; 1859S; 1861; 1862S; 1863S (2); 1864S (2); 1867S; 1868; 1869S; 1870S (2); 1871S (2); 1872 (2); 1872S (2); 1873 (6); 1873S (8); 1874S (7); 1875CC; 1876 (5); 1876CC; 1876S (6); 1877S (17); 1878 (4); 1878S (13); 1879S (11); 1880 (1); 1880S (3); 1881 (8); 1881S (15); 1882S (15); 1883CC; 1883S (11); 1884CC; 1884S (8); 1885S (5); 1887S (3); 1888S (10); 1889; 1889S (10); 1890CC; 1890S (17); 1891S (14); 1892S (9); 1893S (5); 1894; 1894S (10); 1895; 1895S (13); 1896 (4); 1896S (12); 1897 (3); 1897S (15); 1898S (19); 1899; 1899S (20); 1900S (28); 1901S (11); 1902S (17); 1903S (7); 1904 (3); 1904S (12); 1905S (13); 1906D; 1906S (5); 1907D (2); 1907S; 1908 (2); 1908D; 1909; 1910D; 1910S (9); 1911 (2); 1913D (3); 1914S (4); 1915; 1925; 1927 (2)

Included thousands of dollars worth of bonds.

Total value over $200,000; less $29,865 in gold, leaves over $170,000 in silver and paper. The only inventory known is of the gold coins.

Disposition: Silver and paper turned in for face value. Gold sold to James and Meta Lee of Chicago for $29,865.

Bibliography: King 1952.

871. Seymour, Connecticut, USA, October 1950.

Type of find: Hoard.

Date of deposit: 1932.

Container: Tin box.

Contents: AV, P.

Description:
 USA, gold coins

USA, paper money

$5,000 in old American currency and gold coins. Some of the gold coins dated back to 1750 and on several were scratched the initials "J.S." The house was once owned by Dr. John Strapp.

Disposition: Found by workers renovating the house. The money was hidden in a wall in a dust covered tin box. Norman Mackinnon had purchased the house not long before.

Bibliography: "$5,000 Hoard Found in Wall," *New York Times* October 5, 1950, 33.

872. Kingston, Tennessee, USA, August 1941.

Type of find: Hoard.

Date of deposit: 1932.

Contents: AR, 13+AV, 8+ P.

Description:
 USA, silver coins
 USA, gold coins (13+)
 USA, paper money (8+)

Disposition: Hoard of money found by Tommy Burns, a painter, while tearing down an old building. Contained $800 in paper currency, $250 in gold, and several silver pieces. The gold coins were sent to Washington for Federal inspection.

Bibliography: "Cache of Coins Found in Tennessee," *Numismatist* 54, no. 8 (August 1941): 644.

873. 405 Prospect Street, Indianapolis, Indiana, USA, August 1941.

Type of find: Hoard.

Date of deposit: 1933.

Container: Trunk.

Contents: 509 AV.

Description: USA, gold coins, some as old as 1842.

Found by two junk dealers, Charles Franklin Keller, 41, and Mack Winters, 19, in a trunk. The coins were examined by the Indianapolis

Secret Service and the face value totalled $4,885.

Disposition: Anna Dehler and Edward F. Crossen sued on the grounds that they were the owners. The U.S. government sued on the grounds that the gold coins should be forfeited to the government. The coins were held at the Fletcher Trust Company, and then taken by the U.S. Marshal.

Keller and Winters were the finders. Edward F. Crossen had bought the trunk from the Little Sisters of the Poor. The trunk originally belonged to Anna Dehler, who lived with the Little Sisters. The trunk contained $1,996 in coins that were considered to be collectors' items, so the government seized the other $2,889 in gold coin.

Bibliography: "Find $5,000 in Gold Coins. Indianapolis Junk Dealers Uncover Hoard in Old Trunk," *New York Times*, August 10, 1941, 3.
"'Junk' Proves Gold Coin. Indianapolis Dealers Find $4,885 in an Old Trunk," *New York Times*, August 10, 1941, 40.
"Junk Dealers buy Trunk—Find Gold Coins," *Numismatist* 54, no. 9 (September 1941): 682.
"U.S. Sues for $5000 Hoard of Gold," *Numismatic Scrapbook Magazine* 8, no. 4 (April 1942): 170.
"From the Editor," *Numismatic Scrapbook Magazine* 8, no. 7 (July 1942): 317.
"Litigants Divide Hoard of Gold Found in Old Trunk Last Year," *Numismatic Scrapbook Magazine* 8, no. 9 (September 1942): 444.

874. Green Bay, Wisconsin, USA, August 1938.

Type of find: Hoard.
Date of deposit: 1933.
Contents: 9 AV.
Description:
 USA, $5
 USA, $10
 USA, $20 (7)

Disposition: Found by two boys playing in their backyard in a sewer drain in Green Bay.
Bibliography: *Numismatic Scrapbook Magazine* 4, no. 8 (August 1938): 328.
"Buried Gold Coins Found in Green Bay, Wis.," *Numismatist* 51, no. 8 (August 1938): 695.

875. Toledo, Ohio, USA, March 1939.

Type of find: Hoard.
Date of deposit: 1933.
Container: Old canvas belt.
Contents: 26 AV.
Description: USA, $20 (26)
Disposition: Found by Eleanor Johns, aged 10.
Bibliography: Ted Hammer, "Here and There," *Numismatic Scrapbook Magazine* 5, no 4 (April 1939): 177.

876. 717 Tracy Avenue, Kansas City, Missouri, USA, before December 22, 1939.

Type of find: Hoard.
Date of deposit: 1933.
Container: Metal box concealed behind bricks.
Contents: 93 P.
Description:
 USA, gold certificates, $100 (87)
 USA, gold certificates, $500 (4)
 USA, gold certificates, $1,000 (2)

In November 1939 the Bonded Wrecking & Lumber Company purchased 717 Tracy Avenue and commenced to demolish the building. While doing so, a brick wall fell, revealing a metal box containing gold certificates, which was found by the company's employee, Joseph Johnson.

Disposition: The heirs of the previous resident of the building, Louis H. Wyatt, deceased, sued on the grounds that he had hidden the gold certificates. The claim of the finder, Joseph

Johnson, was dismissed on the grounds that since the treasure was mislaid, rather than lost or abandoned, the treasure should vest in either the true owner or the owner of the land, here, the Bonded Wrecking & Lumber Company. The ultimate disposition of the case between the landowner and those who claimed to be the heirs of the true owner is unknown.

Bibliography: Louis W. Evans, "Workman Finds Hoard," *Numismatic Scrapbook Magazine* 6, no. 1 (January 1940): 20.

State ex rel. Scott v. Buzard, 144 S.W.2d 847 (Mo. Ct. App. 1940).

877. New Orleans, Louisiana, USA, 1958.

Type of find: Hoard.

Date of deposit: 1933.

Contents: 222 P.

Description: USA, gold certificates (222)
$22,200 in gold certificates concealed in a mattress by Emily Baron.

Disposition: Found in 1958 when the mattress was sent to a fabric recycling center and a blast of air was directed at the mattress to clean it, thereupon blowing the money into the air. Face value to the heirs of Emily Baron; the U.S. Treasury took possession of the actual gold certificates.

Bibliography: U.S. v. Peter, 178 F. Supp. 854 (E.D. La. 1959).

"$22,000 in gold certificates found in old mattress," *Numismatic Scrapbook Magazine* 26, no. 1 (January 1960): 27.

878. Oak Lawn Section, Dallas, Texas, USA, January 1955, and Carrollton, Texas, USA, May 1971.

Type of find: Hoard.

Date of deposit: 1933.

Containers: Thermos jug and glass jars.

Contents: 4,650+ P.

Description:
USA, $20 gold certificates
USA, $50 gold certificates, in packages with wrappers bearing the stamp of the Federal Reserve Bank of New York

Disposition: Amount of the two finds in 1955 and 1971 totaled $232,500. The initial 1955 find by Jackson Davis in the thermos jug consisted of $45,170 in $20 and $50 bills, 1928 and 1929 series gold certificates, in packages with wrappers bearing the stamp of the Federal Reserve Bank of New York. Further finds discovered by additional digging in the basement in 1955, of more thermos jugs and a glass jar, brought the total found up to approximately $190,000.

The 1955 initial find was concealed in a gallon thermos jug and was found by Jackson Davis while digging a ditch for a sewer line in the basement of the Felder home. It had been concealed during the Depression by William Davis Felder, Sr., an investor in cotton and oil, who died in 1938.

After litigation, the 1955 thermos find was awarded to the owner of the house, William Davis Felder, Jr.

In May 1971 another glass jar was discovered with $42,500 in currency, also dated 1928 and 1929 and in wrappers from the Federal Reserve Bank of New York, on a site in Carrollton, outside Dallas, Texas, that had been filled up with dirt transported from the Felder home after it was sold in 1969. It was found by R. W. Kirkland, while operating a backhoe to construct a storm sewer. C. D. Doolittle and L. C. Stanciel were assisting him.

Custody of the 1971 find was turned over to the local sheriff. After litigation with five people, including the present and past owners of the land, and a jury finding that the money was lost property, District Court Judge Spencer Carver of Dallas ruled on

December 29, 1971 that the trove should go to the finders, with the largest share going to Kirkland. Two families who claimed to be prior owners of the money, the Felders and the Letots, appealed, and the Texas Court of Civil Appeals in September 1972 reversed and remanded for a new trial among the finders and the two families who claimed to be the prior owners. The final disposition of the 1971 find is unknown.

Bibliography: Bowers 1997, 347, 349.
"Texas: Money in a Jug," *Newsweek*, October 24, 1955, 30.
"Finds $50,000 In Gold Certificates," *Numismatic Scrapbook Magazine* 21, no. 11 (November 1955): 1544.
Haynes v. Felder, 239 F.2d 868 (5th Cir. 1957).
"Judge Awards Hoard of Gold Certificates to Workers," *Coin World*, January 12, 1972, 15.
Neale v. Kirkland, 486 S.W.2d 165 (Tex. Civ. App. 1972).

879. 15 miles outside Odessa, Texas, USA, March 1940.

Type of find: Hoard.
Date of deposit: 1933?
Contents: 300 AV.
Description:
  USA, $10 (100)
  USA, $20 (200)
  Exact number of coins not specified, but known to total $5,000 in face value.
Disposition: Found by Riley Smith.
Bibliography: "Buried Treasure," *Numismatic Scrapbook Magazine* 6, no. 3 (March 1940): 184.

880. Lancaster, Ohio, USA, May 1958.

Type of find: Hoard.
Date of deposit: 1933?
Contents: 10 AV.
Description:
  USA, $5 (5)
  USA, $10 (2)
  USA, $20 (3)
Disposition: Found by a 14 year old boy on the roof of a home.
Bibliography: "Gold Find," *Numismatic Scrapbook Magazine* 24, no. 5 (May 1958): 1123.

881. Edgewater Drive, Lakewood, Cleveland, Ohio, USA, May 2006.

Type of find: Hoard.
Date of deposit: 1933?
Containers: Wrapped in pages from the *Cleveland Plain Dealer* and placed in four steel boxes, one of which was tied to a wire nailed to a stud.
Contents: Ca. 15,000 P.
Description:
  USA, Federal Reserve Bank of Cleveland, 1929, $10
  USA, National banknote, Indiana National Bank of Indianapolis, $10
  USA, $50
  USA, $500, apparently including these from the following Federal Reserve Districts: District D (3); District G (2); District H (2)
  USA, $1,000, included one from District H
  Two of the boxes also contained, besides money, religious memorabilia.
  The money was in bundles with P. Dunne written on them. Patrick J. Dunne owned the home during the Depression. The house was built in 1924. Dunne died a widower in 1966, and left the house to his sister Agatha Gannon. She died unmarried and childless in 1974, leaving the estate to her nephews and nieces.
Disposition: Found by Bob Kitts, a contractor, while renovating the bathroom of Amanda Reece. Reece promised Kitts a finder fee

of 10%, but reneged. Myron Xenos, who had a client who was a friend of Reece, was originally supposed to market the currency, but this fell apart after the litigation commenced. Kitts sued Reece and went public with the case, whereupon the Dunne heirs intervened in the litigation.

The litigation ended up in probate court before Magistrate Charles Brown. The lawyer for Kitts was Patrick Farrell; the lawyer for Reece was Skip Lazzaro; the lawyer for the heirs of Dunne is Egidijus Marcinkevicius of Euclid. Reece said in court on February 5, 2008 that she has already spent all but $18,000, and said that if she is not awarded the find, she will have to declare bankruptcy. At a deposition, Reece said she spent some of the money on a trip to Hawaii with her mother, and that $60,000 of the cash in a shoebox was mysteriously stolen from her, although she did not report this theft to the police. By the time of the litigation, only $25,230 remained. Reece later abandoned any claim to the money. In October 2008 Magistrate Brown ruled that the $157,000 marked as Dunne's property belonged to Dunne's heirs; and that the $25,000 not clearly marked would have gone to Reese, but since she had dropped the claim, the money went to Kitts. Of the remaining $25,230, Kitts got, pro rata, $3,457, and the Dunne heirs, $21,773. Reese filed bankruptcy in November 2008.

Bibliography: J. Kroll, "He found $182,000—in her bathroom. Who gets the cash?" *Cleveland Plain Dealer*, December 11, 2007.

Jim Nichols, "Found cash may be nearly gone but claimants are multiplying," *Cleveland Plain Dealer*, February 6, 2008.

Bradley Campbell, "The Wall of Greed. A contractor ripped up a bathroom and found a fortune. Now everyone wants a piece," *Cleveland Scene*, February 13, 2008, available at http://www.clevescene.com/2008–2–13/news/the-wall-of-greed/print.

Damian G. Guevara, "Contractor, ex-homeowner's heirs to split cash found in Lakewood house's walls," *Cleveland Plain Dealer*, October 23, 2008.

"Ohio Cash Hoard Dispersed," E-Sylum 11, no.45, November, 10, 2008, http://coinbooks.org/club_nbs_ esylum_v11n45.html.

"More on the Ohio Cash Hoard," E-Sylum 11, no.46, November 17, 2008, http:// coinbooks.org/ club_nbs_esylum _v11n46.html#article30.

882. 137 East 33rd Street, New York, New York, USA, August 1956.

Type of find: Hoard.

Date of deposit: 1933?

Contents: 23 P.

Description: USA, $100 notes (23)

The bills were behind a brick in an old fireplace in a brownstone. Found by Pearlie Dickens, supervisor of a construction crew who were demolishing three brownstones. The statement in the 1956 article in the *New York Times* that 40 notes were found originally is not borne out by the 1957 article.

Disposition: Dickens claimed the notes as the finder. The Lefcourt Realty Corporation claimed as the owner of the building. The estate of William Masiello claimed it on the grounds that William Masiello had placed the notes behind the fireplace; his mother, Mrs. Josephine Masiello had lived at the address. Walter Ford Murray and Madeleine Murray, tenants at 135 East 33rd Street, claimed the notes on the grounds that the notes had actually been found on the side of 135 East 33rd Street. Justice Joseph A. Boccia, of Part Nine of the Municipal Court, awarded the find to Dickens. In a post-trial settlement, Dickens took $900, the Masiello estate received $1,000, and the Lefcourt Corporation $400. The Murray claim could not be substantiated and was withdrawn.

Bibliography: "Demolition Crew Finds $4,000; Police Recover Only $2,300 of It," *New York Times*, August 9, 1956, 27.

"$2,300 Found Here in Razed Fireplace Is Divided Among 3 Claimants in Court," *New York Times*, June 19, 1957, 37.

"Buried Treasure can Stir Trouble," *New York Times*, August 23, 1959, R1.

883. Scranton, Pennsylvania, USA, April 29, 1952.

Type of find: Hoard.

Date of deposit: 1933?

Container: Tin can.

Contents: 4 AV, 4 P.

Description:

USA, $5 (2): 1895; 1908
USA, $20 (2): 1875; 1880
USA, $20 gold certificates (4)

Bibliography: "Boys Find 'Treasure.' Unearth $130 in Gold Coins and Certificates in Refuse Dump," *New York Times*, April 30, 1952.

884. Eastern USA, early 1980s.

Type of find: Hoard.

Date of deposit: 1933.

Contents: 1,411 AV.

Description:

USA, gold $1 (2): 1850; 1852
USA, $2.50 (585): 1843O (2); 1845; 1845O (2); 1846O (2); 1847O (2); 1850 (4); 1851 (7); 1852 (14); 1852O (2); 1853 (19); 1854 (7); 1854O (2); 1855 (2); 1856 (8); 1857; 1857S; 1859; 1859S; 1861 (15); 1862; 1871S (2); 1873 (12); 1878 (21); 1878S (8); 1879 (13); 1879S (3); 1887 (2); 1890 (4); 1893 (2); 1895; 1896 (2); 1897 (2); 1898 (3); 1899 (6); 1900 (12); 1901 (22); 1902 (23); 1903 (48); 1904 (43); 1906 (56); 1907 (88); 1908 (51); 1909 (11); 1910 (2); 1911 (17); 1912 (3); 1913 (6); 1914 (7); 1914D (11); 1915 (10)

USA, $5 (293): 1834 (2); 1836 (3); 1838 (2); 1839 (2); 1839C; 1840; 1843; 1844O (2); 1845 (6); 1846 (4); 1847 (7); 1848 (3); 1849; 1851; 1852; 1853; 1854; 1855S; 1856S; 1857; 1861 (8); 1863S; 1874 (3); 1877S; 1879S (3); 1880 (5); 1880S (8); 1881 (9); 1881S (5); 1882 (11); 1882S (2); 1884S; 1885S (2); 1886; 1886S (11); 1887S (3); 1888S (2); 1893S (4); 1895; 1897 (5); 1897S (3); 1898 (2); 1898S (8); 1899; 1899S (5); 1900 (10); 1900S; 1901S (12); 1902S (4); 1903S (8); 1904; 1905S (6); 1906D (5); 1906S; 1907; 1907D (5); 1908 (17); 1908S (22); 1909 (6); 1909S (5); 1910 (8); 1911 (9); 1911S; 1912 (8); 1913 (7); 1913S; 1914; 1915 (6)

USA, $10 (263): 1840; 1842O (2); 1844O; 1845O; 1847 (3); 1847O (3); 1849 (4); 1850 (3); 1852 (2); 1853; 1854S; 1856S; 1857; 1879S (2); 1880 (7); 1880S (4); 1881 (9); 1881S (7); 1882 (11); 1882S; 1883; 1884S; 1885 (2); 1885S; 1886S (2); 1887S (6); 1889S (2); 1890; 1892 (3); 1893 (3); 1893S; 1894 (2); 1894O; 1894S; 1895O; 1896S; 1897 (12); 1897S (5); 1898 (3); 1898S; 1899 (6); 1899S (5); 1900S; 1901 (11); 1901S (10); 1902; 1902S (2); 1903; 1903S (2); 1905 (2); 1905S (5); 1906; 1906D (15); 1906S (3); 1907 Liberty (4); 1907D; 1907S (2); 1907 Indian (29); 1908 (7); 1908D (2); 1909 (2); 1909S (2); 1910 (2); 1910D (3); 1910S (5); 1911 (5); 1912 (6); 1912S (2); 1913 (4); 1914; 1914D (2); 1915 (4)

USA, $20 (272): 1878S; 1879S; 1890S; 1895; 1904; 1907D (99); 1923D (154); 1927 (14)

Disposition: Sold by David E. Tripp and Manfra, Tordella & Brookes.

Bibliography: Bowers 1997, 150–51.

885. Border of North Dakota and Minnesota, USA, October 15, 1992.

Type of find: Hoard.

Date of deposit: May 1935.

Container: Coffee can.

Contents: 61+ P.

Description:
  USA, South Dakota, national banknotes, small size (9)
  USA, North Dakota, national banknotes, small size (11)
  USA, Minnesota, national banknotes, small size (21)
  USA, other states, national banknotes, small size (14)
  All small size notes, 57 type I, 4 type II.

Disposition: From the owners to a dealer, then to Charles Parrish of Rosemount, Minnesota. Parrish later stated that there had turned out to be more items in the hoard than he had first thought when he had reported it to the *Bank Note Reporter* in November 1992 (hence the amount of 61 plus).

Bibliography: *Bank Note Reporter*, November 1992, 4.
  Charles Parrish, conversation with John M. Kleeberg, July 1993.

886. Angelina National Forest, Texas, USA, November 1994.

Type of find: Hoard.

Date of deposit: 1930s.

Contents: 50 B.

Description: USA, Texas, Aldridge Lumber Company, tokens (50)
  The cases do not specify the metal of the lumber company tokens, but they are bimetallic with a brass ring and an aluminum insert; however, in all specimens known, the aluminum insert is missing.

Disposition: Found on the site of an abandoned lumber mill company town by Billy Ray Shivers using a metal detector. After litigation, awarded to the U.S. Federal government.

Bibliography: In Re Shivers, 900 F.Supp. 60 (E.D. Tex 1995).
  U.S. v. Shivers, 96 F.3d 120 (5th Cir. 1996).

887. Philadelphia, Pennsylvania, USA, October 25, 1956.

Type of find: Hoard.

Date of deposit: March 25, 1939.

Containers: 3 cans in an iron or lead pipe, wrapped in the *New York Times* of March 25, 1939.

Contents: 300 AV.

Description:
  USA, $2.50 (3)
  USA, $5 (23)
  USA, $10 (6)
  USA, $20 (268)
  Total face value, $5,542. Most coins were dated 1911. The earliest date was 1863 and the latest date 1928. The numismatic value was given as $50,000.

Disposition: If the owner cannot be found, to the junk man who found it, Willie Brassey, who had just finished a 3-Month sentence for vagrancy in Holmesburg Prison. Brassey's claim was contested by the family of Ben W. Kingsdorf, who died in 1958. The Commonwealth of Pennsylvania also claimed it by right of escheat. The finder was awarded $9,000 in June 1959.

Bibliography: "Junk Man Finds $5,542," *Numismatic Scrapbook Magazine* 22, no. 11 (November 1956): 2143.
  "Family Claims Gold Hoard," *Numismatic Scrapbook Magazine* 23, no. 6 (June 1957): 1090.
  "Junkman Who Found Gold Cache to Receive $9,000," *Numismatic Scrapbook Magazine* 25, no. 6 (June 1959): 1585.

888. Montréal, Québec, Canada, August 1982.

Type of find: Hoard.

Date of deposit: 1939–40.

Contents: Ca. 100 P.

Description:
  Canada, Bank of Canada, $5, 1937

Canada, Bank of Canada, $10, 1937

Canada, Bank of Canada, $20, 1937 (65) (mostly signed Osborne-Towers)

Canada, Bank of Canada, $50, 1937 (3) (signed Gordon-Towers)

Canada, Bank of Canada, $100, 1935 (5)

Canada, Bank of Canada, $100, 1937 (22) (signed Osborne-Towers)

The $5 notes were present with serial numbers in excess of 6,000,000, indicating that these notes were originally produced in large numbers.

The 1937 $100 was rare before the discovery of this hoard.

Disposition: Dispersed. One $100 of 1937 acquired by Harold Don Allen.

Bibliography: Harold Don Allen, "On Coin Hoards and Fiscal Paper," *Numismatics International Bulletin* 17, no. 1 (January 1983): 16–17.

889. Reno, Nevada, USA, 1974.

Type of find: Hoard. Called "the Redfield Hoard."

Date of deposit: 1930–65.

Contents: 407,596 AR.

Description: Accumulation of U.S. silver dollars by LaVere Redfield, who died in 1974.

Numbers in the table below are in thousands. These estimates were arrived at by interpreting the estimates of Breen, Highfill, and Akers, which are often adjectival ("several," "a few") rather than numerical, plus Highfill's ranking of the top ten varieties, by quantity, in the hoard. Highfill's top ten list is, in descending order: 1881S, 1880S, 1879S, 1878S, 1882S, 1896, 1898, 1891S, 1897S, 1890S.

Plumbo states that in his first purchase of four Redfield hoard silver dollars in Anchorage, Alaska in 1977 he acquired the mintmarks 1886S, 1887S, 1888S, and 1896S.

Date	No.	Date	No.	Date	No.
1878S	40	'90CC	2	1899S	7
1879S	40	1891	5	1900S	0.3
'79CC	0.09	1891S	20	1902S	7
1880S	40	'91CC	5	1903	0.9
1881S	60	1892	2	1903S	1
1882S	20	'92CC	1.7	1921S	0.9
1883S	1.002	1892O	4	1922S	7
'85CC	0.5	1893	3	1923S	7
1886S	12	'93CC	1	1924S	0.3
1887S	10	1895S	1	1925S	4
1888S	3+	1896	20	1926S	7
1889	2	1897	7	1927S	4
1889S	5	1897S	20	1928S	6
1890	3	1898	20	1935S	0.9
1890S	7	1898S	7		

Disposition: Sold at a courtroom auction, January 27, 1976, to Steve Markoff of A-Mark Coin Company, Beverly Hills, for $7.3 million, who sold it on through Robert Hughes, John Love, and Paramount International Coin Corporation, and who then distributed the coins over the next dozen years. Paramount packaged the coins in sonically sealed black, red, and dark green plastic holders which state that they contain "A Silver Dollar from the Redfield Collection." A final tranche of 6,000 silver dollars was bought by Blanchard in 1988.

Bibliography: Bowers 1997, 313–35; Breen 1988, 444, 449, 451–58, 461–62 (Breen 5530, 5533, 5548, 5561, 5568, 5573, 5598, 5604, 5609, 5615, 5617, 5622, 5624, 5625, 5629, 5630, 5633, 5639, 5642, 5649, 5650, 5652, 5653, 5655, 5661, 5674, 5695, 5715, 5723, 5725, 5728, 5731, 5740); Highfill 1992, 93–95; Miller [1983?], 5–7.

Tom Dougherty, "The Disappearing Cartwheels: Who's Hoarding the Iron Men?" *Numismatic Scrapbook Magazine* 21, no. 2 (February 1955): 306 (citing *Out West magazine*) (a robbery of Redfield in 1954 in

Reno revealed that Redfield had hidden away silver dollars to avoid paying taxes).

Paul M. Green, "The Redfield Hoard Revisited. What happened when over half a million silver dollars hit the market?" *Coinage*, May 1982, 50–52.

Michael R. Fuljenz, "Market Forum: Balance of Redfield Hoard Sold," *Numismatist* 101, no. 12 (December 1988): 2135.

Paul M. Green, "1891 Morgans numerous in Redfield Hoard," *Numismatic News*, January 20, 2004, 53.

Richard D. Plumbo, "It's time for the rest of the Redfield story," *Coin World*, April 26, 2004.

890. 534 Franklin Street, Pontiac, Michigan, USA, October 1979.

Type of find: Hoard.

Date of deposit: 1951.

Contents: 9,000+ AR.

Description:
  USA, 25¢
  USA, 50¢
  USA, silver $1
  The coins were dated 1879 to 1951.

Disposition: Taken to the Police Department to be stored and inventoried. The coins were later transferred to the Pontiac State Bank.

Bibliography: Bowers 1997, 63.

891. Sandusky, Ohio, USA, 1964.

Type of find: Hoard.

Date of deposit: 1957.

Contents: 48+ P.

Description: USA, paper money (48+)

Disposition: $4,467 in currency found in an old piano that the Cesarinis bought at an auction in 1957. They found the currency when cleaning the piano in 1964.

Bibliography: Cesarini v. U.S., 296 F.Supp. 3 (N.D. Ohio, 1969).

892. Keokuk, Iowa, USA, August 1992.

Type of find: Hoard.

Date of deposit: 1957.

Containers: Wrapped in handkerchiefs, tied with string, wrapped in aluminum foil, then hidden in the wing of an airplane and the wing of the airplane screwed shut.

Contents: 600+ P.

Description: USA, $20, paper money (600+)

Two packets of currency wrapped in aluminum foil hidden under a wing of an airplane. The currency was tied with string and wrapped in handkerchiefs. It totaled $18,000, mostly in $20 bills. The bills were pre-1960s, chiefly 1950s; one bill was dated 1934. Found by Heath Benjamin while doing a routine annual inspection at Lindner Aviation.

Disposition: To the State Central Bank, who owned the airplane.

Bibliography: Benjamin v. Lindner Aviation, Inc., 534 N.W.2d 400 (Iowa 1995).

Part II

Treasury Accumulation and Release
of U.S. Silver Dollars

In the last quarter of the nineteenth century, special interest groups persuaded the U.S. government to engage in a price support operation of the silver market. The Bland-Allison Act of 1878 required the government to buy 2 million ounces of silver a month. Since it is easier to strike 30 million dollar coins a year, rather than more coins of lesser denominations, the Mint coined the silver into dollars. Over 600 million dollars of the Morgan type were minted. The general public refused to take the coins, and the coins ended up in the Treasury vaults. The Treasury was able to get the money back into circulation by issuing silver certificates backed by the silver dollars. The financial panics of 1893 and 1895 and the election of McKinley in 1896 brought the price support operation to an end.

This section will give an overview of the release of this gigantic accumulation of silver coins.

Many date and mintmark combinations were thought to be rarer than they actually were, because collectors believed that they had been melted during the First World War. Ever so often the Treasury would release bags of silver dollars with what had been thought to be rare date and mintmark combinations, and the price would tumble. The most notorious was the break in price of the 1903O silver dollar, which had been valued at up to $1,500. In November 1962 the Treasury released 100,000 1903O silver dollars, and the price collapsed in the course of a week. People stormed the Treasury, exchanging their silver certificates for bags of silver dollars. Between January 1960 and March 1964 the Treasury paid out over 152 million silver dollars. This massive outflow of silver dollars was not only because of collectors looking for rare dates and mintmarks, but also because silver provided a hedge against inflationary pressures. This continued until March 25, 1964, when the Treasury ceased to redeem silver certificates in coin, and thenceforth gave bags of silver granules; in 1967, it ceased to redeem silver certificates in silver altogether.

When the Treasury stopped paying out silver dollars, it still had nearly three million silver dollars of numismatic value, mostly from the Carson City Mint. The General Services Administration sold these in a series of mail bid sales from October 1972 through to 1980.

So far as the dates of deposit are concerned, this can be determined with unopened original bags of silver dollars, because these come with tags attached to them, which give the date the bag was sealed by the Treasury, the Mint, or a sub-treasury. A series of tags saved by Howard W. Herz of Minden, Nevada, from bags he went through in 1962–63 have dates ranging from 1889 to 1912;

nothing earlier or later. Herz donated these tags to the American Numismatic Society. The bags were sealed in New Orleans, Philadelphia, or Washington. These tags indicate that the bags of silver dollars were closed and deposited in the Treasury in connection with issues of silver certificates. Later bags sealed by the Federal Reserve in 1918 and 1943 are also known, however, often with unusual contents, such as Liberty seated dollars.

All coins discussed in this section are U.S. silver dollars. The coins are referred to by date and mintmark only.

I. Washington, DC, USA, September 1926.
1882CC (1,000)
Bag found in the Treasury vaults; many were obtained by members of the 1926 American Numismatic Association convention in exchange for silver certificates.
"Convention Notes," *Numismatist* 39, no. 10 (October 1926): 564.

II. San Francisco, California, USA, 1937.
1889S (7,000+)
Several bags of uncirculated 1889S dollars, retrieved from the vaults of the San Francisco Mint.
Breen 1988, 451 (Breen 5548).

III. Washington, DC, USA, late 1938.
1880S, normal date, medium S (20,000)
1880CC (10,000)
1881S (20,000)
1882CC (3,000)
1883 (7,000)
1883O (1,000)
1883CC (1,000)
1884O (1,000)
1884CC (1,000)
1885O (1,000)
"Mint Releases Dollars of the 80's," *Numismatic Scrapbook Magazine* 21, no. 1 (January 1955): 1.
Breen 1988, 451 (Breen 5548).

IV. Washington, DC, USA, 1944.
1926 (10,000)
The *Coin Collector's Journal* wrote in January 1944: "A flood of silver dollars has been loosed on the market by the Treasury Department through the various Federal Reserve Banks. Most of these dollars are in brilliant mint state and probably formed the reserve against which the old silver certificates were issued. Dates formerly considered rare have appeared in large quantities and collectors are warned against paying much premium for such pieces. The disposition among collectors and dealers is to put away a reasonable number of obtainable dates as an investment but considering the large quantities appearing it does not look like such a good bet."
Coin Collector's Journal 11, no. 1 (January-February 1944): 3.
Breen 1988, 462 (Breen 5724).

V. Washington, DC, USA, November 1945.
1923 (10,000)
1925 (10,000)
"Another Peace Dollar Tumbles," *Numismatist* 59, no. 4 (April 1946): 427.
"Mint Releases Dollars of the 80's," *Numismatic Scrapbook Magazine* 21, no. 1 (January 1955): 1.
Breen 1988, 462 (Breen 5717, 5722).

VI. Philadelphia, Pennsylvania, USA, December 1951.
1903S
"Mint Releases Dollars of the 80's," *Numismatic Scrapbook Magazine* 21, no. 1 (January 1955): 1.

VII. Great Falls, Montana, USA, 1952.

1893S (20)
1894S (3,000)
Breen 1988, 444, 455, 456 (Breen 5632, 5636).

VIII. Philadelphia, Pennsylvania, USA, December 1954.

1884
1885 (2,000)
1886 (1,000)
1886O (1,000) (but none of them uncirculated)
1889 (5,000)
"Mint Error Looses Rare Silver Dollar. 3 Million, Valued at $2 to $17, Are Issued –Some Found Here," *New York Times*, December 23, 1954, 1.
Robert K. Plumb, "Mint Error Drops Old Dollar Price. Release of Coins from 1880s Tumbles Market for All but Rarest Specimens," *New York Times*, December 24, 1954, 19.
"Mint Releases Dollars of the 80's," *Numismatic Scrapbook Magazine* 21, no. 1 (January 1955): 1.
Abe Kosoff, "On Silver Dollars," *Numismatist* 68, no. 9 (September 1955): 954.
Breen 1988, 453 (Breen 5581, 5586, 5589).

IX. Great Falls, Montana, USA, October 1955.

1893CC (1,000)
Bag of 1893CC silver dollars. They had been received in a routine shipment from the Federal Reserve Bank of Minneapolis.
Large quantities of 1893CC silver dollars were already available at $5 apiece at the American Numismatic Association convention in August 1955.
"Rare CC Dollars Placed In Circulation," *Numismatic Scrapbook Magazine* 21, no. 11 (November 1955): 1544.
"More Silver Dollars Escape," *Numismatist* 68, no. 12 (December 1955): 1331.

John J. Pittman, "Silver Dollar Releases," *Numismatist* 69, no. 2 (February 1956): 169–70.

X. Ohio, western Pennsylvania, and western New York, USA, October and November 1955.

1903 (10,000)
1922 (10,000)
"large quantities of brilliant uncirculated 1903 and 1922 Philadelphia silver dollars"
John J. Pittman, "1903 Dollars Released," *Numismatic Scrapbook Magazine* 22, no. 1 (January 1956): 20.
John J. Pittman, "Silver Dollar Releases," *Numismatist* 69, no. 2 (February 1956): 169–70.

XI. Great Falls, Montana, USA, 1961.

1894 (1,000)
Bag of uncirculated dollars that was found in Great Falls, Montana, about 1961.
Breen 1988, 444, 456 (Breen 5634).

XII. Allen, Michigan, USA, April 1962.

1840, 1859O, 1872(2), 1871 (2), 1892S (10), 1893S (2), and 1902O (10).
Liberty seated and Morgan dollars of unusual dates found by A. Berman in a sack sealed by a Federal Reserve Bank in 1943. A couple of years earlier a Chicago collector found Liberty seated dollars in a Federal Reserve bag sealed in 1918. Howard W. Herz has also spoken of finding Liberty seated dollars in bags of silver dollars in Las Vegas in 1962–63.
"Liberty Seated Dollars Found in Sack," *Numismatic Scrapbook Magazine* 28, no. 4 (April 1962): 968.

XIII. Washington, DC, USA, 1961–March 25, 1964.

Between January 1960 and March 25, 1964, the Treasury paid out over 152 million silver dollars, including 5–6 million in the very last week (some reports say 18 million in a few days). Since the exact quantities released of each date and mintmark combination were impossible to record accurately among this huge amount of coins, this entry will list only the date and mintmark combinations that are believed to have occurred in large numbers in this release. Some bags had Liberty seated dollars; some had trade dollars; 1869S was found in one bag. The 1903O dollars turned up mixed with 1904O dollars, with the 1903O dollars being in the minority.

1859O	1882S	1889	1898O
1860O	1883	1889O	1899
1878CC	1883O	1890	1899O
1878S	1884CC	1890O	1900S
1879O	1884O	1890S	1901O
1879S	1885O	1891O	1902O
1880CC	1887	1892O	1903O
1880S	1887O	1893	1904O
1881S	1888	1894O	1923S
1882	1888O	1896O	1926S
1882O			

"Rare Coin Falls in Price Sharply. Dealers Puzzled by Flow of 1903 Silver Dollars," *New York Times*, December 1, 1962, 23.

Lincoln Grahlfs, "News of Coins: As to the Crash in 'Rare' Silver Dollar Values," *New York Times*, December 9, 1962, Section 2, 19.

"Trade Dollars in Bags," *Numismatic Scrapbook Magazine* 29, no. 1 (January 1963): 301 (concerning the 1903O dollar).

"Investors Depleting Treasury Dollar Hoard," *Numismatic Scrapbook Magazine* 29, no. 11 (November 1963): 3396.

Edwin L. Dale, "U.S. Has 'Grab Bags' For Coin Collectors," *New York Times*, March 21, 1964, 1.

"Long Lines Form to Buy Silver Dollars at Treasury," *New York Times*, March 24, 1964, 10.

"Treasury Halts Sale of Its Silver Dollars," *New York Times*, March 26, 1964, 10.

"Treasury Will Retain 3 Million Silver Dollars," *New York Times*, March 27, 1964, 10.

"Silver Dollar Stampede," *Numismatic Scrapbook Magazine* 30, no. 5 (May 1964): 1530.

"Treasury Blocks Silver Dollar Run," *Numismatist* 77, no. 5 (May 1964): 586.

"Morgan Dollars Puzzle Treasury. Distribution of Rare Coins Poses Knotty Problems," *New York Times*, May 10, 1964, 47.

"Dealer Claims Rare Dollars in Treasury Vault Switched," *Numismatic Scrapbook Magazine* 30, no. 9 (September 1964): 2388.

Breen 1988, 439, 442, 444–45, 448, 451–58 (Breen 5458, 5464, 5487, 5490, 5519, 5551, 5561, 5574, 5577, 5580, 5592, 5595, 5610, 5613, 5615, 5630, 5635, 5646, 5654, 5656, 5658, 5665, 5683, 5691, 5696, 5701).

Bowers 1993, 8.

XIV. West Point, New York, USA, 1971–74.

1,959,428 AR. The liquidation of the Carson City silver dollar holdings by the General Services Administration. This was conducted in five mail bid sales: October 1972–March 1973, June-July 1973, October 1973, February 1974, April-June 1974. Approximately 1.1 million remained unsold after this round of sales.

Date, mintmark	Amount NSM 1/1965	Amount Bowers
1878CC	60,919	60,993
1879S	2,000	
1879CC	5,015	4,123
1880S	1,000	

1880CC	131,422	131,529
1881S	1,000	
1881CC	147,111	147,485
1882S	2,000	
1882CC	607,374	605,029
1883	1,000	
1883O	1,000	
1883CC	758,810	755,518
1884O	4,000	
1884CC	968,149	962,638
1885	2,000	
1885O	1,000	
1885CC	150,135	148,285
1887	3,000	
1890CC	3,965	3,949
1891CC	4,941	5,706
1922	1,000	

There are at least three different sets of figures as to how many coins there were remaining as of the beginning of 1965; two of these sets of figures are in the table above. One set of numbers was provided by the *Numismatic Scrapbook Magazine* of January 1965. The same numbers, but rounded off to the nearest thousand, appear in the table photographed in the Numismatist in February 1972. Q. David Bowers provides a different set of numbers in his silver dollar *Encyclopedia*. The same numbers that Bowers uses were used by Walter Breen in his *Encyclopedia*, but rounded off in a somewhat inconsistent fashion. The third set of figures is in the New York Times article of December 11, 1972, which gives these numbers for the three major dates: 1882CC (611,000); 1883CC (756,000); 1884CC (965,000).

"Majority of Treasury Dollar Hoard Is Three Dates," *Numismatic Scrapbook Magazine* 31, no. 1 (January 1965): 269.

"From the Editor: Treasury Dollar Hoard," *Numismatic Scrapbook Magazine* 32, no. 5 (May 1966): 1030.

"Cancer-Heart Fund Dollar Bill Introduced in Senate," *Numismatic Scrapbook Magazine* 32, no. 7 (July 1966): 1507.

"Treasury Department Opposes Silver Dollar Legislation," *Numismatic Scrapbook Magazine* 32, no. 9 (September 1966): 2117.

"Congressman Sullivan Gives Reason For Dollar Proposal," *Numismatic Scrapbook Magazine* 32, no. 11 (November 1966): 2365.

"Rare Coins Go to West Point," *New York Times*, December 6, 1971, 78.

"Silver Dollar Transfer is First Step Towards Release," *Numismatist* 85, no. 2 (February 1972): 203–4.

Thomas V. Haney, "Another Look at the Old Dollars," *New York Times*, April 9, 1972, Section 2, 34.

"CC Dollar Errors Heighten Interest," *Numismatic Scrapbook Magazine* 38, no. 9 (September 1972): 814, 816, 818.

"CC Dollars Go on GSA Auction Block," *Numismatic Scrapbook Magazine* 38, no. 12 (December 1972): 1078.

"Stack's Blow Whistle on GSA Silver Dollar 'Investments,'" *Numismatic Scrapbook Magazine* 38, no. 12 (December 1972): 1079–80.

"SEC Refuses to Get Involved In Dispute on Silver Dollar Ads," *New York Times*, December 5, 1972, 12.

John H. Allan, "Personal Finance: Silver Dollar Sale Not Making Dealers Turn Cartwheels," *New York Times*, December 11, 1972, 63.

"SEC: CC Dollars Not Securities; GSA: Dollars Not 'Great' Investments," *Numismatic Scrapbook Magazine* 39, no. 1 (January 1973): 70–71.

"'CC' Dollar Dry Hole?" *Numismatic*

Scrapbook Magazine 39, no. 2 (February 1973): 115.

"Lack of Response Forces GSA To Extend CC Dollar Ordering Period To April 30," *Numismatic Scrapbook Magazine* 39, no. 3 (March 1973): 264, 266.

Herbert C. Bardes, "Numismatics: Offshoots of an Off-Center Cartwheel," *New York Times*, April 15, 1973, Section 2, 34.

"GSA CC Dollar Sale Returns $20 Million," *Numismatic Scrapbook Magazine* 39, no. 6 (June 1973): 570.

Thomas V. Haney, "Coins: GSA Plans Exhibit for New Orleans," *New York Times*, July 23, 1973, Section 2, 23.

"Peace Dollars Jesse James Never Got," *Numismatic Scrapbook Magazine* 39, no. 7 (July 1973): 667.

"Gary Palmer Pans GSA Dollar Sale," *Numismatic Scrapbook Magazine* 39, no. 8 (August 1973): 705.

Herbert C. Bardes, "Numismatics: Carson City Data," *New York Times*, January 13, 1974, 32.

"CC Dollars, 1879, on Block at $300," *Numismatic Scrapbook Magazine* 40, no. 2 (February 1974): 205.

Robert J. Cole, "Personal Finance: U.S. Selling Carson City Silver Dollars But Drops 'Investment' in Promotion," *New York Times*, May 20, 1974, 74.

Herbert C. Bardes, "Numismatics: 'Great Silver Sale' Is Over," *New York Times*, September 8, 1974, Section 2, 41.

Herbert C. Bardes, "Numismatics: Carson City Dollar Dilemma," *New York Times*, February 9, 1975, 38.

"Last of U.S. Collection of Silver Dollars Made In Carson City on Sale," *New York Times*, February 9, 1980, 6.

Breen 1988, 445, 452 (Breen 5574, 5580, 5585, 5617, 5624).

Bowers 1993, 8, 2317, 2332, 2350, 2371, 2389, 2486, 2299, 2259.

XV. West Point, New York, USA, February 8, 1980.

823,287 AR. The mail bid sale conducted by the General Services Administration: February 8–April 8, 1980.

1883CC (195,745)

1884CC (428,152)

Mixed years, 1878CC-1885CC and 1889CC-1893CC (299,308)

"A Coin That Survived the Wild West Is Caught in Washington Crossfire," *New York Times*, November 26, 1978, 70.

"U.S. Lifts Costs Of Silver Coins," *New York Times*, January 8, 1980, D10.

Ed Reiter, "Numismatics: Silver Dollar Sale," *New York Times*, January 20, 1980, Section 2, 41.

"Sale of Old Silver Dollars," *New York Times*, February 8, 1980, D5.

"Last of U.S. Collection of Silver Dollars Made In Carson City on Sale," *New York Times*, February 9, 1980, 6.

Ed Reiter, "Numismatics: Unexpected Sellout," *New York Times*, March 2, 1980, Section 2, 44.

Breen 1988, 445.

XVI. West Point, New York, USA, 1980.

55,847 AR. Mail bid sale conducted by the General Services Administration, July 1980.

1880CC (4,284)

1881CC (18,996)

1885CC (31,567)

"Last of U.S. Collection of Silver Dollars Made In Carson City on Sale," *New York Times*, February 9, 1980, 6.

Breen 1988, 445.

Part III

Finds of American Coins Outside the Americas

A1. Empúries, Alt Empordà Province, Catalonia, Spain, 1908–37.

Type of find: Archaeological excavation.

Date of site: Occupied since the 6th Century B.C.E.

Date of American coin: 1542.

Contents: 49 AE, 12 BI, 6 AR.

Description: 1 American coin:
  Spanish colonies, 4 maravedíes, Santo Domingo
  The 67 coins in this entry comprise only the medieval and modern finds.

Bibliography: Campo and Cinta-Mañé 1986.

A2. Gapinge, near Veere, Zeeland, the Netherlands, April 1969.

Type of find: Hoard.

Date of deposit: 1550.

Contents: 289 AR, 1 AV.

Description: 1 American coin:
  Spanish colonies, Charles and Johanna, 2 reales, México, assayer L
  The Mexican coin is the coin that closes the hoard (assayer L began work in 1548), which is the coin that had to travel furthest from its mint. If the Mexican coin is excluded from consideration, the hoard closes with coins of 1543.

Bibliography: Van Gelder 1969–70.

A3. Groede, Zeeuws-Vlaanderen, Zeeland, the Netherlands, 1943.

Type of find: Hoard.

Date of deposit: 1572.

Contents: Ca. 200 AR, AV, of which Van Gelder saw 48 AR and 4 AV.

Description:
  1 American coin:
  Spanish colonies, Charles and Johanna, 4 reales, México, assayer G, with water

Bibliography: Van Gelder 1964a.

A4. El Arahal, Sevilla Province, Spain, June 1972.

Type of find: Hoard.

Date of deposit: Ca. 1575.

Contents: 338 AR.

Description:
  53 American coins:
  Spanish colonies, Charles and Johanna, reales, México (3)
  Spanish colonies, Charles and Johanna, 2 reales, México (32)
  Spanish colonies, Charles and Johanna, 4 reales, México (18)

Disposition: Museo Arqueológico Hispalense.

Bibliography: Fernández-Chicarro 1972.
  Coin Hoards 2 (1976): 146 (no. 574).

A5. Herpen, near Ravenstein, Noord-Brabant, the Netherlands, early 1969.
Type of find: Hoard.
Date of deposit: 1582.
Contents: 12 AR, 4 AV.
Description:
　1 American coin:
　Spanish colonies, Charles and Johanna, 2 reales, México, assayer L
Bibliography: Van Gelder 1969–70b.

A6. Nieuport, Belgium, October 1952.
Type of find: Hoard.
Date of deposit: 1582.
Container: Purse.
Contents: 206 AR, 53 AV.
Description:
　1 American coin:
　Spanish colonies, 2 reales, México
　Naster numbers each coin in the hoard; the Mexican coin was number 230.
Bibliography: Naster 1953.

A7. Bolsward, Friesland, the Netherlands, 1952.
Type of find: Hoard.
Date of deposit: 1583–84.
Contents: 357 AR.
Description:
　1 American coin:
　Spanish colonies, Philip II, 4 reales, México
Bibliography: Muntvondsten 1952.

A8. Shoals of Judaea, Bassas da India, between Mozambique and Madagascar, 1977.
Type of find: Shipwreck.
Ship: Santiago (a Portuguese ship).
Sank: August 19, 1585.
Contents: 3,000 AR.
Description: Many silver cobs of both Spain and Spanish America have been recovered, some rare.
The American coins included:
Spanish colonies, Philip II, 4 reales, México, assayer O
Spanish colonies, 8 reales, México
Spanish colonies, 4 reales, Panama, assayer Xo (2)
Spanish colonies, 4 reales, Panama, assayer Bo (2)
Spanish colonies, 4 reales, Lima, assayer R
Spanish colonies, 8 reales, Lima
Disposition: The ship was relocated by Ernest Erich Klaar in 1977 and salvaged in 1984 by Paul Valentine, Stephen Valentine and Tubby Melidonis.
Bibliography: Pickford 1994, 144, 178; Ponterio 1995, lots 866–67; Ponterio 1996b, lots 1158–63; Proctor 2005, 148–49, 154, 158; Sebring 1986, 120–21; Sedwick and Sedwick 2007, 152–53 (Sedwick 3).

A9. Southeast of Stromboli Reef, Blasket Sound, County Kerry, Ireland, September 1967.
Type of find: Shipwreck.
Ship: Santa Maria de la Rosa, one of the ships of the Armada. Thompson, however, thinks the ship has been misidentified, and it actually is *Nuestra Señora de la Rosa*, or possibly *Nuestra Señora del Rosario*.
Sank: September 21, 1588.
Contents: 1 AR, 1 AV.
Description:
　1 American coin:
　Spanish colonies, Philip II, 4 reales, México
Bibliography: McDonald 1974, 35–44; Pickford 1994, 171; Potter 1972, 325, 333–37; Thompson 1970, 6; Wignall 1982, 45–75.

A10. Port na Spaniagh, near Port Ballintrae, County Antrim, Northern Ireland, United Kingdom, June-September 1968 and 1969.

Type of find: Shipwreck.

Ship: Girona, a galleon of the Spanish Armada.

Sank: October 26, 1588.

Contents: 122 AE, 789 AR, 414 AV.

Description:

10–11 American coins:

Spanish colonies, Philip II, 2 reales, México, assayer O

Spanish colonies, Charles and Johanna, 4 reales, México, assayer O

Spanish colonies, Charles and Johanna, 4 reales, México, with water

Spanish colonies, Philip II, 4 reales, México

Spanish colonies, Philip II, 8 reales, México (2)

Spanish colonies, Philip II, 8 reales, Lima, assayer oD (4)

May include a fragment of: Spanish colonies, 4 reales, Santo Domingo

Over three quarters of the total derive from most, if not all, of the mints operating in Spain in the third quarter of the 16th century. Seville is most heavily represented. Also present are coins of México, Peru, Naples and Sicily, Portugal and Genoa. The coins were issued by Ferdinand and Isabella, Charles and Johanna, and Philip II.

Disposition: Purchased by the Ulster Museum, Belfast, Northern Ireland, United Kingdom.

Bibliography: Flanagan 1988; McDonald 1974, 44–49; Potter 1972, 322–23, 327–33; Seaby 1972; Sebring 1976, 25–26; Sténuit 1969; Sténuit 1971; Thompson 1970, 6.

"Belfast Museum Seeks Funds to Buy Treasure," *Coin World*, October 25, 1972.

Coin Hoards 1 (1975): 99 (no. 385).

A11. Haanrade, near Kerkrade, Limburg, the Netherlands, 1943.

Type of find: Hoard.

Date of deposit: 1588.

Container: Pot.

Contents: 39 AR.

Description:

1 American coin:

Spanish colonies, Charles and Johanna, 2 reales, México, with water

Disposition: In 1946 the owner placed the hoard on loan at the Museum Ehrenstein in Kerkrade.

Bibliography: Sprenger 1968.

A12. Kerhostin, Saint-Pierre de Quiberon, Département Morbihan, Brittany, France, April 1975.

Type of find: Hoard.

Date of deposit: 1590.

Container: Gray pot.

Contents: 624 AR.

Description:

194 American coins:

Spanish colonies, Charles and Johanna, Santo Domingo

Spanish colonies, Charles and Johanna, México (77)

Spanish colonies, Philip II, México (114)

Spanish colonies, Philip II, Lima

Spanish colonies, Philip II, Potosí

It is not clear how the denominations break down among the individual mints, but within the entire hoard the denominations break down: 2 reales (272); 4 reales (258); 8 reales (94).

The hoard is thought to be connected to the occupation of Brittany by Spanish troops under Don Juan de l'Aguila in October 1590. The Spanish troops did not withdraw from Brittany until 1598.

Disposition: Found in a pot in front of a fireplace by a worker doing repair work in a house. This house may not be the actual find spot; it is possible that the finder may have moved it from one house to another.

Bibliography: André and Dhénin 1975. "Archéologie: Monnaies de Roi. Plus de 700 pièces anciennes mises au jour en Bretagne," *Le Figaro* (Paris), 13/14 September 1975, 22. *Coin Hoards* 2 (1976): 133 (no. 513).

A13. Culemborg, Gelderland, the Netherlands, October 1952.

Type of find: Hoard.

Date of deposit: 1596.

Contents: 110 AR.

Description:
5 or 6 American coins:
Spanish colonies, Philip II, 8 reales, México (3)
Spanish colonies, Philip II, 8 reales, Potosí (2)
Spanish colonies, Philip II, 8 reales, unidentified

Bibliography: Van Gelder 1952.

A14. Niedersachsen, Germany, near the Dutch border, 1960.

Type of find: Hoard.

Date of deposit: 1597.

Contents: 21 AR.

Description:
All coins but one were from Dutch or German mints.
1 American coin:
Spanish colonies, Philip II, 4 reales, México, assayer F

Bibliography: Vinkenborg 1961.

A15. Val di Non (Trentino), near Cles, Italy, 1998.

Type of find: Single find.

Contents: 1 AR.

Description: Spanish colonies, Philip II, real, México

Bibliography: Kleeberg and Bernardelli 1998, 377 n 30.

A16. Formentera, Balearic Islands, Spain, 1930s.

Type of find: Hoard.

Date of deposit: 1600.

Contents: AR 6+, AV 100+.

Description:
3 American coins:
Spanish colonies, Philip II, 4 reales, México (3)

Disposition: Dispersed. The above seen in a private collection, 1975.

Bibliography: *Coin Hoards* 2 (1976): 146 (no. 575).

A17. Gazteluberri, near Cegama, Guipúzcoa Province, Basque country, Spain, April 1960.

Type of find: Hoard.

Date of deposit: 1598.

Contents: 44 AR, 9 AV.

Description:
20 American coins:
Spanish colonies, Philip II, 4 reales, México, NDA
Spanish colonies, Philip II, 8 reales, México (14): assayer F (10); NDA (4)
Spanish colonies, Philip II, 4 reales, Potosí, assayer B
Spanish colonies, Philip II, 8 reales, Potosí (4): assayer A; assayer B; assayer D (2)

Bibliography: de Navascués 1967.

A18. Lleida, Lleida Province, Spain, 1946.

Type of find: Single find.

Contents: 1 AR.

Description: Spanish colonies, Philip II, real?, México

Bibliography: Mateu 1971, 196 (Mateu 1343).

A19. Fortune Island, the Philippines, January-May 1992 and January-April 1993.

Type of find: Shipwreck.

Ship: San Diego.

Sank: December 14, 1600.

Contents: 3 AE, 400 AR, 1 AV.

Description:

400 American coins:

Spanish colonies, reales, México: assayer F; assayer O

Spanish colonies, 2 reales, México, assayer F

Spanish colonies, 4 reales, México, assayer F

Spanish colonies, 8 reales, México, assayer F

Spanish colonies, 8 reales, Potosí, assayer B

Bibliography: Dhénin and Thierry 1996.

A20. Sneek, Friesland, the Netherlands, June 1947.

Type of find: Hoard.

Date of deposit: 1604.

Container: Pot.

Contents: 147 AR.

Description:

40 coins were from Dutch, French, English and Italian mints. 107 were from Spanish mints, including the following 52 American coins:

Spanish colonies, Philip II, 2 reales, México, assayer F (3)

Spanish colonies, 4 reales, México (19): Philip II, assayer O (2); Philip II or III, assayer F (8); Philip III, assayer F (3); Philip III, assayer D (2); Philip II or III, NDA (4)

Spanish colonies, 8 reales, México (14): Philip II, assayer F (2); Philip II or III, assayer F (9); Philip III, NDA (3)

Spanish colonies, Philip II, 2 reales, Potosí, A

Spanish colonies, Philip II, 4 reales, Potosí, assayer B

Spanish colonies, 8 reales, Potosí (12): Philip II, assayer A; Philip II, assayer B (3); Philip II, assayer C; Philip II, assayer R (3); Philip III, assayer R (4)

Spanish colonies, Philip II or III, 2 reales, unidentified American mint (2)

Disposition: Fries Scheepvaart Museum, Sneek (including the pot); some specimens in 1954 were on display in the town hall of Sneek.

Bibliography: Van Kuyk 1946–47 (description of the European coins); Van Gelder 1954 (description of the American coins).

A21. Anreppen, Detmold, Nordrhein-Westfalen, Germany, March 1995.

Type of find: Archaeological excavation of a Roman military camp.

Date of deposit: 1604 (this is the likeliest date of deposit; in this year Spanish mercenaries plundered the Detmold region and killed many inhabitants).

Contents: 1 AR.

Description: Spanish colonies, Charles and Johanna, 2 reales, México, assayer O [1564–72]

Bibliography: Peter Ilisch, letter to John M. Kleeberg, March 13, 1995.

A22. Oud-Beijerland, Zuid-Holland, the Netherlands, 1980.

Type of find: Hoard.

Date of deposit: 1605.

Container: Clay jug marked with the year 1585.

Contents: 167 AR, 24 AV.

Description: There are supposed to be 31 or 32 American coins in the hoard, but only 29 have been cataloged:

Spanish colonies, Philip II, real, México, assayer O

Spanish colonies, 2 reales, México (4): Philip II, assayer F (2); Philip II or III, assayer F; Philip III, assayer F

Spanish colonies, 4 reales, México (7): Philip

II, assayer F (4); Philip II, assayer O; Philip II or III, assayer F; Philip III, assayer F

Spanish colonies, 8 reales, México (9): Philip II, assayer F (8); Philip II, assayer O

Spanish colonies, Philip II, 4 reales, Lima, assayer D

Spanish colonies, Philip II, 2 reales, Potosí, assayer B

Spanish colonies, 4 reales, Potosí (3): Philip II, assayer B; Philip II, assayer L; Philip II, assayer R

Spanish colonies, Philip II, 8 reales, Potosí, assayer B (3)

Disposition: Found by a metal detectorist. Scheduled to be auctioned by Coin Investment B. V., The Hague, the Netherlands, No. 19, November 21, 1983, but withdrawn before the auction.

Bibliography: Bijkerk 1984; Dym 1984.

A23. St.-Martin-de-Beauville, Lot-et-Garonne, France, November 1970.

Type of find: Hoard.
Date of deposit: 1605.
Container: Pot.
Contents: 366 BI, 46 AR.
Description:

2 American coins:
Spanish colonies, Charles and Johanna, real, México
Spanish colonies, Philip II, real, México

Disposition: Bibliothèque National, Paris, (56)
Bibliography: Duplessy 1978.
Coin Hoards 6 (1981): 154–55 (no. 426).

A24. Wilkowo, Reszel Commune, Olsztyn Province, Poland, 1841.

Type of find: Hoard.
Date of deposit: 1607.
Contents: 1,160 AR, 4 AV.
Description:

2 American coins:
Spanish colonies, Philip III, 8 reales, México (2)

Disposition: Berliner Münzkabinett(?) (31 AR and 4 AV).

Bibliography: Kluge 1978, 96–97 (Kluge 4); Męclewska and Mikołajczyk 1983, 81–82 (Męclewska and Mikołajczyk 262); Mikołajczyk 1984, 217 (Mikołajczyk 1).

A25. Near Sevilla?, Sevilla Province, Spain, May 2003.

Type of find: Hoard.
Date of deposit: 1609.
Contents: 269 AR.
Description: Of the 162 coins identifiable by mint, 37 were American coins:

Spanish colonies, 2 reales, México (7): 1607F; assayer F (6)

Spanish colonies, 4 reales, México (19): assayer O (5); assayer F (13); assayer A

Spanish colonies, 8 reales, México, assayer F (10)

Spanish colonies, 4 reales, Potosí, assayer B

A coin described as a 2 reales from México, 1597F, has been assumed to be a misreading for 1607F.

This hoard included coins from Granada, Segovia, Seville, Toledo, and Valladolid, as well as México and Potosí. The largest quantity is from Seville (65). The last dated coin is 1607; however, the hoard does include a coin from México of assayer A, who commenced work in 1608. The later date of deposit is because the hoard is thought to have been buried during the uprising of the Moriscos.

Disposition: Auctioned by Münzzentrum-Rheinland, May 2003.

Bibliography: Münzzentrum-Rheinland 2003, lots 2393–2483.

A26. Near Toledo?, Toledo Province, Spain, July 1972.

Type of find: Hoard.

Date of deposit: 1613.

Contents: 82 AR.

Description:

24 American coins:

Spanish colonies, Philip II or III, 2 reales, México, assayer F

Spanish colonies, Philip II or III, 4 reales, México, assayer F (6)

Spanish colonies, Philip II or III, 8 reales, México, assayer F (2)

Spanish colonies, Philip IV, 4 reales, Potosí (4): assayer Q; assayer B (3)

Spanish colonies, Philip IV, 8 reales, Potosí (11): assayer Q (2); assayer R (4); assayer B (4); assayer S

This hoard included coins from the mints of Valladolid, Toledo, and Seville, as well as México and Potosí. The largest quantity was from Toledo (18), which may indicate the find spot.

Disposition: Auctioned by Sotheby's, London.

Bibliography: Sotheby's 1972, lots 115–38.

A27. Cis, Starogard Gdánski environs, Gdánsk Province, Poland, May 20, 1856.

Type of find: Hoard.

Date of deposit: 1613.

Contents: 3,383 AR, 9 AV.

Description:

1 American coin:

Spanish colonies, Philip III, real, México

Disposition: Berliner Münzkabinett.

Bibliography: Kluge 1979, 94–95 (Kluge 9); Męclewska and Mikołajczyk, 1983, 90–91 (Męclewska and Mikołajczyk 293); Mikołajczyk 1984, 217 (Mikołajczyk 2).

A28. Mauritius Island, Indian Ocean, 1979.

Type of find: Shipwreck.

Ship: Unknown Dutch merchantman.

Sank: 1615.

Contents: 1 AE, 1 AR.

Description:

1 American coin:

Spanish colonies, 8 reales, México, 1607

Photographs on file in the British Museum.

Bibliography: Coin Hoards 6 (1981): 125 (no. 362).

A29. Rill Cove, Kynance, Cornwall, England, United Kingdom, 1975.

Type of find: Shipwreck.

Ship: Called the Lizard silver wreck.

Sank: Ca. 1618.

Contents: 3,000 AR.

Description:

Spanish colonies, 2 reales, México

Spanish colonies, 4 reales, México

Spanish colonies, 8 reales, México, assayer F (Sebring)

Spanish colonies, 8 reales, Potosí

All the coins recovered are cobs of the denominations of 2, 4, and 8 reales. Most cobs recovered are from México, but the wreck also includes some from Potosí and from mainland Spanish mints. Discovered by Ken Simpson and Mike Hall.

Bibliography: Sebring 2004, lot 1623; Sedwick and Sedwick 2007, 153–54 (Sedwick 6); Simpson 1977.

A30. Mozambique, 2003.

Type of find: Shipwreck.

Ship: São José.

Sank: July 22, 1622.

Contents: 20,000 AR.

Description:

Spanish colonies, 4 reales, México

Spanish colonies, 8 reales, México

Spanish colonies, 4 reales, Lima

Spanish colonies, 8 reales, Lima
Spanish colonies, 4 reales, Potosí
Spanish colonies, 8 reales, Potosí

Disposition: Relocated by Arqueonautas in 2003, who, as of 2007, planned to sell the coins as soon as recovery and conservation were complete.

Bibliography: Sedwick and Sedwick 2007, 157–58 (Sedwick 11).

A31. Ooselt, near Doetinchem, Gelderland, the Netherlands, before 1948.

Type of find: Hoard.
Date of deposit: 1622.
Container: Pot.
Contents: 98 AR.
Description:
36 American coins:
Spanish colonies, 4 reales, México (12): 1609F; 1611; NDA (10)
Spanish colonies, Philip II, 8 reales, México (11): assayer F; NDA (10)
Spanish colonies, Philip III, 8 reales, México, assayer F
Spanish colonies, 2 reales, Potosí, NDA
Spanish colonies, Philip II, 8 reales, Potosí (8): assayers B (4); assayer R (2); NDA (2)
Spanish colonies, Philip III, 8 reales, Potosí (2): assayer R; assayer Q
Spanish colonies, real, mint unknown, NDA

Disposition: Acquired before 1948 by Jacques Schulman.
Bibliography: Schulman 1949.

A32. Ulvenhout, near Nieuw-Ginneken, Noord-Brabant, the Netherlands, fall 1975.

Type of find: Hoard.
Date of deposit: 1625.
Container: Pot.
Contents: 36 AR.
Description:
1 American coin:
Spanish colonies, Philip III, 8 reales, México, assayer F

Bibliography: Vermeulen 1975–77.

A33. The Needles, Isle of Wight, Hampshire, England, June 1979.

Type of find: Shipwreck.
Ship: Dutch East India Company ship *Campen*.
Sank: October 1627.
Contents: 8,000 AR.
Description:
Included a few American cobs:
Spanish colonies, 8 reales, México (20)
Spanish colonies, 8 reales, Potosí (20)
Most of the coins recovered were Dutch lion daalders, but a few cobs were recovered too.

Disposition: W. H. Lane & Son, Penzance, England, United Kingdom, Auction, June 1, 1983.
Bibliography: Sedwick and Sedwick 2007, 158 (Sedwick 12).

A34. Abrolhos Islands, Western Australia, Australia, 1963, 1973.

Type of find: Shipwreck.
Ship: The Dutch East India Company ship *Batavia*, from Texel, Noord-Holland, the Netherlands, en route to Batavia, Java, Indonesia.
Sank: June 4, 1629.
Contents: 10,000 AR.
Description:
4 American coins:
Spanish colonies, 8 reales, México (4)

Disposition: Excavated by Hugh Edwards and Max Cramer. Western Australia Museum. However, 11 coins illicitly leaked out and were sold in a Stack's auction, March 1969.

Bibliography: Sebring 1982; Sedwick and Sedwick 2007, 159–61 (Sedwick 14); Wilson 1964, 191–92.

A35. Mombasa, Kenya, 1977.
Type of find: Hoard.
Date of deposit: 1631.
Contents: Ca. 12 AR.
Description:
  Spanish colonies, 4 reales, México (2)
  Spanish colonies, Philip II or Philip III, 8 reales, México, assayer F
  Spanish colonies, 8 reales, México (2)
  Spanish colonies, unidentified coins (7)
Disposition: Fort Jesus Museum in Mombasa (1).
Bibliography: Sassoon 1978 (*Coin Hoards* 5: 350).

A36. Wijchen, Gelderland, the Netherlands, 1975.
Type of find: Hoard.
Date of deposit: 1632.
Container: Pot.
Contents: 28 AR.
Description:
  2 American coins:
  Spanish colonies, Philip II, 8 reales, Potosí (2): assayer B; NDA
Bibliography: Van Gelder 1975–77.
  Coin Hoards 7 (1985): 405 (no. 663).

A37. Fusina (Venezia) embankments, Veneto, Italy, 1994.
Type of find: Single find.
Contents: 1 AR.
Description: Spanish colonies, 8 reales, Potosí
Disposition: Found in excavations in the lagoon; another Spanish colonies coin possibly came from the same area.

Bibliography: Asolati and Crisfulli 1994, 195; Kleeberg and Bernardelli 1998, 377n30.

A38. Gambellara, Veneto, Italy, 1913.
Type of find: Hoard.
Date of deposit: 1633.
Contents: 55 AR.
Description:
  8 American coins:
  Spanish colonies, real, México, assayer D
  Spanish colonies, 2 reales, México, assayer F
  Spanish colonies, 8 reales, México, assayer D (2)
  Spanish colonies, 8 reales, Cartagena, assayer E
  Spanish colonies, 8 reales, Potosí (3): assayer R; assayer P; assayer T
Bibliography: Kleeberg and Bernardelli 1998.

A39. Skołobow, Czerwonoarmeijsk District, Zhytomyr Province, Ukraine, 1970.
Type of find: Hoard.
Date of deposit: 1633.
Contents: 1,000 AR.
Description: Spanish colonies, 4 reales, México
  The publications attribute this coin to the mint of Zacatecas; but the mint of Zacatecas only commenced work in 1810.
Bibliography: Mikołajczyk 1978, 42–43 (Mikołajczyk 63); Mikołajczyk 1984, 218 (Mikołajczyk 6).

A40. Ipatevsky Alley, site of a former market in ancient Kitaï-gorod in the old center of Moscow, Russia, 1970, and at Kolomenskoy along the Moscow River, Moscow, Russia, summer 1972.
Type of find: Hoard.
Date of deposit: 1630s.
Container: Copper pot.
Contents: 4,607 AR.

Description:
  Spanish colonies, 2 reales, México
  Spanish colonies, 4 reales, México
  Spanish colonies, 8 reales, México
  The hoard contained coins of Spain and the Spanish colonies, chiefly from México, but also many from Segovia. The denominations were 2 reales, 4 reales, 8 reales; the rulers went from Ferdinand and Isabella to Philip IV. Cancio suggests that the money was sent to Russia to pay for naval stores that were used to construct ships in Havana, Cuba.

Disposition: The hoard was found in two parcels. The first portion was found in a copper pot at a depth of 6 meters in Ipatevsky Alley in 1970; it consisted of 3,398 coins. The second portion was found in a load of fill along the Moscow River in the summer of 1972; it consisted of 1,209 coins. Acquired by the Muzee Istorii i Rekonstruktsii, Moscow, Russia.

Bibliography: Cancio 1990; Veksler and Mel'nikova 1973 142–44, 202–3 (Hoard number 30) (only refers to the 1970 find).

A41. Manila, the Philippines, August 1957.

Type of find: Hoard.
Date of deposit: 1634.
Contents: 34 AR.
Description:
  Spanish colonies, 8 reales, México, assayers D and P (3)
  Spanish colonies, 8 reales, México, 1630D
  Assayer P commenced work in 1634, providing a terminus post quem.
Bibliography: De Jesus 1965.

A42. Saint-Jean-lez-Saint-Nicolas, Belgium, June 1931.

Type of find: Hoard.
Date of deposit: 1635.
Container: Gray pot.
Contents: 11 AR, 5 AV.
Description:
  3 American coins:
  Spanish colonies, silver coins (2)
  Spanish colonies, gold coins (1)
  The coins were found while demolishing an old stable.
Bibliography: Baillion 1931.

A43. Pange, Moselle, France, 1850.

Type of find: Hoard.
Date of deposit: 1638.
Contents: 85 AR.
Description:
  71 American coins:
  Spanish colonies, 4 reales, México (3)
  Spanish colonies, 8 reales, México (16): assayer F (3); assayer D (4); NDA (9)
  Spanish colonies, 8 reales, Bogotá (3): assayer P; assayer E (2)
  Spanish colonies, 4 reales, Potosí (2)
  Spanish colonies, 8 reales, Potosí (46): assayer B (3); assayer Q; assayer R; assayer T (18); assayer P (5); NDA (18)
  Spanish colonies, 8 reales, Potosí, counterfeit
  Probably connected to the reconquest of the Duchy of Lorraine by Duke Charles IV at the head of Spanish troops in 1638.

Disposition: In the early nineteenth century, the Marquis de Pange used a log from an old oak downed in a storm to form a mantelpiece for his fireplace. This mantelpiece broke open suddenly, almost as if it were exploding, and heavy silver coins dropped out. Still owned in 1974 by the family of the Marquis de Pange.

Bibliography: Dhénin 1998.

A44. Manila?, the Philippines, October 1954.

Type of find: Hoard.
Date of deposit: 1639.
Contents: 48 AR.

Description:
  Spanish colonies, real, México, 1639P
  Spanish colonies, 4 reales, México, 1639P (21)
  Spanish colonies, 8 reales, México, 1639P (26)
Bibliography: De Jesus 1955.

A45. Budgoszcza, Mahilyow Province, Belarus, 1900.
Type of find: Hoard.
Date of deposit: 1643.
Contents: 15 AR.
Description:
  1 American coin:
  Spanish colonies, 4 reales, México, clipped
Bibliography: Mikołajczyk 1984, 218 (Mikołajczyk 10).

A46. Barton, Preston, Lancashire, England, United Kingdom, November 1967.
Type of find: Hoard.
Date of deposit: 1643–44.
Contents: 5 AR.
Description:
  1 American coin:
  Spanish colonies, 8 reales
  This 8 reales could be from the Spanish mainland, but Besley suggests that it is American; the only detailed description of this hoard refers to the coin as a "piece of eight."
Disposition: Apparently given to the Harris Museum, Preston, Lancashire, England, United Kingdom.
Bibliography: Besly 1987, 64, 87 (Besly E3). "A 17th Century Find from Barton, Lancs.," *Seaby's Coin and Medal Bulletin* 1968, no. 5 (whole no. 597) (May): 177.

A47. Anhai Commune, Jinjiang County, Fujian Province, China, 1971.
Type of find: Hoard.

Date of deposit: 1644.
Container: Black earthenware pot.
Contents: 10 AR.
Description: Spanish colonies, 8 reales, México (10): 1644P; 164[-]P; assayer P (8)
Bibliography: *Coin Hoards* 3 (1977): 180 (no. 503.1).

A48. Echternach, Luxembourg, May 1950.
Type of find: Hoard.
Date of deposit: Pieces assembled 1635–36; actual concealment 1645.
Contents: 2,453 BI, AR.
Description:
  1 American coin:
  Spanish colonies, Philip II, 2 reales, México, NDA (catalog number A 43, 1977)
Disposition: Cabinet des Médailles du Musée d'Histoire et d'Art à Luxembourg.
Bibliography: Kleeberg 1993–94, 257; Weiller 1975, 378; Weiller 1996, 39.

A49. Kent?, England, United Kingdom, 1957.
Type of find: Hoard. Called "Bruce Binney's Hoard."
Date of deposit: 1645–47.
Contents: 62 AR.
Description:
  2 American coins:
  Spanish colonies, Philip IV, 8 reales, México
  Spanish colonies, Philip IV, 8 reales, Potosí
Bibliography: Besly 1987, 95 (Besly H5); Kent 1957.

A50. Village of the Guanqiao commune, Nanan County, Fujian Province, China, 1975.
Type of find: Hoard.
Date of deposit: 1647.
Container: Earthenware pot.
Contents: 42+ AR, 4 silver bars.

Description:
   Spanish colonies, real, México, NDA (2)
   Spanish colonies, 2 reales, México, NDA
   Spanish colonies, 4 reales, México, NDA (2)
   Spanish colonies, 8 reales, México (4): assayer D; assayer D?; assayer P (2)
   Spanish colonies, 8 reales, Potosí (2): assayer TR; 1647T
   Spanish colonies, unidentified coins (30+)
Bibliography: Coin Hoards 3 (1977): 180–81 (no. 503.2).

A51. Schönberg chapel, Kehlen, Luxembourg, 1976–77.
Type of find: Hoard.
Date of deposit: 1649.
Contents: 10 AR, 2 AV, 1 gilt ring.
Description:
   1 American coin:
   Spanish colonies, Philip IV, 2 escudo, Bogotá (catalog number A 10, 2)
   The coin was originally cataloged as a coin of Philip II. Upon re-cataloging the piece as a coin of Philip IV, the hoard fits together more tightly, with dates ranging from 1612–28 to 1649.
Disposition: 1982 to Cabinet des Médailles du Musée d'Histoire et d'Art à Luxembourg.
Bibliography: Kleeberg 1993–94, 257; Weiller 1989, 54; Weiller 1996, 39.

A52. Tréport, Arrondissement Dieppe, Seine-Maritime, France, April 8, 1964.
Type of find: Hoard.
Date of deposit: 1649–50.
Contents: 423 AR.
Description:
   1 American coin:
   Spanish colonies, Charles and Joan, México, 2 reales, assayer G, with water
Disposition: Bibliothèque National, Paris (25).
Bibliography: Duplessy 1979.
   Coin Hoards 6 (1981): 155–56 (no. 427).

A53. Off San Francisco, on the coast of Santiago, Cape Verde Islands, 2000.
Type of find: Shipwreck.
Ship: Unknown ship of Portuguese or Spanish origin.
Sank: Ca. 1650.
Contents: 51 AR.
Description:
   Spanish colonies, 8 reales, México (29): 1645P; assayer P (17); NDA (11)
   Spanish colonies, real, Potosí
   Spanish colonies, 4 reales, Potosí, 1646
   Spanish colonies, 8 reales, Potosí (20): assayer T (4); assayer V; NDA (15)
Bibliography: Sedwick and Sedwick 2007, 163–64 (Sedwick 18); Sotheby's 2000, lots 583–87.

A54. North Africa, November 2003.
Type of find: Hoard.
Date of deposit: Ca. 1650.
Contents: 2 AR.
Description: Spanish colonies, 8 reales, México, cob (2)
Bibliography: Jonathan Kern, Advertisement, Coin World, November 10, 2003, 47.
   Jonathan Kern, Advertisement, Coin World, April 26, 2004, 30.

A55. Sevastopol, Crimea, Ukraine, 1862.
Type of find: Hoard.
Date of deposit: Ca. 1650.
Contents: 6 AR.
Description: Spanish colonies, 8 reales, México (6)
Bibliography: Kotlar 1975, 285 (Kotlar 1191); Mikołajczyk 1984, 220 (Mikołajczyk 22).

A56. Lejas Kundzin, Latvia, 1914.
Type of find: Hoard.
Date of deposit: Ca. 1650.
Contents: 239 AR.
Description:
    4 American coins:
    Spanish colonies, 2 reales, México (3)
    Spanish colonies, 4 reales, México
Bibliography: Mikołajczyk 1984, 220 (Mikołajczyk 23).

A57. Loenen, Utrecht, the Netherlands, 1961.
Type of find: Hoard.
Date of deposit: 1651.
Container: Pot.
Contents: 130 AR.
Description:
    1 American coin:
    Spanish colonies, Philip II or III, 2 reales, México
Bibliography: Schulman 1961.

A58. Domont, Seine-et-Oise, France, November 1997.
Type of find: Hoard. Called the "Adrien Hoard," after its finder, Adrien Meszaros, then aged 2.
Date of deposit: 1651.
Contents: 425 AR.
Description:
    4 American coins:
    Spanish colonies, 2 reales, México, 1631
    Spanish colonies, 4 reales, Potosí, 1648Z/TR
    Spanish colonies, 8 reales, Potosí (2): assayer T; 1646V
    Thought to have been buried during the military movements of the Fronde.
Disposition: Sold through a mail bid sale, June 10, 1999.
Bibliography: Comptoir Général Financier 1999; Le Livre du Trésor d'Adrien 1998.

A59. Island of Yell, Shetland, Scotland, United Kingdom, May 19–July 31, 1971.
Type of find: Shipwreck.
Ship: Dutch East India Company ship *Lastdrager*, which left Texel, Noord-Holland, Netherland, February 9, 1653, en route to Batavia (now Jakarta), Java, Indonesia.
Sank: March 2, 1653.
Contents: 500+ AR (only 407 coins were identifiable).
Description:
    53 American coins:
    Spanish colonies, 4 reales (3)
    Spanish colonies, 8 reales, México (4)
    Spanish colonies, 8 reales, American mint other than México (4)
    Spanish colonies, too corroded for further identification (42)
Bibliography: Sténuit 1974a; Sténuit 1974b, 26–27, 34; Sténuit 1977.

A60. Outside the New Gate of Quanzhou, Fujian Province, China, January 1975.
Type of find: Hoard.
Date of deposit: 1654.
Contents: 38 AR.
Description:
    Spanish colonies, reales, México, 1654P (2)
    Spanish colonies, 2 reales, México, 1654P (6)
    Spanish colonies, 4 reales, México, 1654P (7)
    Spanish colonies, 8 reales, México, 1654P (23)
Bibliography: *Coin Hoards* 3 (1977): 182–83 (no. 503.5). *Coin Hoards* 2 (1976): 146.

A61. North of Perth, Western Australia, Australia, 1957–73.
Type of find: Shipwreck.
Ship: Dutch East India Company ship *Vergulde Draeke*.

Sank: April 28, 1656.

Contents: 19,100 AR, of which only 10,678 AR were identifiable.

Description:

4,940 American coins:

Spanish colonies, reales, México (6)

Spanish colonies, 2 reales, México (1,171): assayer O (2); assayer F; assayer D; assayer P; 164[-]P; 1648P; 1649P; 1651P; 1652P; 1653P; 1654P; NDA (1,159)

Spanish colonies, 4 reales, México (1,831): assayer D (3); 160[-]A; 16[-]0D, with chopmark inside oblong (Siam mark?); assayer F; 1649P; 1651P; 1652P; 1653/2P; 1653P; 1654P; NDA (1,809)

Spanish colonies, 8 reales, México, (5,798): assayer O; assayer F; 1608A/F; 1609A; 1610F; 1620D; 162[-]D; assayer D (2); 1640P; 1641P; 1642P; 1646P; 1647P; 1648P; 1649P; 1650P; 1651P; 1652P; 1653P; 1654P (2); assayer P, counterstamped with the golden fleece of Antwerp; NDA (5,775)

Spanish colonies, 2 reales Bogotá (2): assayer R [ca. 1647]; 1653R

Spanish colonies, 4 reales, Bogotá (8): 1645R; 1651R; 1652PoR; 1653PoM; NDA (4)

Spanish colonies, 8 reales, Bogotá (29): shield type, assayer R; 1651PoRM; 1652PoRM; 1653PoRS; NDA (25)

Spanish colonies, 2 reales, Potosí (7): 164[-]R; 1652E (McLean Type IV, obverse B); NDA (5)

Spanish colonies, 4 reales, Potosí (23): 1652E (McLean Type IV, obverse A); 1652E (McLean Type IV, reverse B); 1652E (McLean Type VII, obverse B); 1653E; 1654E; NDA (18)

Spanish colonies, 8 reales, Potosí (271): assayer T with transposed castles and lions on obverse and reverse (dyslexic mint worker)[1619–22] (miscatalogued as assayer R or B, catalog no. PR 1857); assayer O; 1652E (McLean Type IV, obverse A) (2); 1652E (McLean Type V, obverse A); 1652E (McLean Type V, obverse B); 1652E (McLean Type VIII, obverse B); [-]61, but shield type (possibly assayer T [1619–22] with dyslexic mint worker), counterstamped crown; NDA (263)

The following listing of coins from the Vergulde Draek combines those auctioned by Schulman in 1969 and by Downey in 1986:

Spanish colonies, Philip II, 2 reales, México (2): assayer O; assayer F

Spanish colonies, 4 reales, México, 1652P

Spanish colonies, 8 reales, México (14): 1608A; ca. 1612F; 1649P (2); 1650P; 1652P (4); 1653P (2); 1654P (3)

Spanish colonies, 8 reales, Bogotá (2): ca. 1629; 1651 PRMS

Spanish colonies, 4 reales, Potosí, 1653E

Spanish colonies, 8 reales, Potosí (6): 1652E (3); 1653E (3)

Disposition: Western Australian Museum (7,194); in private hands (11,906). Hans Schulman auction, 1969 (12); P. J. Downey auction, 1986 (28).

Bibliography: Green 1973; Downey 1986; Schulman 1969, lots 891–902; Wilson 1964, 191–95; Wilson 1977.

A62. Fulbeck Hall, Lincolnshire, England, United Kingdom, 2002.

Date of deposit: 1659.

Container: Seventeenth century silver box for counters.

Type of find: Hoard.

Contents: 19 AR.

Description: English colonies, Maryland, Lord Baltimore, sixpences, [1658–59] (19)

Included one example of the error with no P in MULTIPLACIMINI. This coin was bought at the auction by Stack's. The grade of the coins varied from About Fine to Extremely Fine on British grading standards; judging by the photographs, this is a very conservative grade by United States standards. In the United States, the coins would grade AU to Mint State.

Disposition: Morton & Eden Auction, November 2002; all examples were bought by United States buyers, notably Stack's and Anthony J. Terranova.

Bibliography: John Andrew, "Hoard of 19 Baltimore sixpence tops Morton & Eden's Nov. 13–14 auction," *Coin World*, January 13, 2003, 56.

A63. Near Bow Church, London, England, United Kingdom, February 1942.

Type of find: Hoard.

Date of deposit: 1660s.

Contents: 20+ AR.

Description:

A mass of clippings from English shillings of James I and Charles I.
1 American coin:
English colonies, Massachusetts, clipping from an Oak Tree shilling, Noe 6

Disposition: Sold by Burdette G. Johnson to the American Numismatic Society, February 11, 1942; item number 1942.50.1.

Bibliography: Burdette G. Johnson coin invoice, February 11, 1942 (provided courtesy of Eric P. Newman).
American Numismatic Society, computerized catalog, www.numismatics.org.

A64. Brighstone Parish, Isle of Wight, Hampshire, England, United Kingdom, December 2004.

Type of find: Single find.

Contents: 1 AR.

Description: English colonies, Massachusetts, oak tree twopence, 1662, Noe 30 (Portable Antiquities Scheme Reference Number IOW-D80EF7)

Disposition: Found by a member of the Isle of Wight Metal Detecting Club. Consigned to auction with Triton in New York, January 2009.

Bibliography: Triton 2009, lot 1107.

A65. Zuid-Holland, the Netherlands, before 1968.

Type of find: Hoard.

Date of deposit: 1662.

Contents: 104 AR.

Description:

1 American coin:
Spanish colonies, Philip II, real, México, assayer O

Bibliography: Van Gelder 1968.

A66. Off Sicily, Italy, April 2004.

Type of find: Shipwreck.

Ship: Unknown.

Sank: Ca. 1667.

Contents: 300 AR.

Description:

Spanish colonies, 2 reales, México, 1663 (unlisted date)
Spanish colonies, 2 reales, México, 1630–65
Spanish colonies, 4 reales, México, 1630–65
Spanish colonies, 8 reales, México
Mostly Spanish cobs, but includes several Mexican cobs as well, including a number of rare dates. Emerged through the ancient coin trade.

Bibliography: Sedwick and Sedwick 2007, 168 (Sedwick 23).
Jonathan Kern, Advertisement, *Coin World*, April 26, 2004, 29.

A67. Harbor, Guadalquivir River, Sevilla, Sevilla Province, Spain, mid-1990s.

Type of find: Possibly a shipwreck.

Ship: Unknown.

Date of deposit: 1671.

Contents: 100 AR.

Description:
> Spanish colonies, 4 reales, Potosí
> Spanish colonies, 8 reales, Potosí
> The coins were found in Sevilla harbor while laying fiber optic cable. None of the coins are dated later than 1671. The coins are sometimes attributed to a wreck, the Señorita de Santa Cristina, which is said to have sunk in 1672 off Cadiz, but Sedwick can find no trace of this wreck or its salvage.

Bibliography: Sedwick and Sedwick 2007, 169 (Sedwick 25).

A68. Gortnaheltia, Newport, County Mayo, Ireland, early June 1945.

Type of find: Hoard.

Date of deposit: Early 1670s.

Contents: 6 AR.

Description:
> 1 American coin:
> Spanish colonies, 8 reales, Potosí, 1666E

Disposition: Found by Michael Lenehan. Donated to the Royal Irish Academy.

Bibliography: Kenny 1981.

A69. Gampola, Sri Lanka, July 1971.

Type of find: Hoard.

Date of deposit: 1674.

Contents: 17 AR.

Description:
> 1 American coin:
> Spanish colonies, probably Philip IV, real, México

Bibliography: Lowick 1977.

A70. Tenneville, Belgium, January 1958.

Type of find: Hoard.

Date of deposit: 1674.

Container: Small gray jar.

Contents: 216 AR, 8 AV.

Description:
> 1 American coin:
> Spanish colonies, 8 reales, Bogotá, PoRS, dated 1662 or 1667, counterstamped with the golden fleece of Antwerp
> The coins were found in the course of excavating the old church of Saint Gertrude at Tenneville. The article is accompanied by a photograph of the Bogotá coin, and of the container. It is cataloged as number 138 in the listing of the hoard.

Bibliography: Mertens and De Donder 1958.

A71. South side of the Anglesey Skerries, close to Holyhead, Wales, United Kingdom, mid-July 1971 and 1976.

Type of find: Shipwreck.

Ship: Mary.

Sank: March 25, 1675.

Contents: 2 AE, 271 AR.

Description:
> 1 American-related coin, 1 American coin:
> Ireland, St. Patrick farthing
> Spanish colonies, 8 reales, Potosí, 1621–24

Bibliography: Dolley and Warhurst 1977; McDonald 1974, 55–57.

Coin Hoards 4 (1978): 120 (no. 391).

A72. Churchquarter Townland, Dundonald, County Down, Northern Ireland, United Kingdom, August 23, 1928.

Type of find: Hoard.

Date of deposit: 1676.

Container: Old black sock.

Contents: 32 AR.

Description:
> 4 American coins:
> Spanish colonies, 8 reales, México (2): 1659P; 1665–70, assayer S
> Spanish colonies, 8 reales, Potosí, pre-1652 type
> Portuguese colonies, Brazil, 8 reales, Potosí,

1660E, with 600 reis counterstamp of 1663 (raising value 25%)

Also found with the coins was a gold posy ring of mid- or late seventeenth century date.

Disposition: Northern Ireland Museum of Finance.

Bibliography: Seaby 1960–61.

A73. Ballyvarley Townland, near Banbridge, County Down, Northern Ireland, United Kingdom, February 25, 1931.

Type of find: Hoard.

Date of deposit: 1677.

Container: Wooden box.

Contents: 20 AR.

Description:

3 American coins:

Spanish colonies, 2 reales, Potosí, 1656

Spanish colonies, 8 reales, Potosí (2): 163[-]; 1662

Disposition: Northern Ireland Museum of Finance. Placed on exhibit at Jordan's Castle, Ardglass, but stolen during the Second World War.

Bibliography: Seaby 1960–61.

A74. Indang, Cavite Province, the Philippines, July 1964.

Type of find: Hoard.

Date of deposit: 1677.

Container: Light gray stoneware jug of bluish tint of Chinese manufacture—late Ming or early Qing (i.e., ca. 1644).

Contents: 21 AR.

Description:

Spanish colonies, 8 reales, México, 1665P

Spanish colonies, 8 reales, México, assayers P, G, and L (20)

Since assayer L (Martin López) only commenced work in 1677, that date provides a terminus post quem for the deposit of the hoard.

Bibliography: De Jesus 1965.

A75. Off Cape Agulhas, the southernmost tip of Africa, near the Cape of Good Hope, South Africa, 1982.

Type of find: Shipwreck.

Ship: English East India Company ship *Johanna*.

Sank: June 8, 1682.

Contents: 23,000 AR.

Description:

Spanish colonies, 4 reales, México (7): 1679L (2); 1681L (5)

Spanish colonies, 8 reales México (23): 1655P; 1660P (2); 1668G; 1677G (2); 1680L (11); 1681L (5); Charles II (Sebring)

Spanish colonies, 8 reales, Potosí, 1664E

The recovery has mostly been of Mexican cobs of Philip IV and Charles II, 4 and 8 reales, dated 1679–81, in low grade.

Disposition: Found by a group of South African divers under the leadership of Gavin Clackworthy.

Bibliography: Ponterio 1993, lot 1932; Ponterio 1995, lots 841–45; Ponterio 1996a, lots 1054–68; Ponterio 1996b, lots 1133–40; Sebring 1986, 119; Sebring 2004, lot 1619; Sedwick and Sedwick 2007, 171–72 (Sedwick 28).

A76. Katwoude, near Monnikendam, Noord-Holland, the Netherlands, January 1964.

Type of find: Hoard.

Date of deposit: 1683.

Contents: 449 AR, 2 AV.

Description:

2 American coins:

Spanish colonies, Philip IV, 2 reales, México

Spanish colonies, 2 reales, Potosí, 1663E

Bibliography: Van Gelder 1964b.

A77. Lleida, Lleida Province, Spain, 1946.

Type of find: Single find.

Date of deposit: 1680s?

Contents: 1 AR.

Description:

Spanish colonies, 8 reales (cob)

Disposition: Seen in the possession of a merchant. It had been found in the city.

Bibliography: Mateu 1967, 56 (Mateu 1197).

A78. Polchówko, Puck Commune, Gdánsk Province, Poland, March 20, 1847.

Type of find: Hoard.

Date of deposit: 1686.

Contents: 3,440 AR.

Description:

1 American coin:

Spanish colonies, Philip III, 4 reales, México

Disposition: Berliner Münzkabinett (3,440 AR).

Bibliography: Kluge 1978, 904–5 (Kluge 20); Męclewska and Mikołajczyk 1991, 138–39 (Męclewska and Mikołajczyk 1195); Mikołajczyk 1984, 219 (Mikołajczyk 16).

A79. Billingsgate Dock, London, England, United Kingdom, 1995.

Type of find: Archaeological excavation.

Date of deposit: 1688.

Contents: 3 SN.

Description: English colonies, James II, 1/24 real for the American Plantations, 1688 (3)

Bibliography: Noël Hume 1995, 22.

A80. Aubel (Kreft), near Liège, Belgium, 1964.

Type of find: Hoard.

Date of deposit: June 1691.

Contents: 31 AR, 11 AV.

Description:

1 American coin:

Spanish colonies, Philip IV, 2 escudos, Bogotá

Disposition: Musée Curtius de Liège.

Bibliography: Dengis 1984.

A81. Enfield, London, England, United Kingdom, summer 1789.

Type of find: Single find.

Contents: 1 AE.

Description: England, elephant halfpenny, reading GOD PRESERVE LONDON

The coin had no diagonals in the central part of the cross, making it the variety Breen 186.

Disposition: Found while pulling down part of the old palace at Enfield.

Bibliography: "Enfield, June 26: Antient Knives, Forks and Spoons," *Gentleman's Magazine* 60, pt. 2, no. 1 (July 1790): 595 (the coin is illustrated on a fold out engraving facing page 596).

"The Elephant Halfpenny," *American Journal of Numismatics* 11, no. 4 (April 1877): 94.

A82. Oudekraal, South Africa, 1950s.

Type of find: Shipwreck.

Ship: Dutch East India Company ship *Huis te Kraaiestein* (or *Cruyenstein*).

Sank: May 26, 1698.

Contents: 1,000 AR.

Description:

Spanish colonies, Charles II, 8 reales, México

Bibliography: Sebring 2004, lot 1607; Sedwick and Sedwick 2007, 172 (Sedwick 29).

A83. Shishan Commune, Nanan County, Fujian Province, China, November 1972, March 1973, and 1975.

Type of find: Hoard.

Date of deposit: 1700.

Containers: 4 white glazed pots.

Contents: 100+ AR.

Description:

Spanish colonies, 4 reales, México, NDA (3)
Spanish colonies, 8 reales, México (12): 164[-]P; 1667G; assayer G (3); assayer L (4);

cut in half; NDA (2)

Spanish colonies, 4 or 8 reales, México, NDA (85)

Bibliography: *Coin Hoards* 3 (1977): 181–82 (no. 503.3).

A84. Plaza de San Juan, Lleida, Lleida Province, Spain, 1946.

Type of find: Hoard. Found during excavations.

Date of deposit: 1700.

Contents: 42 AR.

Description: Spanish colonies, Charles II, 8 reales, Potosí (42)

Bibliography: Mateu 1947–48, 83 (Mateu 319).

A85. Pasay, the Philippines, February 2005.

Type of find: Hoard.

Date of deposit: 1700.

Container: Swatao type jar, late Ming, early Qing (i.e., ca. 1644). Jar is 8 inches high, diameter of 7 inches, diameter of opening 4 inches, diameter of base 4 inches.

Contents: 400–500 AR.

Description:

Spanish colonies, Charles II, reales, México (100)

Spanish colonies, Charles II, 2 reales, México (100)

Spanish colonies, Charles II, 4 reales, México, 1688L

Spanish colonies, Charles II, 4 reales, México (100)

Spanish colonies, Charles II, 8 reales, México (100)

Spanish colonies, Charles II, 4 reales, Potosí (20)

Spanish colonies, Charles II, 8 reales, Potosí, 1683V

Spanish colonies, Charles II, 8 reales, Potosí, assayer VR

Spanish colonies, Charles II, 8 reales, Potosí (20)

The coins were mint-fresh coins of the late 1600s, bright and silvery, characterized by strange shapes and rare as to type.

Bibliography: Labao 2005 (includes photographs of the container and of 5 of the coins) (reference and photocopy of the article courtesy of Daniel Frank Sedwick). Daniel Frank Sedwick, "Silver Cobs of Mexico, 1536–1733," http://www.sedwickcoins.com/silver_cobs_mexico.htm (citing *Bank Note Society of the Philippines Journal* [August 2005]).

A86. Mauritius Island, Indian Ocean, 1979.

Type of find: Shipwreck.

Ship: British privateer *Speaker*, captain John Bowen.

Sank: 1702.

Contents: 1 AR, 4 AV.

Description:

1 American coin:

Spanish colonies, Charles II, 8 reales, México

Photographs on file in the British Museum.

Bibliography: *Coin Hoards* 6 (1981): 125 (no. 363).

A87. Gilstone Rock, off the Isles of Scilly, Cornwall, England, United Kingdom, July 1967–73.

Type of find: Shipwreck.

Ship: HMS *Association*, a British warship en route from Lisbon, Portugal, to Great Britain.

Sank: October 22, 1707.

Contents: 8,000 AR and AV.

Description:

1,237 American coins were sold in the four auctions:

Spanish colonies, 8 reales, México (58): Philip III; Philip IV (51); Philip IV, assayer R; Charles II, assayer L (2); 1687L; 1689L (cataloged as 1869); 1703

Spanish colonies, 8 reales, Lima (132): 1659V; 1684V (9); 1685R (7); 1685; 1686R (11); 1686R royal; 1687R (12); 1688R (6); 1689V (8); 1690R (8); 1691R (7); 1692V (3); 1693V (6); 1694M (14); 1695R (9); 1696H (11); 1697H (3); 1698H (3); 1699R (7); 1700H; 1701H; ND

Spanish colonies, real, Potosí (2): 1699; ND

Spanish colonies, 2 reales, Potosí (2): 1682VR; ND

Spanish colonies, 8 reales, Potosí (323): 1652E transitional (Type IV); 1654E; 1656E; 1657E; 1660E; 1664E(2); 1666E; 1667E; 1668E; 1669E(4); 166[-]E (3); 1670E(2); 1671E; 1672E; 1673E (2); 1674E; 1675E; 1676E (4); 1676E royal; 1677E (2); 1678E; 1678; 1679C (2); 1680V (3); 1681V (7); 1682V (14); 1683V (15); 1684; 1684V (4); 1684VR (4); 1685VR (11); 1686VR (23); 1687VR (21); 1688VR (4); 1689VR (42); 1690VR (26); 1691VR (16); 1692VR (17); 1693VR (21); 1695VR (11); 1696VR (3); 1697VR (3); 1697F; 1698F (5); 1699F (11); 1700F (2); 1701F (2); 1701; 1702Y (2); ND (9)

Spanish colonies, reales, ND (9)

Spanish colonies, Philip IV, 2 reales

Spanish colonies, 4 reales, ND

Spanish colonies, lower denominations and 8 reales, illegible (685)

Portuguese colonies, Brazil, 4,000 reis, Rio (4): 1703, 1704 (3)

Counterstamped coins (16):

Portuguese colonies, Brazil, 8 reales, bearing the counterstamp for 600 reis (11): Spain, 1617; México (2); Bogotá, 1665PRS; Potosí, 1661E; 1662; 1664E(2); 1666E; 16[-]; Spanish colonies

Portuguese colonies, Brazil, 8 reales, bearing the counterstamps for 480 reis and 600 reis (3): México; Potosí, 1622P; Potosí, 1627T

Portuguese colonies, Brazil, 8 reales, bearing the counterstamps for 480 reis and 600 reis, and monogram crowned (2): México; Potosí, 16[-]T

Disposition: Sold at four auctions: Sotheby's (London), July 14, 1969 and January 28, 1970; and W. H. Lane and Sons (Penzance), September 24, 1974, and September 25, 1975.

Bibliography: Lane 1974; Lane 1975; McDonald 1974, 68–81; Sebring 1986, 92–94, 117; Sebring 1995, 13–24; Sebring 2004, lot 1629; Sedwick and Sedwick 2007, 172–74 (Sedwick 30); Sotheby 1969; Sotheby 1970.

"British Divers find a 'Carpet of Silver' in 3 Sunken Ships," *New York Times*, September 21, 1967, 49.

A88. The Isles of Scilly, Cornwall, England, United Kingdom, 1969 and 1975.

Type of find: Shipwreck.

Ship: Originally identified as the HMS *Romney* in 1969, a later, more thorough investigation identified the wreck as the *Eagle*. A sister ship of HMS *Association*, en route from Lisbon, Portugal to Britain.

Sank: October 22, 1707.

Contents: 50 AR, 2 AV.

Description:

22 American coins:

Spanish colonies, 8 reales, México (7)

Spanish colonies, 8 reales, Lima (6)

Spanish colonies, 8 reales, Potosí (7)

Portuguese colonies, Brazil?, gold coins? (2)

Bibliography: McDonald 1974, 80; Sedwick and Sedwick 2007, 174 (Sedwick 31).

A89. Raamsdonk, Noord-Brabant, the Netherlands, April 1970.

Type of find: Hoard.

Date of deposit: 1711.

Container: Pot.

Contents: 559 AR, 17 AV.

Description:

2 American coins:

Spanish colonies, Philip IV, 2 escudos, Bogotá (2): 164[-]; 16[-]

Disposition: Auctioned by A. I. Verhage, Middelburg, Zeeland, the Netherlands, July 21 and 28, 1970.

Bibliography: Van Gelder 1969–70c; Van Gelder 1970.

A90. Twenty miles north of Kalbarri, Western Australia, Australia; discovered April 1927; excavated from the 1960s onwards.

Type of find: Shipwreck.

Ship: Dutch East India Company ship *Zuytdorp*.

Sank: 1–7 June, 1712.

Contents: 103,210 AR.

Description:

Stan J. Wilson's analysis of the coins published in 1985 included 100 American coins:

Spanish colonies, 2 reales, México (12): 1708 (7); 1700–8 (5)

Spanish colonies, 4 reales, México (22): 1660; 1708 (19); 1700–8 (2)

Spanish colonies, 8 reales, México (66): 1652 (5); 1695; 1708 (45); 1709 or 1705; 1700–8 (14)

By 1991 13,210 AR had been recovered from the shipwreck for the Western Australian Museum. The American coins known in 1991 break down according to denomination in this fashion:

Spanish colonies, reales, México (2)

Spanish colonies, 2 reales, México (159)

Spanish colonies, 4 reales, México (140)

Spanish colonies, 8 reales, México (483)

Disposition: Western Australian Museum (13,210). However, some 90,000 coins were looted from the wreck in the period 1980–86.

Bibliography: Playford 1996; Sedwick and Sedwick 2007, 176–77 (Sedwick 34); Twelftree 1971; Wilson 1964, 193–94; Wilson 1985.

A91. Badajoz, Badajoz Province, Spain, 1965.

Type of find: Hoard.

Date of deposit: Ca. 1720.

Contents: AR.

Description:

Spanish colonies, Philip IV, Charles II, Philip V, 2 reales, México

Spanish colonies, Philip IV, Charles II, Philip V, 4 reales, México

Spanish colonies, Philip IV, Charles II, Philip V, 8 reales, México

Spanish colonies, Philip IV, Charles II, Philip V, 2 reales, Lima

Spanish colonies, Philip IV, Charles II, Philip V, 4 reales, Lima

Spanish colonies, Philip IV, Charles II, Philip V, 8 reales, Lima

Spanish colonies, Philip IV, Charles II, Philip V, 2 reales, Potosí

Spanish colonies, Philip IV, Charles II, Philip V, 4 reales, Potosí

Spanish colonies, Philip IV, Charles II, Philip V, 8 reales, Potosí

Bibliography: Mateu 1971, 191 (Mateu 1282) (citing Ricardo Martín Valls, *Boletín del Seminario de Estudios de Arte y Arqueología, Universidad de Valladolid* 31 [1965]).

A92. Merton College, Oxford, Oxfordshire, England, United Kingdom, 1903.

Type of find: Hoard.

Date of deposit: 1723.

Contents: 13 AV.

Description:

1 American coin:

Portuguese colonies, Brazil, John V, 2,000 reis, 1715 Bahia

Disposition: Found during construction. 1 coin to Mr. Axtell, the builder, in consideration of the trouble he took in recovery of the hoard, 12 (including the American coin) to Merton College, deposited on permanent loan at the Ashmolean, 1951.

Bibliography: Thompson 1952–53, 190–91; Robinson 1971, 134.

A93. Porto Santo (now called Porto do Guilherme), Madeira Islands, Portugal, May-August 1974.

Type of find: Shipwreck.

Ship: Dutch East India Company ship *Slot ter Hooge*, en route from Amsterdam, Noord-Holland, Netherlands, to Batavia (now Jakarta), Indonesia.

Sank: November 19, 1724.

Contents: AR.

Description:

American coins:

Spanish colonies, 8 reales, México

The salvors also found brass nested coin weights.

Disposition: John Lethbridge recovered 349 silver bars, most of the 8 reales, and 9,067 guilders worth of smaller coins in 1725, and 190,000 guilders worth of treasure in 1726. He returned again in 1732, 1733, and 1734, but the results were disappointing. The modern salvage was by Robert Sténuit in the summer of 1974.

Bibliography: Earle 2007, 181–82; Pickford 1994, 134, 169; Sebring 1986, 63–66, 121; Sedwick and Sedwick 2007, 182–83 (Sedwick 38); Sténuit 1975.

A94. Rundøy, off the coast of Norway, July 1972.

Type of find: Shipwreck.

Ship: Akerendam, en route from the Netherlands to Batavia (now Jakarta), Indonesia.

Sank: March 8, 1725.

Contents: 5 AE, 49,803 AR, 6,624 AV.

Description:

Included gold and silver ducats and Dutch 2 stuiver coins plus 10,365 American coins:

Spanish colonies, 2 reales, México (13)

Spanish colonies, 4 reales, México (2,200)

Spanish colonies, 8 reales, México (8,121)

Spanish colonies, 4 reales, Lima (6): 1717; 1718 (2); 1721; ND (2)

Spanish colonies, 8 reales, Lima (12): 1686; 1698; 1718; 1719 (2); 1721 (2); ND (5)

Spanish colonies, 2 reales, Potosí (3): 1685; 168[-]; 1700

Spanish colonies, 4 reales, Potosí, 1715

Spanish colonies, 8 reales, Potosí (9): 1716 (2); 1717; 172[-]; ND (5)

Disposition: The coins were divided among Dutch and Norwegian governments, and the divers. The divers' share was auctioned as a whole in 1978, after which those coins were assembled into promotional sets consisting of 23 silver coins and one gold coin.

Bibliography: Marsden 1975, 209; Pickford 1994, 135, 169; Rønning 1973–74; Sebring 1986, 66–67; Sedwick and Sedwick 2007, 184 (Sedwick 40).

"Norway Faces Row Over Sea Treasure," *New York Times*, August 13, 1972, Section 1, 6.

Christopher Batio, "Treasures Surface in Shipwreck Salvage," *World Coin News*, March 1, 1993, 39.

A95. Arbucias, Gerona Province, Spain, 1948.

Type of find: Single find.

Contents: 1 AV.

Description: Spanish colonies, Philip V, 8 escudos, Lima

Bibliography: Mateu 1951, 236 (Mateu 423).

A96. Athens, Greece, 1971.

Type of find: Archaeological excavations in the Athenian Agora.

Date of deposit: 1700–30.

Contents: 6 AR.

Description:

Spanish colonies, 8 reales, México (3): assayer P; NDA (2)

Spanish colonies, 8 reales, Potosí (3)

A photograph of one is reproduced; it is an 8 reales cob of Philip IV, from México, assayer P. A plaster cast of this coin is in the collection of the American Numismatic Society, New York, New York, USA.

Disposition: Agora Museum, Athens, Greece.

Bibliography: Kleiner 1978, 25 no. 23.

Coin Hoards 5 (1978): 93 (no. 255).

A97. Pillaton Hall, Staffordshire, England, United Kingdom, January 15, 1741.

Type of find: Hoard.

Date of deposit: 1724–42.

Contents: 7,366 AV.

Description:

Between 2 and 300 American coins:

Portugal or Portuguese colonies, Brazil, 1,600 reis

Portugal or Portuguese colonies, Brazil, 2,000 reis (2)

Portugal or Portuguese colonies, Brazil, 3,200 reis (14)

Portugal or Portuguese colonies, Brazil, 4,000 reis (197)

Portugal or Portuguese colonies, Brazil, 6,400 reis (69)

Portugal or Portuguese colonies, Brazil, 12,800 reis (15)

Portuguese colonies, Brazil, 10,000 reis

Portuguese colonies, Brazil, 20,000 reis

The silver coins (not enumerated) totaled £639/12/3.

Bibliography: Robinson 1971, 124–35.

A98. Yeste, Albacete Province, Spain, September 1960.

Type of find: Hoard.

Date of deposit: 1729–30.

Contents: 132 AR.

Description:

9 American coins:

Spanish colonies, Philip V, 8 reales, México (7): assayer D; NDA (6)

Spanish colonies, Philip V, 8 reales, Potosí (2): 17[-]Y; 171[-]Y

Bibliography: Vega 1979.

A99. Near the park in Esch-sur-Alzette, Luxembourg, before 1989.

Type of find: Single find.

Contents: 1 AR.

Description: Spanish colonies, 2 reales, México, 1732 (catalog number D 445)

Bibliography: Weiller 1989, 244.

A100. Dorpel Sandbank, Deurloo Channel, in the North Sea, off Texel, Noord-Holland, the Netherlands, 1981–83 and 1992.

Type of find: Shipwreck.

Ship: The Dutch East India Company ship *t'Vliegend Hart*.

Sank: February 3, 1735.

Containers: 3 chests packed with peat (only 2 chests found intact, the second chest to be recovered had smashed on the ocean floor, spreading its contents over the seabed); plus smaller boxes used by passengers to smuggle coin out.

Contents: 7,000 AR, 2,000 AV.

Description:

Spanish colonies, 4 reales, México (7): 1731F (2); 1732F (4); 1733/2F;

Spanish colonies, 8 reales, México (7): 172[9?]; 1730G; 1730R; 1731F; 8 reales, México, 1732F (cob); 8 reales, México, 1733F (recortado); assayer R (cob)

The 4,820 Spanish coins in the third chest found consist of the following:

Spanish colonies, real, México, 17[-]

Spanish colonies, 2 reales, México, 17[-]
Spanish colonies, 4 reales, México, 1729–33 (756)
Spanish colonies, 4 or 8 reales, México, 17[-] (23)
Spanish colonies, 8 reales, México, 1708–33 (4,038)

Disposition: The first chest was found in 1983, and contained several thousand silver coins, and the 2,000 gold coins. The silver coins were chiefly 4 reales and 8 reales from México, dated 1730–33; the gold coins were 1729 gold ducats from Utrecht. The second chest, which had smashed on the bottom of the ocean, contained American coins. These were 4 reales and 8 reales, chiefly from México, dated 1730–33. A third chest was recovered intact in 1992. It contained ducats from West Friesland and Utrecht, and 4,820 Spanish coins, enumerated in more detail above. During 1990 and 1991, several smaller boxes were found that contain silver rijders from Dutch provincial mints; this was money that had been smuggled aboard by private passengers. The excavation was done by Rex Cowan. The shipwreck was analyzed and written up by the Rijksmuseum het Koninklijk Penningkabinet, Leyden, the Netherlands.

Bibliography: Earle 2007, 235–37; Pol and Jacobi 1993; Sedwick and Sedwick 2007, 186–87 (Sedwick 43).

Stewart Westdahl, "The Dutch East Indiaman 'Vliegenthart,'" Ponterio, San Diego, California, USA, Auction Catalog, February 5, 1994.

A101. Sallent, Barcelona Province, Spain, 1968.
Type of find: Single find.
Contents: 1 AR.
Description: Spanish colonies, real, México, 1735
Disposition: Local museum.

Bibliography: Mateu 1971, 199 (Mateu 1370).

A102. Spain, 1946.
Type of find: Hoard.
Date of deposit: 1736.
Contents: 4 AV.
Description:
Spanish colonies, Philip V, 4 escudos, México, 1736
Spanish colonies, Philip V, 4 escudos, Lima, 1736
Spanish colonies, Charles II, 8 escudos, Lima, 1697
Spanish colonies, Philip V, 8 escudos, 1736

Bibliography: Mateu 1945–46, 267–68 (Mateu 212).

A103. Fetlar, Shetland Islands, Scotland, United Kingdom, August–September 1971.
Type of find: Shipwreck.
Ship: Danish Asiatic Company ship *Wendela*.
Sank: December 18–19, 1737.
Contents: 805 AR, 44 AV.
Description:
29 American coins:
Spanish colonies, 4 reales, México, 1735
Spanish colonies, 8 reales, México (28): cobs (3); cob, cut in half; cob 1732; milled, 1733; milled, ND; recortado, 1733 (3); recortado, 1733, fragment; recortado, ND; recoratado, ND, fragment; milled, 1734 (6); milled, 1735 (7); milled, 1736
Spanish colonies, fragment, México

Nearly all the coins on the shipment were bought from two Jewish money changers of Copenhagen, Behrendt Jacob and Berendt Samuel. Most of the coins were probably acquired from Amsterdam (or possibly Hamburg), and thus the shipwreck does not reflect monetary circulation in Denmark, but rather that in the Netherlands (or possibly in Hamburg).

Disposition: Salvage was by Robert Sténuit. Auctioned by Sotheby's, November 8, 1973.

Bibliography: Earle 2007, 238–39; Jensen 1973–74, 31–67; Sedwick and Sedwick 2007, 187–88 (Sedwick 44); Sotheby's 1973; Sténuit 1974b, 34–35.

A104. Goodwin Sands, Kent, England, United Kingdom, December 2004–7.

Type of find: Shipwreck.

Ship: Dutch East India Company ship *Rooswijk*.

Sank: December 19, 1739.

Contents: 555 AR.

Description:

Spanish colonies, 4 reales, México (79):
Cobs (53): 1728D; 1729R (4); 1730/29R (2); 1730R (17); ND (29)
Recortados (6): 1733MF (5); 1734MF
Pillars (20): 1734/3MF (2); 1734MF (2); 1735MF (8); 1736/5MF; 1736MF (3); 1737MF (3); 1738MF

Spanish colonies, 8 reales, México (475):
Cobs (98): 1720; 1725D; 1726D (2); 1728D; 1728D (royal); 1729R (25); 1730/29R (3); 1730R (19); 1731F (3); 1732/1F (2); 1732F (3); 1733; ND (36)
Recortados (48): 1733F (5); 1733MF (34); contemporary cast counterfeit 1733MF; 1734/3MF (6) 1734MF (2)
Pillars (329): 1732F (4); 1733MXMF (2); 1733F; 1733MF (large crown on globes); 1733MF (12); 1734/3MF (9); 1734MF (81); 1735/4MF; 1735MF (66); 1736/5MF; 1736MF (79); 1737MF (with inverted As for Vs in "VTRAQUE" and "VNUM") (3); 1737MF (42); 1738/7MF (3); 1738MF (23); 173[-]MF cut in half

Spanish colonies, 8 reales, Guatemala, 1735/4 (2)

Disposition: Salvaged by Ken Welling and Rex Cowan.

Bibliography: Ponterio 2006; Sedwick and Sedwick 2007, 188 (Sedwick 45).

A105. Isla de Maio, Cape Verde Islands, June 1996–99.

Type of find: Shipwreck.

Ship: English East India Company ship *Princess Louisa*, which departed Portsmouth, Hampshire, England, United Kingdom, March 20, 1743.

Sank: April 18, 1743.

Contents: 60,000 AR.

Description:

English colonies, Massachusetts, pine tree shilling, Noe 1

Spanish colonies, ½ reales, México (5): 1731, 1734–39 (4)

Spanish colonies, reales, México (148): Charles and Johanna, assayer O; 1730; 1734–39 (20); NDA (126)

Spanish colonies, 2 reales, México (58): assayer D (2); assayer F (7); 1729R (5); 1730R (4); 1730F; 1731; 1731F (9); 1734–39 (8); NDA (41)

Spanish colonies, 4 reales, México (2): 1732F, 1733MF (recortado)

Spanish colonies, 8 reales, México, 1733MF (recortado)

Spanish colonies, 2 reales, Bogotá, Philip V, NDA

Spanish colonies, Bogotá, 4 reales, 1721ARC

Spanish colonies, reales, Lima, 1699

Spanish colonies, 2 reales, Lima (53): 1684V; 1686R; 1702H; 1703H; 1705H; 1710H; 1711M; 1717M (2); 1722M; 1723M; 1724M; 1725M; 1726M; 1727M; 1730M; 1731N; 1732N; 1733N (2); 1734N (3); 1735N (2); 1736N; 1737N (2); 1738N; 1739V (2); 1740V; 1741V; NDA (20)

Spanish colonies, 4 reales, Lima (22): 1710H; 1714M; 1715M; 1720M; 1721M (2); 1723M (2); 1724M; 1725M; 1726M; 1727M; 1728N;

1737N; 1739V (2); 1741V (3); NDA (3)

Spanish colonies, 8 reales, Lima (41): 1696H; 1697H (2); 1703H; 1707H; 1710H; 1711M; 1717M (2); 1718M (3); 1720M; 1721M (2); 1722M; 1723M (2); 1724M (3); 1725M (4); 1726M (4); 1727M (4); 1728N (4); 1729N; 1735N; 1737N; 1739V

Spanish colonies, reales, Potosí (2): 1725Y; 1733YA

Spanish colonies, 2 reales, Potosí (47): 1688VR; 1689VR; 1694VR; 1699F; 1707Y; 1713Y; 1717Y; 1719Y; 1722Y; 1724Y; 1725Y (2); 1726Y (2); 1727Y (4); 1728M; 1729M (3); 1730M (3); 1731M; 1732M (2); 1732YA; 1733YA; 1733E (2); 1734E (4); 1735E (2); 1736E (4); 1737; 1737E; 1737M; 1738M

Spanish colonies, 4 reales, Potosí (81): 1684V; 1691VR; 1702Y; 1705Y; 1714Y (2); 1715Y; 1717Y; 1718Y; 1719Y (2); 1720Y (3); 1722Y (2); 1724Y (2); 1726Y; 1727Y; 1732; 1732M; 1733; 1733YA; 1734E (3); 1735E (7); 1736E (5); 1737 (7); 1737M; 1738M (7); 1739M (5); 1740 (5); 1740P; 1741P (8); 1742; NDA (7)

Spanish colonies, 8 reales, Potosí (111): 1658E; 1668E (royal), holed; 1669E; 1676E; 1682V; 1683V; 1688VR; 1690VR; 1691VR; 1692VR; 1693VR (2); 1695VR; 1696VR; 1701F; 1701Y; 1706Y; 1707Y; 1713Y; 1714Y; 1716Y (3); 1718Y (2); 1719Y; 1720Y; 1721Y (2); 1722Y (4); 1723Y (2); 1724Y; 1725Y (3); 1726Y (2); 1727Y (3); 1728M (6); 1736E; 1737E; 1741P; Charles II – PhilipV (58)

Spanish colonies, reales, Lima or Potosí (445)

Spanish colonies, 2 reales, Lima or Potosí (556)

Spanish colonies, 4 reales, Lima or Potosí (10)

Spanish colonies, 8 reales, Lima or Potosí (100)

Spanish colonies, cobs in clusters (177+)

Bibliography: Earle 2007, 188–90, 217–18, 350; Heritage 2001, lots 5418–5553; Sedwick and Sedwick 2007, 189 (Sedwick 46); Sotheby's 2000, lots 543–72.

A106. Gunner Rock, Broad Sound, off St. Agnes Island, the Isles of Scilly, Cornwall, England, United Kingdom, September 1971.

Type of find: Shipwreck.

Ship: Dutch East India Company ship *Hollandia*.

Sank: July 13, 1743.

Contents: 35,000+ AR.

Description:

The London Sotheby's auction offered 2,527 European coins and 3,680 American coins. The Lane auction offered 33 European coins and 446 American coins. The American coins in those auctions were:

Spanish colonies, reales, México (4): 1736MF (2); 1737MF; 1738MF

Spanish colonies, 2 reales, México (9): 1733F (cob) (2); 1736MF (3); 1737MF (2); 1738MF; 1739MF

Spanish colonies, 4 reales, México (267): 1733MF (recortado); 1734MF (recortado); 1732F (pillar); 1733MF (pillar) (3); 1734MF (pillar) (2); 1735MF (6); 1736MF (5); 1737/6MF; 1737MF (3); 1738/7MF; 1738MF (6); 1739MF (4); 1740MF (169); 1741MF; 1742/41MF (2); 1742MF (22); NDA (cob) (39)

Spanish colonies, 8 reales, México (3,897): ca. 1650, assayer P; ca. 1716, assayer J; 1730G (2); 1730F; 1732 (cob) (2); 1733MF (recortado) (6); 1734MF (recortado); assayer MF (recortado) (5); 1732F (pillar) (2); 1733F (pillar) (3); 1733MF (pillar) (10); 1734/3MF; 1734MF (pillar) (88); 1735MF (89); 1736MF (281); 1737MF (183); 1738/7MF; 1738MF (362); 1739MF (325); 1740MF (464); 1741MF (517); 1742MF (229); NDA (cob) (73); NDA (pillar) (1,250)

Spanish colonies, 4 reales, Guatemala (10): 1733; 1734 (2); 1735/4; 1737; NDA (5)

Spanish colonies, 8 reales, Guatemala (31):

1733J (2); 1734J (2); 1735J; 1737J (5); 1738J (8); 1739J; 1740J; 1741J; assayer J (10)
Spanish colonies, 8 reales, Lima (7): 1732 (2); 1738; 1740; NDA (3)
Spanish colonies, 4 reales, Potosí, 1684PV

Disposition: Discovered in 1971 by the London solicitor Rex Cowan. Auctioned by Sotheby's, London, England, United Kingdom; by Sotheby Parke-Bernet, New York, New York, USA, June 1971; W. H. Lane & Son, Penzance, Cornwall, September 1975; also offered by the Houston Numismatic Exchange, Houston, Texas, USA.

Bibliography: Earle 2007, 187–88; Lane 1975; Marsden 1975, 210–17; Pickford 1994, 172; Sebring 1986, 67–69; Sedwick and Sedwick 2007, 189–90 (Sedwick 47); Sotheby's 1972a.
"'*Hollandia*' Yields Silver Coin Hoard after 229 Years on Ocean Floor," *World Coins* 9, no. 5 (whole no. 101) (May 1972): 640, 642, 644.

A107. Off Mauritius Island, diving expeditions in the 1950s.

Type of find: Shipwreck.

Ship: French East India Company slaveship *Saint Geran*, which departed Lorient March 24, 1744, and loaded up with slaves at Gorée Sénégal.

Sank: August 18, 1744.

Contents: 2+ BI, 2+ AR.

Description:
France, 2 sol, 1743A (2)
Spanish colonies, 8 reales, México, 1741 (2)
Divers are also reported to have brought up coins dated 1742.

Bibliography: Arroyo 1972; Bowers and Merena 1983, lots 101–2; Breen 1988, 51 (Breen 396); Sebring 1986, 120.

A108. Gawthorpe Hall, Gawthorpe, Lancashire, England, United Kingdom, 1850.

Type of find: Hoard.

Date of deposit: 1745.

Contents: 91 AV.

Description:
Possibly 37 American coins:
Portugal or Portuguese colonies, Brazil, John V, 1,600 reis
Portugal or Portuguese colonies, Brazil, John V, 4,000 reis, 1709 onwards (19 different years) (33)
Portugal or Portuguese colonies, Brazil, John V, 6,400 reis, 1745
Portugal or Portuguese colonies, Brazil, John V, 12,800 reis (2): 1730; 1732
The date of deposit is believed to be connected with the rising of the Pretender, Bonnie Prince Charlie, in 1745.
The article says that there was a 4,000 reis of 1745. This is an unlisted date. It is more likely to have been a 6,400 reis of 1745. The listing has been emended accordingly.

Disposition: Found under the wooden sill of a mullioned window between the woodwork and the stone and mortar below during the renovation of the house by Sir Charles Barry (the architect of the Houses of Parliament).

Bibliography: Harland 1856–57, Part 2 (41), 328–30; Part 3 (42), 525; Robinson 1971, 134; Victoria History 1911, 464–67.

A109. Meob Bay, Namibia, 1963–64.

Type of find: Shipwreck.

Ship: Unknown Dutch East India Company ship.

Sank: 1746.

Contents: AE, AR.

Description:
1 American coin:
Spanish colonies, Philip V, 8 reales, México, 1743
Thought to be coins washed in from the remains of a Dutch East India Company ship that sank in or after 1746.

The finders also discovered copper duits of the Zeeland chamber of the Dutch East India Company dated 1746.

Bibliography: Marsden 1975, 217–18.

A110. Gaanzecraal, between the Robben and Dassen islands, off South Africa, March 1979.

Type of find: Shipwreck.

Ship: Dutch East India Company ship *Reigersdaal.*

Sank: October 25, 1747.

Contents: 6,800 AR.

Description:

Spanish colonies, 4 reales, México (18): 1732 no assayer; 1735MF; 1736MF (2); 1737MF (2); 1738MF (2); 1739MF; 1740MF; 1741MF; 1742MF (6); 1743MF

Spanish colonies, 8 reales, México (3,443): 1732F; 1733MF (6); 1733MXF; 1734MF (32); 1735MF (54); 1736/5MF; 1736MF (104); 1737 (117); 1738/7MF (7); 1738 3 over 3 MF; 1738MF (197); 1739/8MF (2); 1739MF (425); 1740 4 over 3 MF (14); 1740MF (346); 1741 4 over 3 MF; 1741MF (436); 1742/1MF (75); 1742 4 over 3 MF (2); 1742MF (440); 1743/2MF (113); 1743MF (863); 1744MF (200); 1744/3MF (5)

Spanish colonies, Philip V, 8 reales, México, cobs (2)

Spanish colonies, 4 reales, Guatemala, 1738J

Spanish colonies, 8 reales, Guatemala (10): 1737J; 1740J; 1741J; 1742J; 1743J; ND (5)

Disposition: 3,400 to Arthur Ridge, who sold his portion in its entirety in the 1980s; 3,400 to Jimmy Rawe, of whose portion some were auctioned by Superior, June 2, 1992.

Bibliography: Ponterio 1993, 1944–58; Sedwick and Sedwick 2007, 191 (Sedwick 49); Superior 1992, lots 4024–4373; Superior 1993, lots 1388–1403.

A111. Dunchurch, near Rugby, Warwickshire, England, United Kingdom, September 18, 1961.

Type of find: Hoard.

Date of deposit: 1751.

Contents: 89 AE.

Description:

All halfpennies including a high proportion of forgeries.

1 American-related coin:

Ireland, Wood's Hibernia halfpenny

Disposition: Birmingham City Museum.

Bibliography: Robinson 1972.

Coin Hoards 1 (1975): 104 (no. 406).

A112. Needle Rock, Isle of Wight, England, United Kingdom, 1973, 1976–77, 1980–81.

Type of find: Shipwreck.

Ship: HMS *Assurance*, en route from Britain from Jamaica.

Sank: April 24, 1753.

Contents: 2 AE, 206 AR.

Description:

192 silver American coins:

Spanish colonies, reales, México (54): [1708–24]; [1726–28]; 1729 (2); 1729–30 (5); 1729–31 (3); 1730–31; [pre-1731] (29); 1730; 1731 (5); ND (6)

Spanish colonies, 2 reales, México (5): [pre-1731] (3); 1730; ND

Spanish colonies, 8 reales, México (50): [1708–24]; [pre-1731]; 1730; 1731 (2); [1733–47] (7); 1740 (29); 1745; 1746 (7); 1748

Spanish colonies, reales, Guatemala (2): 1739; 1746

Spanish colonies, ½ reales, Lima (4): 1738; 1739; 1749; 1749–51

Spanish colonies, reales, Lima (3): 1734; 1735; ND

Spanish colonies, 2 reales, Lima (4): 1748;

1751 (3)

Spanish colonies, 4 reales, Lima (10): 1734; 1740 (2); 1742; 1747 (6)

Spanish colonies, 8 reales, Lima (21): [1718–28]; 1719; 1728; 1734; 1740; 1741; 1743; 1746; 1747 (13)

Spanish colonies, reales, Lima or Potosí (2)

Spanish colonies, 2 reales, Lima or Potosí (2): 1749; ND

Spanish colonies, 4 reales, Lima or Potosí, ND (9)

Spanish colonies, 8 reales, Lima or Potosí, ND (10)

Spanish colonies, ½ real, Potosí, ND

Spanish colonies, reales, Potosí (2): 1736; 1748–49

Spanish colonies, 2 reales, Potosí (7): 172[-]; 1725; 1731; 1732; 1735; 1743; ND

Spanish colonies, 8 reales, Potosí (5): 1737; 1743 (2); 1744; ND

Spanish colonies, ½ reales, no mint, ND

The list above is based on that compiled by Joseph E. Cribb of the British Museum. Added to it are the 23 coins, all from Lima, which were auctioned by Sotheby's in 1973.

Disposition: Carisbrooke Castle Museum, Newport, Isle of Wight (172); Royal Naval Museum, Portsmouth (13); Sotheby's auction, London, England, United Kingdom, 1973 (23).

Bibliography: McDonald 1974, 86–94; Sedwick and Sedwick 2007, 192–93 (Sedwick 51); Sotheby's 1973.
  Coin Hoards 4 (1978): 121–22 (no. 400).
  Coin Hoards 5 (1979): 109 (no. 307).
  Coin Hoards 7 (1985): 371–72 (no. 573).

A113. Bird Island, off Port Elizabeth, South Africa, 1994.

Type of find: Shipwreck.

Ship: English East India Company ship *Dodington*. Thought to be carrying the treasure of Robert Clive, and merchandised by some as the "Clive Treasure."

Sank: July 17, 1754.

Contents: AR, AV.

Description:

Spanish colonies, ½ reales, Potosí, 1733–52
Spanish colonies, reales, Potosí, 1733–52
Spanish colonies, 2 reales, Potosí, 1733–52
Spanish colonies, 4 reales, Potosí, 1733–52
Spanish colonies, 8 reales, Potosí, 1733–52
Portuguese colonies, Brazil, 6,400 reis, 1745 (Sebring)

Disposition: Modern salvage is by Dave Allan.

Bibliography: Earle 2007, 189–90; Pickford 1994, 182; Ponterio 1995, lot 833; Sebring 2004, lot 1632; Sedwick and Sedwick 2007, 193–94 (Sedwick 52).
Jonathan K. Kern, Advertisement, *Coin World*, December 22, 2003, 30.

A114. Acequión, Albacete Province, Spain, 1943.

Type of find: Single find.

Contents: 1 AR.

Description: Spanish colonies, Ferdinand VI, real?, Potosí, 1755

Bibliography: Mateu 1945–46, 268 (Mateu 216).

A115. Intramuros, Manila, the Philippines, May 1952.

Type of find: Hoard.

Date of deposit: 1765.

Container: Jar (discarded by the finders).

Contents: 2,590+ AR.

Description:

Spain, ½ real (¼ pistareen), Seville, 1738
Spanish colonies, ½ reales, México (cob) (61): 1715; assayer J (4); assayer D (2); NDA (54)

Spanish colonies, ½ reales, México (milled) (306): 1734 (5); 1735 (7); 1736 (14); 1737 (5); 1738 (11); 1739 (5); 1740 (7); 1741 (7); 1742 (4); 1743 (4); 1744 (9); 1745 (12); 1746 (24); Philip V, 1747 (5); Ferdinand VI, 1747 (8); 1748 (11); 1749 (10); 1750 (7); 1751 (17); 1752 (19); 1753 (11); 1754MF, royal crowns (24); 1755 (8); 1756 (4); 1757 (14); 1758 (6); 1759 (10); Ferdinand VI, 1760 (4); Charles III, 1760 (2); 1761 (2); 1762 (23); 1763 (3); 1764 (2); 1765 (2)

Spanish colonies, reales, México (cob) (1,127): 1703F; 1718J; 1724D; 1729R (3); 1739 (5); 1730F; 1730R (5); 1730 (6); 1731F (10); 1731 (9); 1732; assayer D (31); assayer F (31); assayer G (31); assayer L (6); assayer R (34); NDA (951)

Spanish colonies, reales, México (milled) (249): 1732; 1734 (10); 1735 (15); 1736 (17); 1737 (12); 1738 (14); 1739 (12); 1740 (8); 1741 (9); 1742 (9); 1743 (10); 1744 (13); 1745 (12); 1746 (25); Philip V, 1747 (2); Ferdinand VI, 1747 (11); 1748 (17); 1749 (4); 1750 (8); 1751 (11); 1752 (13); 1753 (3); 1755; 1757 (6); 1759; 1761 (2); 1762 (3); 1763

Spanish colonies, 2 reales, México (cob) (290): 1716; 1729R; 1730R; 1731 (3); 1732F (2); 1732; assayer J (12); assayer D (10); assayer F (20); assayer R (18); NDA (220)

Spanish colonies, 2 reales, México (milled) (201): 1734; 1735 (9); 1736 (8); 1737 (9); 1738 (12); 1739 (6); 1740 (5); 1741 (2); 1742 (8); 1743 (3); 1744 (4); 1745 (11); 1746 (12); Philip V, 1747 (2); Ferdinand VI, 1747 (11); 1748 (26); 1749 (16); 1750 (11); 1751 (13); 1752 (8); 1753 (3); 1754MF, royal crowns (5); 1755 (4); 1756 (5); 1757; 1758 (2); Ferdinand VI, 1760; 1762; 1765

Spanish colonies, 4 reales, México (milled) (4): 1745; 1748; 1751; 1752

Spanish colonies, 8 reales, México (cob) (18): 1729R; 1731F; 1731J; 173[-]R; 173[-] (13); assayer J

Spanish colonies, 8 reales, México (milled) (273): 1738; 1739 (9); 1740 (2); 1741 (4); 1742 (4); 1743 (3); 1745 (8); 1746 (14); Philip V, 1747 (3); Ferdinand VI, 1747 (9); 1748 (4); 1749 (14); 1750 (34); 1751 (21); 1752 (43); 1753 (44); 1754MF, royal crowns (25); 1754MF, imperial and royal crowns (4); 1754MM, imperial and royal crowns (11); 1755 (11); 1756 (2); 1757 (3)

Spanish colonies, 8 reales, Guatemala (24): 1733; 1734; 1739; 1740; 1742 (2); 1743; 1747; 1749 (2); 174[-]; 1751 (4); 1752 (2); 1753 (4); ND (3)

Spanish colonies, ½ real, Lima, 1759JM

Spanish colonies, reales, Lima (8): 1753J (4); 1758JM (4)

Spanish colonies, 2 reales, Lima (3): 1753J; 1755JD; 1757JM

Spanish colonies, 8 reales, Lima (3): 1747V (cob); 1753J (milled) (2)

All the Lima coins are milled, except for the 8 reales, 1747V. All the Guatemala coins are cobs.

De Jesus observed: "It will be noted that among the pillar dollars the year 1744 is not represented. This fact confirms the common observation among local collectors that no importation of 1744 dollar ever reached the Philippines."

De Jesus also noted that he saw no gold or other valuables, but says that it is not improbable that some had been found but not revealed by the finders. He remarks that it is interesting that there are no Potosí coins in the hoard.

Disposition: Found by workers while excavating a foundation. Some (possibly most) of the coins (including the 1747V from Lima) to Pablo I. de Jesus.

Bibliography: De Jesus 1952; De Jesus 1953. "Advanced Report of a Manila Hoard," *Numismatist* 65, no. 5 (May, 1952): 478.

A116. Matadepera, near Tarrasa, Barcelona Province, Spain, July 1966.

Type of find: Single find.

Contents: 1 AR.

Description: Spanish colonies, Charles III, 8 reales, Potosí, 1765

Disposition: Museo Espona.

Bibliography: Mateu 1967, 63 (Mateu 1250).

A117. Villarobledo, Gerona Province, Spain, 1951.

Type of find: Single find.

Contents: 1 AR.

Description: Spanish colonies, Charles III, 8 reales, Lima, 1770
Seen by Mateu in Valencia in 1952.

Bibliography: Mateu 1953, 95 (Mateu 636).

A118. Bataan Province, the Philippines, March 1954.

Type of find: Hoard.

Date of deposit: 1776.

Contents: 93 AR.

Description:

Spanish colonies, 8 reales, México (89): 1772MF (assayers' initials and mintmark inverted); 1772FM (assayers' initials and mintmark inverted) (15); 1773FM (assayers' initials and mintmark inverted) (5); 1773FM (normal) (21); 1774FM (16); 1775FM (23); 1776FM (8)

Spanish colonies, 8 reales, Lima (4): 1772JM; 1773JM; 1775JM (2)

Disposition: Acquired by Pablo I. de Jesus.

Bibliography: De Jesus 1954.

A119. Old city of Huian, Fujian Province, China, October 1973.

Type of find: Single find.

Contents: 1 AR.

Description: Spanish colonies, 8 reales, México, 1786

A small jade carving was found with the coin.

Bibliography: Coin Hoards 3 (1977): 182 (no. 503.4).

A120. Hartwell or Rifona Reef, off Boa Vista, Cape Verde Islands, July 23, 1996.

Type of find: Shipwreck.

Ship: English East India Company ship *Hartwell*, en route from Portsmouth, England, to Guangzhou, China.

Sank: May 24, 1787.

Contents: 35 AR.

Description:

Spanish colonies, ½ reales, México (6): 1773FM; 1774FM; 1779FF; 1780FF; 1783FM; ND

Spanish colonies, reales, México (2): 1781FF; ND

Spanish colonies, 8 reales, México (24): 1756M; 1773FM (2); 1774FM (2); 1776FM; 1777FM; 1778FF (4); 1780FF (2); 1781FF (3); 1782FF (4); 1784FM (2); 1785FM (2)

Spanish colonies, 8 reales, Guatemala, 1779P

The ship had 60 chests of silver belonging to the English East India Company, worth £53,642.

Disposition: About 120,000 8 reales were recovered by the Braithewaites in 1787–90. Over 46,000 8 reales were looted from the wreck by pirates in 1789. Excavated in the 1990s by Arqueonautas.

Bibliography: Earle 2007, 259–70, 355; Pickford 1994, 76–77, 169; Sotheby's 2000, lots 497–98.

A121. Northwest Turkey, 1981.

Type of find: Hoard.

Date of deposit: 1794.

Contents: 17 AR.

Description:
   8 American coins:
   Spanish colonies, 8 reales, México, 1794 (2)
   Spanish colonies, 8 reales, Lima (4): 1788; 1792; 1793; 1794
   Spanish colonies, 8 reales, Potosí, 1794
   Spanish colonies, 8 reales, no mint, ND

Disposition: Çannakale Museum.

Bibliography: Coin Hoards 6 (1981): 169 (no. 498).

A122. Almuñécar, Granada Province, Spain, 1953.

Type of find: Single find.

Contents: 1 AR.

Description: Spanish colonies, Charles IV, 8 reales, Potosí, 1798PP

Disposition: Pedro Gutiérrez del Amo, Lleida, Lleida Province, Spain.

Bibliography: Mateu 1958, 74 (Mateu 929).

A123. Texel, Noord-Holland, the Netherlands, 1800–1938.

Type of find: Shipwreck.

Ship: HMS *Lutine*, en route from London to Hamburg.

Sank: October 9, 1799.

Contents: AE, AR, AV.

Description:
   The following coins and medals were recovered between 1886 and 1938:
   Russia, Catherine II, 5 kopek, 1793
   German states, Prussia, Frederick William III, copper medal
   Great Britain, George III, halfpence (ca. 24) (photographs of one show it to be a counterfeit)
   Great Britain, George III, twopence, 1797
   Great Britain, ½ guineas (6)
   Great Britain, guineas (15): 1790; 1791; 1793; ND
   France, Louis XVI, louis (2)
   France, louis (49)
   France, Louis XVI, 2 louis, 1786
   France, 2 louis (37)
   Italian states, Naples and Sicily, Ferdinand IV, 4 ducati (9)
   Italian states, Naples and Sicily, Charles III, 6 ducati (9)
   Austrian states, Salzburg, thaler
   Unspecified silver coin
   Spanish colonies, reales (2)
   Spanish colonies, 2 reales (17)
   Spain or Spanish colonies, 4 reales (20)
   Spain or Spanish colonies, Charles III and Charles IV, 8 reales, probably including México and Lima (2,205) (date of one recovered in 1938 known to be Charles IV, 1789)
   Spain or Spanish colonies, escudos (6)
   Spain or Spanish colonies, 2 escudos (10)
   Spain or Spanish colonies, 4 escudos
   Spain or Spanish colonies, 8 escudos (8)

Disposition: Recoveries from the *Lutine*, often successful, have been proceeding ever since the ship sank. In 1800 local fishers employed by the Dutch government recovered $273,000 (Thompson says £55,000; van der Molen says 301,721 Dutch guilders; all three figures are very close to each other). This included over 29,248 Spanish 8 reales. In 1814 Pierre Eschauzler recovered a gold louis, an 8 escudo, and eight 8 reales. There was a new attempt in July 1857 and some coins were retrieved. In July 1858 a diver came up with a bag of silver bullion. By the middle of October gold and silver bars, and coin, to the value of $140,000 had been recovered. In 1859 five gold and two silver bars were recovered. From July 1857 until the end of 1860, when the recovery ended, they recovered forty-two gold bars, sixty-four silver bars, and some coins, for a total value of

$220,000. In 1886–89 suction pumps pulled up 11,164 coins, with a value of $4,600. No silver or gold bars were recovered. In 1938 salvors recovered a copper medal of King Frederick William III of Prussia, an 8 reales of Charles IV dated 1789, some other copper and silver coins, and a gold bar. Further on in the same season some gold coins were recovered: an 8 escudos of 1797, a shield guinea, a louis of 1786, an escudo of 1793, and a Sicilian gold coin of 1735. The total found in the summer of 1938 was 10 AE, 123 AR, 8 AV. The recovery technique used in 1938 was a tin dredge, which is believed to have destroyed the wreck entirely.

Eschauzler said that it was the custom of banks at the time to ship bullion in bars marked with their name and serial numbers of 1 to 100. One hundred gold bars, with nineteen different marks, have been brought to the surface in the several recoveries; and ninety-nine silver bars have been found with five firms' initials. A list may be found in Thompson's article. In 1938 a gold bar weighing 3.5 kilograms was recovered, with the inscription 2 F BB 57. Gold bars with similar inscriptions numbered 56 and 58 had been recovered earlier.

Bibliography: Nesmith 1958a, 132–56; Thompson 1963; Van der Molen [1966].

"The Treasure Ship *Lutine* Yields More Wealth. For more than a Hundred Years, Efforts have been made to Recover the Contents of the Frigate that was Wrecked with Probably $6,000,000 on Board, and Much has been Secured," *New York Times*, October 15, 1911, part 6, 1–2.

A124. Ljubostinja, Serbia, 1966.

Type of find: Hoard.

Date of deposit: Ca. 1800.

Contents: 820 AR.

Description:
17 American coins:
Spanish colonies, 2 reales, México (3): Philip III (2); Philip IV
Spanish colonies, Philip IV, 4 reales, México (4)
Spanish colonies, 8 reales, México (5): Philip III, assayer F; Philip IV, [1621–24] (4)
Spanish colonies, 4 reales, Potosí (3): Philip III; 1627; Philip IV
Spanish colonies, Philip IV, 8 reales, Potosí (2)
This was the treasury of a monastery, which is why the contents stretch from the seventeenth to the end of the eighteenth centuries.

Bibliography: Dušanić 1979.

Coin Hoards 7 (1985): 260 (no. 422).

A125. Sleaty, County Laois, Ireland, 1865.

Type of find: Hoard.

Date of deposit: Ca. 1800.

Container: Cow's horn.

Contents: Ca. 100 AR, 400 AV.

Description: Spanish colonies, 8 reales, probably México (100)
Coins in a cow's horn concealed in thatch. Described as about 400 guineas and a considerable number of Spanish dollars.

Bibliography: Dolley 1975.

Coin Hoards 1 (1975): 105 (no. 409).

A126. Donaghadee, County Down, Northern Ireland, United Kingdom, October 1829.

Type of find: Shipwreck.

Ship: Enterprise, homeward bound from South America.

Sank: 1802.

Contents: Ca. 500 AR.

Description:
Spanish colonies, Charles III, 8 reales
Spanish colonies, Charles IV, 8 reales

Recovered by the three Owen brothers of Holyhead, who used a diving bell and reaping hooks.

Bibliography: "Dollar Fishery on the Coast of Ireland," *Worcester (MA) National Aegis*, October 28, 1829, citing the *North Wales Chronicle* (reference courtesy of Q. David Bowers).

A127. Cape Saint Mary, off the Algarve, Portugal, May 2007.

Type of find: Shipwreck.

Ship: Nuestra Señora de la Mercedes, which blew up during a battle with the British fleet, while en route from Spanish America to Cadiz.

Sank: October 5, 1804.

Contents: 500,000 AR, 200 AV.

Description:

Spanish colonies, 8 reales, México (500,000)
Spanish colonies, 8 escudos (200)

Disposition: In May 2007 Odyssey Marine Exploration announced that they had raised 500,000 silver coins and a few hundred gold coins from a "colonial era" shipwreck in the Atlantic. They denied that it was the HMS *Sussex*, which sank in 1686. Rumors suggested that the ship was the *Merchant Royal*, which sank in 1641. However, Colapinto's article in the New Yorker says that the ship was *Nuestra Señora de la Mercedes*, which sank in 1804. The identity of the coins found aboard is an educated guess.

Taken to Tampa, Florida; in litigation between Odyssey Marine Exploration and the Spanish government.

Bibliography: Colapinto 2008.

"Record wreck 'found off Cornwall,'" BBC News Website, May 19, 2007, http://news.bbc.co.uk/1/hi/england/cornwall/6671975.stm.

A128. Leyton Rock, near Boa Vista, Cape Verde Islands, 2000.

Type of find: Shipwreck.

Ship: English East India Company ship *Lady Burgess*, en route from Britain to Madras (now Chennai) and Bengal.

Sank: April 20, 1806.

Contents: 105 AR, 32 AV.

Description:

Included the following American coins:
Spanish colonies, real, México, 1797FM
Spanish colonies, 8 reales, México (34): 1772FM (assayer's initials inverted); 1773FM; 1774FM; 1775FM; 1776FM; 1777FM; 1777FF; 1778FF; 1779FF; 1783FF; 1784FM; 1785FM; 1786FM; 1787FM; 1788FM; 1789FM (2); Carolus IV, 1790FM; Carolus IIII, 1790FM; 1791FM; 1792FM; 1793FM; 1794FM; 1795FM; 1796FM; 1797FM; 1798FM; 1800FM (2); 1801FT; 1802FT; 1803FT; 1803 TH; 1804 TH
Spanish colonies, 8 reales, Guatemala (2): 1777P, 1779P
Spanish colonies, 2 reales, Potosí (2): 1782PR; 1799PR
Spanish colonies, 8 reales, Potosí (23): 1775JR; 1776PR; 1777PR; 1779PR; 1781PR; 1782PR; 1783PR; 1785PR; 1788PR; 1789PR (Carolus III); 1790PR; 1791PR; 1793PR; 1794PR; 1795PP; 1796PP; 1797PP; 1798PP; 1799PP; 1800PP; 1801PP; 1802PP; 1803PJ
Spanish colonies, 8 reales, Santiago (6): 1790DA; 1793DA; 1794DA; 1795DA; 1797DA; 1798DA

Bibliography: Sotheby's 2000, lots 462–67.

A129. Esquierquies Rocks off Sicily, Italy, 1975.

Type of find: Shipwreck.

Ship: HMS *Athenienne*.

Sank: October 20, 1806.

Contents: 4,000 AR.

Description:

The coins, all 8 reales issued under Charles III and IV, mostly come from Lima, Potosí, and México; a few also came from Santiago, Seville, and Madrid. Sebring has a photograph of an 8 reales, México, 1798FM. The following pieces were in the Amsterdam and the Penzance auctions:

Spanish colonies, 8 reales, México (160): 1773FM inverted; 1774FM; 1775FM; 1777FM; 1778FF; 1779FF (2); 1781FF; 1782FF; 1783FF; 1784FM; 1785FM (2); 1786FM (2); 1787FM; 1789FM; 1790FM; 1791FM (3); 1792FM (6); 1793FM (9); 1794FM (11); 1795FM (8); 1796FM (9); 1797FM (9); 1798FM (12); 1799FM (10); 1800FM (12); 1801FT (12); 1802FT (12); 1803FT (12); 1804 TH (16); ND

Spanish colonies, 8 reales, Guatemala (4): 1793M; 1796M; 1798M; 1801M

Spanish colonies, 8 reales, Lima (39): 1778MJ; 1780MI; 1788IJ; 1790IJ (2); 1791IJ (2); 1793IJ (3); 1794IJ (2); 1795IJ (3); 1796IJ (5); 1797IJ (4); 1798IJ (3); 1799IJ; 1800IJ (2); 1801IJ (3); 1802IJ (3); 1803IJ (2); ND

Spanish colonies, 8 reales, Potosí (16): 1773JR; 1775JR; 1783PR; 1787PR; 1790PR; 1792PR; 1793PR; 1794PR; 1795PP; 1796PP; 1797PP (2); 1798PP; 1799PP; 1800PP; 1801PP

Spanish colonies, 8 reales, Santiago (3): 1779DA; 1800AJ; 1803FJ

The wreck was found and salvaged by Robert Sténuit. There may have been originally 40,000 AR on the ship, but only 4,000 were recovered, and sea and sand had reduced 3,500 of these to silver slivers with no numismatic value.

Disposition: Sold by W. H. Lane, Penzance, England, United Kingdom, September 26, 1975, and by Christie's, Amsterdam, March 16, 1983.

Bibliography: Christie's 1983, lots 445–60, 465–66; Lane 1975, lots 1051–1238; Sebring 1986, 104–5, 117; Sebring 1995, 15.

A130. Point Cloates, Western Australia, Australia, October 1978, May 1980, July 1995.

Type of find: Shipwreck.

Ship: Rapid, left Boston, September 28, 1810, en route for Guangzhou, China.

Sank: January 7, 1811.

Contents: 9 AE, 20,000 AR.

Description:

Most of the silver was salvaged in 1811–13. Coins recovered so far in the modern recoveries include thirteen U.S. silver dollars, one Italian tallero, two Chinese cash, a Portugese copper coin, and six U.S. cents. The other coins are all 8 reales from México. One of them, a Charles IV coin, bore the Bank of England counterstamp of the head of George III. The dates break down as follows:

1759	1	1784	8	1799	121
1768	1	1785	3	1800	111
1770	1	1786	15	1801	119
1772	4	1787	12	1802	147
1773	1	1788	20	1803	133
1774	4	1789	25	1803, ctsped 8	1
1775	3	1790	28	1804	151
1776	10	1791	32	1805	69
1777	5	1792	31	1806	93
1778	2	1793	50	1807	32
1779	10	1794	44	1808	66
1780	9	1795	60	1809	4
1781	9	1796	93	ND ctsped W	1
1782	7	1797	99	ND	3,937
1783	4	1798	96	scraps	500

A survey of 3,500 coins, published in 1979, breaks the 8 reales down by mints and sovereigns:

Mint	Chas III	Chas IV	Ferd VII	N/A	Sum
México	119	1,331	9	191	1,650
Potosí	18	239	0	10	267
Lima	21	202	0	21	244
Sant'go	0	13	0	1	14
G'mala	2	7	0	0	9
Madrid	0	16	0	3	19
Seville	3	10	1	0	14
N/A	71	687	3	562	1,283
Sum	234	2,465	13	788	3,500

Disposition: Western Australian Museum. The artifact numbers have the prefix RP, and include the ranges RP1,870–93 and RP2,037–2,181, plus many other individual numbers up through RP13,533.

Bibliography: Balil 1981; Henderson 1980; Henderson 1983; Wilson 1979.

Artifacts database on the Western Australian Museum website, www.museum.wa.gov.au.

A131. Whittys Hill, near Wellington Bridge, County Wexford, Ireland, April 1954.

Type of find: Hoard.

Date of deposit: 1807.

Contents: 143 AR, 199 AV.

Description:

112 American coins. All, except for one 4 reales, were 8 reales.

The following coins were not counterstamped (77):

Spanish colonies, 4 reales, México, 1788

Spanish colonies, 8 reales, México (33): 1778; 1784; 1786; 1788; 1789; 1790 (4); 1791 (3); 1794 (2); 1795 (2); 1796 (2); 1797 (4); 1798; 1799; 1800; 1801; 1802; 1803; 1804 (3); 1805; 1806 (2)

Spanish colonies, 8 reales, Lima (4): 1789; 1800; 1803; 1805

Spanish colonies, 8 reales, Potosí (8): 1791; 1793; 1794; 1798; 1799; 1802; 1803; 1804

Spanish colonies, 8 reales, no mint recorded: Charles III, ND (4); 1798 (7); 1799 (4); 1800 (3); 1802 (4); 1804 (7); 1805 ; 1806; 1807

Counterstamped Spanish colonies 8 reales (the counterstamp is listed first, followed by the mint and date of the host coin) (35):

Head of George III in oval (5): Lima, 1774; México, 1792; Mexico, 1794 (2); México 1795

Head of George III in oval, also 1 CULNAN: Lima, 1794

B: México, 1781

B on obverse, W on reverse: Lima, 1799

Gothic C in obverse field: México, 1804

C and V on obverse, small cross pattée on reverse: Lima, 1799

C.EAD[E?] on neck, small device in front of forehead: México, 1803

CS in oval, on face: México, 1801

E.1: México, 1791

E.1 on neck: México, 1796

EP R(?) 1R1 on obverse, H1 on reverse: Lima, 1797

ICU, G1b on forehead and in field: Lima, 1796

I. H. and V: México, 1783

ID in field: México, 1798

IV: Lima, 1789

IC? and a small device: Lima, 1780

K on neck: Lima, 1796

Retrograde L on obverse, H and a small device (quatrefoil?) on reverse: México, 1802

LP: México, 1779

M or W on neck, letter under, in front of throat: México, 1804

N.J. in obverse field: México, 1804

O on king's nose: Potosí, 1802

O[?]LYNE: México, 1792

TB on neck, in monogram, ID in field on obverse: México, 1798

TS on neck and A+D on cheek: México,

1804
VC or LC, conjoined in obverse field, CER
W on king's neck and hair ribbon: Potosí, 1793
Two small devices, one possibly an arrow head in obverse field: Lima, 1804
Fleur de lis: México, 1780
A device, possibly a plume, on neck: Potosí, 1803
A small device, possibly a rose, on neck: México, 1806
Star within circle on neck, V horizontally behind, two small devices in field: México, 1802

Disposition: National Museum of Ireland (89).

Bibliography: Kenny and Gallagaher 1988.

A132. Fuentes de Andalucía, Sevilla Province, Spain, October 1952.

Type of find: Hoard.

Date of deposit: 1809.

Contents: 182 AR.

Description:

154 American coins:

Spanish colonies, 8 reales, México (82): 1772FM; 1783FM (2); 1790FM; 1791FM (2); 1792FM; 1793FM; 1795FM; 1796FM; 1798FM (2); 1799FM; 1800FM; 1801FM; 1801FT; 1802FT (3); 1803FT (8); 1804 TH (12); 1805 TH (14); 1806 TH; 1807 TH (6); Charles IV, 1808 TH(16); Ferdinand VII, 1808 TH (3); 1809 TH (3)

Spanish colonies, 8 reales, Guatemala (2): 1791M; 1796M

Spanish colonies, 8 reales, Popayán, 1800PP

Spanish colonies, 4 reales, Lima, 1779MI

Spanish colonies, 8 reales, Lima (32): 1785IJ; 1791IJ; 1794IJ; 1796IJ (2); 1797IJ (2); 1798IJ (3); 1799IJ; 1800IJ (5); 1801IJ (3); 1802IJ (2); 1803IJ (2); 1803JP; 1804JP; 1805JP (2); 1807JP (3); 1808JP (2)

Spanish colonies, 4 reales, Potosí (2): 1785PR;

1792PR

Spanish colonies, 8 reales, Potosí (12): 1793PR; 1799PP; 1802PP; 1803PJ (2); 1805PJ; 1807PJ (5); 1808PJ

Spanish colonies, 8 reales, Santiago, 1806FJ

The mint was unrecorded for the following, which went to the finder (6):

Spain or Spanish colonies, 4 reales, 1792

Spain or Spanish colonies, 8 reales (5): 1803; 1804; 1806; 1808 (2)

Disposition: Leonardo Iznar Muñoz (the finder) (6); Museo Arqueológico Hispalense (176).

Bibliography: Fernández-Chicharro 1953, 87–90 (Mateu 713).

A133. Off Needle Rock, Isle of Wight, England, United Kingdom, 1977.

Type of find: Shipwreck.

Ship: Probably HMS *Pomone*.

Sank: October 14, 1811.

Contents: 2 AE, 4 AR.

Description:

3 American coins:

Spanish colonies, 8 reales, México, 1808

Spanish colonies, 8 reales, Lima, 1808

Spanish colonies, 8 reales, mint uncertain, 1772–1825

The coins were found in the same general areas as the Assurance wreck, but must have come from a later wreck on the same site. The most likely candidate is the Pomone.

Disposition: Carisbrooke Castle Museum, Newport, Isle of Wight.

List compiled by Joseph E. Cribb, British Museum; in 1978 D. J. Tomalin was said to be preparing a full publication of the wreck.

Bibliography: McDonald 1974, 182 (information on the Pomone).

Coin Hoards 4 (1978): 123 (no. 404).

A134. Lebrija, Sevilla Province, Spain, April 1986.
Type of find: Hoard.
Date of deposit: 1813.
Contents: 70 AV.
Description:
  7 American coins:
  Spanish colonies, 2 escudos, Bogotá, 1788JJ
  Spanish colonies, 8 escudos, Bogotá, 1795JJ
  Spanish colonies, escudo, Popayán (3): 1777SF; 1789SF; 1795JF
  Spanish colonies, 8 escudos, Popayán, 1786 SF
  Spanish colonies, 2 escudos, Santiago, 1806FJ
Bibliography: De Paula 1987–89.

A135. Cargados Carajos Shoals, Mauritius, 1986.
Type of find: Shipwreck.
Ship: English East India Company ship *Cabalva*.
Sank: 1818.
Contents: AR.
Description:
  Spanish colonies, Charles IV, 8 reales, México
  Spanish colonies, Ferdinand VII, 8 reales, México
  Spanish colonies, Charles IV, 8 reales, Lima
  Spanish colonies, Ferdinand VII, 8 reales, Lima
Bibliography: Sebring 1986, 117–18.

A136. Athenian Agora Excavations, Hadrian Street, Athens, Greece, June 10, 1971.
Type of find: Hoard; archaeological excavation.
Date of deposit: 1818–19.
Container: Cloth purse in a flowerpot.
Contents: 17 AR, 11 AV.
Description:
  2 American coins:
  Spanish colonies, 8 reales, México, 1803FT
  Spanish colonies, 8 reales, Potosí, 1797PP
The hoard includes both Maria Theresa thalers (3) and Spanish colonies 8 reales. The Maria Theresa thalers of 1780, being of lower fineness, should drive out the Spanish colonies 8 reales from circulation in northern Africa, the Red Sea, and the eastern Mediterranean. This hoard indicates that in 1818 the two coinages were still circulating together in mainland Greece. Compare also the Elechnitz hoard from Bulgaria, below, deposited in 1847, which also contains both types of coins (*NFA* A140); and the Himerodendria hoard from Greece, deposited in 1850 (*NFA* A141).
Disposition: Found during the demolition of a house, directly below the basement level. Part of the collection of the Athenian Agora Excavations.
Bibliography: Kroll, Miles, and Miller 1973, 309–11.

A137. Morella, Castellón Province, Spain, 1961.
Type of find: Hoard.
Date of deposit: 1824.
Contents: 3 AR.
Description:
  1 American coin:
  Spanish colonies, 2 reales, México, 1773 MJ
Bibliography: Mateu 1961, 152 (Mateu 1104).

A138. Durham Coast, between Seaton Carew and West Hartlepool, Durham, England, United Kingdom, March 1867.
Type of find: Shipwreck.
Ship: Duck of London.
Sank: 1832.
Contents: 200 AR.
Description:
  200 American coins:

Spanish colonies, Charles III, probably México (200)

Bibliography: Thompson 1970, 140–41.

A139. "Les Comes," Castellbell i el Vilar, Bages Province, Catalonia, Spain, October 16, 1974.

Type of find: Hoard.
Date of deposit: Early 1838.
Contents: 76 AV.
Description:

19 American coins:
Spanish colonies, 4 escudos, México, 1775FM
Spanish colonies, 8 escudos, México, 1810HJ
Spanish colonies, 2 escudos, Popayán (2): 1783SF; 1793/2SF/JF
Spanish colonies, 8 escudos, Bogotá (4): 1788JJ; 1799JJ; 1807JJ; 1809JF
Spanish colonies, 8 escudos, Lima (5): 1777MJ; 1792IJ; 1798IJ (2); 1817JP
Spanish colonies, 8 escudos, Potosí (2): 1788PR; 1798PP
Spanish colonies, 8 escudos, Santiago (4): 1790DA; 1797DA; 1801AJ; 1802JJ

The hoard is noteworthy because all the 8 escudos are from the American mints. Also, although deposited in 1838, 92.1% of the coins date from the reign of Charles IV and earlier. The hoard thus reflects the importance of the American colonies to Spain's economy and how the Peninsular War and the loss of the American colonies impoverished Spain.

Believed to have been deposited during the disturbances of the First Carlist War.

Disposition: Museu Comarcal de Manresa.
Bibliography: Datzira 1981; Mateu 1979, 121–47 (Mateu 1591).

A140. Elechnitz, Blagoevgrad Region, Bulgaria, 1976.

Type of find: Hoard.
Date of deposit: 1847.
Contents: 16 AR, 32 AV.
Description:

7 American coins:
Spanish colonies, 8 reales, México (6): 1778; 1794FM; 1805 TH; 1818JJ (2); 1821JJ
Spanish colonies, 8 reales, Lima, 1804JP
Also included Maria Theresa thalers (3).

Disposition: The Blagoevgrad Regional Museum (16 AR); melted down as bullion (32 AV).
Bibliography: Yurukova 1978, 62.
Coin Hoards 6 (1981): 149 (no. 406).

A141. Himerodendria of Stamma, Messolongi (Aetoloakarnania), Greece, April 1973.

Type of find: Hoard.
Date of deposit: 1850.
Contents: 189 AR, all crown size.
Description:

Between 43 and 60 American coins:
Spanish colonies?, Charles IV, 8 reales, México?, 1795–1808 (6)
Spanish colonies, Ferdinand VII, 8 reales, México?, Lima?, and Potosí?, 1809–25 (11)
Mexico, Republic, 8 reales, 1827–50 (28)
Peru, Republic, 8 reales, 1834–41 (13)
Bolivia, Republic, 8 soles (2): 1830; 1833

The hoard also contained Maria Theresa thalers. The hoard also included one Greek 5 drachmai, a French 5 franc pieces, and thalers from Austria, Baden, Bavaria, Saxony and Württemberg.

Disposition: Athens Numismatic Museum.
Bibliography: Oikonomidos 1975, 4–5.

Coin Hoards 3 (1977): 149 (no. 404) (note that the cross-reference there to *Arhaiologikon Deltion* 31 [1976] is incorrect; the article appeared in the volume of the previous year).

A142. Dhulic Rock, near Galley Head, off Cork, Ireland, June 1983.
Type of find: Shipwreck.
Ship: SS *Crescent City.*
Sank: February 9, 1871.
Contents: AR.
Description: Mexico, peso, Zacatecas, 1870
Date of salvage is a terminus ante quem, derived from the date of the W. H. Lane auction containing coins from this wreck.
Bibliography: Pickford 1994, 172; Sebring 2004, lot 1623.

A143. China, June 7, 1990.
Type of find: Hoard.
Date of deposit: 1875.
Contents: 3 AR.
Description:
Spanish colonies, 8 reales, México, 1800
Spanish colonies, 8 reales, México, 1809
Mexico, 8 reales, Durango, 1875
Bibliography: China Numismatics, no. 42 (1993): 51.

A144. Holm House Farm, near Stockton-on-Tees, Teesside, England, United Kingdom, August 1964.
Type of find: Single finds made on a farm where the sewage from Stockton-on-Tees used to be deposited.
Date of deposit: 1880s.
Contents: 200 AE + AR.
Description:
2 American coins:
British colonies, Lower Canada, bouquet sou
USA, 50¢
Bibliography: Evans 1964.

A145. Bay of Biscay, off France, 1995.
Type of find: Shipwreck.
Ship: RMS *Douro.*
Sank: April 1, 1882.
Contents: 1,115 AR, 11,308 AV.
Description:
The bulk of the cargo was over eleven thousand sovereigns, but it also included 1,366 Brazilian coins:
Portuguese colonies, Brazil, 1,000 reis (4): 1752 (2); 1778; 1787
Portuguese colonies, Brazil, 1,600 reis (2): 1773; 1782B
Portuguese colonies, Brazil, 2,000 reis (5): 1754; 1778 (4)
Portuguese colonies, Brazil, 4,000 reis (17): 1700; 1762 (2); 1771; 1774; 1775 (3); 1777; 1806B; 1808; 1810B; 1811/0; 1812; 1813; 1815; 1816
Portuguese colonies, Brazil, 6,400 reis, Bahia (15): 1765; 1769; 1776; 1783/2; 1784; 1789/8 (3); 1790; 1792 (2); 1793; 1795; 1800; 1802
Portuguese colonies, Brazil, 6,400 reis, Rio de Janeiro (114): 1750 (2); 1756; 1758; 1760; 1762 (2); 1766; 1768; 1769 (2); 1770 (4); 1771 (3); 1772; 1773; 1774 (2); 1775; 1776; 1777; 1778; 1780 (3); 1781 (3); 1782; 1783 (3); 1784; 1785 (5); 1786 (5); 1787 (3); 1788 (5); 1789 widow (2); 1789 toucado; 1790 (5); 1791; 1792 (6); 1793 (4); 1794 (3); 1795; 1796 (5); 1797 (6); 1798 (2); 1799; 1801 (3); 1802 (3); 1803 (2); 1804; 1806 (3); 1807 (2); 1808 (2); 1809 (3); 1810 (2); 1813
Brazil, Peter I, 6,400 reis, Rio de Janeiro (4): 1824; 1832 (3)
Coins issued following the monetary reform under Peter II:
Brazil, Peter II, 500 reis (429)
Brazil, Peter II, 1,000 reis (632)
Brazil, Peter II, 2,000 reis (55)
Brazil, 10,000 reis (65): 1849; 1850; 1853 (13); 1854 (41); 1855 (6); 1856 (3)
Brazil, 20,000 reis (10): 1851; 1852 (2); 1853 (2); 1855; 1856 (2); 1857 (2)

Disposition: Sold at auction, November 20–21, 1996.

Bibliography: Spink's/Christie's 1996.

A146. In the North China Sea, off Luzon, the Philippines, June 1995.

Type of find: Shipwreck.
Ship: USS *Charleston*.
Sank: November 2, 1899.
Contents: AR, AV.
Description:
  Mexico, 8 reales, cap and rays type
  USA, Liberty type gold coins
  Assorted world trade coins

Bibliography: Paul A. Brombal Coins and Jewelry, "Treasure of the USS *Charleston*," http://www.pbrombal.com.

A147. Deidenberg, Elsenborn Region, Eastern Cantons, Belgium, October 1983.

Type of find: Hoard.
Date of deposit: August 1914.
Container: Small metal box.
Contents: 11 AV.
Description:
  6 American coins:
  USA, $10, 1881, 1882, 1893, 1894, 1901S, 1907

At the time of deposit this area (Eupen-Malmédy) was part of Germany, right next to the Belgian border. The date of deposit has been chosen on the basis that the hoard was concealed in connection with the military movements at the outbreak of the First World War. Eupen-Malmédy was ceded by Germany to Belgium after the First World War under the Treaty of Versailles.

Disposition: Found beneath the first step of the stairway to the cellar.

Bibliography: Dengis 1983.

A148. In the Vinh Thanh Mountains, Central Highlands, 35 miles northwest of the Port of Quinhon, Vietnam, July 31, 1968.

Type of find: Hoard.
Date of deposit: 1968.
Container: U.S. Army .50 caliber ammunition can, manufactured in Homerville, Georgia, USA.
Contents: 3,000 P (not including the South Vietnamese currency).
Description: USA, $50 (3,000)

935,000 dongs worth of South Vietnamese notes were also found. The U.S. $50s were in three stacks of a thousand each. Each stack was divided into five packets, tied with vines (so each packet was worth $10,000). All the money was circulated, not fresh. Thirty of the U.S. notes were marked with Chinese characters.

It was suggested at the time that the currency might have been profits from the black market. This, however, is unlikely, since the black market at the time used U.S. $100s rather than U.S. $50s. The hoard almost certainly was a money supply sent by North Vietnam down the Ho Chi Minh Trail to fund Vietcong operations in the Qui Nhon/Military Region 5 Area. North Vietnam set up a "Special Foreign Currency Fund," codenamed B29. B29 bought U.S. dollars in Hong Kong (which explains the Chinese characters on the notes), moved them to an office in Guangzhou, and then couriered the money from Guangzhou to Hanoi. From Hanoi the money was sent south down the Ho Chi Minh Trail. B29 made over U.S. $315 million worth of physical transfers in this manner.

The use of the ammunition can to contain the money is curious; B29 normally used tin-lined steel crates measuring 50 centimeters long, 20 centimeters thick and weighing 12 kilograms. Perhaps this cache was a portion of a larger shipment, broken out of the steel crates.

This information comes from reminiscences about the B29 operation published in Vietnamese newspapers on the occasion of the thirtieth anniversary of the Communist victory on April 30, 2005. The articles were translated from Vietnamese into English and the translations supplied by Merle Pribbenow. Howard A. Daniel III also provided helpful information for this entry.

Disposition: Found in a cave by Dwayne Morrison and the 3rd Platoon of B Company, 1st Battalion, 50th Infantry. After litigation, awarded to the U.S. Federal government.

Bibliography: Joseph B. Treaster, "$150,000 is Found in Vietnam Cave. G. I. Patrols Also Discover Cache of Saigon Currency," *New York Times*, August 5, 1968, 14.

"Army Keeps Cash Found by Sergeant," *Coin World*, March 1, 1972, 62.

Morrison v. U.S., 492 F.2d 1219 (1974) (Ct. Cl.).

Howard A. Daniel III, e-mail message to John M. Kleeberg, December 14, 2006.

Merle Pribbenow, e-mail message to John M. Kleeberg, December 14, 2006.

REFERENCES

Adams, John W. 1999. *The Indian Peace Medals of George III or His Majesty's Sometime Allies.* Crestline, CA: George Frederick Kolbe.

Akers, David W. 1975. *United States Gold Coins. An Analysis of Auction Records.* Vol. 2: *Quarter Eagles, 1796–1929.* Englewood, Ohio: Paramount Publications.

———. 1979. *United States Gold Coins. An Analysis of Auction Records.* Vol. 4: *Half Eagles, 1795–1929.* Englewood, Ohio: Paramount Publications.

———. 1980. *United States Gold Coins. An Analysis of Auction Records.* Vol. 5: *Eagles 1795–1933.* Englewood, Ohio: Paramount Publications.

———. 1982. *United States Gold Coins. An Analysis of Auction Records.* Vol. 6: *Double Eagles, 1849–1933.* Englewood, Ohio: Paramount Publications.

Allen, Leslie. 1982. "Tierra del Fuego." In *Secret Corners of the World,* 68–105. Washington, DC: National Geographic Society.

Allen, W. Frank. 1967. "Previously Unknown Spanish Gold Coins." *Numismatist* 80, no. 2 (February): 139–54.

American Auction Association (Division of Bowers and Ruddy Galleries, Inc.), Hollywood, CA, USA. 1974. *Auction Catalog (Stanislaw Herstal),* February 7–9.

André, Patrick, and Michel Dhénin. 1975. "Le Trésor de Saint-Pierre-Quiberon (Morbihan). Une Page de l'Histoire de la Ligue en Bretagne." *Archéologie en Bretagne,* no. 7 (Third Trimester): 31–33.

"Antiquities and Numismatics of Staten Island." 1868–69. *American Journal of Numismatics* 3, no. 5 (September 1868): 38–40; 3, no. 10 (February 1869): 73–75.

Apolant, Juan Alejandro. 1992. *Cronica del Naufragio del navío Nuestra Señora de la Luz (Montevideo 1752).* 1968. Reprint, Montevideo: Centro de Estudios del Pasado Uruguayo/Instituto Uruguayo de Numismática.

Appleton, William Sumner. 1874. "Newspaper Cuttings." *American Journal of Numismatics* 8, no. 3 (January): 57–58.

———. 1883. "Avalonia Pattern-Piece." *American Journal of Numismatics* 18, no. 2 (October): 42.

———. 1886. "Avalonia Again." *American Journal of Numismatics* 20, no. 4 (April): 93.

Apuzzo, Robert. 1992. *New York City's Buried Past. A Guide to Excavated New York City's Revolutionary War Artifacts, 1776–1783.* New York: R. + L. Publishers.

Archilla-Diez, Efrain. 1990. "Bats, Caves, and Caribbean Treasure." *Numismatist* 103, no. 7 (July): 1087–90.

Arnold, J. Barto, III, and Robert Weddle. 1978. *The Nautical Archaeology of Padre Island. The Spanish Shipwrecks of 1554.* Texas Antiquities Committee Publication, No. 7. New York: Academic Press.

Arroyo, H. 1972. "Peripatetic Pieces of Eight." *Numismatic Circular* 80, no. 9 (September): 320–21.

Asolati, Michele, and G. Crisfulli. 1994. *Ritrovamenti monetali di età romana nel Veneto,* ed. Giovanni Gorini, VI/2, *Venezia/Altino II.* Padua: Editorale Programma.

Atchison, Darryl A. 2007. *Canadian Numismatic Bibliography.* Victoria, British Columbia: Numismatic Education Society of Canada.

Augsburger, Leonard. 2008. *Treasure in the Cellar. A Tale of Gold in Depression-Era Baltimore.* Baltimore: Maryland Historical Society.

Baillion, Fernand. 1931. "Trouvailles: Trouvaille de Saint-Jean-lez-Saint-Nicolas." *Revue Belge de Numismatique et de Sigillographie* 83: 112.

Balil, Alberto. 1981. "Plata Española en Australia Occidental." *Gaceta Numismática* 61 (June): 53–56.

Banning, E. B. 1986–87. "Cache and Bury: The Archaeology of Numismatics." *Canadian Numismatic Journal* 31, no. 11 (December 1986): 473–85; 32, no. 1 (January 1987): 5–12.

Barker, R. B. 1978. "'New' Jamaican Counterstamps." *Numismatic Circular* 86, no. 6 (June): 308–10.

Barnsley, Edward R. 1993. "A Late Date Analysis of the Fairfield Hoard." *Colonial Newsletter* 33, no. 2 (whole no. 94)(July): 1383–84.

Bass, George F., ed. 1988. *Ships and Shipwrecks of the Americas. A History Based on Underwater Archaeology.* New York: Thames and Hudson.

Beals, Herbert K. 1980. "Chinese Coins in Six Northwestern Aboriginal Sites." *Historical Archaeology* 14: 58–72.

Beauchamp, William M. 1891. "Notes on Early Medals, Rings, Etc." *Report of the Proceedings of the Numismatic and Antiquarian Society of Philadelphia for the Years 1887–1889:* 40–49.

———. 1903. *Metallic Ornaments of the New York Indians.* New York State Museum, Bulletin 73 (Bulletin 305), Archaeology 8. Albany: University of the State of New York.

———. 1908. *Past and Present of Syracuse and Onondaga County, New York. From Prehistoric Times to the Beginning of 1908.* New York: S. J. Clarke.

Beck, Colleen M., Eric E. Deeds, Sheila Pozorski, and Thomas Pozorski. 1983. "Pajatambo: An 18th Century Roadside Structure in Peru." *Historical Archaeology* 17: 54–68.

Belden, Bauman L. 1927. *Indian Peace Medals Issued in the United States.* New York: American Numismatic Society.

Bense, Judith A., ed. 1999. *Archaeology of Colonial Pensacola.* Gainesville: University Press of Florida.

Bentley, William. 1905. *Diary.* Salem, MA: Essex Institute.

Bermuda Monetary Authority. 1997. *Coins of Bermuda, 1616–1996.* Edited by Malcolm E. Williams, Peter T. Sousa and Edward C. Harris. Hamilton, Bermuda: Bermuda Monetary Authority.

Berry, Paul S. 2002. "The Numismatic Record of Ferryland." *Avalon Chronicles* 7: 1–71.

———. 2006. "The DK Token—Revisited." *Colonial Newsletter* 46, no. 3 (whole no. 132)(December): 3065–68.

Besly, Edward. 1987. *English Civil War Coin Hoards.* British Museum Occasional Paper No. 51. London: British Museum.

Betts, Charles Wyllys. 1894. *American Colonial History Illustrated by Contemporary Medals.* New York: Scott Stamp and Coin.

Bijkerk, M. 1984. "Een 16–eeuwse muntvondst: Oud-Beijerland 1980." *Jaarboek voor Munt- en Penningkunde* 71: 145–49.

Bissett, Charles P. 1902. "A Find of Louis d'Or on the Coast of Cape Breton," *Canadian Antiquarian and Numismatic Journal* 3rd series, 4, no. 1 (January): 38–40.

Blackman, E. E. 1919. "Ancient Pawnee Medal." *Nebraska History and Record of Pioneer Days* 2, no. 2 (April-June): 5.

Bolton, Reginald Pelham. 1918–19. "The Military Hut-Camp of the War of the Revolution on the Dyckman Farm Manhattan. Explored by the Members of the Committee on Field Exploration of The New-York Historical Society." Pts. 1, 2, and 3. *Quarterly Bulletin of the New-York Historical Society* 2, no. 3 (October 1918): 89–97; 2, no. 4 (January 1919): 130–36; 3, no. 1 (April 1919): 15–18.

———. 1919. "The 'Old Fort,' and Camp Site at Richmond, Staten Island. Explored by the Committee on Field Exploration of the New-York Historical Society, W. L. Calver Chairman." *Quarterly Bulletin of the New York Historical Society* 3, no. 3 (October): 82–88.

———. 1921. "A Pioneer Settler's Home on Spuyten Duyvil Hill." *Quarterly Bulletin of the New York Historical Society* 5, no. 1 (April): 13–18.

———. 1931. "Number 120 Wall Street." *Quarterly Bulletin of the New York Historical Society* (January): 111–21.

Borrell Bentz, Pedro J. 1983. *Historia y Rescate de Galeon Nuestra Señora de la Concepción.* Santo Domingo, Dominican Republic: Museo de las Casas Reales.

Botsford, Robert K. 1935. "A Most Unusual Hoard." *Numismatist* 48, no. 2 (February): 82–83.

Bowden, Tracy. 1996. "Gleaning Treasure from the Silver Bank." *National Geographic* 190, no. 1 (July): 90–105.

Bowers, Q. David. 1979. *The History of United States Coinage As Illustrated by the Garrett Collection.* Los Angeles: Bowers and Ruddy Galleries.

———. 1997. *American Coin Treasures and Hoards.* Wolfeboro, NH: Bowers and Merena Galleries.

———. 1998. *The Treasure Ship S.S. Brother Jonathan: Her Life and Loss, 1850–1865.* Wolfeboro, NH: Bowers and Merena Galleries.

———. 2002. *A California Gold Rush History featuring the Treasure from the* SS Central America. Newport Beach, CA: California Gold Marketing Group.

Bowers and Merena, Los Angeles, California, USA. 1983. *Auction Catalog (George D. Hatie),* August 3–5.

Bowers and Merena, Wolfeboro, New Hampshire, USA. 1987. *Auction Catalog,* March 26–28.

———. 1999. *Auction Catalog (S.S. Brother Jonathan),* May 29.

———. 1999–2000. *Auction Catalog (Harry W. Bass, Jr., Collection),* Part II: October 2–4, 1999; Part III: May 2000; Part IV: November 20–21, 2000.

———. 2000. *Auction Catalog (Paul Mory),* June 22–23.

Bowers and Ruddy, Los Angeles, California, USA. 1977. *Auction Catalog (Harold A. Blauvelt, Iberoamerican and 1715 Spanish Treasure Fleet Collections),* February 17–19.

Boyd, E. 1961. "A Bronze Medal of Sixteenth Century Style." *El Palacio. A Quarterly Journal of the Museum of New Mexico in cooperation with the Archaeological Society of New Mexico* 68, no. 2 (Summer): 124–28.

———. 1970. "17th Century Spanish Medal Found in Estancia Valley." *El Palacio. Quarterly Journal of the Museum of New Mexico* 76, no. 3 (June): 16.
Breen, Walter Henry. 1952. "Survey of American Coin Hoards." *Numismatist* 65, no. 1 (January): 7–24; 65, no. 10 (October): 1005–10.
———. 1958. "Brasher & Bailey: Pioneer New York Coiners, 1787–1792." In Ingholt, *Centennial Publication of the American Numismatic Society*, 137–45.
———. 1988. *Walter Breen's Complete Encyclopedia of U. S. and Colonial Coins*. New York: Doubleday.
———. 1990. "The S. S. *Central America*: Tragedy and Treasure." *Numismatist* 103, no. 7 (July): 1064–72, 1126–30, 1166–67.
Breen, Walter Henry, and Ronald J. Gillio. 2003. *California Pioneer Fractional Gold. Historic Gold Rush Small Change 1852–1857 and Suppressed Jewelers' Issues 1858–1882*, 2nd ed. revised by Robert D. Leonard, Jr., et al. Wolfeboro, NH: Bowers and Merena Galleries.
Breton, Pierre Napoléon. 1894. *Histoire illustrée des monnaies et jetons du Canada*. Montréal: Pierre Napoléon Breton.
Brill, Robert H., I. Lynus Barnes, Stephen S. C. Tong, Emile C. Joel, and Martin J. Murtaugh. 1987. "Laboratory Studies of Some European Artifacts Excavated on San Salvador Island." In *First San Salvador Conference: Columbus and IIis World*, edited by Donald T. Gcracc, 247–92. Fort Lauderdale, Florida: College Center of the Finger Lakes, Bahamian Field Station.
Brown, Frank W. 1966. "The Story of San Antonio Money." *Numismatist* 79, no. 11 (November): 1463–69.
———. 1972. "The Story of the Discovery of the Garza Coins Called 'Jolas.'" *Numismatist* 85, no. 4 (April): 515–18.
Brown, I. D., and Michael Dolley. 1971. *A Bibliography of Coin Hoards of Great Britain and Ireland 1500–1967*. Special Publication No. 6. London: Royal Numismatic Society.
Bugbee, N. Penn. 1927. "The Granby Coin." *Numismatist* 40, no. 11 (November): 680.
Burgess, Robert F., and Carl J. Clausen. 1976. *Gold, Galleons, and Archaeology*. Indianapolis: Bobbs-Merrill.
"Buried Treasures Found." 1885. *American Journal of Numismatics* 20, no. 2 (October): 42.
Butler, J.D. 1882a. "Spanish Silver in Early Wisconsin—a Unique Medallic Find." *Canadian Antiquarian and Numismatic Journal* 10, no. 4 (April): 173–76.
———. 1882b. "The Hispano-Wisconsin Medal." *Canadian Antiquarian and Numismatic Journal* 11, no. 1 (July): 26–28.
Buttrey, Theodore Venn, Jr. 1967. "Cut Coins in Canada." *British Numismatic Journal* 36: 176–78.
Calver, William L. 1920. "The Summer Work of the Field Exploration Committee. 'Connecticut Village' Located." *Quarterly Bulletin of the New York Historical Society* 4, no. 3 (October): 71–73.
———. 1921. "Children's Toys Found in Revolutionary Camps." *Quarterly Bulletin of the New York Historical Society* 4, no. 4 (January): 100–3.
———. 1928. "Consider the Revolutionary Bullet." *Quarterly Bulletin of the New York Historical Society* 11, no. 4 (January): 120–27.
Cammarano, Maurice. 1998. *Corpus Luiginorum. Recueil général des pièces de cinq sols ou douzièmes d'écu dits "Luigini," 1642–1723*. Paris: Bibliothèque nationale de France.

Campo, Marta, and Maria Cinta-Mañé. 1986. "Hallazgos Monetarios Medievales y Modernos en Empúries." *Gaceta Numismática* 81 (June): 67–83.

Canadian Numismatic Company, Québec, Québec, Canada. 2008. *Auction Catalog (Canadian Numismatic Association),* July 19.

Cancio, Leopoldo. 1978–79. "El Tesoro de El Mesuno Corregido y Aumentado." *Gaceta Numismática* no. 51 (December 1978): 32–40; 52 (March 1979): 37–49.

———. 1979. "Una Arras en Santa Fe de Bogotá." *Gaceta Numismática* 47 (December): 31–35.

———. 1981. "Un Tesorillo de Monedas de Potosí." *Gaceta Numismática* 63 (December): 28–34.

———. 1990. "Two Moscow Hoards of Spanish Silver Coins." *Journal of the Russian Numismatic Society* 38 (spring): 6–9.

Cantwell, Anne-Marie, and Diana diZerega Wall. 2001. *Unearthing Gotham. The Archaeology of New York City.* New Haven: Yale University Press.

Carlotto, Tony. 1998. *The Copper Coins of Vermont and Those Bearing the Vermont Name.* N.p.: Colonial Coin Collectors Club.

Carter, John, and Trevor Kenchington. 1985. "The Terence Bay Wreck: Survey and Excavation of a Mid-18th Century Fishing Schooner." In *Proceedings of the Sixteenth Conference on Underwater Archaeology,* edited by Paul Forsythe Johnston, 13–26. Society for Historical Archaeology, Special Publication Series, No. 4. Glassboro, NJ: Society for Historical Archaeology.

Castells & Castells, Montevideo, Uruguay. 1997. *Auction Catalog (Nuestra Señora de la Luz),* November 6.

Chapman, Henry, Philadelphia, Pennsylvania, USA. 1918. *Auction Catalog (Alison W. Jackman),* June 28–29.

Charlton, J. E. 1976. "The Numismatic Treasures of 'Le Chameau.'" *Canadian Numismatic Journal* 21, no. 8 (September): 307–9.

Christensen, Henry, Inc., Teaneck, New Jersey, USA. 1982. *Numismatic Commentary and Auction Sale, #80,* May 14.

Christie's, Amsterdam, Noord-Holland, the Netherlands. 1983. *Auction Catalog,* March 16.

Christie's, London, England, UK. 1992. *Auction Catalog (Maravillas),* May 28.

Christie's, New York, New York, USA. 1988a. *Auction Catalog (Atocha and Santa Margarita),* June 14–15.

———. 1988b. *Catalog (The Research Coin Collection).*

———. 1989. *Auction Catalog (HMS Feversham),* February 7.

———. 2000. *Auction Catalog (Central America),* December 14.

Cibis, Kurt. 1975. "Ein Münzschatzfund mit kurtrierischen Dreipetermännchen aus New York." *Trierer Zeitschrift für Geschichte und Kunst des Trierer Landes und seiner Nachbargebiete* 38: 135–52.

Clark, Joshua Victor Hopkins. 1849. *Onondaga; or Reminiscences of Earlier and Later Times; being a Series of Historical Sketches Relative to Onondaga; with Notes on the Several Towns in the County, and Oswego.* Syracuse: Stoddard and Babcock.

Clarke, John M. 1911. "Results of Excavations at the Site of the French 'Custom House,' or 'General Wolfe's House,' on Peninsula Point in Gaspé Bay." *Canadian Antiquarian and Numismatic Journal* 8, no. 4 (October): 147–69.

Clausen, Carl J. 1968. "The Fort Pierce American Gold Find." *Florida Historical Quarterly* 47, no. 1 (July): 51–58.

Cleland, Charles E. 1971. "Metallic Artifacts." In *The Lasanen Site*, edited by Charles E. Cleland, 19–34. Anthropological Series. East Lansing, MI: Michigan State University.

Clifford, Barry, and Peter Turchi. 1993. *The Pirate Prince: Discovering the Priceless Treasures of the Sunken Ship Whydah. An Adventure.* New York: Simon and Schuster.

Coffman, Ferris LaVerne. 1957. *1001 Lost, Buried, or Sunken Treasures. Facts for Treasure Hunters.* New York: Nelson.

Cogan, Edward, New York, New York, USA. 1875. *Auction Catalog (Mendes I. Cohen),* October 25–29.

Cohen, David H. 1985. "The Randall Hoard." In *America's Copper Coinage*, 41–51. Coinage of the Americas Conference, Proceedings No. 1. New York: American Numismatic Society.

Coin Galleries (Division of Stack's), New York, New York, USA. 1988. *Mail Bid Sale,* November 9.

———. 1994. *Mail Bid Sale,* July 13.

———. 1998. *Mail Bid Sale,* April 15.

Colapinto, John. 2008. "Secrets of the Deep. The dispute over what may be the largest sunken treasure ever found." *New Yorker,* April 7.

Comptoir Général Financier, Paris, France. 1999. *Mail Bid Sale (Trésors I),* June 10.

Cotter, John L. 1958. *Archaeological Excavations at Jamestown, Colonial National Historical Park, and Jamestown National Historic Site, Virginia.* United States, Department of the Interior, National Park Service, Archaeological Research Series, No. 4. Washington, DC: Department of the Interior.

Cotter, John L., Daniel G. Roberts and Michael Parrington. 1992. *The Buried Past: An Archaeological History of Philadelphia.* Philadelphia: University of Pennsylvania Press.

Cox, Joseph A. 1964. *The Recluse of Herald Square. The Mystery of Ida E. Wood.* New York: Macmillan.

Craig, Alan K. 2000a. *Spanish Colonial Gold Coins in the Florida Collection.* Gainesville: University Press of Florida.

———. 2000b. *Spanish Colonial Silver Coins in the Florida Collection.* Gainesville: University Press of Florida.

Cribb, Joseph E. 1977. "Some hoards of Spanish Coins of the Seventeenth Century Found in Fukien Province, China." *Coin Hoards* 3: 180–84.

Crisman, Kevin J. 1988. "Struggle for a Continent: Naval Battles of the French and Indian Wars." In Bass, *Ships and Shipwrecks of the Americas,* 129–48.

Crosby, Sylvester Sage. 1875. *The Early Coins of America.* Boston: Sylvester S. Crosby.

Daley, Robert. 1977. *Treasure.* New York: Random House.

Danforth, Brian J. 2001. "Wood's Hibernia Coins Come to America." *Colonial Newsletter* 41, no. 2 (whole no. 117)(August): 2213–30.

Datzira i Soler, Sebastià. 1981. "Trobalia de Castellbell i el Vilar." *Acta Numismàtica* 2: 282–89.

De Paula Pérez Sindreu, Francisco. 1987–89. "Hallazgo de setenta monedas de oro en una enscombrera pública de Lebrija (Sevilla)." *Numisma* 37–39 (whole nos. 204–21): 183–200.

Deagan, Kathleen A. 1980. "Spanish St. Augustine: America's First 'Melting Pot,'" *Archaeology* 33, no. 5 (September-October): 22–30.

———. 1992. "La Isabela, Europe's First Foothold in the New World." *National Geographic* 181, no. 1 (January): 40–53.

———. 1995. *Puerto Real. The Archaeology of a Sixteenth-Century Spanish Town in Hispaniola.* The Ripley P. Bullen Series, Florida Museum of Natural History. Gainesville: University of Press of Florida.

Deagan, Kathleen, and José María Cruxent. 2002a. *Archaeology at La Isabela. America's First European Town.* New Haven: Yale University Press.

———. 2002b. *Outpost among the Taínos. Spain and America at La Isabela, 1493–1498.* New Haven: Yale University Press.

DeCosta, Benjamin Franklin. 1871. *Rambles in Mount Desert: with Sketches of Travel on the New-England Coast from Isle of Shoals to Grand Menan.* New York: A. D. F. Randolph.

Deetz, James. 1993. *Flowerdew Hundred. The Archaeology of a Virginia Plantation, 1619–1864.* Charlottesville: University Press of Virginia.

De Jesus, Pablo I. 1952. "Buried Hoard in Manila's Walled City." *Numismatist* 65, no. 11 (November): 1082–90.

———. 1953. "Further Report on the Manila Hoard." *Philippine Numismatic Monographs* 9: 1–5. Reprinted in *Numismatist* 68, no. 3 (March 1955): 255–57.

———. 1954. "Note on a Buried Hoard in Bataan Province." *Philippine Numismatic Monographs* 10 (March): 44.

———. 1955. "A Hoard of Mexican Silver Cobs Discovered in the Philippines." *Philippine Numismatic Monographs* 11 (October): 1–5.

———. 1965. "Cavite Coin Hoard." *Philippine Numismatic Monographs* 15: 1–6.

Dengis, J. L. 1983. "Un trésor de monnaies contemporaines découvert dans les Cantons de l'Est." *Revue Belge de Numismatique et de Sigillographie* 129: 208–9.

———. 1984. "Trouvailles d'Aubel." *Revue Belge de Numismatique* 130: 225–230.

Dhénin, Michel. 1998. "Un trésor de monnaies espagnoles du XVIIe siècle découvert à Pange (Moselle)." *Trésors Monétaires* 17: 349–55.

Dhénin, Michel, and François Thierry. 1996. "The coins." In *Treasures of the San Diego,* edited by Jean-Paul Desroches, Gabriel Casal, and Franck Goddio, 184–89. Paris: Association Française d'Action Artistique.

Di Peso, Charles C. 1976. "That Other Revolution." *Archaeology* 29, no. 3 (July): 186–93.

Dickeson, Montroville Wilson. 1865. *The American Numismatic Manual of the Currency or Money of the Aborigines, and Colonial, State, and United States Coins. With Historical and Descriptive Notices of Each Coin or Series,* 3rd ed. Philadelphia: J. B. Lippincott.

Dolley, Michael. 1975. "A Neglected Nineteenth Century Find from the Co. Laois." *Numismatic Circular* 83, no. 2: 60–61.

Dolley, Michael, and Margaret Warhurst. 1977. "New Evidence for the Date of the so-called 'St. Patrick's' Halfpence and Farthings." *Irish Numismatics* 10, no. 5 (whole no. 59) (September-October): 161–63.

Domínguez González, Lourdes. 1995. *Arqueología Colonial Cubana: Dos Estudios.* Havana, Cuba: Editorial de Cicencias Sociales.

Doty, Richard G. 1984. "The North Carolina Railroad Hoard." *Museum Notes* 29: 191–201.
Doty, Richard G., and John M. Kleeberg, eds. 2006. *Money of the Caribbean.* Proceedings No. 15. New York: American Numismatic Society.
Downey, P. J., Pty. Ltd., Melbourne, Victoria, Australia. 1986. *Auction Catalog,* March 25.
Drooker, Penelope B. 1988. "Soundings in Harvard Yard." *Archaeology* 41, no. 1 (January/February): 92.
Droulers, Frédéric. 1980. *Les Trésors de Monnaies Royales de Louis XIII à Louis XVI découverts en France et dans le Monde depuis le XIXe Siècle.* Paris: Feydeau Numismatique and Frédéric Droulers.
Dubois, Patterson. 1884. "Compte Rendu." *American Journal of Numismatics* 18, no. 4 (April): 89–91.
———. 1885. "Hog Money, etc." *American Journal of Numismatics* 19, no. 3 (January): 66–67.
Dubois, William Ewing. 1846. *Pledges of History. A Brief Account of the Collection of Coins belonging to the Mint of the United States, more Particularly of the Antique Specimens.* Philadelphia: C. Sherman.
Dunn, C. Frank. 1939. "New Jersey Cent Unearthed in Kentucky." *Numismatist* 52, no. 1 (January): 20–21.
Duplessy, Jean. 1978. "Le Trésor de Saint-Martin-de-Beauville (Lot-et-Garonne) (Monnaies d'Argent et de Billon des XVe et XVIe Siècles)." *Revue Numismatique,* 6th ser., 20: 157–70.
———. 1979. "Le Trésor Monétaire du Tréport (Monnaies d'argent françaises et étrangères des XVIe et XVIIe siècles)." *Cahiers Numismatiques* 14 (whole nos. 59–61) (March-September): 270–86.
Dušani, Svetozar St. 1979. "Ostava Srebrnog Novtsa XVI–XVIII Veka iz Manastira Ljubostinje u Srbiyi," [A Hoard of Silver Coins of the XVI-XVIII Centuries Discovered at the Monastery of Ljubostinja (Serbia)]. *Numizmaticar [Numismatics]* 2: 191–218.
Dym, Kurt A. 1984. "Hallazgo de Monedas Españolas de los Paises Bajos." *Gaceta Numismática* 74–75 (September-December): 234–45.
Earle, Peter. 1979. *The Wreck of the Almiranta. Sir William Phips and the Search for the Hispaniola Treasure.* London: Macmillan.
———. 2007. *Treasure Hunt. Shipwreck, Diving, and the Quest for Treasure in an Age of Heroes.* New York: St. Martin's Press.
Elder, Thomas L., New York, New York, USA. 1910. *Auction Catalog (Ebenezer Gilbert),* October 12–13.
Esler, Graham. 1977. "The Otterville Hoard." *Canadian Numismatic Journal* 22, no. 3 (March): 103–7.
Evans, David. 1964. "Down on the Farm." *Seaby's Coin and Medal Bulletin* no. 8 (August): 277–280.
Evans, Robert. 2000. "A Wealth of Double Eagle Die Varieties." *Numismatist* 113, no. 7 (July): 740–47.
Ewen, Charles R., and John H. Hann. 1998. *Hernando de Soto among the Apalachee. The Archaeology of the First Winter Encampment.* Gainesville: University Press of Florida.
Falan, William J., and George C. Ingram. 1973. "Gateway to Upper Canada: The Fort at Coteau du Lac." *Archaeology* 26, no. 3 (July): 188–97.
Farris, Glenn J. 1982. "'Cash' as Currency: Coins and Tokens from Yreka Chinatown." *Historical Archaeology* 13: 48–52.
Fauver, L. B. 1980. "An Old Hoard of Blacksmiths." *Canadian Numismatic Journal* 25, no. 1 (January): 18–19.

Ference, Thomas, and Gary A. Trudgen. 2001. "A Pouch Full of Money." *Colonial Newsletter* 41, no. 1 (whole no. 116)(April): 2201–4.

Fernández-Chicharro y de Dios, Concepción. 1953. "Recientes Descubrimientos Numismáticos en Andalucía." *Numario Hispánico* 2: 87–90.

———. 1972. "Hallazgos numismáticos de Sevilla en 1972." *Numisma* 22: 361–80.

Flanagan, Laurence. 1988. *Ireland's Armada Legacy*. Dublin: Gill & Macmillan.

Frossard, Edouard. 1880. "Medals Found in the Arctic Regions." *Numisma* 4, no. 6 (November): 3.

Fuller, Perry W., Baltimore, Maryland, USA. 1935. *Auction Catalog (Theodore Jones and Henry Grob)*, May 2.

García Castañeda, José A. 1938. "Asiento Yayal." *Revista de Arqueología* 1, no. 1 (August): 44–58.

Garrett, Wilbur E. 1987. "Waterway that led to the Constitution: George Washington's Patowmack Canal." *National Geographic* 171, no. 6 (June): 716–53.

Gaspar, Peter P., and Eric P. Newman. 1978. "An Eighteenth Century Hoard from Philadelphia." *Coin Hoards* 4 (London): 127–30.

Gladfelter, David D. 2002. "By Sudden Descent: Discovery of the George Colonial Paper Hoard." *Colonial Newsletter* 42, no. 3 (whole no. 121)(December): 2403–6.

Ira & Larry Goldberg, Beverly Hills, California, USA. 2005. *Auction Catalog (Pre-Long Beach)*, February 20–23.

Gordon, Ralph C. 1987. *West Indies Countermarked Gold Coins*. N.p.: Erik Press.

Graham, R. J. 1986. "An Old Newfoundland Savings Hoard." *Transactions of the Canadian Numismatic Research Society* 22: 60–61. Reprinted in: *Canadian Numismatic Journal* 31, no. 7 (July/August 1986): 316–17.

Gredesky, Todd. 2000. "More on the Circulation of English and Irish Coppers: Small Change Coppers found in Southern New Jersey." *Colonial Newsletter* 40, no. 1 (whole no. 113)(April): 2063–64.

Green, Jeremy N. 1973. "The wreck of the Dutch East Indiaman the *Vergulde Draeck*, 1656." *International Journal of Nautical Archaeology and Underwater Exploration* 2, no. 2 (September): 267–89.

Greenwood, Roberta S. 1978. "The Overseas Chinese at Home: Life in a nineteenth century Chinatown in California." *Archaeology* 31, no. 5 (September-October): 42–49.

Grissim, John. 1980. *The Lost Treasure of the Concepción*. New York: William Morrow.

Gums, Bonnie. 1987. "Remnant of French Colonial Village Excavated at Cahokia." *Historic Illinois* 10, no. 3 (October): 1–3, 5.

Gunselman, Cheryl, and Roderick Sprague. 2003. "A Buried Promise: the Palus Jefferson Peace Medal." *Journal of Northwest Anthropology* 37, no. 1: 53–88, available at http://www.wsulibs.wsu.edu/Holland/masc/temp/buriedpromise.hm.

Handley, L. B. 1943. "Buried Treasure." *Numismatist* 56, no. 6 (June): 459–60.

Hanscom, Dick. 1995. "Willis and Welch: Merchants to a Gold Rush." *Numismatist* 108, no. 4 (April): 437–43.

———. 1998. "A Medal of Exploration and Friendship." *Numismatist* 111, no. 3 (March): 285–87, 321–23.

Hanson, Lee, and Dick Ping Hsu. 1975. *Casemates and Cannonballs. Archaeological Excavations at Fort Stanwix, Rome, New York*. Publications in Archeology 14. Washington, DC: National Park Service.

Hardesty, Donald L. 1988. *The Archaeology of Mining and Miners: A View from the Silver State.* Society for Historical Archaeology, Special Publication Series, No. 6. Pleasant Hill, CA: Society for Historical Archaeology.

Harland, John, ed. 1856–57. *The House and Farm Accounts of the Shuttleworths of Gawthorpe Hall, in the County of Lancaster, at Smithils and Gawthorpe, from September 1582 to October 1621,* Part 2–3. Chetham Society, Remains Historical & Literary Connected with the Palatine Counties of Lancaster and Chester, 41–42. Manchester: Chetham Society.

Harris, N. Neil. 1986. "Coins of the *Nuestra Señora de Atocha*." *Numismatist* 99, no. 10 (October): 2017–40.

Haseltine, John W., Philadelphia, Pennsylvania, USA. 1880. *Auction Catalog,* January 21.

Hayden, Horace Edwin. 1874. "Indian Peace Medals." *American Journal of Numismatics* 9, no. 1 (July): 7–8.

———. 1886. "Various Silver and Copper Medals Presented to the American Indians by the Sovereigns of England, France and Spain, from 1600 to 1800, and especially of five such medals of George I of Great Britain, now in possession of this Society and its Members." Wyoming Historical and Geological Society, *Proceedings and Collections* 2: 217–38.

Hecht, Robert A., Kingsborough Community College, Brooklyn, New York. 1993. Letter to John M. Kleeberg, April 21.

Heldman, Donald P. 1980. "Coins at Michilimackinac." *Historical Archaeology* 14: 82–107.

Henderson, Graeme. 1980. "Indiamen: Traders of the East." *Archaeology* 33, no. 6 (November-December): 18–25.

———. 1983. "Update: The Identification of a China Trader." *Archaeology* 36, no. 3 (May-June): 69.

Heritage Auction Galleries, Dallas, Texas, USA. 2007. *Auction Catalog (Treasures of the Sea Collection),* January 7–8.

Heritage Numismatic Auctions, Dallas, Texas, USA. 1989. *Auction Catalog,* June 15–18.

———. 2001. *Auction Catalog (FUN Signature Sale),* January 4–6.

Highfill, John W. 1992. "The Redfield Hoard." In *The Comprehensive U. S. Silver Dollar Encyclopedia,* edited by John W. Highfill. Broken Arrow, OK: Highfill Press.

Hoare, Jeffrey, Auctions, Inc., Toronto, Ontario, Canada. 1993. *Auction Catalog,* February 26–27.

Hodder, Michael J. 1992. "An American Collector's Guide to the Coins of Nouvelle France." In Kleeberg, *Canada's Money,* 1–35.

Hoge, Robert Wilson. 2002. "Numismatic Materials Recovered from the Fort Vengeance Monument Site (VT-RU-216), Pittsford, Vermont." *American Journal of Numismatics* 14: 97–104.

Holmes, Walter. 1959. "On Old Banknotes Found in Western Ontario." *Canadian Numismatic Journal* 4, no. 11 (November): 444.

Hoover, Oliver. 2007. E-mail message to John M. Kleeberg, November 26.

Hubbard, Clyde. 1993. Face-to-face conversation with John M. Kleeberg, July 29.

Hudgins, Joe D. 1984–86. "A Historic Indian Site in Wharton County, Texas." *Bulletin of the Texas Archeological Society* 55: 29–51.

Hudson, J. Paul. 1979. "Brass Casting Counters (or Jettons) found at Jamestown." *Quarterly Bulletin of the Archaeological Society of Virginia* 34, no. 2 (December): 112–14.

Huey, Paul R. 2004. "A New Look at an Old Object." *New York State Preservationist* 8, no. 2 (Fall/Winter): 22.

Ingholt, Harald, ed. 1958. *Centennial Publication of the American Numismatic Society.* New York: American Numismatic Society.

Irwin, Ross W. 1995. "Hoard of Coins Found." *Transactions of the Canadian Numismatic Research Society* 31: 105.

Jackson, Kevin, and Roger Moore. 2007. "Imitation 1781 British Halfpenny Recovered in Virginia." *Colonial Newsletter* 47, no. 3 (whole no. 135)(December): 3193–94.

Jacobs, Wayne L. 1999. "The Saga of the Pistareen: Part Three." *Canadian Numismatic Journal* 44, no. 3 (March): 118–22.

Jara M., Carlos. 2008. E-mail message to John M. Kleeberg, January 17.

Jensen, Jørgen Steen. 1973–74. "Mønterne fra Ostindiefareren 'Wendela,' forlist ved Shetlandsøerne 1737." *Nordisk Numismatisk Årsskrift*: 31–67.

Johnson, Chester R. 1961. "A Note on the Excavation Of Yunque, San Gabriel." *El Palacio. A Quarterly Journal of the Museum of New Mexico in cooperation with the Archaeological Society of New Mexico* 68, no. 2 (Summer): 121–24.

Jones, John F. 1938. "The Aaron White Hoard of Coins: One of the Many Contributing Causes for the Scarcity of Specie During the Civil War." *Numismatist* 51, no. 2 (February): 111–12.

Jordan, Louis E. 2006. "The DK Token and Small Change in Early Seventeenth Century Settlement at Ferryland, Newfoundland." *Colonial Newsletter* 46, no. 2 (whole no. 131)(August): 3005–59.

———. 2007. "Coinage and Exchange at the Richmond Island Trading Post during the 1630s and the Richmond Island Coin Hoard." *Colonial Newsletter* 47, no. 1 (whole no. 133)(April): 3121–47.

Judge, Joseph. 1988. "Between Columbus and Jamestown: Exploring Our Forgotten Century." *National Geographic* 173, no. 3 (March): 330–63.

Kays, Thomas A. 1995. "Notes from a New Patron and Relic Hunter." *Colonial Newsletter* 35, no. 1 (whole no. 99) (April): 1488.

———. 1996. "More Observations by a Relic Hunter." *Colonial Newsletter* 36 no. 3 (whole no. 103)(September): 1637–45.

———. 2001. "When Cross Pistareens Cut Their Way Through the Tobacco Colonies." *Colonial Newsletter* 41, no. 1 (whole no. 116)(April): 2169–99.

———. 2005. "Second Thoughts on a First Rate Coin Hoard: Castine Revisited." *Colonial Newsletter* 45, no. 2 (whole no. 128)(August): 2837–68.

———. 2007. "Second City in Virginia Also Plans 400th Anniversary of its Founding." *Virginia Numismatist* 23, no. 4 (fall): 9–12.

Keith, Donald H. 1988. "Shipwrecks of the Explorers." In Bass, *Ships and Shipwrecks of the Americas,* 45–68.

Kelso, William M. 1979. "Rescue Archaeology on the James: Early Virginia Country Life." *Archaeology* 32, no. 5 (September-October): 15–25.

———. 1984. *Kingsmill Plantations, 1619–1800. Archaeology of Country Life in Colonial Virginia.* Studies in Historical Archaeology, ed. Stanley South. Orlando, Florida: Academic Press.

———. 1997. *Archaeology at Monticello. Artifacts of Everyday Life in the Plantation Community.* Monticello Monograph Series. Monticello, VA: Thomas Jefferson Memorial Foundation.

———. 2006. *Jamestown: the Buried Truth.* Charlottesville, VA: University of Virginia Press.

Kelso, William M., Nicholas M. Luccketti and Beverly A. Straube. 1995–2000. *Jamestown Rediscovery I-VI.* Jamestown, VA: Association for the Preservation of Virginia Antiquities.

Kenny, Michael. 1981. "English and Spanish Coins, 1594–1666, from Gortnaheltia, Newport, Co. Mayo." *Numismatic Circular* 89, no. 5 (May): 162–63.

Kenny, Michael, and Colm Gallagher. 1988. "The Wellington Bridge Hoard." In *Small Change. Papers on post medieval Irish Numismatics in memory of Michael Dolley M.R.I.A.* edited by Colm Gallagher, 49–52. Numismatic Society of Ireland, *Occasional Papers* No. 36. Dublin: Numismatic Society of Ireland.

Kent, John P. C. 1957. "Mr. Bruce Binney's Civil War Hoard." *Numismatic Chronicle* 6th series, 17: 245–46.

———. 1958. "Gold Bars and Ingots from the Bermuda Treasure." *Numismatic Chronicle* 6th Series, 18: 9–12.

Kessler, Alan H. 1976. *The Fugio Coppers: A Simple Method for Identifying Die Varieties with Rarity Listing and Price Guide.* Newtonville, MA: Colony Coin Corp.

Kiesling, Stephen. 1994. *Walking the Plank. A True Adventure Among Pirates.* Ashland, Oregon: Nordic Knight.

Kinder, Gary. 1998. *Ship of Gold in the Deep Blue Sea.* New York: Atlantic Monthly Press.

King, James B., Jr. 1984. *The Tilley Treasure.* Point Lookout, Missouri: School of the Ozarks Press.

King, Stafford. 1952. "Gold in Curran Hoard totaled $14,235." *Numismatist* 65, no. 5 (May): 475–78.

Kleeberg, John M. 1992a. *Money of Pre-Federal America.* Coinage of the Americas Conference, Proceedings No. 7. New York: American Numismatic Society, 1992.

———. 1992b. "The New Yorke in America Token." In Kleeberg, *Money of Pre-Federal America,* 15–57.

———. 1993–94. Review of *La Circulation Monétaire et les Trouvailles Numismatiques du Moyen Âge et des Temps Modernes au Pays de Luxembourg,* by Raymond Weiller. *American Journal of Numismatics* 5–6: 257.

———, ed. 1994a. *Canada's Money.* Coinage of the Americas Conference, Proceedings No. 8. New York: American Numismatic Society.

———. 1994b. "Introduction." In Kleeberg, *Canada's Money,* ix-xi.

———. 1995. "The Silver Dollar as an Element of International Trade: A Study in Failure." In *America's Silver Dollars,* edited by John M. Kleeberg, 87–110. Coinage of the Americas Conference, Proceedings No. 9. New York: American Numismatic Society.

———. 1995–96. "Reconstructing the Beach-Grünthal Hoard of Counterfeit Halfpence: the Montclair, New Jersey (1922) Hoard." *American Journal of Numismatics* 7–8: 187–208.

———. 1996. "The Shipwreck of the *Faithful Steward:* A 'Missing Link' in the Exports of British and Irish Halfpence." In *Coinage of the American Confederation Period,* edited by Philip L. Mossman, 55–77. Coinage of the Americas Conference, Proceedings No. 11. New York: American Numismatic Society.

———. 1999. "From Regional to National Gold Circulation Patterns: the Evidence of the Hull, Texas (1936) Hoard." *American Journal of Numismatics* 11: 69–83.

———. 2005. "The Stepney Find: Hoard or Collection? The Debate Continues." *Colonial Newsletter* 45, no. 1 (whole no. 127)(April): 2807–31.

———. 2006. "The Law and Practice Regarding Coin Finds: Treasure Trove Law in the United States." International Numismatic Commission, *Compte Rendu* 53: 13–26.

———. 2008. "The Philadelphia Gold Hoard of 1872." *Colonial Newsletter* 48, no. 1 (whole no. 136) (April): 3235–63.

Kleeberg, John M., and Armando Bernardelli. 1998. "The Gambellara, Veneto (1913) Hoard." *Quaderni Ticinesi. Numismatica e Antichità Classiche* 27: 371–85.

Kleiner, Fred. 1978. *Mediaeval and Modern Coins in the Athenian Agora*. Excavations of the Athenian Agora: Picture Book No. 18. Princeton, NJ: American School of Classical Studies at Athens.

Kluge, Bernd. 1978–79. "Znaleziska Monet z XVI-XVIII w. na Obszarze Polski na Podstawie Zbiorów i Archiwum Gabinetu Numizmatycznego Muzeów Pánstwowych w Berlinie." *Wiadomości Numizmatyczne* 22 (1978): 93–109; 23 (1979): 87–115.

Kotlar, Mikołaj. 1975. *Znaleziska Monet z. XIV-XVII. W. na Obszarze Ukraińskej SRR. Materiały.* Wrocław: Polskie Towarzystwo Archeologiczne i Numizmatycne.

Kovach, John. 1993. "Another Visit to Economy, Pennsylvania." *John Reich Journal* 7, issue 4 (July): 26–31.

Kraljevich, Jr., John J. 2007. "Coins in the Jamestown Wilderness." *Numismatist* 120, no. 5 (May): 50–57.

Krause, Chester L., and Clifford Mishler. 2000. *Standard Catalog of World Gold Coins*. 4th ed. Iola, Wisconsin: Krause.

Kroll, John H., George C. Miles, and Stella G. Miller. 1973. "An Early Byzantine and a Late Turkish Hoard from the Athenian Agora." *Hesperia* 42, no. 3 (July-September): 301–11.

Labao, Erni R. 2005. "The Pasay Hoard." *Bank Note Society of the Philippines Journal* (August): 7–11.

Lane, W. H., & Son, Penzance, Cornwall, England. 1974. *Auction Catalog (HMS Association)*, September 24.

———. 1975. *Auction Catalog (Sunken Treasure from Nine Famous Wrecks)*, September 26.

Lange, David W. 1984. "Henry D. Cogswell and His Curious Time Capsule." *Numismatist* 98, no. 1 (January): 26–31.

Laramée, Serge, Boucherville, Québec, Canada. 1989. *Auction Catalog (1989 Canadian Numismatic Association)*, July 28–30.

Lasser, Joseph R. 1989. "The Remarkable *Feversham* Hoard." *Numismatist* 102, no. 2 (February): 234–37, 291, 293–94.

Lasser, Joseph R., Gail G. Greve, William E. Pittman, and John A. Caramia, Jr. 1997. *The Coins of Colonial America*. Williamsburg, Virginia: Colonial Williamsburg Foundation.

Lefroy, John Henry. 1877. *Memorials of the Discovery and Early Settlement of the Bermudas or Somers Islands, 1515–1685 Compiled from the Colonial Records and other Original Sources*. London: Longmans, Green.

———. 1878. "On a New Piece of Bermuda Hog Money of the Value of Twopence." *Numismatic Chronicle* 2nd Series, 18: 166–68.

———. 1883. "On a New Piece of Bermuda Hog-Money of the Current Value of IIId." *Numismatic Chronicle* 3rd Series, 3: 117–18.

Leonard, Robert D., Jr. 2006. "Private mint cleaned up currency in 1783." *Numismatic News,* December 5, 44, 46.

Lepera, Patsy Anthony, and Walter Goodman. 1974. *Memoirs of a Scam Man: The Life and Deals of Patsy Anthony Lepera.* New York: Farrar, Straus and Giroux.

Link, Marion Clayton. 1960. "Exploring the Drowned City of Port Royal." *National Geographic Magazine* 117, no. 2 (February): 151–83.

Le Livre du Trésor d'Adrien. 1998. Domont, Seine-et-Oise, France: Ville de Domont.

Lloyd, Jack M. 1998. "Another Thought on the Stepney Hoard." *Colonial Newsletter* 38, no. 3 (whole no. 109)(December): 1889–90.

Loeffelbein, Robert L. 2003. "Peace Medals: On the Trail of Missing Medals. Where are the commemoratives Lewis and Clark gave to Native leaders?" *Numismatist* 116, no. 8 (August): 29.

López Reilly, Andrés. 2001. *Galeones, naufragios y tesoros: Los hallazgos de Rubén Collado en las costas uruguayas.* Montevideo: Ediciones de la Plaza.

Lorenzo, John. 2001. "The Old Newburgh-Cocheton Turnpike Coin Find." *Colonial Newsletter* 41, no. 2 (whole no. 117)(August): 2231–40.

Lossing, Benson John. 1851–52. *The Pictorial Field Book of the Revolution, or, Illustrations, by Pen and Pencil, of the History, Biography, Scenery, Relics, and Traditions of the War for Independence.* New York: Harper & Brothers.

Low, Lyman H. 1886a. "Coinage of the Mexican Revolutionary General Morelos." *American Journal of Numismatics* 21, no. 1 (July): 17–22.

———. 1886b. *Auction Catalog (H. Allen Tenney and Wilmot D. Porcher),* September 20.

———. 1894. "A Supplement to the Sketch of the Coinage of the Mexican Revolutionary General José Maria Morelos." *American Journal of Numismatics* 29, no. 1 (July): 10–11.

Lowick, Nicholas M. 1977. "A Second 'Gampola' Hoard." *Coin Hoards* 3: 116–19.

Lyall, Bob. 1983. "A Hoard of Tortola Black Dogs." *Numismatic Circular* 91, no. 8 (October): 267–68.

Lyon, Eugene. 1976. "The Trouble with Treasure." *National Geographic* 149, no. 6 (June): 786–809.

———. 1979. *The Search for the Atocha.* New York: Harper & Row.

———. 1982. "Treasure from the Ghost Galleon." *National Geographic* 161, no. 2 (February): 228–43.

MacCord, Howard A., Sr. 1969. "Camden: A postcontact Indian site in Caroline County." *Quarterly Bulletin of the Archaeological Society of Virginia* 24, no. 1 (September): 1–55.

MacDonald, A. M. 1965. "The Halifax Steamboat Token, Fact or Fiction?" *Transactions of the Canadian Numismatic Research Society* 1, no. 1 (January): 28. Reprinted in: *Canadian Numismatic Journal* 11, no. 7 (July 1966): 258.

———. 1969. "The Halifax Steamboat Company." *Canadian Numismatic Journal* 14, no. 11 (November): 346–47.

Marsden, Peter. 1975. *The Wreck of the Amsterdam.* New York: Stein and Day.

Martin, C. H. 1927. "Notes on Money other than United States Issues Used in Lancaster County, Pennsylvania." *Numismatist* 40, no. 1 (January): 5.

Martin, Patrick E. 1977. *An Inquiry into the Locations and Characteristics of Jacob Bright's Trading House and William Montgomery's Tavern.* Arkansas Archeological Survey, Publications on Archeology Research Series, no. 11. Fayetteville, AR: Arkansas Archeological Survey.

Marx, Robert F. 1967. *Pirate Port. The Story of the Sunken City of Port Royal.* Cleveland: World.

———. 1971. *Shipwrecks of the Western Hemisphere 1492–1825.* New York: World.

———. 1973. *Port Royal Rediscovered.* Garden City, NY: Doubleday.

Mateu y Llopis, Felipe. 1945–46. "Hallazgos Monetarios (IV)." *Ampurias. Revista de Arqueología, Prehistoria y Etnología* 7–8: 233–76.

———. 1947–48. "Hallazgos Monetarios (V)." *Ampurias. Revista de Arqueología, Prehistoria y Etnología* 9–10: 55–95.

———. 1951. "Hallazgos Monetarios (VI)." *Ampurias. Revista de Arqueología, Prehistoria y Etnología* 13: 203–54.

———. 1953. "Hallazgos Monetarios (VIII)." *Numario Hispánico* 2: 91–105.

———. 1958. "Hallazgos Monetarios (XV)." *Numario Hispánico* 7: 67–74.

———. 1961. "Hallazgos Monetarios (XIX)." *Numario Hispánico* 10: 141–61.

———. 1967. "Hallazgos Monetarios (XX)." *Numario Hispánico* 11: 45–74.

———. 1971. "Hallazgos Monetarios (XXI)." *Numisma* 21: 177–208.

———. 1979. "Hallazgos monetarios (XXV)." *Numisma* 29: 121–47.

May, Katja. 1999. "Petalesharo." In *American National Biography* 17:383–84. New York: Oxford University Press.

McDaniel, John. 1977. "Liberty Hall Academy. The Applications of Historical Archaeology in the Investigation of an 18th Century Virginia Academic Site. An Interim Report." *Quarterly Bulletin of the Archaeological Society of Virginia* 31, no. 4 and 32, no. 1 (June and September): 141–67.

McDonald, Douglas. 1988. "Temporary Tokens of a Boom Town Saloon." *Numismatist* 101, no. 6 (June): 1008–15.

McDonald, Emmett. 2000. "Nineteenth Century Counterfeit Detection Devices." In *Circulating Counterfeits of the Americas,* edited by John M. Kleeberg, 247–66. Proceedings of the Coinage of the Americas Conference, 14. New York: American Numismatic Society.

McDonald, Kendall. 1974. *Treasure Beneath the Sea.* South Brunswick, NJ: A. S. Barnes.

McKusick, Marshall, and Erik Wahlgren. 1980. "The Norse Penny Mystery." *Archaeology of Eastern North America* 8 (Fall): 1–10.

McLachlan, Robert Wallace. 1884. "Canadian Numismatics: Colony of Newfoundland." *American Journal of Numismatics* 19, no. 1 (July): 11–15.

———. 1885a. "Canadian Numismatics—Miscellaneous." *American Journal of Numismatics* 19, no. 3 (January): 57–61.

———. 1885b. "A Glastonbury Penny of 1812 described as 'a Baltimore Penny' of 1628." *American Journal of Numismatics* 19, no. 3 (January): 52–53.

———. 1886. *Canadian Numismatics. A Descriptive Catalogue of Coins, Tokens and Medals in or Relating to the Dominion of Canada and Newfoundland. With Notes, Giving Incidents in the History of Many of these Coins and Medals.* Montreal: the Author.

———. 1889. "A Hoard of Canadian Coppers." *Canadian Antiquarian and Numismatic Journal* 2nd ser., 1, no. 1 (July): 27–34.

———. 1899. "Medals Awarded to Canadian Indians." *Canadian Antiquarian and Numismatic Journal,* 3rd ser., 2, no. 1 (January): 1–14.

McLean, A. Torrey. 1995. "The Portobelo Treasure Hoard of 1630." *Numismatist* 108, no. 10 (October): 1233–37.

Mease, James. 1838. "Old American Coins." *Collections of the Massachusetts Historical Society* 3rd series, 7: 282–83.

Męclewska, Marta, and Andrzej Mikołajczyk. 1983. *Skarby Monet z Lat 1500–1649 na Obszarze PRL. Inwentarz.* Warsaw: Polskie Towarzystwo Archeologiczne i Numizmatyczne, Komisja Numizmatyczna.

———. 1991. *Skarby Monet z Lat 1500–1649 na Obszarze Polski Inwentarz II.* Wrocław: Polskie Towarzystwo Archeologiczne i Numizmatyczne, Komisja Numizmatyczna.

Menzel, Sewall H. 1987. "Confirmation of the 1750 Lima Mint Quarter-Real Cob." *Numismatist* 100, no. 5 (May): 1011–12.

———. 2004. *Cobs, Pieces of Eight and Treasure Coins: the Early Spanish-American Mints and their Coinages, 1536–1773.* New York: American Numismatic Society.

Mertens, Joris, and Liliane de Donder. 1958. "Trouvaille des Monnaies des XVIe et XVIIe siècles à Tenneville." *Revue Belge de Numismatique et de Sigillographie* 104: 175–89.

Meylach, Martin. 1971. *Diving to a Flash of Gold.* Garden City, NY: Doubleday.

Michael, Rita. 1982. "An Imitation Eighteenth Century Copper Halfpenny." *Canadian Numismatic Journal* 27, no. 6 (June): 254–57.

Mickle, Isaac. 1845. *Reminiscences of Old Gloucester or Incidents in the History of the Counties of Gloucester, Atlantic and Camden, New Jersey.* Philadelphia: Townsend Ward. Reprint. Woodbury, NJ: Gloucester County Historical Society, 1968.

Mikołajczyk, Andrzej. 1978. "Uzupełnienia do Pracy M. Kotlara 'Znaleziska Monet z. XIV-XVII. w. na Obszarze Ukraińskej SRR.'" *Wiadomoci Numizmatyczne* 22: 34–44.

———. 1984. "The Italian Coins in Poland from 16th to 18th Century. Appendix 1: Finds of Spanish and American-Spanish silver and gold coins recorded on the area of the former Polish-Lithuanian state and in the neighbouring regions (in chronological order)." *Revista Italiana di Numismatica e Scienze Affini* 86: 205–20.

Miller, Wayne. 1983. *The Morgan and Peace Dollar Textbook.* Metairie, Louisiana: Adam Smith.

Miner, Charles. 1845. *History of Wyoming, in a Series of Letters to his Son William Penn Miner, Esq.* Philadelphia: J. Crissy.

"Money-digging in Maine." 1871. *American Journal of Numismatics* 6, no. 2 (October): 32–33.

Moogk, Peter N. 1976a. "The Louisbourg Medal of 1720." *Canadian Numismatic Journal* 21, no. 11 (December): 434–40.

———. 1976b. "A Pocketful of Change at Louisbourg." *Canadian Numismatic Journal* 21, no. 3 (March): 96–104.

———. 1987. "When Money Talks: Coinage in New France." *Canadian Numismatic Journal* 32, no. 2 (February): 54–75.

———. 1989. "The Coins of Quebec's Place Royale." *Canadian Numismatic Journal* 34, no. 7 (July/August): 246–49.

Moore, Clarence Bloomfield. 1901. *Certain Aboriginal Remains of the Northwest Florida Coast, Part I.* Philadelphia: P. C. Stockhausen.

Mordecai, Samuel. 1860. *Virginia, especially Richmond, in Bygone Days; with a Glance at the Present: Being Reminiscences and Last Words of An Old Citizen.* 2nd ed. Richmond: West & Johnston.

Morris, Edward. 1960. "The Upper Sackville Hoard." *Canadian Numismatic Journal* 5, no. 5 (May): 229.

Mossman, Philip L. 1998. "The Stepney Hoard: Fact or Fantasy?" *Colonial Newsletter* 38, no. 2 (whole no. 108)(August): 1809–51.

———. 1999. "The Circulation of Irish Coinage in Pre-Federal America." *Colonial Newsletter* 39, no. 1 (whole no. 110)(April): 1899–1917.

———. 2003. "Money of the 14th Colony: Nova Scotia (1711–1783)." *Colonial Newsletter* 43, no. 3 (whole no. 124)(December): 2533–93.

Münzzentrum-Rheinland, Cologne, Nordrhein-Westfalen, Germany. 2003. *Auction Catalog* May 7–9.

Mumford, Will. 2005. "The Search for the Chalmers Mint: A further analysis…" *Anne Arundel County History Notes* 36, no. 2 (January): 1–2, 7–9.

"Muntvondsten: Bolsward." 1952. *Jaarboek van het Koninklijk Nederlandsch Genootschap voor Munt- en Penningkunde* 39: 98–100.

Naster, Paul. 1953. "Trouvailles: Trouvaille de monnaies de XVe et XVIe siècles à Nieuport (1952)." *Revue Belge de Numismatique et de Sigillographie* 99: 114–28.

de Navascués, Joaquín María. 1967. "El Tesoro de Gazteluberri." *Numario Hispánico* 11: 93–114.

Nesmith, Robert I. 1946. "A Hoard of Lima and Potosí 'cobs,' 1654–1689." *Museum Notes* 1: 81–99.

———. 1955. *The Coinage of the First Mint of the Americas at Mexico City.* Numismatic Notes and Monographs, 131. New York: American Numismatic Society.

———. 1958a. *Dig for Pirate Treasure.* New York: Devin-Adair Company.

———. 1958b. "A Hoard of the First Silver Coins of Nuevo Reino de Granada (Colombia)." In Ingholt, *Centennial Publication of the American Numismatic Society*, 513–30.

Nesmith, Robert I., and John S. Potter, Jr. 1968. *Treasure... how and where to find it.* New York: Arco.

Newman, Eric P. 1956. *Coinage for Colonial Virginia.* Numismatic Notes and Monographs 135. New York: American Numismatic Society.

———. 1958. "A Recently Discovered Coin Solves a Vermont Numismatic Enigma." In Ingholt, *Centennial Publication of the American Numismatic Society,* 531–42.

———. 1963. "A Snake Breeds a St. Patrick Farthing." *Numismatist* 76, no. 5 (May): 619–24.

———. 1962. "Additions to Coinage for Colonial Virginia." *Museum Notes* 10: 137–43.

———. 1992. "The Earliest American Publications on Numismatics: A Rediscovery." *Asylum. Quarterly Journal of the Numismatic Bibliomania Society* 10, no. 3 (Summer): 3–9.

Newman, Eric P., and Peter P. Gaspar. 1978. "The Philadelphia Highway Coin Find." *Numismatist* 91, no. 3 (March): 453–67.

Niellon, Françoise, and Marcel Moussette. 1981. *Le Site de l'Habitation de Champlain à Québec: étude de la collection archéologique (1976–1980).* Québec, Québec, Canada: [Province of Québec?], June.

Noe, Sydney Phillip. 1920. *Coin Hoards.* Numismatic Notes and Monographs 1. New York: American Numismatic Society,.

———. 1942. *The Castine Deposit: An American Hoard.* Numismatic Notes and Monographs 100. New York: American Numismatic Society.

———. 1952. *The Pine Tree Coinage of Massachusetts.* Numismatic Notes and Monographs 125. New York: American Numismatic Society.

Noël Hume, Ivor. 1970. *A Guide to Artifacts of Colonial America.* New York: Knopf.

———. 1971. *Willliamsburg Cabinetmakers: The Archaeological Evidence.* Colonial Williamsburg Archaeological Series, No. 6. Williamsburg, VA: Colonial Williamsburg Foundation.

———. 1974. *Digging for Carter's Grove.* Colonial Williamsburg Archaeological Series, No. 8. Williamsburg, VA: Colonial Williamsburg Foundation.

———. 1984. "The Very Caterpillers of This Kingdome: or, Penny Problems in the Private Sector, 1600–1660." In *The Scope of Historical Archaeology. Essays in honor of John L. Cotter,* edited by David G. Orr and Daniel G. Crozier, 233–51. Occasional Publications of the Department of Anthropology, Temple University. Philadelphia: Laboratory of Anthropology, Temple University.

———. 1992. *Martin's Hundred.* Charlottesville, VA: University Press of Virginia.

———. 1994. "Roanoke Island: America's First Science Center." *Colonial Williamsburg. The Journal of the Colonial Williamsburg Foundation* 16, no. 3 (Spring): 14–28.

———. 1995. "For Necessary Change, or, Penny Problems in the Private Sector." *Colonial Williamsburg. The Journal of the Colonial Williamsburg Foundation* 17, no. 3 (Spring): 16–24.

Noël Hume, Ivor, and Audrey Noël Hume. 2001. *The Archaeology of Martin's Hundred.* Philadelphia: University of Pennsylvania Museum of Archaeology and Anthropology.

Oikonomidos, Mantō. 1975 [1983]. "Nomismatikon Mouseion Athinōn: Hevrimata, Neōterika." [Numismatic Museum of Athens: Finds of Modern Coins.] *Arhaoiologikon Deltion [Archaeological Bulletin]* 30, part B1 (Hronika): 4–5.

Olds, Dorris L. 1976. *Texas Legacy From the Gulf. A Report on the Sixteenth Century Shipwreck Materials Recovered from the Texas Tidelands.* Texas Memorial Museum, Miscellaneous Papers No. 5. Texas Antiquities Committee, Publication No. 2. Austin: Texas Memorial Museum and Texas Antiquities Commission.

Olsen, John W. 1983. "An Analysis of East Asian Coins Excavated in Tuscon, Arizona." *Historical Archaeology* 17: 41–55.

Parke-Bernet Galleries, Inc., New York, New York, USA. 1971. *Auction Catalog (Le Chameau),* December 10–11.

Parker, A. G. 1913. "Lincoln Indian Peace Medal." *Numismatist* 26 (March): 132.

Parsons, Usher. 1863. "Indian Relics Recently Found in Charlestown, R. I., with Brief Notices of the Nyantic Tribe of Indians." *Historical Magazine* 7, no. 2 (February): 41–44.

Pastron, Allen G. 1989. "On Golden Mountain." *Archaeology* 42, no. 4 (July/August): 48–53.

Pearson, Charles. 1977. "Evidence of Early Spanish Contact on the Georgia coast." *Historical Archaeology* 11: 74–83.

Pernambucano de Mello, Ulysses. 1979. "The shipwreck of the galleon *Sacramento*—1668 off Brazil." *International Journal of Nautical Archaeology and Underwater Exploration* 8, no. 3 (August): 211–23.

Peterson, Mendel. 1961. "An Early Seventeenth Century Wreck." *Numismatist* 74, no. 6 (June): 761–74.

———. 1962. "Cut Coin in the United States." *Numismatist* 75, no. 5 (May): 582–85.

———. 1975. *The Funnel of Gold.* Boston: Little Brown.

———. 1979. "Graveyard of the Quicksilver Galleons." *National Geographic* 156, no. 6 (December): 850–76.

Pickford, Nigel. 1994. *The Atlas of Shipwrecks and Treasure.* London: Dorling-Kindersley.

Playford, Phillip. 1996. *Carpet of Silver. The Wreck of the* Zuytdorp. Nedlands, Australia: University of Western Australia Press.
Pol, Arent, and Hans Jacobi. 1993. *De Schat van Het Vliegend Hert. Compagniesgeld en Smokkelgeld uit een VOC-Schip.* Leiden, Netherlands: Rijksmuseum Het Koninklijk Penningkabinet.
Ponterio, San Diego, California, USA. 1993. *Auction Catalog, Sale #61,* February 26–27.
———. 1995. *Auction Catalog, Sale #77,* October 7.
———. 1996a. *Auction Catalog, Sale #79,* February 3.
———. 1996b. *Auction Catalog, Sale #83,* September 21.
———. 1999. *Auction Catalog (Capitana), Sale #99,* April 10.
———. 2006. *Auction Catalog (31st Annual Chicago International Coin Fair/Rooswijk),* March 31, April 1.
Potter, John S., Jr. 1972. *The Treasure Diver's Guide.* New York: Bonanza Books.
Prime, William Cowper. 1860. "Coin in America." *Harper's New Monthly Magazine* 20 (whole no. 118) (March): 468–79.
———. 1861. *Coins, Medals, and Seals, Ancient and Modern.* New York: Harper & Brothers.
Proctor, Jorge A. 2005. *The Forgotten Mint of Colonial Panama. A Look into the Production of Coins in America during the 16th Century and Panama's Spanish Royal House for Minting Coins.* Laguna Hills, CA: Jorge A. Proctor.
Proskey, David U. 1873. "Coins Plowed Up." *American Journal of Numismatics* 8, no. 1 (July): 22.
Prucha, Francis Paul. 1971. *Indian Peace Medals in American History.* Madison, WI: Wisconsin State Historical Society.
Reiter, Ed. 1978. "Buried Coin Treasure. A Major Find, Using Metal Detectors in a Philadelphia Dump." *Coinage,* May, 88–90.
Richardson, H. W. 1883. "A Baltimore Penny." *Magazine of American History* 10, no. 3 (September): 194–210.
———. 1886. "A Professional Numismatist: Reply to a Criticism." *Magazine of American History* 15, no. 4 (April): 401–3.
Robinson, John. 1917. "The Boston Numismatic Society in the 70's. Reminiscences of an Older Member, April 1917." *Numismatist* 30, no. 8 (August): 328–30.
Robinson, P. H. 1971. "The Eighteenth Century Coin Hoard from Pillaton Hall, Staffs." *British Numismatic Journal* 40: 124–35.
———. 1972. "The Dunchurch and Stafford Finds of Eighteenth Century Halfpence and Counterfeits." *British Numismatic Journal* 41: 147–58.
Rønning, Bjørn R. 1973–74. "Et funn av mynter blant vrakrestene etter den hollandske ostindiafareren Akerendam, forlist ved Runde I 1725." *Nordisk Numismatisk Årsskrift:* 68–115.
Rolde, Neil. 1995. *An Illustrated History of Maine.* Augusta, ME: Friends of the Maine State Museum.
Rouse, Irving. 1942. *Archeology of the Maniabón Hills, Cuba.* Yale University Publications in Anthropology, no. 26. New Haven: Yale University Press.
Salwen, Bert. 1966. "European Trade Goods and the Chronology of the Fort Shantok Site." *Bulletin of the Archeological Society of Connecticut,* no. 34 (June): 5–39.
Sassoon, H. 1978. "Two Mexican Pieces of Eight Found in Mombasa, Kenya." *Coin Hoards* 5: 129, 143–44.
Saxon, Lyle. 1930. *Lafitte the Pirate.* New York: Century Co.

Scher, Stephen K. 1994. *The Currency of Fame: Portrait Medals of the Renaissance.* New York: Harry N. Abrams.

Schrock, Ulrich E. G. 1987. *Münzen der Stadt Göttingen.* Bremen, Germany: Bieber.

Schulman, Jacques. 1949. "Muntvondst te Oosselt." *Jaarboek van het Koninklijk Nederlandsch Genootschap voor Munt- en Penningkunde* 36: 98–101.

———. 1961. "Muntvondsten: Loenen (Utr.) 1961." *Jaarboek voor Munt- en Penningkunde* 48: 105–6.

Schulman Coin and Mint, New York, New York, USA. 1972. *Auction Catalog,* November 27–29.

———. 1974. *Auction Catalog,* December 2–4.

Schulman, Hans M. F., Gallery, Inc., New York, New York, USA. 1969. *Auction Catalog (Treasures of Two Oceans),* February 6–8.

Seaby, Peter. 1978. "The First Datable Norse Find from North America?" *Seaby's Coin & Medal Bulletin,* no. 12 (whole no. 724)(December): 369–70, 377–82.

Seaby, W. A. 1960–61. "Five Seventeenth-Century Coin Hoards from Ulster." *British Numismatic Journal:* 331–43.

———. 1972. "The *Girona* Coins." *Seaby's Coin and Medal Bulletin ,* no. 8 (whole no. 648)(August): 309–12.

Sebring, Thomas H. 1976. "Treasure Unlimited." *Numismatist* 89, no. 1 (January): 21–27.

———. 1982. "A Taler and a Tale of Horror." *Numismatist* 95, no. 7 (July).

———. 1986. *Treasure Tales: Shipwrecks and Salvage.* Devon, Pennsylvania: Cooke Publishing.

———. 1989. "Two Coins from the Battle of Santiago Bay." *Numismatist* 102, no. 1 (January): 54–57, 142–45, 149.

———. 1991. "Piggybank Shipwrecks." *Numismatist* 104, no. 8 (August): 1212–19.

———. 1995. "British shipwreck sites have produced rich finds." *World Coin News,* August 18, 13–15.

———. 2004. American Numismatic Rarities, Wolfeboro, New Hampshire, USA, *Auction Catalog (Thomas Sebring),* January 5–6.

Sedwick, Daniel Frank, and Frank Sedwick. 2007. *The Practical Book of Cobs.* 4th ed. Winter Park, Florida: Daniel Frank Sedwick.

Sedwick, Frank. 1985. "In Search of Colombian Cobs." *Numismatist* 98, no. 7 (July): 1312–23.

Shelby, Wayne H. 2003. "Survey of Colonial Coins Recovered in Southern New Jersey." *C4 Newsletter* 11, no. 4 (Winter): 7–40.

———. 2005. "Survey of Colonial Coins Recovered in Southern New Jersey—Part II." *C4 Newsletter* 13, no 2 (Summer): 6–44.

———. 2006. "Circulation patterns of small denomination regal Spanish silver in southern New Jersey during Colonial, Confederation and early Federal Times." *C4 Newsletter* 14, no. 3 (Fall): 16–22.

Shepard, Steven J. 1983. "The Spanish *Criollo* Majority in Colonial St. Augustine." In *Spanish St. Augustine. The Archaeology of a Colonial Creole Community,* edited by Kathleen Deagan. Studies in Historical Archaeology, ed. Stanley South. New York: Academic Press.

Shomette, Donald. 1993. *The Hunt for HMS De Braak: Legend and Legacy.* Durham, NC: Carolina Academic Press.

Sigler, Phares O. 1946. "The Coins of Colonial America. Chapter XVI: Nova Constellatio, Immune Columbia and Confederatio Pieces." *Coin Collector's Journal* 13, no. 4 (July-August): 105–12.

———. 1948. "Spanish Coins Found at San Juan, Puerto Rico." *Coin Collector's Journal* 15, no. 5 (September-October): 108–9.
Simpson, K., et al. 1977. "An early 17th Century wreck near Rill Cove, Kynance, Cornwall: An interim report." *International Journal of Nautical Archaeology* 6, no. 2 (May): 163–66.
Sipsey, Everett T. 1964. "New Facts and Ideas on the State Coinages. A Blend of Numismatics, History, and Genealogy." *Colonial News-Letter* 5, no. 5 (whole no. 13)(October): 61–70.
Slack, John A. 1967. *Finders, Losers: The Lucayan Treasure Find.* New York: Holt Rinehart and Winston.
Smith, Marvin T. 1984. "A Sixteenth Century Coin from Southeast Alabama." *Journal of Alabama Archaeology* 30, no 1 (June): 56–59.
Smith, Roger C. 1988. "Treasure Ships of the Spanish Main." In Bass, *Ships and Shipwrecks of the Americas,* 85–106.
Smith, Roger C., et al. 1995. *The Emanuel Point Ship: Archaeological Investigations, 1992–1995, Preliminary Report.* Tallahassee, Florida: Bureau of Archaeological Research, Florida Department of State.
Smith, Watson, and Bernard L. Fontana. 1970. "Religious Sacramentals from Awatovi." *Kiva* 36, no. 2 (Winter): 13–16.
Smythe, R. M., & Co., New York, New York, USA. 2007. *Auction Catalog (El Cazador),* October 30.
Snowden, James Ross. 1861. *A Description of the Medals of Washington; of National and Miscellaneous medals; and of other Objects of Interest in the Museum of the Mint. Illustrated by Seventy-Nine Fac-Simile Engravings. To which are added Biographical Notices of the Directors of the Mint from 1792 to the Year 1851.* Philadelphia: J. B. Lippincott.
Sobin, George, Jr. 1974. *The Silver Crowns of France, 1641–1973.* Teaneck, NJ: Richard Margolis.
Sotheby's, London, England, UK. 1969. *Auction Catalog (HMS Association),* July 14.
———. 1970. *Auction Catalog (HMS Association),* January 28.
———. 1972a. *Auction Catalog (Hollandia),* April 18.
———. 1972b. *Auction Catalog (Lucayan Beach Treasure),* July 26–27.
———. 1973. *Auction Catalog,* November 8.
Sotheby's, New York, New York, USA. 1993. *Auction Catalog (The Uruguayan Treasure of the River Plate),* March 24–25.
———. 1999. *Auction Catalog (Central America),* December 8–9 (original date cancelled and actually held in June 2000).
Soto, Anthony. 1961. "Mission San Luis Rey, California—Excavations in the Sunken Gardens." *Kiva. A Journal of the Arizona Archaeological and Historical Society* 26, no. 4 (April): 34–43.
Spearman, Arthur D. 1948. "Cornerstone Coins of Santa Clara." *Numismatist* 61, no. 1 (January): 44–46.
Spink America, New York, New York, USA. 2001. *Auction Catalog (Santa Maria de la Consolación),* December 10–11.
Spink's/Christie's London, England, UK. 1996. *Auction Catalog (The Douro Cargo),* November 20–21.
Spittal, David. 1993. "Two Centuries of Coinage at Fort York, Ontario." *Canadian Numismatic Journal* 38, no. 7 (July/August): 244–53.
Sportack, Mark A. 2005. "Somers Islands Hogge Money: Rediscovery!" *Colonial Newsletter* 45, no. 2 (whole no. 128)(August): 2875–89.

———. 2006. "The Myths and Mysteries of the Somers' Ilands Hogge Money." In Doty and Kleeberg, *Money of the Caribbean,* 21–115.

Sprenger, J. 1968. "Muntvondsten: Haanrade 1943." *Jaarboek voor Munt- en Penningkunde* 55: 80–81.

Stack's, New York, New York, USA. 1993. *Auction Catalog,* September 8–9.

———. 1994. *Auction Catalog,* June 8.

———. 1999. *Auction Catalog (Americana),* January 12–13.

———. 2004. *Auction Catalog (John J. Ford II),* May 11.

———. 2006a. *Auction Catalog (John J. Ford XIII),* January 16.

———. 2006b. *Auction Catalog (John J. Ford XVI),* October 17.

———. 2007. *Auction Catalog (J. A. Sherman),* August 5.

———. 2008a. *Auction Catalog (Americana),* January 15–16.

———. 2008b. *Auction Catalog (SS New York),* July 27.

Stahl, Alan M. 1990. "Indian Peace Medals, Official and Unofficial." *Médailles*: 38–48.

———. 1991. "American Indian Medals of the Colonial Period." In Kleeberg, *Money of Pre-Federal America,* 159–80.

Stahl, Alan M., and William Scully. 1991. "American Indian Peace Medals of the Colonial Period in the Collection of the American Numismatic Society." In Kleeberg, *Money of Pre-Federal America,* 215–59.

Starbuck, David R. 1993. "Building Independence on Lake Champlain." *Archaeology* 46, no. 5 (September/October): 60–63.

———. 2004. *Rangers and Redcoats on the Hudson. Exploring the Post on Rogers Island, the Birthplace of the U.S. Army Rangers.* Hanover, NH: University Press of New England.

———. 2007. "Commerce of War: Inside a colonial merchant's house." *Archaeology* (July/August): 41–43.

Steffy, J. Richard. 1988. "The Thirteen Colonies: English Settlers and Seafarers." In Bass, *Ships and Shipwrecks of the Americas,* 107–28.

Sténuit, Robert. 1969. "Ireland's Rugged Coast Yields Priceless Relics of the Spanish Armada." *National Geographic* 135, no. 6 (June): 745–77.

———. 1971. *Les Trésors de l'Armada.* Paris: Albin Michel.

———. 1974a. "Early relics of the VOC trade from Shetland: The wreck of the flute *Lastdrager* lost off Yell, 1653." *International Journal of Nautical Archaeology and Underwater Exploration* 3, no. 2 (September): 213–56.

———. 1974b. "Wrecks and Riches: the Lure Below." In *Undersea Treasures,* 8–37. Washington, DC: National Geographic Society.

———. 1975. "The Treasure of Porto Santo." *National Geographic* 148, no. 2 (August): 260–75.

———. 1977. "Appendix One: The Wreck of the V.O.C. *Fluit* Lastdrager lost off Yell (Shetland), 1653." In *The Loss of the Verenigde Oostindische Compagnie Jacht VERGULDE DRAECK, Western Australia 1656. An historical background and excavation report with an appendix on the similar loss of the fluit* LASTDRAGER edited by Jeremy N. Green, 437. BAR Supplementary Series, 36. Oxford: British Archaeological Reports.

Stewart, Frank H. 1924. *History of the United States Mint, its People and its Operations.* [Philadelphia]: Frank H. Stewart Electric Co.

Stokes, Isaac Newton Phelps. 1915–28. *The Iconography of Manhattan Island 1498–1909. Compiled from the Original Sources and Illustrated by Photo Intaglio Reproductions of Important Maps Plus Views and Documents in Public and Private Collections.* 6 vols. New York, R. H. Dodd.

Storm, Alex. 2002. *Seaweed and Gold. True Canadian Treasure Hunting Adventures.* [Louisbourg, Nova Scotia, Canada]: [Alex Storm].

Stubbs, John D. 1992. "Underground Harvard: The Archaeology of Student Life." PhD diss., Harvard University.

Superior Galleries, Beverly Hills, California, USA. 1982. *Auction Catalog (Auction '82),* August 13–14.

———. 1992. *Auction Catalog (Reijgersdaal),* June 2.

———. 1993. *Auction Catalog (Worrell),* December 11–13.

Terranova, Anthony J. 1997. "What's New with the Bank of New York Fugio Hoard?" *Colonial Newsletter* 37, no. 3 (whole no. 106)(December): 1767.

Thompson, J. D. A. 1952–53. "The Merton College Coin Collection." *Oxoniensia* 17–18: 188–92.

———. 1963. "Notes on the Lutine Treasure." *Numismatic Circular* 71, no. 10 (October): 200–2.

———. 1970. "Sea Treasures in the British Isles." *Numismatic Circular* 78, no. 1 (January): 5–7; no. 4 (April): 140–41.

Thompson, Tommy. 1998. *America's Lost Treasure.* New York: Atlantic Monthly Press.

Triton (joint venture of Classical Numismatic Group, Freeman and Sears, and Numismatica Ars Classica), New York, New York, USA. 2009. *Auction XII,* January 5.

Trudgen, Gary A. 1995. "Early American Coins Recovered from the John Bridges' Tavern Site." *Colonial Newsletter* 35, no. 2 (whole no. 100)(July): 1534–40.

———. 2000. "Danielson, CT Hoard." *Colonial Newsletter* 40, no. 1 (whole no. 113)(April): 2067–68.

Tucker, Teddy. 1962. "Adventure is My Life." With Don A. Schanche. Pts. 1–3. *Saturday Evening Post,* February 24, 20–27; March 3, 44–47; March 10, 64–66, 68.

Twelftree, C. C. 1971. "Dutch Shipwreck Yields To Australian Investigation." *Numismatist* 84, no. 7 (July): 1011–13.

Van der Molen, S. J. [1966]. *Goud in de Golven. De Ware Geschiedenis van de "Lutine."* The Hague, the Netherlands: Nijgh & van Ditmar.

Van Gelder, H. Enno. 1952. "Muntvondsten: Culemborg." *Jaarboek van het Koninklijk Nederlandsch Genootschap voor Munt- en Penningkunde* 39: 151–53.

———. 1954. "Muntvondsten: De vondst Sneek 1947." *Jaarboek voor Munt- en Penningkunde* 41: 112–14.

———. 1964a. "Muntvondsten: Groede 1943." *Jaarboek voor Munt- en Penningkunde* 51: 56–57.

———. 1964b. "Muntvondsten: Katwoude 1964." *Jaarboek voor Munt- en Penningkunde* 51: 61–71.

———. 1968. "Muntvondsten: Zuid Holland." *Jaarboek voor Munt- en Penningkunde* 55: 83–85.

———. 1969–70a. "Muntvondsten: Gapinge 1969." *Jaarboek voor Munt- en Penningkunde* 56–57: 143–47.

———. 1969–70b. "Muntvondsten: Herpen 1969." *Jaarboek voor Munt- en Penningkunde* 56–57: 152–53.

———. 1969–70c. "Muntvondsten: Raamsdonk 1967 en Raamsdonk 1970." *Jaarboek voor Munt- en Penningkunde* 56–57: 159–66.

———. 1970. "Muntvondst Raamsdonk." *De Geuzenpenning* 20, no.3 (July): 40.

———. 1975–77. "Muntvondsten: Wychen 1975." *Jaarboek voor Munt- en Penningkunde* 62–64: 171.
Van Kuyk, J. 1946–47. "Muntvondst te Sneek." *Jaarboek van het Koninklijk Nederlandsch Genootschap voor Munt- en Penningkunde* 33–34: 144–50.
Van Loon, Gerard. 1723–31. *Beschrijving der Nederlandsche Historiepenningen.* The Hague, the Netherlands: Christiaan van Lom, 1723–31.
———. 1821–69. *Beschrijving van Nederlandsche Historie-Penningen.* Amsterdam, the Netherlands: Pieper en Ipenbuur, 1821–69. (A continuation of van Loon's work under the same name.)
"Various Coin Finds." 1884. *American Journal of Numismatics* 18, no. 4 (April): 95–96.
Vega de la Torre, José R. 1979. "El atesoramiento de Yeste (Albacete)." *Numisma* 29 (whole nos. 156–61): 93–119.
Veksler, A. G., and A. S. Mel'nikova. 1973. *Moskovskie Klady* [Hoards of Moscow]. Moscow: Mosk. Rabochii.
Vermeulen, M. A. 1975–77. "Muntvondsten: Ulvenhout 1975." *Jaarboek voor Munt- en Penningkunde* 62–64: 170.
The Victoria History of the Counties of England: Lancashire, 6. 1911. London: University of London Institute of Historical Research.
Villiers, Alan. 1975. "Queen Elizabeth's Favorite Sea Dog: Sir Francis Drake." *National Geographic* 147, no. 2 (February): 216–53.
Vinkenborg, J. 1961. "Muntvondsten: Plaats onbekend." *Jaarboek voor Munt- en Penningkunde* 48: 103.
Wagner, Kip, and L. B. Taylor, Jr. 1966. *Pieces of Eight: Recovering the Riches of a Lost Spanish Treasure Fleet.* New York: E. P. Dutton.
Walker, Sansoucy. 1968. "Field Report on an Excavation at Louisbourg, Nova Scotia, Canada." *Quarterly Bulletin of the Archaeological Society of Virginia* 22, no. 3 (March): 91–116.
Walsh, Lorena S. 1997. *From Calabar to Carter's Grove: The History of a Virginia Slave Community.* Charlottesville, VA: University Press of Virginia.
Warren, Edward H. 1938. *Cases on Property.* 2nd ed. Cambridge, MA: Harvard Cooperative Society.
Webb, William S. 1938. *An Archaeological Survey of the Norris Basin in Eastern Tennessee.* Smithsonian Institution, Bureau of American Ethnology, Bulletin 118. Washington, DC: United States Government Printing Office.
Weikert, Jr., Edward L. 1953–54. "Money Hoards." *Numismatic Scrapbook Magazine* 19, no. 12 (December 1953): 1185–86; 20, no. 1 (January 1954): 123–24.
Weiller, Raymond. 1975. *La Circulation Monétaire et les Trouvailles Numismatiques du Moyen Age et des Temps Modernes au Pays de Luxembourg.* Luxembourg: Ministère des Arts et des Sciences.
———. 1989. *La Circulation Monétaire et les Trouvailles Numismatiques du Moyen Âge et des Temps Modernes au Pays de Luxembourg* 2. Publications d'Histoire de l'Art et d'Archéologie de l'Université Catholique de Louvain, 71; Numismatica Lovaniensia, 13. Louvain-la-Neuve: Séminaire de Numismatique Marcel Hoc.
———. 1996. *La Circulation Monétaire et les Trouvailles Numismatiques du Moyen Âge et des Temps Modernes au Pays de Luxembourg* 3. Publications Nationales du Ministère de la Culture. Luxembourg: Ministère de la Culture.

Indices

Index of Find Spots

Argentina:
    Buenos Aires: 530
    Cordoba Province, La Herradura: 626
    Salta or Tucumán: 97
Australia:
    Western Australia, Abrolhos Islands: A34
    Western Australia, Kalbarri: A90
    Western Australia, Perth: A61
    Western Australia, Point Cloates: A130
Bahamas:
    Bahamas Bank: 100
    Grand Bahama: 170
    Lucayan Beach: 64
    New Providence: 553
    San Salvador (Watling Island): 2
Belarus:
    Mahilyow Province, Budgoszcza: A45
Belgium:
    Aubel: A80
    Deidenberg: A147
    Nieuport: A6
    Saint-Jean-lez-Saint-Nicolas: A42
    Tenneville: A70
Bermuda: 25, 37, 50, 56, 75, 558
    Castle Harbor: 54
    Castle Island: 51, 636
    Port Royal: 46
    St. George's: 44, 47, 48, 49
Brazil:
    Bay of All Saints: 63, 81, 134, 172
British Virgin Islands:
    Tortola: 813
Bulgaria:
    Blagoevgrad Region, Elechnitz: A140
Canada: 143, 647

Canada, British Columbia:
    Cuadra Island: 689
    Vancouver's Island: 690
Canada, New Brunswick:
    St. Martin: 352
Canada, Newfoundland and Labrador:
    Labrador, Hamilton Inlet: 317
    Newfoundland: 810
    Newfoundland, Ferryland: 76, 168, 768
Canada, Nova Scotia:
    Cape Breton: 242, 287, 343
    Chignecto Isthmus: 312, 313, 338
    Dartmouth: 595
    Halifax: 315
    Louisbourg: 189, 204, 205, 327
    Saint John River Valley: 346
    Scatarie Island: 185, 632
    Upper Sackville: 492
Canada, Nunavut:
    King William Island: 676
    Utjulik: 678
Canada, Ontario:
    Amherst Island: 482
    Belwood: 806
    Burford: 621
    Fairfield: 563
    Golspie: 703
    Hamilton: 614
    Harrisburg: 624
    Harrison Township: 442
    Kingston: 398
    Kitchener (Berlin): 351
    Massey: 285
    Napanee River: 648
    Norwich: 679
    Penetanguishene: 575
    Staffordville: 840
    Tara: 850
    Toronto: 489, 574, 710
    Wasaga Beach: 440
    York Mills: 663

Canada, Prince Edward Island: 338
Canada, Québec:
  Chambly: 645
  Coteau du Lac: 384
  Montréal: 584, 888
  Peninsula Point, Gaspé Bay: 87
  Phillipsburg: 571
  Québec: 140, 342, 640, 644
Canada, Saskatchewan:
  Moose Jaw: 796
  Regina: 797
Cape Verde Islands:
  Boa Vista: A120, A128
  Maio: A105
  Santiago, San Francisco: A53
Chile:
  Concepción: 576
  Skyring Island: 617
China: A143
  Fujian Province, Huian: A118
  Fujian Province, Jinjiang County, Anhai Commune: A47
  Fujian Province, Nanan County, Guanqiao Commune: A50
  Fujian Province, Nanan County, Shishan Commune: A83
  Fujian Province, Quanzhou: A60
Colombia: 110
  Bogotá: 85
  El Mesuno: 72
Costa Rica:
  Alajulea: 684
Cuba: 40
  El Mango: 4
  El Yayal: 5
  Havana: 184, 283
  Santiago Bay: 827
Dominica: 536
Dominican Republic: 9
  Ambrosia Banks: 78
  La Isabela: 3
  Samaná Bay: 239, 240
  Santo Domingo: 8, 475
Ecuador:
  Chanduy: 93
  Guayaquil: 521
  Isla de Muerto: 148
  Manta: 171
  Punta Santa Elena: 521

El Salvador:
  San Salvador: 669, 863
France:
  Bay of Biscay: A145
  Lot-et-Garonne, St.-Martin-de-Beauville: A23
  Morbihan, Saint-Pierre-de-Quiberon: A12
  Moselle, Pange: A43
  Seine-et-Oise, Domont: A58
  Seine-Maritime, Tréport: A52
Germany:
  Niedersachsen: A14
  Nordrhein-Westfalen, Anreppen: A21
Greece:
  Athens: A96, A136
  Messolongi (Aetoloakarnania), Himerodendria of Stamma: A141
Guatemala: 766
  Guatemala City: 29, 805
  Near the Mexican border: 671
Haiti: 503
  Bayahá: 23
  Habitation Montholon: 10
  Les Cayes: 526
  Mid-region, between Port-au-Prince and St. Marc: 562
  Southern Haiti: 169
Ireland:
  Cork: A142
  County Kerry, Blasket Sound: A9
  County Laois, Sleaty: A125
  County Mayo, Newport, Gortnaheltia: A68
  County Wexford, Wellington Bridge, Whittys Hill: A131
Italy:
  Sicily: A66
  Sicily, Esquierquies Rocks: A129
  Val di Non: A15
  Veneto, Fusina (Venezia): A37
  Veneto, Gambellara: A38
Jamaica:
  Clarendon: 96
  Saint Catherine: 95
  Port Royal: 159
  Spanish Town: 94
Kenya:
  Mombasa: A35
Latvia:
  Lejas Kundzin: A56
Luxembourg:
  Echternach: A48

Index

Esch-sur-Alzette: A99
Kehlen: A51
Mauritius: A28, A86, A107
    Cargados Carajos Shoals: A135
Mexico: 28, 203, 650
    Durango: 479
    Jalisco, Magdalena: 512
    Mexico City: 27, 45, 244, 598
    Oaxaca, Tlacochahuaya: 566
    Puebla: 26
    Sonora, Nogales: 807
    Yucatan: 40
Montserrat: 528
Mozambique: A30
    Bassas da India: A8
Namibia:
    Meob Bay: A109
Netherlands:
    Friesland, Bolsward: A7
    Friesland, Sneek: A20
    Gelderland, Culemborg: A13
    Gelderland, Ooselt: A31
    Gelderland, Wijchen: A36
    Limburg, Haanrade: A11
    Noord-Brabant, Herpen: A5
    Noord-Brabant, Ulvenhout: A32
    Noord-Holland, Katwoude: A76
    Noord-Holland, Raamsdonk: A89
    Noord-Holland, Texel: A100, A123
    Utrecht, Loenen: A57
    Zeeland, Gapinge: A2
    Zeeland, Groede: A3
    Zuid-Holland: A65
    Zuid-Holland, Oud-Beijerland: A22
North Africa: A54
Norway:
    Rundøy: A94
Panama: 33
    Camino Real: 31
    Nombre de Dios: 32
    Old Panama: 30
    Panama City: 713
    Portobelo: 65, 290
Peru:
    Lima: 34, 155
    Pajatambo: 280
    Southern Peru: 70
Philippines:
    Bataan Province: A118

Cavite Province, Indang: A74
Fortune Island: A19
Luzon: A146
Manila: A41, A44, A115
Pasay: A85
Poland:
    Gdánsk Province, Puck Commune, Polchówko: A78
    Gdánsk Province, Starogard Gdánski Commune environs, Cis: A27
    Olsztyn Province, Reszel Commune, Wilkowo: A24
Portugal:
    Algarve, Cape Saint Mary: A127
    Madeira Islands, Porto do Guilherme: A93
Russia:
    Moscow: A40
Serbia:
    Ljubostinja: A124
South Africa:
    Cape Agulhas: A75
    Gaanzecraal: A110
    Oudekraal: A82
    Port Elizabeth, Bird Island: A113
Spain: A102
    Albacete Province, Acequión: A114
    Albacete Province, Yeste: A98
    Alt Empordà Province, Empúries: A1
    Badajoz Province, Badajoz: A91
    Balearic Islands, Formentera: A16
    Barcelona Province, Tarrasa, Matadepera: A116
    Bages Province, Castellbell i el Vilar: A139
    Barcelona Province, Sallent: A101
    Castellón Province, Morella: A137
    Gerona Province, Arbucias: A95
    Gerona Province, Villarobledo: A117
    Granada Province, Almuñécar: A122
    Guipúzcoa Province, Gazteluberri: A17
    Lleida Province, Lleida: A18, A77, A84
    Sevilla Province, El Arahal: A4
    Sevilla Province, Fuentes de Andalucia: A132
    Sevilla Province, Lebrija: A134
    Sevilla Province, Sevilla: A25, A67
    Toledo Province, Toledo: A26
Sri Lanka:
    Gampola: A69
Turkey:
    Northwest Turkey: A121
Ukraine:
    Crimea, Sevastopol: A55
    Zhytomyr Province, Skołobow: A39

United Kingdom:
    England, Cornwall, Isles of Scilly: A88
    England, Cornwall, Isles of Scilly, Gilstone Rock: A87
    England, Cornwall, Isles of Scilly, St. Agnes Island, Gunner Rock: A106
    England, Cornwall, Kynance, Rill Cove: A29
    England, Durham, between Seaton Carew and West Hartlepool: A138
    England, Hampshire, Isle of Wight: A33, A64, A112, A133
    England, Kent: A49
    England, Kent, Goodwin Sands: A104
    England, Lancashire, Gawthorpe: A108
    England, Lancashire, Preston, Barton: A46
    England, Lincolnshire, Fulbeck Hall: A62
    England, London: 809, A63, A79
    England, London, Enfield: A81
    England, Oxfordshire, Oxford: A92
    England, Staffordshire, Pillaton Hall: A97
    England, Teesside, Stockton-on-Tees: A144
    England, Warwickshire, Dunchurch: A111
    Northern Ireland, County Antrim, Port na Spaniagh: A10
    Northern Ireland, County Down, near Banbridge, Ballyvarley Townland: A73
    Northern Ireland, County Down, Donaghadee: A126
    Northern Ireland, County Down, Dundonald, Churchquarter Townland: A72
    Scotland, Shetland Islands, Fetlar: A103
    Scotland, Shetland Islands, Island of Yell: A59
    Wales, Holyhead, Anglesey Skerries: A71

USA, Alabama: 483
    Bay Minette: 622
    Clay County: 759
    Demopolis: 757
    Florence: 720
    Henry County: 19
    Mobile: 213, 628, 773
    Perdido Bay: 17
    Rockville: 760
    Slocomb: 823
    Tuskegee: 758

USA, Alaska:
    Cleary City: 847
    Olnes: 848

USA, Arizona:
    Awatovi: 67
    Flagstaff: 687
    Santa Cruz de Terrenate: 373
    Tucson: 838

USA, Arkansas:
    Amity: 798
    Arkansas Post: 587
    Little Rock: 749

USA, California:
    Anacapa Island: 698
    Bidwell's Bar: 695
    Canyon City: 785
    Carmel: 694
    Chico: 787
    Crescent City: 764
    Donner Lake: 675
    Monterey: 842
    North Fork of American River: 704
    Oakland: 828
    Pasadena: 751
    Placerville: 685
    Point Arguello: 701
    Rincon Point: 693
    San Diego: 510
    San Francisco: 24, 793, II
    San Luis Obispo: 697
    Santa Clara: 413
    Smartsville: 692
    Superior: 737
    Ventura: 683, 819
    Yreka: 809

USA, Colorado:
    Colorado Springs: 844
    Jamestown: 832

USA, Connecticut:
    Berlin: 446
    Bridgeport: 127
    Clinton: 761
    Danielson: 560
    Greenwich: 524
    Hartland: 297
    Middletown: 98
    New Milford: 801
    New Boston: 741
    Norwich: 215
    Northwestern Connecticut: 467
    Seymour: 871
    Stamford: 380
    Stepney: 456
    Stratford: 365
    Windsor: 123

USA, Delaware:
    Cape Henlopen: 507
    Rehoboth: 438

USA, District of Columbia:
    Washington: 534, 613, I, III, IV, V, XIII

USA, Eastern United States: 884

Index

USA, Florida:
    Broward County: 600
    Clearwater: 662
    Conch Key, Florida Keys: 262
    Fernanda: 485
    Fernandina: 597
    Florida Keys: 264
    Fort Pierce: 190
    Hawk Channel, Florida Keys: 261
    Jupiter Inlet: 105
    Lake Eustes: 276
    Little Conch Reef, Florida Keys: 260, 263
    Marquesas Keys: 60, 61
    Pasco: 855
    Pensacola: 18, 299
    Pepper Park: 706
    Saint Augustine: 20, 269
    Spruce Creek: 16
    Tallahassee: 6
    Treasure Harbor, Florida Keys: 259
    Vero Beach: 556
    Wabasso: 53
USA, Georgia: 593
    Flint River, Dougherty County: 241
    Royston: 852
    Saint Catherine's Island: 36
    Saint Simon's Island: 12
    Savannah: 22, 765
    Silas Crossing: 654
USA, Idaho:
    Arrow: 537
    Lewiston: 837
    Sun Valley: 858
USA, Illinois:
    Buffalo: 794
    Cahokia: 206
    Centralia: 660
    Du Quoin: 853
    New Boston: 733
    Prairie Town: 718
    Quincy: 736
    Springfield Township: 699
    Urbana: 821
USA, Indiana:
    Bloomington: 631
    Crawfordsville: 730
    French Lick Springs: 583
    Indianapolis: 873
    New Castle: 792
    Springport: 623
    Tipton: 649

USA, Iowa:
    Dubuque: 625
    Iowa City: 700
    Keokuk: 892
    Marshalltown: 862
    Ottawa: 719
    Selma: 869
USA, Kansas:
    Lawrence: 503
    Stockton: 620
USA, Kentucky:
    Hodgenville: 854
    Lafayette, South Christian: 519
USA, Louisiana: 384, 432, 673
    Bunkie: 535
    New Orleans: 659, 877
    Opelousas: 402
    Pierre Part: 414
USA, Maine:
    Biddeford: 629, 732
    Boothbay Harbor: 132
    Brooklin: 1
    Castine: 178
    Fort Halifax, Kennebec River: 321
    New Vineyard: 656
    Pemaquid: 68
    Penobscot River: 403
    Portland: 74, 99, 578
    Richmond Island: 69
    Searsport: 449
    Sullivan: 226
    Waterville: 564
    West Hampton: 602
USA, Maryland: 103
    Allegany County: 323
    Annapolis: 128, 427
    Baltimore: 702
    Boonsboro: 740
    Frederick: 232
    Fruitland: 672
    Hagerstown: 739
    Ijamsville: 478
    Laurel: 150
    Port Deposit: 341
    Somerset County: 273
    Southern Maryland: 102, 104
USA, Massachusetts:
    Boston: 71, 120, 135, 138, 142, 163, 225, 271, 277, 445, 448, 601, 608, 826
    Brookline: 111
    Cambridge: 73, 447

Cambridgeport: 588
Canton: 272
Cape Ann: 256
Coleraine: 202
Connecticut River: 154
Dorchester: 52
Duxbury: 71, 448
Essex: 121
Fall River: 585
Feeding Hills (West Springfield): 615
Gloucester: 219
Hingham: 106
Longmeadow: 179
Lowell Island: 125
Lynn: 783
Martha's Vineyard: 513
Medford: 77
Nantucket: 599
New Bedford: 508
Northborough: 515
Oak Bluffs: 396
Pittsfield: 294
Plymouth: 117, 674
Roxbury: 138, 445
Salem: 133, 176, 303, 454, 505
Saugus: 118
Scituate: 637
Southwestern Massachusetts: 468
Waltham: 490
Wellfleet: 198
Wellingsley: 122
West Springfield: 126
Western Massachusetts: 337, 450
Willemansett: 612
Williamstown: 129
Worcester: 664

USA, Michigan:
Allen: XII
Bronson: 839
Coldwater: 839
Delton: 735
Fort Michilimackinac: 255, 344
Fort Saint Joseph: 362
Lima: 550
Marine City: 678
Marshall: 817
Milan: 630
Muskegon: 731
Pontiac: 890
Presque Isle: 388
Saint Ignace: 145
Saint Joe's River: 387

USA, Minnesota: 542
Duluth: 857
Green Isle Township: 870
Mayhew: 833
Red Wing: 688

USA, Mississippi:
Fort Adams: 554
Jackson: 744
Natchez: 745
Tupelo: 417, 487
Vicksburg: 747

USA, Missouri:
Kansas City: 876
Kingston: 777
New Haven: 435
Saint Joseph: 665
Saint Louis: 542, 738
Sedalia: 771
Waynesville: 753

USA, Montana:
Great Falls: VII, IX, XI
Helena: 822
Milk River: 543
Missoula: 667

USA, Nebraska: 539, 861
Geneva: 779
Genoa: 742
Gilead: 772
Hastings: 546
Lincoln: 865
Spring Creek: 711

USA, Nevada:
Carson City: 780
Genoa: 820
Lovelock: 851
Pyramid Lake Indian Reservation: 714
Rawhide: 849
Reno: 889
Shoshone Wells: 750
Virginia City: 767

USA, New Hampshire: 231
Exeter: 131
Haverhill: 182
Lempster: 329
Merrimack River: 119
Portsmouth: 332, 379
Warner: 639

USA, New Jersey:
Asbury Park: 433, 491
Barnegat: 180
Bergen: 212

Index

Brown's Mills: 238
Camden: 480
Burlington County: 279
Elizabeth: 802
Elizabethport: 161
Freehold Township: 412
Gloucester and Salem Counties: 517
Harrison Township: 494
Highlands: 357
Hoboken: 609
Holgate: 504
Hudson County: 212
Mantoloking: 520
Monroe: 402
Montclair: 476
Morristown: 458
New Brunswick: 518, 783
Newton: 149, 402
Nutley: 484
Rancocas: 466
Somerville: 533
Southern New Jersey: 114, 231
Sparta Township: 428
Trenton: 525
Walker's Creek: 39
Washington: 439
Wildwood Gables: 808

USA, New Mexico:
    Albuquerque: 859
    Fort Fillmore: 727
    Moriarty: 137
    Pecos: 436
    Silver City: 360
    Yunque: 38

USA, New York:
    Addison: 434, 567
    Albany: 62, 174, 237, 265, 268, 509, 547, 658
    Baldwinsville: 302, 318
    Ballston Spa: 336
    Bronx: 230, 254, 316, 381, 451
    Brooklyn: 282, 310, 419, 516
    Castleton Island State Park, Papscanee Island: 82
    Cayuga County: 101
    Clermont/Germantown: 247
    Cold Spring Village: 406
    Colonie: 166
    Crown Point: 334
    Dutch Kills, Queens County: 377
    Easthampton: 91
    East Moriches: 217, 399
    Elmsford: 278
    Florida: 187
    Flower Hill: 486
    Fort Brewerton: 405
    Fort Edward: 322
    Fort George, New York: 378
    Fort Montgomery State Historic Site, Popolopen Creek: 375
    Fort Niagara: 353
    Fort Ticonderoga: 339
    Garrattsville: 400
    Glen Cove: 59
    Hamptons: 136
    Hart's Corners: 424
    Hempstead: 845
    Hunter Island: 164
    Johnstown: 348
    Kaneenda: 173
    Knowlwood: 359
    La Fayette: 258
    Manlius: 335
    Massena: 646
    Middletown: 607
    Montgomery: 763
    Mount Vernon: 606
    Munnsville: 88, 308
    New Rochelle: 216, 319
    New Windsor: 385, 453
    New York: 80, 84, 92, 113, 162, 177, 183, 230, 245, 254, 286, 310, 311, 316, 333, 345, 364, 377, 378, 381, 382, 383, 390, 404, 419, 420, 425, 426, 451, 457, 501, 516, 565, 653, 691, 708, 769, 805, 816, 845, 882
    Newburgh: 306, 477
    Newtown, Queens: 113
    Onondaga Valley: 291
    Oriskany: 266
    Oswego: 324
    Otsego County: 397
    Patchogue: 641
    Peebles Island State Park: 460
    Pompey: 89, 90, 167, 295, 307, 415
    Port Chester: 502
    Rensselaer: 188, 224
    Rensselaer or Saratoga Counties: 340
    Rockland County: 197
    Rome: 330
    Sackets Harbor: 499
    Sag Harbor: 643
    Saratoga Springs: 288, 815
    Sayville: 728
    Schuylerville: 296
    Scipioville: 153
    Setauket: 376
    Shinnecock: 175
    Staten Island: 92, 162, 177, 245, 333, 404, 691, 769

Stony Point: 393
Union Springs: 309
Upstate New York: 218, 577
Victor: 841
Warwick: 864
West Point: XIV, XV, XVI
Western New York: X
Westhampton: 552
Wurtsboro: 743

USA, North Carolina: 270, 707
Currituck County: 409
Gouldsborough: 374
Kitty Hawk: 788
Manteo: 35
New Bern: 186
Raleigh: 762
Ramseur: 422
Statesville: 251, 252
Wilmington: 755

USA, North Dakota:
Border with Minnesota: 885
Dickinson: 638

USA, Ohio: 748, X
Beatty: 289
Burton: 605
Cincinnati: 776, 866
Cleveland: 812, 830, 881
Hillsboro: 544
Lancaster: 880
Milford: 867
Norwalk: 668
Raridon: 572
Sandusky: 891
Scio: 568
Springfield: 680
Toledo: 875

USA, Oregon: 593, 800
Fort Clatsop: 540
Gladstone: 443, 627
Heppner: 831
Jackson County: 799
Lane County: 782
Powers: 506
Rainier: 442
Sullivan's Island: 726
Umpqua River Valley: 592
Warren: 442

USA, Pennsylvania: 248, 652
Allegheny County: 778
Bloomsburg: 814
Chester: 151

Danville: 633
Delaware River: 391
Eastern Pennsylvania: 709
Easton: 464
Economy: 670
Falls of Schuylkill: 734
Fort Ligonier: 158, 370, 452
Franklin: 331
Germantown: 514, 611
Huntingdon: 657
Lower Merion Township: 407
Mahanoy City: 559
Manheim Township: 423
Natrona: 192
New Bethlehem: 682
Philadelphia: 115, 165, 250, 282, 298, 328, 349, 371, 386, 437, 481, 523, 527, 531, 532, 551, 569, 618, 619, 635, 655, 686, 774, 781, 786, 811, 829, 843, 887, VI, VIII
Prymus: 358
Scranton: 883
South Mountain: 596
Sunbury: 194, 325
Topton: 825
Tunkhannock: 196
Valley Forge: 394
Washington: 208, 461
Western Pennsylvania: X
Wilkes Barre: 193
Wrightsville: 191

USA, Puerto Rico: 7
Mayagüez: 790
Sabana Seca: 11
San Juan: 705
San Juan Harbor: 459

USA, Rhode Island: 109
Charlestown: 108
Newport: 124
Somerset: 214

USA, South Carolina:
Charleston: 209, 444
Chester: 803
Columbia: 368, 756
Hancockville: 409
John's Island: 257
Myrtle Beach: 651
Orangeburg: 301
Parris Island: 21
Yorkville: 696

USA, South Dakota: 868
Deadwood: 818
Mandan Territory: 545

Index

USA, Southern United States: 469, 473
USA, Tennessee: 723
    Bedford County: 717
    Brownsville: 293
    Caryville: 455
    Jackson: 712
    Kingston: 872
    Knoxville: 464
    Loudon: 350
    Monroe County, Fort Loudoun: 326
    Stewart County: 715
USA, Texas: 634, 673
    Angelina National Forest: 886
    Clarksville: 642
    Corpus Christi: 721
    Dallas: 878
    Gordonsville: 725
    Hull: 789
    Hungerford: 274
    Kerens: 770
    Odessa: 879
    Padre Island: 13, 14, 15
    San Antonio: 579, 580, 581, 795
USA, Utah:
    Heber: 856
USA, Vermont:
    Alburgh: 395
    Bakersfield: 354
    Bennington: 210
    Carver's Falls: 392
    Lake Champlain, near Fort Ticonderoga: 347
    Mount Independence: 372
    Pittsford: 431
    West Brattleboro: 498
USA, Virgin Islands:
    St. John: 570
USA, Virginia: 195, 243, 275, 836
    Alexandria: 235, 522, 529, 549, 586, 616
    Bacon's Castle, Surry County: 140
    Bermuda Hundred: 56
    Bloxom and Hallwood: 661
    Charles City County: 160
    Camden: 146, 147
    Charlotte Court House: 410
    Chesapeake Bay: 356
    Clarke County: 418
    Culpeper: 207
    Deep Creek: 724
    Dumfries: 229
    Dunkirk: 249
    Falls Church: 236
    Fauquier County: 363
    Fredericksburg: 227, 228, 495, 496, 497, 716
    Greenville: 488
    Guinea Station: 470
    Haymarket: 355
    Henricus: 141
    Hopewell: 222
    James River: 253, 279
    Jamestown: 43, 116, 304
    Leedstown: 500
    Martin's Hundred: 58, 66
    Matildaville: 556
    Middlesex County: 130
    Monticello, Charlottesville: 361
    Natural Bridge: 752
    New Kent County: 200, 223, 493
    Norfolk: 267, 430
    North Anna River: 211
    Northern Virginia: 429, 549
    Osbourne: 141
    Portsmouth: 199
    Powhatan Courthouse: 292
    Prince Edward County: 234
    Prince George County: 55
    Richmond: 284, 320, 462, 471
    Roanoke: 754
    Rosewell Plantation: 201
    Salem: 157
    Shenandoah Valley: 220
    Southeastern Virginia: 42
    Spotsylvania Courthouse: 610
    Stafford County: 83, 181
    Stafford Court House: 369
    Surry: 300
    Varina: 152
    Virginia Beach: 79
    Wakefield: 144
    Warm Springs: 472
    Waynesboro: 681
    White Post: 474
    Williamsburg: 41, 107, 156, 233, 421, 465
    York County: 86
    Yorktown: 112, 305, 366, 411
USA, Washington:
    Bridgeport: 775
    Elma: 589
    Goat Island: 538
    San Juan Island: 834
    Seattle: 835
    Stevenson: 591
    Vancouver: 590
USA, West Virginia:

Kanawha County: 722
Morgantown: 561
Point Pleasant: 367

USA, Wisconsin: 389
Green Bay: 874
Hudson: 729
LaCrosse: 824
Levis: 604
Milwaukee: 791
Mineral Point: 666
Oconowomoc: 746
Prairie du Chien: 416, 582
Valmy: 860

Uruguay:
Gorriti Island: 246
Montevideo: 314

Venezuela:
Cumana Bay: 573

Vietnam:
Vinh Thanh Mountains: A148

West Indies: 511

Index to Special Types of Finds and to Named Hoards

Adrien Hoard: A58

Archaeological excavations: 1, 2, 3, 4, 6, 10, 11, 12, 17, 18, 20, 21, 23, 24, 30, 35, 36, 38, 43, 51, 55, 58, 62, 66, 67, 68, 73, 76, 79, 80, 82, 84, 86, 87, 89, 116, 139, 140, 145, 147, 151, 159, 160, 165, 166, 168, 174, 187, 188, 189, 201, 206, 213, 215, 224, 233, 246, 255, 265, 267, 269, 274, 280, 298, 299, 304, 305, 306, 312, 313, 315, 316, 321, 322, 324, 325, 330, 334, 342, 344, 347, 348, 349, 361, 370, 372, 373, 383, 384, 393, 394, 398, 403, 404, 406, 407, 411, 421, 427, 430, 431, 436, 437, 440, 441, 442, 443, 453, 455, 460, 465, 481, 488, 489, 499, 509, 510, 531, 547, 553, 554, 557, 563, 574, 575, 582, 587, 619, 621, 627, 635, 641, 655, 693, 710, 726, 750, 767, 768, 786, 797, 809, 819, 837, 838, A21, A79, A84, A96, A136

Baltimore Gold Hoard: 702

Bank of New York Fugio Hoard: 457

Butternut Hoard: 709

Castine Deposit: 178

Crib hulks: 425, 653

Dashiell Payroll: 706

Donner Party: 675

Economite Hoard: 670

Finds discovered in containers: 69, 101, 112, 131, 143, 159, 176, 180, 183, 204, 244, 300, 310, 331, 358, 363, 368, 377, 385, 390, 400, 402, 408, 439, 456, 457, 466, 475, 479, 484, 490, 491, 501, 505, 512, 513, 514, 515, 519, 524, 535, 558, 560, 565, 566, 572, 578, 585, 592, 602, 606, 610, 615, 633, 639, 642, 644, 656, 657, 659, 671, 672, 674, 680, 681, 691, 692, 699, 702, 707, 712, 715, 717, 720, 724, 725, 727, 730, 732, 736, 737, 739, 744, 748, 752, 753, 755, 756, 760, 761, 763, 769, 777, 779, 781, 782, 783, 785, 787, 792, 794, 799, 801, 802, 803, 804, 806, 808, 815, 817, 820, 824, 829, 830, 833, 839, 841, 842, 846, 850, 851, 853, 855, 857, 858, 861, 862, 868, 871, 873, 875, 876, 878, 881, 883, 885, 887, 892, A6, A11, A12, A20, A22, A23, A31, A32, A36, A40, A42, A47, A50, A57, A62, A70, A72, A73, A74, A83, A89, A100, A115, A125, A136, A147, A148

Fort Pierce American Gold Find: 706

Foundation deposits: 184, 204, 205, 292, 413, 480, 527, 551, 553, 601, 608, 609, 613, 614, 617, 618, 635, 663, 664, 680, 705, 774, 780, 783, 793, 805, 811, 812, 815, 821, 825

Funerary deposits: 12, 16, 17, 67, 68, 108, 145, 175, 191, 192, 266, 350, 386, 387, 388, 416, 417, 442, 443, 487, 546, 592, 627, 667, 676, 677, 711, 742, 837

George Hoard: 412
Goodhue-Nichols Find: 505
Louisbourg expedition payment: 303
Mohawk Valley Hoard: 658
New Orleans Hoard: 659
Oat Bin Hoard: 777
Otterville Hoard: 840
Philadelphia Highway Find: 282, 371, 686
Randall Hoard: 594
Redfield Hoard: 889
Richmond Island Hoard: 69
Saltwater uncs: 706
Seawater uncs: 706
Shipwrecks (arranged by date):
1554 Plate Fleet: 13, 14, 15
Espíritu Santo (1554): 14
San Esteban (1554): 15
Tristan de Luna Expedition (1559): 18
Portuguese wreck (1580): 25
Santiago (1585): A8
Santa Maria de la Rosa (1588): A9
Girona (1588): A10
San Pedro (1596): 37
San Diego (1600): A19
Walker's Creek shipwreck (1600): 39
Central American shipwreck ("Golden Fleece?")(1600): 40
Sea Venture (1609): 44
Dutch Merchantman (1615): A28
Lizard silver wreck (1618): A29
San Martin (1618): 53
Warwick (1619): 54
San Antonio (1621): 57
São José (1622): A30
Nuestra Señora de Atocha (1622): 60
Santa Margarita (1622): 61
Hollandia (1627): 63
Campen (1627): A33
Batavia (1629): A34
Van Lynden (1629): 64
El Mesuno (1635): 72

Viga (1637 or 1639): 75
Nuestra Señora de la Pura y Limpia Concepción (1641): 78
Utrecht (1648): 81
Unknown Spanish or Portuguese ship (1650): A53
Lastdrager (1653): A59
Jesus Maria de la Limpia Concepción (La Capitana) (1654): 93
Nuestra Señora de las Maravillas (1656): 100
Vergulde Draeke (1656): A61
San Miguel el Arcángel (1659): 105
Unknown shipwreck on Lowell Island, Massachusetts (date unknown): 125
Unknown shipwreck off Sicily (1667): A66
Santíssimo Sacramento (1668): 134
Unknown shipwreck in Seville harbor (1671): A67
Mary (1675): A71
Santa María de la Consolación (1681): 148
Johanna (1682): A75
Memory Rocks Wrecks (1697): 170
Huis te Kraaiestein (1698): A82
Santo Ecclesiastico (Standing Cannon Wreck)(1699): 172
The Speaker (1702): A86
HMS Association (1707): A87
HMS Romney (1707): A88
HMS Feversham (1711): 185
Zuytdorp (1712): A90
1715 Plate Fleet: 190
Nuestra Señora de la Regla (Capitana de Flota) (Cabin Wreck)(1715): 190
Urca de Lima (Wedge Wreck)(1715): 190
Santo Cristo de San Roman (Corrigan's Wreck)(1715): 190
Carmen (Capitana de Tierra Firma) (Rio Mar Wreck) (1715): 190
Nuestra Señora del Rosario (Almiranta) (Sandy Point Wreck)(1715): 190
Nuestra Señora de las Nieves (Douglass Beach Wreck) (1715): 190
Whydah (1717): 198
Nuestra Señora de Guadalupe (1724): 239
Conde de Tolosa (1724): 240
Slot ter Hooge (1724): A93
Akerendam (1725): A94

Le Chameau (1725): 242
Seahorse (1728): 246
1733 Plate Fleet: 259, 260, 261, 262, 263, 264
El Rubi Segundo (Capitana) (1733): 259
Nuestra Señora de Balvaneda (El Infante) (1733): 260
San Pedro (1733): 261
El Sueco de Arizón (1733): 262
San José de las Animas (1733): 263
Nuestra Señora de las Angustias y San Rafael (El Charanguero Grande) (1733): 264
t'Vliegend Hart (1735): A100
Shipwreck off the coast of the Carolinas (1737): 270
Wendela (1737): A103
Rooswijk (1739): A104
Invencible (1741): 283
Princess Louisa (1743): A105
Hollandia (1743): A106
Saint Geran (1744): A107
Saint Michel (1745): 287
Dutch East India Company ship (1746): A109
Golgoa (1746): 290
Reigersdaal (1747): A110
Nuestra Señora de la Luz (1752): 314
Terence Bay Wreck (1752): 315
HMS Assurance (1753): A112
Dodington (1754): A113
HMS Tilbury (1757): 327
L'Auguste de Bordeaux (1761): 343
Boscawen (1763): 347
Augusta (1777): 391
Carver's Falls Shipwreck (1777): 392
Penobscot River Shipwrecks (1779): 403
El Cazador (1784): 432
Faithful Steward (1785): 438
Hartwell (1787): A120
San Juan Harbor Shipwreck (1788): 460
Long Beach Island Shipwreck (1797): 504
HMS De Braak (1798): 507
HMS Lutine (1799): A123
Mantoloking Beach Shipwreck (1800): 521

Santa Leocadia (1800): 522
Enterprise (1802): A126
Nuestra Señora de las Mercedes (1804): A127
Lady Burgess (1806): A128
HMS Athenienne (1806): A129
"Coconut Wreck" (1809–10): 555
Roberts (Holden Wreck or Frank Gordon I Site)(1810): 556
Rapid (1811): A130
HMS Pomone (1811): A133
San Pedro de Alcantara (1815): 573
Cabalva (1818): A135
Sunrise Wreck (1823): 600
Duck of London (1832): A138
Leonidas (1832): 632
SS North Carolina (1840): 651
SS New York (1846): 673
Winfield Scott (1853): 698
Yankee Blade (1854): 701
Ship's boat from William and Mary (1857): 706
SS Central America (1857): 707
SS Brother Jonathan (1865): 764
SS Republic (1865): 765
SS Crescent City (1871): A142
USS Huron (1877): 788
RMS Douro (1882): A145
Infanta Maria Theresa (1898): 827
Cristobal Colon (1898): 827
USS Charleston (1899): A146
Stepney Hoard: 456
Tilley Treasure: 753
Votive deposits: 34, 85, 403
Wood, Ida E.: 845

Index to Contents of Finds

Ancient coin: 281, 501
Argentina, coin: 617
Argentina, La Plata, 8 reales: 675
Austria, kreuzer: 80
Austria, Maria Theresa thaler: A136, A140, A141
Austria, other type of thaler: A141
Austrian states, Salzburg, thaler: A123
Barbados, side cut pistareen: 470, 471
Bent coin: see witch piece
Bolivia, ½ sol: 510
Bolivia, 2 soles: 659
Bolivia, 8 soles: 602, 626, 659, 675, A141
Bolivia, scudo: 810
Brazil, coin: 617
Brazil, 500 reis: A145
Brazil, 1,000 reis: A145
Brazil, 2,000 reis: A145
Brazil, 6,400 reis: A145
Brazil, 10,000 reis: A145
Brazil, 20,000 reis: A145
British colonies: for coins minted before 1707, see under English colonies
British colonies, Bahamas, penny: 553
British colonies, Bermuda, halfpenny: 421
British colonies, Bermuda, penny: 346
British colonies, Canada, 1¢: 189, 640
British colonies, Canada, 10¢: 806
British colonies, Connecticut, Higley threepence: 270
British colonies, Hudson's Bay Company Territories, Northwest Company token: 589, 590, 591, 592, 593
British colonies, Lower Canada/Canada East, banknote: 584
British colonies, Lower Canada/Canada East, token: 168, 281, 384, 571, 574, 589, 590, 591, 592, 593, 640, 644, 645, 646, 734, A144
British colonies, Lower and Upper Canada, blacksmith copper: 346, 574, 640, 644, 647
British colonies, Lower and Upper Canada, North American token: 574, 741
British colonies, Montserrat, counterstamped 8 reales: 528
British colonies, New Brunswick, cent: 189
British colonies, New Jersey, paper money: 380, 412
British colonies, Newfoundland, 1¢: 768
British colonies, Newfoundland, 5¢: 768
British colonies, Newfoundland, 20¢: 840
British colonies, Newfoundland, $2: 810
British colonies, Nova Scotia, token: 189, 595, 608, 797
British colonies, Nova Scotia, cent: 189
British colonies, Prince Edward Island, token: 574, 644, 735
British colonies, Rosa Americana: 189, 208, 209, 741
British colonies, Rosa Americana halfpenny: 189, 421
British colonies, Rosa Americana penny: 321, 421, 476
British colonies, Rosa Americana twopence: 189, 214, 338, 421
British colonies, Saint Vincent, black dog: 570
British colonies, Tobago, 2¼ pence: 421
British colonies, Tortola, black dog: 813
British colonies, Upper Canada/Canada West, banknote: 679
British colonies, Upper Canada/Canada West, token: 574, 614, 640, 648, 735, 806
British colonies, Virginia, halfpenny: 281, 361, 370, 421, 427, 461, 462, 463, 464, 465, 497
British colonies, William Pitt halfpenny token: 281
British colonies, Pennsylvania, Kittaning destroyed medal: 328
British colonies, Indian peace medal: 191, 192, 193, 194, 195, 196, 197, 248, 266, 317, 318, 328, 335, 336, 337, 350, 351, 353, 367, 386, 387, 388, 389, 503, 546
Canada, 1¢: 189, 710, 768
Canada, 5¢: 710, 840
Canada, 10¢: 710, 840
Canada, 25¢: 840
Canada, 50¢: 189, 840
Canada, paper money: 840, 850, 888
Canada, Yukon, token: 847
Central America, silver coin: 738
Central American Republic, sun and volcanoes counterstamp: 669
Central American Republic (Costa Rica), 8 reales: 671
Central American Republic (Guatemala), 8 reales: 671, 673
Central American Republic (Honduras), coin: 671

Chile, 50 centavos: 707

Chile, escudo: 810

Chile, 8 escudos: 673

Chile, paper money: 835

China, cash: 159, 421, 441, 442, 443, 506, 627, 690, 693, 726, 735, 750, 775, 809, 819, 838, A130

China, 10 cash: 838

China, Hong Kong, 1¢: 809

China, Hong Kong, 10¢: 838

Coin weight: 43, 80, 189, 190, 198, 623, A93

Colombia, 2 escudos: 673

Confederate States of America, paper money: 754, 762, 763

Costa Rica, 8 reales: 671

Costa Rica, escudo: 684

Costa Rica, 2 escudos: 684

Costa Rica, ½ onza: 684

Costa Rica, counterstamped coin: 669, 671

Counterfeit coin: 76, 78, 79, 80, 151, 168, 177, 189, 222, 223, 281, 282, 312, 316, 321, 338, 345, 346, 370, 371, 374, 383, 384, 406, 418, 421, 423, 425, 431, 438, 439, 452, 456, 476, 477, 481, 496, 517, 536, 555, 560, 608, 669, 686, 813, 819, A43, A123

Counterstamped coin: 43, 60, 76, 77, 78, 80, 82, 93, 95, 96, 100, 134, 140, 178, 185, 189, 255, 259, 281, 312, 326, 330, 343, 344, 421, 452, 473, 474, 517, 528, 536, 555, 565, 566, 569, 586, 658, 669, 671, 707, 790, 813, A61, A70, A72, A87, A130, A131

Courland, Riga, silver coin: 43

Cut or clipped coin: 35, 42, 43, 58, 76, 83, 107, 130, 157, 181, 185, 189, 199, 200, 211, 223, 207, 253, 256, 279, 281, 299, 300, 304, 305, 322, 330, 344, 347, 361, 369, 370, 421, 427, 465, 470, 471, 474, 488, 496, 497, 499, 500, 531, 536, 554, 555, 563, 569, 587, 603, 636, 723, 822, A45, A83, A87, A103, A104, A130

Danish colonies, 12 skillings: 281

Danish colonies, 24 skillings: 281

Denmark, ½ skilling: 735

Denmark, skilling KM: 384

Denmark, 2 skillings: 281, 421

Denmark, frederik d'or: 673

Denmark, 2 frederiks d'or: 673

Denmark, 2 christians d'or: 673

Dominican Republic, ¼ real: 790

Egypt, 5 qirsh: 793

England: for coins minted after 1707, see under Great Britain

England, farthing: 43, 58, 62, 73, 76, 79, 86, 108, 112, 133, 147, 168, 189, 281, 421, 517, 686

England, copper and tin halfpenny: 73, 76, 139, 151, 164, 165, 166, 168, 177, 187, 272, 281, 282, 316, 326, 334, 344, 380, 381, 404, 421, 427, 517, 686

England, elephant halfpenny: A81

England, silver halfpenny: 43

England, silver penny: 68, 76, 552

England, threehalfpence: 43, 69

England, ½ groat: 43

England, twopence: 185

England, Maundy twopence: 151

England, threepence: 76

England, groat: 41, 69, 76, 83

England, sixpence: 24, 35, 42, 43, 55, 56, 69, 74, 76, 107, 144, 152, 168, 189, 380, 421

England, shilling: 42, 43, 69, 76, 130, 178, 185, 365, 369, 421

England, ½ crown: 160, 185

England, double crown: 69

England, ¼ laurel: 76

England, ½ guinea: 343

England, guinea: 142, 365

England, laurel: 69

England, unite: 69

England, token: 43, 76, 114, 115, 116, 135, 136

England, jeton: 189

England, medal: 43, 158

England, coin weight: 43

English colonies: for coins minted after 1707, see British colonies

English colonies, James II 1/24 real: 116, A79

English colonies, Maryland, Lord Baltimore, denarium: 102, 103, 104, 130

English colonies, Maryland, Lord Baltimore, sixpence: A62

English colonies, Massachusetts, New England sixpence: 91

English colonies, Massachusetts, New England shilling: 185

English colonies, Massachusetts, willow tree shilling: 131, 185

English colonies, Massachusetts, oak tree twopence: 111, 138, A64

Index 351

English colonies, Massachusetts, oak tree threepence: 138

English colonies, Massachusetts, oak tree sixpence: 138, 185

English colonies, Massachusetts, oak tree shilling: 109, 131, 132, 138, 185, 253, 322, A63

English colonies, Massachusetts, pine tree threepence: 117, 118, 119, 138

English colonies, Massachusetts, pine tree sixpence: 68, 120, 121, 122, 123, 124, 138, 178, 185

English colonies, Massachusetts, pine tree shilling: 68, 125, 126, 127, 128, 129, 130, 131, 132, 133, 138, 176, 178, 179, 185, 188, 281, 465, A105

English colonies, Newfoundland, lead token: 76

English colonies, Somers Islands (Bermuda), twopence: 46, 47

English colonies, Somers Islands (Bermuda), sixpence: 48, 49, 51

English colonies, Somers Islands (Bermuda), shilling: 50, 51

English colonies, Indian peace medal: 146, 147

France, coin: 692

France, denier tournois: 140, 189

France, double tournois: 62, 76, 87, 88, 140, 168, 189

France, liard: 87, 89, 98, 101, 140, 189, 281, 313, 338, 339, 421

France, Anglo-Gallic gros: 689

France, douzain: 52, 76, 77, 82, 140, 189, 312

France, silver coin: 37, 143, 343, 670

France, 6 deniers, "dardennes": 189, 338

France, ½ sol: 189, 281, 370, 421, 517

France, 15 deniers sols: 189, 255, 312

France, 30 deniers: 189, 313, 338

France, sol: 80, 82, 168, 189, 281, 330, 346, 370, 493, 608

France, 5 centimes: 168, 793

France, 2 sols: 189, 255, 281, 313, 338, 343, 347, A107

France, 10 centimes: 810

France, 4 sols: 76, 87, 140, 178

France, 20 centimes: 810

France, 15 sous: 198

France, 20 sous: 198

France, 30 sous: 198, 281

France, 1/20 écu: 189, 338

France, 1/12 écu: 185

France, 1/10 écu: 189

France, 1/6 écu: 242, 343

France, 1/5 écu: 189, 338, 343

France, ¼ écu: 92, 178, 189

France, 1/3 écu: 242, 338, 343

France, ½ franc: 640, 810

France, ½ écu: 108, 178, 189, 198, 201, 226, 242, 343

France, franc: 810

France, 5 francs: 631, 673, 675, 761, 776, A141

France, écu: 87, 178, 189, 198, 226, 242, 281, 297, 319, 329, 331, 343, 385, 438, 491, 596, 602, 607, 659, 686

France, louis d'or: 162, 189, 242, 287, 343, 357, 422, 555, 569, 673, 686, A123

France, 2 louis: 242, 343, 555, 569, A123

France, 20 francs: 673, 692, 707

France, 40 francs: 673

France, jeton: 189, 213

France, medal: 145, 153, 167, 173, 204, 205, 301, 307, 308, 309

French colonies, 9 deniers des colonies françoises: 166, 189, 206, 212, 213, 338, 522

French colonies, 12 deniers: 213

French colonies, sol tampé: 281

French colonies, 2 sous: 421

French colonies, 3 sous: 416

French colonies, Gloriam Regni, 5 sols: 143

French colonies, Cayenne, 2 sous: 570

French colonies, Guadeloupe, counterstamped 6,400 reis: 536

French colonies, Martinique, counterstamped 6,400 reis: 536, 555

French colonies, Windward Islands, 12 sols: 421

French states, Burgundy, douzain: 189

French states, Dauphiné, douzain: 343

French states, Navarre/Béarn, sol: 189

French states, Navarre, 2 sols: 189

German states, copper coin: 383

German states, pfenning: 735

German states, 2 pfennings: 735

German states, Baden, thaler: A141

German states, Bavaria, thaler: A141

German states, Bayreuth, heller: 347

German states, Brunswick-Lüneburg, 5 thalers: 655
German states, Brunswick-Lüneburg, 10 thalers: 673
German states, Brunswick-Wolfenbüttel, ducat: 405
German states, Electoral Palatinate, 20 kreuzers: 421
German states, Frankfurt/Main, kreuzer: 396
German states, Göttingen, 1/24 thaler: 378
German states, Hanover, 5 thalers: 673, 707
German states, Hanover, 10 thalers: 673
German states, Hesse-Cassel, thaler: 484
German states, Lübeck, sechsling: 43
German states, Nuremberg, pfennig: 313
German states, Prussia, frederick d'or: 532
German states, Prussia, 2 fredericks d'or: 673
German states, Saxony, thaler: 322, 675, A141
German states, Saxony, 10 thalers: 673
German states, Schwarzenberg, thaler: 411
German states, Soest, 3 pfennigs: 281
German states, Trier, dreipetermännchen: 183
German states, Württemberg, thaler: A141
German states, Nuremberg, jeton: 24, 35, 43, 44, 58, 66, 76, 269, 421, 430
German states, medal: 71, 258, 302, 311, A123
Germany, mark: 810
Germany, 10 marks: 810
Great Britain: for coins minted before 1707, see under England
Great Britain, coin: 617
Great Britain, farthing: 73, 168, 174, 189, 278, 281, 303, 322, 326, 338, 344, 347, 360, 362, 370, 421, 427, 477, 489, 517, 632, 686, 735
Great Britain, halfpenny: 62, 68, 73, 157, 166, 168, 174, 187, 188, 189, 224, 230, 247, 254, 256, 265, 272, 279, 281, 286, 288, 303, 306, 310, 312, 313, 315, 316, 321, 322, 324, 325, 326, 330, 334, 337, 338, 342, 344, 345, 346, 348, 349, 359, 362, 370, 371, 374, 375, 380, 381, 383, 384, 390, 393, 394, 400, 404, 406, 418, 420, 421, 423, 427, 431, 437, 438, 439, 452, 456, 467, 476, 477, 485, 489, 501, 508, 517, 532, 560, 563, 608, 611, 632, 640, 646, 663, 686, 687, 810, A123
Great Britain, penny: 168, 281, 563, 632, 710
Great Britain, twopence: 517, A123
Great Britain, sixpence: 80, 189, 198, 574
Great Britain, shilling: 168, 278, 639, 672, 806

Great Britain, ½ crown: 168, 198, 400
Great Britain, crown: 198, 400, 810
Great Britain, ½ sovereign: 630
Great Britain, sovereign: 630, 673, 707, 788
Great Britain, ½ guinea: 343, A123
Great Britain, guinea: 271, 281, 327, 343, 352, 368, 377, 390, 391, 392, 400, 422, 438, 440, 473, 491, 507, 515, 519, 575, A123
Great Britain, 5 guineas: 368
Great Britain, Bank of England, small head of George III counterstamp on 8 reales: A130, A131
Great Britain, evasive halfpenny: 346, 421, 621, 653
Great Britain, Washington Liberty and Security penny: 560
Great Britain, token: 281, 489, 564, 640, 686, 741
Great Britain, jeton: 473, 520, 686
Great Britain, medal: 277, 291, 282, 293, 310, 333, 337, 405, 494, 527, 534, 617, 637, 676, 677, 686
Great Britain, decoration: 678
Greece, drachma: 810
Greece, 5 drachmai: A141
Guatemala, 8 reales: 671
Guatemala, 16 pesos: 804
Holed coin: 12, 19, 35, 42, 43, 84, 85, 185, 189, 200, 268, 322, 337, 346, 347, 360, 383, 404, 432, 476, 517, 589, 590, 591, 592, 593, 669, 686, 722
Honduras, coin: 671
Hungary, poltura: 421
India, copper coin: 686
Indian peace medal: 146, 147, 191, 192, 193, 194, 195, 196, 197, 248, 266, 317, 318, 328, 335, 336, 337, 350, 351, 353, 367, 386, 387, 388, 389, 416, 417, 469, 483, 487, 503, 537, 538, 539, 540, 541, 542, 543, 545, 546, 604, 620, 638, 665, 666, 667, 688, 711, 742, 837
Ireland, farthing: 168, 215, 281
Ireland, St. Patrick's farthing: 150, 186, A71
Ireland, Wood's Hibernia farthing: 68, 232, 281, 517
Ireland, St. Patrick's halfpenny: 149
Ireland, copper halfpenny: 43, 68, 168, 189, 247, 281, 312, 342, 344, 346, 361, 393, 407, 419, 421, 423, 425, 427, 438, 439, 456, 476, 477, 489, 517, 640, 653, 686
Ireland, Wood's Hibernia halfpenny: 68, 166, 174, 189, 210, 216, 217, 218, 219, 220, 221, 224, 225, 231, 233, 234, 235, 236, 238, 265, 281, 298, 338, 345, 421, 560, 686, 741, A111

Index

Ireland, copper penny: 43, 189
Ireland, sixpence: 76
Ireland, shillings: 76
Ireland, gun money: 76, 156, 157, 281
Ireland, Voce Populi halfpenny: 340, 341
Ireland, token: 144, 281, 346, 482, 489
Ireland, medal: 574
Italian states, tallero: A130
Italian states, Aquilea, soldo: 3
Italian states, Fosdinovo, luigino: 796
Italian states, Genoa, minuto: 3
Italian states, Naples and Sicily, 4 ducati: A123
Italian states, Naples and Sicily, 6 ducati: A123
Italian states, Napoleonic Kingdom of Italy, 20 lire: 673
Italian states, Parma and Piacenza, medal: 163
Italian states, Sardinia, 20 lire: 673
Italian states, Tuscany, tollero: 322
Italy, coins: 617
Italy, lira: 810
Japan, mon: 838
Japan, 4 mon: 838
Japan, 100 mon: 793
Love token: 76, 454
Mexico, silver coin: 738, 804
Mexico, real: 566
Mexico, 2 reales: 566, 658, 659
Mexico, 8 reales: 566, 602, 619, 624, 631, 633, 654, 659, 660, 671, 672, 673, 675, 721, 776, 807, A141, A143, A146
Mexico, peso: A142
Mexico, gold coin: 730
Mexico, escudo: 810
Mexico, 8 escudos: 622, 650, 673, 804
Mexico, 10 pesos: 804
Netherlands, cent: 735
Netherlands, ½ duit: 174
Netherlands, duit: 168, 281
Netherlands, stuiver: 43, 76
Netherlands, 2 stuivers: 43, 62, 78, 82, 90
Netherlands, 6 stuivers: 76, 421
Netherlands, schelling: 172
Netherlands, ½ lion daalder: 185

Netherlands, lion daalder: 63, 99, 161, 178, 185
Netherlands, 3 gulden: 178
Netherlands, ducaton: 81
Netherlands, gold florin: 81
Netherlands, 5 gulden: 673
Netherlands, 10 gulden: 673
Netherlands, jeton: 43, 84
Netherlands, medal: 55, 113, 295
Norway, silver penny: 1
Peru, 2 reales: 659
Peru, 8 reales: 659, 673, 698, A141
Peru, North Peru, 8 reales: 659, 673
Poland, medal: 373
Portugal, ceitil: 3, 5, 6
Portugal, copper coin: A130
Portugal, silver coin: 134
Portugal, 5 reis: 189, 281
Portugal, 10 reis: 168, 189, 268, 281, 427
Portugal, 40 reis: 281
Portugal, 60 reis: 76
Portugal, ½ tostão: 76
Portugal, 100 reis: 76, 172
Portugal, 120 reis: 76
Portugal, 200 reis: 172
Portugal, 400 reis: 172, 185, 433
Portugal, tostão: 76, 172, 178
Portugal, ½ cruzado: 172
Portugal, ½ San Vicente: 25
Portugal, cruzado: 25, 172
Portugal, 1,600 reis: A97, A108
Portugal, 2,000 reis: A97
Portugal, 3,200 reis: A97
Portugal, 4,000 reis: A97, A108
Portugal, 4 escudos (6,400 reis): 327, 332, 343, 555, A97, A108
Portugal, 12,800 reis: A97, A108
Portuguese colonies, Brazil, 5 reis: 281
Portuguese colonies, Brazil, 10 reis: 281
Portuguese colonies, Brazil, 20 reis: 281
Portuguese colonies, Brazil, 300 reis counterstamp: 178, 185

Portuguese colonies, Brazil, 600 reis counterstamp: A72, A87

Portuguese colonies, Brazil, 640 reis: 172

Portuguese colonies, Brazil, gold coin: A88

Portuguese colonies, Brazil, 1,000 reis: A145

Portuguese colonies, Brazil, 1,600 reis: 395, 474, A97, A108, A145

Portuguese colonies, Brazil, 2,000 reis: A92, A97, A145

Portuguese colonies, Brazil, 3,200 reis: 410, 474, A97

Portuguese colonies, Brazil, 4,000 reis: 271, 569, A87, A97, A108, A145

Portuguese colonies, Brazil, 6,400 reis: 289, 314, 327, 332, 357, 359, 410, 422, 474, 507, 536, 555, 558, 569, A97, A108, A113, A145

Portuguese colonies, Brazil, 10,000 reis: A97

Portuguese colonies, Brazil, 12,800 reis: 245, 271, A97, A108

Portuguese colonies, Brazil, 20,000 reis: A97

Rome, Constantine era coin: 281

Rome, Nero coin: 501

Russia, 2 kopeks: 281, 421, 563

Russia, 5 kopeks: 354, A123

Russia, 5 roubles: 532

Scotland, bawbee: 198, 421

Scotland, twopence: 112

Scotland, plack (4 pence): 43

Scotland, 20 pence: 76

Scotland, sword and scepter: 69, 76

Siam, counterstamp: A61

Spain, ardite: 184

Spain, dinero: 184

Spain, maravedí: 4, 6, 20, 43, 60, 106

Spain, 2 maravedíes: 60, 189, 281

Spain, 4 maravedíes: 5, 6, 43, 60, 61, 76, 78, 189, 281

Spain, 8 maravedíes: 60, 61, 76, 78, 80, 189, 338, 452

Spain, silver coin: 78, 134, 186, 670

Spain, 40 centimos: 827

Spain, ½ real: 3, 21, 76

Spain, ½ real (¼ pistareen): 157, 189, 300, 314, 344, 421, 603, 716, A115

Spain, real: 15, 22, 39, 60, 75, 185

Spain, real (½ pistareen): 68, 73, 189, 199, 207, 243, 257, 267, 273, 281, 283, 314, 338, 375, 421, 438, 496, 603, 648

Spain, peseta: 602

Spain 2 reales: 60, 61

Spain, 2 reales (pistareen): 157, 181, 182, 189, 200, 202, 211, 222, 223, 227, 228, 229, 238, 241, 256, 279, 281, 294, 296, 304, 305, 312, 314, 327, 330, 338, 355, 361, 370, 377, 395, 403, 421, 433, 465, 470, 471, 488, 496, 497, 499, 504, 535, 565, 603, 641, 659, 661, 673, 793, 810

Spain, 2 pesetas: 827

Spain, 4 reales: 60, 61, 151, 178, 189

Spain, 4 reales de vellon: 603

Spain, 5 pesetas: 827

Spain, 8 reales: 57, 60, 61, 75, 602, 603, A87, A130

Spain, 20 reales: 705

Spain, ½ escudo: 432

Spain, escudo: 60, 198

Spain, 2 escudos: 60, 61, 93, 190, 198, 673

Spain, 25 pesetas: 828, 853

Spain, 4 escudos: 159

Spain, 8 escudos: 60, 190, 198, 239

Spain, medal: 36, 38, 67, 137, 240, 385, 510

Spain, decoration: 240

Spanish colonies, silver coin: 43, 61, 636, 670, 752, A35, A42

Spanish colonies, ½ real: 157, 185, 189, 198, 261, 281, 299, 312, 322, 324, 338, 370, 421, 489, 532, 582, A112

Spanish colonies, real: 61, 189, 198, 261, 281, 299, 312, 322, 330, 421, 488, 565, 658, 669, A31, A87, A123

Spanish colonies, 2 reales: 25, 61, 157, 185, 189, 198, 281, 299, 322, 330, 338, 496, 501, 554, 561, 565, 636, 658, 659, 810, A20, A123

Spanish colonies, 4 reales: 25, 61, 185, 189, 190, 198, 299, A59, A87, A123, A132

Spanish colonies, 8 reales: 25, 61, 176, 178, 185, 189, 190, 198, 260, 281, 300, 326, 330, 344, 359, 366, 375, 385, 427, 454, 484, 485, 490, 491, 500, 501, 504, 507, 513, 515, 516, 518, 521, 524, 526, 535, 573, 574, 589, 595, 600, 607, 625, 626, 629, 656, 658, 659, 669, 672, 721, 722, 723, 761, 822, A13, A46, A59, A77, A87, A121, A123, A126, A130, A131, A132, A133

Spanish colonies, gold coin: A42, A127

Spanish colonies, escudo: 398, A123

Spanish colonies, 2 escudos: 250, 264, 518, 810, A123

Spanish colonies, 4 escudos: 180, 264, 518, 558, 810, A123

Spanish colonies, 8 escudos: 190, 271, 377, 422, 459, 479, 511, 512, 558, 569, 572, 596, 622, 625, 629, 810, A102, A123

Spanish colonies, Indian peace medal: 416, 417, 546

Spanish colonies, Bogotá, ¼ real: 110

Spanish colonies, Bogotá, ½ real: 85, 110

Spanish colonies, Bogotá, real: 110, 603

Spanish colonies, Bogotá, 2 reales: 60, 78, 110, 185, A61, A105

Spanish colonies, Bogotá, 4 reales: 60, 61, 78, 110, 185, A61, A105

Spanish colonies, Bogotá, 8 reales: 60, 61, 78, 100, 105, 110, 178, A43, A61, A70

Spanish colonies, escudo, Bogotá: 190

Spanish colonies, Bogotá, 2 escudos: 60, 72, 100, 185, 190, 198, 263, 314, 327, 555, A51, A80, A89, A134

Spanish colonies, Bogotá, 8 escudos: 432, A134, A139

Spanish colonies, Cartagena, real: 110

Spanish colonies, Cartagena, 2 reales: 78, 105

Spanish colonies, Cartagena, 4 reales: 78, 105

Spanish colonies, Cartagena, 8 reales: 60, 65, 78, 100, 105, A38

Spanish colonies, Cuzco, 8 reales: 603

Spanish colonies, Cuzco, escudo: 190

Spanish colonies, Cuzco, 2 escudos: 171, 185, 190

Spanish colonies, Durango, 8 reales: 603

Spanish colonies, Guatemala, ¼ real: 603

Spanish colonies, Guatemala, ½ real: 281, 669

Spanish colonies, Guatemala, real: 189, 556, 603, 669, A112

Spanish colonies, Guatemala, 2 reales: 281, 314, 556, 565, 603, 669

Spanish colonies, Guatemala, 4 reales: A106, A110

Spanish colonies, Guatemala, 8 reales: 327, 343, 556, 562, 603, 669, 671, 673, A104, A106, A110, A115, A120, A128, A129, A130, A132

Spanish colonies, Lima, ¼ real: 34

Spanish colonies, Lima, ½ real: 34, 185, 189, 190, 281, 322, 603, A112, A115

Spanish colonies, Lima, real: 60, 169, 185, 190, 299, 312, 338, 421, 496, 556, 603, 669, A87, A105, A112, A115

Spanish colonies, Lima, 2 reales: 60, 61, 169, 185, 190, 322, 346, 421, 492, 496, 529, 603, A91, A105, A112, A115

Spanish colonies, Lima, 4 reales: 40, 60, 61, 159, 169, 185, 190, 492, 603, A8, A22, A30, A87, A91, A94, A105, A112, A132

Spanish colonies, Lima, 8 reales: 39, 60, 61, 148, 155, 159, 170, 178, 185, 190, 263, 314, 327, 343, 492, 521, 556, 562, 603, A8, A10, A12, A30, A87, A88, A91, A94, A105, A106, A112, A115, A117, A118, A121, A123, A129, A130, A131, A132, A133, A135, A140, A141

Spanish colonies, Lima, escudo: 190, 259

Spanish colonies, Lima, 2 escudos: 190, 259

Spanish colonies, Lima, 4 escudos: 190, 314, A102

Spanish colonies, Lima, 8 escudos: 190, 198, 314, 507, 573, A95, A102, A138

Spanish colonies, México, 4 maravedíes: 12

Spanish colonies, México, ¼ real: 421

Spanish colonies, México, ½ real: 26, 27, 62, 78, 168, 185, 190, 189, 244, 275, 281, 299, 310, 314, 320, 322, 360, 361, 372, 375, 382, 393, 404, 413, 421, 431, 432, 489, 496, 510, 556, 567, 568, 603, 633, 686, 716, A105, A115, A120

Spanish colonies, México, real: 15, 16, 17, 26, 27, 28, 40, 45, 58, 59, 61, 78, 85, 94, 185, 190, 244, 269, 281, 299, 312, 314, 322, 346, 361, 364, 382, 413, 414, 421, 431, 432, 436, 452, 477, 556, 603, 608, 633, 669, 671, 686, A4, A15, A18, A19, A22, A23, A27, A38, A44, A50, A60, A61, A65, A69, A90, A100, A101, A105, A106, A112, A115, A120, A128

Spanish colonies, México, 2 reales: 13, 14, 15, 26, 40, 45, 60, 61, 64, 68, 78, 85, 178, 185, 189, 190, 275, 281, 314, 327, 346, 413, 421, 432, 492, 495, 496, 522, 549, 556, 587, 603, 633, 669, 686, 782, A2, A4, A5, A6, A10, A11, A12, A19, A20, A21, A22, A25, A26, A29, A38, A40, A48, A50, A52, A56, A57, A58, A60, A61, A76, A90, A91, A94, A99, A100, A105, A106, A112, A115, A124, A137

Spanish colonies, México, 3 reales: 14

Spanish colonies, México, 4 reales: 13, 14, 15, 16, 19, 26, 29, 37, 40, 45, 60, 61, 64, 78, 100, 105, 185, 190, 262, 263, 322, 356, 432, 492, 556, 669, 675, A3, A4, A7, A8, A9, A10, A12, A14, A16, A17, A19, A20, A22, A25, A26, A29, A30, A31, A35, A39, A40, A43, A44, A45, A50, A56, A60, A61, A75, A78, A83, A85, A90, A91, A94, A100, A103, A104, A105, A106, A110, A115, A124, A131

Spanish colonies, México, 8 reales: 37, 39, 45, 53, 54, 60, 61, 64, 65, 75, 78, 100, 94, 159, 172, 178, 185, 189, 190, 203, 206, 259, 260, 262, 263, 274, 276, 281, 285, 290, 310, 314, 322, 323, 327, 338, 343, 345, 346, 358, 363, 376, 383, 391, 395, 399, 401, 402, 408, 409, 421, 432, 435,

465, 475, 486, 492, 496, 514, 528, 548, 556, 559, 562, 563, 578, 586, 603, 631, 633, 642, 654, 657, 659, 669, 671, 673, 675, 686, A8, A10, A12, A13, A17, A19, A20, A22, A24, A25, A26, A28, A29, A30, A31, A32, A33, A34, A35, A38, A40, A41, A43, A44, A47, A49, A50, A53, A54, A55, A59, A60, A61, A66, A72, A74, A75, A82, A83, A85, A86, A87, A88, A90, A91, A93, A94, A96, A98, A100, A103, A104, A105, A106, A107, A109, A110, A112, A115, A118, A119, A120, A121, A123, A124, A125, A126, A128, A129, A130, A131, A132, A133, A135, A136, A138, A140, A141, A143

Spanish colonies, México, escudo: 190, 263

Spanish colonies, México, 2 escudos: 190, 263

Spanish colonies, México, 4 escudos: 190, 252, A102, A139

Spanish colonies, México, 8 escudos: 190, 251, 263, 314, 409, 410, 507, 579, 598, 633, 657, 804, A139

Spanish colonies, Panama, ½ real: 30, 31, 32

Spanish colonies, Panama, real: 30, 31, 32, 33, 34

Spanish colonies, Panama, 2 reales: 30, 31, 33, 60

Spanish colonies, Panama, 4 reales: A7

Spanish colonies, Popayán, 2 reales: 603

Spanish colonies, Popayán, 8 reales: A132

Spanish colonies, Popayán, escudo: A134

Spanish colonies, Popayán, 2 escudos: A139

Spanish colonies, Popayán, 8 escudos: 673, A134

Spanish colonies, Potosí, ½ real: 148, 185, 189, 314, 322, 421, 521, 556, 603, A112, A113

Spanish colonies, Potosí, real: 60, 61, 70, 75, 76, 78, 85, 93, 97, 100, 105, 141, 147, 148, 169, 185, 190, 249, 280, 281, 284, 299, 312, 338, 496, 521, 603, 636, 669, 671, A53, A87, A105, A112, A113, A114

Spanish colonies, Potosí, 2 reales: 57, 60, 61, 70, 75, 78, 85, 93, 97, 100, 105, 148, 169, 178, 185, 190, 280, 421, 492, 496, 521, 556, 603, 669, A20, A22, A31, A61, A73, A76, A91, A94, A105, A112, A113, A128

Spanish colonies, Potosí, 4 reales: 40, 57, 60, 61, 64, 65, 70, 75, 78, 93, 97, 100, 105, 148, 159, 169, 172, 185, 189, 190, 220, 314, 432, 492, 556, 603, 634, 669, 725, A17, A20, A22, A25, A26, A30, A43, A53, A58, A61, A67, A91, A94, A105, A106, A112, A113, A124, A132

Spanish colonies, Potosí, 8 reales: 53, 57, 60, 61, 64, 65, 70, 75, 76, 78, 93, 97, 100, 105, 148, 154, 155, 159, 161, 170, 172, 175, 178, 185, 189, 190, 198, 246, 259, 263, 314, 327, 343, 492, 530, 556, 562, 603, 654, 669, A12, A13, A17, A19, A20, A22, A26, A29, A30, A31, A33, A36, A37, A38, A43, A49, A50, A53, A58, A61, A67, A68, A71, A72, A73, A75, A84, A87, A88, A91, A94, A96, A98, A105, A112, A113, A116, A121, A122, A124, A128, A129, A130, A131, A132, A136, A141

Spanish colonies, Potosí, hearts: 148

Spanish colonies, Potosí, 8 escudos: A139

Spanish colonies, Santiago, ¼ real: 576

Spanish colonies, Santiago, real: 576

Spanish colonies, Santiago, 2 reales: 603

Spanish colonies, Santiago, 8 reales: 603, A128, A129, A130, A132

Spanish colonies, Santiago, 2 escudos: A134

Spanish colonies, Santiago, 4 escudos: 314

Spanish colonies, Santiago, 8 escudos: 314, A139

Spanish colonies, Santo Domingo, 4 maravedíes: 5, 7, 8, 9, 10, 11, 12, 15, 23, 94, 95, 96, A1

Spanish colonies, Santo Domingo, 4 reales: 14, 15, A10, A11

Spanish colonies, Texas, San Antonio, Garza jola: 579, 580, 581

Spanish colonies, Zacatecas, 8 reales: 603, 673

Spanish Netherlands, liard: 281

Spanish Netherlands, ducatoon: 239

Spanish Netherlands, Antwerp, golden fleece counterstamp: A61, A70

Spanish states, Castile and Leon, blanca: 2, 3, 18

Spanish states, Castile and Leon, ½ real: 3

Spanish states, Castile and Leon, real: 3

Spanish states, Castile and Leon, seisén: 3

Spanish states, Navarre, ½ blanca: 3

Sweden, 2 öre: 735

Sweden, ½ skilling: 281, 517

Thailand, counterstamp: A61

USA, California, fractional gold: 582, 698, 707

USA, California, private gold: 582, 682, 685, 694, 698, 704, 708, 772

USA, Confederatio copper: 446

USA, Connecticut, copper: 166, 189, 224, 281, 342, 346, 370, 406, 427, 439, 447, 451, 452, 456, 467, 477, 489, 552, 560, 741

USA, Georgius Triumpho copper: 281

USA, Immune Columbia/Nova Constellatio copper: 686

USA, Maine, banknote: 708

USA, Maryland, John Chalmers, threepence: 427

Index

USA, Maryland, John Chalmers, sixpence: 428

USA, Maryland, John Chalmers, shilling: 429

USA, Massachusetts, 1¢: 312, 346, 450, 741

USA, Massachusetts, paper money: 445

USA, Massachusetts, North Swansea, bungtown halfpenny: 476

USA, New Hampshire, pine tree copper: 379

USA, New Jersey, copper: 62, 281, 338, 346, 370, 443, 452, 455, 458, 466, 476, 477, 489, 686, 741

USA, New Jersey, paper money: 412

USA, New Jersey, banknote: 606, 784

USA, New York, paper money: 412

USA, New York, banknote: 668

USA, New York, Ephraim Brasher, counterstamped guinea: 473

USA, New York, Ephraim Brasher, doubloon: 569

USA, New York, Brasher & Bailey/Mould & Atlee/Machin's Mills halfpenny: 281, 370, 406, 452, 453, 456, 460, 476

USA, New York, Nova Eborac copper: 456, 741

USA, North Carolina, Bechtler, $1: 696

USA, North Carolina, Bechtler, $5: 673

USA, Nova Constellatio copper: 281, 370, 424, 425, 426, 427, 560, 741

USA, Vermont, copper: 281, 324, 346, 431, 456, 467, 468, 477, 560, 741

USA, bar copper: 383

USA, Washington piece: 478, 480, 560

USA, regulated (counterstamped) gold coin: 252, 473, 474, 536, 555, 569

USA, Fugio 1¢: 281, 448, 449, 457, 508, 552, 741

USA, coin: 591

USA, copper coin: 869

USA, ½¢: 189, 281, 361, 421, 477, 481, 550, 552, 563, 605, 616, 686, 741, 774

USA, 1¢: 73, 80, 188, 281, 310, 361, 406, 421, 427, 431, 460, 477, 481, 488, 497, 498, 502, 505, 508, 509, 531, 532, 533, 547, 551, 557, 574, 585, 588, 594, 608, 609, 613, 635, 646, 653, 664, 673, 686, 709, 710, 722, 735, 741, 752, 753, 805, 809, 811, 819, 825, 826, A130

USA, 2¢: 361, 710, 741, 786

USA, nickel 3¢: 361, 783, 805, 811

USA, nickel 5¢: 73, 361, 655, 686, 783, 805, 809, 811

USA, silver coin: 733, 782, 788, 808, 817, 830, 834, 855, 860, 870, 872

USA, silver 3¢: 281, 722, 738, 752, 756, 793, 814

USA, silver 5¢: 281, 361, 481, 493, 497, 525, 587, 618, 640, 664, 672, 686, 706, 707, 738, 745, 752, 756, 786, 793, 806

USA, 10¢: 73, 281, 361, 557, 585, 587, 608, 613, 618, 641, 661, 664, 672, 673, 680, 686, 722, 738, 745, 750, 752, 756, 783, 793, 805, 806, 809, 811, 843

USA, 25¢: 361, 613, 641, 658, 659, 661, 664, 670, 672, 673, 680, 686, 706, 707, 718, 738, 752, 753, 756, 765, 783, 793, 795, 805, 806, 809, 811, 818, 843, 862, 890

USA, 50¢: 80, 281, 481, 488, 561, 565, 577, 609, 610, 611, 612, 613, 624, 631, 634, 643, 651, 652, 656, 657, 658, 659, 660, 661, 662, 663, 664, 670, 672, 673, 674, 675, 680, 686, 703, 706, 707, 718, 721, 722, 738, 741, 751, 752, 753, 756, 760, 765, 766, 776, 783, 793, 795, 805, 806, 809, 811, 862, 869, 890, A144

USA, silver $1: 281, 612, 659, 661, 670, 672, 673, 680, 686, 741, 746, 752, 774, 776, 780, 783, 791, 793, 795, 805, 811, 812, 818, 821, 822, 825, 860, 862, 889, 890, I, II, III, IV, V, VI, VII, VIII, IX, X, XI, XII, XIII, XIV, XV, XVI, A130

USA, gold coin: 674, 724, 729, 731, 739, 758, 782, 795, 830, 831, 835, 851, 852, 856, 860, 871, 872, 873, A146

USA, gold $1: 698, 702, 706, 707, 727, 741, 748, 752, 776, 781, 793, 794, 798, 803, 805, 811, 884

USA, gold $2.50: 651, 673, 681, 695, 698, 702, 706, 707, 712, 718, 722, 733, 748, 767, 770, 776, 781, 794, 803, 805, 810, 811, 816, 884, 887

USA, gold $3: 707, 751, 776, 794, 803, 805, 811

USA, gold $5: 481, 544, 612, 655, 673, 681, 698, 700, 702, 704, 706, 707, 712, 714, 715, 717, 718, 720, 747, 748, 764, 769, 770, 773, 776, 781, 792, 794, 798, 803, 805, 811, 816, 824, 831, 839, 853, 857, 858, 859, 862, 864, 870, 874, 880, 883, 884, 887

USA, gold $10: 525, 673, 691, 702, 706, 707, 718, 746, 747, 764, 765, 769, 770, 773, 776, 781, 787, 792, 794, 798, 800, 803, 805, 808, 811, 816, 824, 839, 853, 854, 856, 858, 859, 862, 864, 870, 874, 879, 880, 884, 887, A147

USA, gold $20: 700, 701, 702, 704, 706, 707, 712, 713, 715, 718, 720, 733, 736, 737, 744, 746, 747, 748, 749, 757, 759, 760, 764, 765, 769, 770, 773, 776, 779, 781, 787, 789, 792, 794, 798, 799, 801, 803, 805, 811, 814, 815, 816, 817, 818, 820, 823, 824, 831, 832, 833, 834, 836, 839, 841, 842, 853, 854, 857, 858, 859, 862, 863, 864, 867, 870, 874, 875, 879, 880, 883, 884, 887

USA, Humbert/USAOG $10: 698, 707

USA, Humbert/USAOG, $50: 697, 699, 707, 785

USA, paper money (including national banknotes): 397, 412, 588, 719, 755, 777, 778, 793, 802, 834, 845, 846, 861, 862, 865, 866, 867, 868, 869, 870, 871, 872, 876, 877, 878, 881, 882, 883, 885, 891, 892, A148

USA, obsolete banknote: 588, 606, 615, 668, 683, 708, 730, 734, 784

USA, gold bars: 707

USA, coin weight: 623

USA, token: 188, 281, 649, 653, 686, 687, 722, 728, 741, 743, 774, 809, 829, 847, 848, 849, 886

USA, Indian peace medal: 469, 483, 487, 503, 537, 538, 539, 540, 541, 542, 543, 545, 546, 604, 620, 638, 665, 666, 667, 688, 711, 742, 837

USA, medal: 168, 523, 527, 583, 599, 601, 628, 732, 740, 741, 771, 774, 793, 805, 844

USA, decoration: 789

Vietnam, Annam, cash: 819

Vietnam, Annam, dong: 809

Vietnam, United Dai Viet, dong: 838

Vietnam, South Vietnam, paper money: A148

Witch piece (bent coin): 42, 76, 345